THE AFRICAN POOR

AFRICAN STUDIES SERIES 58

Published in collaboration with
THE AFRICAN STUDIES CENTRE, CAMBRIDGE

OTHER BOOKS IN THE SERIES

6 *Labour in the South African Gold Mines, 1911–1969* Francis Wilson
14 *Culture, Tradition and Society in the West African Novel* Emmanuel Obiechina
18 *Muslim Brotherhoods in Nineteenth-century Africa* B. G. Martin
20 *Liberia and Sierra Leone: An Essay in Comparative Politics* Christopher Clapham
23 *West African States: Failure and Promise: A Study in Comparative Politics* John Dunn
24 *Afrikaners of the Kalahari: White Minority in a Black State* Margo and Martin Russell
25 *A Modern History of Tanganyika* John Iliffe
26 *A History of African Christianity 1950–1975* Adrian Hastings
28 *The Hidden Hippopotamus: Reappraisal in African History: The Early Colonial Experience in Western Zambia* Gwyn Prins
29 *Families Divided: The Impact of Migrant Labour in Lesotho* Colin Murray
30 *Slavery, Colonialism and Economic Growth in Dahomey 1640–1960* Patrick Manning
31 *Kings, Commoners and Concessionaires: The Evolution and Dissolution of the Nineteenth-century Swazi State* Philip Bonner
32 *Oral Poetry and Somali Nationalism: The Case of Sayyid Muhammad 'Abdille Hasan* Said S. Samatar
33 *The Political Economy of Pondoland 1860–1930: Production, Labour, Migrancy and Chiefs in Rural South Africa* William Beinart
34 *Volkskapitalisme: Class, Capital and Ideology in the Development of Afrikaner Nationalism 1934–1948* Dan O'Meara
35 *The Settler Economies: Studies in the Economic History of Kenya and Southern Rhodesia 1900–1963* Paul Mosley
36 *Transformations in Slavery: A History of Slavery in Africa* Paul E. Lovejoy
37 *Amilcar Cabral: Revolutionary Leadership and People's War* Patrick Chabal
38 *Essays on the Political Economy of Rural Africa* Robert H. Bates
39 *Ijeshas and Nigerians: The Incorporation of a Yoruba Kingdom, 1890s–1970s* J. D. Y. Peel
40 *Black People and the South African War 1899–1902* Peter Warwick
41 *A History of Niger 1850–1960* Finn Fuglestad
42 *Industrialisation and Trade Union Organisation in South Africa 1924–55* Jon Lewis
43 *The Rising of the Red Shawls: A Revolt in Madagascar 1895–1899* Stephen Ellis
44 *Slavery in Dutch South Africa* Nigel Worden
45 *Law, Custom and Social Order: The Colonial Experience in Malawi and Zambia* Martin Chanock
46 *Salt of the Desert Sun: A History of Salt Production and Trade in the Central Sudan* Paul E. Lovejoy
47 *Marrying Well: Status and Social Change among the Educated Elite in Colonial Lagos* Kristin Mann
48 *Language and Colonial Power: The Appropriation of Swahili in the Former Belgian Congo 1880–1938* Johannes Fabian
49 *The Shell Money of the Slave Trade* Jan Hogendorn and Marion Johnson
50 *Political Domination in Africa: Reflections on the Limits of Power* edited by Patrick Chabal
51 *The Southern Marches of Imperial Ethiopia: Essays in History and Social Anthropology* edited by Donald Donham and Wendy James
52 *Islam and Urban Labor in Northern Nigeria: The Making of a Muslim Working Class* Paul M. Lubeck
53 *Horn and Crescent: Cultural Change and Traditional Islam on the East African Coast, 500–1900* Randall J. Pouwels
54 *Capital and Labour on the Kimberley Diamond Fields 1871–1890* Robert Vicat Turrell
55 *National and Class Conflict in the Horn of Africa* John Markakis
56 *Democracy and Prebendal Politics in Nigeria: The Rise and Fall of the Second Republic* Richard A. Joseph
57 *Entrepreneurs and Parasites: The Struggle for Indigenous Capitalism in Zaire* Janet MacGaffey

THE AFRICAN POOR

A history

JOHN ILIFFE

Reader in African History, University of Cambridge,
and Fellow of St John's College

CAMBRIDGE UNIVERSITY PRESS

CAMBRIDGE

NEW YORK NEW ROCHELLE MELBOURNE SYDNEY

Published by the Press Syndicate of the University of Cambridge
The Pitt Building, Trumpington Street, Cambridge CB2 1RP
32 East 57th Street, New York, NY 10022, USA
10 Stamford Road, Oakleigh, Melbourne 3166, Australia

First published 1987

Printed in Great Britain at
Redwood Burn Limited, Trowbridge, Wiltshire

British Library cataloguing in publication data

Iliffe, John, *1939–*
The African poor: a history. – (African
studies series; 58).
1. Poor – Africa – History
I. Title II. Series
305.5′69′096 HC800.Z9P6

Library of Congress cataloguing in publication data

Iliffe, John.
The African poor.
(African studies series)
Bibliography.
Includes index.
1. Poor – Africa – History. I. Title. II. Series.
HC800.Z9P625 1987 305.5′62′096 87–14622

ISBN 0 521 34415 8 hard covers
ISBN 0 521 34877 3 paperback

RB

In memory of my mother, Violet Evelyn Iliffe

Contents

Preface

This book draws largely on the magnificent resources of the University of Cambridge Library. The Managers of the African Studies Centre, Cambridge, and its Librarian, Dr Janet Seeley, were also especially helpful in obtaining materials. I am indebted to archivists and librarians at many institutions: Archives Nationales (Section Outre-Mer), Paris; Bayero University Library, Kano; University of Birmingham Library; British Library; British Newspaper Library; Chancellor College Library, Zomba; Church Missionary Society Archives, London; University of Edinburgh Library; Institute of Development Studies, Nairobi; Malawi National Archives; National Library of Scotland; Rhodes House, Oxford; School of Oriental and African Studies, London; Seeley Historical Library, Cambridge; Tanganyika African National Union; Tanzania National Archives; University Library, Dar es Salaam; and Zimbabwe National Archives. The British Council financed a visit to Malawi. David Beach, Ms Alison Izzett, Steven Kaplan, Paul Richards, Robert Ross, Megan Vaughan, Dr Jean-Luc Vellut, and Nigel Worden supplied unpublished material. Books by Dr Polly Hill and Professor Olwen Hufton provided many ideas. Seminars at Birmingham, Cambridge, London, and Zomba made suggestions. Peter Kinyanjui, Lorne Larson, and John McCracken helped with travel in Africa. Tony Hopkins, Gilbert Lewis, and Michael Twaddle gave advice. Jack Goody provided the stimulus. John Lonsdale and the Cambridge University Press showed me their habitual kindness. I am grateful to all those who have helped me.

St John's College, Cambridge JOHN ILIFFE
October 1986

1

The comparative history of the poor

There are three reasons for writing a book on this subject. One is that poverty is growing today in sub-Saharan Africa, terribly in the form of mass famine and insidiously in the declining living standards of remote villages and urban shanty towns. Contemporary poverty has become an important subject of research, notably in Nigeria,[1] in the numerous country studies sponsored by the International Labour Office and the World Bank,[2] and in the massive Carnegie Inquiry into poverty and development in southern Africa.[3] The hope that research and practical thought about poverty may benefit from a historical perspective is one reason for this first attempt to provide one.

A second reason for writing the book is a belief that Africa's splendour lies in its suffering. The heroism of African history is to be found not in the deeds of kings but in the struggles of ordinary people against the forces of nature and the cruelty of men. Likewise, the most noble European activities in Africa have been by those – often now almost forgotten – who have cared for the sick and starving and homeless.

The third reason is academic. The old imperial history was marred by an elitism which, because the elite was often a tiny white minority, could degenerate further into racialism. The national histories that have replaced it, by contrast, are marred by their parochialism. To escape both defects requires a comparative social history which treats peoples on a basis of equality rather than subjection. The history of the poor permits an experiment on these lines. Historians of Africa have much to learn from recent work on the history of poverty in Europe. They can also draw something from parallel work in other continents, although this is more fragmentary. In particular, European historians have identified major questions about the poor which need to be asked in Africa: their identity, numbers, characteristics, and location; the reasons for their poverty; what they thought and did about it; and what the larger society thought and did about them.

Yet a comparative history of the African poor must first surmount three obstacles. One is to find a usable definition of poverty. This could be discussed at great length, debating the advantages of analysing absolute poverty (measured against the minimum necessary to maintain a person's physical efficiency) or relative poverty (measured against the average living standards of a particular society).[4] Yet beyond showing that the superiority once attributed to the notion of relative poverty is no longer obvious,[5] such a discussion would have little value for the history of Africa because both definitions rely on measurements which were not made there until the 1930s. For earlier periods the historian must rely largely upon descriptions of behaviour which either the describer or the historian identifies as indicating poverty. Moreover, the poor are diverse, poverty has many facets, and African peoples had their own varied and changing notions of it. A precise and consistent definition is not feasible. Nevertheless, poverty has an inescapable connotation of physical want, especially in poor countries. Examination of the sources suggests that two levels of want have existed in Africa for several centuries. On one level have been the very large numbers – perhaps most Africans at most times – obliged to struggle continuously to preserve themselves and their dependants from physical want. These will be called the poor. On another level have been smaller numbers who have permanently or temporarily failed in that struggle and have fallen into physical want. These will be called the very poor or destitute. Of course, there was no sharp dividing line between them. Yet the distinction has cross-cultural validity. It existed in ancient Greece.[6] It was identified by Charles Booth's pioneer study of London during the 1880s, which defined the poor as those 'living under a struggle to obtain the necessaries of life and make both ends meet' and the very poor as those who 'live in a state of chronic want'.[7] The distinction between *pauvre* and *indigent* was drawn in early modern France, where 'Both *pauvre* and *indigent* knew hunger, but the *indigent* were never free from it.'[8] In Africa the distinction existed in some, but not all, pre-colonial languages[9] and has appeared frequently since, most recently in accounts of South African resettlement sites during the early 1980s.[10] Because a history of the African poor in the wider sense would be almost a history of Africa, this book is chiefly about the very poor, but it is also about the circumstances in which the ordinarily poor became very poor, either temporarily or permanently.

The second obstacle facing a history of African poverty is the inadequacy of the sources. This is true in any continent: the poor leave only sporadic traces in the record. In Africa the problem is doubly difficult because literacy was rare until modern times. The impressions of poverty to be gathered from oral traditions and from generalised descriptions by foreign observers can be seriously misleading.[11] More reliable are the incidental references to the poor in contemporary or near-contemporary records: Ethiopian hagiographies, Islamic chronicles, missionary letters, travellers' journals, anthropologists' observations, administrators' reports. The list looks impressive and sources for the social history even of the poor are richer in Africa than is often realised, but the subject can be studied seriously only where written sources survive. Moreover, Africa characteristically lacked the charitable institutions whose records have provided much material for the history of poverty in Europe. It happens, too, that this book has been written under circumstances which have made it difficult to study unpublished sources surviving in Africa. It rests largely on published sources and certain documents available in Europe. For this and other reasons, it attempts only to rough out a subject for further study.

The third obstacle to this project is the widespread belief that until recently there were no poor in Africa, because economic differentiation was slight, resources were freely available, and the 'extended family' supported its less fortunate members. Only with the coming of colonial rule, market economies, and urbanisation, so it is often claimed, did things begin to fall apart. This 'myth of Merrie Africa'[12] was widely held during the colonial period. 'The rules and regulations of every African Community leave no ground for idle women, prostitutes or vagabonds, and create no possibility for the existence of waifs and strays', a Lagos newspaper explained in 1913. 'No Barnado's Homes, no Refuge for the Destitute grace the cities; because the conditions producing them are absent.'[13] Black South Africans often agreed:

> There were no poor and rich; the haves helped those who were in want. No man starved because he had no food; no child cried for milk because its parents did not have milk cows; no orphan and old person starved because there was nobody to look after them. No, these things were unknown in ancient Bantu society.[14]

White South Africans, colonial officials, and anthropologists widely accepted this view and transmitted it to nationalist intellectuals and international agencies. The United Nations Regional Adviser on Social Welfare Policy and Training, Economic Commission for Africa, explained in 1972:

> In rural Africa, the extended family and the clan assume the responsibility for all services for their members, whether social or economic. People live in closely organized groups and willingly accept communal obligations for mutual support. Individuals satisfy their need for social and economic security merely by being attached to one of these groups. The sick, the aged and children are all cared for by the extended family. In this type of community, nobody can be labelled as poor because the group usually shares what they have. There is no competition, no insecurity, no big ambitions, no unemployment and thus people are mentally healthy. Deviation or abnormal behaviour is almost absent.[15]

When expressed in so simplistic a form, this view of the African past or present is scarcely worth refuting. Yet there is a more penetrating claim that poverty existed but was relatively rare in pre-colonial Africa. The most important statement is Professor Jack Goody's attempt to isolate the main differences between African societies and those of pre-industrial Europe and Asia. Generally, so he has argued, Africa lacked stratified classes with distinct subcultures, because it lacked the plough, intensive agriculture, literacy, and world religions, but possessed ample land and practised exogamous polygyny.[16] Since 'poverty ... implies the opposite, riches, in the same way that slavery implies freedom',[17] poverty was generally absent from these unstratified societies, along with such ancillary phenomena as asceticism, religious charity, and systematic begging.[18] Only those exceptional regions – notably Ethiopia and perhaps the Central Sudan – which did have intensive agriculture, literacy, and world religions also possessed stratified subcultures and, by implication, conditions breeding numerous poor.[19] This book neither challenges Goody's general analysis of Africa's distinctiveness nor disputes that both differentiation and poverty were especially overt in Ethiopia and the Central Sudan. Rather, it argues that in normal circumstances the forms of poverty existing there had little to do with technology, landownership, intensive agriculture, or even (in a direct sense) the pattern of social stratification, although these did affect the behaviour of the poor. The point is that the nature and causes of poverty in pre-colonial Africa – and indeed most of Africa to this day – were not those implied either by Goody's analysis or by those of historians who have written on the subject.[20] This explains why very poor people existed widely in pre-colonial Africa, not only in Ethiopia and the Central Sudan. It also explains the manner in which poverty has changed in Africa during the twentieth century.

In order to introduce this argument and the main themes in the history of the African poor it is useful to compare their experience with that of the poor in Europe and other continents. Two initial distinctions are valuable. One is Dr Gutton's dichotomy of structural poverty, which is the long-term poverty of individuals due to their personal or social circumstances, and conjunctural poverty, which is the temporary poverty into which ordinarily self-sufficient people may be thrown by crisis.[21] The second distinction is between the structural poverty characteristic of societies with relatively ample resources, especially land, and that characteristic of societies where such resources are scarce. In land-rich societies the very poor are characteristically those who lack access to the labour needed to exploit land – both their own labour (perhaps because they are incapacitated, elderly, or young) and the labour of others (because they are bereft of family or other support). In land-scarce societies the very poor continue to include such people but also include those among the able-bodied who lack access to land (or other resources) and are unable to sell their labour power at a price sufficient to meet their minimum needs. The history of the structural poor in Western Europe during the medieval and early modern periods turns on this distinction. Until perhaps the twelfth century Europe was a land-rich continent which nevertheless contained many structural poor, who were predominantly the weak, especially those bereft of labour. 'The poor of North Italy, in the tenth century', it has been written, 'are the unfortunate, the disinherited, "widows, orphans, captives, the defeated, the infirm, blind, crippled, feeble". There is no poor class but men in a situation of poverty.'[22] Landless labourers with varying degrees of freedom certainly existed in many areas, but they were generally absorbed into the labour-hungry rural economy.[23] During the twelfth and thirteenth centuries, by contrast, Western Europe's growing population pressed upon the available land in many regions. To the incapacitated poor were added men who lacked viable landholdings and could not sell their labour.[24] Many migrated to towns, where by the early fourteenth century wages were so low that even men in regular employment might not be able to support themselves and their families.[25]

During the fourteenth century Europe's population declined again and the pressure on resources eased. Two centuries later, however, demographic growth once more transformed the pattern of poverty. In England, for example,

> In the villages and towns of the fifteenth and early sixteenth centuries, poverty had not been regarded as a major social problem. It was limited in extent and generally the result of particular misfortune – the death of a spouse or parent, sickness or injury – or else a phase in the life cycle, notably youth or old age ... By the end of the sixteenth century and still more by the mid seventeenth century, the poor were no longer the destitute victims of misfortune or old age, but a substantial proportion of the population living in constant danger of destitution, many of them full-time wage labourers. In both town and country a permanent proletariat had emerged, collectively designated 'the poor'.[26]

In later eighteenth-century France, similarly, the incapacitated still formed a large proportion of the poor, but observers were more concerned by the poverty of the able-bodied who lacked land, work, or wages adequate to support the dependants who were partly responsible for their poverty. Whereas in early medieval Europe the most common beggar had been aged or blind, in later eighteenth-century France, by one account, the most common beggar was a child.[27]

This transition from land-rich to land-scarce poverty has taken place in other continents. Most poverty in Asia today is due to land shortage, unemployment, and low wages. Poverty in India is closely associated with large families.[28] Only in Europe, however, has the history of the transition been written systematically. This book is a first attempt to chart it in Africa. It argues that the structural poor of pre-colonial Africa were mainly those lacking access to labour. Because poverty took this form, attempts to relate it to landholding systems, agricultural technology, or world religions have little relevance. Historical record of those lacking labour in pre-colonial societies is uneven, partly because vulnerability to misfortune varied with time and place, partly because mechanisms to prevent such unfortunates from falling into extreme poverty varied, and partly because the availability of sources is uneven. Yet the structural poor of this kind appear to have been numerous everywhere. They appear most frequently in folktales, which often identified a category of weak individuals – the old, the handicapped, and the very young – who lived in destitution but triumphed over the strong, usually by magical means. To help such unfortunates might bring praise and fortune to the helper.[29]

By contrast, structural poverty resulting from land scarcity appeared only slowly in Africa. This gave the history of poverty there its special character when compared with Europe or Asia. That Africa was a land-rich continent is a commonplace of African studies, but its implications for the poor have been overlooked. Although historians have claimed that certain pre-colonial rulers used political power to deprive subjects of access to land, thereby reducing them to poverty, the sources for these claims are questionable. There is stronger evidence for landlessness due to personal misfortune and for poverty resulting from lack of cattle in societies heavily dependent upon them. Extensive landlessness first emerged in South Africa during the eighteenth century. In colonial Africa it was limited to certain areas of ruthless alienation or unusual population density. Both there and in the south, however, land scarcity was slow to breed extreme poverty because many of the landless could sell their labour at wages which at least ensured subsistence. Only slowly during the twentieth century did Africa – and chiefly southern Africa – see numerous able-bodied men lacking land, work, or wages sufficient to maintain physical efficiency. Only slowly did possession of a family, rather than lack of one, become a cause of structural poverty. By the 1980s southern Africa had certainly entered a resource crisis as acute as that of thirteenth-century Europe. Even there, however, the new poor had only been added to the older category of incapacitated and unprotected. Structural poverty has been a cumulative phenomenon which has displayed the same continuity over long periods as in Europe.[30]

Conjunctural poverty, by contrast, has exhibited greater change. In pre-colonial Africa, as in Europe until the seventeenth century, the chief cause of conjunctural poverty was climatic and political insecurity which might culminate in mass famine mortality. It was at these moments that resources were acutely scarce and exclusion from them by political or other means became the chief determinant of poverty. With time, however, these crises grew less common. In England the last famine to cause mass deaths occurred in 1623, in France early in the eighteenth century.[31] Devastating famine mortality generally disappeared from Western Europe during the 1740s, from India (with one exception) at the beginning of the twentieth century, and from China somewhat later in this century.[32] It was not that food shortages ceased, but that they ceased to kill great numbers. This book argues that twentieth-century Africa experienced a similar change in conjunctural poverty, although unevenly and incompletely.[33] The chief reasons for it were broad increases in wealth, diversified sources of income, more effective government, better transport, wider markets, and improved hygiene and medicine.[34] The cost, in Africa as at times elsewhere, was that epidemic starvation for all but the rich gave way to endemic undernutrition for the very poor.[35] Conjunctural and structural poverty converged.

As in understanding the nature of poverty, so in studying the means by which the poor survived, much is to be learned from historians of Europe and Asia. They have emphasised four means of survival. Their sources have attracted them especially to institutions which the wider society created either to care for the poor, to confine them, or to help them escape from poverty – in Europe the history of institutions broadly followed that sequence.[36] Informal and individual charity offered a second means of survival.[37] A third was organisation by the poor themselves, either by underworld groupings[38] or by the Untouchable communities which characterised Asian poverty.[39] Finally, historians have stressed that the poor relied less on institutions or organisations than on their own efforts, 'devious, ugly, cruel, and dishonest as these might be'.[40]

These means of survival existed also in Africa, but the balance among them differed. A scarcity of formal institutions characterised poverty there. Even where they existed, as in Ethiopia and the Islamic regions of West Africa, they were secondary to an individual charity attuned to the personalised character of mobile, colonising societies. Where institutional provision existed outside Christian or Islamic influence, it often sought to conceal the poverty of beneficiaries. The scarcity of institutions not only makes the history of charity difficult to recover in Africa but also meant that Africans had, and often still have, much hostility to institutional care for the poor. Informal benevolence, on the other hand, did flourish in some societies little touched by Islam or Christianity, implying indigenous evolution of the idea that the poor merited special sympathy – a notion virtually absent from Greece or Rome.[41] Organisations created by the very poor were rare in pre-colonial Africa and in the twentieth-century countryside, although more common in modern towns. Although stigmatised groups of untouchables are often held to be associated with world religions,[42] they existed in several parts of Africa but were a far smaller proportion of the poor than were the Untouchables of India or Japan.[43]

Given the scarcity of institutions and organisations, the African poor sought their survival in two directions. One was the family. Although much nonsense has been written about African families as universal providers of limitless generosity, it is nevertheless true that families were and are the main sources of support for the African poor, as much for the young unemployed of modern cities as for the orphans of the past. In several African languages the common word for 'poor' – *umphawi* in the Chewa language of modern Malawi, for example – implies lack of kin and friends,[44] while the weak household, bereft of able-bodied male labour, has probably been the most common source of poverty throughout Africa's recoverable history. Equally important, however, is the fact that Africans lived in different kinds of families, from the Yoruba compound with scores of related residents to the elementary households of Buganda. Each kind of family had its particular points of weakness and exuded its particular categories of unsupported poor – orphans in one case, barren women in another, childless elders in a third. Moreover, family structure was not an immutable ethnic characteristic but could change to meet changing needs. The intimate connection between poverty and family structure has been neglected by historians of Europe and may be Africa's chief contribution to the comparative history of the poor.

Yet in another respect the African and European poor were entirely at one. Both relied for their survival chiefly on their own efforts. Like pre-industrial Europe, Africa was and is a harsh world for the weak. By protecting themselves from famine, by exploiting the resources of the bush, by hawking or begging or stealing, by endurance or industry or guile, by the resourcefulness of the blind or the courage of the cripple, by the ambition of the young or the patience of the old – by all these means the African poor survived in their harsh world. These are their inheritance amidst the harshness of the present.

2

Christian Ethiopia

Ethiopia to the end of the nineteenth century is the logical place to begin a history of the African poor. Its hagiographies of saints and chronicles of kings are early written sources of a quality unique in Africa. Its Christian inheritance facilitates comparison with both medieval Europe and the rest of Africa, illuminating the distinctively African and the distinctively Christian elements in Ethiopia's pattern of poverty. Such comparison reveals that the Ethiopian poor were not unique products of a social order unique in Africa – plough-using, stratified, Christian, literate – but were chiefly the poor to be found in any pre-industrial society rich in land. In the long term it should be possible to write a true history of the Ethiopian poor, showing how their identity and experience changed between the thirteenth and the nineteenth centuries, but this will need a knowledge of Ethiopian languages not available here. Instead, this chapter indicates the broad character of the poor and their means of survival over some 700 years as a basis for comparison and change in sub-Saharan Africa as a whole.

The Ethiopian poor were innumerable and ubiquitous. In 1520 Francisco Alvares, the Portuguese priest who wrote the first European account of Ethiopia, described 'more than 3,000 cripples, blind men, and lepers' at a miraculous shrine close to the ancient capital at Axum.[1] Although he and other Portuguese visitors came from a society familiar with extreme poverty, they were appalled by its prevalence in Ethiopia. 'Their Charity to the Poor', Father Jerome Lobo observed in the seventeenth century, 'may be said to exceed the proper Bounds, that prudence ought to set to it, for it contributes to encourage great numbers of Beggars, which are a great Annoyance to the whole Kingdom, and . . . afford more exercise to a Christian's Patience, than his Charity.'[2] Nineteenth-century Europeans, less accustomed to mass poverty, experienced in Ethiopia the fascinated revulsion recorded by the extravagant Cornwallis Harris at a religious festival in the early 1840s:

> In the adjacent enclosure a crowd of horrible and revolting objects formed

> the most miserable of spectacles. The palsied, the leprous, the scrofulous, and those in the most inveterate stages of dropsy and elephantiasis, were mingled with mutilated wretches who had been bereft of hands, feet, eyes, and tongue, by the sanguinary tyrants of Northern Abyssinia, and who bore with them the severed portions, in order that their bodies might be perfect at the Day of Resurrection. The old, the halt and the lame, the deaf, the noseless, and the dumb, the living dead in every shape and form, were still streaming through the narrow door; limbless trunks were borne onwards upon the spectres of asses and horses, and the blind, in long Indian file, rolling their ghastly eyeballs, and touching each the shoulder of his sightless neighbour, groped their way towards the hum of voices, to add new horrors to the appalling picture.[3]

The important point about these descriptions is that in Ethiopia, as in early medieval Europe, the very poor were chiefly the incapacitated. Prominent among them were cripples, who were frequently described as paralytics and may often have been victims of the poliomyelitis which in the early 1960s was found to have attacked 85 per cent of infants in Addis Ababa.[4] The healing of cripples was a miracle often ascribed to Ethiopian holy men. 'There was a shrine of our father Takla Haymanot', it is recorded of the greatest thirteenth-century saint,

> and on the day of his commemoration a woman who was a paralytic came there to beg for alms; now her head and neck were bent down to her knees, and she was unable to turn either to the right or to the left. Now she could not drink water from out of a cup, but only from a plate, and as she was drinking, our father Takla Haymanot laid hold upon her head and neck, and drew them back behind her with an unseen hand, and her body was made straight.[5]

The same account, possibly written about 1515, describes the saint visiting the Wifat district of Shoa: 'They collected all the sick folk who were with them, and their numbers were thus:– dumb folk, twelve; paralytics, thirteen; epileptics, seven; blind, ten.'[6] The dumb were occasional beneficiaries of miracles,[7] while the prevalence of eye diseases struck not only Alvares and Harris but twentieth-century doctors.[8] Another incapacitating malady was epilepsy, known as 'the slaves' disease',[9] which was thought infectious and greatly feared. In the twentieth century epileptics not cured by spirit exorcism 'are almost certain to end up as demented and disfigured beggars around the churchyards and cemeteries'.[10]

Leprosy sufferers formed a special category among the poor. The disease was less common than in many parts of Africa. It was concentrated, as is usual, among the poorer people of isolated rural regions like Gojjam,[11] but its victims tended to leave their homes for centres of wealth and population. Many lived as beggars, often clustering into distinct communities.[12] They had their own patron saint, Gebre Christos, the son of a rich king who gave away his wealth and prayed successfully for leprosy in order to suffer like Christ.[13] Ethiopians viewed leprosy with ambivalence. They thought it incurable.[14] The church taught that it was a punishment for sin or a test of faith: there is a twentieth-century account of monks refusing treatment because 'The more miserable their bodies the purer their souls would grow.'[15] Other sufferers at that time blamed heredity, sorcery, evil spirits, or breach of taboos. In Gojjam leprosy was apparently thought hereditary in certain families with whom others did not intermarry, but sufferers were not otherwise isolated because their complaint was not considered contagious.[16] Others were less certain and combined a degree of avoidance[17] with a charity which won European admiration. 'There are many lepers in this country', Alvares reported, 'and they do not live away from the people; they live all together; there are many people who, out of their devotion, wash them and tend their sores with their hands.'[18]

In early medieval Europe the structural poor included many who were incapacitated by old age, but in Ethiopia, although the unreliable Harris mentioned them, there is otherwise no evidence that old age as such caused destitution, perhaps because age was much respected and there were institutions to which the elderly could retreat.[19] Widowhood, on the other hand, was a common consequence of insecurity and early marriage which led many women into poverty. During persecution in the 1620s, Portuguese priests were 'continually crouded with Widows and Orphans, that subsisted upon our Charity'.[20] As elsewhere in Africa, childless women were probably especially to be pitied; modern study has found a positive correlation between female sterility and conspicuous psychiatric morbidity, while the helplessness of unmarried women is a recurrent theme of modern Amharic literature.[21] Orphaned or abandoned children existed, as the Portuguese priests and later travellers found. In Adwa in 1818 Nathaniel Pearce recorded several children abandoned at rich men's doors by women who hoped to reclaim them after escaping from poverty, not always with success.[22] By European standards, however, such children were rare[23] and it is striking that the family poverty so prevalent in early modern Europe appears to have been absent from Ethiopia, except during famine. 'Curiously with patriarchal people living in communities', a British traveller wrote during the 1890s, 'a large family is a source of wealth; just the reverse to what it is in England.'[24] What worried Ethiopians was not that children were born but that so many died. A missionary who had visited Jerusalem, the earthly paradise of Ethiopian imaginations, was asked 'whether it was true that children did not die there'.[25]

Ethiopia's poor also differed from their European contemporaries in that some belonged to stigmatised, endogamous groups more common in Asia. Among those who lacked 'clean bones' were craftsmen. 'Literally spit on, cursed at, and considered lesser men',[26] they were often suspected of sorcery and forbidden to own land, but were not necessarily poorer than their neighbours. Several rural communities had simiiar outcaste groups performing tasks considered degrading.[27] Their status had some parallels among small ethnic groups on the edges of the Christian kingdom who were reduced to dependence as it expanded. By 1900 Addis Ababa contained depressed slave communities from many southern groups, supplementing the 'Shanqala' from the western lowlands who were the main historic source of slaves.[28] Some slaves held high positions of trust and they cannot all be numbered among the very poor.[29] Rather, a distinct lower stratum existed among them, at least by the early twentieth century:

> Among the rich, and especially in the palaces of the Negus, the Rases, and other important chiefs, there is a class of especially disinherited slaves who are designated by the soubriquet *tchintcha-achker*, 'servants of the waste-land'.[30] They have hardly any share in the affluence of the house. Subject to the most degrading tasks, they are despised by all, even by their more fortunate companions. They clothe and feed themselves as they can. What everyone else disdains is abandoned to them. They do, however, receive a regular distribution of grain. They are the dregs of the class: infirm, aged, sick of disease or from birth.[31]

That slaves should have included a destitute stratum which exactly paralleled the very poor stratum among freemen supports the hypothesis that incapacitation was the chief reason for severe structural poverty in this society.

Visitors to Ethiopia could not escape the structural poor. They might also be so unfortunate as to witness one of the natural catastrophes which temporarily reduced ordinary Ethiopians to conjunctural poverty. Famines were the most common. Most were due to drought, although locust invasions caused eleven recorded famines between 1647 and 1900, while one, in 1611, resulted from excessive rain and cold.[32] Perhaps the most terrible, in 1889–92, was chiefly due to cattle plague. Menelik II's secretary described it:

> All the large stock had been exterminated by sickness; and, since this was an unprecedented occurrence, the people, instead of hoeing the ground, remained inactive. Hence the following year . . . a general famine broke out. Since there was no grain, people began to eat roots. Believing that the King's house was bursting with grain, the people arrived from the four corners of the land . . . and the town of Entotto was full of the poor and famished.
>
> Atie Menelik and the Echege,[33] unable to endure the sight of so much suffering, had a large rectangular shed constructed to the right of the church of St Mary of Entotto. All the poor found a refuge there. They were so numerous that the porches of the three churches of St Mary, St Raguel, and St Uriel, the constructions raised on the tombs, and the environs of the neighbouring houses overflowed with unfortunates . . . To acquire merit, leading men each took five or six to feed at his home.
>
> At this time, bread was cut and enclosed in serving baskets; beans, corn and peas were put together in iron pots where they were cooked. It was all served in large baskets and the stewards of the King and the Echege caused this food to be carried out and themselves distributed it in equal portions. But, as food in times of famine can scarcely conserve life, the number of those who died exceeded that of the survivors . . .
>
> Seeing that the herds were destroyed and that the famine still raged, the King said: 'The cattle have completely disappeared, and now, until the Lord turns His face towards us, I have prepared for myself a hoe to dig the ground

> and an axe to cut wood, in order to give you an example.' He then sent several small hoes and axes to King Takla Haymanot, Ras Mikael, and Ras Walie, telling them: 'Imitate me!' . . .
>
> But the famine still continued. People ate the flesh of horses and donkeys.[34] Men ate one another. A woman of Wollo ate her own child. In another region named Ensaro a woman ate seven children. The wild animals, for their part, took control everywhere. Lions, leopards, hyenas came to devour men where they stood . . .
>
> Since the famine and plague continued to rage, the King and the Echege passed day and night in the prayer house raised beside the reception house, appealing to Mary, in the company of their friends the monks . . .
>
> In speaking of this famine, we have wished to say that the plague ravaged the whole country, but we must add that at the court, as before, nothing was lacking.[35]

This account illustrates the recurrent features of Ethiopian famine behaviour: initial resort to famine foods; abandonment of homes when local resources were exhausted; convergence on churches, monasteries, houses of great men, and especially the court; wholesale but ultimately inadequate distribution of relief in expectation of spiritual reward; the king's recourse to prayer and symbolic encouragement of self-help; the collapse of men's control of nature and themselves; and the fact that even so widespread a catastrophe weighed most heavily on the poor. Although other accounts state that in 1889–92 even the court experienced austerity,[36] nevertheless certain categories were especially vulnerable during famine. There were regional differences: deaths in 1889–92 were most numerous in the dry lowlands,[37] while the arid lands of Tigre in the north suffered repeatedly.[38] There were occupational differences: herdsmen suffered especially when their cattle died or could no longer be exchanged for grain, as did those who had recently adopted agriculture and were still unskilled in it.[39] And there were social differences: children were often abandoned or sold during famine, for their own good, and missionaries found that the aged, the infirm, and the very poor who could not take the road to church or capital were most in need.[40] In Shoa during 1831 the price of grain rose until only the rich could buy it, 'whilst the wretched poor were left to die'.[41]

Not only did the poor throng public places in good times and overflow them in bad, but Ethiopians placed poverty at the centre of their culture. Fasting, self-mortification, and charity occupied quite special places in Ethiopian Christianity. 'Abyssinians consider fasting to be the essence of religion', wrote an acute observer, for ordinary Christians were supposed to fast (usually until midday) on 165 days of the year, while for zealots the figure might rise to 250 days.[42] The self-mortification of ascetics, although similar to that throughout the Eastern Church, astonished even Portuguese priests, themselves no sybarites. 'The Life of a Religious among them is a perpetual Abstinence', wrote Jerome Lobo, while Alvares tried a hermit's diet and pronounced it 'the most dismal food in the world'.[43] Even the black

Jews of Ethiopia, the Falasha, contrary to Jewish custom, had borrowed monastic and eremitic practices from Christians.[44]

The problem is why the poor were so numerous and visible in Ethiopia and why poverty was so central to its culture. The most suggestive answer lies in Professor Goody's argument that Ethiopia 'lies geographically inside the African continent but culturally outside', sharing with pre-industrial Europe certain cultural features which bred both a poor stratum and a reaction against conspicuous privilege by elite members who instead practised charity or asceticism. These cultural features were the plough, a large agricultural surplus, wide differences of landownership, a culturally distinct ruling class, literacy, and a world religion.[45] The difficulty with this argument is that in Ethiopia, as in early medieval Europe, the very poor were impoverished less by lack of access to land than by lack of access to labour: they were chiefly those incapacitated and bereft of care, as the preceding description has shown. Only in times of disaster did Ethiopia see the destitute families which characterised the land-scarce poverty of early modern Europe. Tigre was a partial exception, for its density of population struck early travellers, its poor seem to have been most numerous, and by the nineteenth century it contained paid agricultural labourers and exported them to other regions.[46] Able-bodied poor certainly existed, for a homily attributed to emperor Zara Yaqob (1434–68) distinguished 'the poor and needy in worldly goods who, besides their poverty, are sick in their whole body and feeble in all their limbs' from 'those who are poor in worldly goods but healthy in their bodies, who even possess nothing whatever . . . they stand in service to the rich'.[47] Almost nothing is known of the second category, but, as elsewhere in Africa, they may have been victims of insecurity and personal misfortune rather than of lack of access to resources, given that direct evidence of land shortage is absent even in Tigre, while in the Amhara highlands landlessness was rare even in the twentieth century.[48] Ethiopian noblemen were not primarily landlords but tribute-consumers. They probably took a larger proportion of the crop than was normally extracted from African cultivators, but much less than in land-scarce societies. Professor Crummey has estimated that highland peasants in the eighteenth and nineteenth centuries may on average have lost at least 30 per cent of their produce by exactions of all kinds, but he has stressed that their *average* loss was not the point, for the important thing was that they lost their produce irregularly, through the random exactions of the powerful.[49] As everywhere in Africa, and perhaps also in early medieval Europe,[50] insecurity was more important than land pressure as a cause of poverty. The insecurity could take the form of great natural disasters or it could be the recurrent physical insecurity of a turbulent and violent society.

Armies were the curse of the Ethiopian peasantry. 'The Poverty of the Souldiers impoverishes the Countries through which they march', Ludolphus recorded in the seventeenth century. 'For in regard it is a difficult thing to carry Provisions over such steep and rugged Mountains, and long wayes, they take by force what is not freely given them; and by that means lay wast their own Countries no less than their Enemies: whereby the poor Countrey people are constrain'd to turn Souldiers, and so taught to deal by others, as they were dealt with themselves.' The Emperor Tewodros put it more tersely two hundred years later: 'Soldiers eat; peasants provide.'[51] Repeated depredations discouraged agriculture or the accumulation of famine reserves. They also bred intense anxiety. During the 1840s a traveller was directed to lodge with an elderly widow:

> She half in her dotage, mistaking us for soldiers or robbers, set up such piercing cries, that the whole population was in a short time about our ears. The matter was soon understood, and the old crone's fears were in some measure explained away; but she was still anything from happy, and I felt pity for her, as, remaining near the hut, she kept prowling about on some excuse or other, and (as she thought unobserved) making off with sundry little articles of her property, which she had carefully concealed in holes of the thatch or elsewhere, and then returning for others, talking to herself and sobbing all the while in a most piteous manner.[52]

A twentieth-century student of the drought-free but much-pillaged Gurage people noted their unnecessarily labour-intensive agricultural practices, their obsessive hoarding of food, the austerity of their public eating habits, and the massive clandestine feasts by which poor men exorcised the *awre* spirit whose symptoms – loss of appetite, nausea, and stomach pains – suggested intense anxiety.[53] Nor was insecurity confined to warfare. The *shefta* or bandit was more common in Ethiopia than elsewhere in sub-Saharan Africa. Although often admired for defending their honour or property and defying authority, most were led by dissident noblemen who used banditry as a means of political competition and preyed ruthlessly on the poor. 'For most peasants', a recent study concludes, '*sheftenat* was a burden of tribute and fear.'[54] 'O God', bandits were said to pray, 'give us the property of old weak men, the property of the blind and limping, the property of orphans and women, the property of him who has no power and who does not remember, the property of him, who curses [but does not act].'[55]

Insecurity helps to explain why the very poor were numerous in Ethiopia, but it does not explain why they were more visible than in other African societies which also suffered insecurity. For this there were perhaps two reasons. One lay in the family structure of the dominant Amhara people.[56] They were a bilateral people who reckoned descent and inheritance from both father and mother. Instead of being bound into a corporate descent group, each individual therefore had a range of social identities and rights from which he could choose the most advantageous. Bilateral societies are characteristically individualistic and mobile, both socially and geographically. This was so among the Amhara. At marriage, Amhara commonly left their parents' homes to establish a new elementary household wherever their manifold claims to inherit land could be realised most conveniently.

As a proverb said, 'A fire and relatives warm best from a distance.'[57] Extended kinship ties had little significance, except among noblemen.[58] Observers of twentieth-century towns were to find that the Gurage were the only Ethiopian people with an extended family system which assisted its members.[59] Like other bilateral peoples in Africa, therefore, Amhara who were threatened by poverty found little support from kinsmen. Their vulnerability was intensified by marriage patterns. Amhara married young: boys at about eighteen, in the early nineteenth century, and girls at fourteen or fifteen. Even in Alvares' day marriage was unstable and divorce common.[60] This probably bred numerous people bereft of support: divorced (especially barren) women, childless widows, solitary aged men. It could also have bred numerous abandoned children, as was the case in the twentieth century, but in earlier periods children were said generally to remain with one or other parent.[61] That Amhara family structure provided unusually little support for the poor is suggested by the fact that European travellers rarely eulogised family solidarity (as was common elsewhere in Africa) and gave the impression that the poor were exceptionally solitary.

Yet the main reason why the Ethiopian poor were so visible was probably not that they were especially numerous but that they clustered together where they could be noticed. In studies of European poverty it is a truism that the poor were made in the countryside but seen in the town.[62] The same principle applied in Ethiopia. Its hagiographies show that poor people abounded in the countryside,[63] but Ethiopia was by African standards a large-scale society and possessed institutions which attracted the poor from wide areas and made them visible. Leprosy was most common in the remote highlands, but its victims were *noticed* in towns, at healing shrines, at festivals, or wherever the emperor might be.[64] Handicapped people, who in many African societies would have remained unseen in their villages, were led in Ethiopia to display their sufferings in order to benefit from Christian charity. They were not necessarily more numerous than in Africa's small-scale societies, only more visible. This point is at the heart of the history of the African poor.

For the present, however, it has been argued that the centrality of the poor in Ethiopian culture was due not only (and perhaps not primarily) to the social distribution of resources, but also to insecurity (both climatic and political), family structure, social scale, and the existence of institutions and charitable practices. These practices and institutions are best considered from the viewpoint of the poor.

Poor people have two strategies of survival. They can struggle for independence, scraping a living by any available means. Or they can struggle for dependence, seeking the favour of the fortunate. In practice, of course, many alternate between the two strategies, which are not entirely distinct. But for analytical purposes it is well to consider them separately.

In Africa as a whole, as in Europe, the poor survived chiefly by their own efforts and ingenuity. In Ethiopia, however, it is the lack of evidence of such enterprise that is striking. There was, of course, the land, and one must assume that it was the first recourse of those who could work it. Yet the very poor were usually either incapacitated or had been ruined by agricultural disaster. Wage-labour – a crucial resource during famine in twentieth-century Africa – was virtually confined to Tigre until the mid nineteenth century.[65] An able-bodied man could often find employment as a soldier, but many of the poor were not able-bodied. A gifted man, even if blind, might become a bard or remembrancer, but most of the poor were not gifted. They could indeed exploit bush produce, for there has been an intimate connection throughout African history between the poor and the wild.[66] In 1891, for example, a missionary watched hundreds of famine victims 'spread into the villages, carrying a little wood, water, straw, hay, to sell them and buy grain'.[67] In Addis Ababa at that time urchins made a living by collecting cakes of dung from the streets to sell as fuel, 'and you can see poor old women, Galla or Shanqala, who carry them on their backs, in high pyramids, to sell them in the market'.[68] Old women also supplied Addis Ababa with much of its firewood – the environs of Ethiopian towns were deforested even in the 1620s – while surrounding peasants brought in their food crops and the women of the lower classes sold bread in the streets each evening.[69] By the 1840s there were also women obliged to subsist by prostitution, in addition to a long-established pattern of more prestigious courtesanship.[70]

Yet the striking point is how few were the urban pickings available to the poor, for Ethiopia was almost uniquely bereft of substantial towns. 'In all the country', Alvares reported in the 1520s, 'there is no town which exceeds 1,600 households, and of these there are few, and there are no walled towns or castles, but villages without number.'[71] Gondar, established as the imperial capital in 1636, may have housed up to 80,000 people at its peak, when one of its quarters was a refuge for courtesans, outlaws, *déclassés*, wandering monks and nuns, and the indigent of all kinds.[72] By the early nineteenth century it was much decayed, however, and probably the only other town with over 10,000 people at that time was the Muslim commercial centre at Harar.[73] Substantial urbanisation began only with the foundation of Addis Ababa in 1886.

Thus the Ethiopian poor lacked many means of independent survival which towns provided in other cultures. This may partly explain why they relied so heavily on begging. In polite Amhara society it was shameful to solicit a gift, but the ritualised context of begging appears to have dissipated the shame, so that a man with 'clean bones' would rather beg than practise a despised trade.[74] This was one means by which Christianity robbed poverty of some of the shame which caused it to be hidden and disguised in other African societies. Ethiopia's beggars were extraordinarily diverse. At their core were the incapacitated and largely immobile, such as those described unsympathetically at the Shoan court as 'two rows of noisy beggars, male and female, old, middle-aged, and young; who, leprous, scrofulous, and maimed, exhibited the most disgusting sores, and implored charity for the sake of Christ and the Virgin Mary'.[75] These permanent beggars were supplemented at intervals by the victims of famine and insecurity, as a visitor saw them at Massawa in the early 1830s:

> The number of beggars is relatively very large and most of them perish from hunger or other distress. To be precise, they are mostly people from the neighbouring mountains who have lost their cattle, their sole source of income, through some robbery or sickness, and have come to Massawa to earn themselves the most necessary means of subsistence by carrying firewood or drinking-water. However, since foodstuffs, as imported articles, are rather dear here and great competition exists among the people engaged in any kind of work, their earnings are not sufficient to satisfy their hunger. If then one becomes sick or weak, he can maintain himself only by begging, but gifts come so sparsely that day by day the unfortunate grows leaner and loses strength, until at last starvation at a street-corner ends his life.[76]

Generally, however, Ethiopians impressed observers by their generosity to beggars. 'They sit at every street corner', it was remarked in Addis Ababa in 1906, 'and I noted that the natives seemed rather generously disposed towards them. The people going to the market . . . rarely passed these beggars without dropping something at their feet; it might be a few sticks of firewood, something to eat, or whatever they were taking to the market.'[77] Food was the normal, but not invariable, gift. Generosity could be stylised:

> Sometimes, when the mendicant goes from one house to another in a country which he does not know, he is conducted to the neighbouring house; thence he is led again to another house, and thus in sequence to the exit from the village.
>
> The rich give not only dollars but, if they meet a leper on their road, they may even be seen to make him a present of their mule with the saddle and all the harness.[78]

Emperor Tewodros was remembered for distributing horses to leprosy sufferers.[79]

The Ethiopian church distinguished the deserving poor from able-bodied vagrants. The *Fetha Nagast* ('Law of the Kings'), a Coptic legal code in use in Ethiopia by the seventeenth century, outlined an elaborate machinery to ensure that charity was given only to 'those who truly have need'; to give alms to others, it warned, was to rob the poor.[80] Ethiopians ignored the distinction. 'It is the Abyssinian doctrine to give, according to your means, to all that come, without distinction', a careful observer wrote in the 1840s.[81] Consequently, although 'sturdy beggars' were probably less numerous than among West African Muslims, they were nevertheless common. They included students at religious schools, often peasant boys far from their homes who lived by begging food in the villages, crying, 'For the sake of the name of Mary, for the sake of God the generous, please remember (to give me) my daily bread.'[82] For them begging was a spiritual training, as in the Islamic and Buddhist traditions. 'The life of mendicant students is a model of comradeship based on humility and concern for one another's welfare', a twentieth-century teacher has explained. '... Students are taught to practice humility and hospitality, to wash the feet of the "guest of God". They visit the old and the feeble with food and clothing; they visit the sick and those confined in prisons, and thus perform the Six Commandments of the Holy Gospels.'[83] Their teachers might also be mendicants, as were many poor monks and priests, whose training for ordination included a year or more wandering from church to church, sleeping in churchyards or the open, and begging their living. Other churchmen begged through the towns in a quasi-ceremonial way at festivals.[84] Yet no special merit seems to have attached to charity given specifically to a churchman, nothing comparable to that attending gifts to Indian ascetics, for in Ethiopian thought the virtue lay simply in the generosity. Gifts might as well be made to the servant who had broken a household utensil and was driven out to beg until he had replaced it, to the manacled debtor obliged to beg until he could repay his creditors, or to the murderer who begged his blood-money in the market, crying, 'For my life! For my life!'[85]

Because Ethiopia had no inns, villagers were legally obliged to entertain passing strangers, a provision eagerly exploited by vagabonds.[86] 'The beggar's trade has its ruses', visitors reported,

> and travelling deacons know them thoroughly. When the heat distresses them and they see an attractive village, they hide in the neighbourhood to await sunset, because they know that travellers who stop early are accused of idleness and receive hospitality only with difficulty. As night approaches, they cover their clothes with dust and, feigning to be harassed by fatigue, they present themselves before the villagers, who are not always deceived by their stratagem.[87]

Minstrels and praise-singers were a special category whose entertainment value was ambiguously joined with moral blackmail of the wealthy; they were classed as women and were the most despised group in Ethiopia's social hierarchy.[88] The strangest beggar of all was the *lalibäla*, who was descended from a leprosy sufferer and could escape the complaint only by begging and singing in the villages before dawn.[89]

The *lalibäla* was notoriously importunate. 'They sometimes even openly plunder in the market', it was reported, '... and generally their insolence is beyond belief.'[90] As in other cultures, begging often contained a latent menace. Leprosy sufferers were said to abuse even a district governor with impunity.[91] 'The pauper may show himself exigent, have menace on his lips and sometimes "daggers in his eyes"', a missionary wrote; 'one gives to him just the same.'[92] One traveller claimed that it was not unusual for a beggar to ride up to a house on horseback and send in his servant to demand alms.[93] Once gratified, however, the mendicant should show humility. A visitor noted that noblemen were expected to eat noisily, beggars with 'unostentatious quietness'.[94] Whatever their approach, beggars couched it in religious terms, asking alms for the sake of God, Mary, St Takla Haymanot, or another saint rather than referring to their infirmities. It is particularly noteworthy that, with the exception of a single reference to an orphan, accounts of Ethiopian mendicants do not appear to mention child beggars (other than religious students) until Addis Ababa was founded, when begging by street urchins became common.[95] This contrast with the prevalence of child beggars in early modern Europe is perhaps further evidence that family poverty due to scarcity of land and employment was not yet common in Ethiopia.

Those among the poor who sought not independence but protection might turn to religious institutions. This did not necessarily mean the Christian church. The *zar* spirit possession cult, which incorporated survivals from Ethiopia's pre-Christian religions, probably provided limited support for some poor people. Little is known of it before the twentieth century, but it attracted many deprived people, especially barren or unhappy women and marginal men with sexual difficulties.[96] In addition to cathartic satisfaction, the cult, especially in the Gondar region, provided initiates with membership of a community. This may have been little material advantage to most, for initiates had to make offerings. The poorest, however, could work off their dues by 'serving the tray', and in the twentieth century it was common for informal 'assistants' – often unattached and impoverished women – to cluster around a cult leader, living in his compound, performing services, spinning cotton, and receiving their subsistence from offerings made by initiates and patients. Occasionally the leader might find employment for a cult-member.[97] Similar informal clientage relationships existed in rural spirit cults outside the Amhara highlands.[98] They were typical of the subtle and disguised means by which Africa's indigenous institutions often provided for the very poor.

Nevertheless, it was chiefly to the Christian church that the very poor turned for religious protection. Parish churches were almost the only meeting-points in the Ethiopian countryside and were very numerous. 'It is not possible to sing in one Church or Monastry without being heard by another, and perhaps by several', Jerome Lobo reported in the 1620s.[99] Churchyards, although haunted by dangerous spirits, were places of refuge for the very poor. Researchers described such a 'churchyard community' in Addis Ababa in 1973. It comprised 97 people living in 55 burial houses, which were mud huts with tin roofs over or around a tomb. Each hut housed either men or women of similar age. There were no young women. Young men, who formed the larger groups, were mostly students. Many men and most women were elderly. Of the 48 residents studied, 45 were sick and 29 were seriously disabled (6 were paralysed, 4 had leprosy, 3 were blind, and 5 had chronic eye diseases). Only 22 had ever married and 15 of those had no living children. One-half had lived in the churchyard for more than ten years. They saw it as a place of security. 'People were mainly dependent on begging: all of the nuns, and the majority of the monks, students and the lay-people', the researchers noted. 'Only 13 of the 32 people who were begging ever left the church-yard for this purpose. The others just stayed inside and went to the gate whenever there was a celebration.'[100] No earlier description of a churchyard community survives, but they certainly existed, for the chronicle of the Emperor Galawdewos (1540–59), written before 1605, records that 'by his power he delivered the captives and the afflicted who dwelt among the tombs', while the account of the famine of 1889–92, quoted earlier, also refers to them.[101] Several early travellers describe the unfortunate making their homes in church porches or on the broad verandahs surrounding the circular churches of central and southern Ethiopia.[102] As in early Christian Europe, these resident poor were expected to attend services and were fed after them. Alvares, in 1520, noted that two of the famous rock churches at Lalibela each had at its entrance 'a good big house, with a bench which goes all round it on the inside', where 'alms are given to the poor, who sit on these benches'.[103] The resident poor were periodically joined at times of danger by whole communities taking refuge in the supposedly inviolable grounds of church or monastery. Even in normal times it was common to deposit valuables in a priest's house.[104]

The church provided many services. Its *dabtara* (broadly, deacons) included many medical experts, while miraculous healing – always especially attractive to the poor, because cheap and quick – could be sought from a living holy man or a saint's shrine. 'Who was there, man or woman, who came to him to be healed, carried on a bed, and who, having left his bed, did not go forth upon his feet?' demands the hagiography of Marha Krestos, fifteenth-century abbot of Debra Libanos, the greatest of Ethiopian monasteries.[105] Since the monastic tradition stretched back continuously to the fifth century in Tigre but developed only from the thirteenth century in Shoa and neighbouring provinces,[106] one unanswered question about the history of poverty in Ethiopia – a question needing expert knowledge – is whether the monastic contribution to poor relief changed significantly with time and place. Taking the period and the country as a whole, however, monasteries certainly provided much institutional care. Their rules required monks to practise charity towards the poor and detailed the provision to be made.[107] Some charity was casual, for travellers frequently sought hospitality at a monastery. Much was more permanent. An early sixteenth-century document from Dabra Wagag in eastern Shoa records the existence of a *hospice* for the poor, close to the church,[108] while Alvares wrote at the same period of Debra Bizan in Tigre: 'In my opinion there were in all always a hundred monks in this monastery, most of them old men of great age, and as dry as wood, very few young men [, and many boys whom they bring up from the age of eight, and many of the lame and blind].'[109] As this passage indicates, monks not only cared for the poor, many of them *were* the poor. At Debra Damo in Tigre, in the twentieth century, the monastery was divided into two sections, one being significantly poorer and confined to those coming from a distance.[110] More commonly, however, the monks included many orphans and especially the aged, for it was common for elderly people of all ranks to retire into a monastery either after the death of a spouse or, by agreement, when both partners saw death approaching:

> When the Abyssinians arrive at an advanced age, most of them become monks or nuns, whether they be rich or poor, married or unmarried: the rich then deliver over their possessions to their children, who support them till their death with much filial piety. The poor live on the bounty of others. The men become monks at any period of life; but the women seldom become nuns till they are forty-five or fifty years of age.[111]

In this manner Ethiopia's monasteries and convents provided some solution to the problem of old age in a society whose elementary family structure rendered it acute. Nor was it only the aged who found such refuge. Alvares was appalled to find even the priesthood used as a form of social welfare:

> A monk had come [for ordination] entirely blind: how was he, who had never seen nor had eyes, to be made a priest for the mass: also another entirely crippled in the right hand, and four or five who were crippled in the legs: these also they made priests, and a priest had to be sound in his limbs. The answer came, that . . . with respect to cripples, I should speak to the Ajaze Raphael . . . He asked me what such as these would do if they had not alms from the church.[112]

The practice was still common three centuries later.[113]

The poor who sought dependence might also look to lay charity. During the famine of 1889–92 corpses lay not only around the churches but along the roads to the capital and the houses of the rich. Emperor Menelik opened his granaries and ordered noblemen to care for the famished.[114] Iyasu I had taken the same steps during the famine of 1701 and Susenyos in 1627. When his home was plundered by royal troops during the mid nineteenth century, Gabru Dasta joined those waiting at court for the emperor to distribute largess.[115] Royal generosity extended also to the structural poor. That Emperor Amda Seyon was 'especially kind to the poor' was known to a writer in the Arab world as early as the 1340s. Five centuries later the King of Shoa fed some 200 persons daily and reserved certain articles of tribute (notably a coarse black cloth) partly for the poor.[116] Alvares reported that tribute from certain royal estates was designated for charitable purposes. At his accession Yohannes I (1665–82) is said to have distributed the precious metals and clothes he found in the treasury, while his successor outdid him by breaking up his crown and giving the gold fragments to the poor.[117] Once a fixed capital was established in 1636, emperors organised feasts which the poor could sometimes attend.[118] Zara Yaqob (1434–68) ordered that Christian festivals should be sanctified by the distribution of alms and once gave the abbot of Debra Libanos a thousand loaves and a hundred pots of beer to distribute to the poor on the feast of St Takla

Haymanot,[119] which became an especially popular occasion for largess. 'On this day', a missionary wrote from Shoa in 1839, 'the King gives money and salt to the poor, and mules to those who cannot walk, in memory of Tecla Haimanot, who cured cripples and other sick men.'[120] Emperors also distributed alms when they or those close to them were sick, but their charity was expected to surround them wherever they went, for the hordes accompanying their progress included many beggars and at every place of pilgrimage or ceremony the poor were assembled to await largess.[121]

This flow of charity was not confined to the emperor. His empress, in particular, was expected to personify female compassion.[122] Provincial governors shared the obligation. A district official in Shoa fed 80 religious students and orphans every day during the 1830s.[123] 'In their Villages', Ludolphus learned in the seventeenth century, 'they appoint the Chiefest of the Inhabitants for the Relief of the Poor.'[124] Individual noblemen had reputations for generosity or miserliness, while Gondar's merchants, who prided themselves on their charity, made weekly distributions of alms. Every pious man was expected to give an annual feast for the poor on the festival of his patron saint.[125] On St Takla Haymanot's day in 1830, for example, the Echege

> had from three hundred to four hundred persons in his house, to whom he caused bread and beer to be distributed; which is looked upon as almost equal to the bread and wine of the Lord's Supper . . . I had my house full of people; and the silence with which they drank their beer, and the vows which they offered up from time to time for all the individuals in the house, although mixed with superstition, were edifying to me, and reminded me of the love-feasts of the first Christians.[126]

When Menelik II appointed Ethiopia's first modern ministers in 1907, he granted two the special honour of holding a celebratory feast for the poor.[127]

One sixteenth-century hagiography of a fifteenth-century saint records that his parents 'built two dwellings: one for the monks, the other for the poor'.[128] Generally, however, private charity was less institutionalised. A wealthy man expected the poor to be present at the major rites of his life – at his marriage, for example, and especially at his funeral. Almeida reported in the 1620s that alms were given to the clergy and the poor on the third, seventh, thirtieth, and fortieth days after a man's death, and on its anniversary.[129] The most important distribution, however, was at the *teskar* banquet some six months after the death:

> Before any one of them [the clergy] can taste a morsel, the 'haioh', which is the feeding of the numerous poor who may be congregated outside the gates, must take place. On such occasions these poor people never allow any one to eat till after they have been served. With loud voices they adjure the assembly, for the sake of the Saviour or one of the saints, not to commence eating till they shall have first had their perquisite. A man then counts them, tapping each on the head with a stick; and to every one of them is handed a bit

> of the entrails, liver, or meat, rolled up in a cake of bread. When all have been served they hold their portions in both hands under their mouths, and then shout 'Hai-oh!' with a long *sostenuto*[130] on the last note. Liberally translated, this would express a prayer for the resurrection of the dead to a new and better life. This part of the ceremony is very important. Few persons would dare to neglect it, or to hazard the maledictions of the assembled poor, by treating their importunities in any way harshly, as such conduct would be a perpetual reproach and a lasting source of annoyance.[131]

Perhaps the most remarkable forms of Ethiopian philanthropy were charitable clubs, which existed at least by the early nineteenth century.[132] The *sembete* was a club whose members took turns to bring food and drink to their church on Sundays and distribute them to travellers and the poor, eating the residue themselves. Club members helped one another in misfortune, while the poor whom they aided were expected to repay an unfortunate benefactor, perhaps by collecting timber to rebuild a house destroyed by fire. The *serkehebest* functioned in a similar manner except that the food was displayed beside a road and travellers were pressed to partake of it.[133]

Behind these forms lay a theology of charity. It was set out most systematically in the *Fetha Nagast*.[134] Alms, this explained, were 'a loan made to God . . . secure and advantageous'. The reward to the giver was remission of sin in proportion to his intention. Alms must be given gladly, either publicly or in secret, the latter being more admirable. Only the truly needy should be helped, but they should be aided regardless of faith or character: the chronicle of Iyasu I records that he 'always had something in his hands to give, and at the moment of granting charity did not say "this one is a Jew, that is unfaithful or a murderer".'[135] In return, the recipient's chief duty was to pray for his benefactor. Yet even the poorest could themselves earn merit by giving, as was explained in Zara Yaqob's beautiful homily on Christ's Nativity:

> The poor shall not say, 'I am but poor, with what shall I celebrate his [the Archangel's] memory? I have nothing of the things of this world.' Poor man, you do not lack cold water or edible, not bitter, wild plants and fruits to celebrate his memory . . . These are more acceptable to the Lord than splendid cattle or any kind of mead or wine, as once the widow's mite was more acceptable than the sacrifice of the Jews . . . Among the poor there are two kinds: Those who are poor in worldly goods but healthy in their bodies, who even possess nothing whatever, man or woman. These certainly do not lack food to celebrate a festival. For they stand in service to the rich and earn from their work for the rich, so as to be able to celebrate a festival. Such are all those poor who chop wood or carry stone and wood and make clean the houses of the rich. All these healthy poor have no lack of means to celebrate a festival. Listen, then, we will tell you of the poor and needy in worldly goods who, besides their poverty, are sick in their whole body and feeble in all their limbs! They too can celebrate the memory of the guardian Archangel . . . for they receive alms from good men, friends of the poor, be it that one gives them half a loaf or even a whole loaf, be it that one gives them half

> a cup or a full cup. Whoever thus receives alms, great or small, and gives another poor person a little of his food, fulfils the prescribed celebration of his festival.[136]

This passage is especially revealing of Ethiopian attitudes towards poverty. Although men welcomed the prayers of the poor, there was no notion that the poor were especially close to God, in the sense developed in later medieval Europe by St Francis of Assisi and his contemporaries. Rather, in this and in other ways, Ethiopian attitudes towards poverty resembled those of early medieval Europe. In the hagiographies of Ethiopian saints, miracles benefiting the poor are jumbled together with all kinds of wonders, often wholly trivial. Poverty, like famine, was seen as an act of God. The poor served a purpose by enabling others to be charitable, but there was nothing virtuous or honourable about poverty as such. Virtue and its reward lay rather in the act of giving, so that Zara Yaqob exhorted even the poorest to give. The idea was embodied in the popular legend of Balaya Sab, a notorious cannibal who was saved from perdition purely by giving a goblet of water to a beggar.[137] Perhaps this stress on giving was linked to the heroic ethic and notion of honour pervading Ethiopian society[138] and many other African cultures.

To Ethiopians, poverty was noble not in paupers but in holy men. They were the spiritual heroes, the counterparts of warrior kings. In their hagiographies, poverty had almost stereotyped places.[139] The story began with the holy man's parents. They were already charitable people. 'They gave alms of what they had to the poor and needy. For this the Lord gave them great wealth; they were rich in gold and silver, in servants and serving-maids.'[140] But they were poor in children. St Takla Haymanot's mother told her husband of her desire for a son: 'Come now, and give unto the church whatsoever it hath need of, and that of which the poor have need give thou unto them . . . and let all the furniture which we have left in our house be for the poor, so that God Almighty may be our creditor.' When her husband agreed, the future saint was conceived and the pair celebrated with 'a feast for the poor and needy'.[141] When he grew to maturity, the holy man himself marked his vocation by distributing his possessions:

> He gathered together all the goods which were in the house and in the field, and he began to distribute them among the poor and needy, and among the widows, and those who were ready to die of misery . . . until at length there was left unto him nothing whatsoever. And when the men of the city and all his kinsfolk saw that he was giving away broadcast all his possessions, they gathered together round about him, and said until him, 'Wherefore dost thou scatter abroad all this property at one time?' Then our father the holy man Takla Haymanot said unto them, 'I am not scattering my property, on the contrary I am multiplying it so that it may become a bond for me.'[142]

From this moment of abnegation, the holy man entered a career of self-mortification. Towards the end of his life St Takla Haymanot withdrew to the desert, where he ate and drank only on the Sabbath and occupied a cell which was just large enough to stand in and had eight iron spikes sunk in the walls. 'Now when he had remained standing up for a long time', the hagiography tells, 'one of his thigh bones broke and dropped off . . . and afterwards he stood upon one leg for seven years, during four of which he drank no water whatsoever.'[143]

To such heroes the sick came for healing and the hungry for food. When the thirteenth-century abbot Iyasus Mo'a prayed during a famine, God promised 'that neither in your monastery, nor in your town, nor in your cave shall anyone ever suffer either hunger or thirst, either affliction or distress'.[144] Nor did the holy man's death put an end to his blessings. A list of the miracles wrought at his shrine or by invoking his name generally concluded a hagiography, along with a promise, made by God to the holy man during his lifetime, of the benefits guaranteed to those who honoured him:

> Whosoever receiveth a wandering beggar in thy name, him will I receive when he beggeth before Me, and I will make him to abide in the mansions of My house. Whosoever satisfieth the hungry man in thy name, him will I receive and him will I satisfy with the bread of life; and whosoever giveth drink unto the man who is athirst in thy name, to him will I grant to drink of the fountain of blood which floweth from My side . . . And whosoever comforteth any man that is poor, or any man whom affliction hath visited, on the day of thy commemoration, or who shall send, according to his means, a load of garden herbs, or a bundle of wood, or a supply of water, or if he help him in any way whatsoever, him will I place in the kingdom of the heavens.[145]

Reading these wonderful legends, it is well to mark the relationship they reveal between the holy man and the afflicted.[146] The poor enter the story purely as recipients. Their functions are to display the hero's sanctity and receive the charity of those who would imitate him. The holy man, for his part, is generally of aristocratic birth and, in addition to his personal asceticism, is a powerful abbot. He does not *share* the poverty of the afflicted.[147] St Takla Haymanot (d.1313) belonged to the same century as St Francis of Assisi (1181/2–1226), but he exemplified that aristocratic condescension towards the poor which St Francis sought to replace by participant fraternity.[148] In terms of physical austerity, as Alvares observed, the Ethiopian ascetic was incomparably the more self-sacrificing, but it was the austerity of a heroic ethos, whereas St Francis sacrificed nothing less than the heroic ethos itself. This contrast between heroic and participant charity was to run through the history of poverty in Africa.

The general pattern of Ethiopian society was a loose and limited institutionalisation allowing for much individualism. Its monks, for example, were not characteristically the individual ascetics who dominated Syrian monasticism, but nor did they necessarily live the cenobitic life of the Benedictine rule. Monastic organisation showed much diversity, but the predominant pattern, taken from a Byzantine model, was for monks to inhabit individual huts or cells scattered around a church, kitchen, and assembly hall, attending these with varying regularity.[149] The poor sought aid both from the institutional resources of the monastery and from the personal charity of the individual holy man. Institutions exclusively designed for the poor did not exist. When Alvares complained that the halt and blind were ordained, and was asked 'what such as these would do if they had not alms from the church', he answered

> that in our country such as these, being given to the church, might serve and would have alms in the churches and monasteries, and such as the blind would be [organ players and] organ blowers and bell ringers, and do other things which there are there, and which there are not in this country. And if they did not serve in monasteries or churches, that the kings of the country had in their cities and towns large hospitals, with big revenues, for the blind and cripples, and sick and poor. The Ajaze answered that this all seemed very good, and that the Prester[150] should know it, and would be very pleased.[151]

Nothing happened. 'Ethiopians have an instinctive aversion for civil or administrative uniformity', a nineteenth-century French visitor observed; 'they see it as a means and also an effect of tyranny'.[152] When foreigners urged Menelik II (1889–1913) to segregate leprosy sufferers, he replied, 'Haven't I enough crimes on my conscience?'[153] Moreover, the poor themselves were remarkably unorganised. Some beggars lived and travelled in groups, especially if they had leprosy, and a distinct colony of leprosy sufferers lived outside the walls of Harar.[154] But there is no further evidence of organisation and certainly nothing on the scale found among West African Muslim beggars and in many parts of Europe and Asia.[155] Almsgiving, in the main, was similarly unstructured, for the *Fetha Nagast* was largely ignored. Imperial charity was controlled by a Grand Almoner, at least by the late sixteenth century.[156] The degree of institutionalisation involved is suggested by a description of the Feast of St Takla Haymanot at the Shoan court during the early 1840s:

> An annual muster-roll being kept as a check, all who were ascertained to have been participators in the distribution of the preceding year were unceremoniously ejected by the myrmidons of the purveyor-general, who has the interests of the state revenues warmly at heart. The mendicants were next classed in squads according to their diseases, and the dwarf father confessor . . . proceeded, in capacity of King's almoner, to dispense the royal bounty with a judicious hand. Sheep, clothes, and money, were distributed according to the apparent necessities of the wretched recipients, whilst each donation made was carefully registered by the scribes in attendance; and half-baked bread, raw beef, and sour beer, in quantities sufficient to satisfy every monk and beggar in the realm, having been heaped outside the palace gate, all ate their fill, and dispersed.[157]

Shoa was the best-administered province at that time.

Poverty and charity were themselves only loosely defined. The terms used for these and related concepts over several centuries would repay expert study, but to an unskilled eye it appears that by the seventeenth century, at least, Ethiopians used two words (apparently interchangeably) to mean poor, *meskin* and *deha*,[158] in addition to a rich vocabulary describing various kinds of poor (orphans, blind, etc.). It is interesting that neither *meskin* nor *deha* specifically connoted lack of wealth, power, or kin, as was often the case with African terms for poverty. *Deha* could mean anyone who worked the land and did not possess a fief.[159] *Meskin* seems to have had an implication of destitution, at least by the twentieth century,[160] but there is no indication that a clear distinction was drawn between the two. Almsgiving, similarly, was not clearly distinguished from other forms of generosity, either in language[161] or in practice. At his coronation, for example, Menelik II spent several hours distributing 'alms', but the recipients included European residents.[162] Begging, similarly, merged indistinguishably into gift-exchange between clients and patrons, so that a nineteenth-century visitor listed, as one of his four categories of beggars, 'respectable persons who would not dream of begging or singing in public, but made gifts of clothing or other small presents to the nobles in order to obtain in return a present of twice the value'.[163]

In a fluid society where the poor were so strongly involved in unequal personal relationships, it is not surprising that criticism of inequality itself was rare. Peasants were certainly conscious of their exploitation and revolt was common, often with millenarian elements. The most serious social protest was led by Isaac the Inciter, a stigmatised metal-worker who told his judges that 'not finding anybody . . . who could pay me enough to clothe and feed myself, driven by poverty, I departed for Shoa', where his insurrection began in 1686–7. 'After him', the royal chronicle recorded, 'went all the foolish and wicked who were escaping from poverty. All the people from the borders rebelled with him.'[164] Yet the fact that Isaac claimed to be the rightful emperor shows that inequality as such was not at issue, any more than it was at issue in the miracles of saints whose intervention transferred the wealth of the evil rich to the pious poor. Moreover, rebellion by 'all the people from the borders' illustrated the regionalism – often in social alliance with local noblemen and priests – which characterised protest and allowed it to be suppressed piecemeal. 'Abyssinian social history is markedly less turbulent and markedly more stable than that of medieval Europe', an authority has written.[165] That is true, but only if it is remembered that major social protest was also rare in Europe before the thirteenth century.[166] In this Ethiopia again shared the patterns of early medieval Europe.

Ethiopians did not criticise poverty, but nor did they idealise it. They saw it with the weary realism of those who lived with it every day and had no thought that it might be prevented. 'When he sees a poor man, his eye closes', ran a proverb. 'Thinking that I would be righteous, I put her on my back, but she remained hanging there', said another. Excessive benevolence was thought to bring madness.[167] The poor were often brutally treated and there are accounts of respectable citizens petitioning that the swarms of mendicants should be dispersed as a public nuisance.[168] Yet visitors were almost invariably struck by the generosity and kindness shown to the poor.[169] They were simply a normal part of society.

If Christian Ethiopia is compared with its closest Christian parallel – early medieval Europe – certain similarities and contrasts appear. The poor were equally visible and central in both societies, yet their poverty was rarely a result of land shortage, so that both family poverty and child beggars were rare. Instead, the structural poor were mainly the incapacitated, while the conjunctural poor were especially numerous in Ethiopia because drought and famine bred destitution there, in addition to the consequences of insecurity which both societies shared. In both, however, the poor were individuals; categorisation remained imprecise and unimportant. With regard to means of survival, land was available but the poor were almost by definition those prevented from exploiting it. Other means of independent survival were notably lacking in Ethiopia, owing to the scarcity of towns. This partly explains the proliferation of beggars and the extensive recourse to charity. As in Europe, Ethiopian Christians saw charity as a means of winning merit, 'a loan to God', and practised it indiscriminately, with a panache which matched the heroic ethos. Yet individualism and the legacy of the Eastern Church bred in Ethiopia a lack of specialised institutions for the poor which was the most important difference (along with the prevalence of drought-induced famine) between poverty there and in early medieval Europe.

If, on the other hand, Christian Ethiopia is compared with other pre-colonial African societies, a different pattern of similarities and contrasts emerges. Ethiopia's poor were broadly similar in origin to those elsewhere in Africa: they were the incapacitated, outcaste groups, and victims of climatic or political insecurity. But the Ethiopian poor were probably more numerous and unquestionably more visible than anywhere else except in Muslim Africa, because insecurity was extreme in Ethiopia, bilateral kinship provided little family support, and the scale of Ethiopian society created both a large reservoir of rural poor and institutions which attracted them and made them visible. The most important such institution was Christian charity, but even in terms of physical institutions – parish church, monastery, court – Ethiopia was generously endowed by African standards. Elsewhere in Africa, except in Islamic regions, the poor had fewer opportunities for dependent survival and, therefore, a greater incentive to independent struggle.

This, however, is to anticipate later arguments. For the present, the important point is to have shown that even if Ethiopian treatment of the poor was distinctively Christian, the poor themselves were mainly products of a land-rich society. For this means that they may equally have existed in other land-rich societies of pre-colonial Africa.

3

The Islamic tradition

The written sources from the Islamic societies of the West African savanna before the twentieth century are less numerous than from Ethiopia but more abundant than from most other parts of sub-Saharan Africa. In both regularity of contact and similarity of social organisation, the savanna was closer to the wider Islamic world than Ethiopia was to the rest of Christendom, so that patterns of poverty within Islam had much in common. Nevertheless, abundant land, political and environmental insecurity, lack of institutionalisation, distinctive family systems, and a pervasive personalism characterised poverty in the savanna as elsewhere in Africa. What most distinguished the region from Ethiopia was that towns were more important in the savanna.

Both in number and origin, the very poor of the West African savanna were similar to those of Ethiopia. In normal times most were incapacitated. Early in the twentieth century a scholar named Imam Imoru wrote that in the Kano Emirate, the heartland of the Hausa people in what became Northern Nigeria,

> there are rich people, *tajirai*, and there are poverty-stricken people, *matsiyata*, who barely eke out a living.
>
> Kano has more diseases and illnesses than any other Hausa land. There is a vast number of sick people there: many lepers, *kutare*, cripples, *guragu*, blind people, *makafi*, and people with spinal deformities, *kusanti*. There are also mentally ill people, *mahankata*, some of whom walk about spitting. Some of these sick people drag themselves about on their bottoms while others lean on sticks.
>
> In all the towns there are many sick people who sleep in the markets; when the market closes they remain there as if it were their home.[1]

An Ethiopian who observed these unfortunates might have found leprosy sufferers less prominent than in his own country, for leprosy was not especially common in the savanna and although its victims were tolerated and allowed to live within some savanna towns – as they were not in North Africa – they held a less central place in Islamic tradition than in Christianity.[2] The blind, by contrast, were more visible and culturally central than in Ethiopia, although blindness itself was not exceptionally prevalent.[3] Kano city alone was said to contain 1,300 blind people in the later nineteenth century,[4] while in Kukawa, the capital of neighbouring Bornu, a traveller remarked in 1870

> the unbelievable number of blind people, who sit beside the road, half-naked and half-starved, in strident tones appealing for their wretched sustenance to the kindheartedness of passers-by, or in long rows of ten or more, one behind the other, grope their way along the busiest streets with the most experienced among them as their guide.[5]

Islam offered the blind sympathy, charity, and imaginative fulfilment. One wrote:

> O my Lord, answer my prayer,
> That I may behold myself praying for [Muhammad] at [Medina]
> And raise my eyes and look
> And see the dark sheen of the Ka'ba there,
> And be happy without boasting.[6]

With the exception of the relative importance of leprosy sufferers and the blind, however, an Ethiopian would have found the incapacitated of the savanna familiar enough. It would not have surprised him to find few destitute families or children, except during famine.

Like Ethiopia, savanna societies also contained endogamous castes of artisans, but they were not necessarily the impoverished outcastes of India or Japan. They were indeed stigmatised and polluting, but even among the despised entertainers and praise-singers known to the French as *griots*, 'towards whom every insult is permitted',[7] the only specifically poor group were those who directed their praises to 'people of common status like cultivators, hunters, herdsmen, strangers passing through the country' and dressed in rags to emphasise their need.[8] The same principle applied to slaves, who were more numerous in the savanna than in Ethiopia. They practised almost as wide a range of occupations as did freemen, extending from the slaves who held one-quarter of the titled offices in nineteenth-century Maradi (in modern Niger) to the great majority of slaves who, as cultivators, labourers, and domestic servants, formed part of the working poor.[9] Acquired chiefly by raids on non-Islamic peoples to the south, slaves were most destitute when newly captured:

> A single horseman rode first, showing the way, and the wretched captives followed him as if they had been used to this condition all their lives. Here were naked little boys running alone, perhaps thinking themselves upon a holiday; near at hand dragged mothers with babes at their breasts; girls of various ages, some almost ripened into womanhood, others still infantine in form and appearance; old men bent two-double with age, their trembling chins verging towards the ground, their poor old heads covered with white wool; aged women tottering along, leaning upon long staffs, mere living skeletons; – such

> was the miscellaneous crowd that came first; and then followed the stout young men, ironed neck to neck![10]

Slaves could generally expect their material condition to improve with time, but there were exceptions: in brutal slave-dealing chiefdoms like Damagaram (in modern Niger), where in the mid nineteenth century 'the slaves of the Sarkee [ruler] of Zinder are double-ironed, like convicts, and in this condition jump through the streets';[11] among profit-orientated traders like the Maraka of the middle Niger, whose slaves were found by early twentieth-century French officers to be 'poorly fed, mistreated, and poorly clothed', receiving well under half the grain ration they needed;[12] in the harsh environments of the desert fringes and oases such as Tibesti, where men were known to kill themselves rather than become slaves;[13] or in the hell-on-earth of the Saharan salt-diggings.[14] These circumstances were exceptional, however, and there are indications that slaves – especially when incapacitated – were treated better than in the brutal frontier conditions of nineteenth-century East Africa. Yet one must not minimise the degradation of slavery. 'People have nothing but contempt for slaves in Hausaland', Imam Imoru wrote, and when the French emancipated slaves in Senegal in 1848 many immediately bathed in the sea to wash away their past.[15]

Beggars were as numerous in the savanna as in Ethiopia. The most ubiquitous were religious students who supported themselves by begging, in a tradition found throughout the Islamic world and said, like the Ethiopian begging tradition, to be an apprenticeship in humility. In Timbuktu they toured the town each evening, crying, 'A foreign student, friend of God'.[16] Kukawa alone was thought in 1865 to have 2,000–3,000, varying in age up to 25:

> In place of all clothing they wear a goatskin slung about their hips. A wooden board, a small earthenware inkwell, a few reed-pens, and a gourd bowl make up all their belongings. Thus they traverse the streets begging all day long, making special demands on those who sell foodstuffs, for only a proportion of them receive board and lodging in the houses of the notables, among whom it is the custom to have their sons instructed together with a few students.[17]

These young men came from societies where youthful violence was expected and institutionalised: youths from different quarters of Hausa towns competed for girls and fought one another, in neighbouring Nupe age-grades fought annual battles on New Year's Day, the four quarters of Timbuktu celebrated the end of the rains by playing a kind of mass hockey, and pitched battles governed by elaborate rules were fought by young men of rival villages in Wadai, Nupe, and Maradi.[18] Given these traditions, the religious students – educated, rootless, and numerous – were potentially the most radical social group in pre-colonial Africa. When a jihad in 1818 made Hamdallahi, on the middle Niger, a major educational centre, its notables were so harassed that they demanded that the students be expelled, only for the jihad leader, Shehu Ahmadu, to join the column, carrying his bundle and writing-board, 'since I am the doyen of these undesirables'. He agreed to stay only when the notables promised that each family would provide food for students three times a day.[19]

Adult beggars, by contrast, were dispersed less evenly across the savanna, with the exception of the *griots* who were found everywhere among the longer-Islamised peoples. French accounts of Senegal in the eighteenth and nineteenth centuries emphasise that although beggars were common, all were either *griots*, religious students, blind, or cripples. 'I never saw a single poor beggar', a traveller wrote after touring the coast from the Senegal to Sierra Leone in 1785–7. '. . . In Africa, the only men who demand charity are the blind', who were treated with great generosity.[20] 'The only unfortunates are the blind and the crippled', Abbé Boilat confirmed in the early 1850s, although he also mentioned *griots* and students.[21] The same pattern existed in the Mande-speaking region centring on modern Mali. As René Caillié found when he walked through this region in 1827, begging was relatively rare and confined to important towns such as Jenne, where 'a number of beggars, reduced to mendicity by old age, blindness, or other infirmities', were found especially around the mosque.[22] By contrast, further east in Hausaland was probably the largest concentration of beggars in Africa. Heinrich Barth, who had travelled widely in Mediterranean lands, found 'the most troublesome beggars in the world' at Sokoto during 1853.[23] As elsewhere, Hausa beggars were generally those disabled by blindness, leprosy, crippling, or simple-mindedness. 'The beggar's best friend is his cough', said a proverb, and Kano had a special officer to bury those who died in the market.[24] It is not certain that pre-colonial Hausaland also possessed the able-bodied professional beggars common in the Islamic world, but it is likely, for they existed there as a small but well-rewarded category in the early twentieth century.[25]

There were several reasons why beggars flourished in the savanna. They performed a necessary function where almsgiving was a religious obligation. Savanna societies were highly commercialised, admired lavish generosity, and (unlike Ethiopians) used a currency of cowrie shells which lent itself to largess. Yet these considerations do not explain why beggars were more numerous in Hausa than Mande areas. The reason probably lay in different family systems. Mande-speaking peoples lived in large patrilineages which could provide strong support for unfortunate members. 'In all these countries I never saw a mendicant', Caillié reported. 'The aged who are unable to support themselves are always maintained and treated with respect by their children.'[26] Hausa, too, often lived in complex patrilocal families, but their kinship system had a bilateral element which narrowed the range of significant kinship relations, encouraged individualism, and perhaps – as Professor Cohen has argued – bred numbers of unfortunate people who found begging better than family support as a means of survival.[27] That two bilateral peoples – Hausa and Amhara – should have produced Africa's most numerous beggars was a revealing example of the importance of family systems in the analysis of poverty.

Moreover, the same societies, probably for the same reasons, bred exceptional numbers of unsupported women. Many were widows, for early marriage of girls (commonly at thirteen or fourteen), polygyny, the notion that old age began at menopause, and the special misery of childless women meant that Hausaland had far more solitary widows than widowers, at least in the twentieth century. Other unsupported women were those 'who have refused to marry', as Imam Imoru chauvinistically described them.[28] Known as *karuwai* and often misleadingly called prostitutes, they were women of marriageable age who had not yet remarried after divorce or widowhood and chose to live apart from their kin. To support themselves they might take presents from lovers, their houses were recognised centres of a bohemian lifestyle, and in the twentieth century most were not well-off, but they were distinct from prostitutes, who accepted any client for a fixed fee and were known by a different term. Regarded with an amalgam of admiration, envy, and contempt, *karuwai* were products of early marriage, easy divorce, a commercialised economy which gave women much economic independence, and a bilateral system which provided little scope for an unmarried woman within the family.[29] Among Mande-speakers, by contrast, there appear to have been no counterparts to *karuwai* except among trading groups.[30] Probably the cohesive Mande patrilineages gave women a more dependent but secure status. In modern times Mande-speaking Bambara homesteads have eagerly welcomed even elderly women.[31]

In twentieth-century Hausaland *karuwai* existed in both town and countryside, but little is known of rural poverty in the West African savanna at earlier periods, for indigenous written sources are of urban origin and European travellers passed swiftly from town to town. Some modern studies of Hausaland which have attempted to penetrate into the nineteenth century have stressed that a grain-based agriculture dependent upon a short and unreliable wet season bred numbers of very poor cultivators whose condition resulted less from shortage of land or accident of birth than from ill fortune, personal inadequacy, or, no doubt, incapacitation.[32] On the other hand, the countryside as a whole was probably more prosperous in the nineteenth century before modern transport systems concentrated trade and industry in towns,[33] while many devices existed to preserve even the poorest from starvation, save during severe famine. Apart from inherited skills in agriculture and crafts, poor Hausa could establish a client relationship with a wealthier patron, working on his farm and performing menial tasks in return for subsistence and help in establishing an independent household. Poor men could hope that rulers would forgo taxes and open granaries in bad years. The incapacitated might have their fields cultivated by kinsmen or a work team of young villagers.[34] Sheer self-interest encouraged reciprocity. As an early British officer in Hausaland wrote, 'The fact that a man can always get a handful of grain here and there is probably due to the simple charity inherent among peasant folk; but it may perhaps be also due to an instinctive feeling . . . that bad times may place them, too, in a position dependent on other humanity.'[35] Yet the extent of rural poverty must not be minimised. Hausaland was the savanna's most favoured region – 'one of the most fertile spots on earth', according to Barth[36] – yet only three days west of Kano, in 1825, a traveller found 'a small wretched looking village' whose inhabitants 'were miserably clad, and exhibited signs of extreme poverty'.[37]

Elsewhere such poverty was more pervasive. It might be due to shortage of good land, as in the upper Senegal floodplain, or to insecurity, as with non-Muslim peoples huddled into mountain retreats, or to extreme environmental conditions, as with the 'ragged Tubu, struggling with extreme poverty and constant hunger' in their desiccating Saharan outcrop.[38] Nor was community support always forthcoming. The most miserable villagers were often elderly people, male or female, who were either childless or abandoned by their children. Early missionaries had to open refuges for them.[39] In Mande-speaking villages, dominated by large founder-families who controlled access to land, more recent settlers were often severely deprived.[40] Agricultural slaves might suffer similar deprivation. In some areas the expansion of slavery and of the use of firearms during the eighteenth and nineteenth centuries tended to reduce free cultivators towards slave status. When the Mande-speaking Vakaba Toure created the Kabadougou chiefdom (in the north-west of modern Ivory Coast) in 1848, his subjects complained that he converted all the free villagers into slaves.[41]

This was only one instance of the political insecurity which caused much rural poverty, if perhaps not so brutally as in eighteenth- or nineteenth-century Ethiopia. Some was the work of bandits. Highwaymen infested the forested areas separating settled regions, pirates operated on the Niger near Jenne in the eighteenth century, the internal delta of the Niger (like the British Fens) was a traditional refuge for outlaws, and the wonderful masquerade of the Dogon (of modern Mali) included a highwayman equipped with arms and leather beer bottle.[42] Yet, as elsewhere in pre-colonial Africa, insecurity owed less to outlaws than to the forces of 'order'. As Dr Hill has written, the rural savanna world of 1900 was 'harshly inegalitarian, heavily-taxed'.[43] The Muslim warriors who ruled it believed, as Sokoto's first caliph wrote, that 'man is urban by nature', and they had little but contempt for rustics whose faith was, at best, susceptible to syncretism.[44] Nineteenth-century Hausaland may have had the best government in pre-colonial Africa, but the governors' chief rural activity was not patronage and largess but the despatch of horsemen – 'lazy, vicious plunderers', as a missionary described them[45] – to bring in the annual grain tax, from which each level of the ruling class took a share.[46] In 1892 the Emir of Kano responded to an epidemic of cattle plague by raising the cattle tax.[47] The rest of the savanna was convulsed by warfare throughout the nineteenth century. Jihad brought famine to the Senegal Valley in 1859–60 and bred a generation of hunger in Senegambia thereafter.[48] When Shehu Ahmadu's successors quarrelled with Timbuktu and its Tuareg allies, the resulting violence plunged the middle Niger into 'an abyss of anarchy and misrule'. 'Great numbers . . . were hovering round us, all of them begging for food', a traveller reported in 1854.[49] Thirty years later the borders of Samori's Mande-speaking kingdom were wastelands of hunger and devastation.[50]

Political insecurity was only one cause of the periodic famine which was the chief form of conjunctural poverty in the savanna. Locusts were first recorded on the coast of Senegal in 1606 and were occasionally responsible for dearth, as were other insect infestations.[51] Cattle disease could reduce pastoralists to destitution. An unprecedented Niger flood destroyed crops around Timbuktu in 1616, while both Senegal and Bornu experienced food shortages in 1872 owing to excessive rainfall.[52] Yet the most common cause of famine was drought. Within the generally dry and cool climatic phase which began in the third millennium before Christ and still continues, there have been shorter cycles of better or worse rainfall in the savanna. The sixteenth and seventeenth centuries appear to have enjoyed generally good rainfall until the 1680s, when acute drought affected the savanna from Senegambia to Darfur.[53] So severe was the famine of 1697 that a chronicle from Agades records with horror that men even ate their herds and sold their books.[54] Several decades of climatic instability culminated in the mid eighteenth century in the savanna's worst recorded drought and famine. The chronicles of Timbuktu state that rich as well as poor suffered and that half the town's people died, while Senegal's slave exports reached an unprecedented peak.[55] Major famines occurred again throughout the region during the 1790s and 1830s, although most of Hausaland may have escaped the latter crisis. Thereafter no very extensive drought afflicted the savanna until the end of the nineteenth century.[56] Smaller regional catastrophes did take place. Hausaland experienced severe famine in 1855, localised shortages occurred there almost every year, and a careful study of the upper Senegal Valley has shown repeated food shortages between 1858 and 1897 but only a single major famine in 1867–9.[57]

Agriculturalists took elaborate technical and social precautions to minimise the risk of famine. Their rain-making rites ranged from the humble 'drought *salla*' of Hausa Muslims to the transvestite dances of some Senegalese women.[58] If rain and crops failed, women exploited their knowledge of wild plants. During Timbuktu's terrible famine of 1741, 'The most distinguished people ate nothing but . . . seeds of grasses . . . or of any other grain which ordinarily were eaten only by the most vile and impoverished people.'[59] When all food resources were exhausted, women and children might concentrate on conserving energy, while men, helpless and dishonoured, might abandon their families, seek work or a benefactor, or sell themselves into slavery.[60]

What is not clear is whether the rural peoples of the savanna flocked to the towns during famine, as in Ethiopia they flocked to monasteries, provincial noblemen, and the emperor. The savanna was much more urbanised than Ethiopia, but, especially in Hausaland, it was the urbanisation of numerous small towns and large villages rather than the great agglomerations which dominate the African countryside today, so that there was a marked rural–urban continuum[61] and little historical evidence of rural hostility to towns, except among pastoralists. Even Kano, the commercial capital of Hausaland, was thought to house only 30,000–40,000 residents in 1824. Timbuktu, for all its fame, had only 10,000–12,000 residents four years later. Saint-Louis, capital of the French colony of Senegal, numbered some 15,000 in 1865.[62] The larger towns were chiefly governmental centres and places to trade with foreign merchants.[63] Their high mud walls often enclosed large unbuilt areas where crops were sometimes grown and countrymen and their stock could take refuge in emergency. A chronicle states that when the ruler of Jenne converted to Islam he prayed 'that he who, driven from his country by indigence and poverty, may come to inhabit this town, may find here in exchange, by the grace of God, abundance and wealth',[64] and the towns did indeed give sanctuary to unfortunate individuals of all kinds. In Saint-Louis, where written sources survive, these refugees included famine victims. In 1794 its Governor sought to deport them back to the mainland, while seventy years later dearth and disorder in Saloum 'led to Dakar a crowd of people devoured by hunger and poverty. They were to be met with in every street, eating grass or earth and struggling against death.'[65] Towns in Kano province closed their gates to countrymen during famine in 1908, while a greater catastrophe five years later brought hordes of starving people into Hausa towns.[66] This suggests that such behaviour may have been normal during dearth, but there does not appear to be a single account from the pre-colonial savanna (excluding Senegal) of a mass influx to town during famine.[67] This may be because no European traveller in the region described a major (rather than localised) famine,[68] but the indigenous chronicles are also silent. The alternative explanation would be that there was little advantage in migrating to town in famine because food was as scarce there as in the countryside, given the limited economic domination exercised by towns. Food prices certainly rose dramatically in Hausa towns during famines, despite the existence of officials to control prices.[69] Whether towns attract the starving depends on the towns: in the large Tswana towns of nineteenth-century southern Africa, which were artificial political creations, the normal response to famine was for townsmen to disperse into the countryside.[70] There is no evidence of that in the West African savanna. Perhaps an equilibrium between town and country existed there. Certainly the region had the best animal transport system in sub-Saharan Africa. Legend said that Kano's prosperity rested on the grain trade.[71] Nineteenth-century Hausaland, at least, may have made some progress towards establishing control over famine mortality.

If the poor of the West African savanna were broadly similar to those of Ethiopia, their means of survival were often different. This was not so in the countryside. There agriculture was, of course, the chief resource and land was scarce only within the close-settled zones around the major Hausa towns, in certain areas of flood-irrigation, and in the most densely packed mountain refuges. Many marginal roles in village economies fell to the poor. Most villagers practised a craft during the long dry season. In the twentieth century, at least, those performed by the poor often used reeds, grass, wood, dung, or other bush products, which here as elsewhere were a precious resource.[72] In 1827 Caillié saw women carrying firewood into Jenne from 12 or 15 miles away. Later in the century a missionary met 'a woman from Egga [in Nupe], who had been deserted by her husband, made her way to the Binue, and took to collecting india-rubber for a livelihood'.[73] Between foraging and petty trade the line was thin. Traversing the impoverished region within the Niger Bend in 1853, Barth met

> from 150 to 200 people, all tall slender men, half naked, with nothing but a poor ragged cloth round their loins, and another rag still poorer round their heads, and each armed with a couple of spears and a ragged shield . . .
>
> They were poor people from G'ao . . . and the neighbourhood . . . carrying as merchandise on a couple of asses and bull oxen nothing but cotton strips, or 'tari', rice, and a few mats.[74]

Trade also merged into porterage, an important resource for the able-bodied poor. At Wanangi, the river port which supplied Bida with firewood, a missionary saw 'little girls [and] old negresses with unsteady steps gaily supporting loads which would have made our most vigorous European workers tremble'.[75] Other wage employment was rare in the countryside, but some poor villagers earned food by agricultural labour, while by the end of the nineteenth century labourers were migrating from Bornu as far as Tunisian farms.[76]

It was the proliferation of small towns that gave the poor of the savanna opportunities for independent survival lacking in Ethiopia. The only existing estimate of the numbers of poor comes from Nema, in the north of modern Mali, where at about the time of the First World War the population of 1,167 included 'a hundred poor (*miséreux*), a floating population who come to seek some pickings (*quelques ressources*) in the town'.[77] Skilled urban craftsmen were not poor, but most crafts employed apprentices, who probably lived close to subsistence, and unskilled rural migrants who did heavy or dirty labouring jobs which even slaves despised. In late nineteenth-century Jenne these labourers earned only one-half as much as journeymen, while in Kano the man who mixed mud for building earned less than one-third of a mason's wages. Such migrants were employed in Kano Emirate's highly capitalised indigo-dyeing industry, alongside religious students.[78] Moreover, certain crafts were specialities of the poor.

'Hausa people say, "Calabash mending is the last way to make a living"', Imam Imoru wrote; '"after that, may God give one the means to survive!"'[79] In Bida rope-making was a speciality of the blind. Poor elderly women in Jenne had a reputation for medical skill. Presumably they were also the majority of Senegambia's hired mourners. Brick-making was a poor man's trade in many pre-industrial cultures; bricks could be bought ready-made in nineteenth-century Kano.[80] The most important means of survival, however, were scavenging and hawking. Firewood was a major problem for savanna towns, then as now. The country around Salaga and Sikasso was denuded of timber for 5 or 10 miles. The firewood sold in Hausa towns was so expensive and poor in quality that it had to be supplemented with other fuels.[81] 'In some places they leave the [millet] stalks and whoever likes can gather them', Iman Imoru recorded, 'but in Kanoland, where there is no "bush" and firewood is scarce, the stalks are valuable and one does not touch those which do not belong to him. People sell these stalks in towns and villages for a high price.' In return, the city exported its nightsoil to fertilise surrounding fields, transporting it in head-borne baskets or fibre sacks slung on the backs of donkeys.[82] Fodder for horses was expensive, especially late in the dry season; in Zaria many young boys lived by collecting it. Others sold water from house to house or retailed it from large pots to passers-by.[83] Foraging thus merged imperceptibly into hawking. 'The people of Soccasso [Sokoto] cry their provisions round the city', Richard Lander noted in 1825; 'and milk, fish, &c are daily hawked through the streets by the lower orders.'[84] Along with the cries for grain, mutton, beef, and camel-meat, he listed that for wheat-cakes, because urban Hausa bought much of their food in the streets ready-cooked, providing employment for both children who hawked it and mothers who cooked it. In Timbuktu, similarly, most trade (except in cloth, salt, meat, and shoes) was in the hands of women, commonly slaves or lower-class Africans.[85] Whether the poor also found a means of survival in crime is unknown, but a study of eighteenth-century Daura hints at the existence of an underworld, while Kano closed its fifteen gates at sunset, enforced an 8.00 p.m. curfew, and was said to harbour many thieves.[86]

Not only did savanna towns provide means of independent survival rarely available in pre-colonial Africa, but Hausaland and neighbouring Nupe (much influenced by Hausa culture) were the only areas of sub-Saharan Africa where organisations of the poor existed. These may in part have imitated models elsewhere in the Islamic world, where there were both underworld gangs and official guilds of beggars, whose purposes included taxation.[87] But there were also models nearer at hand in the craft organisations found in savanna towns. Nupe had true guilds, 'closed occupational groups, the members of which live together in one locality and practise certain hereditary crafts'; as elsewhere in the Islamic world, but not in medieval Europe, 'the guild-heads receive their titles . . . from the *Etsu* [ruler]'.[88] The situation in Hausa emirates is less clear; they may not have had true guilds, but each craft had an appointed chief (*sarki*) whose functions often included collecting occupational taxes throughout the emirate.[89] Each craft tended to concentrate in one quarter of a Hausa town. Although a craft structure could exist – as in Bornu and Timbuktu[90] – without being imitated by the poor, it was nevertheless probably the pattern for their organisations in Hausaland and Nupe. In 1824 Kano city had distinct villages for the blind and for the lame, within the walls but separate from other built-up areas. 'The lepers' quarter of Kano is very near our house', Imam Imoru reported. '. . . The blind have their separate quarter . . . That section is like a small town. There is even a "ruler of the blind", *sarkin makafi*.' Bida too had a special quarter for blind people in 1891, with their own *sarki* and chief *mallam*, both blind.[91] Among Hausa immigrants to Ibadan in the twentieth century, the *sarki* of each group of incapacitated organised its begging activities, taking for himself the alms collected on Fridays but performing onerous duties of hospitality and representation.[92] Nothing is known of such organisation in earlier centuries.

The other group of marginal people who were organised were the *karuwai*. Those of a Hausa town had either a woman chief recognised by the ruler or were subject to the chief woman grain-seller, whose compound was a recognised hostel for unattached women. Since *karuwai* commonly lived together in separate compounds, they doubtless practised much mutual aid. In addition, they provided many devotees of the *bori* spirit possession cult which survived from indigenous Hausa religion as a cult of affliction closely comparable to *zar* in Ethiopia.[93] Like *zar*, little is known of *bori* before the twentieth century and there is no direct evidence that it served welfare functions, except in the sense that its rites were believed able to cure barrenness, leprosy, or other afflictions.[94] Yet its informal services were probably substantial. Thus a twentieth-century *séance* involved much exchange of gifts, a sacrificed beast might be distributed as alms, and there is evidence that the cult and the *karuwai* compounds were sanctuaries not only for marginal men but also for the widowed and forsaken.[95] In Tunis, shortly before the First World War, the *bori* cult provided accommodation for newly arrived Hausa members, sometimes found work for them, cared for them when destitute, and protected them from the final indignity of a pauper's funeral.[96] No such functions are recorded in West Africa.

Despite this limited degree of organisation, there is no evidence that the poor had any political role in savanna towns, not even the menace of riot which they exerted in Muslim cities elsewhere.[97] Notables might fear religious students, but the only evidence even of a food riot seems to have come from Kano in 1908, when a missionary (himself a hundred miles away) reported during a famine that 'a mob of people infuriated and in despair of ever getting justice or relief, infuriated with hunger went to attack the Residency'.[98] No popular action is recorded during Kano's civil war of 1893–5. There were several reasons for this quiescence. Like the North African towns which were their chief models, those of the savanna were not autonomous commercial communities but administrative centres dominated by political rulers.[99] They had no representative institutions: 'public apathy . . . is the Hausa criterion of a successful regime'.[100] There were no popular military units of the kind found in Syrian towns, no carnivals to mock authority, no tradition of 'town riot' such as was so vigorous in the Yoruba area of West Africa.[101] The Islamic teachers who provided popular leadership in North African towns did occasionally denounce misrule in the savanna[102] but may have been too vulnerable to organise popular protest. One in nineteenth-century Daura who declared, 'Courtiers belong to kings; the peasant belongs to our Lord God', was promptly driven from the town.[103] Moreover, many clerics accepted the established structure of society. Even Shehu Ahmadu, despite his sympathy for mendicant students, responded to a suggestion that the caste system should be abolished by offering the proposers a meat stew mixed with lizards.[104] Within the small savanna towns, moreover, there was a 'manifold gradation of social rank'[105] bound together by ties of patronage and charity which gave positive status even to the poorest. Writing of Nupe in the 1930s an anthropologist noted 'the ambiguous attitude of many individuals in the lower classes, vacillating between bitter resentment against the ruling class and readiness to identify themselves with its glory'.[106]

These constraints on popular action were reinforced by the very structure of savanna towns. As in North Africa,[107] they were usually divided into two zones. The central zone consisted of wards with occupational or ethnic specialities, but it was not divided economically between rich and poor, who lived jumbled together. The peripheral zone, by contrast, was generally occupied by the straw huts of recent immigrants and casual labourers. This was the pattern of Timbuktu, for example, while in Sokoto Barth noticed 'the part nearest the wall being rather thinly inhabited, and the people being evidently reduced to a state of great poverty and misery'.[108] Saint-Louis had a similar structure until the mid nineteenth century, when the French authorities sought to clear temporary housing from the central zone and create 'a fine central quarter fit to compare with those of our towns in France and Algeria'.[109]

Most savanna peoples distinguished linguistically between two broad classes of the powerful and the weak. Indeed, in the Malinke language of the Mande family the normal word for both 'poor' and 'indigent' in the late nineteenth century, *fangantan*, was the negative form of a word, *fanga*, meaning both 'power' and 'wealth'.[110] This was a particularly clear example of the categories used by a people with strong traditions of militarism and centralised power, as was the Wolof word for commoners, *baadoolo*, which meant 'powerless'.[111] Elsewhere, however, both language and categorisation were more complex. The chronicles of Timbuktu, as a religious and commercial centre, distinguished a class of notables, who included clerics and merchants as well as rulers, from a broad lower class including both artisans and slaves.[112] In Bornu, by contrast, the state dominated stratification and a sharp distinction existed between office-holders and commoners. In a loose sense the commoners were the poor, but Bornu also recognised a stratum of destitute who approximated closely to the very poor as understood in this book:

> To be poor is one thing, but to be destitute (*ngudi*) is quite another, since it means the person so judged is outside the normal network of social relations and is consequently without the possibility of successful membership in ongoing groups, the members of which can help him if he requires it. The Kanuri say that such a person is not to be trusted.[113]

This identification of destitution with lack of normal social relations, and hence lack of support (other than charity) when incapacitated, is helpful when seeking to understand the nature of poverty in the savanna. The neighbouring Hausa used similar categories. They distinguished office-holders (*masu sarauta*) from commoners (*talakawa*); the latter word connoted humility and was derived from an Arabic term meaning to be subordinate.[114] But Hausa also distinguished *talakawa* from the destitute (*matsiyata*), not without ambiguity but with a clear difference of emphasis. The earliest Hausa dictionary, published in 1876, translated *talautši* as poverty, humility, meekness, and *matsiata* as distress, poverty, anxiety, care.[115] Imam Imoru put the contrast more vividly: 'The common people, *talakawa*, make their soup [i.e. relish] without meat, and the destitute, *matsiyata*, are forced to make it without salt.'[116] Thus while formal poetry contrasted poverty with riches,[117] ordinary usage contrasted it also with sufficiency.

In providing for the poor, savanna societies showed a characteristically African preference for personal relationships over institutions which was as unique within Islam as Ethiopian practice was unique within Christendom. In Islamic towns elsewhere – and especially in North Africa – the chief form of philanthropy was *waqf*, a permanent endowment in property or money to support a mosque or provide schools, hospitals, public baths, bread for poor students and prisoners, or a host of other services. In some North African towns most shops and many houses were *waqf*, as was one-fifth of Egypt's cultivated land in the late eighteenth century.[118] In West Africa, by contrast, *waqf* appears to have been confined to the single region of Timbuktu, Jenne, and Masina. According to the chronicles of Timbuktu, Askia Mohammed of Songhai, who controlled the region, founded a hostel for West African pilgrims at Medina while on pilgrimage in 1498 and then, on his return, presented a casket to the central mosque of Timbuktu as *waqf* to hold copies of the Koran.[119] Later in the sixteenth century a successor especially rich in slaves, Askia Daoud, 'founded, for the poor of Timbuktu, a plantation which was maintained by thirty slaves and carried the name of "garden of the poor"'.[120] He also presented the central mosque at Gao with 27 slaves to undertake its upkeep. In the early twentieth century a few *waqf* still existed in Timbuktu for the support of mosques and the distribution of food to the poor. In Jenne and Masina, too, the chronicles recorded *waqf* – in the form of houses, cattle, or books – for the support of mosques, students, and the poor, although they had disappeared by the early twentieth century.[121]

These are the only indications that *waqf* existed anywhere in West Africa.[122] In some parts of the region it is specifically said not to have been practised, in one area even the notion was unknown,[123] while in Hausaland – a major centre of Islam – the silence of the sources implies that *waqf* did not exist.[124] Its absence appears to have been unique in the Islamic world and is difficult to explain. Dr Trimingham suggested that West African land tenure made permanent endowments of property impossible,[125] while an endowment of slaves was obviously ephemeral. The difficulty with this explanation is that the most common forms of *waqf* elsewhere were business properties and urban houses.[126] Even if such houses were relatively easy to build in savanna towns, they were not valueless, for although there was not a single rented house in Kano in the late nineteenth century, houses were bought and sold.[127] Nor was there any obvious impediment to *waqf* established by the means employed in Jenne and Masina or by endowments in money, such as were often made in Istanbul.[128] It is true that many features of savanna life – insecurity, polygyny, partible inheritance – militated against the use of private wealth to create charitable institutions, but that was presumably also true in other Islamic lands, where *waqf* was designed precisely to counter such tendencies towards impermanence. Perhaps the answer lies more in the strength of West Africa's traditions of personalised largess.

The consequences are clearer. The rarity of *waqf* encouraged mendicancy. Religious students begged in the streets because, unlike their counterparts in Fez and Tunis, they were not fed from endowments.[129] The old and handicapped, lacking institutional provision, clustered around the mosques and relied on informal means of support, much as others relied on the *bori* cult. Caillié observed that mendicants were always to be found around the Great Mosque at Jenne, while blindness was a qualification for appointment as *muezzin* in some savanna mosques and elderly women earned a pittance as sacristans.[130] Above all, the absence of *waqf* gave special importance to almsgiving.

Islamic law divided alms into two categories. One was the compulsory *zakat*, which was partly a poor-rate, normally payable to the state for redistribution, and was fixed at one-tenth of the annual harvest and a comparable proportion of other wealth above a certain minimum. The other category was voluntary almsgiving (*sadaka*) to the needy.[131] Whereas *zakat* was necessarily institutionalised, *sadaka* was characteristically personalised. Their relative importance was therefore a valuable indicator of the nature of charity in Islamic West Africa.

At one extreme, *sadaka* was an act of personal generosity designed to procure worldly prosperity in an instrumental manner. Hausa gave wheat to the poor to drive away fever epidemics, while in 1940 an anthropologist heard an elder tell a child in Timbuktu, 'Give half your earnings to your parents and alms to the old and the poor and you are certain of success in life.'[132] Almsgiving was also a source of social prestige. A chronicle of Timbuktu tells that the ruler of Songhai's chief slave once exceeded his authority by giving the produce of a royal slave farm to its poor residents in order to win himself honour. In the twentieth century the town's Arabs claimed special rights to give alms as a concomitant of the aristocratic status they asserted.[133] Rulers especially used voluntary almsgiving to display power and win popularity. Nineteenth-century emirs of Zaria were said never to wash their clothes but to give them away after wearing them a week.[134] As the Emir of Nupe returned from the mosque in 1879, 'a man threw to the crowds of people cowries for which they scrambled; and all the way, the people greeted their King by loud cries of Father! Father!! and prostrated themselves in the dust'.[135] Eighteenth-century Daura had an official who 'administered the distributions of *sadaka* (alms) and chiefly largesse to malams and presided over distributions of *sadaka* that accompanied the rites of death, naming, and marriage at the palace'.[136] Largess reached its peak at Sallah, which marked the end of Ramadan and was the savanna's great annual festival. A sixteenth-century ruler of Songhai is said to have asked at Sallah whether a single person at his capital had not received a gift from him during Ramadan, and to have been met by silence.[137] Here almsgiving was absorbed into the whole network of redistribution which tied these societies together.

Yet good men knew that the Koran taught that alms were best given in secret.[138] When Caillié visited the mosque at Timbuktu disguised as a poor Muslim, 'a middle-aged Moor stepped up to me gravely, and without saying a word slipped a handful of cowries into the pocket of my coussabe. He withdrew immediately, without affording me time to thank him.'[139] Scholars taught that specific acts of generosity could atone for specific sins. A peck of grain to each of sixty poor persons was recompense for breaking the Ramadan fast, according to a tenth-century legal authority, while a peck to each of ten persons atoned for a broken oath.[140] More broadly, almsgiving had its reward in Paradise. 'The Prophet said', the jihad leader Uthman dan Fodio reminded his followers, '"The generous man is near to God, near to men, near to Paradise and far from Hell."'[141] 'Give alms frequently', a Senegalese preacher exhorted his congregation, 'for alms avert calamities and unhappy accidents. They attract good fortune, and on the day of the Last Judgment they form a shade to shelter him who has given them.'[142] Dying men were exhorted to a final generosity, while popular belief in northern Ivory Coast at the beginning of the twentieth century held that pagans would be tormented in hell by a serpent formed from the alms they had neglected to give.[143] Among the evils which would prefigure the Mahdi, so Uthman dan Fodio wrote, was that 'men will beg from the rich in vain'.[144]

As in Ethiopia, there is little to suggest much discrimination between deserving and undeserving poor. Only the destitute had a legal right to receive alms – and even, in dire necessity, to steal – but Islamic tradition was ambiguous on this point and it does not seem to have been the duty of a pious man to make enquiry.[145] As in Ethiopia, too, almsgiving was part of many domestic rites. A Hausa family might make a rule of leaving enough at each meal to feed a beggar.[146]

These acts of charity were voluntary and personal, but a particular obligation to care for the poor lay on Muslim clerics. Some benefactors sought merit by making them gifts to distribute. The chronicles of Timbuktu tell of a fifteenth-century *mallam* who promised paradise to anyone who gave him a thousand *mithqals* of gold to distribute to the poor during a famine; he received both the gold and a dream warning him, 'In future make no more promises in Our name.'[147] Where there was no Islamic state to collect *zakat*, the *imam* might call for an annual *sadaka* from all believers and distribute it himself, as was the practice among the Maraka of Banamba *cercle* (in modern Mali) at the beginning of the twentieth century.[148] In the area of Jenne and Masina, at that time, *sadaka* and *zakat* were combined and the clergy and notables of a village distributed them in the mosque 'to the poor of the village, travellers bereft of resources, the clergy and their students, old women left without husbands or children, the imam, the muezzin, etc.'[149]

Collection and distribution of *zakat* by the secular authorities was an accurate indicator of their administrative capacity and commitment to Islam. It was normal in the area of Timbuktu and Jenne before the French conquest and also to varying degrees in the theocracies created by eighteenth- and nineteenth-century jihads. In Futa Jalon it was collected by village chiefs, who theoretically sent it to the central government but actually distributed it themselves. Centralised collection was more effective in Futa Toro, where it was a critical test of political power.[150] *Zakat* was collected in at least parts of Hausaland before the early nineteenth-century jihad; in Daura much of it was distributed to officials, royal slaves, and clerics. The jihad made it theoretically the only tax collected from Muslims in the Sokoto Caliphate. Most seems to have been disbursed at emirate level, as was legally correct, but it also continued to feed the rulers' households and supporters; by the 1840s Uthman's successors were accused of failing to distribute it as alms.[151] In the Hamdallahi Caliphate *zakat* was the chief tax and seven-thirtieths are said to have been given to the poor. There was also a levy of grain at the end of Ramadan – a kind of obligatory *sadaka* – four-fifths of which are said to have gone to the poor and the clergy.[152] Following the Tukulor jihad of 1854, *zakat* was collected in Kaarta, the most thoroughly governed province, but perhaps not elsewhere.[153] In Samori's military empire *zakat* appears to have been simply a 10 per cent tax, while pious purposes were met by an obligatory *sadaka* at the end of Ramadan.[154]

West African reformers did not regard the canonical regulations as exhausting a true Muslim's charity. Writing of his hero, Uthman dan Fodio stressed the Caliph Umar's personal acts of mercy: 'He used to take care of the blind, the chronically ill, the decrepit and the children by night; he carried water and wood to them by himself and removed dirt from them.'[155] We do not know whether Uthman himself performed such acts of mercy, but Shehu Ahmadu concentrated the poor of Hamdallahi around him. 'The whole western part of the compound', it was remembered, 'was reserved for lodging passing strangers, for orphans, for the old, for all the people without resources who were housed and fed at the state's expense.'[156] Shehu Ahmadu came closer to a Franciscan participant approach to the poor than did St Takla Haymanot. Yet, in striking contrast to Ethiopia, Islamic holy men were not expected either to heal the poor or to perform miracles on their behalf. A list of miracles associated with the Tukulor leader al-Hajj Umar does not contain a single work of mercy, while those attributed to Uthman dan Fodio are wholly banal.[157]

Savanna Muslims viewed poverty with much ambivalence. Their traditions stressed the values of wealth and generosity. At their best, these traditions evoked the largess of the rich and the hospitality of common people which many European travellers admired.[158] At their worst, the same traditions bred contempt for poverty, both in others, expressed sometimes in mockery of the handicapped, and in oneself, for the shame of poverty could lead men (but apparently not women) to suicide.[159] Like Ethiopians, savanna Muslims lived too close to poverty to idealise it. 'Beg from a beggar and you will see the blackest miserliness', said a Hausa proverb. 'Poverty you hate it and are hated for it', added the Fulani.[160] Yet Fulani combined display of wealth with admiration of altruism and the cultivation of a personal austerity[161] which probably explained why the Islam of their state in Futa Jalon was so joyless[162] and why they took the leading role in Islamic reforming movements. Certainly their jihads were directed in part against the conspicuous consumption of Jenne and Alkalawa. Once Islam dominated, it coexisted uneasily with the hedonistic traditions and commercial materialism of savanna towns. It bred much shallow verse about the world as 'an abode which passes away',[163] but it bred also a serious admiration of self-abnegation. Was it not the Prophet who 'took upon himself poverty [*talauchi*], it was better to him than wealth, that all his people might look at him, that we may follow his example'?[164] Ascetics vowed to spend their lives in the shadows of mosques in Futa Jalon. Sufi mystics in Bornu were reported to 'dig a hole and make a tunnel and provision it with a little flour and water . . . and the reason for their staying forty days underground is so that they may perform Sufism'. Uthman dan Fodio was said to own only one pair of trousers and one cap.[165] Theoretically, at least, rich and poor were equal in the mosque. They were certainly equal in death – Islam's simple and uniform funerary rites found rapid acceptance – in the severe mortification of the fast,[166] and in the appalling rigours of the Pilgrimage, which the exceptionally pious occasionally made as voluntary beggars.

There is an account of a crippled mendicant from Kano who walked to Mecca and immediately gave away anything he received as alms. 'A pilgrim for Mecca is a dead man', said Fulani.[167]

The spiritual uneasiness of these mercantile and acquisitive societies was soothed by the professionally poor. This was especially the function of ascetic *mallams*. Abbé Boilat, who hated them, wrote that the *mallam*, 'in the eyes of the public, is a man of privations, he rigorously observes his fasts and vigils'. In Hausaland, too, he was expected to shun wealth and office. Some were truly poor: the Fulani term for teachers, *torodbe*, means 'those who solicit together in groups'.[168] To give alms for their support was an act of special merit. In 1352–3 Ibn Battuta noted that on the night of 27 Ramadan the King of Mali – still somewhat unschooled in the Faith – 'distributed among the qadi and the khatib and the faqihs a sum of money which they call *zakah*'. Several centuries later, in 1892, a Christian missionary found that even non-Muslims saw superstitious value in giving alms to a *mallam*.[169] Yet ambivalence surrounded even these gifts. Unlike much Indian practice, it was not meritorious for a *mallam* to live by charity. A tradition attributed to the Prophet declared that 'the upper hand is better than the lower hand', i.e. that charity was better than begging. Uthman dan Fodio urged his hearers to 'give up going about begging for anything' and supported himself by making rope, as did several of his successors.[170] The chronicles of Ṭimbuktu tell of a fifteenth-century scholar who took to trade late in life because 'I do not wish to be a charge on anyone', although this meant seeing the Prophet in his dreams only once a year instead of every night.[171] In the chroniclers' view, the greatest merit attached to *mallams* who were both ascetic *and* generous, who gave away to the poor what they received as alms.[172] It was a satisfying blend of traditional and Islamic values, comparable to the heroic Christianity of Ethiopia.

Poverty was as central to the large-scale societies of the savanna as to Ethiopia. The very poor were similar in origin: they were the handicapped and unfortunate individuals who lacked family care, supplemented periodically by victims of political or climatic insecurity. They survived by similar means, except that towns gave the savanna poor more opportunities for independent survival. In both regions the wider societies aided the poor chiefly by personal generosity rather than the institutional provision found in other Islamic and Christian lands. This, it appears, was the broad pattern of poverty in those areas of pre-colonial Africa from which indigenous written sources survive.

4

Poverty and power

In those areas of pre-colonial Africa beyond the influence of Christianity or Islam, the chief problem in reconstructing the history of the poor lies in the sources. Many regions have no written records until late in the nineteenth century, while most oral traditions focus on dominant groups rather than marginal people. For this reason, this and the two following chapters concentrate on areas with especially rich sources.

Even in these regions, however, the records are difficult to use. They are chiefly of three kinds. One category contains the formal accounts of African peoples written by European visitors, ranging from sixteenth-century traders and missionaries to nineteenth-century travellers and the earliest anthropologists. As the work of foreigners, these accounts may contain misunderstandings. More seriously, as formal accounts they may be coloured by the preconceptions with which the writers approached both Africans in general and the poor in particular, preconceptions often drawn from notions of poverty current in Europe. These sources, it will be suggested, offer stereotypes of African poverty which can be misleading. The same is true, for different reasons, of the oral traditions which form the second category of sources. Where these say anything of the poor, it is often coloured either by ethnic or social stereotypes or by the social conditions existing when the traditions were recorded.

Formal written accounts and oral traditions, taken alone, suggest that poverty was widespread in pre-colonial Africa but differed from that in Ethiopia or the West African savanna. These sources depict the poor as social categories rather than individuals. They view them as those excluded from resources rather than as victims of incapacitation or insecurity. In some regions they suggest a more institutionalised care of the poor than existed in Ethiopia or Islamic West Africa.

These three chapters do not deny that this picture contains truth. Pre-colonial Africa was large and diverse enough to embrace many kinds of poor. It will be argued, however, that the picture is heavily coloured by stereotypes and anachronisms, that it obscures the distinction between the ordinary poor and the very poor which is central to poverty in Africa, and that a more accurate picture can be obtained only by examining also the third available source: the references to poor individuals contained, often in passing, in contemporary letters, diaries, and other papers – references inevitably made chiefly by foreigners, but without much of the categorising and conceptualising which marked their formal accounts. These scattered references suggest that the very poor were closer to those found in Christian and Muslim Africa: individual victims of misfortune and insecurity. Yet the similarity was not complete. Poverty in Africa varied with time and place.

The three chapters follow a broad progression from societies known chiefly from formal written accounts and oral traditions to those whose documentary sources have been searched for individual cases of poverty. By chance, this progression partly coincides with a chronological sequence. But the unevenness of the sources and the labour required to search them mean that only scattered case studies have been attempted. A comprehensive history of the African poor is still decades away.

One of the first parts of sub-Saharan Africa to be described in detail by Europeans was the West African coast, especially the Gold Coast and Benin where much trade was concentrated in the sixteenth and seventeenth centuries. In the small commercial states which composed this region, towns dominated the countryside and each state was controlled by an urban nobility of hereditary political and military leaders, successful merchants, and priests. Noblemen headed coresident descent groups which might number scores or hundreds of people. In clothing, demeanour, and sometimes food, noblemen distinguished themselves sharply from commoners, whose poverty was emphasised by most observers.[1] 'The remainder of the negroes of this kingdom', a traveller wrote of Issiny (in modern Ivory Coast) early in the eighteenth century,

> are very wretched and impoverished (*gueux et misérables*), having not a cloth to cover themselves, nor rightly anything but what the Brembis [nobles] choose that they should have. Most of the time they die of hunger, which obliges them to work every day, and often even to engage themselves as perpetual slaves to the nobles in order to have the means of life.[2]

Most free commoners were rural cultivators. According to Dr Kea's study of the Gold Coast in the seventeenth century, they were continuously threatened by the exactions levied by urban rulers, who possessed military forces and exercised political control over access to land. On admittedly slender evidence, Dr Kea believes that cultivators may have paid between one-quarter and one-half of their output to the ruling class.[3] They paid in gold, which required them to market much produce and expose themselves to market risks. In addition, cultivators were subject to corvée labour, military service, and other exactions. Inability to meet these exposed the cultivator to legal penalties or loss of access to land. Unsuccessful cultivators often joined the urban strata who formed a minority of free commoners.[4]

Free townsmen ranged from the modestly prosperous, through the skilled craftsmen, the numerous fishermen, and the wage-earning day-labourers (who 'were scorned by all'[5]) to the lowest-paid domestic servants, water-carriers, charcoal-burners, and the like. The payroll of the Dutch West Indies Company for 1659 shows that its highest-paid local employee on the Gold Coast earned 32 times as much as the lowest-paid.[6] Day-labourers were especially rootless, for many were young, they often moved to new towns in search of employment, and a proportion were probably dispossessed cultivators or runaway slaves and freedmen. Active discontent took several forms: 'fishermen rioting against the fish tax, impoverished peasants abandoning their farms and becoming bandits, mutinous militiamen unwilling to lay down their arms, and hungry urban paupers stealing crops from farms'.[7] Several towns held annual festivals at which the poor 'may freely sing of all the Faults, Villanies and Frauds of their Superiours'.[8]

The final element in the seventeenth-century Gold Coast population were slaves. They could be acquired by capture, purchase, or legal process. Although the distinction between slave and free was firmly maintained, slaves were as sharply differentiated as commoners, some acquiring wealth and exercising authority while others lived miserably. As retainers to noblemen slaves were joined by a semi-free category of bonded commoners, who might be debtors, pawns for debt, those condemned to bondage by legal process, or those who had chosen bondage as a source of protection. There is no evidence of slave revolts, but some of small-scale defiance.[9]

For the free poor, the first lines of defence were cultivation and wage-labour. Banditry is recorded, while many 'vaggabones' were recruited into state armies. 'Common whores' existed in several towns.[10] Collecting bush produce brought the lowest recorded earnings, and it is an indication of the exceptional degree of exploitation on the Gold Coast that those collecting firewood owed fees to the nobleman owning the bush concerned.[11] Visitors said there was no professional begging,

> The Reason of which is, that when a Negroe finds he cannot subsist, he binds himself for a certain Summ of Money, or his Friends do it for him; and the Master to whom he hath obliged himself keeps him in all Necessaries, setting him a sort of Task, which is not in the least slavish, being chiefly to defend his Master on occasion, and in sowing time to work as much as he himself pleases.[12]

Dr Kea believes that these bonded commoners who swelled the retinues of noblemen included many indebted peasants and families impoverished by dearth.[13] An early seventeenth-century visitor to the Gold Coast mentioned 'young children who are sold by their parents because they lack the means to feed them and to provide for them',[14] while pawning of children was common in Benin.[15] Noblemen were expected to be liberal. A self-made man who purchased a noble title had to feed the whole town for three days, while a rich nobleman would hold several festival days each year on which he would display his wealth and dispense food and drink to all comers.[16] Royal charity was especially conspicuous in Benin:

> The king being very charitable, as well as his subjects, has peculiar officers about him, whose chief employment is, on certain days, to carry a great quantity of provisions, ready dressed, which the king sends into the town for the use of the poor. Those men make a sort of procession, marching two and two with those provisions in great order, preceded by the head officer, with a long white staff in his hand.[17]

On the Gold Coast, however, Dr Kea believes that during the seventeenth century individual largess was unable to support the growing numbers of destitute and was supplemented by institutional provision. As early as 1600 a traveller recorded that 'Those who are blind or who have some physical defect such as being crippled or lame, so that they cannot make their own living, are put by the king with the blacksmiths to work their bellows, or with those who press palm oil or grind dyes . . . or to similar tasks in which they can be useful and earn their living.'[18] A later account added that the state also provided for young men by enlisting them as soldiers.[19] Priests supported poor people from offerings made at shrines.[20] In 1645 the town council at Kormantse imposed a fine on the town's ruler and distributed one-third of it 'for the poor'. Elmina town council distributed a fine to 'the poor' in 1646 and another 'for the use of the common people' in 1659. European companies occasionally distributed to the poor either confiscated merchandise or fines levied on company employees.[21] From a single anonymous statement of 1665 that after the main harvest the cultivators 'furnished the poor for gold' Dr Kea has suggested the existence of a poor tax.[22] However that may be, descriptions of the seventeenth-century Gold Coast suggest institutional poor relief at least as elaborate as in Ethiopia or the West African savanna.

In contrast to those two areas, however, accounts of poverty on the Gold Coast and in Benin, chiefly during the seventeenth century, suggest that the poor were victims of political exclusion from the means of production. As Dr Kea writes,

> Urban paupers constituted a propertyless group of *manouvriers* or *adwumafo*[23] without 'corporate' ties to the production (and reproduction) of their means of subsistence. They did not own or have direct access to the means of production and were therefore separated from the conditions of production which would have made their social existence as self-supporting producers possible ... Paupers were dependent upon public relief assistance; their economic conditions compelled them to live on a day-to-day basis.[24]

This account presents two problems. One is whether it is distorted by its sources. Not only did European travellers read and plagiarise one another extensively, but there seems to have been an oral tradition of the European forts which attributed stereotyped behaviour and characteristics to Africans, despite much real ignorance of them.[25] Moreover, the travellers came from European societies which habitually distinguished small upper and large lower classes, rarely described the latter precisely,[26] expected poor people to be victims of land scarcity, and were accustomed to institutional poor relief. The second problem is whether it was the poor, as described, who benefited from the poor relief system, for the only recipients whose identity is mentioned were not the working poor but handicapped people who received either sheltered employment or charity.[27] The very poor, it would appear, lacked access to labour rather than access to land.

Where so much uncertainty exists, all that can be said is that the poor of the West African coast in the sixteenth and seventeenth centuries appear to have been unusually numerous and more commonly the victims of political exploitation than was normal in Africa. However, the stereotyping tendency of the sources obscures the distinction between the poor and the less numerous very poor, who were probably often victims of incapacitation. The latter were probably the chief beneficiaries of an unusually institutionalised poor relief system.

The tendency for formal European descriptions to obscure the nature of poverty recurs in the Kongo kingdom (in the north of modern Angola), which in the sixteenth and seventeenth centuries was the other area of sub-Saharan Africa best known to Europeans. A summary of missionary reports on Kongo prepared in the Vatican around 1590 put their conclusion concisely: 'There are no poor among them, because all are so. Nobody, however, lacks what is necessary to life, for they are content with little.'[28] The missionaries were struck by how little that was. 'The poverty is extreme', one wrote on arriving at the coastal province of Sonyo in 1645. 'Foodstuffs are in very little abundance. The blacks content themselves with some provisions and vegetables, with millet, panic[29] and manioc roots. The most fastidious drink of the rich is only a little palm wine, and they do not have much of that.'[30] Conditions were worst during drought, which afflicted the kingdom each decade between 1640 and 1720, and during the great famines which tended to occur once in each man's lifetime.[31] Yet it was the lack of *storable* wealth that most struck the missionaries. During the mid seventeenth century one listed the possessions left by two 'people of inferior condition' for whom he had acted as notary. One left three pieces of cloth, a 'beggar's wallet' (*besace*), some calabashes and clay dishes, and a cooking pot. The other left an imported clay bottle, two cloths, a bow, some household utensils, and two cooking pots.[32] Dr Thornton has argued that these repeated accounts of extreme poverty are misleading, because analysis of baptismal records shows that infant mortality rates and average life expectancy were comparable to those of other pre-industrial societies of the time.[33] That may be true, but its implication is significant: such pre-industrial societies had many paupers.

Amidst this common poverty, the missionaries identified two special categories. Slaves were the lowest stratum, for here there was no suggestion, as on the Gold Coast, of a free stratum impoverished by denial of access to land. Some formal accounts gave slaves a wholly distinct status – 'The slaves alone work and serve', declared the summary of c.1590[34] – but missionaries on the spot realised that this was an over-simplification. Kongo social structure rested on the *kanda*, an exogamous, corporate, territorially based, matrilineal descent group controlling land.[35] Slaves were people torn from their own kin groups and made dependants of a *kanda*. Their status could improve with time and they were not always sharply distinguishable from junior freemen.[36] Yet slaves performed the most burdensome tasks, especially long-distance porterage. 'If these people could offer to God the work and poverty they suffer, they would derive great merit from it', a Jesuit wrote in 1625, 'for I do not know a saint reputed for his poverty who was poorer than they.'[37] There are records of strikes by seventeenth-century caravan porters, and of their severe repression.[38]

The second category whom missionaries distinguished from general poverty were aristocrats. They clustered in the capital, São Salvador, and the nine provincial centres, for towns dominated the countryside in Kongo as on the Gold Coast.[39] Missionaries stressed that even aristocrats were poor. 'The greatest gentleman when most gravely ill has no other bed than the hard earth and a poor straw mat', one wrote, adding that during a severe famine in the 1640s even the provincial ruler of Sonyo – the second man in the kingdom – was virtually without food.[40] Yet aristocrats practised a distinct subculture. They 'infinitely despise any sort of work and of occupation there may be, even those which are in some fashion honourable', a missionary reported in the 1660s.[41] Contact with the Portuguese strengthened the cultural distinction by providing new sources of power and exotic goods. Slave holdings expanded. First the king and then other noblemen created slave armies. By the seventeenth century aristocrats were raiding the Kongolese countryside itself for slaves, while the concentration of their interests on the capital increased the impoverishment of the provinces.[42] Tribute was recorded in writing and became less flexible. Villagers withdrew from the roads and occasionally rebelled, as in a rising against over-taxation in Mpemba in c.1652[43] or more famously in the millenarian Antonine movement of the early eighteenth century whose followers, as an unsympathetic missionary wrote, came chiefly 'from the forests and the wilds, ruder than rudeness itself, more ignorant than ignorance itself'.[44] The common people of the towns apparently took advantage of royal deaths to riot and plunder.[45] While aristocrats continued to eat the preferred millet, common people adopted higher-yielding crops introduced by the Portuguese, especially manioc (a symbol of poverty in many parts of Africa) and maize (which in the sixteenth century was thought fit only for pigs).[46] The sources do not suggest an indigenous tradition of aristocratic largess, although missionaries – like other Europeans in pre-colonial Africa – found commoners generous to them and to one another.[47]

Although many missionaries to Kongo were ascetics – sometimes barefoot mendicants eager to share the life of the poor[48] – and although they came from southern Europe where poverty was widespread, they were nevertheless shocked by the material poverty of the Kongo countryside. And yet their formal accounts never moved beyond stereotyped categories: all Kongo save aristocrats formed the poor, among whom only slaves were distinctly unprivileged. That there was such a gulf between aristocrats and commoners, and that commoners in general were poor, seems beyond dispute. The problem, as always in Africa, is whether the poor were distinct from the very poor. The linguistic evidence suggests that they were not,[49] but there are occasional references to people in special need. A missionary in the Bamba province in 1666–7 reported, for example, that 'several Cripples came to beg of me, and I gave them some of those [cowrie] Shells that serve instead of Mony'.[50] Abandoned infants are also mentioned.[51] Emphasis on the expansion of the *kanda* may have put barren women at special risk; a missionary reported that they were repudiated by their husbands and there is evidence from the early twentieth century that unwanted widows could be harshly treated.[52] The *kimpasi* spirit possession cult provided some support for the unfortunate, for a missionary described a *kimpasi* enclosure as a 'place of superstition destined to the care of the ill and other pagan ceremonies' and its officers included cripples, dwarfs, twins, albinos, and others considered abnormal, who were regarded as incarnations of the spirits.[53]

Stronger evidence of the very poor comes from missionary charity. The earliest accounts of almsgiving for the poor in São Salvador date from the arrival of Jesuit missionaries in 1548.[54] A diocese of São Salvador was created in 1596. By 1612 the King of Portugal gave its bishop 80,000 *reis* each year to distribute as alms.[55] In 1631 the bishop also received almost as much – 175 *cofos* of cowrie shells – from the King of Kongo as tithes.[56] In Sonyo in 1688 a missionary distributed (presumably to the poor) the baskets of food which Christians brought to honour their ancestors on All Souls' Day.[57] That such almsgiving was a European innovation may be indicated by the fact that the late nineteenth-century phrase for alms, *lukau luankenda*,[58] seems unconnected with the ordinary vocabulary for generosity or wealth. But the great emphasis which missionaries laid on works of charity had the result that in the mid seventeenth century an exhortation to 'be a friend of the poor, give alms for the redemption of captives and slaves, help the afflicted' was part of the coronation ceremony,[59] while as late as 1813 King Garcia V of Kongo assured his brother of Portugal that 'we are very charitable to the poor'.[60]

The earliest suggestion of more institutionalised charity is a statement by an ambassador from Kongo in 1595 that there were six confraternities in the kingdom whose functions included 'works of mercy' and whose members included 'benefactors'.[61] In the early seventeenth century they were supplemented at São Salvador by a Confraternity of the Misericordia, the traditional Portuguese institution caring for the poor and sick. 'Not only

Portuguese, but also Ethiopians [i.e. Africans]' took part in its charitable works, the bishop explained in 1619.[62] Twelve years later the bishop (whose see had been withdrawn to Luanda in 1625) reported that the confraternity had its own church and 'is administered in common by the Portuguese and the blacks ... It has its regulations for the exercise of charitable works, spiritual as well as temporal, but it has no hospital, as its constitution requires, because the blacks are very poor and the kings not very powerful. The Portuguese living in the town, on the other hand, are very few at present and do not volunteer to guarantee the costs.'[63]

However, the question of the hospital is more complicated. There was none in São Salvador in 1609, but one witness affirmed that there was a 'House of Compassion' (*Domus Misericordiae*), and this was repeated in 1621 and 1626. The term might have been used loosely to mean the confraternity itself rather than a building, were it not that the witness in 1626, who was exceptionally knowledgeable, described it as 'a House of Compassion in country fashion' (*domus Misericordiae ad modum terrae*).[64] Presumably, then, for a few years the confraternity supported a building for works of mercy in São Salvador, although it may have disappeared by 1631. Perhaps it existed only during and shortly after the brief period when a bishop resided at São Salvador.

By the later seventeenth century missionary work was concentrated in the coastal province of Sonyo, where a missionary described elaborate care of Christians at the provincial capital in 1682:

> During their Sickness, and after they are confess'd, we frequently furnish them with Refreshments out of Charity ... Besides this we have several Slaves belonging to our Church which are skill'd in Phlebotomy, Surgery, Physick, and what not, who all do what lies in their power to recover these People when sick, or out of order: This we take care is done for them *gratis*, to the end they may have no occasion to run to the Wizards for help. For those that are poor and old, fatherless, lame, blind, or the like, there is an Hospital built near to our Convent, where both their spiritual and temporal Wants are supply'd by us as often as there is found occasion, or that it consists with our Abilities. This is a Charity which has not a little promoted the increase of Christianity in these parts.[65]

Surprisingly, no other record of this institution has been found.[66]

This analysis of the Kongo kingdom in the sixteenth and seventeenth centuries suggests that the missionaries were probably right to see the broad and growing gulf between aristocrats and commoners as the main social division. Yet the formal picture they gave of the common people – that, with the exception of slaves, 'there are no poor among them, because all are so' – is belied by fragmentary evidence, especially the provision which missionaries themselves made for very poor individuals. As on the Gold Coast at this time, exclusive reliance on formal European accounts gives only a partial and misleading picture of poverty.

The Kongo kingdom was one of a group of states known as the Kingdoms of the Savanna which occupied the grasslands spread in an arc around the Congo forest. These small kingdoms were the major states of Central Africa, but few were visited by Europeans until the nineteenth century. For accounts of poverty in this region, therefore, we rely more on oral traditions recorded by anthropologists or historians than on formal European descriptions such as exist for Kongo and the West African coast. In addition, some scattered references to individual poor people exist in late nineteenth-century publications. Unpublished sources have not been examined.

Amid much local variety, the picture of these kingdoms taken largely from oral accounts closely resembles the formal picture of Kongo given by early missionaries. The chief feature was a sharp distinction between rulers and subjects, a distinction created and maintained by force. In his account of the wealthy and culturally sophisticated Kuba state of central Zaïre, for example, Professor Vansina has stressed the contrast among freemen between the small minority of conquering Bushoong patricians and the far more numerous commoners. Among free commoners the chief distinction, as in Kongo, was between people of the capital, where power was concentrated, and rustics in the villages. Below the free commoners was a large category of 'menials'.[67] The structure was held together by force, ideological domination, and tribute. 'Surplus grew out of political demand', writes Vansina.[68] An equally sharp distinction between rulers and ruled, capital and village, marked the Lunda Kazembe kingdom in the Luapula Valley of modern Zambia. 'The first class in the nation . . . are the Chilolos [chiefs]', a Portuguese visitor remarked in 1832, 'and the second and lowest are the Bashya or servants, among whom are counted the peasantry, craftsmen, etc.'[69] In the Bulozi kingdom, also in Zambia, patricians grew long fingernails to demonstrate that they did no manual labour.[70] Since free commoners throughout this region had access to land, stratification rested on political power,[71] a pattern taken to its extreme in the Bemba kingdom, again in Zambia, where an exceptionally autocratic polity was imposed on an exceptionally crude agriculture. Because these kingdoms occupied varied environments, the material prosperity of ordinary people ranged from the relative security of Kuba country, where only one pre-colonial famine is remembered, to the extreme vulnerability of Lunda and Luba regions or the bleak aridity of Bembaland where food was a constant source of anxiety.[72] In terms of consumption, the advantages of power might therefore be expressed in conspicuous luxury, as among the Lozi, or merely a more secure food supply, as among the Bemba.[73]

Within the lower stratum there was generally a significant distinction between free commoners and a servile category who, in contrast to the slaves of Ethiopia or Islamic West Africa, seem to have had no chance of high office. In the Kuba kingdom these 'menials' included inhabitants of subjected villages (who paid more tribute and had less autonomy than free commoners), pawn wives (who had fewer rights than free wives and did the most menial household tasks), and slaves (who were obtained by capture or trade and did 'all the hard work or all the boring tasks', including those otherwise reserved for women). Slaves could be sacrificed at patrician funerals, but their descendants gained freedom after two generations.[74] This pattern was characteristic of kingdoms with rich environments and complex economies. In the Zambezi floodplain, for example, the labour-intensive Lozi economy depended on numerous slaves, who were harshly treated and barred from access to advantageous economic resources.[75] Lozi, like Kuba, were slave importers, whereas the simpler economy of Bembaland used relatively few slaves and exported many. 'No one would know the difference between a slave and a poor relative', Bemba told an anthropologist, '. . . except that the former worked harder and only ate the food left over by the household.'[76] Outlying non-Bemba tributaries seem to have borne a greater weight of exploitation.[77]

As in Kongo, these distinctions between rulers and ruled are thought to have widened as a result of long-distance trade. The exploitation of slaves in Bulozi appears to have increased in the late nineteenth century as agricultural produce became marketable in exchange for firearms, so that the king created a police force armed with whips to supervise slaves. Atrocity stories about Kuba kings increased during the nineteenth century.[78] In the Tio kingdom around Stanley Pool, long-distance trade reduced slaves and poorer freemen towards a single lower class, a process paralleled up-river among the Bobangi trading peoples and with some analogies in Bulozi.[79] As earlier in Kongo, such changes could provoke the poor to resistance. Rebellions by 'menial' groups in the Kuba kingdom were severely repressed on several occasions.[80] 'When I tried to explain to King Liwanika [of Bulozi] . . . that a poor "matlanka" (lowest slave) might be seated in the palace of God, and a king or chief shut out, he got very excited, forbade me ever to say such a thing again, or ever to teach such things to his people', a missionary recorded in 1883. '. . . "Those are not *people*", they say; "they are our dogs."'[81] A slave rebellion took place ten years later. When European control was established, the first concern of Bulozi's rulers was to assure their subjects that 'you are still our slaves'.[82]

As in Kongo, unprivileged commoners and servile groups clearly formed the poor of savanna kingdoms. If, however, one asks who were the very poor among them, then the broad social categories which are the language of oral traditions are little help. It is revealing, for example, to compare Professor Vansina's account of poverty among the Kuba, which is expressed in terms of social categories, with his analysis of the more commercialised Tio, where rich written sources and individual life histories identify poverty as 'not having many kinsmen, being alone and powerless . . . The role of kinship as a system of social security is clear.'[83] This identification of poverty with weak families is an important early example of a pattern which was to be widespread in twentieth-century Africa, but it is unlikely to have exhausted the causes of extreme poverty. Certainly the scattered references to very poor people in European descriptions of other savanna kingdoms suggest a wide range of individual misfortunes. Livingstone's account of Bulozi in 1855 suggests that orphans were especially at risk. He described 'poor boys going about picking up grains of corn which [had] fallen in the kotla [meeting place] – almost skeletons . . . Boys and girls may be seen undergoing absolute starvation when their masters or rather owners are scarce of food.'[84] In Msiri's kingdom in modern Shaba a late nineteenth-century missionary quickly accumulated a 'little family of waifs and outcasts', while others acquired many infants whose mothers had died.[85] There are references to aged paupers in Bulozi.[86] Its climate favoured leprosy and its tributary peoples, especially the Lovale, had exceptionally high proportions of leprosy sufferers. Among the Lozi these were rusticated to an area where they would not threaten the purity of the royal court, as also were the insane.[87] In several remote regions early missionaries found leprosy sufferers or epileptics abandoned to die.[88] Kazembe's kingdom segregated leprosy sufferers and also, like Bulozi, had unusually large numbers of blind people, although there is no record of how they were treated.[89]

Just as stratification in these kingdoms was politically imposed to a remarkable degree, so provision for the poor rested more completely on political authorities than anywhere else in Africa. There is some evidence that secret societies cared for their members. The widespread Butwa society's 'help in sickness or need' was 'much to be desired'.[90] But there is no evidence that the numerous spirit possession cults – studied with special care in this region – had welfare functions other than treating such conditions as childlessness.[91] References to family care are surprisingly rare, although doubtless it was common. There was no begging tradition, but among Bemba there was a recognised procedure, *ukupula*, by which anyone in straits could offer temporary labour to a wealthy person in return for food.[92] Rich Lozi also practised patronage, but, as Livingstone saw, it had limits:

> There is not among them that constant stream of benevolence flowing from the rich to the poor which we have in England, nor yet the unostentatious attentions which we have among our own poor to each other. The rich show kindness to the poor only in expectation of services in return; while a poor person who has no relatives will seldom be supplied even with water in illness, and when dead will be dragged out to be devoured by the hyaenas, instead of being buried. Relatives alone will condescend to touch a dead body . . . Having thus far noticed the dark side of the native character, I must not omit to add that I have witnessed frequent acts of kindness and liberality. I have seen instances in which both men and women have taken up little orphans, and carefully reared them as their own children.[93]

Nevertheless, it was to the chief that men normally turned. Kuba kings kept huge storehouses.[94] Bemba chiefs, too, were expected to maintain food reserves against scarcity and to support those too old or young to provide for themselves. There, 'To give with a flourish was the glory of chieftainship.'[95] Livingstone wrote that Sebituane's generosity to the poor was one reason for his popularity in Bulozi in the early 1850s.[96] Another alien conqueror, Msiri, 'would befriend a down-and-outer for no other reason than his poverty, giving him a house, a wife, and a granary of food. He was accustomed daily with his own hands to distribute cooked food to the lepers and the aged who would gather in his compound.'[97] At the capital and in each province of Kazembe's kingdom, tributary labour cultivated cassava fields which could be allocated to people in need or used as food reserves for those facing starvation.[98] Even in Nsama's relatively small Tabwa chiefdom, east of Lake Mweru, an experienced missionary found in 1905 'a very large grain store – the largest I have seen among natives. It is 15 to 18 feet high and about the same in diameter . . . His big grain store was explained as due to the fact that he is expected to feed the poor, the outcast and the stranger – it is in fact the first African poor law supply or better the patriarchal principle of the Shepherd of his people.'[99]

The welfare functions performed by political authorities in the kingdoms of the savanna certainly exceeded those practised in the interlacustrine kingdoms of East Africa. In Buganda, for example, late nineteenth-century sources reveal both a poor stratum and very poor individuals, as in Central Africa, and show that a growing cultural gulf separated the capital from the countryside.[100] Numerous foreign slaves formed the lowest stratum, supplemented by a few Baganda, 'men and women who had been sold by a relative in trouble, children who had been kidnapped, or who had been pawned to raise money in an emergency'.[101] 'The poor eat sweet potatoes without salt or relish of any kind generally, to them plantains are a great treat', a missionary reported, and there is evidence that poor men without relatives were especially vulnerable to the state's indifference to human life.[102] The Luganda oral literature was exceptionally rich in proverbs about poor men, emphasising their isolation as individuals: 'A poor man is like a yam; he creeps alone.'[103] To judge from twentieth-century evidence, these solitary individuals probably included many elderly people, who often enjoyed little respect and were barred by custom from living with their married children.[104] Solitary individuals certainly included men destituted by debt, women widowed by violence (the common word for a widow connoted a woman seized in war), victims of famine, epileptics, and especially leprosy sufferers, who were treated with a ruthlessness unusual in Africa.[105] According to an idealised missionary account, poor individuals could seek support from kinsmen or patrons:

> The Baganda were charitable and liberal; no one ever went hungry while the old customs were observed, because every one was welcome to go and sit down and share a meal with his equals.
>
> Real poverty did not exist . . . when a person got into debt, the clan

> combined to assist him to pay it, or if a clansman was fined, the clan helped to pay the fine. There were no orphans, because all the father's brothers were fathers to a child; and the heir to a deceased person immediately adopted and became responsible for the children of the latter . . .
>
> Chiefs . . . had the care of many women related to them who had lost their husbands, or who had never been really married, and, as they grew old, had been turned away or made into household drudges; such oppressed women escaped from their former homes and took refuge with their relations.[106]

From the king, however, the Baganda poor could expect nothing. He does not appear to have fed them ceremonially, as did Msiri, nor to have kept granaries or special plantations to provide for them. The poor did not throng his court, as they did in Ethiopia, but avoided it as a place of danger. In the neighbouring and related kingdom of Bunyoro the coronation oath included promises to treat poor and rich equally and to care for orphans, but a king of Buganda was told rather that 'The peasants are like sorghum – whosoever mows it down, owns it.'[107]

The most interesting evidence of poverty in the interlacustrine region comes from Rwanda and Burundi. It raises again both the reliability of oral traditions and the question whether numerous Africans were impoverished by lack of access to land imposed by political power. That this did happen in Rwanda was asserted in traditions which Dr Vidal collected there during the late 1960s, a decade after the revolution in which the Hutu cultivators (over 80 per cent of the population) destroyed the predominance of Tutsi pastoralists.[108] Her informants explained that the crucial issue for most Hutu in pre-colonial Rwanda was access to arable land. This was controlled by Hutu lineages until King Kigeri Rwabugiri (1860/5–95) – the real creator of Rwanda as Europeans knew it – forcibly asserted Tutsi control over arable land, first at the centre of the kingdom and then increasingly in its newly conquered peripheries. Tutsi chiefs gradually broke the autonomy and solidarity of Hutu lineages, leaving the elementary families vulnerable to exploitation. The chiefs gained direct control over unoccupied land and indirect control over occupied lineage land which they asserted by demanding tribute in return for the right of continued occupation. The tribute was paid partly in kind and partly in labour on the chiefs' fields. In the most fully dominated regions, this corvée, known as *ubuletwa*, amounted to two days' work in every five, according to Dr Vidal's informants.

With regard to the poor, the informants claimed that under Rwabugiri a large proportion of Hutu lost their economic independence and even their possession of land, not generally because land itself was scarce but – as Dr Kea argues for the seventeenth-century Gold Coast – because they could not meet the politically imposed qualifications for access to land.[109] *Ubuletwa* was imposed on the holding rather than the individual, so that a landholder with no other adult male in his family might find it especially difficult both to meet this obligation and to grow his family's food. The difficulty was compounded in time of famine, which was common in nineteenth-century

Rwanda. Moreover, any misfortune or failing – sickness, civil violence, victimisation by the chief, personal idleness, or irresponsibility – might prevent a man from meeting his tributary obligations and threaten him with dispossession and dependence.

The wholly landless man became a day-labourer (*umucancuro*) cultivating for another from dawn to noon in return for a day's food, conventionally defined as a basket of beans. Those slightly better situated combined a proportion of day-labour with a plot of land inadequate to provide independent subsistence. 'It was shameful to be a day-labourer', Dr Vidal was told:

> The wife had no clothes and must go and cultivate to obtain a used cow-skin. The day-labourer was a pauper who cultivated for everything: milk, clothes, food. He ate no matter what: a goat which had died suddenly, an aborted heifer. They were truly poor. They were the very lowest people in the society . . .
>
> The day-labourers were despised. Look: I am drinking beer with you and other people of my rank; a day-labourer could not come and sit with us; he stayed on one side waiting for someone, moved by compassion, to call him and give him the dregs left at the bottom of the pot.[110]

Because land itself was not scarce, day-labourers were generally held responsible for their own misfortunes. 'They were dogs', the informants declared. 'Nobody prevented them from cultivating for themselves!'[111] Individuals did indeed escape their condition by hard work, but Dr Vidal concluded that this was difficult, for the labourer's reward provided so little margin over his daily subsistence needs.[112] Nor was the class small or marginal. Dr Vidal's informants declared that day-labourers – defined as those who worked for others but never employed others – were about half of all cultivators in central Rwanda.[113]

If this account is correct, Rwanda's labourers and poor peasants were the most numerous and clearly defined class of poor people in sub-Saharan Africa, and they were created chiefly by the use of power to exclude men from land. In early twentieth-century Rwanda, Dr Vidal wrote, 'the social formation was such that the wealth of some provoked the poverty of others',[114] a qualitative difference from the poverty created by incapacitation which existed widely elsewhere. The distinction correlated with the fact that Rwanda had no slaves.[115] Instead the kingdom had created a dependent labouring class which was formally free.

Dr Vidal knew that her information might be contaminated by experience of the colonial period and especially by the Hutu revolution. She devised means to counteract this, discovering, for example, that Hutu and Tutsi informants gave similar accounts of stratification.[116] Yet she found only a single individual who confessed to having been a day-labourer.[117] The claim that half the cultivating population were labourers finds little support in the first written accounts of Rwanda. The most interesting study was made in 1907–8, when European control was still slender, by a Polish ethnographer, Jan Czekanowski. He identified four strata (*Stände*): royal officials; *ngabo* warriors (who occupied their own land, did not perform *ubuletwa*, and were most numerous in outlying provinces); *biletwa* (whom he described as 'free peasants without landed property [*Grundbesitz*]. They cultivate the land of the Crown and pay the chiefs a two- or three-day compulsory labour [*Frondienst*] during the five- or six-day week'); and the Twa pariah group.[118] As a Pole, Czekanowski was quick to see that the Tutsi ruled Rwanda as conquered territory in which *ubuletwa* was the core of subjection:

> In Mulera the clans have been subjected by the King and pay taxes. The Tutsi have driven the natives from some hills and have permitted homeless members of fragmented clans to settle themselves there. This rabble must render compulsory labour and support their master in return for the protection they are guaranteed. These are new communities which one must really regard as analogous to proprietary districts (*Gutsbezirken*).[119]

Nevertheless, Czekanowski never used the word *umucancuro* or described day-labourers as a substantial class. Some sub-chiefs, he noted, had their fields cultivated by 'their clients, whom they have made serviceable through loans of cattle, as also by wage-labourers, who are paid with butter and milk'.[120] This was his only reference to such labourers, although 'poor folk who needed something to eat or who worked for beer' are mentioned in recollections of early twentieth-century Rwanda.[121] In general, Czekanowski described a rather undifferentiated *biletwa* class of tributary but land-occupying peasants. Indeed, he thought that because there was still ample land, 'power in Rwanda can be exercised much more simply by monopolising cattle', as was Tutsi practice.[122] He added, moreover, that 'The power-holders must show consideration for their subordinates or run the risk that, abandoned by their followers and subordinates, they may be worsted by their rivals.'[123]

Czekanowski's picture of a much-oppressed class of land-occupying peasants with a smaller number of very poor people dependent upon labour was broadly confirmed by Dr Vanwalle's oral research in western Rwanda during the late 1970s. She found that Kigeri Rwabugiri had subjected Hutu lineages to *ubuletwa* service. She also identified the *umucancuro*, but as a man temporarily obliged to undertake day-labour, especially during famine or the hungry season before harvest, and able to abandon this status or change his employer at will.[124] The picture also has a parallel in Dr Botte's work on nineteenth-century Burundi. This, too, is based on oral sources which are difficult to use. 'Informants present two irreconcilable and contradictory versions of labour tribute', Dr Botte writes: '*corvée* for some, it is without importance for others. And why be astonished at that, seeing that they reflect existing social relationships, the division of society into social classes, and therefore the manner in which surplus labour weighs on one and the other?'[125] Moreover, leading Barundi historians reject Dr Botte's analysis, insisting that tribute was levied only by the monarchy and not the aristocracy.[126] And it is especially dangerous to draw parallels between Burundi and Rwanda because Burundi did not experience the degree of centralisation and aristocratic domination which Kigeri Rwabugiri imposed on Rwanda.[127]

Nevertheless, Dr Botte's analysis deserves careful attention. Like Dr Vidal, he holds that the terms of access to land were the basis of society in nineteenth-century Burundi and that in the central provinces, at least, Tutsi succeeded in the late nineteenth century in making land tenure contingent on the provision of tribute, mainly in periodic gifts to the chief but also perhaps in labour service at one of the many royal demesnes scattered through the country.[128] Such demesnes had staffs of permanent cultivators, servants, and retainers who were landless men who had volunteered to enter royal service. In addition, at peak seasons each demesne employed neighbouring Hutu 'recruited from the poorest stratum of the peasantry: people too poor to offer a pot of beer to the chief in order to escape the *corvée*'.[129] Outside the royal demesnes was a category of poor peasants (*abagererwa*) who cultivated a plot of land belonging to a richer man in return for a certain number of days' labour each year.[130] Finally, *abashumba* were landless men – perhaps orphans, victims of famine or civil war, debtors, men with uneconomic plots or inadequate sources of labour, victims of dispossession, or those simply unwilling to meet tributary obligations – who attached themselves as servants to a patron, living in his enclosure, subsisting at his expense, and performing whatever duties he directed.[131] The earliest dictionary of the Rundi language defines *umushumba* as 'one who is in the service of a master who in return gives him food and lodging, a domestic, a slave (in the Barundi sense).'[132] The word had connotations of taking to the road and of poverty, while the standard Rundi words for poverty, *ubworo* and *ubukene*, had implications of humility and labour.[133] The *umushumba* could leave his master, which no doubt reduced antagonism, as perhaps did the use of kinship terminology to describe the relationship, but in practice a landless man found it difficult to free himself, and proverbs said, in effect: Once servile, always servile.[134] Yet the *abashumba* were permanent servants rather than day-labourers and they were fewer than Dr Vidal's informants held day-labourers to have been in Rwanda.[135] Burundi, it appears, had a stratum of landless *individuals* who supported themselves by dependent labour, much as in early medieval Europe. A proverb recorded in the mid twentieth century suggests an awareness of family poverty rarely found in tropical Africa: 'The poverty of the solitary is exceeded by that of the woman with a child on her back.'[136]

Dependent labourers were not the only poor people in Rwanda and Burundi. There were bandits on the edges of the kingdoms, 'roving girls' who were either widows or unmarried women and might end up as concubines or prostitutes, and especially the victims of warfare and famine.[137] Generally, however, the poor were absorbed into relations of dependence. 'I went to offer a gift to an overlord in hopes of getting a cow . . . I was dressed in rags . . . My job was to clean the drinking gourds', a Hutu later remembered of the early twentieth century. A woman recalled that 'I was in such poverty I had nothing to put on but a goat skin, the skin of the poor,' when her father sent her against her will to serve his overlord's wife.[138] Relationships of dependence were all-pervasive. 'To disengage from clientship was impossible', Dr Linden has written. 'No sooner did the missionaries weed out one set of patron–client relationships than another sprang up.'[139]

Clientship was the normal context for provision for the poor. The royal rituals of Rwanda and Burundi did not mention this as a royal obligation,[140] but Kigeri Rwabugiri is remembered in western Rwanda as a generous king whose residence attracted the poor and needy and whose storehouse, *rutsindamapfa* ('conqueror of famine'), was opened in time of dearth.[141] Smaller men, not surrounded by the legend which clothes Rwabugiri, were remembered less charitably. 'Who desires a *corvée* goes to the chief', said a cynical Rundi proverb.[142] 'Those who were content to come and beg something to eat, without working for the *shebuja* [patron], were not received by him', Dr Botte was told. '. . . He said this: "Are these my own children? Too bad for them if they die of hunger. It's nothing to me."'[143] The royal courts of Burundi are said to have burned their unused sorghum stocks at the end of each year 'in making fire for the cattle'.[144] There could be no more vivid illustration of the brutality with which poverty was made overt in these kingdoms, in contrast to its concealment in less stratified societies. Rwanda and Burundi were among the worst parts of Africa in which to be poor.

This chapter is necessarily inconclusive. That poverty existed in these precolonial states, despite the absence of land shortage or world religions, is clear enough, but the extent and nature of that poverty remain uncertain because of the scarcity of sources and the difficulty of interpreting those that exist. Generally, the poor were probably rendered so by the use of political power; on the Gold Coast and in Rwanda and Burundi this power may have acted by limiting access to land, but the sources may exaggerate this point. The very poor, by contrast, are less well evidenced but seem mostly either to have suffered personal misfortune or to have lacked access not to land but to the labour of themselves (through incapacitation) or others (through solitude or neglect). Certainly poverty here was, as ever, complex. With regard to the survival and care of the poor, the striking feature was the importance of power-holders in providing relief. That was a natural corollary of their importance in creating poverty. Here too, however, the sources may mislead, for they probably neglect the less spectacular but perhaps more important actions both of family members and of the poor themselves. Problems of evidence dominate the study of poverty in these societies.

5

Poverty and pastoralism

Unlike land, livestock were a scarce resource in pre-colonial Africa. Pastoralists did not live in the egalitarianism often attributed to herdsmen but instead provided some of the continent's clearest evidence of poverty, defined – as they themselves defined it – by lack of livestock. Differentiation was accentuated by the riskiness of pastoral environments and the impossibility for a domestic unit to practise pure pastoralism unless it possessed a minimum number of animals.[1] The importance of pastoralism in breeding poor people was a distinctive feature of poverty in Africa when compared with many other regions.

This chapter pursues these issues in three pastoral areas: the Saharan edge of West Africa, the Rift Valley and its environs in the east, and the cattle-keeping areas of southern Africa. Two problems receive special attention. First, pastoral peoples had to choose between two diametrically opposed strategies for dealing with their poor members. They could incorporate them into openly inegalitarian societies, as was the practice of Tuareg and Moors in West Africa and Tswana in the south, or they could exclude them from ostensibly egalitarian societies, as was done by East African herdsmen and the Khoi of southern Africa. The reasons for choosing one or other strategy are obscure, but the result was two quite different patterns of social organisation. The second problem concerns evidence. Pastoralists rarely attracted early literate observers, so that their history is especially dependent upon oral traditions and the stereotyping to which these are liable when discussing the poor. In West and East Africa it is rarely possible to escape this constraint. In southern Africa, however, literate observers lived among cattle-keeping peoples long before European conquest. There, and especially among the Tswana, something of the complexity of poverty can for once be glimpsed.

The inegalitarianism of pastoral societies was especially blatant in West Africa. The Tuareg people of the Sahara and Sahel pursued the strategy of incorporating all levels of wealth into a hierarchical society. As a desert people who had spread southwards into better-watered regions, however, their hierarchy varied in detail from one region to another. The best-known desert group were the Kel Ahaggar of the mountain massif in southern Algeria which dominates the central Sahara.[2] Kel Ahaggar society was controlled by a small minority of camel-owning warrior-nobles (*ihaggaren*). Its most numerous members were vassal warriors known as *kel ulli*, 'goat people'. From among the vassals had emerged specialised clerics (*ineslemen*). Blacksmiths (*ineden*) formed a distinct caste. The pastoral camps also contained black slaves (*iklan*). Finally, during the 1860s, but apparently not before, the Kel Ahaggar incorporated sedentary, dependent cultivators (*izeggaren*, called *haratin* in Arabic).

Further south, in the Sahel, Tuareg groups differed from one another in social organisation, but all displayed one major difference from the Kel Ahaggar. Although the nobles remained a pastoral (and commercial) group, pastoral vassals were less numerous; indeed, the most southerly Kel Gress and Kel Ewey of modern Niger had no pastoral vassals at all by the nineteenth century.[3] Instead, the most numerous group were the freed slave cultivators known as Bella in the western Songhai-speaking regions and Buzu in the eastern Hausa-speaking areas. Tuareg penetrating the Sahel had presumably found themselves a small minority among cultivators and had adapted Tuareg social organisation to assimilate and dominate them.[4]

Accounts of the Kel Ahaggar in the late nineteenth century show that the least privileged category were the *izeggaren* cultivators, a relatively small group of share-croppers who kept only one-fifth of their produce and paid the rest to noble landowners. Kel Ahaggar despised agricultural labour, did not intermarry with *izeggaren*, and regarded them with contempt. By contrast, the *kel ulli* vassals, although tributary, enjoyed some reciprocity with nobles. So to a lesser extent did the slaves. These were true slaves of individual Tuareg, did the heavy household work and much herding, could be inherited but rarely sold, and could not marry without consent nor bequeath possessions to their heirs. But they were raised with their masters' children, incorporated into their masters' households as fictive kinsmen, bore arms and accompanied their masters on raids, adopted their masters' tribal loyalties and enmities, and had important pastoral and commercial functions. Among the desert Tuareg, therefore, the economic status of a dependent category correlated with its social proximity to the masters and the antiquity of its incorporation into their society.[5]

This pattern also applied in the Sahel. The status of Bella or Buzu cultivators varied widely. Those who spoke the Tuareg language, acknowledged Tuareg superiority, and claimed no other origin enjoyed higher status than those more recently incorporated. A study of a Bella community in modern Niger has shown that long-assimilated dependants were proud to have served heroic Tuareg warriors and despised more recent slaves.[6] Bella and Buzu are said to have owed their masters an annual leather sack containing 80–100 kilograms of grain and to have been obliged to lodge them when they moved south in the dry season.[7] Perhaps worse – because less predictably – exploited were those agricultural communities such as the Hausa of Adar in modern Niger who were preyed upon by competing Tuareg groups without being incorporated into their society.[8]

It is known that among the Kel Ahaggar the elected chief (*amenukal*) had the duty of charity to the poor of all strata and that among the Kel Ferwan of Aïr the vassals owed their master an annual *sadaka* in stock which were sold for the benefit of the poor.[9] Apart from this, however, no evidence is available on individual distress among Tuareg, so that the study of poverty can penetrate no further than these generalities about social strata.

Among their desert neighbours to the west, the Moors of modern Mauritania and its environs, slightly greater detail is available. They too incorporated the poor as dependants into a blatantly inegalitarian society. Warrior-nobles (*hassanis*) chiefly exploited free pastoral tributaries (*zanegha*), whom René Caillié thought in 1825 'the most wretched of the Moors'.[10] They paid an annual tribute in grain, stock, and services, as well as other exactions, in return for the doubtful benefits of 'protection'. Clerical tribes (*zawaya*) who shared power with the nobles chiefly exploited slaves (*abid*), whose treatment Caillié described in terms which contrast sharply with those used by twentieth-century anthropologists for Tuareg slavery:

> They treat their slaves with barbarity; calling them by insulting names, beating them, and requiring a great deal of service in return for very little food, and having no other garment than a sheep-skin. I sometimes protested against the cruelty with which these wretches were treated. 'They are slaves, they are infidels', was the reply.[11]

Both nobles and clerics also drew exactions from *haratin* comparable to those among Kel Ahaggar: freed slaves, either Africans or with much African blood, used as dependent cultivators or herdsmen. According to an early French report, 'the tribute (*horma*) which *haratin* pay is generally lighter than that paid by the *zanegha*. The normal rate is two cloths a year, i.e. the same as that paid by the slaves living in the tribe.'[12] It may be an indication of the harsher social order of the Moors that, unlike Tuareg, their exactions do not seem to have varied with the social proximity of dependants.

As to individual poverty, Caillié noted that among clerical tribes 'The poor who have no herds of their own are maintained by their tribe, every inhabitant of the camp in turn giving them the milk of one cow.'[13] A poor stratum also existed among nobles:

> There are amongst the Moors a sort of vagabonds called *Wadats*; these are the very poorest hassanes, who have often neither tents to lodge in, nor cattle to feed them; and being too idle to work, which indeed they consider as a disgrace, they like better to run from tent to tent and beg for a living . . . The parties of Wadats are chiefly composed of women and children; there are

> seldom any men amongst them: they travel on foot and mounted on asses, and always apply to the chief of the camp, who is obliged to find them provisions.[14]

Among servile categories, too, women and children were especially liable to poverty. Mungo Park, who lived in great misery among the Moors in 1796, thought the lot of female slaves especially wretched.[15] Caillié pointed also to the neglect of young boys:

> Such of the Moors as have young slaves ten or twelve years old, send them to the enclosure where the calves are, at milking time; and from every cow they let them drink a mouthful of milk; which is all the food they receive, so that they suffer much from hunger.[16]

In all pre-colonial Africa perhaps only elsewhere in the Sahara was the condition of the poor so wretched as among the Moors.

In contrast to Tuareg and Moors, East African pastoralists incorporated only certain poor people into their societies and obliged the remainder to seek their livelihood outside the pastoral economy. The most important evidence here comes from Dr Waller's study of the Maasai of the Rift Valley during the nineteenth century.[17] Although Maasai obtained food from surrounding agriculturalists, they did not themselves cultivate but relied upon a ratio of stock to human beings which had to be unusually high if the pastoralists were to survive periodic drought.[18] Marked differences of wealth resulted. 'Rich (*il karsisi*) and poor (*il aisinak*) had always coexisted and, to some extent, complemented each other within Maasai society', Dr Waller writes. 'The herds of the wealthy provided a local surplus for redistribution in the form of hospitality and stock loans; and the poor might seek some security as the clients of the rich. The two were particularly linked through the demand for labour.'[19] Large stock-owners kept the delicate balance between their herds and the labour needed to shepherd them by recruiting dependent herdsmen, chiefly from poorer families lacking the stock to support their members. Early in the twentieth century, for example, most Maasai elders on the Laikipia Plateau of Kenya had up to three or four herdsmen. 'The relationship between the herder and his employer was originally conceived of in quasi-kinship terms', Dr Waller explains. '. . .It can best be seen as a form of patronage.'[20] While the rich formed a stratum with some permanence, the poor were only mobile individuals, especially as some herdsmen were young non-Maasai who might be adopted into Maasai families or return to their homes when they had earned a beast or two. Maasai claimed that any energetic man could build a herd. 'One heifer is worth a man's head', said a proverb.[21] In practice it was more difficult, especially after the mid nineteenth century when repeated civil wars concentrated stock into relatively few hands and reduced the status of herdsmen towards that of 'menials', as they came sometimes to be called.[22]

Only a proportion of poor Maasai were herdsmen. Others who lost the struggle for stock, grazing, and water might join one of the agricultural groups – either Maasai- or Bantu-speaking – who surrounded the Rift Valley; they might even resort to the common expedient of the African poor and exploit the free resources of the bush as 'Dorobo', a Maasai word which had come to mean 'poor folk without cattle or other possessions'.[23] As Dr Waller writes, 'The two ideas of poverty and hunting are closely linked in Maasai history and thought.'[24] Yet the successful hunter or agriculturalist who acquired enough stock to pursue a pastoral life could return to the Rift Valley arena and become Maasai once more. Like Tuareg society, Maasai identity contracted in drought as poor men were forced to hunt or cultivate, then expanded again with the rains when the milk supply could support larger numbers. By excluding many of the poor, Maasai maintained among themselves an egalitarian ideology which harmonised with their acephalous age-set organisation and contrasted with the explicitly hierarchical ideology of Tuareg or Moors. The reasons for the contrast are obscure. One may have been the relative richness of the Rift Valley environment which enabled a minority to live as almost pure pastoralists, whereas on the desert fringes of West Africa pastoralists depended more on vegetable food and needed direct control over servile groups to grow or trade for it.[25]

Comparable evidence for other East African pastoral societies is not available before the mid twentieth century. It then shows that all included identifiable categories of poor people. Destitute families generally existed only in those societies which also practised agriculture,[26] for such families simply could not survive among more specialised pastoralists, whose poor were individuals. These might become dependent herdsmen in richer households, as among the Karimojong, or 'eke out existence on wild fruits and occasional labour for more wealthy people', as among the Turkana, or seek to recoup their fortunes by raising small stock at the cost of partial loss of status, as among the camel-herding Rendille.[27] The notion that no industrious man need remain poor for ever was strong among pastoralists and some studies showed greater mobility and egalitarianism than existed among the nineteenth-century Maasai.[28]

The tendency for livestock to differentiate extended beyond pastoral peoples to those East African agriculturalists who possessed cattle. It was at least elegant that the Common Bantu root meaning poverty, *–danda–*, was not found in the Proto-Bantu language originating in West Africa but took form among the Eastern Bantu, whose interaction with pastoral peoples was more intense.[29] Among the Kikuyu of modern Kenya, who interacted extensively with Maasai, marriage required livestock and poor young men seeking livestock were the chief source of labour for the wealthy. They might become dependent herdsmen (*ndungata*) rewarded in sheep or goats; roving voluntary servants (*njaguti*) who were often the feckless; temporary agricultural labourers working for their food; or men adopted into a colonising group and permitted to use a portion of its land in return for labour service, in which case they were called *athomi ahoi*, a term connoting 'poor beggars'.[30] That the vocabulary of poverty should have been exceptionally rich[31] among an acephalous, ostensibly egalitarian, but intensely competitive people may say much about societies of this type throughout Africa,[32] although in the Kikuyu case differentiation was accentuated by possession of livestock.

In southern Africa the existence of early European sources permits at least a glimpse of the true complexity of poverty in pastoral societies. As early as 1632 Dutch seamen reported contact at the Cape with *Strandlopers* or beachcombers, a group of 40 or 50 people with 'nothing else to eat but some rock mussels and greens off the land'.[33] Bereft of stock, they were excluded from pastoral Khoi (Hottentot) society and provided a sanctuary for 'refugees, outcasts, orphans, and other persons without family'.[34] They were, in fact, an epitome of pre-colonial Africa's most common categories of poor, and they immediately attached themselves to the Dutch settlers as dependants.[35] Further inland, destitute Khoi either herded cattle for richer men or resorted to hunting and became San or 'Bushmen', who were, as an early Dutch governor observed, 'the same as the poor in Europe'.[36] Khoi were pure pastoralists and highly differentiated by wealth.[37] So, too, were the Bantu-speaking Herero of modern Namibia. 'One who possesses a herd of cattle which he calls his own, is called a master', an early missionary to the Herero reported. 'One who has not acquired or inherited cattle is of no importance. It is compulsory for such a person to throw in his lot with an owner of property . . . The poor led a wretched life.'[38]

Most Bantu-speaking peoples of southern Africa combined stock-keeping with cultivation. Early accounts of these peoples – especially the most southerly, the Xhosa – described high levels of reciprocity and mutual aid which protected the unfortunate from poverty. Ludwig Alberti, who served on the Cape frontier from 1803 to 1806, put this most strongly:

> The Kaffir [Xhosa] gladly and willingly renders assistance to his neighbouring fellow-creatures which they may stand in need of, and appears to feel the necessity for this powerful social tie deeply.
>
> If someone is completely impoverished and asks for assistance from a strange horde, he is immediately provided with nourishment; he then remains there for several days, and renews his petition every morning, when he adds that he is compelled thereto by the hunger and want of his family. After a few days, one believes it to be necessary to create a feeling of confidence in the petitioner, as he would otherwise, as one says, not look for assistance so abjectly and persistently; so the impoverished person receives a head of cattle from this one and that one, and in this way is enabled to satisfy the wants of his family.[39]

Alberti's views were publicised by the traveller Henry Lichtenstein, who likewise reported that if the elderly 'become sick and helpless, every one is eager to afford them assistance. Poor relations are not less kindly treated', he added, quoting a Xhosa saying, 'We must not let even our enemies die with hunger.'[40] Several nineteenth-century missionaries gained the same impression. 'The ties of friendship among the natives are very strong, and a poor man is generally assisted', one told a commission of enquiry in 1883.[41] The African Christian elite took the same view,[42] as has the most recent historian of the Xhosa, Dr Peires, who has described a society ordered by reciprocity and has stressed the welfare functions of chiefs whose authority depended on their following. 'Like a father, the chief provided refuge for culprits, bridewealth for young men and assistance for all who needed it', he writes. '. . .If enemies swept off the cattle or if the rain declined to fall, it was the chiefdom as a whole which acted . . . When misfortune struck an individual or when a young man lacked bride-wealth, the chief provided for him.'[43] Studies of peoples related to the Xhosa have also stressed the chief's responsibility for the poor. 'It is when distress and misfortune fall upon the people that the economic position of the chief is most clearly illustrated', states the standard work on the Zulu. 'At such times he is expected to use his wealth to help his people, and he will hand out cattle and grain to those of his subjects who have not sufficient food to eat.'[44] The comparable work on the Swazi quotes a saying: 'The goods of the king are the goods of the nation.'[45] Accounts of the southern Sotho make the same point.[46] Political authorities among the South African Bantu clearly had welfare functions paralleled elsewhere in Africa only in Ethiopia and the Kingdoms of the Savanna.

Yet reciprocity disguised inequality. In 1848 the authorities in newly-created British Kaffraria conducted a census of the Ngqika section of the Xhosa living west of the Great Kei River. It revealed marked inequality. Of the 5,765 households, 40 per cent belonged to the 14 per cent of homesteads which contained 9 or more households, while 19 per cent of homesteads contained only 1 or 2 households and were probably the poorest. While 20 per cent of household heads were polygynists, no fewer than 32 per cent of adult men were unmarried, suggesting that younger and poorer men had difficulty in finding wives. Marriage depended on access to cattle for bride-wealth, and cattle were most unevenly distributed. While 32 per cent of households had no cattle, the wealthiest 20 per cent had between 5 and 160 cattle each.[47] By 1848 the Ngqika had been in contact with Europeans for at least 70 years and were increasingly short of land, which may have accentuated differentiation among them. Yet they had only recently been brought under European rule and their pattern of inequality is unlikely to have changed beyond recognition. Xhosa society may have been reciprocal, but it was certainly not undifferentiated.

For the poor Xhosa, as for the poor Maasai or Kikuyu, advancement lay through clientage. 'If a man be poor and has no cattle', wrote the first missionary in the region, 'he goes to the King, and to the Captains, who always give him more than a sufficient quantity.'[48] Dr Peires describes two varieties of clientage. In one an individual – characteristically a young man seeking bridewealth – attached himself to a rich man and tended his cattle for reward. In the other an unfortunate man – perhaps a refugee or a victim of drought – obtained cattle on extended loan, keeping a share of the progeny. Both forms, Dr Peires emphasises, bred ultimate independence, and neither implied unfreedom.[49] There was probably also a third situation. Here a survivor from an unsuccessful homestead became a more permanent adherent to a larger one, in a pattern of competition for people common in African societies with strong lineage organisation.[50] 'In a rich man's kraal' among the closely related Zulu, 'cooking and other housework used to be done by dependants (*abantu abakhonzile*), who lived there in a state of voluntary servitude',[51] and although 'servitude' may be too strong a word, 'dependence' may not be. Very poor Xhosa families certainly existed. 'They never eat fish', wrote the first missionary, 'except some kraals, which are very poor, but they are, as it were, separated from the common society, and on that account despised.'[52]

Apart from those impoverished by lack of stock, Xhosa society also contained incapacitated and unprotected individuals. 'The converts', Dr Peires writes of the first Xhosa Christians,

> were mainly people who lived in Xhosaland, but were out of place there. There were large numbers of women rejecting various oppressions, such as unwanted husbands, the levirate, and *upundlo*.[53] Some were accused witches and others were disfigured – blind, albino, leprous, or just too old . . . All of these were peripheral to Xhosa society.[54]

Such 'peripheral' people formed a large proportion of the poor everywhere in pre-colonial Africa. Among the Xhosa they appear to have come from certain rather clear categories. Foundlings or destitute children were rarely mentioned, for cow's milk was available if the mother died in childbirth and among these strongly patrilineal people, as Lichtenstein reported, 'orphan children are educated by the brothers of their father', although mistreatment by a dead mother's co-wives was a stock theme of folklore.[55] There is no mention of impoverished elderly men; as in other cattle-owning societies, they could perhaps claim the produce of their beasts.[56] Several early observers reported that cripples were rare. Those with leprosy, on the other hand, were quite numerous; advanced cases were ostracised, as also were many victims of smallpox.[57] Yet the chief characteristic of 'peripheral' Xhosa, as Dr Peires makes clear, was the preponderance of women. That they should have formed so large a proportion of the poor in this patrilineal, male-dominated society illustrates the importance of family structure in shaping forms of poverty. By the late 1820s the pioneer Methodist missionary to the Xhosa had erected 'three rows of small cottages' at his station 'as an asylum for unfortunate and persecuted widows'.[58] Young brides also often suffered much misery,[59] but it was childless women who were especially vulnerable. In 1883 several European witnesses told the Cape

Commission on Native Laws and Customs that bridewealth was 'a kind of poor-law' for widows, but the Paramount Chief and Councillors of the Thembu flatly denied it in the case of childless widows – 'The father of the husband gets the cattle back if she has no children; even if she has and they die, the ikazi goes back' – and showed complete indifference to the fate of such women.[60] There are several nineteenth-century case-histories of destitute and maltreated Xhosa women.[61]

If women were especially insecure in this cattle-owning society, its other main source of poverty was its vulnerability to natural or man-made disaster. Southern Africa experienced quite regular rainfall cycles and could expect a famine during each phase of drought.[62] Xhosa suffered drought in 1804–5, 1829, 1833, 1842–3, 1850–3, the early 1860s, and 1878–9.[63] Yet their greatest nineteenth-century disaster was self-inflicted, for in 1856–7 many destroyed their cattle and grain reserves at the behest of prophets who promised that it would ensure the return of the ancestors and the restoration of Xhosa prosperity and power. In April 1857 a missionary wrote from the eastern bank of the Kei:

> Large numbers of people, the whole populations of kraals, may be seen daily in the open country digging for roots, others gathering the inside bark from the mimosa thorn, and all presenting an abject appearance . . . Crowds of beggars are here every day, with most touching tales of children starving, and old men dying . . . Kreli, the chief, is hungry himself, and comes to beg of me . . . He gave leave to all his people to eat *new* food, and to work as much as they liked; would consider making application to the Governor for work for his people on this side, or near, the Kei river.[64]

According to a contemporary estimate, 20,000–25,000 Xhosa may have died.[65]

Although sections of Xhosa resisted white control for another generation, the cattle-killing of 1856–7 destroyed the nation as a coherent and autonomous people. Long-standing inequalities were now exacerbated by European exactions. As the administrator of the Ciskei wrote in 1865:

> This distribution of stock leaves the mass of people entirely destitute and they have nothing but their grain for subsistence and the payment of their taxes. Corn, when they are able to sell it, brings about 5 shillings a bag and in many cases a woman or man will have to travel 20 miles with a bag of corn on their heads for which they will receive 9 pence or 1 shilling and then have to travel back again for 20 miles and thus raise the tax.[66]

Later administrative reports suggest increasingly extensive destitution. In 1880, for example, Tamacha District of the Ciskei reported 'many invalids, aged and feeble, widows and paupers'.[67] Three years later Mfengu leaders in the Ciskei urged the government to create an Orphan Chamber on the Dutch model.[68] The poor were entering the new world of colonial institutions.

Despite the evidence of poverty amongst them, Xhosa occupied a relatively favoured region. To their north and west, on the arid highveld, the risk of destitution was more acute. Attention here will focus on the Tswana peoples, for they are exceptionally well documented by travellers from the first years of the nineteenth century and by resident missionaries from 1816. These sources make it possible to study a cattle-owning people in detail and to observe not only the existence of poverty but changes in its nature. Here, moreover, it is possible to glimpse something of the complexity of poverty, for the poor and very poor were drawn from at least four sources: servile strata of non-Tswana origin; incapacitated and unprotected individuals; impoverished but able-bodied Tswana; and victims of climatic or political insecurity. Poor categories and poor individuals, the structural poor and the conjunctural poor, coexisted in a confusion which indicates that one is at last dealing with the real world.

During the nineteenth century the Tswana held several non-Tswana groups in subjection. Among them were the Kgalagadi, a related Sotho-speaking people who occupied the region before the Tswana entered it but were then broken up, subjected, and incorporated as hereditary servants, although some broke free again early in the nineteenth century and established themselves independently in the Kalahari.[69] Some Kgalagadi servants lived in the desert or on its fringes, hunted or kept their own cattle herds, and paid tribute in hunting produce to an 'overseer' appointed by a Tswana chief. Others lived closer to a Tswana settlement, herded their masters' cattle, and might be summoned to perform seasonal agricultural labour.[70] 'I have known chiefs take armed men', a missionary wrote in 1842, 'and travel a hundred miles into desert places, in order to bring back Balala,[71] whom they wished to assist them in watching and harvesting the gardens of their wives.'[72] A master might also take Kgalagadi children into his household as servants or distribute them among his friends. 'The Bakalahari children', Livingstone wrote in 1850, 'are usually distinguished by the large protruding abdomen and thin ill-formed legs and arms. The listless eye shews that youth has few joys for them.'[73] Their cultural similarity to the Tswana meant, however, that Kgalagadi could advance themselves. 'Within the memory of those now living', a missionary wrote in about 1870, 'tribes once independent have been reduced to the condition of Bakalahari; while others who had been long Bakalahari have been called, through the grace of their chief, to the privileges of citizenship, and appointed a place in the town of the tribe.'[74]

The second non-Tswana servile group were known as (Ma)Sarwa. They were sections of the San whom both white and black were exterminating elsewhere in southern Africa at this time, chiefly because San were hunters who often regarded domestic livestock as game.[75] Tswana leaders later claimed with justice that they had treated San better than had other southern African peoples, for Tswana, like Tuareg, incorporated such subject groups rather than excluding them, partly perhaps because San mastery of the neighbouring desert made them an asset in this region. Assimilation of San had probably begun several centuries earlier, but their subjection accelerated from about 1820 when trade with the Cape Colony made hunting products valuable and supplied Tswana with firearms which for the first time gave them superiority over San bows.[76] In the 1820s most San were still independent and their status could be compared favourably with that of Kgalagadi. Thirty years later the major western Tswana groups had subjected most San in their vicinity, while by the 1880s and 1890s Tswana frontiersmen were penetrating the remote Kalahari to trade with San and eventually establish suzerainty over them.[77]

In the mid nineteenth century San status was shaped chiefly by the great herds of game which ranged the west and north of Tswana territory. Especially expert hunters could establish a relatively privileged status. Such were the Dennassena, described by James Chapman in 1852 as 'the pride of their masters the Bamangwato,[78] for whom they had swept this country of all the elephants with their spears alone'.[79] Next day, however, Chapman met a more typical San group:

> The Bushmen here, though a finer race of people, are just as degraded in all their notions as the worst I have seen. They call themselves dogs, pack oxen and horses of Sekomi [the Ngwato chief], and never think of aspiring to any other position. Dogs because they hunt and kill game for their masters, pack oxen because they must carry home the proceeds of their hunts for hundreds of miles, and horses because they must act as spies and run from one post to another with the least information.[80]

San exploited in this manner lived in extreme poverty. From one Chapman 'endeavoured to purchase the whole of his worldly possessions, which consist of a bow with quiver containing about 20 arrows . . . a small and worn-out spear, a sharpened stick to grub roots with, and in a knapsack 2 pieces of wood for making fire, an awl, a needle, some medicine roots, and some gum and sinews'.[81] 'The greater portion of these people were skeletons', he wrote of another group among the Kwena, 'the legs, arms and head bare of flesh, a big belly on account of the roots they eat. The joints of the knees and arms very large and the marrow bones thin . . . The natives were watching the locusts and at night, when they are unable to fly owing to cold, they gather large bags full and kill them with a slow fire, and pack them away after drying in the sun, for winter consumption.'[82] For such beings Tswana had only contempt. 'The Bamangwato are very cruel to the Bushmen, whom they flog with sticks every 10 minutes', Chapman recorded. 'They hold the Bushmen as beasts, term them bulls and cows, heifers and calves. In speaking of a female who has borne a child, they say she has calved.'[83] In the event of war between Tswana groups or even conflict between individual notables, 'it is quite fair . . . to kill all the vassals, as it would be to lift the cattle, of him who cannot be displaced from his chieftainship'.[84]

Most San were hunters, but masters occasionally seized children to serve in their households. These were occasionally bartered for goods, most often with Afrikaners but sometimes among Tswana. Women, too, were taken into domestic servitude.[85] San could not leave their master's service, they could be transferred from one master to another, they had no access to Tswana courts, and their status was hereditary.[86]

The position of San appears to have improved during the later nineteenth century. Tswana traditions generally ascribe this to the great Ngwato chief, Khama (1875–1923), who is said to have removed many disabilities from servile groups and encouraged them to own cattle.[87] 'Upon becoming Chief', he declared in 1916, 'I renounced the right to accept any tribute from these tribes, and at the same time declared them free to use their property to their own advantage.'[88] There was truth in this: Khama prohibited the sale of San children or the transfer of San from one master to another, while his own San were among the first to own stock.[89] But Khama remained the largest employer of servile dependants, was capable of ruthlessness towards them, and appears to have shared the general Tswana view that San were less susceptible to assimilation than other dependants.[90] Perhaps more profound reasons for changes in San status were that wild game was declining, so that San were becoming more valuable as herdsmen, and that Tswana masters had difficulty in preventing San from trading hunting produce with the growing numbers of white men entering the country.[91] In 1887 an official among the southern Tswana reported that dependants could escape subjection by working for a European or appealing to a Resident Magistrate.[92] Servitude remained most rigorous in the remote Tawana area further north, but there the most servile groups were not San or Kgalagadi but Yei and Noka cultivators and fishermen.[93]

These non-Tswana subjects were only one section of the poor. In addition, as everywhere in pre-colonial Africa, there were individual victims of misfortune and family breakdown. Those most often mentioned were children. Two of the earliest European visitors to the Tlhaping group of southern Tswana – Lichtenstein in 1803–4 and Burchell in 1812 – were invited to buy small ill-nourished boys, as was a pioneer missionary to the neighbouring Rolong.[94] Missionaries took into their homes a girl abandoned by her parents, a boy orphaned by the execution of his parents for theft, and a small hungry boy whose hand had been burned by his stepfather for repeatedly stealing food. They also rescued occasional foundlings and infants exposed to die.[95] 'When a *poor* woman dies and leaves a young infant, it is killed and buried with her as a rule', a missionary wrote. 'No one will be troubled with the bringing up of it.'[96] 'An orphan can learn the law at his place of service', said a proverb, and an early dictionary translated the common word for orphan, *khutsana*, as 'an orphan; a fatherless or motherless child, or both; one stricken with grief; a person of low degree'.[97]

The second major category of very poor individuals were unprotected women, for, like the Xhosa, this was a male-dominated patrilineal society. Among the Tlhaping in 1812 Burchell described

> *a woman with her two children* . . . Her eldest child was a girl about six years old; the other was much younger. She appeared to be about thirty, and told us that she had long been deserted by her husband, who left her that he might take another wife. Since that time she had wandered about with her two children from place to place, making any hut her quarters as long as its owners were willing, or able, to share their food with her. . .
>
> This poor creature possessed, she said, nothing on earth, but the clothes she wore . . . She was however, besides her cloak, the owner of a *pitsa* . . . or *earthen pot*.[98]

Such deserted wives appear to have had little legal redress.[99] The other documented category of unprotected and destitute women were widows.[100] Although Tswana women had much independent responsibility for agriculture, this did not give them economic autonomy, for they had access to land only through males and were probably more vulnerable to exclusion from the means of production than were male commoners in the Gold Coast or Rwanda. A Tswana widow normally entered the household of her eldest son or of a male relative of her husband. She had a right to support from her husband's estate, but the property belonged to her sons.[101] Consequently, 'A bitter sorrowful lot is that of a Mochwana woman who has no children!'[102] 'She receives little sympathy as a rule', an anthropologist later reported:

> her husband neglects or ill-treats her; she is scorned by other men and ridiculed by her own sex. Barrenness is attributed variously to sorcery, to some deficiency in the woman's 'blood', to some abnormality of her womb, to some former abortion, and, above all, to the fact that before marriage she had led a very promiscuous life.[103]

Livingstone pictured a Tswana woman saying: 'I am getting old . . . and I have no child; you know how Bechuana husbands cast their old wives away; what can I do? I have no child to bring water to me when I am sick.'[104] In 1823 a missionary to the Rolong noted the deaths of two elderly women, one neglected despite having served the chief's sister, the other dying of hunger 'at a time when the people abound in milk'.[105] Old men, by contrast, were rarely mentioned among the poor, probably because they could depend on their cattle for sustenance until death.[106]

A third category of very poor individuals were the incapacitated. A few were cripples or mentally ill, but these were quite rare, while leprosy was almost unknown.[107] By contrast, the blind were numerous, because the arid environment bred eye complaints and repeated smallpox epidemics left many sightless. 'I have never seen so many blind people as in the Kaffir town of Taung', a missionary reported in 1897: 'in one day I have counted 75 close to the church, all victims of smallpox.'[108] The first baptised Tswana Christian was a blind girl, attracted, so the missionaries feared, by 'the loaves and fishes'. In 1868 missionaries took in a young woman whose husband had turned her away when she lost her sight through smallpox. Twelve years earlier they had reported an 'old blind and almost destitute' woman.[109]

Apart from servile groups and incapacitated individuals, the poor included also a number of able-bodied 'true Tswana'. They are especially difficult to identify because observers easily confused them with Kgalagadi, but indications exist.[110] 'The poor, as my interpreter informed me, are always kept poor', Burchell wrote of the Tlhaping; 'and if I might judge by appearances, there are many of that description. Those whom I supposed to be free or without a master, were always emaciated.'[111] A later visitor to the Tlhaping wrote of 'the poor amongst them who live in the fields', whilst missionaries mentioned 'poor or field Batlarus'.[112] To live permanently outside a town was thus one likely indication of poverty. Another was not to own cattle, for although cattle loans were common, twentieth-century analogies suggest that they were probably seldom made to men wholly without stock.[113] A missionary distinguished two categories of Tswana by their reactions to the appearance of locusts: whereas the rich were appalled lest the locusts ate the grass needed by their cattle, the poor who had no cattle rejoiced because they could themselves eat the locusts.[114] In 1818 a missionary heard for the first time that a thief had been executed because he had been too poor to pay a fine. Others believed that 'orphans and the children of the very poor' were especially vulnerable during initiation rites.[115]

The structural poor of nineteenth-century Tswana society were thus a complex stratum and perhaps an unusually large one by African standards. This was echoed in the rich vocabulary of poverty recorded in the twentieth century. An early dictionary lists five words for destitute. One, *humanega* – also the standard word for 'poor' – shared the same root, *huma*, as the word for 'rich',[116] so that a Tswana proverb could say 'Where there is no wealth there is no poverty' with a succinctness found elsewhere in Africa only perhaps among Mande-speakers.[117] The starkness of the dichotomy of rich and poor among the Tswana probably owed much to the existence of despised servile categories, whose position depressed that of poor freemen, much as the existence of slaves in the Cape Colony depressed the status of the Africans.[118] Another reason for the dichotomy was probably the pastoral emphasis of Tswana economy. And a third reason was that Tswana lived in an exceptionally risky environment which bred conjunctural poverty. 'This is a land', a missionary wrote in 1834, 'where the natives may be said to keep (from necessity) one perpetual fast and their manner of living in general is far beyond what may be termed abstemious. They live a starving life and scarcely ever can say that they have had a full meal of wholesome food. In fact they seem to live in a kind of middle state between the dead and the living.'[119] The customary greeting, according to a colleague, was, 'What are you eating?' and the reply was, 'Nothing whatever.'[120] The whole process of Tswana history, with groups repeatedly incorporated in subordinate capacities, suggests recurrent disaster and destitution.

Tswana country shared southern Africa's cycle of good and bad rainfall, but accentuated by the fact that the area lay between several rain-bearing air masses. Acute droughts are recorded in 1825, 1833–4, 1845–51, 1858–62, and 1876–9, interspersed with years of excellent rainfall.[121] 'I have never seen anything like this drought', Livingstone wrote in 1849. 'The very trees seem to feel it. The leaves crumple together, and we hear that there are some tracts of the Bakalahari country in which the trees are killed.'[122] People collected berries and roots. Men hunted. Women sold their ornaments for grain. Locust swarms were 'like the manna to the people'.[123] When local resources were exhausted, the whole population abandoned the towns for the interior in search of rain or bush produce.[124] The poor generally suffered most. San were an exception, for their social organisation was designed to resist drought and their foraging skills were invaluable.[125] Other dependants might be discarded as a burden during famine. In 1856 'The Batuana were bordering on starvation, and some of the Macobas and poor people, besides many children taken in battle, were dying.'[126] Among Rolong, those without cattle suffered especially during the 1820s. Women, children, the old, the infirm, and the Kgalagadi were said to be the chief victims of the southern Tswana famine of 1898. Missionaries found the aged especially vulnerable. Those trekking in search of food might have to abandon the weak and helpless.[127] Disease also took a special toll of the poor. 'The careless and heedless who had not been inoculated, the poor people and the vassals, died every day' during the smallpox epidemic of 1862.[128]

Yet natural disaster was only one calamity that created and destroyed poor people. The other was political insecurity and violence. During the first half of the nineteenth century successive invasions devastated Tswana country. Starving Sotho refugees attacked the Tlhaping in 1823. Tswana groups then beggared one another or lost land, cattle, and often children to the Ndebele.[129] From the 1820s frontiersmen from the Cape Colony with guns and horses looted Tswana herds, scattered and impoverished a previously prosperous people, and converted the pioneer mission station at Kuruman into 'the assylum of the destitute and forlorn'.[130] They were followed twenty years later by Afrikaners who raided and subjected the eastern Tswana. The population of the desert edge, so a missionary wrote in 1842, had been swollen 'by fugitives from other towns and villages, which have been reduced by devastating wars from peace and plenty, to the most abject poverty, and the inhabitants forced to flee to the desert for sustenance'.[131]

That Tswana took refuge on the desert edge during famine and war indicated how artificial were the large capital towns which characterised their chiefdoms. The earliest account of Latakoo, the Tlhaping capital, in 1801 thought it 'fully as large as Cape Town', with a population of 10,000–15,000.[132] Later in the century the Ngwato capital was generally reckoned to house some 30,000 people, which made it twice as populous as Timbuktu and almost as large as Kano.[133] Yet these towns were population concentrations rather than urban centres. They were built beautifully but impermanently of wood and reeds, moved quite frequently in response to political and environmental crises, and had neither markets nor economically specialised quarters.[134] Fields surrounded the towns, hyenas might prowl their streets at night, and many inhabitants were often away tending herds or supervising dependants. Only fear of attack and the political will of chiefs held the towns together.[135] Such artificial and undifferentiated conglomerations offered poor Tswana few opportunities for independent survival, which is doubtless why townsmen dispersed during famine. This may also explain their eagerness to accept wage employment. After some initial difficulty, Kuruman was by 1829 'overstocked not being able to employ the one tenth of the applicants'.[136] By 1824 a few 'individual plebeians' had already visited the Cape Colony. Their numbers gradually increased during the nineteenth century, especially during famines, until by 1880 there were 2,135 Tswana at the Kimberley diamond mines alone.[137] There is some evidence that many migrants were poor. Khama occasionally sentenced men to migrant labour in order to earn a fine. In 1877 he apologised to a recruiter for sending only 'a very few Veldt people' – that is, serfs – not 'from my own town'. An unsympathetic observer in Kimberley dismissed Tswana migrants as 'dwarfed little fellows, three of whom are scarcely able to lift a common bag of meal'.[138]

Where few specifically urban means of independent survival were available, the poor were obliged, as in Ethiopia, to seek dependence. Their first recourse was no doubt to kinsmen and especially, as in all societies, to the younger women who carried the chief burden of family care. 'To the daughter they cling for protection and shelter in their helplessness', a missionary wrote of elderly widows, '. . . and I have seen instances of tender reverence and devotion in such daughters.'[139] A generous man might support a host of 'destitute persons, widows and orphans, more or less connected with him by blood or by marriage'.[140] If kin failed, public begging seems not to have been an option. Instead, as Livingstone wrote, 'A poor man attaches himself to the kotla of a rich one, and is considered a child of the latter.'[141] The largest benefactors were chiefs, who were expected to support needy subjects and act as 'upper guardians' to widows and orphans.[142] 'To be begged from is one of the marks of chieftainship among Bechuanas', a missionary declared, and a generous chief like Sekgoma I of the Ngwato might be hailed as 'food-giver'.[143] In famine, especially, a chief was expected to open his granaries, while communities had 'chief's fields' worked communally as famine reserves.[144] Public festivities also supported the poor:

> During the circumcision of the boy cattle must be killed every day. The poor people come together to the chief's kraal and he must feed them during the ceremony; those that possess cattle take perhaps each an ox and give it to the chief leaving it with him when it is to be killed. In former times Bushmen and all sorts of people used to assemble on such occasions to partake of the feast

> but now they are not so liberal, restricting their gifts to the parents of the children.[145]

This report of 1835 is the only direct suggestion that liberality may have declined as stratification increased during the early nineteenth century, but pioneer missionaries were less impressed than later anthropologists by Tswana benevolence. 'The standard of feeling is surely at a low ebb amongst the natives of this part [of] S. Africa towards the aged, sick and young', one noted in 1823. 'The characteristic of the native character', another wrote after twenty years in the country, 'is want of compassion to his fellow, his brother, and his friend.'[146] Given the relatively large scale of Tswana society, the importance of chieftainship, and the extreme environmental insecurity, the nineteenth-century sources contain remarkably little evidence of public care for the poor. Perhaps, as in the twentieth century,[147] much was provided only in return for dependent labour.

The relatively rich sources describing the Tswana people in the nineteenth century give some indication of the extent and complexity of poverty in a cattle-keeping society. Equally, as later chapters will show,[148] the sources reveal a remarkable continuity between the pre-colonial poor and those of the late twentieth century. Nothing illustrates the continuity of the African past more vividly than the study of poverty.

6

Yoruba and Igbo

This survey of the poor and their means of survival in pre-colonial Africa will end with two special cases, the Yoruba and Igbo peoples of modern Nigeria. Their interest is partly that they are especially well documented. Anglican missionaries and evangelists lived among the Yoruba from 1845. Many were themselves Yoruba and the daily journals they kept are unique sources. Anglican missionaries also settled among the Igbo in 1857, although few were Igbo and their knowledge of the country was less profound. Later in the century Roman Catholic missionaries also worked in both regions.

Among Yoruba and Igbo poverty can be studied at a level deeper than mere stereotypes. Moreover, the two societies were distinctive. Although both were only marginally touched at this time by Islam or Christianity, both had cultural traditions which were among the richest in Africa. Many Yoruba lived in towns, with populations ranging up to 100,000, and had an unusually strong kinship structure of large coresident descent groups. Igbo, by contrast, were a classically stateless people whose egalitarian ideology made the status and care of the poor matters of special delicacy.

The Anglican missionaries and evangelists who served in Yorubaland between 1845 and 1900 recorded encounters with exactly 100 identifiable individuals who were very poor in the sense that they were in a state of chronic want.[1] Other persons in similar circumstances are mentioned, but without comparable detail. The 100 individuals fell into four categories. Thirty-five were elderly, of whom 17 were men and 18 women – a higher proportion of men than would have been found among the cattle-owning Tswana. Most of the elderly men were incapacitated: 3 were dying, 7 were sick, 3 were blind, and 1 of the blind was also deaf. Characteristically, they either had no relatives or had been abandoned by them. Of the elderly women, only a minority were incapacitated: 5 were dying, 2 were sick, and 1 was blind. The remainder were generally widows without attendant relatives, for Yoruba women enjoyed much economic independence from their husbands but, as a corollary, became especially dependent on their children in old age, so that lack of children or neglect by them could cause great insecurity. 'O thou god Shongo, my maker and preserver in life', an elderly woman prayed, 'thou hast caused me to wake again this morning, I thank thee. Thou knowest I am old, and child less, thou knowest also that I am a widow, and have no husband to care for me. Send me kind persons to do me favour today, and guide me through the day not to fall into any evil.'[2] Early Roman Catholic missionaries found it necessary to establish a refuge for old people of both sexes in Abeokuta.[3]

The largest category of very poor – 42 of the 100, equally divided between males and females – are mentioned either as adults or without indication of age, which probably implies adulthood. Of the 42, 35 were incapacitated: 4 were dying, 21 were sick, 9 were blind, and 4 were insane.[4] Among mature Yoruba, it appears, the chief cause of severe structural poverty was incapacitation, as elsewhere in pre-colonial Africa. The greatest misery appears to have been suffered by strangers and unwanted slaves, but there were cases of extreme poverty among women with small children who had been abandoned by their husbands – the only form of family poverty which appears in these sources. The most common incapacitating disease was guinea worm. Less prevalent but more feared was leprosy. In contrast to Ethiopians or Hausa, Yoruba expelled leprosy sufferers from their towns with a ruthlessness rare in Africa:

> There are several villages which are composed solely of lepers. They marry among themselves and form families whose children are born lepers,[5] but this terrible disease ordinarily carries away these little ones very quickly . . . Those who become very sick are pitilessly expelled from the villages and condemned to wander here and there and to take refuge where they can. They ordinarily retire into caves in the rocks. Abandoned to the sadness which is the inseparable companion of this disease, they die of sufferings and hunger.[6]

Ten children and adolescents formed the third category of poor. Seven were sick, which suggests that children, like adults, were reduced to poverty chiefly by incapacitation. Disease appears to have been the most common reason why these children were rejected by their kin, although a few were turned away for mystical reasons. 'In this country', wrote a Yoruba pastor, 'a child who has unfortunately lost father and mother is supposed to be possessed of the witchcraft and is frequently reproached for killing the parents.'[7] Similar thinking partly explained the fourth category of identifiable poor: the 13 abandoned infants, not one of whom is mentioned as being sick. Most appear to have been children of mothers who died in childbirth, for apart from the difficulty of nursing such babies where only human milk was available, they were often blamed for their mothers' deaths. Early missionaries cared (with limited success) for many such infants, although others were no doubt brought up by their kin.[8]

Thus severe structural poverty in later nineteenth-century Yorubaland chiefly affected those among the incapacitated – the old, sick, and very young – who were bereft of family care. Less is known of the ordinarily poor. They doubtless included those impoverished by debt, who were often forced to pawn themselves or their dependants, and also the inhabitants of isolated towns and villages who were either preyed upon by stronger groups or suffered from sheer remoteness. 'This town Ado ... is a very nasty town', an evangelist wrote of one such backwater, 'the people themselves are very poorly cladded and the majority of the people are invalids. Of course the town is unhealthy. The population is not above 120.'[9] Beyond such general descriptions, however, very little is known of this kind of rural poverty. Nor is much known of social differentiation among the able-bodied inhabitants of larger towns. Their poor no doubt included those who practised such low-status occupations as porterage,[10] but the ample availability of land and the near absence of taxation among the Yoruba meant that the impoverishing pressures found on the Gold Coast or in Rwanda were lacking. What is clear is that the poorer townsmen and villagers, along with the incapacitated, were the chief victims of the one major cause of conjunctural poverty experienced by nineteenth-century Yoruba: the civil wars which racked the country and may have swollen the numbers of poor and influenced their social identity in ways which are now difficult to detect. Each crisis in the civil wars spawned its destitute refugees. When Ile-Ife was destroyed in 1882, 'Old-men, women, and children, who could not escape, were enslaved.'[11] 'As the famine increased, many little homeless, starving wanderers came into the mission compound at [Ijaye]', a missionary recalled of the appalling siege of 1860–2. 'Some of them appeared to be demented by sickness and hunger, and when we were not watching, returned to the streets to perish.'[12] By interrupting trade, warfare also bred unemployment. 'Poverty is great in Abeokuta', a missionary reported in 1892. 'All the canoeists, all the porters who have no farms and who have been without work since the roads were closed, are dying of hunger.'[13] Fortunately, however, Yorubaland's climate rarely caused serious famine, especially during the nineteenth century.

It is noteworthy that only 10 of the 100 identifiable poor were described as slaves, although some orphan children of slave mothers should be added. There were abandoned and maltreated slaves – the Roman Catholic refuge at Abeokuta admitted them[14] – but Yoruba slave owners had a strong paternalist ethic, favoured slaves could attain high rank, and slavery was probably a less important cause of poverty than in the Kingdoms of the Savanna.[15] Apart from leprosy settlements and perhaps a few especially impoverished villages, no distinct groupings of the poor are discernible. There seems to have been no underworld. Yoruba had strong traditions of 'town riot' in which out-groups sought to overthrow those monopolising power, but such riots seem to have been the work of descent groups (which had military functions) and do not reveal any action specifically by the poor.[16] There is no indication that the social order was criticised. The only evidence of the destitute behaving with any cohesion was when 'Lepers, Epileptics, the Deaf, the Dumb, and the Blind' of Abeokuta, together with many of the able-bodied, flocked to a self-proclaimed miracle healer.[17] Otherwise the Yoruba poor were individuals – as a proverb said, 'A poor man has no relatives.'[18] The evidence is too slight to show whether a distinct subculture of poverty existed, but Richard Lander, the most plebeian of early European travellers in Yorubaland, described the poor of Oyo as markedly underprivileged in food and dress.[19] The Yoruba language had a moderately rich vocabulary of poverty. Both Crowther's vocabulary of 1852 and Bowen's dictionary of 1858 have separate words of Yoruba origin for a poor person (*osise, otosi, oluponju*) and a destitute person (*alaini*). A later dictionary, in the early twentieth century, suggests that *alaini* connoted moral worthlessness, but this dictionary also eroded the distinction between poor and destitute, so that only expert linguistic study would permit a conclusion beyond the obvious point that the poor were a fact of Yoruba life.[20]

Nevertheless, the destitute were less numerous and visible in Yoruba towns than in Ethiopia or Hausaland. Part of the reason was probably that Yorubaland was exceptionally rich in opportunities for independent survival. This was true, most unusually, for both sexes. A Yoruba 'agrotown' combined access to land with a high degree of occupational specialisation. Just as elderly men cultivated to the last moment of their physical capacity, so aged women took their places in the market, where, an observer of Lagos noted in the 1950s, they 'will sit over a dusty tray of rusting tins, "just so as not to be sitting for nothing"'.[21] Yoruba bought even more of their food ready-cooked in the streets than did Hausa, providing both nourishment for single men and income for women. Many thousands, chiefly women, found ill-paid casual employment as porters.[22] Young men joined warbands. Old men practised basketwork. Old women spun cotton. Plaiting hair was a professional occupation. Perhaps the lowest in the hierarchy of jobs, as so often in Africa, was the arduous task of collecting bush produce. 'Many poor women . . . obtain a living by supplying the market with firewood, which they sometimes bring from a distance of six or eight miles', a missionary reported. 'Others gather large leaves, which they sell by the basketful to the market women to be employed as wrapping paper.'[23] When a British official estimated the annual profit from occupations in part of the Ilorin province in 1918, he put at the bottom, in ascending order: female spinners; female petty traders, firewood sellers, and preparers of cooked food; female weavers; dyers, potters, and makers of palm oil and shea butter; mat-makers; and male weavers, drummers, honey collectors, and barbers.[24] Crime does not appear in the records as a resource of the poor; in peacetime it was generally attributed to redundant 'warboys' and in wartime to such unemployed workers as canoemen.[25] Nor is there any reference to prostitution, save for the occasional individual harlot. Yoruba culture seems to have had no place for the 'free woman' found in Hausaland, presumably because the young widow or divorcee returned to her powerful kinship group or made a living by trade. However, there were professional prostitutes in Lagos, where many poor Yoruba took refuge.[26]

The wealth of opportunities for independent survival was a distinctive feature of poverty in Yorubaland. Another was the fact that Yoruba had an indigenous tradition of begging which may have been unique in Africa outside Christian or Islamic regions. Begging in Yorubaland, as in Ethiopia or Hausaland, was an exploitation by the poor of prevailing religious practices. The Yoruba beggar – *alagbe* in nineteenth-century vocabularies – was customarily described by missionaries as a 'devil-monger'. This was because the beggar normally carried or sat next to a figurine of Eshu, who was the intermediary between men and Olorun (Owner of the Heavens) but was misinterpreted by missionaries as the devil. The beggar either offered the figurine for passers-by to touch, or invoked Eshu's blessings on them, or simply sat and waited for them to place a cowrie shell or two beside the figurine. 'We met an Elesu woman (Devil Priestess) sitting under a tree in his street blessing the passers by, and receiving a cowry or two from different individuals', it was reported from Oyo.[27] Many of these beggars were probably recent mothers of twins, who were sometimes instructed by diviners to spend a short period in this way.[28] Some beggars used representations of other divinities. A few used no representation at all. It was common for priests and cult-groups to demand offerings from passers-by in honour of a divinity. Yet there were also impoverished beggars who exploited the religious tradition as a means of survival. 'There is no other means by which I can earn my livelihood', one told a passing evangelist.[29] An elderly woman carrying a representation of Oya (wife of Shango, god of thunder) and begging from door to door explained: 'I take up this goddess to go about to ask for cowries, because I have no helper. I am too old to have a husband, I have had many children at Oyo, but they are all dead, hence I have no supporter and none to look to again but to the goddess Oya that is now supporting me.'[30] Some beggars were elderly people who apparently made a modest living from it. A few were able-bodied 'sturdy beggars', to whom there seems to have been no popular hostility, for almsgiving appears to have been undiscriminating. Scarcely any beggars were children, in contrast to the family poverty of early modern Europe. The use of cowrie shells as currency probably encouraged begging, as in Hausaland; indeed, alms seem to have been given almost solely in cowries, in contrast to the food often given in Hausaland, and there was no parallel to the Ethiopian practice of regularly feasting paupers. The possibility that the Yoruba begging tradition was copied from Islamic models in societies to the north cannot be ruled out, but its intimate connection with the indigenous religion argues against this.

Yorubaland had not only beggars but ascetics, another category often thought peculiar to world religions. Again the practice had religious roots. A pastor in Ibadan recorded in 1873

> the death of my cousin Otunbaloku, one of the members of the Ake Church [at Abeokuta], who had been my high priest in the worship of the goddess Obatala in 1842 . . . He had 72 disciples or followers of this god. He was also a great farmer by which he made himself a gentleman. But in process of time this Orisa[31] forbad him from the lawful trade of farming for about 25 years, that he was obliged to carry about, long iron staff which was known to belong to this Orisa, the use of which was to carry about every five days as a day set apart for this Orisas worship. He went therefore with this long staff from street to street, house to house, dancing and blessing people. He received from individuals a cowry or two, but a generous giver may give 4 cowries for his arduous labour; and the result of a whole day route in this way amounts sometimes to 2 strings sometimes to 4 strings.[32]

Such ascetics operated as individuals and lived in public; Yoruba culture would have had little room for Ethiopian hermits. Yet there was a notion that religious experts should be poor, while the association between religious merit and physical suffering was clear in the mutual flagellation practised at the festivals of certain divinities.[33] That the prayers of the poor were especially acceptable to the gods was implicit in the begging tradition. It was explicit in the belief that the blind, lame, mad, and other unfortunates were fashioned thus by the divinity Obatala and enjoyed his special protection.[34] Yet there is also evidence of some deliberate cruelty to the unfortunate,[35] as well as callous neglect. Like Ethiopians, Yoruba lived too close to poverty to idealise it.

Yoruba evidence is weak on the care of the poor. One reason may have been that many supported themselves either through the manifold opportunities for independent survival or by begging. Another reason was probably that the large coresident descent groups – which might contain scores or even hundreds of people – cared for their unfortunate members more frequently than the missionary sources reveal. 'Parents are respected by their children by whom they are cared for and provided in their old age', the Yoruba bishop Crowther reported; 'they think their duty towards their parents is not completed till they can give them honourable burial.'[36] By contrast, institutional provision was totally lacking. The many religious cults had temples, priests, initiates, and funds, but descriptions of them never suggest institutionalised welfare roles,[37] although, like spirit cults elsewhere, they did provide offices (and presumably access to donations) for many elderly people.[38] Yoruba also had innumerable voluntary societies providing mutual aid to members, notably the savings clubs of which there were said to be 300 in Abeokuta alone in 1861.[39] These must have done much to prevent members falling into poverty, but they seem unlikely to have helped the already impoverished.

In Ethiopia, Kazembe's kingdom, or a Tswana town a destitute man might turn to the king. Some accounts suggest that this was so in Yorubaland. Crowther's vocabulary of 1852 quoted a proverb, 'A poor beggar never perishes from want in Oyo (the capital)', and Professor Ojo has stated that so many of the deformed took refuge at any royal palace that 'the Yoruba regarded it as a circus'.[40] Yet of the many descriptions of courts and palaces in the missionary sources only one makes even the vaguest reference to destitutes.[41] Yorubaland as a whole was characterised by the strength of social groups and the relative weakness of the state. Its towns lacked not only public buildings but often planning and public services of any kind. In the absence of convincing evidence, one must doubt whether the authorities had the institutional capacity to provide regularly for the poor, who probably looked instead to individual largess. Here the great compounds which dominated urban geography went together with the embracing generosity which was not only the expected behaviour of great men but the very source of their power. Several leading Christians of this period had large households where many impoverished people found refuge.[42] Yet no Christian remotely approached the wealth of great chiefs. The size of their households is clouded by legend, but an evangelist thought that the most powerful chief of Ode Ondo had perhaps 1,000 followers in 1875, while Ogunmola of Ibadan, perhaps the greatest Yoruba of his time, is said to have *lost* 1,200 of his slaves during the Ijaye war of 1860–5.[43] The records say nothing of charity by such men to the poor. It must surely be the records that are at fault.

Yorubaland provides sub-Saharan Africa's best evidence of the existence of poverty, begging, and asceticism among people who did not practise a world religion, literacy, or intensive agriculture. Yet Yorubaland was a very unusual part of Africa: urbanised, wealthy, culturally sophisticated, large in scale. It is necessary also to investigate the existence and nature of poverty among small-scale communities.

The Igbo, eastern neighbours of the Yoruba, received their first missionaries in 1857 when Anglicans settled at Onitsha on the Niger. These missionaries say much less about poverty among the Igbo than did their colleagues among the Yoruba. The obvious explanation would be that there was less to write about because poverty was rare among a stateless people less stratified than the Yoruba and living chiefly in villages or loosely agglomerated towns. Yet the study of pastoralists showed the danger of assuming that poverty did not exist among stateless peoples.

In reality, as in the Kongo kingdom, the relative silence of the Anglican missionaries was largely a matter of perception. Unlike their counterparts in many parts of Africa, they were not alerted by mass conjunctural poverty, for famine was almost unknown[44] and Igboland's endemic inter-village violence did not breed refugees like the progress of an Ethiopian army. Moreover, there were fewer missionaries than in Yorubaland, fewer still were native to the area, and their different terms of employment did not oblige them to submit daily journals. Onitsha itself was Igbo-speaking, but otherwise the nineteenth-century Anglican missionaries worked along the River Niger rather than penetrating Igboland proper, of which they knew little. Nor did Igbo come to the Europeans. Onitsha was the largest town on the river, but with only some 13,000 people in 1859[45] it was small by Yoruba standards and attracted rather few poor people. In this it exemplified a larger problem of perception. Igbo concealed their poor. Whereas the rulers of Rwanda and Burundi deliberately emphasised differences of wealth and power, and whereas an Ethiopian court or a Hausa town attracted the poor into the open and made their numbers visible, the few institutions by which Igbo provided for the poor were designed to disguise their condition in a society where equal opportunity was the prevailing ideology and poverty was considered shameful. If missionaries wanted to see the Igbo poor, therefore, they had to attract them into the open by offering them genuine relief.

This was clear from the first category of poor people whom Anglican missionaries noticed: unwanted babies. Almost all Igbo groups killed twins at birth, as unnatural creatures. If a mother died in childbirth the infant was often buried with her.[46] Both the Anglicans and the Roman Catholics who also settled at Onitsha in 1885 attempted to rescue and rear such infants, often against the fervent opposition of parents and relatives.[47] These attempts extended their attention to other orphans, who were generally represented in art and folklore as deprived and ill treated.[48] 'We have no less than 65 children to raise and feed', a sister reported from Onitsha in 1898; 'the majority are children abandoned on account of diseases or sores.'[49] Concern with infants also alerted missionaries to the fate of the mothers. 'A little distance on the outside of the town', Bishop Crowther reported from an Igbo village in the hinterland of Bonny, 'is a village of the outcast mothers whose misfortune was to give birth to twins: after the infant twins had been barbarously destroyed as unnatural beings, the mothers are cast out, and forbidden to go into the town to have any dealings in the community.'[50] Supposed witches – predominantly old women – were another outcast group. 'A number of elderly women who have been driven out of their own towns on the charge of witchcraft' lived in an impoverished community on the waterfront at Onitsha, while another group took refuge with the Roman Catholics at Asaba.[51]

Apart from caring for infants, the early Anglican missionaries in Igboland had little training with which to offer aid to the poor. By contrast, Roman Catholic missionaries – especially sisters – were trained and eager to undertake works of mercy. Soon inundated by poor people seeking aid, they described Igboland as a place of extensive misery, and although their accounts were designed to stir consciences and purses in Europe, they also expressed a difference of experience which followed from a difference of approach to a society where poverty was habitually concealed.

Almost as soon as Holy Ghost Fathers reached Onitsha in 1885 they built 'a house of refuge for the old and the despised'. West of the Niger, the Society of African Missions had four such refuges for the aged in 1909, and generally Catholic missionaries in this region found more need to provide for the elderly than was normal in Africa.[52] Old men were especially vulnerable when childless, but missionaries reported that others lost respect once their health was broken, and later anthropologists were surprised by the lack of deference for age.[53] Elderly women, too, were at special risk when childless – a barren woman's body might be mutilated before burial[54]– but they also seem generally to have suffered more and were certainly more common among those seeking mission care:

> 'I am alone', she said to me; 'I built this hut myself. You see this banana? It is all I have. I spin cotton which I sell in order to have something to eat. Often I do without food; I cannot go to find wood, and my legs are not strong enough to support me. When it rains I am soaked through, for the water comes through the banana leaves which I heap up around my hut.'[55]

Since widows remained with their husbands' kin, divorce was relatively easy,[56] and women had considerable economic independence, it is possible that an unusual number of women were left destitute when no longer able to support themselves. The pioneer anthropologist, Northcote Thomas, found in the Awka area in 1911 that nearly one-fifth of all the widows he surveyed were living alone, a pattern confirmed by later enquirers.[57]

Roman Catholic missionaries also found leprosy especially common. Indeed, it was its prevalence that made poverty among the Igbo comparable in scale to that among the Yoruba, for Igboland and its environs had one of the greatest concentrations of leprosy in the world, with over 3 per cent of the population infected in certain divisions during the 1930s and figures of up to 15 per cent recorded for certain clans.[58] Treatment of leprosy sufferers probably varied with the severity of their visible symptoms and the importance of their social positions. While some missionaries reported them living freely within the community, others found many advanced cases abandoned in great misery in the bush.[59] A doctor later wrote of Igboland:

> The leper meets with no sympathy whatever from healthy people. If he is a child he is commonly driven from the village and his fate can be imagined. If he is a strong adult he will be tolerated in the village as long as his disease is not very noticeable, especially if he is well-to-do. If, as is usual, his disease advances, toleration gives place to ostracism, and he is either forced to leave the village and live in the bush, or else he remains in the village, an object of scorn, blamed for every evil that befalls the community. Women, like children, often receive short shrift and are liable to expulsion.
>
> There is of course considerable variation in this treatment of lepers from one village to another. On one extreme a village may be found where every leper is expelled as soon as his sickness is known to his fellows. On the other hand I have found villages where no efforts whatever are made to remove lepers, but all villages are united in the total lack of sympathy which lepers may expect. The end of the story is pitiful. Neglected by his friends, fed for a time perhaps by his companions in trouble, the leper is fortunate if some intercurrent infection supervenes and saves him from starvation.[60]

Igbo believed leprosy to be hereditary, but thought that it manifested itself only in those who offended the gods, were attacked by sorcery or poison, or were in contact with manifest leprosy. Prospective marriage partners were carefully investigated and one doctor claimed in 1937 that in some towns the elders held periodical inspections of all inhabitants.[61] Sufferers in the early stage of the disease tried innumerable remedies:

> The patches are treated with native preparations intended to cause blistering of the skin; or burnt by rubbing with hot ashes; or fire in some other form; or scraped, with or without some form of premedication. When the wounds are healing, pigments or dyes may be rubbed in, to help to restore the normal colour.[62]

It was the advanced and destitute cases living alone in the bush who drew the attention of Catholic missionaries. 'I no longer have anyone', an adolescent sufferer in a squalid hut complained: 'they put me here after my father's death. When I am hungry, I cry, and the people, tired of hearing me, bring me something to eat . . . Nobody comes to see me; all the people of the neighbourhood keep a distance when talking to me.'[63] Such outcasts sometimes created distinct villages. There are accounts of sufferers being killed because of their condition, but these are naturally impossible to verify.[64] During the 1890s Catholic missionaries began to give refuge to abandoned sufferers.[65]

The Igbo poor were visible only to those who penetrated beyond public places. 'We have no beggars', an Igbo wrote in the eighteenth century, and although there was an Igbo word for a beggar in the early twentieth century and an occasional proverbial reference to begging, not a single beggar is mentioned in the missionary sources.[66] Yet Igbo were intensely aware of poverty, for the absence of other forms of stratification made the distinction between rich and poor especially important. 'The Igbo model for viewing their social stratification is based on wealth', an Igbo anthropologist has written. '. . . they distinguish between *ogbenye* or *mbi* – the poor – from *dinkpa* – the moderately prosperous – and the latter from *nnukwu madu* or *ogaranya* – the rich.'[67] In 1911 Thomas listed *obiam* and *obwenye* as words for 'poor', while the largest section of his collection of Igbo proverbs referred to wealth and poverty: 'The rich man puts down his basket in the market, the poor man fears'; 'The poor man gets a friend; the rich man takes him away'; 'If one man walks alone, a fly bites and kills him'; 'Those who have money are friends of each other.'[68] A later anthropologist reported 'an almost hypertrophied sense of property' and an extreme execration of theft. 'Property, money, honesty are constantly recurring motifs', she wrote, and the Igbo stress on industry and achievement became a commonplace to students of Africa. 'The only cure for poverty is industry', warned a proverb.[69] In such a society, as among the Kikuyu, poverty incurred a special moral odium.

Given this ethos, it is not surprising that there were many ways of being poor in Igboland, and again it is the complexity of poverty in a stateless rural society that is striking. Land was becoming scarce in several regions by the late nineteenth century. In 1896 there was 'a kind of civil war' in the Onitsha area when two villages disputed a tract of land.[70] While the traditional staple crop, yams, required good land and was expensive to plant, cassava was cheap to plant, flourished in poor soil, spread quickly in the nineteenth century, and was especially the food of the very poor. 'Those who through poverty cannot afford to plant yams, plants cassada as a substitute', an evangelist in Onitsha noted in 1863.[71] Yet when Thomas sought a criterion of wealth and poverty in 1911 he chose not food but marriage. Children were the consolation of the poor. 'A rich man never takes away a poor man's child', said the proverb.[72] But not every poor man could have children. 'It is possible', Thomas reported, 'to find men of 40 or 45 who have never married because they have been too poor to buy a wife', and he added that bridewealth ranged up to £40, depending largely on the girl's qualities. Such unmarried adult males were known as 'male women'.[73] Thomas's survey of certain quarters of Awka – a rich town famous for iron-working – revealed 33 married men who were monogamous and 103 who were polygynous. By contrast, nearby Agolo village had 356 monogamists, 198 polygynists, and 258 unmarried male householders. As a poor village, Agolo exported women to Awka.[74] One means by which a poor man could respectably secure a wife was to pawn himself in order to raise the bridewealth. Pawning or even enslaving oneself or a relative was also used to meet debts.[75]

Before a man reached the depths of self-enslavement, however, he could try many means of independent survival. His first defence was, of course, the land, and especially the fact that although land was sometimes scarce it was under lineage control and every male lineage member had a right to a plot.[76] Women enjoyed fewer land rights; for them, as in Yorubaland, the market was an important means of survival. Crafts were mainly performed by men, but mat-making was a women's occupation, while an investigator in one area in the 1930s found that custom reserved trade in pots to barren or elderly women. He also found many women collecting and selling bush produce.[77] Young, able-bodied men worked for the prosperous for payment in kind or cowrie shells. Labour migration from barren areas to more favoured parts already existed in the nineteenth century.[78] After a brief initial hesitation, early missionaries found it markedly easier to recruit paid labourers than was normal in Africa. 'The population is so great and it is so difficult to live from their farms', one reported from the Owerri region, 'that if they hear we shall want carriers they come in great numbers begging to be used', even during the farming season.[79]

As everywhere in Africa, there were also opportunities for dependent survival. Family care was the norm, despite individual cases of neglect. The wealthy man was expected to display generosity, especially towards a struggling junior, although proverbs questioned the reality.[80] Largess was displayed especially by those taking the titles which marked a man's success.

'On those days', an informant recalled, 'you will feed everybody, you will give alms to everybody who calls on you for it. You will be cooking, not only for Awka people, but any passer-by . . . The poor man crawling will come to you. I haven't a singlet, you give him a singlet. I haven't shoes. You look at him, he requires shoes, you give him shoes. Until everybody is satisfied.'[81] In 1906 a missionary described a second funeral ceremony in which the empty coffin was carried through the town so that people could throw money into it; the money was then scattered in the market-place.[82] It was characteristic of the concealment surrounding poverty that charity should have appeared as a by-product of other social activities.

Even by African standards, Igbo markedly lacked institutional provision for the poor. Igbo were capable of community action, as was displayed in the Owerri area by the periodic erection of Mbari houses, often at great expense.[83] Yet where social welfare was concerned, concealment was the rule. One remarkable illustration – much in need of historical study – was *osu* slavery, which existed widely in central Igboland and had striking similarities to some Asian outcaste institutions, notably the pagoda slavery of Burma.[84] In principle, *osu* were slaves bought and dedicated to a divinity as propitiatory offerings, 'a living sacrifice'.[85] They occupied 'the lowest rank imaginable in Igbo society', lived in separate communities, were unthinkable as marriage partners, defiled by their very touch, might not be buried lest they anger the earth, and passed their outcaste status to their children.[86] The interesting point, however, is that freemen could take refuge in this marginal community, at the cost of remaining there for life. Criminals could find sanctuary there. So could widows anxious not to be inherited, and it is said that women especially used this means of escape.[87] Observers noticed that a disproportionate number of *osu* were handicapped, and although some thought that a number were deliberately crippled to prevent them escaping, it seems more likely that the handicapped were sold into slavery as children or themselves later found refuge in this way.[88] 'A man might find himself so weak and helpless that he could not earn a living by himself alone', an Igbo scholar has written. 'By declaring himself an *Osu*, he became entitled to feed by the charity of the people, to appropriate certain things as it were by force, and make them his own, and above all, to a share of the food and articles offered in sacrifice to the divinity to which he belonged.'[89] Although *osu* lived chiefly by cultivating the land, they also possessed the privileged right to charity.[90] In 1878 a pastor found a widowed slave dedicated to a divinity living on the outskirts of Onitsha and subsisting 'on the gifts of passers by'. Some forty years later a missionary observed a handicapped *osu* at a market near Onitsha who 'begged or stole from all and sundry, and because of his calling nothing was denied him'.[91] Houses near the village market often belonged to *osu* and it is interesting that the earliest reference to begging in Igboland states that 'At the entrances to the market were weather-beaten, hungry beggars who asked the traders for alms.'[92]

Just as begging in Yorubaland appears to have grown out of indigenous religious practices, so had the most clearly institutionalised provision for the Igbo poor. It is a fitting point to end a discussion designed to demonstrate that while the poor were as much part of pre-colonial Africa as they were of other pre-industrial societies, their identity and means of survival were shaped by the particularity of each culture in which they were found.

7

Early European initiatives

In 1482 the Portuguese established the first permanent European settlement in sub-Saharan Africa at Elmina on the Gold Coast. During the next four centuries European powers created trading posts, mission stations, and colonies in many parts of the continent. This chapter describes the measures they took to care for the poor, both European and African. Unlike previous chapters, this is concerned less with the identity of the poor than with provision for them.

In contrast to the legend that pre-colonial Africa had no poor, European rulers and merchants were generally concerned to avoid being overwhelmed by them. This they attempted by introducing poor relief institutions from their own countries, so that sub-Saharan Africa – itself so lacking in formal institutions – now experienced early modern Europe's diverse approaches to poverty. These institutions were already designed to exclude all but the most deserving. In Africa the filter was even more rigorous lest embryonic services be swamped. Occasionally this parsimony was relieved by private philanthropy. Often it coexisted with a more generous benevolence practised by missionaries, especially by the sisterhoods which during the nineteenth century brought a new quality of charity to the African continent.

The fort at Elmina does not appear to have provided for the poor. Its hospital was 'staffed by two to three Portuguese female nurses, a male attendant, a physician, a barber-bloodletter, and an apothecary',[1] but its inmates were mainly Portuguese troops and sailors. Other European trading companies on the West African coast in the sixteenth and seventeenth centuries confined themselves to distributing among the poor a proportion of confiscated merchandise or fines levied on their employees.[2] Much the same was true on the other side of the continent, in Mozambique, where in 1507 the Portuguese built the first hospital in sub-Saharan Africa, for those taken sick on the voyage between Europe and India.[3] Despite periods of decay, this hospital survived for the next two centuries. For a time it was managed by a Superintendent and 'Brothers of the Misericordia', the charitable institution which in Portuguese towns cared for the poor and sick, but there is no evidence that the hospital in Mozambique cared for poor Africans.[4] Accounts of the colony in the nineteenth century, however, show survivals of other patterns of charity, whether the largess of wealthy patrons[5] or the team of blind people whom a missionary saw sing, dance, and play from door to door in Tete in 1889. 'The oldest have preserved the memory of a few words of the Ave Maria and Salve Regina', he wrote, 'but it takes good will to recognise them as a prayer!'[6]

Portuguese models took firmer root in Angola, but there also poor relief was confined by colonial circumstances. When Paulo Dias de Novais and his men founded Luanda in 1576 they built a hospital which became known as the Hospital of the Misericordia. By the seventeenth century it was managed by the 'Superintendent and Brothers of the Misericordia', but it was chiefly financed by the Crown, whose concern was the medical care of troops.[7] The institution was therefore 'always and principally a military hospital',[8] although the bishop who restored it around 1630 'attended personally to the good care of the poor sick Portuguese, blacks, and coloureds' and the Dutch who took it over in 1641 found that it contained 'lodgings for the poor'.[9] Recaptured by the Portuguese, the institution still survived in 1837, when it was secularised.[10] For Portuguese towns possession of a Misericordia was a coveted symbol of municipal status. Massangano jealously defended the Misericordia established there around 1661 to care for casualties in war against the Kongo kingdom. Benguela later created another. The Misericordia which existed in São Salvador in 1626, with both Portuguese and African brothers and a hospital 'in country fashion', has already been mentioned.[11] There was another at Cape Verde in the 1620s, while at the same period the Emperor of Ethiopia gave missionaries 'a large Present for the finishing of an Hospital, which had been begun in the Kingdom of Tigre', although this was doubtless abandoned in the warfare which soon afterwards swept the Portuguese from the kingdom.[12]

Even in Luanda, however, almost all the inmates of the hospital were said in 1664 to be soldiers.[13] The African poor probably benefited more from the personal charity which sporadically alleviated Angola's brutality and provincialism. Among the plantations of the Bengo Valley during the 1630s a Jesuit, Pero Tavares, performed a ministry of Franciscan poverty, sleeping on a mat, using the discipline, eating local food, and refusing both the planters' hospitality and gifts offered by Africans. 'It is well to do good to these poor people without accepting their presents, on account of their great poverty', he wrote. 'I believe that if the blessed Saint Francis came to these regions, he would see that his poverty was nothing in comparison with theirs.'[14] In Luanda the Jesuit College was reported in 1625 to give alms extensively, while in the 1750s a Capuchin friar, Andrea da Burgio, regularly distributed charity to 'a crowd of poor blacks who came to beg alms at the door of the friary'.[15] Missionaries entertaining African guests sometimes found themselves also feeding uninvited strangers.[16]

Poor relief systems in Portuguese colonies – clergy and lay confraternities jointly managing an all-purpose 'hospital' and providing out-relief in alms – followed a southern European Catholic tradition. Elsewhere in sixteenth-century Europe the organisation of poor relief changed as civic authorities sought to control and rationalise the heterogeneous charities inherited from the Middle Ages. The first part of Africa to experience these changes was the colony founded by the Dutch East India Company at the Cape of Good Hope in 1652. Its first purpose was to nurse sick seamen landed from passing ships. The tented hospital for this purpose established during 1652 was replaced four years later by a permanent institution.[17] A formal poor relief system began in 1665 when the first Calvinist minister arrived.[18] It was modelled on the organisation created in Calvin's Geneva, where laymen entrusted with the care of the poor were made deacons of the church, thereby integrating secular and religious philanthropy.[19] This system survived in essence until the end of Dutch control at the Cape in 1806. Funds came from collections after the communion service, legacies, fines, penances, burial fees, and the like. In 1779 the deacons possessed reserves of 234,155 guilders; their expenditure in 1792 was 15,900 guilders. They investigated claims of poverty to ensure that they were deserving – a requirement which became increasingly rigorous during the eighteenth century.[20] In contrast to the vast General Hospital at Geneva, however, the Cape poor received aid in their own homes or in those of individuals who undertook their care, since the numbers were small and the community sense of a small colony was strong. Most expenditure went to provide food for the elderly, handicapped, widowed, sick, wives of prisoners, and the like, who also received clothing, specially built cottages, and funeral expenses. Those too old to care for themselves were entrusted to a paid attendant. The deacons also paid a retainer to a 'surgeon' and ran a school for the children in their care.[21] Orphans were a special concern, for Cape law allocated property to children if either one or both parents died. By 1673 an Orphan Chamber existed, on Dutch models, to administer this property.[22] The deacons boarded out poor orphans, paid for their education, and then commonly apprenticed them or put them into service, which some observers criticised as giving such children scant hope of advancement. In the early days the Church Council occasionally required neglectful parents to hand their children over to the deacons for proper upbringing.[23]

White paupers were few. In 1732, for example, the governor listed 114 'poor, indigent, decrepit' Europeans in the colony, probably excluding children.[24] 'There are no beggars in the whole colony', a British visitor observed in 1797–8; 'and but a few who are the objects of public charity . . . Where the mere articles of eating and drinking are so reasonably procured as in the Cape, it is no great degree of charity for the rich to support their poor relations, and, accordingly, it is the common practice of the country.' He added, however:

> Those who come under the denomination of poor are, for the most part, emancipated slaves, who may not have the benefit of such relations. Nor does the church provide for such on uncertain grounds. Every person manumitting a slave must pay to the church fifty rix dollars or ten pounds, and at the same time give security that such slave shall not become burdensome to the church for a certain number of years.[25]

Sick male slaves were initially admitted to the hospital, but from 1685 they were generally removed to join sick female slaves in the Slave Lodge, an appalling structure which housed all Company slaves, whether incapacitated or healthy.[26] Individual masters were responsible for their slaves' welfare. 'Free Blacks' – in practice chiefly emancipated half-breed or Indonesian slaves, their children, and a few incorporated Khoi – were initially treated by the deacons on equal terms with whites when seeking poor relief, but during the eighteenth century their position deteriorated, as in other respects. In 1705 the relief paid to them was reduced to roughly half that given to the white poor.[27] A resolution of 1777 required anyone freeing a slave to pay a deposit to the deacons, lest a 'stream of paupers' threaten the welfare system.[28] Impoverished free blacks were in fact supported chiefly from legacies for that purpose, just as others left funds for 'decrepit and sick slaves'. The deacons generally found other free blacks to care for those in need, but racial segregation was still limited at this time. It was not unusual in the late eighteenth century for black orphans to share school classes with children of white burghers.[29]

In 1798 the Dutch colony contained 21,746 'Christians', 25,754 'slaves', and 14,447 'Hottentots'.[30] Slaves could be savagely treated, but poverty was probably more common among Khoi labourers and herdsmen, for by this time few Khoi within the colony possessed land.[31] They were the first numerous group in sub-Saharan Africa who were indisputably pauperised by exclusion from access to resources. 'A Hottentot can now seldom get away at the expiration of his term', an official report explained in 1809:

> If he should happen not to be in debt to his master . . . he is not allowed to take his children, or he is detained under some frivolous pretence . . . In the distant parts of the colony a male Hottentot receives no more in the year than twelve or fourteen Rix-dollars, which may be paid either in money, clothes, or cattle. A female obtains much less.[32]

Legislation in that year declared any Khoi travelling without a pass to be a vagrant who could be assigned to an employer.[33] 'It is now become a received opinion', a commission reported in 1828, 'that a Hottentot found anywhere without a pass is a vagrant.'[34] In Cape Town 'every Hottentot (who has not a contract of Service) is sent to Prison to be kept there till he gets Service'.[35] These measures, designed in part to meet the labour shortage caused by the abolition of the slave trade in 1807, initiated a generation of misery for the Khoi. By 1828 some 5,963 of them had taken refuge at mission stations in the interior.[36] Bethelsdorp, near modern Port Elizabeth, supported many orphans and an asylum for the elderly and indigent. 'All the old and infirm fly thither', the missionary wrote in 1827,

> and there are but few families that have not an infirm father, mother, grandfather or grandmother, uncle or aunt, or some other helpless relation to support, which is a very heavy tax ... I suppose there is no people where our society have sent missionaries who have been and still are in more abject circumstances than the Hottentots ... they have been scattered and peeled.[37]

A year later new legislation removed most special legal disabilities suffered by Khoi, but difficulties of enforcement and failure to make land available ensured that most Khoi remained dependent labourers held down by informal arrangements.[38] In this they were joined after 1838 by those newly freed slaves who did not move to the towns, by some 4,000 liberated slaves landed by the navy, and by growing numbers of destitute Bantu workers who entered the colony from the eastern frontier and accepted wages so low that the condition of farmworkers improved only slowly during the next half-century.[39] In 1875 the average wage of a Coloured agricultural labourer in the Western Cape was 15 or 20 shillings a month plus his keep and the use of a garden. A housemaid in Cape Town earned the same and a male domestic servant about twice as much.[40]

Cape Town had its poor. Ms Judges' invaluable study of the town during the 1830s found that total destitution was quite rare – in 1840 only about 170 of Cape Town's 20,181 people passed through the Pauper Establishment[41] – but many occupations paid a family man much less than the sixpence per person per day reckoned as the minimum for survival. At that rate a labourer's monthly wage (£1.16.0) could have supported only 2.4 people. Often, no doubt, his wife worked as a laundress (at £1.10.0 a month) or wet nurse (at £1.17.6), but family life was barely possible for an unskilled man, even when in full-time work.[42] Should he be sick or injured, should he be unemployed or imprisoned, should he father many children, or should he spend his earnings unwisely in a town where thirsts were deep and alcohol cheap, then his household faced a form of family poverty common in early modern Europe but not previously recorded in sub-Saharan Africa. Most such families were probably Coloured, for although neither Cape Town nor its occupations were racially segregated, the Coloured people – the emerging amalgam of free blacks, ex-slaves, and Khoi – did most low-wage jobs.[43] Newly emancipated slaves – nearly one-third of the total population in the late 1830s – were especially vulnerable, for they often had neither kin nor savings.[44] Among poor whites, Irish immigrants were prominent, as were boatmen and fishermen. A smallpox epidemic in 1840 infected only 5 per cent of those living in the suburban Ward XIII but over 34 per cent in Ward I, where Coloured fishermen clustered around the port and 87 per cent of houses were overcrowded, a problem recently exacerbated by the influx of newly freed slaves into the slums and the first arrival of impoverished

Bantu.[45] As the nineteenth century progressed, Cape Town's multiracial slums became places of sickening squalor.

Poor whites had existed in the Dutch colony almost from its formation, often taking refuge on the frontier.[46] During the nineteenth century their numbers were swollen by unsuccessful settlers, immigrant labourers, and the more feckless of the Trekboers who had penetrated the interior. The Cape census of 1875 listed nearly 10 per cent of the adult white population in four especially ill-paid categories: over 2,000 domestic servants, nearly as many 'undefined' labourers, some 4,000 transport workers, and 2,500 *bywoners* (squatters), herdsmen, farm servants, and agricultural labourers – the last often earning no more than Coloured workers.[47] *Uri-San* (White Bushmen), as Khoi described them,[48] were also found beyond the Cape frontier. 'I think I never saw white people in Africa so poor', a missionary wrote in 1867 of Afrikaners living among the Tswana of Molepolole. 'They are brown and weather-beaten as gipsies, and wear rags such as few of the [African] women on this place who dress, would wear.'[49] Yet Afrikaners, like Igbo, were essentially a stateless people with elaborate ways of disguising poverty. 'The family instinct is particularly strong among the farming population', it was reported from the Transvaal in 1908, 'and the aged, the infirm, and the destitute can usually obtain assistance or a home from their relatives.'[50] Orphans were quickly adopted. *Bywoners* grazed stock on their patrons' land, performed tasks ostensibly as favours, and scrupulously avoided asking for work. As one later boasted, 'Never in my life have I worked for another man *for money*.'[51] The republican governments gave them jobs and building plots, while the Transvaal Volksraad long made grants to poor petitioners much as a Bemba chief might feed his subjects.[52]

Like their Dutch predecessors, the British authorities who occupied the Cape in 1806 were first concerned with hospital facilities. Civilian needs were first met by what became known as the Old Somerset Hospital, opened as a private institution by Dr Samuel Bailey in 1818 but taken over by the government in 1828. 'A large straggling building', over 100 metres square, it was designed as a receiving hospital for merchant seamen, slaves, and lunatics, but it developed into a repository for the incapacitated of all kinds who were bereft of family support and too poor to escape hospitalisation. During the 1820s one wing housed the sick while the others accommodated leprosy patients, paupers, emancipated slaves, and lunatics, the last being 'confined in cells better calculated for the confinement of wild animals'.[53]

The degeneration of the Old Somerset Hospital into a poorhouse paralleled a shift of policy away from the out-relief given to the poor in Dutch times and towards the institutionalisation of the poor which was embodied in Britain in the New Poor Law of 1834.[54] The first institution at the Cape, an Orphan House opened in 1814 for 'poor white, not illegitimate [*nie onegte*] children' by private benefactors led by Widow Möller, long faced 'the prejudice of the people generally to allow their relatives to be supported by public charity'.[55] Other races had less choice. When government slaves were freed in 1827 the former Slave Lodge was converted into a hospital for the aged and infirm among them. Twelve years later it was renamed the Pauper Establishment and admitted paupers of all kinds. In February 1841 it contained 11 white and 77 Coloured inmates, who were supposed not to leave the gates without written permission but in practice often used it as a base for begging.[56] Outside Cape Town the new regime ordained that paupers of all races should be treated only in gaol infirmaries.[57]

This incarceration of sick paupers conformed with the principle of 'less eligibility' which underlay the New Poor Law. It assumed that no able-bodied person need be destitute.[58] In Cape Town, according to Ms Judges, the assumption of the 1830s was that people would work until they could no longer do so and would then either live on savings or be supported by relatives. 'Those who had neither were consistently treated as exceptional cases whose admission to government institutions had to be individually approved by the Governor.'[59] A further corollary was extreme parsimony in providing out-relief, which was available in the countryside only to the permanently incapacitated – 'friendless people, who are physically incapable of earning a living', 'sick persons with young children, widows with young children, or girls only'.[60] This policy was applied during the cattle-killing crisis of 1856–7, when thousands of starving Xhosa entered the colony and Governor Grey refused food to the able-bodied unless they contracted to work for a European employer for three to five years. Children were separated from their parents and apprenticed. Private charitable relief was deliberately sabotaged on the grounds, as a newspaper put it, that it was 'a premium on idleness, and prevented the Kaffirs from becoming what we would find it so much to our and their interest for them to be – labourers'. By the end of 1857, 29,142 Xhosa had been registered for service.[61] Similar principles underlay vagrancy legislation of the 1860s and 1870s which threatened three months' hard labour to anyone wandering abroad without adequate means of support. The Transvaal enacted similar legislation in 1881.[62]

For the deserving poor, by contrast, the nineteenth-century Cape recommended self-help institutions and private charity. The first voluntary welfare society outside the purview of the Dutch Reformed Church appears to have been the European Sick and Burial Society, founded in Cape Town in 1796. It had 150 members in 1830, mostly respectable poor Afrikaners.[63] By 1845 Cape Town had two benevolent societies, one benefit society of English tradesmen, a society 'for giving pecuniary aid to poor and distressed old women of a better class', a European sick and burial society, and four sick and burial societies for Coloured people organised by missions.[64] The Coloured Muslims known as the Cape Malays had no formal institutions but made such careful provision for their poor that it was an important motive for conversion among freed slaves.[65] The biggest charitable organisation was the Dutch Reformed Church, which appears to have maintained its out-relief work among its members throughout the nineteenth century, as did other Christian denominations.[66] Nineteenth-century British models of charity first appeared in 1810, when a deaconess formed the Cape Ladies' Society for the Relief of the Poor, which by 1843 had fourteen district visitors in Cape Town. Among Roman Catholics the first branch of the Society of St Vincent de Paul began to distribute alms in 1858.[67] Privately financed institutions – apart from the Orphan House – came only during the later nineteenth century, in parallel with a trend towards specialised institutions in Britain. Anglicans founded Zonnebloem College with 40 starving orphans from the cattle-killing of 1856–7. In 1862 they opened St George's Orphanage in Cape Town. A year later Dominican sisters pioneered schooling for the deaf and dumb.[68] The Dutch Reformed Church began to create specialised institutions during the 1880s.[69] The Salvation Army's very successful work at the Cape began in 1883; sixteen years later its institutions included five men's shelters in the main towns.[70]

One of the earliest institutions was Hemel en Aarde (Heaven and Earth), east of Cape Town, originally designed as an asylum for Khoi leprosy sufferers from the Swellendam area but enlarged in 1817 into a settlement to which non-whites with leprosy could be sent from all parts of the colony. It was the first leprosy institution south of the Sahara. In 1822 it housed some 120 leprosy sufferers in conditions 'squalid and wretched beyond description', with no useful medical treatment.[71] Moravian missionaries then agreed to supervise the institution, but it remained too remote to permit proper treatment and not remote enough to prevent healthy family members mingling with the sick. Another location was found only in 1843, when an official inspected Robben Island, a barren and windswept sandbank, some 14 kilometres from Cape Town, then used as a penal settlement. 'As the salubrity of Robben Island has long been acknowledged', he reported,

> . . . I would strongly recommend . . . the expediency of removing the leper and pauper establishments of Hemel-en-Aarde and Port Elizabeth, to Robben Island, also the pauper establishment of Cape Town, and the lunatics at present confined in the Somerset Hospital at Cape Town. The leper and pauper establishments which I have referred to, are, I am informed, wretchedly conducted, at a very heavy annual expense to the public.[72]

The move was made in December 1845. Three years later Robben Island housed 73 leprosy patients, 78 lunatics, and 92 chronic sick and paupers.[73]

Although the Robben Island settlement was designed as a humanitarian measure, it was created as an undifferentiated repository for unwanted people at exactly the moment when British administrators and medical men were rejecting such institutions. It was in 1845, for example, that Britain's Lunatics Act required each county to establish an asylum specifically for the insane and created Commissioners in Lunacy dedicated to the new doctrine that insanity could be cured by 'moral treatment' in purpose-built institutions.[74] The conflict between these approaches to the unfortunate was to be played out at Robben Island for over half a century.

Initially, however, the settlement had more urgent problems. 'The lepers moved to the stable sheds, the male lunatics to the late convict station and the female ones to the officers' quarters, a mere labyrinth of cells and passages',[75] while the chronic sick and paupers occupied the former military barracks. As listed in 1855, the three categories differed markedly. The lunatics were socially a cross-section of the general population. They were evenly divided between men and women, came equally from Cape Town and elsewhere, and included 26 ex-slaves, 23 Khoi, 16 Britons, 14 Afrikaners, and 8 'Kafirs'. Twelve were described as 'better-class patients'. Although one-third had arrived during the previous two years, another one-third had spent at least seven years on the island and formed the bulk of its longer-term residents. Among the leprosy patients, by contrast, two-thirds were men, three-quarters came from outside Cape Town, and nearly three-fifths were Khoi, the remainder being chiefly ex-slaves or Afrikaners. Only one leprosy patient was British and only two were described as 'better-class patients' – clearly those who could afford it kept infected relatives at home. Like lunatics, leprosy patients tended to die in their thirties and forties, but 'long-stay' patients were few. The paupers and chronic sick differed in several ways. Nearly five-sixths were men, two-thirds came from Cape Town, and they were mainly either British or former slaves, with fewer Khoi and Afrikaners. The British paupers may often have been derelict sailors. Nearly three-fifths of the chronic sick and paupers had spent less than two years on the island. Their deaths were more numerous than those of other categories, mostly took place after the age of 55, and were frequently ascribed to phthisis, old age, or paralysis. Yet there were also 24 'better-class patients' among them, suggesting a surprisingly high level of genteel poverty.[76] Although lunatics, leprosy patients, and chronic sick and paupers were separated from one another, there seems to have been no segregation by race or class within each category at this time.

The Robben Island settlement disturbed humanitarian opinion almost from its inception. In 1852 a committee of enquiry was deeply affected by the isolation, misery, and squalor it found and concluded that each category of inmates needed separate provision.[77] Further committees of enquiry in 1855 and 1861 urged the complete removal of the settlement to the mainland, but expense deterred the authorities. The inmates themselves had little luck. One 'lunatic' who paddled himself to the mainland on a plank was recaptured and sent back into solitary confinement.[78]

Among the inmates, the lunatics attracted most sympathy, perhaps because they came from all classes and were the only category who might be curable. Humane methods of treatment were gradually introduced from Europe, especially after the appointment of an expert on lunacy as medical superintendent in 1862. Mechanical constraint was abolished in 1863. Incoming lunatics – who were generally committed on the signature of a single district surgeon and arrived with no indication of origin or medical history – were classified and located in appropriate sections. Greater order and cleanliness were achieved. Those capable were employed, 'Constant occupation being the best relief and means of removing and keeping off mental excitement'.[79] During the 1870s, however, most doctors became convinced that Robben Island was unsuitable for lunatics, although, as a leading medical man put it, 'it does very well for lepers and for paupers'.[80] Concern also grew at the apparent increase in the number of insane people for whom no accommodation could be found – a consequence, perhaps, of declining tolerance of abnormality[81] – and at the fact that lunatics were not racially segregated.[82] In 1891 a new asylum for Europeans was opened at Valkenberg on the mainland, but by then the number of institutionalised lunatics in Cape Colony had increased so greatly – from 354 in 1880 to 1,248 in 1898 – that those on Robben Island had to remain there until all were finally removed to the mainland in 1913.[83]

The paupers left the island some fifteen years earlier. Mostly elderly, incurable, apathetic, and mutually supportive, they were exceptionally frustrating to doctors. 'It is no use putting those who won't work on short allowance', the medical superintendent complained in 1871, 'because their friends would supply them with half of their own share.'[84] Nineteenth-century officials and doctors had no time for such derelicts. 'I would certainly keep *them* there', a doctor declared when asked about the settlement's future:

> The very fact of their disliking the Island is in favour of their being kept there, because it prevents unduly numerous applications to get into the chronic-sick wards. Those applications are very numerous as it is, in spite of all we can do. The friends of the chronic sick are always bothering the Executive to get them into the wards of the Old Hospital; but when they have to go to the Island, their friends make extra exertions to care for them at home.'[85]

In the event, however, the paupers were the first to leave the island, chiefly because the doctors there wanted to be rid of them. By 1898 only a single pauper remained.[86] The women were transferred to Grahamstown, while the men were shipped back to the Old Somerset Hospital, which resumed its career as 'the place of the broken down, many there from their own fault – the place of idiocy, a place the whole surroundings of which are depressing'.[87] In 1898 it housed 256 chronic sick. 'Many patients are admitted suffering from no specific disease', the superintendent reported, 'but having become debilitated by their habits and mode of life and by old age. Hence it appears that many are sent in with no hope of recovery, but merely to have peace to die. Of that class a larger number than usual was admitted, 19 of whom died within a week, and 61 within three months of admission.' In that year there was still no separate accommodation for syphilitics, cancer patients, or even children.[88] Although the whites were gradually moved out, the Old Somerset Hospital was still virtually the only pauper institution for non-Europeans in the Cape Province in 1927, when it had 512 beds and was officially characterised as 'indescribably bad'. It was finally demolished in 1937.[89]

The removal of the paupers during the 1890s and the lunatics in 1913 left Robben Island to leprosy patients. Predominantly Africans from poor rural backgrounds suffering from an incurable disease, they were at first left much to themselves, apart from elementary care and feeding. 'They are a peculiar class of people, wedded to their own habits', a committee reported in 1852, 'and it is perhaps better to let them continue to enjoy themselves in their own way rather than impose regulations which might irritate and annoy them.'[90] The result was much squalor, misery, and neglect. Attempts at control arose chiefly from the mistaken belief of the time that leprosy was hereditary rather than contagious, which led to the retention in the wards of healthy children and to grotesque attempts to separate the sexes.[91]

After 1874, when Hansen first observed the leprosy bacillus, doctors again began to suspect that leprosy was contagious. From there it was a short step to believing that it was prevalent, increasing, and demanded rigorous segregation. The Cape enacted compulsory segregation in 1884 and began to enforce it in 1892. A search for leprosy sufferers identified unexpected numbers: whereas the Cape census of 1891 showed 625 leprosy sufferers, enforcement of the Act revealed some 3,000.[92] Robben Island was flooded. Between 1891 and 1893 the number of leprosy patients there rose from 113 to 497.[93] They were customarily picked up without warning, lest their friends should hide them. 'So they came', a missionary recalled,

> disfigured and full of pain and sad of heart, yet some were happy; they had been told that they should soon return strong and freed from the dread disease, if only they would come to the island; and they had not had time to probe the cruel mockery of the promise. The awakening came; and was it wonderful that anger and despair combined to bring about a rising that was only quelled by the crack of pistol against an unarmed leper mob?[94]

For many leprosy sufferers, the deepest cause of bitterness was compulsory rustication to so desolate a spot. 'We are mostly farmers', one protested, 'and we have been put in a place intended for penguins.'[95] Doctors insisted that only 'better-class patients' were eager to get away, whereas 'speaking generally the pauper patients are satisfied with the Island',[96] but the evidence shows that Africans hated the isolation. 'We are dissatisfied at having to remain on the Island', a Thembu explained. 'We Kaffirs are not accustomed to live in a place with water all around it. Then, secondly, we do not know what is happening to our children in our own country, especially in times of drought.'[97] He died on the island after nineteen years there,[98] having been sent as a punishment for leading a protest at a leprosarium on the mainland. Such men became obsessed by their isolation. 'We often used to walk up to near the lighthouse', one explained, 'and from there one can get a good view of Cape Town. It is the only view we can get of civilization. On a clear day, and with a good glass, we can even manage to see the time on the City Hall clock.'[99] 'The only future in store for us here', another protested, 'is blindness, rheumatism and consumption.'[100] A few tried to escape and a handful succeeded. Some killed themselves.[101] Others ignored regulations, tore down notices, brewed illicit liquor, brought in prostitutes and marijuana, and refused any task unless paid. The segregated whites complained that the operating theatre was in the Coloured ward. The Coloured inmates protested at being obliged to mix with Africans.[102]

Few leprosy patients could accept that their misery might be for the public good. 'They do not stop to consider the dangers of contagion, and it is of little use arguing with them', a missionary explained.[103] 'Are your wives and families not afraid of getting the disease you are suffering from?' an African patient was asked. 'Why should they be afraid now', he replied, 'when they lived with us for many years before.'[104] Some were so disfigured that they did not wish to leave, but others had no such reason:

> You have no sores on your body or any outward sign that you have the disease? – No. I feel as healthy as any of you.
>
> Do you want the Committee to believe that the four doctors who have seen you are mistaken? – I cannot say that, but I do not feel ill. I cannot say what a doctor can see. He is more clever than I am.[105]

Some knew how little the doctors understood their complaint. As one insisted, in words with which many doctors would have agreed, 'If our disease is contagious, then this Island is the means of spreading it, because any man who gets leprosy is more afraid of this place than he is of the disease.'[106] Above all, patients knew that doctors could not cure them. 'The longer I stay here the worse I am getting', one complained.[107] Extraordinary drugs were tried – 'gurgun' oil, arsenic, potassium iodide, icthyol, chaulmoogra oil, various supposedly native remedies – and the patients themselves were devotees of patent medicines.[108] Nothing worked. 'What is the use of keeping me here', one asked, 'if they cannot give me medicine to make me well.'[109]

Many faced their fate with courage, most with resignation:

> They have all their times of depression; fortunately most of them have also a blessed gift of forgetfulness and live for the most part in the present without much thought of past or future, and so there is much more cheerfulness and lightheartedness than might be expected. Many of them have a firmer and deeper source of comfort than they care to speak much of, and that one can only learn by getting to know them well; there have been and are some saintly lives among them, rising immeasurably above the general tone, which alas, is certainly a low one . . .
>
> Listlessness and apathy are the besetting infirmities of most. They have lost the self-reliance which comes of fighting the battle of life; their wants are provided for; they have no hope, at least, on this earth. There is no need for them to work, and they become enervated, so that it is difficult to rouse in them more than a passing interest in anything . . .

> Death comes as a blessing to all, even though sometimes it may come painfully, and at the end they are laid to rest in the bleak little cemetery, amid the nameless graves, in sight of the continent to which they so longed to return, at peace – and cured.[110]

It was not until 1931 that the last leprosy patients left Robben Island[111] and it became available for other forms of misery.

The changing European systems of poor relief which had so profound an effect in nineteenth-century South Africa made less impact in tropical colonies. In Sierra Leone, for example, government provision mainly took the form of out-relief, distributed initially through the Freetown Poor Society, founded in 1810, and later as an annual sum voted by the Legislative Council and administered first by the Colonial Chaplain, then by the churches, and finally by lay Charity Commissioners.[112] Private benefactors also contributed. 'The aged and destitute would assemble on Saturdays', Dr Fyfe has written, 'receive a small dole, voted by government, at the Secretariat, and process round the town seeking charity at private houses. These "Saturday militias", as they were called, went on parading the streets into the twentieth century.'[113] Freetown was close to the Islamic begging tradition, but it also possessed a hospital, established early in the century, which took in destitute European sailors, recaptured slaves, and those of the local poor who were beyond outdoor relief. Widows and orphans, the Governor explained in 1845, were 'almost a sacred duty on their country people, who willingly undertake and strictly perform this duty'.[114]

Yet the chief provision against poverty in Sierra Leone was made by self-help organisations. These were of two kinds. The 'Creole' immigrants from Britain and the Americas who created the colony formed their first mutual benefit society only a few years after their arrival in 1787. The churches, which were the core of Creole society, imitated this model; by 1817 one 'compin', as these associations were known, had 70 communicant members paying regular subscriptions in return for aid in sickness or distress. Another society, formed in 1824 by a demobilised soldier, was so successful in forming branches and acquiring quasi-administrative functions that the authorities suppressed it. By the 1890s each compin generally had a galaxy of officers from King, Queen, King's Son, and Governor downwards. It helped its members in need, organised communal labour, and sometimes effectively controlled a whole village.[115] The second kind of self-help organisation was created by the more numerous Liberated Africans who were resettled in Sierra Leone after the abolition of the slave trade. Since they had never reached the Americas, their models were mainly African. Yoruba, especially, recreated the *esusu* savings clubs of their homeland, while several ethnic groups established associations which both preserved indigenous cultures and performed welfare functions.[116] No doubt Islamic charity also flourished, but no evidence on this point has been found.

If nineteenth-century British models had little influence in Sierra Leone, the same was broadly true of French models in Senegal. In France the Revolution of 1789 secularised charitable institutions, brought them under state control, and attempted to replace charity by a sharp distinction between relief for the incapacitated and work for the able-bodied, while important initial steps were also taken towards classifying the unfortunate and providing more humane and specialised care.[117] Senegal, however, had no charitable institutions to secularise. Like Portuguese colonists, the eighteenth-century French had chiefly cared for their own personnel by establishing primitive military hospitals in Saint-Louis and Gorée. Whether these also admitted local civilians is unclear, but the hospital in Saint-Louis did so in the mid nineteenth century, although the poor rarely applied owing to the bureaucratic formalities needed to secure free admission.[118] Both during and after the Revolution the authorities also banned food exports, sold grain below cost price, fixed prices and wages, and fought a long campaign to repress begging, which both disturbed civic tranquillity, increased pressure on food supplies, and was thought to conceal spying and subversion. From the 1790s governors repeatedly ordered mendicants and *griots* back to the mainland, threatening to flog defaulters in the market-place.[119] In 1856 Governor Faidherbe tried to ban Koran school pupils from begging their livelihood in the streets,[120] doubtless with little success. Beyond controlling prices, the authorities appear not to have provided for the poor before 1848, although prosperous *habitants* had a reputation for philanthropy.[121]

The emancipation in 1848 of Senegal's 6,359 slaves brought the first major change in these *ancien régime* policies. Some slaves continued to live with their former masters. More became independent traders. Employment on public works was made available for the able-bodied and a *village de liberté* was established outside Saint-Louis. Orphan children were entrusted to guardians who did little more than allocate them as 'apprentices' to local residents, often their former masters.[122] The elderly and infirm were provided with a *hospice civil* which, as described in 1861, was a miniature version of the Old Somerset Hospital, housing 'the aged, the infirm of both sexes, and women infected with venereal disease', as well as a number of prisoners.[123] Special provision for venereal patients resulted from a marked expansion of prostitution after the ending of slavery, when former slave-owners refused to make special provision for young girls, many of whom found no other way of making a living.[124] The *hospice civil* was still functioning in 1887,[125] a monument to the failure of nineteenth-century principles to establish themselves in Senegal. By then, moreover, the principle of secularisation had also been lost, for the care of the poor had passed mainly to religious sisterhoods.

The six sisters who arrived in Senegal in 1819 as the first female religious in sub-Saharan Africa (outside Ethiopia) were members of the Order of

St Joseph of Cluny. This was a French sisterhood founded fourteen years earlier by Anne-Marie Javouhey,[126] whose anti-revolutionary upbringing had been followed by training among the Sisters of Charity, an order created in the seventeenth century to care for the poor of France. Having established her own community, Mère Javouhey's attention was attracted to French colonies by the need to prepare for the anticipated ending of slavery. This drew her nuns to Senegal. Although they worked mainly as teachers, they brought to Africa a tradition of female care which had been designed for the traditional poor of Europe, especially the incapacitated, and was therefore equally appropriate to Africa.

The Frenchwomen who dominated the work of sisterhoods in nineteenth-century Africa were products of a reaction against the Revolution which revived vocations and ensured that France had more religious in 1877 than in 1777.[127] The movement was personified by Marie de Villeneuve, a young aristocrat from an anti-revolutionary family who in 1836 founded the Congregation of the Immaculate Conception of Castres (popularly known as the Blue Sisters), an order modelled on the Sisters of Charity and dedicated to 'the beautiful work of foreign missions, above all missions to the negroes, and generally to the most forsaken and despised peoples'.[128] Established at Dakar in Senegal in 1848 and at Libreville in Gabon in 1849, the Sisters of Castres became the first religious to concentrate their work among the African poor. This was especially true at Libreville, whose murderous climate and brutal slaving justified their reason for choosing it, which was that it was the most miserable place they could find.[129] Twelve sisters died there in the first eighteen months and the remainder could long do little but survive. By 1868, however, they were caring for a handful of incapacitated people.[130]

As the sisters' care gradually attracted the poor of Libreville and its environs, the needy proved to be those most characteristic of pre-colonial Africa, the incapacitated, with the special feature that an unusually large proportion were slaves in an area where slave-owners habitually carried whips. 'Slaves, whom old age or sickness renders incapable of continued service, are ordinarily most unfortunate', a missionary reported in 1873. 'The master no longer maintains them, or he even expels them from the house and the village, and causes them to languish in the forest, where they die abandoned.'[131] For the next twenty years the missionaries took into their hospitals each year between 60 and 200 sick or destitute slaves:

> I had just said Holy Mass when one of our Christians came looking for me to lead me to a poor slave abandoned by her masters. She had passed the night in the wood close to his dwelling. I had her led to the sisters' hospital, where she was baptised.
>
> A week ago the Sister Nurse [*soeur infirmière*] similarly met a slave who was dying abandoned in the middle of the Glass plains. She had her carried to

> her hospital, where she expired the same night, after having been regenerated by baptism.
>
> Last week, when visiting Saint-Michel to catechise, I again found on my way an old negro woman who had great difficulty in dragging herself along. I asked her where she was going. 'But', she replied, 'I am going to seek refuge in the Sisters' hospital. My master has driven me from his house with the blows of a stick, because I can no longer work as he would wish.'[132]

Yet slaves were not the only unfortunates received into the settlement. Almost every kind of serious illness and handicap could be found.[133]

The central figure in this work was Sister Saint-Charles, who served at Libreville, mostly as Soeur Infirmière, from 1860 until her death in 1911:

> From 1872 she secured the construction of two houses in the native fashion, one full of incurables: 'cancerous women with large sores bound with a rotten banana leaf, adolescent girls covered from head to foot with a hideous scattering of *abouke* (pustules forming large scabs), old women disfigured with leonine leprosy, consumptives, ulcerous, cripples, even mad'.
>
> At first she herself hunted out these pitiable clients. But soon the natives brought them to her establishment in return for a few leaves of tobacco.
>
> These women, embittered by sickness and of debased intelligence, were a heavy moral burden. They stole from the sister, escaped, resisted discipline. Sister Saint-Charles treated them with a semi-divine patience, never rejecting them, pardoning all, and discharging towards them the most repulsive of duties.[134]

Her counterpart among the Spiritan Fathers who also worked at Libreville was Brother Henri, whose hospital cared for the male destitute, sick, and orphaned.[135]

In East Africa similar works of charity began in 1860 when a Roman Catholic mission was founded in Zanzibar Island. It included six sisters from a French order based in Réunion who established an orphanage for freed slave children and found the same overwhelming suffering as in Gabon:

> Neither in the whole island of Zanzibar nor in its vast dependencies is there a single asylum for the unfortunate. The sick poor are abandoned in the streets. Along the ramparts you see the aged dying, extended on the ground . . . In the filthy lanes you meet young people, children, women of the people, whose eyes and legs are eaten by hideous sores. Swarms of flies pounce upon these poor creatures and torment them all day long. Nobody troubles himself.[136]

To care for the sick the mission opened first a dispensary, which was soon thronged, and later two hospitals for Europeans and Africans. To launch their work in Ngambo, the crowded African quarter, they found a wealthy laywoman, Madame Chevalier, who financed and ran a dispensary and pauper hospital there from 1884 until her death in 1897. In 1904, with a subsidy from the British authorities, this hospital was moved outside the town to Walezo. As a settlement for the poor under the care of Sisters of Cluny,

Walezo became one of the largest and most enduring charitable institutions in the continent.[137]

Behind the pioneer sisters of Cluny and Castres came religious women who gradually penetrated all of sub-Saharan Africa. Among Roman Catholics, each male missionary order generally established a female counterpart. The first Protestant women workers were generally wives of missionaries or evangelists – women such as Anna Hinderer who pioneered the care of abandoned babies in Yorubaland during the 1850s[138] – but by the end of the century the increase in female missionaries was the fastest-growing branch of Protestant work and the Anglican church in southern Africa had established several congregations of nuns.[139] European sisterhoods were soon supplemented by African congregations. The earliest were the Daughters of the Holy Heart of Mary, founded in Senegal in 1858 by Thérèse Sagna and Louise de Saint-Jean, the first African nuns outside Ethiopia to make vows.[140] The subsequent remarkable growth of African sisterhoods throughout the continent probably testified to the extent of female dissatisfaction within African societies. It certainly brought to the Christian church a power of female charity which no other institution could rival. 'Engrave in your memory', Marie de Villeneuve had told the first Sisters of Castres, 'the words which have often been repeated to you during retreat: *efface yourself, impoverish yourself, suffer*.'[141] In Europe at that time the Sisters of Charity were perhaps becoming old-fashioned. In Africa they met the kind of poverty for which they were designed, and there – as in twentieth-century Calcutta – it was they who cared for the wretched of the earth.

Although vowed to poverty, the sisters rarely attempted to share the deprivation of those they served. It would certainly have made their death-rate even more dreadful. Yet some missionaries did seek this form of mortification, as had Pero Tavares two centuries earlier. The first ministers of the London Missionary Society to sail for South Africa in 1798 chose to do so in a convict ship, 'that they might begin the scene of their labours among the most miserable and abandoned of their fellow-men'.[142] Perhaps the most remarkable practitioner of Franciscan poverty was the Lazarist bishop, Justin de Jacobis, who served in north-eastern Ethiopia from 1839 to 1860 and adopted the lifestyle of an Ethiopian itinerant teacher rather than the heroic manner of St Takla Haymanot. An Ethiopian priest recalled:

> Another day, he received in this way a man sick of dysentery. He lodged him in his own room. Perceiving eventually that the majority displayed a repugnance to approach him, he had him put on the terrace of his house and cared for him himself day and night for three months, rendering him the most repugnant services ... In all the letters that he wrote, he preferred to all honorific titles that of 'Jacob the Poor'.[143]

On the Protestant side the model of self-abnegation – in a strikingly different idiom – was Mary Slessor, a mill-girl from Dundee who ministered alone on the Cross River in eastern Nigeria from 1880 until 1915, living for a time among the wives of a local chief and then surrounded by a household of sick and abandoned children.[144] Some Africans were impatient of this approach. The hierarchical and competitive Baganda, a later observer wrote, 'wish Europeans not to adopt their standard but to raise it. The Franciscan model is seen not as a challenge to the rich but as a threat to the poor.'[145] Yet more egalitarian peoples may have understood the model better, especially where missionaries like John White and Arthur Shearly Cripps in Southern Rhodesia chose an African lifestyle in preference to that of white settlers.[146] Nor were some Africans deterred from following the Franciscan ideal. At Asaba, on the Niger, Ignatius Bamah was prevented by defective sight from becoming a priest and instead lived in poverty and chastity as a voluntary lay brother amidst the striving competition of Igboland and the bewildered incomprehension of his kinsmen.[147] That was in the twentieth century, but there were earlier examples of Christians who 'went to live with society's rejects – lepers, witches and so on – in a Christian village', took the gospel to such remote peoples as the pygmies of the Ituri forest, or held to their posts as evangelists during the horrors of a sleeping sickness epidemic.[148] In South Africa a missionary who trained former independent church ministers seeking to join the Anglican church found them 'astonishingly careless of money advantages. They reminded me of the Preaching Friars. If they wanted anything extra they asked a friend for it – 15s. for a pair of boots, or 10s. for a pair of trousers – but otherwise they went on merely asking for food, and content if they might but live.'[149] Professor Isichei has written of the Igbo monk, Michael Tansi:

> The sacrifice of a man who leaves relative comfort and security for poverty is easy to recognise and applaud. The sacrifice of a man who was raised in poverty and chooses a poverty from which he could escape, who chooses, in fact, to be poorer than those around him who are really poor, this is something different.[150]

It was not a common African choice, but it was one choice.

To concentrate on the poor was the strategy of most nineteenth-century missionaries, not only in Africa, and it was among the poor and marginal that they generally found their first converts. 'Hardly had we taken our light meal', the first Roman Catholic missionary to reach the East African mainland during the nineteenth century reported, 'than there arrived a crowd of sick people, some afflicted by leprosy, others by ophthalmia.'[151] Most early Igbo converts were 'the poor, the needy, and the rejected: the mothers of twins, women accused of witchcraft, those suffering from diseases such as leprosy which were seen as abominable'. In Kasai they were 'the marginal men in African society: the flotsam and jetsam of the Kasai, men without position, children without parents, women without husbands, slaves without roots, and old people without hope'.[152] For such people the missionaries created enclosed settlements on the pattern of Bethelsdorp or Libreville. By 1911 the White Fathers' vicariate of the Upper Congo, west of Lake Tanganyika, possessed 20 asylums or orphanages and 16 hospitals or refuges, as well as treating over 200,000 patients each year. Kibanga, their largest settlement, contained over 2,000 people in 1890.[153] Perhaps the most remarkable institution was established in 1892 by Capuchin missionaries in the backstreets of Berbera on the Somali coast, where pastoral insecurity and the hope of pickings in coastal towns combined to attract swarms of homeless boys. When disease drove this community from the town in 1903, the missionaries and their young charges lived a quasi-nomadic life in the interior for the next seven years.[154]

Throughout the nineteenth century missionaries insisted that care for the poor was only a means towards the greater end of spiritual salvation. 'To reach the soul', one explained, 'we must first concern ourselves with the body.'[155] Robert Laws, who established Presbyterian work on Lake Nyasa during the 1870s, was a qualified doctor but avoided difficult operations lest failure should jeopardise religious work.[156] Others, notably Livingstone, were less cautious, as generally were Roman Catholics, but Protestant missions were long suspicious of medical work and the Church Missionary Society despatched its first doctors to Africa only with a warning 'that the medical work should always be subordinate to the spiritual'.[157] The first Roman Catholic order specifically devoted to medical missions, the Medical Mission Sisters, was not formed until 1925 – in Philadelphia.

Yet by then the secondary place given to relief of suffering was already in question. The turning-point was 1913. That was the year when Albert Schweitzer settled at Lambaréné in Gabon, choosing it, as had the Sisters of Castres, as the worst place in the world. In renouncing a career of astonishing brilliance, Schweitzer obeyed the Christian ideal of self-abnegation, but he went to Lambaréné not to convert the heathen but to heal their pain.[158] He personified a new approach to African suffering and poverty.

8

Poverty in South Africa, 1886–1948

Pre-colonial Africa was a land-rich continent. Its very poor were chiefly the incapacitated. During the late nineteenth and twentieth centuries, however, the very poor also came to include numbers impoverished by competition for resources. This took place most quickly in South Africa, where inequality was greatest and economic change most rapid. Deprivation of resources was not entirely new there, for many Khoi lacked property even in the eighteenth century and Cape Town in the 1830s already knew the family poverty of the ill-paid or jobless proletarian.[1] Nor was the process fully worked out even in South Africa, for in the mid twentieth century those who lacked property but were able-bodied could usually escape extreme poverty by working for others, except during temporary crises of unemployment, so that the worst poverty of propertylessness was still conjunctural. Nevertheless, between the discovery of gold on the Witwatersrand in 1886 and the National Party's electoral victory of 1948 a new pattern of deprivation was added to the old.

Two other changes accompanied this transition. One was the gradual identification of the poor with the black and Coloured. This had not been the case in Cape Town or Robben Island during the nineteenth century, but by the mid twentieth century few whites were very poor. One reason for this was action by the state, whose ever greater control of property relations and poor relief was the other theme of the period. It culminated during the 1940s in the near-simultaneous creation of a state welfare system and the Apartheid programme, which together were to provide the framework for the evolution of poverty in South Africa for the next forty years.

The multiracialism of South African poverty in the late nineteenth and early twentieth centuries was most obvious in the towns. In the 1830s Cape Town's poor had included Coloured people of Khoi origin, freed slaves, and impoverished white men, all huddled into multiracial slums. During the next forty years inter-racial marriage declined, residential segregation increased, and the wages, voting rights, and educational opportunities of white men all became superior to those of Coloured people, but these changes probably had least effect among the poor, whose numbers were moreover swollen from the late 1830s by the first substantial immigration of Africans.[2] Although many lodged separately in the port area where they worked or squatted on the edges of the town, other Africans settled in the multiracial slums, especially the area known as District Six which during the later nineteenth century became the centre of Cape Town's working-class culture. In 1900 District Six housed the largest group of Africans living in the city.[3]

The African influx was one reason for demands during the 1880s and 1890s for greater segregation and social control. Responsible government in 1874, over 1,000 deaths from smallpox in 1882, racial competition for unskilled jobs, and doctors anxious to introduce current public health doctrines added to the pressure. In 1898 ratepayers in Districts Five and Six demanded measures 'to prevent them being rendered unfit for the habitation of the respectable working classes by reason of the herding of Kaffirs therein'.[4] When bubonic plague struck Cape Town in 1901 the authorities blamed it on 'these uncontrolled Kafir hordes' and implemented a plan to create a segregated African location at Ndabeni near the sewage farm on the Cape Flats 6 kilometres from the city centre. Some 6,000–7,000 Africans were immediately moved there, many at bayonet-point.[5] Yet Ndabeni did not destroy multiracial poverty, for it was soon so crowded that further immigrants had to swell the multiracial slums. 'Natives still throng to Cape Town from the country districts in search of work', it was reported in 1922, 'and make their homes in the slums, *where it is a quite common experience to find fifty or sixty of them herded in small four-roomed houses at night surrounded on all sides by the demoralising attractions of illicit liquor dens and brothels.*'[6]

Most South African towns attempted at this time to destroy multiracial poverty. The most effectively segregated was Durban, whose proximity to reserves enabled it to accommodate Africans (with rare exceptions) only as bachelors, controlling their influx by an elaborate administration financed by a brewing monopoly.[7] This 'Durban system' became one model of urban administration, but at this time it was more common to accept permanent African townsmen but confine them (except domestic servants) to a location and leave them to provide their own housing. Grahamstown had possessed such a location since about 1830.[8] East London's location of wood and tin shacks had in 1916 some 9,500 people, 11 water standpipes, massive rack-renting by African landlords, and (in 1921) a child death-rate fifteen times higher than that of the town's Europeans, but it was designed to make a profit for the town council, as did 191 of the 217 locations in towns reporting to the Secretary of Native Affairs in 1916–17.[9] Unless closely controlled, however, such settlements could develop into multiracial sanctuaries for the poor. When Port Elizabeth's Africans were expelled from the central town during the plague of 1901–2 they settled on peri-urban freehold land, especially at Korsten, and created a multiracial freehold shanty town, dominated by extortionate African landlords and described by the Secretary for Public Health as 'the worst slum in the world', 'inhabited by Europeans, Natives, Indians, Chinese, and other coloured persons, who live cheek by jowl in the closest proximity'.[10]

The most revealing illustration of multiracial urban poverty in the late nineteenth and early twentieth centuries was Johannesburg. Only two years after its creation in 1886 its Sanitary Committee marked out a separate African location, but its remoteness and the absence of legal compulsion to move there meant that many Africans settled close to the city centre in racially mixed slums – Ferreira, Vrededorp, Newclare, Fordsburg, Brickfields – alongside Indians, Coloured people, and the most impoverished white men, who were chiefly Afrikaners.[11] Brickmaking was an occupation in which the poor of all races found employment, along with domestic service, transport, and prostitution – a very incomplete survey in 1896 suggested that Johannesburg had 91 white, 83 Coloured, and 48 African full-time prostitutes, although the true total was probably over 1,000.[12] In that year, however, the relatively high wages hitherto earned by Africans were decisively reduced. A year later demonstrations by needy Afrikaners obliged the authorities to abandon the old distinction between deserving and undeserving poor and create a public works programme and relief fund confined to whites.[13] British victory in the Anglo-Boer War enabled capitalist enterprises to supplant some occupations hitherto performed by the poor.[14] The British authorities were eager, as the Chief Inspector of the Native Affairs Department explained in 1902, 'to enforce the residence of all native employees either in the property of their employers or in a licensed location. All unemployed natives found living elsewhere than in a licensed location should be arrested and punished under the vagrancy law.'[15] Yet multiracial poverty survived. In 1908 there were 2,403 registered white unemployed in Johannesburg and perhaps 2,000 'poor whites'. Numerous white people, especially women, begged in the streets.[16] Eleven years later the slumyards close to the city centre still housed over 20,000 people.[17] 'It is not only the Bantu races . . . which are represented in these yards', a missionary explained. 'There are hundreds, perhaps thousands, of Mohammedans of various races; of half-castes; of low whites and Indians and Chinese, and other heterogeneous species of humanity.'[18] Multiracial poverty had also spread to two freehold settlements on suburban land which whites did not want: Sophiatown to the west of the city (because it adjoined a refuse dump) and Alexandra to the north (because it was too remote). In 1921 Sophiatown and the adjoining Martindale housed 1,457 Africans, 878 Coloured people, 557 whites, and 79 Asians.[19] These slumyards and freehold settlements were already breeding a vigorous working-class culture.

South Africa's rulers identified multiracial poverty as the Poor White Problem. Although destitute white men had long been numerous, they were first seen as a social problem – rather than as victims of their vices – during the

1880s and 1890s, when new European notions of poverty as a social phenomenon mingled with South Africa's growing concern with racial categorisation.[20] Publicised by the Dutch Reformed Church, the Poor White Problem became in 1929–30 the subject of a report, funded by the Carnegie Foundation, which remains a key document in the history of poverty in Africa.[21] Investigating before the international depression was seriously felt, the Carnegie Commission reckoned that 17.5 per cent of white families with children at school – or a total of 300,000–400,000 people – were 'living in great poverty'. Not quite every one of these was a Poor White, whom the Commission defined as 'an impoverished European of rural origin', a definition which revealed its view that the problem originated in the countryside.[22] The main categories of Poor Whites, the Commission reported, were 'poor "bywoners",[23] hired men on farms, owners of dwarf holdings or of small undivided shares of land, poor settlers, and the growing group of unskilled or poorly trained labourers and workers outside of farming'.[24] They were concentrated in the rural Cape and Transvaal, but the Commission was most disturbed by those who had moved to towns, where a minority lived in multiracial slums.[25]

The Carnegie Report and other accounts show that Poor White poverty was of a kind not hitherto seen in sub-Saharan Africa except among Khoi and in nineteenth-century Cape Town. It was structural poverty, long-standing and not due to the international depression or any other conjuncture, although certainly exacerbated by political and climatic insecurity. Of 139 poor landless men investigated by the Commission, 83 were sons of landless fathers.[26] Poor Whites were poor rather than very poor, and they were poor because they were propertyless rather than because they were incapacitated. The destitute, it was stressed, were a separate category and were still generally 'the sick, the infirm, and especially widows and others who had lost the family breadwinner'.[27] Disease was not an important reason for the Poor Whites' condition, nor were more than a minority (one estimate suggested 10 per cent) victims of personality defects, although poverty tended to encourage mental and educational retardation and thus perpetuate itself.[28] Poor Whites were overwhelmingly the landless. Distribution of land among Afrikaners had long been extremely unequal, but this had been masked in the nineteenth century when wealthy patrons had welcomed *bywoners* and the frontier was still open.[29] Now capitalist farming was converting *bywoners* into sharecroppers or labourers or driving them from the land, war and cattle plague especially afflicted small men, and international boundaries had closed the frontier. Between 1911 and 1926 the white rural population changed little, but its natural increase left the countryside.[30] Some of these were victims of partible inheritance under Dutch law, which could fragment land into uneconomic plots where, as was often the case, the poor married early and sought security in large families. The Carnegie Commission found that 77 per cent of Poor White families contained more than four children, against 54 per cent of all white families.

Unlike the poverty of pre-colonial Africa, Poor White poverty was family poverty. 'It was obvious everywhere', the Commission's chairman reported, 'that the most helpless people in the towns were those that brought a family with them.'[31]

Poor White poverty was the poverty of low wages rather than of unemployment. Investigating before the depression, the Commission found few whites unemployed, but it found that wages were often far below a level acceptable to a racial aristocracy.[32] The *bywoner* who had become a herdsman or shepherd often earned only 10 to 30 shillings a month. In certain districts, the chairman wrote, 'there are white men who are ordinary farm labourers and shepherds. I know of a farm in Piketberg near the sea, where only white men are employed. They are paid £12 a year with rations, less than the coloured labourers round about Malmesbury.'[33] 'I worked with a lot of poor whites', an elderly Coloured farmworker recalled fifty years later. '. . . I got 2 shillings a day there but the white workers got 2 shillings and sixpence, 3 shillings on some farms, for the same work . . . There were a lot of poor whites in Rietbron who worked for day wages.'[34] Some employers no longer troubled to disguise inequality in the manner expected by a stateless people:

> The 'bywoner' and farm labourer are in many cases no longer received as social equals by the land-owner and his family. They are very often allowed only in the kitchen of the house. The labourer's wife comes in the house only to work as a servant . . . Thus the poor white in time comes to associate with non-Europeans. The result is that the respect of the coloured man for the European fellow-worker disappears, and from social intercourse to miscegenation is but a step.[35]

The chairman recorded his shock on first hearing a white man call his employer *baas*. This growing *relative* impoverishment was probably one reason why white poverty was more visible than in the past.[36] Another was that poverty is always more visible in towns than in the countryside:

> The rural poor had in many cases been there for a long time, widely scattered in our thinly populated country. When the exodus in search of something better began, and particularly when they drifted in ever increasing numbers to the cities and towns, then for the first time was the fact seriously brought home to the nation as a whole.[37]

Afrikaner society offered the poor many means of survival. There were still nomadic Trekboers on the north-western Cape frontier and others who lived chiefly from hunting. Transport-riding had been undercut by railways, but some men still drove wagonloads of firewood to the cities. Itinerant Afrikaners with donkey wagons still acted as traders or blacksmiths to African communities.[38] A few desperate Afrikaners even ceased to be Poor *Whites* at all and converted themselves into high-status Coloureds.[39] Yet these were extreme solutions. Enterprise usually took more resolute forms. The frontier was not yet entirely closed. The white population of Bechuanaland grew by 93 per cent between 1911 and 1931, the immigrants often subjecting San hunters much as Tswana had done before them. Poor White families flocked into Swaziland during the 1920s, each with a gun, a swarm of children, a black servant, and a bitter hostility to Africans.[40] Those who stayed in settled areas took relief work, sought farm employment, joined with others in opening new land, or tried their luck amid the squalor of the diamond diggings.[41]

Only most unwillingly did Poor Whites leave the countryside. Some moved to small towns in the hope of starting independent enterprises, but these 'village paupers' rarely prospered.[42] The cities, by contrast, might at first mean the squalor of a multiracial slum, but at least they offered work and wages. Against most previous opinion – including that of the Prime Minister – the Carnegie Commission concluded that agriculture offered no solution to the Poor White Problem and that 'the best prospects for the family as a whole are offered by the bigger industrial centres'. Of the indigent urban families they interviewed, 77 per cent said that their move to the city had been 'a change for the better in all respects'.[43] Admittedly the Commission found misery, begging, and a disturbing dependence upon charity, but crime, drunkenness, and immorality were rare, few urban immigrants had 'gone Kaffir', and resistance to working alongside Africans was still strong – one town in the Orange Free State had an all-white staff of sanitary labourers.[44] Family structure survived in the towns, mutual aid societies like burial clubs and Pentecostal churches flourished,[45] and above all there was work, especially for the young. An enquiry in the Transvaal in 1908 had reported, with much exaggeration, that most Poor Whites lived on their children's earnings, the girls characteristically working in laundries and the boys selling newspapers.[46] Twenty years later at least 10,000 white women were working in factories. Often Poor White children went to town first and then attracted their parents.[47] The Congress convened in 1934 by the Dutch Reformed Church to discuss the Carnegie Commission's report resolved that the solution to the Poor White Problem required 'the complete segregation of the towns, and the repatriation of all male natives'.[48]

The Carnegie Commission's optimism about urban opportunities was based on research in 1929–30, before the depression seriously affected South Africa, and on a study which ignored the white poverty caused by incapacitation and unemployment.[49] A less optimistic picture emerged from a study made during the first half of 1933 of those receiving assistance from the Cape Town General Board of Aid, the city's all-purpose charity. Some 78 per cent of those assisted were non-Europeans (predominantly Coloured people), who were only 48 per cent of the city's population. In all, 8.7 per cent of Cape Town's non-Europeans and 2.3 per cent of its Europeans received aid. Recipients were not usully recent immigrants from the countryside: 70 per cent of the Europeans and 84 per cent of the non-Europeans had lived at least ten years in Cape Town. Many were incapacitated: 26 per cent of the Europeans and 29 per cent of the non-Europeans – mostly single persons or childess couples – were aged, disabled, chronically sick, or otherwise permanently dependent, and others were temporarily sick or only semi-fit.[50] In contrast to the Poor Whites of 1929–30, most poverty in Cape Town in 1933 was conjunctural, for 58 per cent of those receiving aid were able-bodied unemployed, although a study in the late 1930s, after the depression had ended, found that poverty among Coloured people was mostly due to low wages.[51] Of those unemployed in 1933, 36 per cent of Europeans and 65 per cent of non-Europeans were unskilled labourers, while 17 and 12 per cent respectively were skilled building workers whose trade was notoriously insecure.[52] In one respect Cape Town's poor were closely similar to Poor Whites: their poverty was chiefly family poverty. Roughly four-fifths of the Europeans and five-sixths of the non-Europeans assisted had families, averaging 5.2 and 5.6 people respectively, and poverty was especially common among people in their thirties burdened with young children who both needed sustenance and prevented the mother from earning – the classic form of poverty in early modern Europe which had been rare in pre-colonial Africa. This finding was confirmed by further study in the late 1930s. As a banner carried during a Coloured hunger march in Cape Town in 1938 proclaimed: 'One room, no food, eight kids.'[53]

The Carnegie Commission and the Cape Town enquiry agreed that existing attempts to alleviate white poverty by charity and relief were inadequate, misguided, and unnecessarily complicated. Under the South Africa Act of 1909 poor relief was a provincial responsibility. Each province had its own system. In the Cape, provincial and municipal administrations jointly financed the Cape Town General Board of Aid and matched in grants the sums spent by charitable organisations, which in 1933 numbered over 150 in Cape Town alone.[54] The Transvaal spent large sums on poor relief but left the Rand Aid Association and other private charities to operate in Johannesburg and devoted only £2,000 of its £96,397 expenditure in 1937–8 to Africans. The Orange Free State was also generous with poor relief, roughly one-quarter of it going to Africans, but niggardly towards private charities. Natal, always different, insisted that poor relief for Africans should be a Union matter and distributed nearly all its funds to charitable bodies operating among Europeans in Durban and Pietermaritzburg.[55] The Carnegie Commission estimated that in 1929 the provincial administrations spent £374,664 on poor relief and grants to charitable societies.[56]

The Union Government's welfare role was at first limited. Its most important service (in conjunction with the provinces) was medicine, which was in effect free to the poor, although often difficult of access. The Union Government also bore responsibility for miners' phthisis and workmen's compensation. Under the Children's Protection Act of 1913 it made maintenance grants to white and Coloured destitute children, orphanages and children's homes, and eventually needy mothers and grandmothers. Old age pensions for indigent whites and Coloureds were introduced in 1928, making the Union Government for the first time a larger contributor to social welfare than the provinces.[57]

Among private charities the most extensive system was that of the Dutch Reformed Church, which in 1937 (with much help from public funds) maintained 14 homes for dependent children, 6 for the aged, and 5 for the sick and crippled, while its women's organisations specialised in child welfare and had over 12,000 members. At parish level, Dutch Reformed Church deacons made monthly grants to the poor, averaging at least £11,000 a year in direct food relief during the 1920s in the Cape Province alone.[58] The range of other charitable provision for white people was bewildering. Almost every religious body provided some institutional care. In 1935, for example, the Salvation Army's facilities included 8 homes, shelters, or hostels for men, 3 for women, 3 for boys, and 4 for girls; a low-cost temperance hostel (The People's Palace) in Cape Town; 2 'social farms' for derelict and alcoholic men; and 2 'rescue homes' for women and girls in trouble.[59] National Councils to coordinate charitable work were established for child welfare in 1924, the blind and the deaf in 1929, and cripples in 1939.[60] A survey of South Africa's more than 1,000 voluntary welfare societies in 1939 showed that roughly one-half dealt with general relief and welfare, more than three-quarters concerned themselves only with Europeans, and there was a heavy concentration in large towns.[61]

This uncoordinated welfare provision attracted much criticism during the early 1930s. The Carnegie Commission complained that amateur relief bodies pauperised Poor Whites by indiscriminate charity. It pointed instead to American social welfare practices, themselves derived from London's Charity Organisation Society, which had stressed the need to investigate each case and grant relief only in a form which would rehabilitate rather than pauperise. The Cape Town enquiry made the same criticism of the Board of Aid, adding that it did nothing to combat the causes of poverty. South Africa, so experts complained, still assumed that poverty was natural and inevitable rather than eradicable.[62] In response to their insistence that the Union Government must establish 'a state bureau of social welfare' to coordinate provision and organise research and rehabilitation, Government created a Department of Social Welfare within the Department of Labour in 1933, linked them as the Department of Labour and Social Welfare in 1935, and then established an autonomous Department of Social Welfare in 1937.[63] It was an important aspect of the growth of central government power.

Critical of indiscriminate charity, the Department of Social Welfare adopted rigorously 'scientific' American principles. Its function, as the Cabinet defined it in 1938, was 'to rehabilitate the socially unadjusted or poorly adjusted individual or family'.[64] In 1940, when the Department took over poor relief from the provinces (except Natal), it ordered that every application must be thoroughly investigated, only one agency must provide relief in any area, relief must normally be given in kind and only to those wholly destitute and without close kin, recipients must where possible render some return service, and assistance must not be made attractive.[65] The directive reduced the numbers receiving poor relief in Kimberley by 60 per cent.[66] The Department also strove to encourage and rationalise the work of private charities, discouraging them from providing general relief and urging them instead to care for particular categories of poor. The Department's staff increased between 1939 and 1949 from 257 to 1,278.[67] They spent much time administering the enlightened Children's Act of 1937, which made child welfare second only to old age pensions as a state responsibility. Moreover, during the Second World War the welfare system was extended in imitation of welfare state models in Britain and New Zealand. In 1944 a Social Security Committee proposed unemployment, invalidity, and other benefits. Europeans, Coloured people, Asians, and long-term African wage-earners who elected to join were to receive full benefits at rates graduated by race, while most Africans were to receive only old age, blindness, or invalidity pensions and certain minor benefits. The total cost was estimated at £30,000,000 a year. Parliament drastically reduced the proposals, especially for non-Europeans, and in 1945 Government abandoned a comprehensive scheme in favour of *ad hoc* improvements. For Europeans the chief gains were unemployment benefits and family allowances.[68]

One reason for parliamentary scepticism towards the welfare state proposals of 1944 was that the Poor White Problem was fading. Exactly why it disappeared is still uncertain. It was not eradicated by Afrikaner nationalist mobilisation: of the £150,000 collected as a *reddingsdaad* (act of rescue), less than 30 per cent was spent on the poor.[69] Nor, probably, was the problem resolved by social welfare measures, which were palliatives. It was ameliorated, but no more, by providing jobs for whites at African expense – 36,000 of them by August 1933, according to a government claim.[70] Rapid industrialisation after 1933 certainly created much new employment and wealth, but in 1939 some 298,000 white persons were still reported to be living in 'terrible poverty' with monthly incomes below £12.[71] In little over a month of 1939 the police rounded up 142 European beggars in central Johannesburg, while a study of the city's prostitutes in 1939–41 showed that they included about 1,000 impoverished white street-walkers. 'Ninety per cent. of full-time professional prostitutes', it reported, 'were originally ill-paid unskilled workers employed in factories, shops, tea-rooms, domestic work and similar occupations. A high proportion of these girls were genuinely unable to live on the wages which they received for their legitimate employment.'[72] A survey in 1938 found that 40 per cent of white schoolboys were to some extent malnourished.[73] Like other poor people, Poor Whites no doubt escaped their condition chiefly by their own efforts, but these remain unexplored. They were helped in the short term by wartime employment and in the long term by the fact that they had the vote and succeeded after 1945 in pressuring their rulers into transferring their poverty to Poor Blacks.[74] 'You know we had many friends who were poor whites', a Coloured labourer later recalled. 'They came to our place to eat and we used to go to their houses for meals. This was on the farms. But these poor whites got better, and better, and better . . . We couldn't improve because we were oppressed, kept down.'[75]

Two things distinguished the African rural areas of South Africa from those of colonial Africa during the early twentieth century. One was an exceptional degree of land alienation which, under the Land Act of 1913, eventually left Africans with only 13 per cent of the territory. The other was that the African population appears – on admittedly inadequate evidence – to have grown continuously from at least the late nineteenth century, without experiencing the decline common in early colonial Africa. The population of the Transkei, for example, apparently increased between 1891 and 1904 from 640,000 to 800,000, while the African population of South Africa as a whole almost doubled between 1904 and 1936 and more than trebled between 1904 and 1960.[76] Land alienation and population growth meant that black South Africans experienced demographic pressure on resources a generation earlier than other Africans.

It was not that the countryside escaped natural disasters. Cattle plague reached South Africa in 1896 and is thought to have killed over 2,500,000 cattle there, probably including a disproportionate number owned by Africans.[77] 'The pride bender', as the epidemic was known in the Ciskei, left the more pastoral peoples close to starvation, children malnourished for lack of milk, farmers bereft of plough-oxen, everyone bereft of transport to carry food.[78] Nor was this an isolated plague. Early in the new century East Coast Fever struck the barely recovered herds. By 1914 nearly three-quarters of Pondoland's cattle were again dead.[79] Drought, too, was recurrent. In the north and east, rainfall cycles initiated periods of dearth in 1893, 1911, and 1931, although only the first appears to have caused deaths.[80] The southern Cape, by contrast, suffered unpredictable droughts, especially after the two world wars. In 1945, for example, emergency feeding arrangements were needed in the Ciskei, 'a high proportion of the people assisted being widows and orphans', while the Middledrift district reported extensive infant starvation and the Lovedale hospital recorded no deaths from actual starvation but 25 per cent of its deaths from malnutrition.[81]

South Africa's pattern of famine, like its demography, was about a generation in advance of tropical Africa's.[82] Whereas deaths from famine were common in tropical Africa until the 1920s, they were rare in South Africa after the 1890s. As at earlier periods in Europe and contemporaneously in India, famine mortality was being brought under control by more efficient transport and government, wider markets, improved medicine, and better opportunities to earn wages. On the other hand, the dearth of the 1940s, although caused by drought, was exceptionally prolonged, almost chronic, suggesting that improved measures for combating famine coincided with increased susceptibility to it. Unchecked by famine, population growth on the limited land available to Africans was precipitating the reserves into endemic undernutrition, exactly a generation before the countries to the north.[83]

This conclusion must be tentative, however, because the agricultural history of the reserves is controversial. One authority holds that their output of grain fell between the early 1920s and the late 1940s by 13 per cent, while their population grew by 41 per cent.[84] Another believes that their total agricultural production was maintained until the mid 1960s, even production per head suffering little until the later 1950s, partly because land was added to the reserves during earlier decades.[85] Beneath the controversy, however, it is clear that even in the 1920s the reserves produced no more than one-half of their food needs and that output in some more arid and densely populated areas, especially in the Ciskei and the Northern Transvaal, suffered catastrophic decline thereafter to less than one-quarter of their needs.[86] These were the areas that suffered the chronic dearth of the 1940s.

The clearest evidence of agrarian crisis was landlessness. Scarcity of land was already apparent in the Ciskei during the 1890s and in the more favoured parts of the Transkei by 1910. In 1928 only 61 per cent of adult males in the Victoria East district of the Ciskei had plots.[87] Twenty years later some 30 per cent of all people in the Ciskei were thought to be landless, although both indigenous practice and government policy encouraged fragmentation of holdings. In 1943 nearly 10 per cent of households in the Transkei were landless and nearly one-half had no cattle.[88] Differentiation was very marked. A survey of the Keiskammahoek area of the Ciskei in 1949–50 revealed annual family expenditures ranging from £2.15.4 to £251.5.4, the richest families being those with a member holding a skilled off-farm job.[89] Cattle ownership remained a special source of inequality. Of 253 families surveyed in Keiskammahoek, 80 had no cattle but 16 owned more than 10 beasts each, while in Pondoland, early in the 1930s, some individuals owned 500 cattle and others none, although late-conquered Pondoland still had adequate land and was an oasis of prosperity when contrasted with such remote and arid regions as the northern Cape.[90]

The poverty of the reserves was accentuated by a lack of opportunities to earn cash except by peasant farming or labour migration. South Africa had fewer rural crafts than many tropical regions – there was no weaving, for example – and under European rule they atrophied, as did such activities as supplying firewood and bush produce to towns, perhaps owing to the exhaustion of supplies, effective government controls, and urban alternatives such as paraffin. South Africa exemplified Dr Hill's claim that towns have impoverished the African countryside during the twentieth century by absorbing all occupations except agriculture.[91] Moreover, rural poverty was self-reinforcing. The reserves were too poor to support prosperous local traders or craftsmen. They were probably too poor even to provide a market for local labour, if the absence of evidence on this subject is any guide.

Both black and white assumed that the African rural poor could rely upon kin and neighbours for support. Some evidence substantiated this. The Keiskammahoek survey found that it was only through the generosity of neighbours that a family with an annual expenditure of £2.15.4 survived. 'Real charity', it concluded, 'is a virtue which still shines brightly in the Reserves.' The survey also found, however, that westernised Mfengu complained that less acculturated Xhosa were too benevolent and filled the area with poor relations.[92] In Pondoland twenty years earlier Hunter had heard old men criticise 'School people' for being 'unwilling to have poor and uneducated people in their houses'. She had also noted that Mpondo chiefs no longer had the resources to provide for the poor as popular memory (perhaps with exaggeration) believed they had in the past.[93] Such new rural institutions as independent churches provided some support, chiefly for the handicapped who were also the main recipients of government assistance, for it was policy to aid only those who were incapacitated and bereft of family support, except during serious famine. The South African state in the 1930s still held to the principle of the New Poor Law: the remedy for poverty was work.[94]

In the late nineteenth century labour migrants appear to have sought cash chiefly to pay bridewealth, expand the homestead, or relieve famine, but during the first half of the twentieth century taxation, land shortage, and lower real wages gradually converted migration into an essential means of family survival. 'It is, without question, the income from the labour centres that keeps the congested areas going', a missionary wrote from the Ciskei in 1925.[95] The proportion of able-bodied men from Pondoland absent at work rose between 1911 and 1936 from 25 to 45 per cent. In Lesotho the figures for the same years were 20 and 47 per cent. The highest proportion recorded may have been the 72 per cent of taxpayers absent from the Middledrift district of the Ciskei in 1928–9.[96] Migration often meant a weary journey, squalid living conditions, hard work, brutal supervisors, and the possibility of incapacitation or death – between 1902 and 1914, 43,484 men from Mozambique alone died in employment on the Rand.[97] From the migrant's viewpoint, however, the greater danger was that he might not find work. 'If when they arrived in Kimberley there was a glut in the labour market', an early account recalled, 'then these poor descendants of Ham were to be seen on the outskirts of Kimberley starving to death.'[98] Such periods of unemployment recurred, especially during the depression of the early 1930s and the Cape famine of the early 1940s,[99] but the demand for labour was generally high during this period and the farms and gold mines offered reliable employment for those needy enough to take it. African poverty here was predominantly the poverty not of unemployment but of low wages or incapacitation.

As its exemplar of poverty, the Keiskammahoek survey took a family with no migrant labourer to send remittances. 'All last year is very hard through no food', its head complained. 'I can only say that if my Lord God had not opened the hearts of my neighbours we would have been in a very bad condition.' She was a widow, like some 38 per cent of the region's homestead heads in 1949–50.[100] Women's economic status was declining with the land available for agriculture, their chief economic function. White laws recognised only male rights over land. Monogamy – encouraged by Christianity, land shortage, and the taxing of plural wives – left many women alone, especially when widowed or when deserted by migrant men.[101] It was true that complex households still provided protection for the poor and were positively encouraged by land shortage and labour migration. Keiskammahoek had two kinds of large households in 1949–50: those of the rich, who could afford them, and those of the poor, who clustered together for mutual support.[102] Nevertheless, economic and social pressures on family structure was confirming the historic African poor – the incapacitated, aged, orphans, solitary women – as the new poor of a world where labour was almost the only defence against poverty. Dr Beinart has described this process in Pondoland during the 1930s:

> Families with migrants were not necessarily the poorest in Pondoland; a significant number of homesteads could not even be assured of any wage income. The size of such homesteads was usually smaller than the average . . . Poverty was closely linked to the process of homestead disintegration. Old couples could find their children marrying and leaving them with no means of support; those who were already poor were probably more vulnerable to isolation. Widows could be left with children and no paternal home to return to . . .
>
> Those men who were too old to migrate and those of all ages who were too weak or ill for the heavy manual work in the mines and sugar fields could still find casual daily labour, or sometimes more regular work, on council road gangs . . . Wealthier kin or larger homesteads in the neighbourhood sometimes absorbed the poor, providing them with keep to do odd jobs around the homestead, or took on boys to herd cattle. Those who were dependent on poorly paid local employment or on wealthier homesteads and those who were coming to the end of their lives, had little chance of breaking out of the trap of poverty . . .
>
> Those families without migrants had little chance of raising themselves out of poverty.[103]

The impoverishment of the reserves deprived Africans employed on white farms or industries of their bargaining power. Before the First World War, full-time farm labourers were normal only in the Cape, where Africans earned an average wage of 10 shillings a month in cash and perhaps as much again in kind. Elsewhere cash wages were somewhat higher: the average cash paid in Natal in 1910 was nearer 20 shillings a month than 10, while in the Transvaal the figure of 1 shilling a day was often quoted.[104] At this time, however, most African farmworkers could insist on being rewarded for their labour not in cash but by the right to use land, while many Africans occupied white land as sharecroppers or cash-tenants rather than workers. Yet like white *bywoners* they were gradually being proletarianised by the capitalisation of farming. In Natal over half the African population lived on white land in 1913, but increasingly as labour-tenants rather than sharecroppers or cash-tenants.[105] In the Orange Free State several Resident Magistrates reported in 1910 that sharecropping was increasing, but a minority declared that it was giving way to labour-tenancy as land values rose, while 'the more progressive farmer pays his servants a regular wage and expects a daily service'.[106] In the Transvaal, sharecropping or cash-tenancy was still normal in 1910, but farmers were gradually imposing labour-tenancy, often on very exploitative terms.[107]

The Land Act of 1913 sought to prohibit sharecropping but not labour-tenancy. Sol Plaatje's famous account of the Act's effects – 'that a Kafir who refused to become a servant should at once be consigned to the road' – caught the immediate misery for a minority, especially the elderly and especially in the Orange Free State, but it obscured the fact that sharecropping died slowly and was destroyed only in the 1960s and 1970s.[108] The intervening half-century saw a bitter struggle through which Africans on white farms were reduced to an exceptionally miserable proletariat. By 1930, when the Native Economic Commission investigated the question, a labour-tenant in the Cape, Transvaal, or Orange Free State normally worked three months a year in return for arable and pasture, while in Natal six months' labour was normal.[109] During the next decade wage employment further replaced labour-tenancy, while terms grew more onerous for those tenants who survived. The Native Service Contract Act of 1932, for example, required labour-tenants in Natal and Transvaal to work six months a year at the farmer's will, forbade them to leave the farm without written permission, empowered them to contract to the farmer any female or juvenile dependant, and prohibited farmers from keeping labour-tenants except on these terms.[110]

As sharecroppers, cash-tenants, and labour-tenants were driven towards the proletariat, wages froze at conventional levels which varied enormously from one locality to another. In 1925, for example, the ruling wage in cash and kind in the Eastern Cape was £12 a year, whereas mineworkers averaged £32 a year in cash alone. Wages in cash and kind on maize farms in 1928–9 ranged from £15.10.0 a year on the smallest farms to £26.2.0 on the largest.[111] A careful study showed the total annual earnings of male farmworkers in the Border area of the Cape in 1933–4 to be £16.10.0 and family income to be probably less than £36 for an average of 6.34 people.[112] Government reckoned in the late 1930s that the average farm wage from all sources for the whole country was about £20 a year.[113] Many labourers were indebted, often paying interest at over 100 per cent a year. Some were addicted to alcohol through the tradition of serving out daily pilchard tins of local wine.[114] Few farmworkers had any chance of advancement, for farmers rarely graded wages even by experience – only 5 of 29 prosperous farms studied in the Grahamstown area did so – and the law made it difficult for workers to leave farms.[115] Many observers noted the sullen and hopeless air of farmworkers. One recorded 'bitter anti-European feeling'.[116]

Whether African farmworkers were worse off than those living in towns or reserves was much debated. The Native Economic Commission of 1930–2 thought that urban Africans suffered most because their expenses were greatest, but many observers felt that farm conditions were worst. Haines, in 1933–4, compared the £3 or less earned each month by a whole family on a Border farm with the monthly wage of £3–5 earned by an unskilled labourer in the bigger Cape towns. Hunter, who studied all three environments in the early 1930s, concluded that farms combined the disadvantages of reserves and towns and that farmworkers were 'the most consistently poor' of the three communities.[117]

In the towns the interwar years were the age of *marabi*. Obscure in origin, the word described a specifically urban, working-class culture which was spawned by the slumyards of Johannesburg, colonised the locations of smaller towns, spilt over into freehold townships like Sophiatown, and had an uncle in District Six. Marabi meant many things. It meant first a syncretic style of music, blending the Afrikaans and Coloured traditions of the Cape with local African rhythms and imported Black American modes; the result could be played on almost anything but characteristically on a piano and a banjo or violin, or in more sophisticated form by small jazz groups. Individuals or couples danced to this, with no fixed steps but any way the music moved provided it was sexy. The locus was a shebeen. The atmosphere was alcoholic, sometimes criminal. Dress was as modern and stylish as funds allowed: red for the ladies, by one account from 1932, with black Japanese shoes and hair in 'the French cut'; the men in 'black shirts, black Japanese shoes and baggy trousers'. Marabi also meant low-class people who behaved this way, and by extension anything the respectable thought disreputable. 'Marabi love' was illicit, a 'marabi girl' wanted a good time. But marabi meant more. It meant youth and modernity. It meant the freedom of the town. It meant the freedom of towns not yet in the grip of the state. It meant hope and ambition not yet crushed. 'It was not all just shebeeny, smutty, illegal stuff', one who enjoyed it recalled. 'Some places it was as dreams were made on.'[118]

In 1927 the slumyards of Johannesburg which had spawned marabi culture were thought to house at least 40,000 people.[119] Six years later the anthropologist Ellen Hellmann wrote a magnificent account of one, 'Rooiyard' as she called it, in Doornfontein, less than 2 kilometres from the city centre. Rooiyard was owned by a European landlord. It consisted of 107 rooms, a shop, 6 latrines, and one working water-tap. Of the rooms, 29 were of brick, the rest of wood and corrugated iron, the whole 'in a state of shocking neglect'.[120] Rooiyard housed 235 adults and 141 children at an average of 3.58 persons per room, but it had also a large shifting population of relatives and friends. Of 100 families, 60 had lived there for an average of 5 months, the rest for an average of 37 months, but all regarded themselves as temporary residents and treated the compound fecklessly. Rents averaged 28s 6d a month for each room, or roughly 40 per cent of the breadwinner's wage, yet rooms were keenly sought, for Rooiyard was central and offered many opportunities for informal earnings.[121]

'The leitmotiv of Rooiyard life', Hellmann wrote, 'is the economic struggle. The Natives of Rooiyard are poor. And their daily activities are, to a large extent, motivated by the drear struggle for survival.'[122] Poor indeed they were: too poor even to be in debt, since nobody would lend to them. Yet they were not the very poor, the destitute. Of 33 families studied, 17 had a bicycle, 17 a sewing machine, 4 a gramophone, often bought on hire purchase, for Rooiyard people spent every penny available because, as one explained, 'If I buy things I save. If I don't buy I don't save, because the money goes just the same.'[123] Meat was usually eaten daily and took roughly one-quarter of all expenditure on food. Tea, sugar, and coffee were in general use. Bread was popular. Most residents thought they ate better than in the countryside.[124] In other senses, too, Rooiyard people – and marabi people generally – were poor but not very poor. They certainly did not practise an anomic 'culture of poverty'. Family life survived vigorously, if in urban forms. Only 3 of the 107 rooms housed more than one family and women took immense care of their rooms.[125] 'Somehow', a visitor wrote, 'those paper frills made me feel more ashamed than anything else I saw.'[126] While older people clung to rural values, the young adopted the marabi style and pursued money and advancement with cheerful ruthlessness. Ironically, South Africa's racialism probably helped African townsmen to endure their poverty: at least they need not see themselves as failures.

Race also helped to preserve a sense of community. Marabi culture was not a conscious working-class culture: it had no political content, it was alcoholic, and the sprawling townships encouraged cross-fertilisation between elite and plebeian cultures.[127] Yet, as a denizen remembered, 'although people didn't seem to be interested in one another, they spoke with a subtle unity of voice. They still behaved as a community.'[128] Slumyard dwellers were not ripe for revolution, but they might repel a police liquor raid. Hellmann mentioned a two-year-old child who would not allow his policeman father to caress him while in uniform. Their 'undeclared guerrilla warfare' with the police[129] was one reason why slumyard people were not like the apolitical, instinctively conservative casual poor of outcast London but more like the slum-dwellers of Latin America, realistic, striving, and self-reliant. They were the poor in Booth's sense, struggling to avert destitution.[130]

Marabi people escaped extreme poverty chiefly through employment in the formal sector. In 1933, 89 of Rooiyard's 100 male family heads had regular employment, earning an average of £3.12.0 a month, chiefly as store workers, delivery men, and laundry workers. Their average wage was the norm for unskilled urban workers during the 1930s. African urban poverty was thus the structural poverty of low wages, the poverty of those who were poor even when employed. It was exacerbated by high price levels resulting from the protection of agriculture and infant industries. A study in Durban in 1946 showed that malnutrition and undernutrition were common even among the best-paid African workers.[131]

The path from poverty to destitution lay through insecurity. Illness might throw a family into indigence. Many unskilled occupations were inherently unstable: of immigrant workers entering Johannesburg between 1936 and 1944, 47 per cent took first jobs lasting less than six months, and although it was often the workers who found something better, turnover was especially high in such insecure occupations as domestic service (55 per cent) and building (52 per cent).[132] Cyclical unemployment peaked during the early 1930s, when the international depression was exacerbated in South Africa by drought and mistaken economic policies. 'Go to the Native Affairs Department, Johannesburg', an African wrote in May 1932, 'and [see] the thousands of thin, hungry young men looking more dead than alive . . . Never was there such hunger and unemployment before.'[133] Early in 1934 officials estimated that there were 10,000 unemployed Africans in the Johannesburg area. Their children were seen scavenging in dustbins or 'prowling round the market trying to pick up rotten fruit and vegetables for food'.[134] The Communist Party organised violent confrontations with the police and encouraged the unemployed to coerce shopkeepers into subsidising relief kitchens. Agitation secured official aid for Johannesburg's unemployed whites, but the issue of relief food to Africans was quickly halted lest it attract even more into the city.[135] Several municipalities provided relief work for a few long-resident Africans, but the potential demand was almost limitless and the work provided can scarcely have outweighed the loss of African jobs through the white labour policy.[136]

'For all that it mattered', a victim later reflected, 'the depression of the early thirties did not seem on the surface to add an ounce of pressure more to the poverty of the Black man.' He remembered that 'there was much less to eat at home', but scrabbling in dustbins was nothing new in his family.[137] White liberals, too, stressed the resilience of marabi society. 'Native workers have shared jobs as well as food', it was reported.[138] But one observer added a caveat:

> During the depression years of 1930–1932 there was much unemployment, but little actual suffering was reported, no actual cases of starvation on the Witwatersrand. The unemployed found food at the homes of relatives and friends and ate from their meagre stores. The whole Native population simply sagged down to a still lower sub-economic level. Indications point, however, to a gradual yielding to stern necessity's law here, an acceptance of the man *versus* man scramble for material goods. The old ties are giving way.[139]

Nor did the return of economic 'normality' in 1934 entirely clear the streets of the 'unemployed Bantu who linger with glaring eyes of a hungry wolf outside the chief Pass Office . . . hungry and fatigued, subdued and unsure of themselves and hardly able to raise their voices above a whisper', showing 'all the weariness and despair brought about by hunger and a fruitless job hunt and dodging of the pick-up cruising the streets'.[140]

For those without formal-sector jobs, an alternative was one of the small-scale, commonly self-employed activities which economists call the 'informal sector'. The search for these opportunities was feverish, for in South Africa's towns, as in the countryside, the informal sector was unusually small. In East London in 1932, for example, Hunter recorded 9,451 male and 3,210 female African employees but only 131 men and 71 women who were self-employed, although she omitted certain categories such as women brewers. A survey of the less impoverished African areas of Johannesburg in 1940 found only 12 per cent of men working 'in African industry either on their own account or as assistants'.[141] The most important reason why the informal sector was small was that the state discouraged African traders. In the Orange Free State, Africans were simply banned from trade, as they were also in East London until 1952.[142] Elsewhere Africans had little prior commercial experience and faced competition from expert trading communities. During the early 1940s, for example, Kimberley had 'six African grocers, two milk sellers, two cafe owners, one baker and two woodsellers. They all, however, lead a very precarious existence, particularly the grocers who have to compete with Chinese and Indian storekeepers on the outskirts of the Locations.' African traders were most successful on the Rand, where there were 500–600 African retailers in 1936, many allegedly in debt. Ten years later only 891 of South Africa's 33,065 retail businesses were in African hands.[143] Similar obstacles faced hawkers, who were anathema to municipal councillors elected by white businessmen and obsessed by hygiene, but hawking was the most common informal-sector activity for Africans. Of East London's 131 self-employed men in 1932, 40 sold fresh produce, 35 tobacco, 14 wood, and 12 cakes. In Johannesburg the growth of industrial employment and the removal of African residences from the city centre to outlying townships during the 1930s created a market for cooked food which was met by a proliferation of mobile 'coffee carts', built of scrap and often operated by ill-paid assistants.[144] Another obstacle to informal enterprise was the scale and vigour of its formal competitors. Even filthy occupations like collecting scrap were often controlled by capital. In East London even bottle-collectors might be employees. A comparison of Hunter's list of informal-sector activities there in 1932 with Reader's survey in the mid 1950s shows that many activities – skin-dressing, mattress-making, sack-repairing – had meanwhile largely disappeared. During the same period Sophiatown's washerwomen were driven out of business and District Six saw its exceptionally lively informal sector undermined by the mechanisation of laundering and the clothing industry.[145] The only male rural craft which flourished steadily in towns was herbalism. Artisans were few, probably owing to official controls and competition from machinery and other races. East London's 20,000 Africans included only 6 tinsmiths in 1932, while its 49 carpenters were partly employees.[146] The most vigorous centre of informal activity at that time was the Salisbury compound in Johannesburg, better known as Mayimayi:

> Here are to be found a battery of barbers whose charge for a hair-cut is sixpence. Here are carpenters who will make trunks and suitcases from packing cases for from ten to thirty shillings apiece. Bootmakers do a thriving business, as do the tailors, bicycle repairers, snuff vendors, dry-cleaners and leather and metal workers. The latter make 'bangles' from brass or copper wire. Furriers also do a good business in monkey tails, skins, and trimmed hats. These craftsmen and salesmen pay rental for their stalls and living quarters in the compound.

Mayimayi, however, was already scheduled for demolition. Its foodstuff section had been closed, as unhygienic.[147]

The dominant informal activity in South African towns was brewing. It was a woman's enterprise. In 1911 Johannesburg contained 4,357 female Africans; in 1936, over 60,000.[148] Because male wages were designed to support only single migrants, the influx of women bred the first family poverty among Africans that the continent had seen. 'Childless couples have a decided advantage over couples who have to provide for children', Hellmann wrote of Rooiyard. 'The women are keenly alive to the additional economic burden of feeding an extra child.' 'Requests for contraceptives and abortive measures', she added, 'were the most frequent of all those addressed to me.'[149] In these circumstances, many women – especially those with small children – turned to brewing for unmarried townsmen, earning average profits higher than a normal manufacturing wage. In the Marabastad location of Pretoria in 1934 about 70 per cent of women derived some income from brewing.[150] Some towns permitted brewing for domestic consumption, but all prohibited Africans from selling beer and many banned its production altogether. The shebeens which sold beer and bred marabi culture were therefore surrounded by the crime, danger, crudity, and squalor of Prohibition. 'They drank and drank and drank', a denizen recalled. 'In case the police should come, they drank the beer without taking the measure from their mouths and held on to their stomachs as though they were in pain.'[151] The pain may have been real. To get drunk on traditional beer needed quantities so conspicuous that Shebeen Queens laced it with carbide or worse to make 'Kill me quick' or a hundred other concoctions, hiding their stocks in holes dug beneath slumyard floors:

> Your Commissioners inspected an illicit liquor yard in Johannesburg. From the car to the yard was a matter of two minutes. There were some twenty Natives, men and women, in the yard. There was an all-pervading smell of alcohol, but no drop of liquor, no utensils which might have contained it, were to be seen.[152]

Undeterred, the police destroyed 568,807 gallons of illicit brew during 1933. In 1935, 6,041 African men and 7,761 women were convicted of possessing liquor.[153] Illegality bred close supportive ties among women neighbours and friends. It also bred resentment of the authorities and their municipal beerhalls. Sophiatown's major political action between the wars was a beer-hall boycott.[154] Apart from their criminality, shebeens also attracted a penumbra of destitute alcoholics, unemployable men, barren or deserted women, the deformed, and the degenerate. A survey of East London in 1955 found over 130 women and nearly 100 men sleeping rough in the bush where illicit drinking took place, sharing an undiscriminating, tolerant life of failure. Their counterparts on the Rand were the *simbamgodi*, the derelicts who earned beer by digging the holes in which women hid it.[155]

The attraction of brewing, despite its accompanying violence and squalor, can be understood only by comparison with other jobs available to working-class women. Those with small children could take in washing and earn all of £1–2 a month in Sophiatown during the 1930s. Those with more freedom might become domestic servants, as did 80 per cent of the economically active women enumerated by the census of 1936 (which did not, of course, enumerate brewers).[156] Female domestic servants in East London in April 1932 earned an average of 25–30 shillings a month, plus food, and were the worst-paid workers in a notoriously ill-paid town. In Kimberley in 1942 African women worked in Coloured families for 5 shillings a month.[157] So badly was domestic service paid that it was increasingly confined to African women,[158] whereas in the late ninteenth century both men and women of all races had entered service. It was one of the most important fields in which the multiracial poverty of the late nineteenth century gave way to the black poverty of the mid twentieth.[159]

For African parents with rural values, marabi culture was of the devil. The proportion of recorded African births described as illegitimate was 59 per cent in Pretoria in 1934–5, 51 per cent in Germiston in 1936–7, and 46 per cent in Bloemfontein in 1932, while Hellmann found in the late 1930s that one-third of Johannesburg's African girls aged over 16 had borne 'illegitimate' babies.[160] 'Soshal Senta and baiskopo will give you a baby and no father', a mother warns in Dikobe's *Marabi dance*, but the stigma attached to 'illegitimacy' in the wider society was often small, except among aspiring bourgeois.[161] Marriage was not easy either to define or to complete in a slumyard. Hellmann reckoned that 20 per cent of Rooiyard's couples lived in informal 'town marriages', while a survey of part of Durban in the mid 1940s found that less than half the couples living together were 'properly' married.[162] Since women married later in town – at 22 in East London as against 16–18 in rural Pondoland – pre-marital sexual activity was inevitably common, indeed universal in Rooiyard. Illegitimacy was due as much to frustrated marriage as to rampant promiscuity. Many young townspeople saw marriage as a personal rather than family contract.[163]

Their attitudes merged with the more powerful impact of labour migration to create independent urban women, often heading their own households. Ezekiel Mphahlele's account of his childhood in the Marabastad location of Pretoria during the 1930s – a rare account of an unhappy African childhood – describes a brutal, drunken father abandoning his all-enduring wife to bring up her turbulent but deeply attached children.[164] Hunter noted women in East London in 1932 living alone with their children, 'keeping the household with their own earnings'. Two decades later more than half the owners of wood-and-iron shacks in the town were women, 59 per cent of them widows. What a South African historian of the period called 'the most general type of poverty in the world, the poor and solitary woman' was already a feature of South African towns.[165]

Missionaries devoted much energy to protecting urban women, especially domestic servants who might contaminate white families. African women themselves created organisations ranging from the Bantu Women's Self-Improvement Association (1918) and the Purity League (1919) to the *manyano* prayer unions which began in Natal in 1912 and expressed parental concern with their daughters' 'immorality'.[166] Such formal, western-style welfare institutions attracted middle-class Africans. A Bantu Relief Committee was formed in Johannesburg in 1932 to assist the unemployed, a 'Social Service Committee of Bantu teachers, nurses, and others' undertook the same function in East London, and Bloemfontein had a similar organisation in 1940.[167] In 1935 James Ntshinga created the Blind and Crippled League in Port Elizabeth 'to consider how to combat the daily occurrence of the Native blinds and crippled, begging from door to door for necessities of life', whereby they 'become a reproach to us and an affliction to our European friends'. It was imitated in Johannesburg two years later.[168] An African Blind Welfare Association was founded in 1940 and a Handicapped African Welfare Association in 1945, its chairman explaining:

> The crippled and blind African beggars who daily stand at City street corners are just where they ought not to be . . . Among the important signs that a race has passed out of barbarism is that which is characterised by the earnest efforts of that race to take care of its less physically or mentally privileged members.[169]

The first Bantu burial society was founded on the Rand in 1932, in imitation of long-established white and Coloured institutions. In 1944 some 65 per cent of households in Western Native Township subscribed to burial societies.[170] Little is known of the urban welfare activities of African churches or tribal associations at this period. In 1937 a Bapedi Union was planned on the Rand with the intention, *inter alia*, 'to make some means to those who are homeless of getting jobs and to deal with matters which affect them',[171] but this subject awaits study. The evidence of *ad hoc* mutual aid is stronger. In the slumyards, for example, funerals were financed mainly by collections among neighbours and friends.[172] Institutionalised African welfare activities were probably even more limited in South African towns than in tropical cities, partly perhaps because South Africa's pre-colonial societies had possessed few institutions transferable to towns and because white repression made institutions difficult to create. Whatever the reason, the effect was to throw the burden of poor relief on to kinsmen, neighbours, and informal arrangements.

Educated Africans welcomed this. East London's Social Service Committee, for example, 'was troubled lest attempts to give relief to the unemployed should make persons who were still in employment cease to relieve their kin, which the Committee considered it was their duty to do'.[173] Reference to this tradition accompanied any appeal for funds to aid the poor. 'In ancient Bantu Society', it was explained when the Bantu Relief Committee was formed, 'the poor and the needy were not allowed to starve by the community in which they lived . . . This generosity of our forefathers must be perpetuated and put into practice from now.'[174] Nor was it only ideologically important. Hellmann stressed the pervasiveness of family support in Rooiyard, where there was little begging but much sponging on relatives, who were willing 'to share [their] last pot of mealie meal with destitute tribesmen'. Krige's study of Marabastad in 1934 revealed 'a wonderful spirit of co-operation and generosity among Natives which largely accounts for the fact that Europeans seldom become aware of the extent of poverty in the locations'. 'No one need starve in a location', a missionary reported from Bloemfontein. 'One young man of seventeen keeps a bedridden father by (I regret to say) rack-renting two rooms, and by sawing tree-boughs into lengths for firewood. He said he made at best 5s. a month by this, but that when he made no profit the neighbours helped him with gifts of food.'[175] Others were less sanguine. Hunter drew a nuanced picture of East London in 1932:

> In spite of this loosening of mutual economic responsibilities it is still considered obligatory that kin should provide for one another in need, and I found a number of cases where persons had been supported by their kin in sickness or unemployment . . . Nevertheless, the fact that the economic struggle is keener under town conditions, and that everything is on a cash basis, is breaking down the old sense of the mutual obligations of kin. The strain of supporting impoverished relatives is undue. A trained Native nurse, who has been ten years working in the location, told me that she knew of several cases in which persons had died of starvation, although they had relatives in the location.[176]

Alongside kinship, the most important institution of mutual aid, the *stokfel*, drew upon neighbourhood and occupational ties. *Stokfel* (from the English 'stockfair') embraced much diversity, but its core was a rotating credit club which originated in the Cape but flourished especially among the women brewers of Johannesburg. Like hire purchase, it was a means of saving where the pressures to spend cash immediately were compelling.

Members contributed a weekly sum to a pool which each received in turn. The week's recipient used it to organise a party which the public paid to attend. The takings were hers to use. If a member suffered a bereavement or went to gaol, her fellows might support her or care for her family. In Western Native Township in 1944 some 20 per cent of households belonged to such clubs. They combined profit, mutual aid, entertainment, and corporate solidarity in a manner epitomising marabi culture.[177]

One novel feature of South African urban poverty was that the poor included many children. Child poverty had been rare in pre-colonial Africa, except in famine. In South African towns it was blatant. 'A few months ago' a missionary reported in 1921,

> a few Johannesburg men investigated some stables in a disreputable part of town. In two or three of these stables, sleeping in lofts above the animals in air which choked the raiders, were found fifty children, both boys and girls, native children who have run away and are drifting into ways of vice. It is estimated that here in the heart of Johannesburg could be rounded up over two hundred children who have no homes and who are living by their wits.[178]

Such *amalalapipe* ('those who sleep in pipes') provided sub-Saharan Africa's first child beggars, other than religious students. Trevor Huddleston described them in the 1950s:

> Sometimes in Johannesburg at night when the cinema crowds are flooding out on to the pavements, I have watched African children – some of them certainly not more than eight years old – hanging about the lighted entrances, darting through the legs of the emerging throng, watching the Greek shops with their brilliant windows. They are filthy dirty. They are hungry. They hold out their hands – 'Penny, baas, penny, baas' – and sometimes they get what they ask and run off in search of more. But nobody cares what happens to them or from where they come.[179]

Public concern for child welfare first became acute shortly before the First World War, largely in response to infant mortality statistics, and led to the formation of the National Council for Child Welfare in 1924 and to the Children's Act of 1937, which provided maintenance for children needing care.[180] Yet this provision rarely benefited Africans, for they and their rulers long assumed that the 'extended family' cared for all African children. Government explained in 1939:

> Having regard to the fact that under Native law it is the natural duty of the head of the kraal or guardian-at-law to support any minor belonging to his kraal or under his care, and that the granting of maintenance by the State will probably lead to an evasion of the responsibility resting upon the Natives under their own customs, grants will not be made in the case of Native children residing in rural areas.

In towns Government would 'endeavour, where circumstances permit, to repatriate the child to the care of relatives living in rural areas'. Consequently only 197 of the 14,760 children then receiving maintenance grants were Africans.[181] Only 27 of South Africa's 120 orphanages and kindred institutions admitted non-Europeans at that time. Ten years later the number had risen to 57.[182]

Given the lack of public care, African children and youths found their own means of survival. Selling newspapers was a highly organised youth activity from the late nineteenth century. Coloured boys of seven could earn 6 shillings a week from it in Cape Town in 1918, while twenty years later Sophiatown lads made £2 a month in central Johannesburg. Others caddied, scavenged, or sang, danced, or played the penny-whistle at street corners, creating a child culture, *kwela* culture, the juvenile counterpart of marabi.[183] Crimes against property were especially common among juveniles of less than sixteen years old. Child gangs existed at least by the 1930s and culminated in the Vultures, a huge gang founded in Sophiatown in 1950 which ran protection rackets on rich children and Asian traders but, like most gangs, was chiefly concerned with territoriality.[184]

Children borrowed gang organisation from their elders. In order to understand the 'juvenile delinquency' which obsessed South Africans from about 1933, one must remember that young Africans were expected to be violent, although they were also expected to moderate their behaviour as they grew older. Among the Xhosa even adult women deliberately encouraged aggression in small boys. Almost everywhere village youths habitually sparred or fought pitched battles with sticks.[185] Gangs of young men known as Amalaita – often domestic servants – took this tradition to town in the early 1900s, holding bloody public contests on Sunday afternoons,[186] and 'juvenile delinquents' subsequently preserved the tradition of violence, probably to rather later ages, while their elders switched to softer urban values. Much juvenile delinquency also resulted from inability to gain full adult status owing to lack of education and jobs. In 1951 Johannesburg had 20,000 male African teenagers in neither school nor work. In the mid 1930s some 72 per cent of juvenile offenders before the Johannesburg courts came from unsatisfactory homes.[187] 'The background of almost every confirmed skolly', an authority wrote of Cape Town's delinquents in 1950,

> is one of filthy slum or pondokkie[188] housing; perpetual neglect and hunger while an infant because both parents are working; the gnawing pain of veld sores, septic wounds and rotting teeth all his life; no supervision over his schooling so that he never passed anything higher than standard three or four; continued idleness while a youngster because there was nobody to make him go to school or work; filthy streets for play-grounds because the house is locked while parents are away at work; illiterate, drunken and often demoralized parents.[189]

Yet although the link between deprivation and delinquency was as clear as in tropical Africa,[190] South Africa's juvenile delinquents were immensely more violent.

The main reason for this was probably exposure to adult criminals in prison – South Africa's prisons contained 2,554 juveniles aged under eighteen in 1938 and were already notorious for gangs and homosexuality – and to hardened juvenile offenders in the few brutal reformatories which existed before the 1930s, especially the Porter Reformatory in the Cape which was truly a school of criminality for the Coloured people.[191] These institutions especially bred juvenile gangs, apparently in two traditions. One was African and originated from an adult criminal society known as the Ninevites, formed around 1890; this spawned the Amalaita groups of the 1900s which were imitated by children and youths in the 1930s and probably bred the juvenile *tsotsi* gangs, such as the Berliners, which terrorised the Rand from the later 1940s.[192] The other tradition concerned the Coloured people of the Cape. There were adult Coloured gangs in Kimberley in the 1870s and juvenile gangs in Cape Town by 1906, but they became more violent and organised between the wars, possibly in response to increasingly violent policing, and culminated during the 1940s in street warfare in District Six between the Globe, representing long-established townsmen, and the Jesters and other gangs formed by recent immigrants.[193] The poor survived by preying on the poor.

For a generation after the First World War South Africa's rulers struggled ineffectively to control black urban poverty. Legislation in 1923 and 1937 empowered municipalities to require Africans to live in designated areas, authorised them to deport the 'idle, dissolute or disorderly', obliged Africans entering towns to leave again if still unemployed after fourteen days, and facilitated municipal financing of low-cost accommodation.[194] Yet the few municipalities that seriously attempted slum-clearance found it hopeless. Korsten was 'cleared' from 1936 and an 'almost idyllic' new township replaced it, but in 1948 more Africans than ever were living in Korsten, many in shacks made from packing-cases.[195] Cape Town opened a model African township at Langa in 1927 but could not keep pace with an African population which increased between 1921 and 1948 from 8,684 to 31,258. In 1936 some 37 per cent of the city's residential area was still racially mixed.[196] Durban's housing policy was even less successful. In 1921, when the city contained 46,000 Africans, most were still housed in bachelor hostels and barracks, but in 1946 half the 114,000 Africans were living in shanty towns, the best-known being Cato Manor.[197]

Johannesburg had the most acute problem, especially in the slumyards close to the city centre. Its solution was to build a massive township 15 kilometres away at Orlando to house 80,000 Africans. The first moved in during 1932. The slumyards were then cleared: Rooiyard was largely demolished in 1934. Yet in 1938 Orlando housed only 26,000 of the 105,445 more permanent Africans living in Johannesburg, let alone the 93,000 Africans on the Witwatersrand who 'live by their wits, sleep with their friends at night, and are not included in the census'.[198] Many clustered ever more densely into the surviving slums. Pimville, created 15 kilometres from the city centre in 1904 as an emergency camp during a plague epidemic, housed 15,000 people in the late 1930s in 'a heterogeneous collection of closely packed wood, iron and brick buildings, constructed about small yards where humans and animals share the restricted space'.[199] Sophiatown, Martindale, and Newclare housed 5,823 people in 1921 and 28,502 in 1937, including 100 whites, 1,377 Asians, and 3,215 Coloured people. The mostly white landlords often accommodated over 80 people in 16 rooms on a 'stand' 50 × 100 feet. Bourgeois and proletarian, social club and shebeen jostled one another. Marabi culture, uprooted from the slumyards, flourished again in the more sophisticated form of jazz orchestras. Residents of Sophiatown called it Little Harlem.[200] And further out, beyond the city's northern border, the population of the freehold township at Alexandra rose between 1930 and 1943 from 7,200 to 45,000.[201]

By the late 1930s the white electorate was acutely alarmed at its leaders' inability to control black urbanisation. Johannesburg's ratepayers campaigned for the demolition of Sophiatown, Alexandra, and their satellites. The Purified Nationalist Party made complete urban segregation part of its platform.[202] Yet in reality the problem was only beginning, for between 1939 and 1952 the African urban population almost doubled. In March 1942 the Minister of Native Affairs admitted that it was for the time being beyond control.[203] One response was to abandon restraints, accept African urbanisation as irreversible and even as the best answer for Poor Blacks as well as Poor Whites, and argue that the real problem of low wages could best be met by recognising African trade unions. This was the view of the influential wartime Secretary of Native Affairs, D. F. Smit, and the energetic Minister of Finance and Social Welfare, J. H. Hofmeyr.[204] It was encouraged by the first systematic study of non-white poverty carried out in sub-Saharan Africa: Professor Edward Batson's survey of Cape Town in 1938–9, which found that some 53 per cent of the city's Coloured people and 48 per cent of its Africans lived below the Poverty Datum Line (the minimum needed to preserve mere physical efficiency), chiefly owing to low wages.[205]

While Government confessed its helplessness, wartime urbanisation swamped housing and other facilities. By 1942 some 10,000 Africans were living outside Cape Town on the Cape Flats, mostly in *pondokkies* made of 'pieces of corrugated iron, old tins and drums, rough bows, sacking, anything which can possibly offer protection against the weather'. Six years later the Council estimated that the city had 150,000 squatters. Port Elizabeth and East London were thought in 1949 to share the highest tuberculosis rate in the world.[206] The urban influx brought whole families in unprecedented numbers, owing to growing rural population pressure and widespread food shortages. Early in 1946 a Johannesburg baker 'had several times seen an African so hungry that he had eaten his half loaf of bread[207] before receiving his change. In another shop, an African who had come in to buy bread after the day's stock had been exhausted collapsed on the doorstep.'[208] Yet the war also brought expectation. The years 1942–5 were the only period between 1910 and the 1970s when wage differentials between black and white workers narrowed. Recognition of African trade unions encouraged activity which climaxed in the mineworkers' strike of 1946. Five times between 1940 and 1945 the people of Alexandra organised bus boycotts to prevent fare increases. This wartime ferment culminated in the squatter movement of 1944–7, when nearly 100,000 Africans – mostly from overcrowded urban locations – settled in self-built camps around Johannesburg, living in 'shacks of hessian, tin, poles, tattered canvas or mealie stalks', 'no go' areas roughly controlled by popular leaders of whom the most spectacular was the ex-murderer, lawyer's clerk, and schoolteacher James Sofasonke Mpanza.[209]

As the urban crisis deepened, the one point on which South Africans agreed was that its solution required central government intervention. For Afrikaner Nationalists this conviction pointed towards the Apartheid programme. For liberals it necessitated the extension to Africans of welfare benefits hitherto confined to other races. Until the 1940s the chief forms of state aid to the African poor were food rations for the permanently destitute and short-term emergency relief given in food or work, all administered until 1940 by the Native Affairs Department at a cost of £50,000–100,000 a year.[210] Institutional care long centred on subsidising the Bantu Refuge at Germiston, established in 1927 in an abandoned mine compound as 'a Home for aged, infirm and maimed Natives and for children who have no relatives capable of supporting them'. In 1940 the Refuge had accommodation for 200 men and 54 women but actually housed only 60 and 21 respectively, for its depressing cheerlessness encouraged the poor 'to make their living on the streets'.[211] African dislike of institutions also extended to the Elandsdoorn rural settlement for the aged and infirm, which was only half full in 1949, and to insane asylums, whose dreadful conditions were an added disincentive.[212]

Most aid to the African urban poor was left to municipalities – some large towns formed social welfare branches and established almshouses during the 1930s and 1940s – and to a few private charities which relied heavily on public funds. In 1936 only 5 per cent of charitable expenditure in Johannesburg was by organisations catering for Africans to any considerable extent.[213] Ezekiel Mphahlele's recollection of Marabastad – 'a white woman came to put up a soup-kitchen. After a few months she disappeared with the kitchen'[214] – captured one kind of charity, but others did enduring work. Among them were pioneer African nurses like Sister Dora Nginza, who worked in Port Elizabeth as a health visitor from 1920 to 1955 and virtually created the public health service in the New Brighton location. In 1941 the Jan H. Hofmeyr School of Social Work in Johannesburg began to train the first African social workers.[215]

Alongside poor relief, the state granted African miners compensation for phthisis and silicosis from 1911, while the Workmen's Compensation Act of 1934 extended compensation to disablement and death in other industries. The Blind Persons Act of 1936 excluded Africans from the pensions then established, but shortly afterwards the Native Affairs Department began to pay a monthly pension of 10 shillings to blind Africans, increased in the early 1940s to 15 shillings in towns and 20 shillings in cities, subject to a means test and a minimum age of nineteen. In 1943 some 20,600 blind Africans received pensions.[216] A year later the Act of 1936 was extended to them. These initiatives were the work of Hofmeyr, who became Minister for Social Welfare in 1937 and retained oversight of domestic policies for most of the next eleven years. Until the vital administrative history has been written, Hofmeyr's personal role in the expansion of welfare benefits to Africans will remain uncertain, but it was undoubtedly important. Although a parsimonious Finance Minister, he 'found it intolerable that any social welfare scheme should apply to white people only'.[217] In addition to blind pensions, he insisted on extending the Social Welfare Department's functions under the Children's Act to small numbers of Africans in 1940, an important step because it broke the South African tradition that services for Africans must be provided separately and through the Native Affairs Department, which in 1940 also lost its responsibility for poor relief.

The centrepiece of Hofmeyr's work emerged from the report of the Social Security Committee of 1944. It proposed that permanently employed or urbanised Africans should receive the same range of benefits as other races, although generally at lower rates. The chief benefits should be old age pensions, family allowances, invalidity pensions, and unemployment benefits. All other Africans should pay lower taxes and receive fewer benefits, but these should include invalidity payments and old age pensions.[218] When parliamentary criticism caused Government to abandon a comprehensive scheme, Hofmeyr salvaged the most important African benefits by including them in his budget.[219] The pensions hitherto paid to the blind were extended to other incapacitated or elderly Africans, so that in 1947–8 some 27,264 received disability grants, 21,864 received invalidity grants, and 196,846 received old age pensions. Provision for the elderly was to have a profound effect on the subsequent history of poverty in South Africa.[220]

At the time, however, controversy centred on unemployment benefits, which were introduced in 1947 for permanent urban employees, including Africans. These evoked furious opposition from white men who insisted that the unemployed should be assigned to labour-hungry farms and that white men were paying for most of the 74 per cent of benefits which went to non-whites. 'It is now really a joy for the native to be unemployed', a National Party member told the House of Assembly in April 1947.[221] A month later the Government suspended the Act as refusals to contribute grew and an election approached. The victorious National Party then amended the legislation to exclude all lower-paid Africans, thereby terminating the reforming impulse of the 1940s.[222]

Ironically, during the next forty years the National Party was to elaborate the most extensive welfare system in Africa, a system which, like the Apartheid programme, was born of urbanisation, inequality, state power, and rampant technocracy. For the present, however, the point to emphasise is that the welfare measures of the 1930s and 1940s provided for the incapacitated who had historically provided most of Africa's poor – the old and young, the blind and disabled – rather than the new poor, the propertyless and conjuncturally unemployed, who had first become numerous in South Africa during this period.

9

Rural poverty in colonial Africa

During the one long lifetime which elapsed between the partition of tropical Africa and its liberation, immensely complicated changes took place in the nature of rural poverty. Until many local studies have been made it would be idle to pretend that any overall understanding is possible. All that can be done at this stage is to indicate certain patterns of change which are already documented for particular regions.

Yet two generalisations may be made. One is that conjunctural poverty changed most. With certain exceptions, the great famines which in the past had periodically decimated populations ceased in the mid colonial period and were replaced by more subtle problems of nutrition and demography. The second generalisation is that no such dramatic change transformed structural poverty. Here, as so often in the history of the poor, continuity predominated. With rare exceptions, colonial Africa remained rich in land. Its very poor continued to be chiefly those who lacked labour and family support. Where especially unprivileged strata had existed, they often survived. A few escaped poverty. Certain new categories of poor were created by colonial rule and economic change. They included groups impoverished by land alienation, but these were less numerous than in South Africa and the able-bodied among them were generally able to escape extreme poverty by working for others, for the means of survival for the poor were also changing. All these developments deserve analysis, but they often ran counter to one another, and even when taken together they did not outweigh the underlying continuity of structural poverty in the colonial countryside.

The experiences of slaves illustrate the complexity of change in structural poverty. Under colonial rule a minority found themselves instantaneously freed, partly as a punishment to their masters for resisting European control, as in Benin in 1897 or following the Tuareg rebellion of 1916,[1] but more often because slaves took advantage of colonial invasion to free themselves. As French troops marched into Dahomey in 1892, thousands of Yoruba slaves fled home, while in 1905 newly captured slaves in Banamba (in modern Mali) deserted their hated Maraka masters *en masse*.[2] Here, however, the French authorities imposed a temporary compromise between slaves and masters, for colonial rulers generally desired a gradual emancipation which would convert slaves into wage-labourers. In the West African savanna, which contained the largest concentration of slaves, both French and British abolished the legal status of slavery and left it to slaves to assert their rights, while creating *villages de liberté* for those needing sanctuary, who were chiefly the old, sick, or very young.[3]

Discrimination against former slaves probably waned most quickly in those non-Islamic societies of West and Central Africa where kin groups customarily assimilated slave descendants, but even there some stigma usually survived. In Asante it was insulting to refer to slave ancestry, but nobody forgot it. Familiarity with agricultural labour could enrich former slaves in the colonial period,[4] as could early access to education, but more often slave status left a legacy of deprivation. One form emerged in Zanzibar, where the British abolished the legal status of slavery in 1897 and tried to convert the slaves into plantation labourers by punishing unemployed freedmen as vagrants, only for the freedmen to escape full proletarianisation and instead become squatters on the clove estates, cultivating food plots in return for seasonal labour and personal deference to the landowner.[5] Elsewhere freedmen provided many early labourers and soldiers. Three-quarters of the troops recruited in French West Africa during the First World War were former slaves, by one account, and much heavy work in West African towns fell to former slaves of Tuareg masters.[6] Freedmen and their descendants often suffered discrimination in access to land. In the internal delta of the Niger the French negotiated an agreement in 1908 by which freed slaves obtained land rights by paying one-sixth of their crop to their former Fulbe masters. In Futa Jalon, Nupe, and parts of Hausaland, too, Fulbe demanded rent from freedmen until the end of colonial rule.[7] 'Under every chief there are considerable numbers of persons who give him half of every day's work, and who receive no compensation for it', it was reported from Dahomey in 1931. 'These helots are the descendants of slaves who were released when the territory was conquered by the Europeans.'[8]

Two of the most oppressive slave regimes in pre-colonial Africa had been those of Tuareg and Moors. Tuareg slaves had diverse experiences under colonial rule. In the Sahel, some acculturated slaves deliberately clung to dependent relationships, but the newly enslaved fled to their homes whenever possible and Bella and Buzu cultivators gradually loosened their ties to Tuareg masters, while *iklan* slaves in nomadic camps lacked resources and found emancipation more difficult but were by the 1950s widely abandoning their masters.[9] Among the Tuareg of Ahaggar in the Sahara, however, a study in 1948 found that dependent *haratin* cultivators averaged only about two-fifths of the income enjoyed by their masters, 7 per cent of the sedentary population lived in abject poverty, the normal accommodation for *haratin* was a hut of reeds or branches housing about 10 people in 15 or 20 square metres, and between 20 and 100 people died each year directly or indirectly from famine. Only during the 1950s did *haratin* manage to raise their share of the crop from the traditional one-fifth to about one-half.[10] In Mauritania many *haratin* abandoned the desert oases for the Sahel and the Senegal Valley from the 1930s, but they remained dependent on their masters for access to land and a survey in 1957–8 showed that nobles had cash incomes 60 per cent above those of *haratin*. The position of slaves in the camps of nomadic Moors is obscure but may have changed little throughout the colonial period.[11]

Slavery survived in Ahaggar and Mauritania because French policy rarely challenged it, because colonial rule created few economic alternatives for dependants, and because masters clung to slavery in the knowledge that their pastoral economy and social order could not survive without it. These considerations generally determined the fate of slaves in the colonial period. It was because so few economic alternatives were open to them that slave women often found emancipation more difficult than men.[12] It was partly because their claim to racial superiority was threatened that Fulbe resisted emancipation so strongly. The same considerations may also explain the paradox that – as in other continents[13] – the inferior status of Africa's stigmatised groups survived more vigorously than its slave systems. Colonial governments were less concerned about the stigmatised, their specialised economic roles left them few alternatives, and their stigma aroused an especially emotional resistance to emancipation.

This was illustrated by the experience of Igboland's *osu* cult slaves. Christian missionaries were exceptionally successful among the Igbo and denounced discrimination against *osu*, who often responded by accepting Christianity and seeking to use education to escape inferiority. A number became wealthy or gained important colonial posts. Yet in the 1930s *osu* were still almost totally segregated. Marriage with them was nearly unthinkable, even for Christians. They were barred from town unions and improvement associations. An anthropologist was astonished by the strength of the revulsion. When the Eastern Region legislature formally abolished the special status of its estimated 60,000 *osu* and prescribed penalties for discrimination in 1956, it did so against the vigorous opposition of a *diala* (free-born) movement.[14]

Change was almost as difficult among the Tswana, where pre-colonial inequalities of wealth and status had been especially marked. Their Kgalagadi subjects were already improving their condition during the nineteenth century and the little that is known of their history during the colonial period suggests that their advancement continued. Two observers writing in 1945 thought that the Kgalagadi had benefited especially from labour migration. 'Many Kgalagadi are indeed still attached to the families of their traditional masters as cattle-herds and domestic servants', they wrote, 'but they are now usually paid for their services, and need not remain against their will', although they added that there was still political and social discrimination against Kgalagadi, marriage with whom was thought demeaning, and that 'The very term "Kgalagadi" is often still used as an insult or sign of contempt.'[15] During the next thirty years much of this contempt dissipated. 'The Bakgalagadi are Bamangwati in the way that any Mongwato is a Mongwato', a Tswana declared in 1971, and eleven years later intermarriage was said to be common.[16] By contrast, the San were culturally more alien from their rulers and enjoyed less advancement. Those in western Bechuanaland were freed from subjection to Tswana chiefs during the 1890s, but land in the Ghanzi area was alienated to Afrikaner farmers and many San became farmworkers. In the east, European rule offered sanctuary from the worst oppression and provided opportunities for wage-labour, but from 1887 it was British policy to avoid sudden interference with San status while announcing 'that Government refused to recognise any difference between the natives of the country; that . . . all were free agents'.[17]

How far from the truth this was in practice emerged during the 1920s, when enquiries revealed cases of homicide and brutality and the Medical Officer who examined labour migrants from the Ngwato chiefdom reported that many showed marks of flogging. Many San were still held in subjection as unpaid domestics, hunters, or herdsmen. Those who took refuge in labour migration or otherwise deserted their masters without permission might be pursued on horseback and dragged back, but others were required only to offer their earnings to their masters, who might take token sums before allowing their dependants to invest the remainder in cattle.[18] An official enquiry in 1931 found that the administration had been so deferential to Tswana chiefs as to have done almost nothing for the San.[19] Further investigation in the Ngwato chiefdom in 1937 enumerated 9,505 San, with perhaps another 1,000 overlooked. Some had no masters, but most were dependants of 213 masters, of whom at least 141 were Ngwato and 38 were Kgalagadi. The Ngwato chief, Tshekedi Khama, had 1,395 San dependants, while 24 other men each had between 100 and 400. Subjection was generally mild: 'a very small percentage of them actually render services to the masters, and fewer still render continuous service'. Hunting on behalf of masters had almost ceased. Most San lived at cattle-posts, cared for their masters' stock in return for free milk and an occasional beast, and were visited only rarely from the town. Many were summoned to aid in ploughing their masters' fields and then had use of the plough teams for their own fields. An estimated 35 per cent of San attempted to cultivate, often with little success. Permanent service was largely confined to girls employed as domestic servants. San status varied with location. Those in the east had access to wage employment and were the most independent and acculturated. In the north they were more backward. In the west they were very primitive indeed. The enquiry found few attempts by masters to interfere with San who migrated as labourers but recorded brutal responses to the ancient complaint of cattle-theft. It noted many children of Bantu men and

San women, observed that it was Ngwato policy to incorporate San into the tribe, and believed that progress was satisfactory.[20]

The issue of San status then slumbered until the late 1950s, when their position in a future independent state aroused concern and led to a new enquiry.[21] This described the condition of San living in Tswana villages or cattle-posts in terms almost identical to those used in 1937, but accounts of those living in western Bechuanaland under Kgalagadi masters were more reminiscent of the nineteenth century and suggested both that the investigations of the 1930s had overlooked the more remote areas and that all but the most elusive San were being subordinated.[22]

The Hutu cultivators of Rwanda and Burundi experienced contradictory patterns of change under colonial rule. In Rwanda, during the early twentieth century, Tutsi chiefs with German backing extended their demands for *ubuletwa* services – two days' work in five as a condition for occupying land – into the peripheries of the kingdom. It was during the First World War, for example, that *ubuletwa* reached the northern provinces. Population growth increased the power exercised by chiefs who controlled land. In 1927 the Belgian regime reduced *ubuletwa* to one day's work in seven, and in 1933 to thirteen days a year, but also extended it to many hitherto exempted and added new demands for poll tax and corvée labour – with the chiefs selecting the labourers.[23] In Burundi, where nothing so oppressive as *ubuletwa* had existed, the Belgians extended tribute and added their own exactions.[24] These pressures eased after the Second World War, when *ubuletwa* was commuted to a tax payment in Rwanda and the *abashumba* farm-servants of Burundi were replaced by wage-labourers.[25]

The poverty of such subject peoples was revealed by studies made in the 1940s of the Hangaza of Bugufi, a small chiefdom in north-western Tanganyika which had once been part of Burundi. Bugufi had two sources of cash: labour migration to Uganda and coffee-growing. Both were ruthlessly exploited by Tutsi chiefs and nobles, who controlled land but grew little coffee, instead extracting the earnings of the Hangaza. Between the 1920s and 1944 the fee charged for allocation of a plot rose from a token sum to three times the annual tax. Tribute in pots of beer (and increasingly in cash) was 'a continuous burden' on Hangaza, whose standard nourishment was one meal of grain or bananas a day. Hangaza had no security of tenure because chiefs could allocate land to any aristocrat, reducing resident Hangaza to tenants. Lacking security, Hangaza avoided cultivating or even inheriting coffee plots, preferring to earn a maximum of 12 shillings a month in Uganda, whither at least two-thirds of the men went each year. Should a Hangaza offend his chief or landlord, he could be evicted and replaced from among the 800 families who entered Bugufi each year from overcrowded Burundi and accepted the even lower status of squatters. In 1944 there were some 3,700 squatters in Bugufi.[26]

Colonial rule not only preserved some existing forms of poverty but created new forms. The most blatant resulted from alienation of land to European settlers in parts of southern and eastern Africa. In the extreme case of South-West Africa the entire Herero people was deprived of its land and cattle following a rebellion.[27] Elsewhere land alienation impoverished particular categories of people. The contrast between Southern Rhodesia and Kenya is revealing. Europeans seized nearly 6,500,000 hectares of Southern Rhodesia – one-sixth of the entire country – within a decade of their invasion in 1890, occupying most of the desirable highveld.[28] Yet absolute landlessness emerged only slowly, for European farmers long permitted many Africans to remain on alienated land as tenants, government limited the acreage which wealthier Africans could cultivate in the reserves,[29] and African land remained communal property to which each local family had a claim. Information on landlessness in Southern Rhodesia is scarce, but in part of the Karanga reserve during the 1960s some 6 per cent of men aged over 45 were landless, as against 81 per cent of those under 30. The burden of propertylessness was thrown on to the young.[30]

By contrast, the Kikuyu of Kenya lost little land to Europeans – perhaps only 6 per cent of Kikuyuland[31] – but experienced greater differentiation, because a circle of European land prevented expansion of the Kikuyu reserve to accommodate population growth, government did not prevent wealthy Kikuyu from acquiring a disproportionate share of land, and the tenurial system of the stateless Kikuyu threw the burden of land shortage on to the unprivileged. Kikuyu land was not communally owned but controlled by families descended from members of *mbari* colonising groups. Land alienated from the Kikuyu was therefore alienated from particular families who had no claims elsewhere. 'If a certain *githaka* [plot] owner had a slice taken off', a witness told the Kenya Land Commission of 1931, 'it was bad luck for him but he didn't get any more given him from other *githaka* owners.'[32] Moreover, many *mbari* included dependants – *ahoi* and *athami* – without full land rights, while the markedly inegalitarian society of precolonial Kikuyuland had also contained many propertyless young clients.[33] When land became scarce, it was expropriated families, *ahoi, athami*, clients, and many women who chiefly suffered. In the early twentieth century many temporarily acquired access to land as labour-tenants on European farms, until the capitalisation of white farming during the 1940s led to their expulsion. In the later colonial period women and former clients provided many of Kikuyuland's hired labourers, while former *ahoi* were often without land.[34] Many forest fighters during the Mau Mau rebellion of 1952 were landless and Dr Kershaw has shown a correlation between intra-Kikuyu violence and conflict between *mbari* members and *ahoi*.[35] Very uncertain figures suggest that at Independence in 1963 some 23 per cent of rural households were landless in Central Province, which included Kikuyuland.[36]

For poor Kikuyu, as for many former slaves, wage employment was often a new means of survival, but for others the compulsory labour of the early

Index of real wages in European agriculture in Southern Rhodesia and Kenya (1914 = 100)

Year	Southern Rhodesia	Kenya
1911	80	
1914	100	100
1921	45	35
1930	92	76
1938		78
1939	99	
1946	72	77
1951	98	61
1961	140	
1964		104

Source: Paul Mosley, *The settler economies* (Cambridge, 1983), p. 116.

colonial period could be a cause of impoverishment. In southern Uganda in 1914 a peasant might legally owe the equivalent of five months' labour each year to chief, landlord, and colonial government, although in practice this was exacted chiefly from the poorest.[37] Forced labour ceased in most colonies during the 1920s, but in Mozambique the *shibalo* system of conscription at very low wages lasted for another 40 years. 'The people have to work almost beyond human endurance', a missionary reported from Alto Moloque in Quelimane Province in 1925:

> The men at forced labour, often hundreds of miles away, for at least six months of the year, and the women and children for varying periods at the boma. The latter two get nothing for their work (except abuse) while the former get a few miserable shillings. Of 400 men who left here in Jan. last for forced labour, 50 are dead and the rest mostly skin and bone.[38]

The people he described were Lomwe, who were then the lowest-paid compulsory workers on sugar estates in the Zambesi Valley, where they earned one farthing a day plus rations, while volunteer Ngoni cane-cutters, the labour elite, earned some 10 shillings a month.[39] Such differentials were an important means by which wage-labour benefited some Africans and impoverished others during the colonial period. In Kenya, for example, skilled workers invested in land and labour in the reserves, while low-paid labourers had to leave their land in the hands of their wives, who might in adverse circumstances be forced to sell it or seek ill-paid employment themselves.[40] Juveniles received the lowest wages of all. In 1955 some tea estates in Nyasaland paid children only one penny a day.[41]

The real value of wages varied over time. Accurate statistics are scarce, but wages were usually quite high during the early colonial period when

Africans still had the alternative of cultivating their own land. A major decline followed the First World War, owing to international economic instability and the compulsion widely exercised by governments at that time. The table on p. 149 shows that 1921 was probably the nadir of wages on European estates in Kenya and Southern Rhodesia. Real wages recovered during the prosperous 1920s and survived the depression of the 1930s because prices generally fell at least as much as wages – for those in employment. Thereafter local circumstances varied but real wages generally fell during the 1940s, owing to war and price inflation, before rising markedly during the 1950s as a result of general prosperity, trade union action, and official steps to stabilise labour. Yet these increases left many workers deprived. In 1973 farm labourers and their dependants were over 20 per cent of Rhodesia's population but earned only 3 per cent of its Gross Domestic Product, the worst wages being given by African farmers, who sometimes paid only a food ration and no cash wage at all. It is an effort to realise that one-third of Rhodesia's farm labourers were immigrant volunteers from the even lower-wage economies of Malawi and Mozambique.[42]

Even where European settlement and land alienation did not occur, the greater integration of African economies with the world market bred new categories of poor. Migrant labourers on African cash-crop farms were one such category. Mossi and other migrants from Upper Volta provided between one-half and two-thirds of Ivory Coast's plantation workers during the 1960s. Excluded from minimum wage regulations and forbidden to form trade unions, they were an exploited under-class. 'They are good workers from Volta', an Ivoirian chief explained in 1966. 'We call them slaves.'[43] What had obliged these men from one of the most prosperous areas of the pre-colonial savanna to undertake migrant labour was that the French authorities had demanded tax but had constructed a transport system which left Mossi country remote and neglected. Other once-prosperous regions suffered similar decay. Railways from Lagos and Dakar to Kano and Bamako helped to destroy the trans-Saharan trade, ruined the Tuareg, and left their former dependants to become unskilled labourers in colonial towns. Isolated by colonial transport systems but protected by colonial laws, the servile groups of Bulozi and the Upper Senegal migrated to work elsewhere, leaving irrigation-based economies to decay. Peace, remoteness, and taxation forced predatory peoples such as the Bemba of Northern Rhodesia and the Fulbe of Futa Jalon into migration.[44]

Income statistics collected at the end of the colonial period showed wide regional variations. In Tanzania in 1967, annual Gross Domestic Product per head varied from 1,186 shillings in the sisal-growing Tanga region near the coast to 177 shillings in the remote Kasulu region.[45] Differentials between town and country were equally marked and tended to widen. Estimated annual per capita income of Africans in Northern Rhodesia in 1946 was £16 in towns and £4 in peasant areas; the equivalent figures in 1964 were £43 and £12. Average earnings of Senegalese groundnut producers, expressed as a proportion of those of Dakar's unskilled workers, fell from 73 per cent in 1890 to 50 per cent in 1927–31 and 38 per cent in 1957–61. Dr Hill's claim that motor transport and modern technology enabled Hausa towns to drain trade, industry, and wealth from the countryside was supported by evidence that per capita income in Northern Nigeria was highest in villages furthest from cities,[46] but elsewhere rural wealth increased during the colonial period – in 1938 the Gold Coast had an estimated 37,000 small cocoa traders – and the most prosperous villages were those nearest the capital.[47] Rural Africa had no universal economic experience during the colonial period.

Migrant labourers often came from the poorest strata: Bella dependants of Tuareg, for example, or servile categories in the Ndebele and Lozi kingdoms.[48] Some Voltaic migrants to the Gold Coast in the early twentieth century claimed to be former slaves robbed of their land by the chiefs. Labour migration was also a means of escape from colonial or indigenous oppression.[49] Often, like those from the northern Gold Coast in 1930, migrants arrived in appalling condition:

> Generally speaking they are dirty, lousy, ill fed, and of very poor physique. They are veritable museums of helminths of all descriptions, yaws and guinea worms.
>
> A high proportion of these people arrive in Kumasi and are unable to work. They cannot obtain food and arrive at the hospital in semi-dying conditions. Consequently they have to be admitted and the hospital is over-crowded with these poor starving creatures.[50]

Yet not all migrant labourers were poor. A careful study of Bechuanaland in 1943 found that the poor, especially those without land or cattle, were most liable to migrate, but that nearly 90 per cent of all men in several chiefdoms had migrated at some time, including many from wealthy families. Among migrants from Futa Jalon, Fulbe were proportionately more numerous than their former slaves because Fulbe had fewer alternative means of earning cash honourably.[51] Moreover, labour migration was a means of survival open only to the able-bodied. As in South Africa, the poorest were often those who could not migrate. As a missionary in Katanga complained, 'The boys go off, even the girls follow and the cripples remain to cripple the town.'[52]

African farmers employed not only migrants but poor local workers. Normally in a cash-crop area only a proportion of cultivators adopted the new crops on a substantial scale. The remainder became the ordinarily poor, with a very poor minority. A study of a Hausa village in 1939 identified these three categories by their access to food: rich families had 3.3 lb of grain per head per day, with condiments and meat in addition; ordinary families had 1.3 lb per head per day; and poor families had 0.83 lb per head per day for only five months of the year. To work for a neighbour as a hired labourer was still 'a stigmatised sign of abject poverty' in Hausaland at that time, but twenty years later it was relatively common.[53] A study of six Yoruba cocoa-growing villages in 1951–2 found that 67 per cent of hired agricultural labour was local, although that proportion was probably unusual.[54] Little is known of these casual workers. Some were poor young men, but they often preferred the anonymity of migration. Others were victims of misfortune. In Basutoland, for example, 'paid labourers are usually people whose own crops have failed or whose ploughing equipment was insufficient to till their lands, or who have few or no lands of their own'. Many of these were women.[55] The same pattern existed in Yakö villages in south-eastern Nigeria during the 1930s:

> There are 'poor relations', generally members of small households who, through disability or misfortune, have outputs well below the general level. In many such cases both the men and women offer their labour at times of planting and harvesting in return for payments in yams which enable them to make up the deficiencies in their own farm outputs.[56]

One unusually detailed study was made in an Igbo village in 1938–9 and showed that casual labourers represented the whole range of personal circumstances which created the rural poor. While the highest annual male income recorded was £19.1.9, one of the lowest was the £3.8.9 earned by a man of 35 with a wife, two small children, and an idle brother. His cash came chiefly from selling yams and working for others. He was poor because he was at the most burdensome stage of his domestic cycle. Yet some female villagers were much poorer. The lowest cash income was earned by a widow with three sons aged fifteen, eleven and seven. Her Christian brother-in-law had refused to marry her and she received £1.3.5 in the year studied, 8s 6d from selling crops, 4s 6d from making and selling pots and mats, 4s 2d from selling bush produce, and 1s 3d from working for other women. The two next poorest women were a barren wife and another widow with a Christian brother-in-law and two infant children. All these women received income chiefly from selling crops but supplemented it with small earnings from handicrafts, bush produce, and casual agricultural labour at a wage of threepence a day.[57]

Christian marriage laws which deprived a widow of care or prevented a neglected woman from divorcing and remarrying were among the many ways in which colonial change damaged the situation of women, just as other changes improved it. The most important new source of female poverty was labour migration, which often left women to support their children and meet obligations to the state. Migrants' wives probably fared best in uxorilocal societies, common in Central Africa, where they lived in their natal villages as members of sorority groups owning land and sharing food,[58] but Lala villages of this kind in Northern Rhodesia in 1947 nevertheless contained women obliged to sell their labour:

> In the larger villages there are usually one or two women who have no family ties there and consequently no one from whom they can demand food; but in these villages there is always more possibility of a woman who has plenty of food giving it to one who will work in her garden for her. In several villages women were questioned, usually widows or divorcees, who obtained most of their food in this manner.[59]

In Nyasaland growing population and land shortage reduced women's economic autonomy, increased their dependence on male earnings, and created a category of women with inadequate land and family support who depended on casual labour and other income-earning devices. Such women generally lived alone or with only their young children, forming probably the most common category of poor people in the villages of colonial Africa, where wealth and large households commonly went together.[60] On the outskirts of Kano city, however, Dr Hill described during the 1960s a pattern of large complex households formed by the poor where land scarcity obliged them to cluster for mutual support.[61] This phenomenon, already reported in Keiskammahoek,[62] suggested that new forms of poverty were emerging in rural Africa at the end of the colonial period.

Yet old and new patterns of rural poverty mingled. This was well illustrated in Buganda. By the 1950s most Baganda peasants grew cotton or coffee, often employing immigrant workers from Rwanda and its environs who by 1959 were three-sevenths of the population. Except when labour was scarce, immigrants earned little: in 1966 Baganda paid them only one-third or one-quarter of the rates commonly paid by other employers. A few poor Baganda also undertook agricultural labour. Observers in the 1950s reported an emerging class of cottagers who needed wage employment for cash income.[63] A decade later an anthropologist 'came across several younger Baganda peasants who did not have any land at all and were doing odd jobs such as pruning, desuckling [*sic*], coffee picking, or brewing Kiganda beer, while waiting for an opportunity to find a tenant plot'.[64] A proportion of these immigrant workers and poor Baganda were reduced to destitution by personal circumstances. In 1961–4 a survey of 26 villages showed that 10 per cent of all homesteads housed people living alone, a condition unusually common in Buganda – where adults of adjacent generations were expected to live separately – and associated closely with poverty.[65] These solitaries numbered 210 men and 78 women. The 64 who were immigrants fell mainly into two groups. One contained older men who had contracted such serious diseases as epilepsy, tuberculosis, or leprosy, knew that if they returned home they would be rejected, and had grown accustomed to solitude. The other consisted of failures, often alcoholics – 30 men and 3 women in the whole sample drank too much and 5 men smoked marijuana. Among the solitary Baganda the most common reasons for isolation were old age – 30 per cent of the whole sample were aged over 60 – poor health, and personality defects. Of all those living alone, 5 suffered from leprosy, 3 were blind, and 11 were epileptics or mentally ill. The interaction between the old poverty of incapacitation and the new poverty of migrant labour was especially clear in this case.

Money itself, the need to pay tax, and economic fluctuations emanating from the world market all bred new types of rural poverty. In itself neither money nor taxation was always novel, but the level of colonial taxation could be very high, especially in the early days. In the Teso district of Uganda in 1927 an unskilled labourer earned 5 shillings a month and paid an annual tax of 21 shillings. In northern Nigeria the initial British tax was simply added to that already paid to emirs.[66] Few colonial administrations had the capacity to relate taxation to earnings in an equitable manner. Most levied flat-rate taxes which fell especially heavily on the poor. Among the Tukulor of the Senegal Valley in 1957–8, tax absorbed 24 per cent of the expenditure of the poorest households, as against 7 per cent for all households. Yet the burden had been much heavier during the depression of the 1930s, when people in Futa Jalon pawned their crops and children or sold their stock, grain, pots, and even their Korans to pay their taxes.[67]

Taxation drained money from rural communities and contributed to that 'cash hunger' so widespread in the Third World.[68] For poor villagers money had a rarity value far above its face value. In the remote Mbulu area of German East Africa in 1906 'a rupee was placed on a stone in the house for fear that it might sink into the ground'. As late as the 1950s Rwandan peasants spoke of 'buying money' with labour or produce.[69] 'Peasants will walk for three days to sell an item for a profit of 100 francs [20 pence]', an anthropologist wrote from Niger, 'because walking *costs* them nothing.' She added, in some bewilderment, that they then seemed to spend the money instantly and irrationally,[70] but perhaps the point – as for the slumyard dwellers of Rooiyard – was that money was so scarce that unless spent immediately it was begged away.[71] A study in the late 1960s showed that Hausa villagers had immense difficulty in obtaining the money to pay tax, buy essential consumer goods, and make the obligatory gifts to neighbours at domestic crises which in one village totalled £900 a year. There the 'search for money' was met partly by its rapid circulation and partly by borrowing, which in turn meant selling much of the harvest to repay debts and then repurchasing food later at higher prices and on credit.[72]

Debt pervaded rural life, as in any agricultural society. Often it was an ancient practice. Moneylenders existed in the Katsina area of Hausaland by the eighteenth century and the Akan peoples of Ghana have pledged almost anything – cloths, farms, children, themselves – for as long as anyone can remember. In East African villages most borrowing seems to have taken place among neighbours and without interest charges,[73] but in West Africa it was often at very high interest rates which expressed not only the difficulty of securing repayment but also the extreme scarcity of cash. Following the abolition of slavery, the pawning of children into a relationship regarded as particularly degrading was a common resource for the poor throughout West Africa until governmental interference and the growth of wage-labour largely ended it during the 1930s. At least 3,000 human pawns existed in the Nupe emirate alone in 1933, commonly deposited in return for loans averaging £3.10.0. Young girls were still pawned as housemaids in the Gold Coast in the late 1940s as a substitute for interest charges of £2–3 a year.[74] The need for such loans was revealed by a study of a Gold Coast cocoa-growing village in 1932–5, which showed that the average family spent £21.14.0 a year, of which £11.10.0 was taken in debt charges, while its income included £6.11.6 from interest on debts. Studies also showed, however, that most creditors were other cocoa-farmers and that indebted households spent more than solvent ones.[75] Debt was not a particular characteristic of the poor but a normal part of village life, the reverse side of saving. As a later student of Hausaland observed, it was the inability to borrow, except from fools or strangers, that was the acid test of poverty.[76] Yet in savanna regions, especially, the need to sell their harvest to meet their debts did hold many peasants in a vicious cycle of poverty and hunger. Studies in Northern Nigeria in 1937 and 1957 both showed that 68 per cent of the population had to seek loans. In contrast to the Gold Coast, 47 per cent of loans in 1957 were to buy food. The annual interest rate was 90–100 per cent.[77]

That debt and pawning excited much concern during the 1930s was in part due to the general economic depression of the time. Conjunctural poverty caused by the trade cycle was one indisputably new form of misery which the colonial period brought. African producers were especially vulnerable. While world prices of cocoa and most other tropical crops fell by roughly two-thirds during the depression, the price paid to cocoa producers at Abengourou in Ivory Coast fell by 86 per cent and tenants at the Gezira scheme in the Sudan had no net income at all in 1930, 1931, and 1933.[78] Import prices also fell, but less. To buy 1 tonne of cotton cloth, Ivory Coast had to export 5.8 tonnes of cocoa in 1929 and 10.3 tonnes in 1932.[79] For the poor, food at least was cheap. Senegalese groundnut growers could buy more food per pound of groundnuts in the mid 1930s than at any time before the 1950s, and it has been seen that the real earnings of agricultural labourers generally rose during the depression.[80] But this did not necessarily meet the need for cash, for the great novelty of the depression was tropical Africa's first serious experience of unemployment. Between 1930 and 1933 the Katanga copper mines reduced their African workforce from 73,000 to 27,000. 'We scan the sisal prices anxiously each week', a Tanganyikan district officer wrote in 1931 as he watched disconsolate migrant labourers return without finding work.[81] Some colonial governments threw the burden of the depression on to the poor. Although Nigeria's estimated gross income fell by nearly 66 per cent between 1928 and 1934, direct tax revenue rose by 19 per cent. The Belgian authorities salvaged the Congo's mining sector by forcing Africans to grow low-priced food crops in a manner which radically widened the differences of wealth between town and countryside, a pattern seen in many parts of the continent at this time.[82] Although ironic, it was in the logic of the colonial economy that the trade cycle should have its greatest impact in areas most remote from trade.

As a cause of conjunctural poverty in rural Africa, the international depression was trivial when compared with famine. This was where the colonial period had its most important consequences for the poor. Environmentally, the middle decades of the nineteenth century had generally been prosperous, but the 1880s initiated nearly half a century of natural disasters. In eastern Africa the relatively high rainfall of the 1870s gave way during the 1880s to erratic precipitation and a decade of famine before any substantial European invasion. Lake levels began to fall in both East and West Africa during the 1890s, while in 1899–1900 the Nile flood was the lowest yet seen. In 1913–14 it was lower still, however, and it remained low until the 1920s.[83] Tropical African rainfall as a whole was low and exceptionally erratic during the first half of the colonial period but began to increase and stabilise between the wars and reached relatively generous levels during the 1950s.[84]

Drought was only one catastrophe of the early colonial period. Locusts ravaged crops throughout the continent during the 1890s, often for the first time for several decades.[85] Cattle plague, probably introduced by the Italian army, precipitated the terrible Ethiopian famine of 1889–92 and then swept westwards and southwards, reaching the Gambia in 1892 and South Africa in 1896. Often it killed more than 90 per cent of cattle,[86] reducing pastoral peoples such as the Maasai to destitution:

> There were women wasted to skeletons from whose eyes the madness of starvation glared . . . 'warriors' scarcely able to crawl on all fours, and apathetic, languishing elders. These people ate anything. Dead donkeys were a feast for them, but they did not disdain bones, hides, and even the horns of the cattle . . . Parents offered us children to buy for a scrap of meat, and when we refused the exchange they cunningly hid the children near the camp and made off.[87]

Famine as a result of drought, locusts, and cattle plague was almost universal in tropical Africa during the late 1890s, as also in India. 'The Great Famine', as Kikuyu called it, killed two-thirds of the people in one *mbari*.[88] As usual, most died not of starvation but of disease, in this case smallpox. 'Corpses and skeletons lay along the caravan route from Nairobi and Fort Smith', a veterinary officer recalled, 'while natives in the eruptive stages of the disease knelt by the roadside mumbling appeals for help.'[89] Venereal diseases spread widely in equatorial Africa at this time, while sleeping sickness devastated the Congo Basin.[90] And to all these natural catastrophes were added deaths from warfare and the movement of peoples which accompanied colonial invasion.

This period of disaster extended into the twentieth century. Between 1911 and 1927 there was not a single year without major famine over some large area of Africa. The sequence began when the rains failed in the Sahel region of West Africa during 1911. The great famine that followed in 1913 and 1914 killed tens or hundreds of thousands,[91] if not the 25–50 per cent of the whole population suggested by some administrators:

> The stricken people tore down the ant-hills in the bush to get at the small grains and chaff within these storerooms . . . The great city of Kano drew the starving thousands from the country in the faint hope of scouring in the streets or markets to pick up what they might, or beg the charity of the townsfolk . . . They died like flies on every road. One came across them in the town markets, emaciated to skeletons, begging feebly for sustenance, or collapsed into unconsciousness where they sat.[92]

This famine was exacerbated by new tax systems, crop exports, declining trans-Saharan commerce, and labour migration.[93] Yet drought was its chief cause, for like other great Sahelian droughts it extended not only eastwards to Ethiopia and western India but southwards through the arid lands of East Africa as far as Basutoland and Angola.[94] Just as it was ending, the First World War campaign bred famine in many parts of East Africa, including the devastating Rumanura famine of 1916–18 in Rwanda.[95] While East Africa was recovering, French Equatorial Africa experienced the greatest famine in its history from 1918 to 1926, probably owing to excessive demands for labour and food.[96] Then in 1926–7 famine returned, more briefly, to the West African savanna, as a result of drought and locusts, perhaps accentuated by taxation, labour migration, and cash-crop production.[97]

From 1927 to the end of the colonial period major 'famines that kill', as many Africans described them, were confined to three sets of circumstances. First, there were a few severe but localised famines, the most serious taking place in Rwanda and its environs in 1928 and in Niger in 1931.[98] Second, Ethiopia is reported to have experienced serious famine in 1927–8, 1934–5, 1947–50, 1953, and 1957–9; the severity of these disasters is unknown, but it was probably greater than elsewhere in tropical Africa.[99] Third, there was widespread famine during or immediately after the Second World War, when drought combined with wartime exactions and a breakdown of administrative capacity, perhaps especially in Rwanda, where 300,000 people are alleged to have died, and in parts of French West Africa.[100] Apart from these three sets of circumstances, famines causing great mortality ceased in colonial Africa from the later 1920s.

This fact is of great importance to an understanding of modern Africa and its poor, but it has not yet received adequate study. One reason for the decline of famine mortality was probably a higher and less erratic rainfall than during the earlier colonial period.[101] Yet later colonial Africa also experienced many of the changes which had previously eradicated 'famines that kill' from other continents.[102] The idea that effective government, good transport, wider markets, and some increase in average wealth could reduce famine mortality was not new to Africa. In Rwanda, for example, the densely peopled, closely governed central regions had long been less liable to famine than the newly settled borderlands, and these advances had taken place in South Africa at the beginning of the twentieth century.[103] During the 1920s they became widely evident in tropical Africa. Stable and competent administrations were increasingly able to foresee famine and prevent or alleviate it – the French neglect to do so in Niger in 1931 reinforces the point.[104] In the Teso region of Uganda, thousands of people died during famine in 1918 before Government intervened to provide relief and control prices for the first time, but when famine returned in 1928 the relief provision was quickly in place.[105] Colonial regimes also pressed root-crops like manioc which resisted drought and locusts.[106] They broke a vital link between food shortage and death by using vaccination to end epidemic smallpox, which was generally accomplished by the 1920s. In Mozambique, for example, smallpox epidemics frequently coincided with major famines before 1900 but not thereafter.[107] Global improvements in hygiene and medical control may also explain why cholera – a great killer in nineteenth-century Africa – was absent between 1923 and 1970. There is evidence that access to wage-labour was important in preventing deaths from starvation.[108] It was during the 1920s that motor vehicles became widely available to assist in controlling famine mortality, not only by transporting relief food but, perhaps more importantly, by creating wider grain markets, sometimes territorial in scope, and releasing the immense quantities of labour hitherto consumed by human porterage. Albert Schweitzer noted the consequences of the old transport system during Gabon's terrible dearth of 1925. 'Along the navigable portion of the Ogowe', he wrote, 'the provision of rice from Europe and India is possible. But in the interior to which the rice would have to be transported for hundreds of kilometres by porters, it can only to a very limited extent be reckoned on as a means of feeding the population. So in those parts there is severe famine, while here the famine is mild.' By contrast, Nyasaland's food shortage of 1926 – its last of the colonial period, with an isolated exception in 1949 – was also the first partly relieved by motor transport.[109] Rwanda's disaster of 1928 was due in part to the fact that, although food existed in certain regions of the country, there were only nine motor vehicles in all Ruanda-Urundi in 1927.[110] Informants in Niger remembered that 1931 was the last famine year of the colonial period because 'From then on the communication systems . . . were so far developed that it became possible to move in very substantial quantities of food from elsewhere.' The commoditisation of the Hausa grain crop, which lay behind the growth of indebtedness among the poor, had its reverse side in the lorry-loads of food whose arrival during shortages in the 1950s was later remembered by Northern Nigerian peasants.[111] By contrast, the survival of mass famine mortality in Ethiopia was probably due to its lack of modern transport, medicine, and government, while one reason for widespread deaths from famine during the 1940s was, as an observer wrote of Futa Jalon, that 'the dearth of lorries put us back into the age which preceded the era of roads'.[112] One advantage of this analysis of the decline of famine mortality is that it explains those severe famines which still took place.

The analysis also finds support in the one colony examined in detail, Southern Rhodesia, although control of famine mortality was established there earlier than in most African territories. Southern Rhodesia's first famine after the European conquest was a classic early colonial famine due to the devastation wrought by the Ndebele and Shona rebellions of 1896–7 and their suppression, exacerbated by drought, locusts, and cattle plague. Faced with this crisis the British South Africa Company's administration experienced immense transport difficulties and could provide only limited aid. As its head explained to Ndebele leaders, 'Hunger moves more quickly over the veldt than the wagons of the Company.'[113] The result was heavy mortality from starvation and disease in Ndebele country.[114] During the next three decades Southern Rhodesia experienced four serious droughts and food shortages – in 1903, 1912, 1916, and 1922 – any of which might have caused numerous deaths. In fact none did, because indigenous survival techniques were supplemented by an efficient administration which gave early warning of famine, provided medical protection against epidemics, and organised the supply of grain, using the railway and European traders with wagons drawn by oxen, mules, or donkeys. It was because Southern Rhodesia was more intensively governed than other colonies and had better trade and transport systems that it controlled famine mortality relatively early. Yet small numbers did die during the famines of 1903, 1912, and 1922. They were chiefly old, very young, or feeble people living in remote areas or where drought or flooding hampered animal transport. As the responsible official telegraphed amidst the crisis of 1912, 'No difficulty about grain it is transport that presents trouble.'[115] After 1923, however, motor transport and better roads combined with further administrative and commercial development to eradicate famine mortality from Southern Rhodesia. Although the colony experienced widespread harvest failures in 1928, 1933, 1942, 1947, and 1960, no deaths are recorded except a few doubtful cases during the 1940s.[116]

Yet the control of famine mortality had a corollary. In France it brought a growing endemic poverty, while in Asia it led experts to claim that the inability of the poor to purchase available food was the very nature of famine.[117] This development was logical. When improved transport expanded grain markets, it ensured that few people in a locality died when their harvest failed, but it also condemned the poor of that locality to indigence even in good years, when their harvest was extracted (often through debt) and transported to areas where prices were higher. Feast and famine waned together. Famine had always borne most heavily on the poor and continued to do so during the late colonial period,[118] but it was no longer true – as in mid eighteenth-century Timbuktu – that even the rich struggled to survive during the most severe famine,[119] while in addition the poor now remained hungry even in good years. 'Before the 1954 main crops began to come on the market', an official reported from the Nupe area of Nigeria, 'food prices were high and some hardship was suffered by the lower income groups such as daily paid labourers. This was due to the heavy demand for foodstuffs from the North, where partial crop failures had occurred and from the South, where cash is plentiful.'[120]

Undernutrition and malnutrition were not new to Africa, but from the middle of the colonial period they replaced periodic famine mortality as the chief problems of subsistence, and it may not have been accidental that European concern with nutrition in Africa began at precisely this moment: Belgian authorities in the Congo discussed the issue in 1923, kwashiorkor (the most dangerous deficiency disease) entered medical knowledge around 1930, and during the 1930s most colonial governments mounted investigations.[121] These studies generally concentrated on two points. First, certain especially disadvantaged regions experienced endemic undernutrition. The worst situation described was that of the Bemba of Northern Rhodesia, where in 1933–4 Richards and Widdowson recorded an average intake of 1,706 calories per head per day in the Kasama area, as against 2,077 for the closely comparable Lala in 1947 and the 2,530 which nutritionists recommended for active adult men in the late 1970s. Bemba also suffered an exceptionally long hungry season each year, but their protein intake was almost certainly adequate at 50 grammes a day.[122] Bemba experienced acute food shortage because they had been a predatory people with a crude agriculture much harmed by labour migration, especially during the depression years when Richards and Widdowson studied there. Although the first investigators often thought that nutrition was even worse in towns, this view was soon abandoned.[123]

The other nutritional problem widely identified during the 1930s was malnutrition: shortage not of food but of certain nutrients, especially proteins. This is a complicated subject, but early nutritionists certainly exaggerated the amount of protein which human beings needed.[124] They were on stronger ground in believing that protein supplies were threatened by the destruction of game, the death of cattle from disease, and the expansion of drought-resistant root-crops such as manioc at the expense of grains with higher protein contents. In Burundi in 1927, for example, the Belgian administration responded to the sequence of early colonial famines by pressing manioc so vigorously as to threaten serious protein deficiency.[125] Many Africans despised manioc – 'cassava and maize are only the poor relations of yam', said a Yoruba poem – and regarded it as the food of the poor, who indeed often grew relatively more of it than did the rich. Peoples especially associated with a manioc diet, such as the Lomwe of Mozambique, were not only ill nourished but ill regarded.[126]

As knowledge of nutrition grew during the later colonial period it became clear that not only certain regions but certain social groups were especially at risk. By the 1950s concern was focussed on infants. During their first year of life they were most threatened by marasmus, which was simply a form of starvation from total calorie deficiency. During their second and third years they were most vulnerable to kwashiorkor, which was caused by protein deficiency following weaning and not only killed advanced cases but could cause lasting retardation – 'An empty stomach means an empty head', ran a later slogan.[127] Both conditions were exacerbated by disease and parasitism, but their chief immediate cause was a lack of suitable foods to replace human milk. Protein-energy malnutrition of infants was therefore 'a problem which is knit into the very pattern of the life of culturally retarded and socially depressed classes'.[128] Such notoriously impoverished, manioc-dependent regions as the Kwango area of the Belgian Congo had exceptionally high kwashiorkor rates. Often a high proportion of cases came from homes where the father was absent. 'Poverty played an important part' in cases of kwashiorkor at Maseru hospital, a doctor reported, 'and I was frequently told that the family had no cows, or money to buy milk. I did not see a case of malnutrition in the children of the educated or wealthier Basuto.'[129] A later study of the Chagga of Tanzania, with many implications for other regions, showed that they attributed kwashiorkor in infants to the moral failings of parents, especially mothers. Scientific evidence also suggested that infant malnutrition had its roots in maternal malnutrition.[130] Women as well as children were at risk.

This was indeed one conclusion of a nutritional study made in Nyasaland during the late 1930s, the most elaborate investigation of the mid colonial period.[131] Although it found a debilitating poverty afflicting all villagers, the worst-affected were those bereft of labour and family support, who included many whose breadwinners were absent as migrant labourers. The poorest rural people encountered were elderly widows in a land-short Christian village who did not enjoy the care which widows normally received. More generally, however, the worst-nourished were women, infants, and boys aged between ten and sixteen who often fended largely for themselves. Other studies showed similar inequalities within families.[132] Nutrition was not only the most important food problem of late colonial Africa but also a sensitive indicator of poverty. Its history in particular regions is one of the most urgent tasks awaiting students of Africa.

The decline of famine mortality during the later 1920s and 1930s removed one of tropical Africa's chief constraints on population growth.[133] After catastrophe and widespread population decline during the early colonial period, a general demographic expansion now became apparent. It began at different times in different regions. Perhaps because Southern Rhodesia established control of famine mortality so early, its population appears to have increased continuously from the beginning of the twentieth century.[134]

The forest region of West Africa also escaped most early colonial disasters and may have experienced continuous demographic increase.[135] Equatorial Africa, by contrast, was devastated by sleeping sickness and by the long-term effects of venereal diseases, which in the early 1960s still left one-half of all women aged 26 years permanently infertile among the Nzakara of the Central African Republic.[136] Not only did this cause perhaps the greatest misery and neglect to be found in colonial Africa, but it meant that equatorial population levels did not begin to recover until the 1950s.[137] For tropical Africa as a whole, however, the 1920s probably initiated a population growth which was to accelerate through the late colonial period into the first decades of independence.

Given that pre-colonial Africa had been a land-rich continent and that the early colonial period had further depopulated it, the demographic expansion of the late colonial period was probably a source of prosperity for most Africans and certainly for the continent. On the eve of independence, however, indications existed that new forms of poverty were arising from pressure on resources. They were clearest in the Kikuyu area of Kenya because land alienation and the local system of tenure bred exceptional numbers of landless people.[138] A more common problem was the fragmentation of holdings in constricted areas of high fertility and dense population, especially mountain outcrops. Such problems could usually still be met by intensifying cultivation, as in the Kigezi area of Uganda, by resettling surplus people elsewhere, as with the Kabre of Togo, by exporting migrant labourers, as did the Igbo of Nigeria, or by all these methods, as among the Bamileke of Cameroun.[139]

For the future, however, these problems were ominous. Their implications were best revealed by the most detailed study of a rural community ever made in Africa: Dr Haswell's investigation of the Maninka village of Genieri in the lower Casamance area of the Gambia, which she studied in 1949–50, 1961–2, and 1973–4.[140] During this period Genieri's population increased from 483 to 771 while its cultivated area per head fell from 0.58 to 0.47 hectares. The village experienced major agricultural innovations, taking up cattle-keeping, extending swamp-grown rice, and adopting ox-ploughs for dry cultivation. While the village population grew between 1949–50 and 1973–4 at an average of 1.9 per cent a year, its food production grew at 2.0 per cent and its total crop output at 3.0 per cent. The traditional hungry season largely disappeared. Genieri outpaced its demographic explosion – but at the cost of greater inequality. Increasingly the village was dominated by the 22 per cent of larger, longer-settled, wealthier households which owned draught-oxen, had access to swamp-ricefields, and controlled relations with the outside world. On the other side stood households without access to swampland who depended on their betters for the loan of draught-oxen and were often indebted at interest rates ranging up to 157 per cent over eight months. The poorest of these households – drawn, it appears, chiefly from recently settled or ex-slave families – were being proletarianised. 'With growing pressure of population on land', Dr Haswell reported in 1974, 'the beginnings of a class of landless agricultural labourers are emerging; casual labour seeking cash wages and food during the peak season of demand found employment especially on groundnut crops among the farmers in the highest income bracket.'[141] 'While fear of hunger has been largely dispelled because of the greater ease with which surpluses can be mobilised', she explained, 'fear of poverty has become the new area of darkness.'[142] Genieri was the colonial African countryside in microcosm.

10

Urban poverty in tropical Africa

The poor of pre-colonial Africa were bred in the countryside but seen in the town. That is why they were so often overlooked: pre-colonial Africa had few towns. During the colonial period towns grew quickly. Observers, white or black, noticed more and more poor people and assumed that their numbers were increasing and that towns created them. Colonial Africa – in contrast to the Africa of the 1980s – regarded poverty as an urban problem. The children picking over Nairobi's dustbins or the destitutes sleeping in Kumasi's markets were seen as products of urban degeneration. In reality most were countrymen hoping to exploit urban opportunities.

Yet if towns rarely created poverty, they gave it new forms. The crowded squalor of a slum, exhausting and repugnant labour, hunger amidst plenty, a prostitute's life or a pauper's death, the humiliation of prolonged unemployment, the discovery that even kinsmen were not infinitely hospitable – all these were lessons for the urban poor to learn. As new forms of poverty – proletarianisation, unemployment, prostitution, delinquency – supplemented older forms of incapacitation, servitude, and hunger, so towns pioneered the transition in the nature of poverty which is a central subject of this book.

Late nineteenth-century Lagos provides a starting-point, for it is richly documented and was an indigenous town brought under British rule in 1861 at an early stage of colonialism. Most of its ordinarily poor people were long-established townsmen. Of 32,508 people enumerated in 1891, 12,040 were traders.[1] Clustered into compounds on a low, unhealthy island, they were racked by diseases of damp and dirt: ulcers and abscesses, rheumatism, digestive disorders, malaria, diarrhoea, dysentery. Certain groups were poorer than most: the 818 fishermen and their families, for example, whose crowded quarter at Offin had exceptionally high infant mortality.[2] Heavy manual labour had hitherto fallen to slaves. Under the British it was left to young male immigrants: men from Cape Coast, Kru from Liberia and, increasingly, escaped slaves or freemen from the Yoruba mainland.[3] These immigrants formed distinct low-status communities. 'Low in their habits and extremely worldly minded', according to a Yoruba clergyman, Kru clustered into temporary shacks, brawled with local residents and the police, predominated in the prison, had a separate and insalubrious ward in the hospital, undertook hard and dangerous jobs which others refused, and earned substantially less than the minimum wage accepted by other workers.[4] Almost equally encapsulated were the Hausa, who came as traders, clerics, and mercenary soldiers. By 1903 their quarter accommodated 1,548 people and was denounced as 'a rendezvous for the scrum [*sic*] of the Hausa population'.[5]

The Hausa quarter was a stronghold of traditional poverty. 'Apart from being old and infirm', a spokesman explained in 1906, 'your petitioners rely mostly for a livelihood upon selling brushwood gathered from the bush as fuel and in tending herds.' Some took in lodgers or washing. Others retired to outlying farms. While poor men fished, 'poor women . . . hawk pepper, salt, cocoanut and boiled corn and such like things about the streets . . . These women's earnings in the majority of instances, do not exceed a shilling per week, and from this small sum she has to manage a livelihood often for herself and very often for a child.'[6] Like other Yoruba towns, Lagos also had a vigorous craft sector. The census of 1891 showed 1,026 dyers, 186 weavers, 424 tailors, 291 sempstresses, 93 blacksmiths, 20 snuffmakers, 33 bamboo- and thatch-cutters, 22 thatchers, 22 barbers, 9 hair-plaiters, 439 washers and ironers, 470 canoemen, 8 hunters, 100 'fetish priests', 102 'native doctors', and 39 drummers.[7] There was also much theft, including a lively trade in purloined building materials. Of 313 persons committed to prison during 1878, 159 were convicted of larceny or theft, 154 were aged over 30, and 231 were described as labourers.[8] Serious crime was thus committed chiefly against property by poor men of mature age.

The poorest Lagosians were those equally at risk in the nineteenth-century countryside. In Yorubaland, unusually, they included many children. Of 2,695 children registered as having been brought into Lagos between 1877 and 1887, 60 per cent were girls – many doubtless sent to be 'fostered' by relatives needing child labour – and 568 were from distant Ilesha, where warfare not only bred captives but 'necessitated in some instances, the sale of freeborn children to get the means to prolong the struggle'.[9] Beggars were also numerous. Some practised the Yoruba tradition of religious begging, others 'travel from house to house on Saturdays, or stand at the corners of streets and in the market places begging alms, and . . . in the majority of cases are maimed or infirm', while by the end of the century Hausa professional beggars had arrived and 'The town is simply inundated with begging impostors, mostly from the interior – stout, hale, hearty fellows who, feigning blindness or pretending to suffer from some imaginary malady tramp from street to street and from house to house, chanting some doleful ballad.'[10] More disturbing were those too helpless even to beg. They slept in the markets, survived briefly on refuse or charity, and eventually died unnoticed in the streets. Some were mentally disturbed. Many were strangers like the unknown woman 'discovered in a dying state in one of the public markets at Faji' or the 'pauper . . . found dead in the market place at Ereko'. Several were former slaves or servants abandoned in Lagos by their masters, but Lagosians, too, could starve to death unheeded, as did Lucy Johnson, 'found dead in the piazza of a house at Cow Lane' at a time of high food prices owing to drought and disorder on the mainland.[11] A newspaper observed:

> Indigence among the natives may be traced in almost every instance to the unfortunate individual becoming incapacitated either through sickness or accident and thrown upon the liberality of his relations and friends, who speedily become tired of him and neglect him altogether and thus compel him to seek from the public that support which is refused him in the bosom of his family. Reluctant to become a public pauper, the unhappy individual endeavours to make shift and procure food as best he can, living upon what he can pick and scrape till at the last he is driven by starvation to solicit alms on the street.[12]

The case that outraged Victorian Lagos concerned Adeola, a slave woman aged about sixty from the mainland whose husband, child, and master were dead, 'and there being no one else in the village to care for her, she resorted to this place for care and help – but not knowing anyone here, she was obliged to take shelter in one of the sheds', where in June 1888 she 'was found in a helpless and friendless condition by the Police', suffering from incurable elephantiasis, long-standing diarrhoea, and extreme emaciation.[13] Because Lagos had no poorhouse, she was admitted to the Colonial Hospital, but there the doctors – observing a principle relentlessly pursued in Britain – were determined 'to prevent the Hospital being used in a considerable measure as an Alms House to the injury of its usefulness as a General Hospital'.[14] Finding that Adeola was incurable and made the ward offensive, a doctor ordered her discharge. She was carried on a stretcher to bushes 100 metres from the gate and dropped on the ground, where she remained for the next 24 hours. 'I was turned out of the Hospital', she told passers-by, 'because I was sick.'[15] Nearby householders gave her a mat, covering, fire, and food, but nobody took her in. Eventually the police returned her to the hospital, where she died. Subsequent outcry revealed that several other incurable paupers had been ejected from the hospital to crawl into the town or die in the bush. '*These persons*', it was asserted, '. . . *were each and every one of them altogether friendless*.'[16]

Adeola personified the ancient poverty of Africa, the poverty of age and sickness and slavery and friendlessness, a poverty so often relegated to the bush. It was still the chief form of poverty in late Victorian Lagos. Alongside it, however, new forms of poverty were also appearing. 'Groups of labourers may be seen daily congregated in the vicinity of the public works department and other places where Government employment is procurable, and who stoutly refuse to work for anything less than the sum fixed per diem by the Government', the press reported in 1895. Four years later, at a time of international recession, it noted 'the large number of Hinterland natives loafing about the streets in quest of work'. Another five years and it described 'labourers rushing to the shop doors whenever a person enters a shop to purchase anything, in the hope of getting the job of carrying the purchased goods'.[17] Change in urban poverty had begun.

As the British built their new town alongside it, old Lagos came to exemplify the city centre slum, 'a rabbit warren of shanties and rickety wooden "upstairs"'.[18] It had counterparts in the Ga settlement at the core of Accra, the Douala waterfront, or the Old Town of Mombasa. Yet there were other kinds of popular quarters in early colonial towns, especially where these were new creations. As soon as it became a municipality in 1897 Salisbury set aside land 4 kilometres from the town centre for a distinct African location, known to its inhabitants as 'MaTank' from the corrugated iron sheets of which it was built. Other towns were less efficient. Unless prevented, the poor occupied central locations because access to work was easiest. In Dar es Salaam, for example, they created a central 'red light' quarter at Kisutu. Generally, however, early colonial officials prohibited this but could not afford planned locations, so that Africans instead created what Blantyre's Medical Officer called 'collections of badly built, insanitary and densely packed huts of a temporary character springing up around the margins of the township'.[19] This happened even in such a bastion of white power as Nairobi, whose government offices were in 1910 separated from African village settlements only by a river valley occupied by mud or iron huts alleged to house numerous prostitutes. Bamako, similarly, soon had a quarter called Kolikotobougou, 'the hooligans' place'.[20] Some towns almost spontaneously divided into privileged and popular quarters. Zanzibar was an early example, but the clearest case, ironically, was Monrovia, where the thatched huts of Krootown were in 1930 ten times as densely occupied as 'Monrovia Proper' where the Afro-American settlers lived. Outside Southern Rhodesia the first towns to be planned from the start with distinct European reservations and native quarters seem to have been Lugard's new settlements in Northern Nigeria, which followed Indian models.[21]

Because initial urbanisation was ineffectively controlled, the next generation of officials faced the same problems of urban squalor and slum-clearance as their South African contemporaries, with whom they shared fears of epidemic disease and racial mingling. Nearly a century of attempts to sanitise the old town of Lagos culminated in the mid 1950s in a slum-clearance scheme which caused riots and much hardship but still left untouched some of Africa's most distressing squalor and poverty.[22] Some administrations were more successful. In Luanda, Lourenço Marques, and Ouagadougou the authorities gradually squeezed Africans out to the edges of the town by building rules, tax levels, property values, and discreet pressure.[23] Brazzaville, by contrast, was systematically rebuilt on segregated lines in 1909 and Bamako in 1917–19, while after the First World War the British adopted a German plan to divide Dar es Salaam into racial zones and a governor-general impressed by Johannesburg provided Elisabethville with a distinct *cité indigène*.[24] Other reconstructions were less effective. Blantyre, for example, was too poor to build the native location which its South African models dictated.[25] Several schemes met vigorous opposition. A German attempt to shift the Africans of Douala from the waterfront to a location at New-Bell provoked appeals to the Reichstag and was never completed. When the French took advantage of a plague epidemic in 1914 to attempt to relocate all Dakar's Africans to a new township called the Medina, riots, strikes, and the political rights enjoyed by *citoyens* ensured that it was only slowly and partially effected.[26] Given such opposition, some colonial governments chose discretion. No other Yoruba town was attacked with the energy devoted to Lagos, so that in the 1960s less than one-tenth of Ibadan's houses had running water.[27] The Islamic towns of the savanna were either left to decay or new quarters were built outside their walls.

Even where energetic reconstruction took place during the early twentieth century, it often created only a new problem. By the 1950s New-Bell was a place of extreme overcrowding and poverty. The Medina became an obstacle to all further attempts to modernise Dakar.[28] The location created for Nairobi's Africans between the wars at Pumwani was originally on the town's periphery but soon became relatively central, and since it was also too small it soon displayed a squalor and overcrowding which earlier informal settlements had never matched – an investigation one night in the late 1930s revealed 492 Africans sleeping in 11 houses designed to accommodate 163. Similar conditions were then common in Southern Rhodesia, where employers were responsible for housing their workers.[29]

Behind these plans and their repeated failure lay the growth of urban populations. Statistics are unreliable, but the experiences of different towns varied. Ouagadougou's population halved before 1930 but then expanded again. Yoruba towns little affected by colonial rule grew no faster than the general population.[30] The most rapid growth in Lourenço Marques took place during the heady days of the Portuguese Republic (1910–26) and in French West African towns during the depression of the 1930s, while Léopoldville, whose African population fell by nearly 40 per cent between 1929 and 1935, then experienced great expansion during the 1940s, as did other towns such as Douala and Nairobi which were of special importance during or after the war.[31] From 1950, however, urban growth – especially in capital cities – became almost universal as a result of Africa's general population increase, economic and educational expansion, and widening differentials between urban and rural incomes. Between 1952 and 1963 metropolitan Lagos swelled from 329,000 to 1,090,000 people and was the fastest-growing city, rivalled by Abidjan (which grew between 1948 and 1965 from 48,000 to 265,000) and Addis Ababa (which numbered 306,766 in 1950 and 912,090 in 1972).[32]

Just as interwar population growth subverted urban planning, so the accelerated increase after 1950 outran building schemes. Leaving aside elite areas, the 'typical' African city had four zones of housing at independence, although each real city naturally varied to some degree. The city had an old indigenous core or a location built before 1939; either was likely to be dilapidated and overcrowded but to contain a range of services and social strata. Either alongside this or beyond it was a belt of rented accommodation, generally owned by municipalities in East and Central Africa and by private landlords in West Africa. Still further from the city centre working people erected their own housing, either legally and with some planning – as in Dagoudane-Pikine, carved out of the bush 13 kilometres from central Dakar in 1952 and containing 28,780 people eight years later[33] – or illegally in what became known as unauthorised or squatter settlements. Some cities, notably Lusaka,[34] had possessed numerous unauthorised settlements since early colonial days, but everywhere they expanded during the 1950s as young married working people with children failed to find accommodation in overcrowded city centres. The drawbacks of unauthorised settlements – distance and lack of services – were even more pronounced in the peri-urban villages which formed the fourth ring of settlement.

Each of these zones had its distinctive kinds of poor and means of survival. The elderly, for example, concentrated in old city centres. In Yoruba towns 3–4 per cent of inhabitants were generally 65 or older, whereas the equivalent proportion in Nairobi in 1979 was only 1.1 per cent.[35] Unemployed bachelors clustered in rented accommodation, often as lodgers with more fortunate kinsmen or friends. Whereas central settlements often had vigorous crafts and markets, rental zones demanded cheap furniture, informal settlements created construction jobs, and peri-urban villagers brewed. As in Victorian Lagos, so in Elizabethan Lusaka, the poor survived by exploiting the ecology of the city.

Most of the poor in colonial towns were unskilled labourers. They became very poor in one of four circumstances: when they were unemployed; when they worked in especially ill-paid occupations; when they had unusually large families; or when general wages were especially low. To understand severe urban poverty therefore requires a discussion of wages and conditions of work.

Early colonial towns were often appalling environments. In Elisabethville in 1911 most African workers were forcibly recruited and lived in camps whose death-rate was 24 per cent a year.[36] This was an extreme case, but the young migrants who made up early colonial workforces suffered much privation. In Dakar, so it was reported in 1908, they 'sleep no matter where, eat no matter what, crowd together in a narrow hut'.[37] Their real wages, on the other hand, were relatively high, because most had to be attracted from viable agricultural economies. In Katanga, for example, the real wages of unskilled Congolese miners were higher in 1914 than at any time during the next decade.[38] The same circumstances ensured that unemployment was rare – indeed virtually unrecorded, it appears, except in Lagos. Immediately after the First World War a combination of depression and inflation damaged both employment and real wages, provoking the first large strikes in several colonies, notably Nigeria, the Gold Coast, and Mozambique.[39] Wages and employment soon recovered, however, to make the 1920s an especially prosperous period until the depression of 1929 intervened. Although many French colonies created jobs by investing in public works, elsewhere the depression brought Africa's first serious unemployment. By 1934, 41 per cent of able-bodied men in Elisabethville's *cité indigène* lacked jobs. Nairobi's male unemployment rate was estimated at nearly 25 per cent in 1933.[40] An invitation to the unemployed of Lagos to register themselves in 1935 produced some 4,000 responses. Over one-half were Lagos-born. More than one-quarter had at least five years of schooling and the largest single category contained 969 men, mostly aged 18–25, who had never been employed. It was probably the first time in tropical Africa that educated young men were numerous among the poor. The authorities and the African elite merely advised them to return to the land.[41]

Apart from an unsuccessful dock strike and riot in Lourenço Marques, riots in Katanga and Lusaka, and a single stoppage in the Gold Coast gold mines, the depression provoked remarkably little resistance among workers, chiefly because they lacked bargaining power, but perhaps also because food prices often fell more than money wages.[42] For those in employment the crisis came in the later 1930s when money wages lagged behind prices in regaining pre-depression levels. Numerous strikes resulted.[43] In Nairobi, for example, the average African monthly wage in 1939 was Shs. 23.57, while the reasonable minimum cost of living was reckoned to be Shs. 38.25 for a family of four and Shs. 20.75 for a single man. Even these figures concealed the differentials which were so important in creating poverty. While the average monthly wage (including rations) of a bus driver was Shs. 79.50, a labourer earned Shs. 15.16 and a male children's nurse (probably a young boy) employed by non-Europeans earned Shs. 6.87.[44] 'The skilled Africans are robbing the unskilled ones', an association in Dar es Salaam protested in 1936.[45]

The Second World War and its aftermath further worsened these conditions. In Douala the purchasing power of the official minimum wage halved between 1938 and 1944. In Accra the real wages of unskilled workers fell by one-third between 1939 and 1945.[46] Workers replied with numerous strikes – there were seventeen stoppages in the Gold Coast's gold mines between 1938 and 1944 and eight dock strikes in Mombasa alone between 1939 and 1945[47] – but they were generally localised actions quickly repressed under wartime regulations. More serious industrial unrest occurred immediately after the war, its high points being major violence in Douala in 1945, general strikes in Nigeria (1945), Tanganyika (1947), and Southern Rhodesia (1948), a rail strike in French West Africa in 1947–8, and dock strikes in Mombasa in 1947 and Lourenço Marques in 1949. The Gold Coast experienced 118 strikes between 1947 and 1950.[48] This militancy was provoked by continuing inflation. Douala's minimum wage, after nearly doubling in real value between 1944 and July 1946, was halved again by March 1948. In Accra, similarly, real unskilled wages rose 30 per cent between November 1945 and November 1947 but then fell back again below their 1945 level. For Kenyan workers this was the worst phase of the colonial period as falling real wages coincided with increasing urbanisation and unemployment.[49]

This period of hardship ended during the prosperous 1950s, when colonial Africa entered its brief 'compassionate period'. Fearing unrest and nationalism, and animated by the reforming zeal of the postwar world, colonial governments encouraged 'responsible' trade unions, instituted minimum wages, and sought to create skilled, settled, better-paid labour forces. Between 1954 and 1960 average real African earnings in Nairobi rose by 38 per cent to levels which purely market forces could not have sustained.[50]

Amidst this new prosperity, however, four forms of poverty survived among wage-earners. First, although skill differentials were narrowing, they remained wide. A survey of Nairobi in 1957 showed that only the best-paid 10 per cent of workers could save and invest in their homesteads. The lowest 34 per cent depended on rural subsidies and appeared to eat scarcely anything during the last days of the month.[51] Early Poverty Datum Line studies revealed the same picture in Central African towns. They also showed that certain colonies like Nyasaland had exceptionally low wages for all urban workers and that the increasing stabilisation of labour was creating new forms of family poverty. 'It is the presence of the wife and children which creates the poverty', one investigator concluded.[52]

The fourth form of poverty apparent during the 1950s was a rapid increase in unemployment, both structural and conjunctural. Mechanisation, a recession in the late 1950s, rapid growth in the number of young adults, an expansion of primary schooling, and in some cases land shortage in the countryside all contributed to it.[53] Yet the most important reason, ironically, was the increase in urban wages favoured by governments, which attracted people into towns, encouraged employers to replace workers by machinery, and bred the unemployment, overcrowding, and ancillary problems which the authorities had intended to prevent. Rising unemployment rates attracted attention in Lagos in 1952, in Léopoldville in 1955,[54] and almost everywhere at the end of the decade. Most figures ranged between 8 and 15 per cent: 8 per cent of adult males in Monrovia in 1959; 10 per cent in Dakar in 1955; 14 per cent of the workforce in 27 Nigerian towns in 1963; perhaps 15 per cent of male wage-labourers in Ghana in 1960.[55] Rates could be especially high in rapidly expanding capital cities (18 per cent in Abidjan in 1955, 22 per cent in Lagos in 1964), in squatter settlements (29 per cent of adult males in Dagoudane-Pikine in 1960), and especially during times of crisis (52 per cent of the workforce in Léopoldville in September 1960).[56]

These figures were exceedingly unreliable, for unemployment was difficult to measure, or even to define, and some calculations (such as that for Léopoldville) counted only those with formal-sector jobs as employed. Yet the alarm of the late 1950s was not groundless. Unemployment, especially of a structural kind, was adding new categories of people to the urban poor.

Unemployment was high in all age groups. Some of the jobless were aging, hopeless, and probably unemployable. Others were family people: of 72 women with children interviewed by the Nairobi City Council Welfare Office during July 1962, 26 attributed their poverty to their own or their husband's unemployment.[57] Yet the largest category of unemployed were young men with primary schooling, not normally ex-schoolboys in their early teens but young men of 16–25 seeking their first job. In Léopoldville in 1961 some 57 per cent of all men of that age were neither at work nor school. In Kampala and Jinja in 1965–6, 29 per cent of the unemployed were teenagers and another 40 per cent were aged 20–24. Such young immigrants often lacked family responsibilities and could wait quite long periods for posts whose rewards would hopefully outweigh temporary privation, especially if they had homes in or close to the town. In the meantime they frequently survived at the expense of kinsmen or friends – a study of Luluabourg in 1957 showed that workers spent no less than one-quarter of their earnings on this *impôt de solidarité*.[58] Their hosts naturally viewed the unemployed with much hostility. In 1961 Léopoldville's 20,000 young unemployed were blamed for most crimes and regarded as the city's lowest social category. Asked to describe the poor, townsmen in Accra in 1975 commonly referred to the unemployed – an indication of how greatly urban poverty had changed.[59]

While some were wholly parasitic, other unemployed men sought temporary jobs. Much work in colonial towns was casual, often fluctuating with the fishing seasons or the agricultural cycle. In the late 1950s some 10,000–15,000 migrants flocked to Bamako each year during the eight-month dry season in an ancient pattern found throughout West Africa. Many became temporary water-carriers or porters, so little committed to the town that often they did not even seek accommodation but slept rough in markets or on verandahs.[60] Much work was in unstable service occupations. In the 1960s nearly half the men of Old Ibadan worked in building or transport, both notoriously fickle trades. Many major towns were ports, where casual labour was both necessary and often preferred by men who valued their freedom. A man might well have a dozen occupations before he was 35. Wages were often especially low in these casual occupations, as also in retailing, hotel and bar employment, and domestic service.[61]

The scramble for cash was even more frantic in towns than in the countryside. So valuable was it that during the 1960s Ouagadougou's traders could buy articles from European stores on credit, sell them for cash at a loss, and lend the cash at a profit before repaying their debt. During the Second World War more than 80 per cent of Freetown's workers were indebted. In

1957 low-paid Africans in Dar es Salaam borrowed 27 per cent of their monthly income.[62] Moneylenders often charged 25 per cent or more a month and still failed within a few years.[63] To escape such charges, one Nigerian or Gambian townsman in six belonged to a rotating credit society during the 1970s. Such associations had many relatively wealthy members, but there was an especially elaborate one in Monrovia composed of Kru labourers, while shoe-shiners in Addis Ababa possessed an association to which they contributed 10 cents a day.[64]

Once the appalling conditions of the early colonial period were remedied, most African townsmen were healthier and better nourished than countrymen, but often this was not true of the poorest. The detailed nutrition survey in Nyasaland in the late 1930s found that what distinguished Ndirande, an African township in Blantyre, from rural villages was a wider difference between food consumption by rich and poor. Similar differences were observed in late colonial towns, where kwashiorkor was often more common than in the countryside, the unemployed were especially ill nourished, and low-paid families in Central Africa were found to spend only two-thirds of the Poverty Datum Line requirement for food.[65]

Thus the unskilled workers who predominated among the poor of twentieth-century towns became very poor when unemployed, especially ill paid, burdened with families, or in periods of declining real wages. Yet seldom were they the majority of the very poor. Many people in colonial towns never received a regular wage at all.

When compared with South African towns, those of tropical Africa were often rich in informal means of survival. In 1953 some 46 per cent of Accra's household heads were self-employed, although the proportion fell to only 3 per cent of the African labour force in settler-dominated Nairobi in 1957.[66] Some townspeople still had access to 'Sunday farms', as they were known in Kumasi. In 1962 Ouagadougou's farmers were twice as numerous as any other occupational group, while Kampala, Blantyre, and Bangui merged almost imperceptibly into the countryside, and many smaller Yoruba 'towns' were still chiefly agricultural settlements.[67] As cities grew, however, peri-urban food plots often gave way to commercial market-gardening, just as fishing-grounds were destroyed by the draining of swamps and inlets and fuel came from ever greater distances. In the late 1890s the Africans who had long supplied Lourenço Marques with firewood and charcoal were supplanted by Portuguese wholesalers using railway transport (and later lorries). Yet the old woman with her load of sticks did not entirely disappear into folktale, for consumers bought firewood and charcoal in tiny quantities from African hawkers, even in Lourenço Marques. Kampala's beer supplies arrived on bicycles and trucks from rural areas where suitable bananas grew. In the early 1970s some 3,500 donkeys brought rural produce into Kano each day.[68]

This process of destruction and re-creation was the general experience of the urban informal sector. Modern industry destroyed many petty occupations but created others. Nigeria's highly capitalised baking industry, for example, flourished only through 'the vigor of the hawkers' response'. The multiplicity of petty traders was itself a symptom of poverty, for poor consumers could only buy in minute quantities and poor sellers would compete relentlessly for minute rewards.[69] Traders were most numerous in West Africa because of its tradition of female marketing. In 1960 Ghana had 323,900 traders, or slightly under 5 per cent of the population; of these, 83 per cent were women. In central Lagos in 1958–9, 87 per cent of women traded.[70] In other regions the trading tradition was weaker, but it grew quickly. In 1954 Lusaka had some 280 market traders; in 1970, some 2,000, including many women. This increase was probably connected with political independence, for colonial governments in East and Central Africa had often discouraged petty traders, banning them from locations in Southern Rhodesia and squeezing them relentlessly in Lourenço Marques.[71]

Urban growth created many opportunities for petty traders to supply the poor. Accra's cooked-food business, once a residual occupation, expanded during the late colonial period into the city's most important trade, although ease of entry made it also the least profitable. In the 1970s Nairobi's markets did a brisk trade in *sukuma wiki* ('stretch out the week'), the outer leaves of cabbages tied together to form an artificial cabbage costing a penny.[72] The *tablier* – known in Eastern Nigeria as the 'article man' – set out his tiny stock of manufactured goods on a table beside the road, just as his nineteenth-century predecessor had spread his goods on a mat or carpet. Abidjan had 3,884 *tabliers* in 1957; they sold cigarettes singly, raising the price when the shops closed.[73] Streetside selling was often the least-rewarding urban occupation, but not the least prestigious. Nairobi's shoeshiners had a history stretching back before Mau Mau, but when studied in 1978 they numbered some 500–600, mostly Kikuyu in their twenties with primary education seeking permanent jobs. It needed about Shs. 100 in equipment, plus contacts and a strong right arm. Men in their twenties might have those. Boys in their teens did not.[74]

For a newly arrived youth with only primary schooling, the best hope was often apprenticeship. In the early 1960s Nigeria alone had about two million apprentices, four times its labour force in large organisations. Apprenticeship was strongest there, flourished in most of West and Equatorial Africa, and developed in less structured forms in East Africa during the colonial period, but not apparently in Central Africa.[75] Nearly all West African apprentices were less than 25 years old; one study in Yorubaland found an average age of 12 in indigenous crafts and 17 in newly introduced crafts, but that was probably younger than normal. The period of apprenticeship there was usually between three and five years, but in Abidjan in the 1970s it averaged six years and in Nairobi only one year.[76] In West Africa the only apprentices paid a regular wage were printers. Many worked unpaid in return for accommodation, a daily meal, occasional presents, and whatever skill they could pick up – for formal tuition was rare.[77] Many paid fees, which were usually modest in West Africa – the longer the apprenticeship, normally, the lower the fee – but higher in East Africa, especially in modern trades, and so high in Brazzaville that apprenticeship was closed to the poor. A ten- or eleven-hour day, six days a week, seems to have been normal.[78] The arrangement could be thoroughly exploitative, for many crafts survived only through this cheap labour. It also held down wages for skilled adult workers. On the other hand, it gave great numbers of men a cheap training and it was better than no craft regulation at all. In the very poor Nima quarter of Accra in 1975 the worst-paid jobs for young people were in informal occupations without apprenticeship.[79]

Older and better-educated apprentices paid higher fees in the new trades of the colonial period because here, too, economic change was destroying old occupations and creating new ones. Leatherwork and blacksmithing decayed, tailoring was overcrowded and ill paid, but there was opportunity in photography, electrical work, vehicle repair, and metal manufacture.[80] Repair work flourished among the poor. New townsmen needed cheap furniture and domestic appliances. Kampala's entrepreneurs made charcoal stoves from old car doors. Nairobi's street-corner craftsmen made lamps from oil-tins and bicycle-carriers from metal rods annexed from building sites.[81] Boys at Hargeisa in Somaliland

> have organised themselves into an engineering firm on a rubbish dump. With home-made tools and materials which others have thrown away, they make tin mugs and tambourines and tumblers from bottles. In this way from twenty-five to thirty boys support themselves. They live, rent free, in a disused shed, and grew four sacks of millet on a piece of land lent them for the purpose.[82]

Whereas the very poor of Yoruba towns had scoured the bush, the very poor of colonial towns scavenged industrial wastelands. Sanitary workers in Lourenço Marques reworked collected trash and resold bottles, plastic bags, rope, metal, old clothes, and a host of other articles.[83] Ibadan had an Association of Worn Out Tyre Traders. In Abidjan men toured the streets with bathroom scales offering to weigh people for twopence a time. They joined the continent's bizarre occupations: the lotto professors, the parking boys, the money doublers, the professional queuers.

Scavenging and crime are hard to separate. Crime was an important source of income for poor townsmen, but its history has not yet been studied and statistics chiefly illustrate the changing sizes and preoccupations of police forces.[84] Contemporaries naturally noticed the spectacular. Lagos recorded organised gangs terrorising the town in the 1860s, predictably from bases on the mainland.[85] This stereotype long survived, as did the image of the master criminal, desperate, magically protected, and living outside society like the hunters of the past.[86] By the 1950s Lagos had an elaborate criminal underworld with its own jargon and meeting-places. Nairobi, too, had an underworld of particular nastiness, especially during the extreme overcrowding and unemployment of 1945–52, when armed Kikuyu gangs dominated the townships.[87] There was evidence that crime flourished in unstructured quarters which lacked community control, and not simply in the poorest areas. Yet there was also evidence that most urban crime grew out of poverty. It was crime by individuals against property, rather than the gang violence of South African cities,[88] and most of the individuals were poor. Of those tried for robbery in Brazzaville in 1935–6, 42 per cent had no trade and 40 per cent were unemployed. 'I was without work and destitute of resources', one explained. 'I stole to eat', said another. The same was true in Timbuktu in 1940, in Cotonou in 1952, and in Kinshasa during the 1960s. Of all males arrested for property offences in Kampala during 1968, 61 per cent were recorded as unemployed.[89]

In their struggle to survive the urban poor drew upon many relationships and institutions. The first sociologists to study African towns stressed the importance of voluntary societies, especially ethnic and other 'primary' associations. More recent research has questioned this.[90] In fact there was probably much variety. The most interesting research has concerned Elisabethville, where the most important associations before the First World War were not new urban societies but the indigenous village associations of Katanga and surrounding regions, notably the Butwa society whose urban cells provided food and care for sick members.[91] This pattern awaits study in other towns. Butwa was supplanted in Elisabethville after the First World War, first by dance societies with welfare functions – as also in Lusaka[92] – and then by specifically tribal associations which were especially active in feeding unemployed members during the 1930s. In West Africa tribal associations had a longer history. Nineteenth-century Freetown's ethnic benefit societies have been mentioned and the various Yoruba sections had societies in Lagos at that time.[93] Perhaps the most enduring tribal association was the Kru Corporation in Monrovia, where public welfare services scarcely existed, immigrants were administered by tribal headmen, and there was overt antagonism to the Afro-American elite among 'we Kru', 'we tribal people', 'we poor people'. In 1958–9 a Kru stevedore might give one-third of his wages to kin and fellow-tribesmen before even reaching home.[94]

The most embracing ethnic communities were the *zongo* quarters which Muslim northerners created in many towns of the West African coast and forest. Like the Hausa quarter of Lagos, they usually contained numbers of elderly people, beggars, and destitutes, for whom the *zongo* chief often cared generously.[95] Formal tribal associations were frequently more ambivalent towards the poor. Many gave high priority to burying the dead, partly to escape the squalor of the pauper funeral often performed by convicts. Their next most common objects of aid were sick members. Many ethnic societies paid to repatriate destitute tribesmen, not only from charity but lest they discredit the tribe. Compulsion might be used, as also in deporting prostitutes.[96] Some associations gave the poor more positive help. The *edder* self-help groups pioneered by Gurage immigrants to Addis Ababa admitted both rich and poor members and initially concentrated on funerals – the poor dug the graves – but later also helped the unemployed. Akwamu women in Accra in the 1950s ran a society encouraging the adoption of destitute children. The Wanyamwezi Association owned rest houses in Zanzibar and Pemba for immigrant clove-pickers. The Ogbomosho Union in Jos in the early 1960s owned rent-free flats to accommodate new arrivals. The Ibo State Union, although in many respects a paper tiger, was an active employment agency.[97] The most highly organised group were perhaps the Moba, a small and conservative tribe from northern Togo numbering 2,000–3,000 in Lomé in the late 1970s. All Moba employed there paid a percentage of wages to community funds, from which a council of elders gave loans in sickness or unemployment to the victim and his clansmen, who were jointly responsible for repayment. Corpses, the mentally ill, juvenile delinquents, and those endangering the community were repatriated at its expense. Whereas most tribal associations neglected women, Moba had a female assembly regulating their behaviour. Most remarkably, the community ran a collective farm 60 kilometres from Lomé for those tribesmen who had difficulty in adapting to urban life and needed a transitional period. The farm sold food to Moba tribesmen at wholesale prices.[98]

This was an extreme example. Most tribal unions were too loosely organised and short of funds to aid more than a small minority of the poor, few of whom were usually members.[99] Sometimes, as among the Luo in Kampala, clan associations of 10–40 members helped the needy more than did the larger tribal union, but even these generally ended in disillusionment.[100] Tribe was chiefly useful to the poor in less formal ways. It was within groups of four or five fellow-tribesmen that the immigrant factory workers of Lagos or the young unemployed of Brazzaville sought to survive, while Tukulor migrants to Dakar lodged in wooden barracks named after their village of origin.[101] Tribe could also give privileged access to an occupation, for colonial towns were full of 'tribal specialities'. It was not surprising that Kikuyu from heavily forested Nyeri supplied Nairobi's charcoal, nor that Fulbe pastoralists sold Dakar its milk, nor even that Kamba living astride the Mombasa–Nairobi road almost monopolised the manufacture of rubber sandals.[102] But it took more organisation to ensure that everyone selling indigenous cloth in Niamey market came from a single Zarma village or that all collectors of empty bottles in Accra were Zabrama.[103] And little but custom and late entry into the labour market explained why sanitary work was monopolised by Frafra in Accra, Chopi in Lourenço Marques, or Lovale in Lusaka.[104] Sanitary workers veiled themselves in Lagos to avoid recognition, but everywhere they showed much corporate solidarity and some achieved considerable economic success.[105] The commercial advantages of stigma were well illustrated in Senegalese towns, where both casted artisans and griots formed associations to defend the caste system and its economic preserves. The Dorze weavers of Addis Ababa suffered extreme insult and discrimination but earned perhaps three or four times the national average in 1970.[106] Generally, however, caste monopolies gave way to economic change, although caste origin continued to obstruct intermarriage or social advancement, as sometimes did slave origin. In Mombasa, for example, free and slave cultures mingled during the twentieth century, but free women still did not marry men of slave ancestry.[107]

Apart from primary associations, the poor could seek support in religious groupings. Religious charity is considered in the next chapter, but religious activities conducted by rather than for the poor seem to have given only limited assistance. Among indigenous institutions, spirit possession cults treated many disabilities, such as sterility and mental disorders, but the only evidence that cults made regular provision for the urban poor is the informal care provided by *bori* among the Hausa and *zar* in Ethiopia. *Zar* may have become increasingly a cult of the poor,[108] but otherwise there is little to suggest change in these institutions. Some Christian sects and independent churches specifically presented themselves as churches of the poor. Many concentrated on healing and gave status to marginal people such as elderly women. Some provided a home for those undergoing healing, gave temporary shelter to the homeless and solitary, or made special provision for such unfortunates as prostitutes and unmarried mothers.[109] Yet the detailed evidence is slender and independent churches, like spirit cults and tribal unions, probably lacked the organisational and financial resources to operate regular poor relief systems and were most effective as networks for informal, sporadic, and personalised aid of the kind characteristic of Africa.

The same was probably true of trade unions. Their chief service to the poor, of course, was to organise them to resist the low wages and unemployment which would reduce them to destitution. Where this failed and men experienced extreme poverty, however, trade unions were probably little help. Many small craft associations had welfare aims and provided assistance with sickness and funerals, but the large unions formed after 1945 rarely had the resources for anything but wage-bargaining and job-protection.[110] Men unemployed during the 1960s complained that trade unions would do nothing for them because they could not pay dues. Only in Accra in 1950 are trade unions known to have organised the unemployed.[111]

The poor were not easy to organise. Their interests and views were diverse and not necessarily radical, for their urgent need and their vulnerability to change generally dictated action which was conservative in objective, if sometimes tumultuous in form. In Lagos, for example, the Yoruba art of 'town riot' was first employed against the British in 1889 when they proposed to introduce municipal government and its attendant taxation. 'Who does not remember', a newspaper recalled, 'the raging mobs, the "madding crowd" that besieged the Government House and paraded the streets with their wild songs insulting those who dared to express their sympathy with the proposed Bill?'[112] During the next two decades agitation opposed taxes to finance street lights and a public water supply. In 1911 women besieged the Provincial Commissioner and threatened Government House when the authorities attempted to ban domestic animals from the streets.[113] Women traders were especially vigorous opponents of taxation and 'modernisation'. Elsewhere in Nigeria they were prominent in tax riots in Abeokuta in 1918 and Aba in 1929. In Togo and Cameroun they successfully resisted the introduction of poll tax. In Accra they prevented a ban on smoking fish in the town.[114] Behind these protests lay a moral economy which asserted the right of the poor to cheap food, cheap housing, and traditional trades in city centres. In 1914 Dakarois took up arms against those seeking to evict them during a plague. Food shortage in 1919 led to riots in Freetown, where Lebanese shops were sacked on suspicion of hoarding. Bulawayo's police liquor detachment had to travel in armoured vehicles.[115] Where the moral economy was not threatened, public excitement generally needed an external stimulus. Religion was one. The poor were eager followers of wonder-workers, whether child prophets in Lagos or witchcraft eradicators in Dar es Salaam. Christian or Muslim teachers could generally excite mass action only when they preached a traditionalist message, as in the riots against the modernising Wahhabi community of Bamako in 1957.[116] Socialist ideas reached the poor chiefly through the minority of workers in modern enterprises, whose existence helped to give the popular politics of late colonial cities more diversity and radicalism than was normal in the towns of early modern Europe. The workers' influence was greatest in Ghana where the radical railway strikes of 1961 and 1971 won support among market-women and the unemployed.[117]

Unemployment did not generally provoke collective action, except at moments during the 1930s when large numbers of workers were laid off. At least five associations of unemployed men appeared in Lagos between 1929 and 1966, but none came to anything. A careful study in Accra in the 1970s noted 'the consistently acquiescent stance of the unemployed'.[118] Among the young unemployed of the 1950s, however, there was more ambivalence, for they both expected eventual success in the established order and were embittered against the rich and powerful who currently denied it to them.[119] Everything depended on the leadership offered to them. Amilcar Cabral observed in 1964 that they 'have proved extremely dynamic in the struggle' to liberate Portuguese Guinea and had provided many of its cadres.[120] But that experience appears to have been unique.

More often the urban poor acquiesced in inequality, provided that the rich had acquired their wealth by means open to others and distributed it generously. This attitude was rooted in a rural background, where inequalities of wealth and status were normal and hard work was seen as the route to success.[121] It was encouraged by the extreme social mobility of the colonial period. Belief in the possibility of self-advancement, reinforced by fear of sharing their condition, also explained the contempt with which the ordinarily poor regarded the unemployed and the destitute.[122] Another reason for acceptance of the existing order was that African residential areas were as yet rarely segregated by wealth. In Addis Ababa 'rich mansions and poor hovels abut each other all over the city'. In Lagos 'rich and poor live side by side, in the same crowded quarters. In one house, for instance, the head of one household made about six thousand a year, and another seven pounds a month: a casual visitor would not have recognised which was which.'[123] Together with widespread self-employment, this meant that class divisions were blurred, the possibility of success was ever visible, the rich were constrained to be generous, the poor were wise to seek patrons, and rich and poor were often joined by family ties.[124]

The family was both a reason for acquiescing in the social order and the chief source of security within it. Sociologists used to think that kinship ties weakened in towns, but more recent research has shown their continuing vigour while stressing that their character often changed, diffuse relationships replacing corporate groups.[125] To this one must add that different family systems responded to urbanisation in different ways. Generally, there was much evidence that urban families supported their poor, the practical burden falling chiefly on younger women. In central Lagos 70 per cent of family heads helped at least one person outside their household in 1958–9. In one area of Accra during the 1970s, 75 per cent of daughters and 70 per cent of sons were helping their mothers. To support aged parents was 'an absolute duty' in Abidjan in the 1960s, while 49 per cent of new arrivals in one quarter of the city went immediately to a relative.[126] This was a normal pattern:

> As I understand that Seth Mgaya, my brother-in-law, and who is a relative and close friend to you has obtained an employment at Dar es Salaam . . . I am writing to request you to be kind as to accept his company to your unity especially in matter of food. Because as he is a stranger and very new to town-life or on depending, he won't be able to support himself with 25/- pay unless some bodies like you his relatives are his leader.[127]

Over one-half of a group of Ghanaian factory workers interviewed during the 1960s had stayed with a relative on first arrival, mostly for over ten weeks. Of the unemployed in Kampala and Jinja in 1965–6, 51 per cent were living with relatives, 27 per cent with employed friends, and only 2 per cent were sleeping rough.[128] Yet kinsmen were not infinitely generous. Aid to kin in Accra in the 1970s was heavily concentrated on those with whom one lived. New arrivals to Lagos or Nairobi in the 1960s who sought hospitality from relatives would be accommodated somehow, but might be coldly received:

> I told my uncle that I had no bed anywhere and did not know where I could sleep. At first he told me to go home or to sleep at the race track where a lot of

> other people sleep at night. But I told him that I would go home and tell my father that he was treating me badly. I only wanted some help and I was willing to work for him [i.e. to help him in the house]. When I told him that he allowed me to stay with him. Later his wife came home and she cursed me. I stayed for seven days and slept in the kitchen. I then left and moved to the house of a friend who was glad to see me.[129]

To turn to friends, preferably of the same age, was a common second step; in the Highfield township of Salisbury in 1969 people preferred *not* to live with relatives because it was too burdensome and constraining. When even friends would no longer support an unsuccessful job-seeker, he could only take refuge with other unemployed or drift into solitude and degradation.[130]

Exactly how far family responsibility extended caused much anguish and resentment. Unemployed men often complained that they were treated more as servants than kinsmen, while Ghanaian workers stated in the 1970s that prosperous relatives showed much hostility when approached. Much depended on the town: Copperbelt families in strictly controlled housing could be less hospitable than most.[131] Much depended on the applicant: a youth with education or a prosperous father could often expect a favourable reception.[132] Much also depended on the host. In Abidjan in the mid 1960s the newly urbanised, who hoped to return to the countryside, struggled to support a wide range of kinsmen while the more permanently urbanised defined their obligations more narrowly.[133] The wealthier townsmen generally bore the main burden, which was one reason why they commonly had the largest households.[134] 'Friends and relatives come expensive', they said in Abidjan, where the poor led narrow and isolated lives.[135] Occasionally, however, the poor clustered into large family units. The biggest households in Lagos in the early 1970s were in the poor areas of the old town, while a small sample in Kinshasa in 1968 showed that the largest and poorest families were those of mature unemployed men.[136]

Much depended, too, on family structure. Luo immigrants to Nairobi in 1968–9 could expect more hospitality than other tribes – as indicated by the number of lodgers per household – because they had an exceptionally strong system of corporate descent groups. In Addis Ababa the only community with such a kinship system were the Gurage, whose young immigrants consequently prospered in the informal sector.[137] By contrast, the shallow bilateral kinship and unstable marriage of the Amhara, which had bred so much poverty in the past, provided little urban protection. In 1960 only 121 of 600 family heads interviewed in Addis Ababa 'supported members of their family living outside of the household or contributed to the upkeep of some relatives', while 12 per cent of children under fifteen were fatherless, 22 per cent of women were divorced, and 41 per cent of families had disintegrated. A survey in 1972 indicated 189,000 divorced women but only 39,000 divorced men in Ethiopian towns.[138] Such figures raise many difficulties, but they suggest both the importance of diverse family systems and the categories which might face destitution should family support fail.

Women were at special risk in towns. Of 91 needy people interviewed by Nairobi City Council's Welfare Office during July 1962, 72 were women, all of whom had children, averaging nearly five each.[139] The nature of female poverty varied with types of town, family systems, and available means of livelihood. Whereas Salisbury contained seven African men for every African woman during the 1950s, Addis Ababa had a female majority.[140] It is tempting to assume – as perhaps in Ethiopian figures for 'disintegrated' families – that women were best situated as wives in elementary families, but there is evidence that this situation could create much unhappiness among urban immigrants, wives often bearing the chief brunt of male unemployment and responding to crisis more positively than their husbands.[141] Yet it is equally dangerous to assume that women were necessarily best situated when most independent of men, for men controlled so much wealth and power. A study of Kampala in the late 1960s showed that solitary women were usually very poor.[142]

Perhaps the most important determinant of female poverty was the range of economic opportunities open to women. In Kampala trade was virtually barred to a respectable woman,[143] whereas in much of West Africa it was the core of female survival. In 1948 some 89 per cent of all economically active women in Accra were traders and a study has suggested that market-women generally prospered during the colonial period, at least until the 1950s. The same study also found, however, that other occupations for women declined under European rule in face of male control of education and large-scale enterprise.[144] Women factory workers were uncommon and sometimes despised. Of those studied in Kinshasa in 1966, only 1.5 per cent were currently married, although most dreamed of a 'good' husband. 'Factory work is the last means of subsistence for women in distress', the researcher reported.[145] Addis Ababa may have been the only tropical city where women were numerous as factory workers, although in 1973–4 they earned as little as one-quarter of the wages paid to men there. Ethiopian women were also domestic servants, an occupation generally confined in tropical Africa to males or young girls.[146] Many women everywhere escaped poverty by practising crafts. Lagos in 1948 had a thousand women dyers, several hundred hairdressers, probably as many washerwomen, and smaller numbers who boiled soap, sewed dresses, pierced ears, or carried on a hundred other occupations.[147] In East and Central Africa, as in the south, brewing was a vital female occupation. In the low-income Mathare Valley area of Nairobi during the 1970s it employed 75 per cent of women surveyed, while one peri-urban village near Blantyre earned over half its income from illicit maize-spirit during the 1950s.[148]

The most successful brewers were often women living without husbands. In strongly controlled colonial towns, such as those of the Copperbelt, they might be prohibited from occupying houses, but elsewhere female-headed households were increasingly common: 21 per cent in Addis Ababa in 1960,

42 per cent among the Creoles of Freetown in the early 1950s, and 59 per cent in the old Ussher Town area of Accra in 1958 – although there the pattern was traditional.[149] Some were prosperous, but many were among the poorest. 'Incomplete households of the "scratch-collection" type are often headed by selfemployed women or men, engaged in petty trade and petty commodity production', it was reported from Cape Coast in the early 1970s. 'This type of household appears to be closely associated with conditions of misery.'[150] Strictly matrifocal families were most extensively reported from Mathare Valley, where some women deliberately limited their families on account of poverty and lack of male support, a concern also reported for very poor women in Addis Ababa, although it was probably more common for the poorest women to seek security in numerous children, as in Accra.[151] Female-headed households often accompanied a preponderance of consensual and unstable marriages. Divorce rates were high in West Africa: some 20 per cent in Lagos in 1958–9, for example, owing not only to infidelity and polygyny but to poverty and unemployment, and there was evidence from Accra that divorce increased when economic conditions worsened.[152] Divorce was also frequent in Addis Ababa, especially among women married at their parents' behest in their early teens to men whom they generally remembered with bitter hatred.[153] Temporary 'town marriages' were common everywhere. In Mathare Valley they normally lasted a few months and gave the woman her rent and food in exchange for domestic and conjugal duties. Ethiopia recognised a temporary marriage in which the (usually poor) woman received almost a monthly salary. In Brazzaville in the early 1950s town wives successfully sued in court for financial recompense.[154]

Town marriage merged imperceptibly into prostitution, best seen as an extreme point on a continuum of sexual relationships in which gifts changed hands. Prostitutes are diverse in most cultures and were certainly varied in colonial Africa, where, moreover, different peoples displayed an extraordinary (and unexplained) variety of sexual mores. West Africa was generally more tolerant of extra-marital sex by women than East or Southern Africa.[155] The richest and most prestigious courtesans were therefore found in the west, notably among the *vedettes* of Kinshasa and the *karuwai* of Hausaland and its environs.[156] Less prestigious but still successful were westernised girls willing to go with any man for money, or the *toutou* who worked in many West African cities, essentially as migrant labourers, and specialised in ephemeral encounters solicited from their own rooms.[157] The latter were also the predominant patterns in East African towns during the later colonial period.[158] Prostitutes of these categories were not generally compelled by poverty; rather, they sought to prosper in the city by gaining access to male earnings.[159] Their profession lacked both the association with outcaste status common in Asia and the exploitation and criminality associated with the semi-legality of organised prostitution in modern Europe. Although a few brothels existed in African cities, the *madame* was important only in Addis Ababa. Africa's impatience of institutionalisation was an advantage here, as was the tolerance of colonial governments except where their troops' health was threatened. In Africa, unlike eighteenth-century France, prostitution was certainly not a one-way ticket to poverty.[160]

Yet it was for some. Alongside entrepreneurial prostitution there was also a subsistence prostitution by women driven by poverty. Like unemployment, it grew more common as the colonial period progressed,[161] although it had existed in both Ethiopia and Senegal in the mid nineteenth century and among freed slaves and other destitute women in the early colonial period.[162] Many Hausa *karuwai* were forlorn women making a poor living, while Kinshasa's *vedettes* were few compared with its despised *chambres d'hôtel*, one of whom told an anthropologist, 'I am a woman and have no learning; what work is there for me except prostitution?' Of factory workers interviewed there in 1966, 72 per cent said they had formerly prostituted themselves but grown sick of it.[163] Abidjan's *toutou* included some said by their leader to be 'sent by their family, which is generally poor', while 'the eldest daughter in a large family with a very uncertain income' and an elderly or unemployed father was a common type of prostitute in Douala.[164] Kinshasa's prostitutes multiplied with the unemployment surrounding independence. The Hutu revolution of 1959–61 left Kigali flooded with Tutsi bar-girls 'waiting for an aeroplane'. During the 1970s drought-stricken Tuareg daughters were sent to earn their keep in savanna towns.[165] By that time Nairobi's estimated 4,000 professional prostitutes earned markedly less than their predecessors half a century earlier and included a category of very young girls, often dull, neglected, and from large but broken families, who gave themselves for a shilling or two or for food or shelter.[166] The exploitation and even outright sale of young girls on the West African coast had been a scandal for several years.[167]

The most disturbing growth of prostitution took place in Addis Ababa. Ethiopia's subsistence prostitution expanded greatly in the twentieth century, especially during the Italian occupation. In 1938 the capital alone was said to have 1,500 prostitutes. 'I had no job and had lost my husband and had nothing to feed my children', a woman later explained. 'I had a number of friends whose husbands had also died. So we all started to prostitute ourselves. The Italian soldiers used to give us 20 lire each time.'[168] Continued urbanisation after the Second World War extended the trade and reduced its profitability. In 1973–4 Dr Dirasse counted 14,789 drinking-places in Addis Ababa with perhaps 27,000 prostitutes working from them. Perhaps another 35,000–45,000 prostitutes operated independently. Altogether it was reckoned that 80,000 women in Addis Ababa were prostitutes.[169] Even if this number seems barely credible,[170] prostitution was more widespread than anywhere else in Africa.[171]

The initial reason was the insecurity of women resulting from Amhara social customs. They married very young: the average age at first marriage of the prostitutes interviewed by Dr Dirasse had been fourteen. Divorce, sterility, and abortion were common. Peasant women rarely owned land. The bilateral kinship and elementary households of the Amhara offered little refuge in misfortune. Young women consequently flocked to the city, swelling its own complement of forsaken girls. Yet employment for women was scarce. Some worked as domestic servants. Others brewed, begged, traded, or became ill-paid factory workers. For the rest, prostitution was the only means of survival, especially as it carried little stigma for Amhara. Of those whom Dr Dirasse interviewed, 40 per cent said lack of employment was their chief reason for becoming prostitutes, 30 per cent cited divorce, and 13 per cent said they wanted to improve their income. Of all those interviewed, 38 per cent worked from their own rooms or kiosks. On average they had become prostitutes at age 21 and earned E$44 a month. Below them were the street-walkers, generally runaway girls of 13–17 who earned a maximum of E$20 a month and either clubbed together to rent a shack or, in desperation, joined other destitutes sleeping in churchyards. 'During the day we wear our old clothes and go begging', one told Dr Dirasse. 'At night we go out with men.'[172]

That prostitutes were most common in the city with the continent's highest proportion of women threw a flood of light on the nature of African poverty in the mid twentieth century.[173] Other groups also risked pauperisation. One was the young. Orphaned, abandoned, or vagrant children had existed in pre-colonial societies, although they were probably less numerous than in some other cultures. Many found refuge at early missions. During the late colonial period, however, child poverty appeared to increase. The chief reason was probably that the social welfare officers appointed in many colonies during the 1940s actively looked for poor children and – as so often with poverty in Africa – found what they were looking for. In addition, European views of how children should be treated were changing, some African methods of providing for children were perhaps breaking down, and broader patterns of socio-economic change were breeding child poverty.

Like most pre-industrial peoples, Africans regarded children not merely as adults-in-training but also as family members with specific contributions to make to the household economy, especially in poor households.[174] In the countryside this might mean herding goats or minding babies. In the colonial towns it might mean paid employment. This was rarely in large enterprises. There were exceptions: between the wars young boys handled coal on the dock at Lourenço Marques, while Gold Coast mines employed boys of thirteen or less underground on firewood trains at sixpence a day and paid girls of the same age one shilling for carrying 25 barrels of sand or 100 kerosene tins nearly half a kilometre. Generally, however, the problem was that children were *not* employed in modern enterprises but rather had to scrape a penny however they could.[175] For girls, especially in West Africa, this often meant hawking food, which was regarded as an admirable preparation for adult life. Roughly one-fifth of Accra's schoolchildren doubled as hawkers during the 1950s, although fewer than one in ten kept the money she earned. When social workers in Lagos tried to ban girl hawkers in 1948, lest they be exploited, there was violent popular opposition.[176] In Hausaland the seclusion of adult women during the colonial period increased reliance on child hawkers, for a woman with a child to sell her cooked food earned about three times as much as one without. Lagos hawkers in the 1950s included twelve-year-old girls and boys working quite independent of adults.[177] In Eastern Nigeria boys acted as night-watchmen in stalls and canoes. Everywhere they might sell newspapers, collect scrap, carry parcels, or work as 'small boys' on building sites or in workshops. But boys were less useful in town than girls, and as competition grew they invented ever more marginal 'jobs', culminating in the 'parking boys' who charged motorists for not molesting their vehicles.[178] Social workers saw all this as either exploitative or delinquent.

Child labour often merged with the West African practice of fostering, where children were given to other adults to be trained in skills which their parents lacked.[179] Rural foster parents were usually kinsmen, but urbanisation, schooling, and new skills led some parents to turn to non-kinsmen, sometimes recompensing them by payment or the child's labour. Fostering thus merged with pawning and apprenticeship, and like both it was open to abuse. As the Gold Coast sociologist K. A. Busia put it in 1950, 'The practice of assigning the training of one's children to other relatives is apt to fail under the new and tempting conditions of urban life.'[180] His main concern was for young girls sent to town as housemaids in return for schooling or payment either to the girl or (more often) her parents. The practice was widespread on the West African coast and became common in Addis Ababa, Nairobi, and Kampala during the twentieth century. Child servants were probably most of the 1,000 girls and 500 boys under nine years old recorded as gainfully employed in Lagos in 1950.[181] Busia was one of many who thought they were often grossly exploited, especially when they were pawns. 'They are poorly fed', he reported, 'are not given adequate clothing, often sleep without pillows, on mats, rags, or the bare floor, in kitchens or verandahs, and may work continuously from 4 a.m. till bed-time, which may be as late as 10 or 11 p.m.'[182] Housemaids have been among the most exploited of the poor in many cultures. In Africa – perhaps because of polygyny and early marriage – they were also exceptionally young.[183] Yet there were worse fates. In Eastern Nigeria the 'fostering' of children as servants or labourers, in some cases apparently to complete strangers, merged into child slavery and prostitution. Many of the children so abused were said to be *osu*. In 1957 one Karimu Adisa received ten years' imprisonment for his twenty-fifth conviction for child-stealing.[184]

When such children escaped or were abandoned, they might join the waifs wandering the streets of colonial towns. Such children had existed in nineteenth-century Yorubaland and were doubtless absorbed into the bands of religious students found in Ethiopia and the West African savanna. Children of eight or ten from Hausaland pilfering food on account of 'hunger and sheer necessity' were reported in Lagos in 1916. Forty years later they were almost certainly more numerous there: twenty were picked up each month sleeping in the streets and markets, and more could not be handled.[185] 'I arrived at Niamey at night', one vagrant recalled, 'and I knew nobody in Niamey . . . I stumbled on the market and I saw the *kayakaya* [casual porters] who slept on the tables and benches, and I too joined them . . . I had 150 francs left in my pocket and I was hungry.'[186] Several West African governments had to forbid vehicle-owners to carry unaccompanied juveniles.[187]

This increase in child vagrancy probably had many causes. One was the hope of schooling in town – Addis Ababa's street-boys were more interested in education than jobs. Another, perhaps exaggerated at the time but nevertheless real, was a degree of family disintegration in urban conditions; of 59 children under twelve years old found sleeping rough in central Accra one night in 1953, every one had at least one parent in the city.[188] A third reason, in certain circumstances, was rural dislocation owing to competition for resources or the disorder accompanying the recovery of political independence. In Nairobi, for example, the Salvation Army set up a welfare centre for destitute children in 1934. Fourteen years later juvenile vagrants were 'one of the most urgent social problems in the Colony'. But the crisis came with the Mau Mau insurrection, in which, according to one account, 10 per cent of the 430,000 Kikuyu children either were orphaned or lost touch with their families.[189] Most were eventually taken in by relatives, but in 1954 some 300 were accommodated in an 'orphan village', another 300 were with their mothers in prison, and more than 1,000 were believed to be homeless in Nairobi. 'They sleep in doorways, drains, anywhere they can find shelter', it was reported. 'They scrounge food just where they can get it. Almost before they arrive in the towns they are on the natural path to delinquency.'[190] Provision for Nairobi's vagrant boys culminated in the formation in 1959 of the Starehe Boys Centre. Of its 400 inmates in 1961–2, 112 had slept in rough shelters around the city, 44 had begged in the streets, and 214 had appeared in court.[191]

Juvenile delinquency was an obsession of the late colonial period. Vagrant youths were nothing new. In the nineteenth century they had joined East African warbands or the 'swarms of ragamuffins' around the Freetown docks.[192] Lagos and Freetown had youth gangs in the 1920s, Dar es Salaam in the 1930s. Several colonies established reformatories between the wars and Southern Rhodesia appointed an official to handle European juvenile delinquents in 1936.[193] Yet it was the Second World War that made juvenile delinquency a 'problem'. The key step was the appointment of Donald Faulkner to study the vagrant boys of Lagos in 1941. He found hundreds of them sleeping in gutters, parks, railway yards, markets, mosques, and graveyards:

> Here at night come stealthy figures. Small and agile, they scale the walls quickly and, dropping lightly on the other side, disappear into the gloom. Some carry fowls under their arms, some yams, while others come swaggering, smoking cigarettes, with money chinking in their pockets. They are desperadoes of 12–14 years of age who make this graveyard their home, stealing food from the market places, cooking and eating it communally in the evening, later sleeping out under the stars. Their days are spent in gambling and loafing, pimping for prostitutes, and picking pockets. Criminal – because that is the way to live, carelessly, irresponsibly, among good companions.[194]

One boy in three had a home in Lagos. The rest were quite recent immigrants. Those under twelve 'have been left stranded in Lagos, are orphaned, truants from school or runaways from home'. They lived by begging and petty theft. Older youths fell into three groups: newly arrived, inexperienced boys who found themselves destitute and lived rough; boys entirely adapted to a vagrant life of petty theft; and older, generally unemployed 'boma boys' who acted as guides or touts for brothels. Faulkner believed that the root problem was neglect and destitution. He established youth clubs and a remand home, juvenile court, probation services, and approved school which provided a model for the rest of tropical Africa.

Other colonies soon followed: Kenya in 1944, the Gold Coast in 1946, Uganda in the early 1950s, all urged on by a Colonial Office influenced by contemporary concern with juvenile delinquency in Britain.[195] The French had a similar obsession which issued in approved schools in Senegal in 1946 and other colonies a decade later.[196] The extent of 'delinquency' was often exaggerated, especially in the late 1950s and 1960s. In Upper Volta in 1964 only 0.22 per cent of males aged 10–18 appeared in court, while Southern Rhodesia's delinquency rate in the mid 1950s was only 6 per cent of Britain's.[197] The problem had much more to do with the rapid increase of the juvenile generation owing to population growth – of all Kenyan African males aged over 15, the proportion aged 15–24 increased between 1948 and 1962 from 20 to 32 per cent – and with its attraction into town by the 'compassionate' policies of the 1950s and 1960s.[198] Nevertheless, the obsession revealed much about poverty in late colonial Africa.

That poverty was the root cause of delinquency, as Faulkner insisted, was generally confirmed by later studies. Of the 600–800 adolescents living by their wits in Ouagadougou in 1965, for example, two-thirds were strangers, chiefly from the most densely peopled and impoverished rural areas, who came seeking work but, finding every avenue closed, drifted into marginal occupations like cigarette-selling and often ended in petty crime.[199] In Niamey in the early 1970s the typical 'delinquent' was a youth of 18–20 living on the streets and stealing in order to eat.[200] Everywhere the bulk of juvenile crime was against property rather than persons. In Kampala in 1968, 40 per cent of thefts by juveniles were worth less than 3 American dollars.[201]

Yet poverty was not all that brought young people before a court. Cultural traditions were important. Many rural societies expected youths to be both aggressive and mobile, so that it was logical that delinquency peaked in savanna towns during the dry season. Nor was it odd that Ethiopian street-boys blamed their misfortunes on failure to find a patron.[202] Family structures were also important. Only 49 of the 222 juveniles who passed through Naguru Remand Home in Kampala during 1956 had both parents living together. Of 271 Yoruba admitted to Lagos Remand Home in 1950–1, 209 came from homes broken by death or separation of parents. Social workers there blamed the problem chiefly on the Yoruba family system, with its large compounds, extensive fostering, and very authoritarian discipline – whips cost a penny each in Lagos in 1948.[203] The chief emotion of juveniles found in the Lagos streets during the 1950s was fear: fear of punishment at home or school, fear of the cruelty or supposed witchcraft of stepmothers, fear of sleeping alone in the open, fear of being kidnapped and killed for medicine, fear of what awaited them if they went home:

> A common sight in Lagos is to see a child hawker, who has dropped her tray because some adult has collided with her, surveying the damaged articles in a paroxysm of fear and grief, while she shrieks and howls piteously, terrified of the punishment she knows will follow . . .
>
> The Yoruba young delinquent is an outcast from the family, not from society: he is running away from the parent-figures, not from 'the cops'; he is flouting the rules of the home, not the laws of the land; he is failing to measure up to the family standards, not to social demands; he is conscious of parental disapproval, not moral guilt.[204]

Juvenile delinquency, as two Ugandans observed, was better defined as juvenile misfortune. Yet there was 'true delinquency': deviant, anti-social, criminal.[205] As in South Africa, it was usually associated with gangs formed initially for mutual aid but developing into criminality. In Lagos this happened under the influence of adult criminals, in Ouagadougou as a result of brutal prison experience.[206] Gang leaders (known in Ouagadougou as *Docteurs en droit*) were usually educated and urban-born – 'sugar boys', as they called themselves on the Copperbelt, used to the sweets of urban life.[207] The most violent gangs operated in Kinshasa in the early 1960s. They included both educated and uneducated youths, used a distinct costume and argot (Kindoubil = Ki + Indian + [Buffalo] Bill), smoked cannabis, imposed 'curfews', fought with weapons over territories and girls, raped women, and preyed especially on the squatter settlements.[208] It was fitting that delinquency should have been greatest where social pathology was most acute.

Those at risk in towns also included the aged, incapacitated, and destitute. Their numbers varied with the town, its rulers' policies, and its people's cultural traditions. Indigenous towns often had three or four times as large a proportion of old people as did new colonial towns.[209] European legislation generally criminalised destitution and mendicancy. Northern Rhodesian laws empowered magistrates to deport the unemployed as vagrants and instituted six different kinds of passes to move around Lusaka. This was the normal pattern in settler territories and also in the tidy-minded Belgian Congo, whose first vagrancy law dated from 1896.[210] French officials, with an ingrained fear of urban riot, made a 'banal and daily' but ineffective practice of deporting the *population flottante*, which meant almost any unemployed immigrant. In 1944 Dakar's courts punished 853 people for simple vagabondage, 41 for vagabondage with associated crime, and 250 for lacking identity cards, with the aim of 'ridding the Federal Capital of useless people'.[211]

Yet in some colonies local opinion restrained the authorities. Lagos had vagrancy legislation from 1911, but even during the depression only a few dozen were deported under it. Freetown, by long tradition, regularly gave out-relief to some hundreds of paupers.[212] Pre-colonial begging traditions proved impossible to uproot. Yoruba religious beggars still operated in the early 1970s, some making a living by it.[213] They were few, however, when compared with the Hausa beggars who flooded Yorubaland during the twentieth century. By 1921 Lagos had an elected Head of the Blind, clearly modelled on a Hausa *Sarkin Makafi*. A survey in the mid 1940s found that 139 of the city's 153 beggars were Hausa. Thirty years later a sample found 259 Hausa and only 28 Yoruba among 366 beggars.[214] A similar pattern existed in Ibadan, where the 421 beggars counted one Friday morning in the early 1970s included 234 blind (a few of them women with children) and 102 leprosy sufferers or cripples, almost all of them Hausa, as were the 40 apparently able-bodied people, most of whom were temporarily down on their luck. Only 18 were mothers of twins, the traditional characterisation of Yoruba beggars.[215] A survey[216] in eleven Gold Coast towns in 1954 had found that Hausa were 273 of the 379 beggars and 80 of the 217 destitutes counted, or 59 per cent of the whole. No less than 110 of those counted were able-bodied. Social workers reckoned that professional beggars earned about as much as unskilled labourers. By contrast, the 217 destitutes were the traditional poor of Africa, Adeola's people, the old, the sick, the handicapped, the feeble-minded. In 1953–4, 58 destitute people were found dead in Gold Coast streets and markets. Although a few destitutes were handicapped people abandoned by relatives, most were strangers. As beggars they were ineffectual. The most degraded were the feeble-minded, who were also those most unpopular with the public. Leprosy sufferers also seldom received much in alms.

The expansion of the Hausa begging tradition was paralleled by its vigour within Hausaland. One morning in 1974 a sociologist counted 4,591 beggars in Zaria (population c.150,000), although the authorities told him there were 7,650.[217] Of those he counted, two-thirds were under twenty years, chiefly Koran school pupils. Of the adults, two-thirds were men, mostly either blind or professional beggars. Most adult women beggars were incapacitated. Any large Hausa town would have shown the same picture.

Africa's other major begging tradition, in Ethiopia, also flourished in the twentieth century but perhaps changed more, chiefly owing to the novelty of urbanisation there. Thus a small sample of disabled beggars in Addis Ababa in 1962 showed that 91 per cent were immigrants to the city and 54 per cent had come to seek medical treatment. In other respects they were a stable and professional group. One-third were literate. The same proportion were married, averaging 2.4 children. Some 53 per cent lived in owned or rented houses, 35 per cent in accommodation provided by the municipality, churches, or individuals, and 14 per cent slept in the streets. More than half 'expressed their satisfaction with begging' and had no desire to return home. Another survey found that even beggars with serious mental illnesses showed 'a quite adequate capacity for survival'.[218] These surveys did not include the numerous child beggars who came to seek schooling much as their elders sought medicine.[219] Outside the capital, begging and destitution doubtless kept much of their traditional form, but even in small towns official pressure obliged the very poor to cluster together. In Dire Dawa, for example,

> Beggars and other poor people used to live in the market and on the verandahs of shops and small hotels, but the municipality wanted them to move to a more remote place and join the poor who were living there. These people had built their houses on the slopes of a hill. The leprosy patients started to occupy its top. At present [1975] the population counts approximately 1000 poor of whom 100 have leprosy. This settlement is called Ganda Miskina (village of misery, village of the poor).[220]

At least 27 of these communities existed in Hararghe province at that time, with 2,867 inhabitants.[221]

While old begging traditions survived and restrained colonial regimes, new begging practices were rare. Most African societies continued to conceal their poor in the countryside. Western education and mission teaching encouraged them. Newspapers and elite associations repeatedly demanded that the destitute be confined or deported.[222] John Chilembwe, that independent African, 'warned his country men against the habit of begging, he explained that begging was very much disgraceful system on the face of the world'.[223] The unemployed rarely begged. As a result there was little begging in African towns, except where pre-colonial traditions survived, until perhaps the late 1930s, when mendicancy was more widely reported. The expulsion of all beggars from Nairobi in 1946 may have been one symptom of a growing problem; another was that by 1962 there were again 255 in the city.[224] As colonial towns grew older they bred increasing numbers of aged, incapacitated, and destitute people. Bulawayo first noted the problem in 1933. Sixteen years later its Native Commissioner reported that 'the number of people too old to work who have lost all ties with the Reserves is increasing. The plight of these people and their families is pathetic as they can no longer live in the Location or at Luveve [Township] when they stop working. Many of them squat illegally on plots round the town, making a living as best they can.' Shortly afterwards Southern Rhodesia's Land Husbandry Act accentuated the problem by cancelling the land rights of long-term townsmen and their widows and dependants.[225] Northern Rhodesia's problem was less acute but growing. There a survey of Broken Hill in 1959 showed that although most aged and handicapped people had retired to their villages, nevertheless 38 per cent of all disability was due to age and was concentrated in the oldest and most permanent locations.[226] Because women married earlier than men they were especially vulnerable. Of persons aged over 56 in Stanleyville in 1952–3, 81 per cent of women but only 34 per cent of men were living without a partner. Aged former prostitutes were particularly at risk, as was any elderly woman without surviving children.[227] The aging unemployed were another growing category:

> In the industrial area of Lagos, and near the docks, these older men often stand together in groups outside factory gates while some younger boys jeer at them and tell them that only younger men with education and skills have the right to get jobs.[228]

As the colonial era ended, African urban poverty was changing. The traditional poor were still there. Blind beggars still felt their way through the streets. Market-women still jostled for tiny profits. Babies still wasted from malnutrition. But now new categories of poor joined them in the swollen towns. Unemployed youths sat on the kerbs awaiting the chance to unload a lorry. Unmarried women sat in their rooms awaiting the sound of a man's approach. Policemen with street urchins and old women with nothing sat in the shade awaiting the arrival of the social worker. Poverty in Africa has been a cumulative phenomenon.

11

The care of the poor in colonial Africa

Previous chapters have identified the poor of colonial Africa and described their efforts to survive. This chapter is about the provision made for them by others. Much of it is about institutions. Because these were rare in pre-colonial Africa, the institutions created to assist the poor during the colonial period generally embodied the traditions, preconceptions, concerns, and circumstances of the foreigners who devised them. They were therefore diverse: independent Africa was to inherit a welfare system of baffling fragmentation and complexity. Partly for that reason, but more because the needy were so numerous, institutions cared for only a minority of poor Africans. Most continued to survive either by the care of their families or by their own efforts.

Victorian Lagos displayed the personalised nature of provision for the poor in early colonial Africa. The provision was made chiefly by Africans. The main benefactors were probably wealthy patrons who adhered to Yoruba religion – as did 74 per cent of the population in 1871[1] – and practised largess according to a code in which honour accrued from generosity either to the poor or to the community at large. This is speculation, however, for such largess left no evidence except echoes in the behaviour of Christian and Muslim notables. Chief Taiwo, for example, was a trader and early Christian 'noted for his readiness always to help those who appealed to him, and he was instrumental in relieving many from difficulties, and his house became a sort of house of refuge for natives of the Hinterland in distress . . . Chief Taiwo was a true type of the African "big man".'[2] Mohammed Shitta Bey, the leading Islamic philanthropist, not only spent £2,000 on a mosque and gave generously to clerics but 'is reported to have relieved in a most liberal manner several people who were in distress, and some of whom he did not know personally'.[3] He insisted on anonymity, but others held to the older tradition. In December 1902 'a Moslem gentleman Mr Disu Ige . . . began from early morning to give alms in the shape of five yards of cloth to each poor and continued to do so throughout the whole day, and in this way gave away hundreds of pieces of cloth'.[4] Both individual Muslims and the Islamic community distributed alms at festivals and special occasions. When the government proposed to rid Lagos of beggars, Muslims 'cried out that the poor should always be with us and larges [*sic*] freely given to them'.[5] Although the community was said to own 21 properties in 1885, presumably as *waqf*, there is no indication that they were used to care for the poor.[6]

The Yoruba tradition of largess influenced even the British authorities, who distributed alms on state occasions such as the Queen's Jubilee, when some 150 poor people received 'a sum of forty pounds in money and a quantity of tin bowls'.[7] Yet Victorian Englishmen generally deprecated largess and preferred institutions, either the workhouses and hospitals of the New Poor Law or the specialised institutions and charitable societies of the later nineteenth century. Lagos saw attempts at both. The Colonial Hospital built soon after British occupation admitted the poor freely, although, as Adeola's case demonstrated, it also discharged them if incurable.[8] In 1873 'sick and starving female paupers' were lodged in the gaol. Their male counterparts were housed successively in the debtors' prison, the Contagious Diseases Hospital, and the gaol, before a poorhouse was opened during the 1890s. This accommodated about a score of paupers at the end of the decade, but apparently lapsed shortly afterwards. Destitute children, meanwhile, were cared for either by indentures or by the Hussey Charity Institution, founded for the industrial training of orphans in 1882 with money bequeathed to benefit slaves.[9]

The Christian-educated Yoruba recaptives known as Saro also inherited the tradition of public largess. In 1896, for example, one of their leaders 'made a public distribution of alms on New Year's Day at his villa to the poor of Ebute Metta and the surrounding villages. Over 400 persons assembled to receive charity, which was dispensed for over several hours, and included food and money to the extent of about thirty pounds.' Two months earlier the wealthiest Saro, R. B. Blaize, had given £100 to the Wesleyan Poor Fund on his fiftieth birthday.[10] Others marked important occasions in this way. Saro often contributed generously towards public purposes. The businessman J. H. Doherty gave £2,000 towards the building of Christ Church Cathedral and £1,284 was quickly subscribed for a public hall.[11] Yet attempts to collect funds for pauper institutions met repeated failure. It was not that Saro opposed institutionalisation. Unlike Muslims, they were eager to clear the poor from the streets.[12] But they saw poor relief institutions as government responsibilities. A plan to build a poorhouse in memory of a respected physician had to yield to a less expensive stained-glass window. When a Yoruba clergyman with an exceptionally westernised cast of mind again proposed a poorhouse, only some £30 was subscribed. A third proposal was made in 1897, to mark the Queen's Jubilee, but the sponsors decided instead to complete the public hall.[13] When the governor inspired Saro women to form a Ladies' League 'for the purpose of visiting our poor and our uneducated sick people, and doing what you could for them', they took up the idea eagerly – during 1901 members attended 799 people – but within four years the League was extinct.[14] With regard to the poor, imported institutional models had as yet made little headway against the Yoruba tradition of individual largess.

Institutional provision for the poor in the early colonial period came chiefly from missionaries. In 1931 the Holy Ghost Fathers alone managed 132 orphanages and 176 hospitals or dispensaries in tropical Africa. During the following year 648 people passed through the poor asylum run by the Sisters of Cluny at Walezo in Zanzibar. Missionaries also provided most of the rapidly expanding institutional care of leprosy.[15] No other organisations operated on this scale, and because the African poor remained predominantly those of a land-rich continent, these traditional forms of care retained all their value. Generally they were conducted on the ancient principle that material aid was chiefly a means towards spiritual salvation. A study of Roman Catholic periodicals published in Belgium has found no change in this approach between 1889 and 1940,[16] while a reading of the main French missionary journal suggests that concern for poverty in Africa actually declined after 1914 in favour of interest in education.[17]

Beneath the surface, however, missionary charity was changing. The catalyst was Albert Schweitzer, who went to Lambaréné in Gabon in 1913 and worked there, with intervals in Europe, until he died in 1965. His motive was Christian: he went to Lambaréné to obey his vocation and save his soul. But he chose to do it by healing rather than preaching, for he believed that suffering lay at the heart of all life, that it was the Christian's duty to relieve and atone for it, and that action was superior to thought.[18] 'This new form of activity', he explained, 'I could not represent to myself as being talking about the religion of love, but only as an actual putting it into practice.'[19] Schweitzer's self-sacrifice was in the heroic style of St Takla Haymanot, and like his predecessor he gave without taking or learning from his beneficiaries.[20] But he was the pioneer of modern philanthropy in the Third World. To finance his hospital required discreet fund-raising, international publicity, and explanation to a secular audience. To this end Schweitzer appealed not to religious duty or merit but to what he called 'The Fellowship of those who bear the Mark of Pain', by whom he meant those in the prosperous, medically skilful West who had experienced pain in themselves or others and recognised a duty to relieve it elsewhere.[21] Like Livingstone, Schweitzer's self-sacrifice caught European imaginations and validated European civilisation. He sanctified secular philanthropy and secularised missionary work. He was a vital bridge from nineteenth-century charity to modern secular relief.

Pressures for change came also from other quarters. Among Roman Catholics, one stimulus was Social Catholicism, which emerged in European cities but influenced missionaries from the 1920s, especially in the mining towns of Katanga, where it bred a paternalistic concern with social welfare.[22] Social Catholicism stressed the lay apostolate, whose most important manifestation in Africa was Ad Lucem, an organisation founded at the University of Lille in 1932 to encourage laymen to exercise professional vocations in the mission field. Led by the remarkable Dr Aujoulat, it began work in 1936 in Cameroun and eleven years later had 78 members working in 19 countries.[23] Even the normally conservative sisterhoods experienced change. In 1937, for example, an Irish nurse and religious, Marie Helena Martin, founded the Medical Missionaries of Mary in response to a Vatican decree authorising the full medical training of nuns. The sisterhood explained:

> Medical Mission work presupposes doing physical good to all who ask us – as Our Blessed Lord did. The question of conversion or change of life may come later . . . It is not for us to go out preaching the Gospel – although we are always ready to answer our patients' enquiries – we pave the way for the acceptance of Our Lord's teaching . . . True, we baptise infants in danger of death, unless we have been expressly asked not to by fervent Mohammedans or Hindus, but the paediatrician goes all out to save life and with modern scientific nursing the results seem almost miraculous the cure rate is so high.[24]

From their base near Calabar, the Medical Missionaries of Mary spread throughout south-eastern Nigeria, concentrating especially on the treatment of leprosy, and thence to eastern Africa, Angola, and to other continents, until by 1962 they had 28 major foundations throughout the world.[25]

On the Protestant side, Social Catholicism had its counterpart in the social gospel which American missionaries in particular preached during the 1920s, especially in South Africa.[26] The most active body, however, was the Salvation Army, which was always strongest in settler territories but entered tropical Africa between the wars. There it largely shared the evangelistic and educational preoccupations of other missions, but it also undertook pioneer welfare work among Africans, running a welfare centre in Nairobi, a poorhouse in Lagos, approved schools in Nigeria and the Gold Coast, and several other institutions. In 1955 the Salvation Army had 1,562 officers in sub-Saharan Africa. At that time its strength in personnel, its concern with suffering, and perhaps its far-sighted leadership enabled it to become the continent's pioneer in providing specialised care for the handicapped. In Kenya alone, in 1981, the Salvation Army managed four schools and two workshops for the blind; two schools, a hostel, and a workshop for handicapped children; a children's home; two boys' training centres; two girls' centres; a home for destitute persons; two feeding programmes for the destitute; and a host of other activities.[27] Specialisation was a general feature of missionary charity in the last years of colonial rule. The White Fathers in Upper Volta gave special attention to vagrant children, opening a craft school for them near Bobo-Dioulasso in 1956, a *garderie* in 1958, and a children's village outside Ouagadougou in 1959. In 1958 specially trained Roman Catholic sisters opened a home for mentally defective children at Bulawayo. Four years later missionaries staffed a new mental hospital in

Northern Rhodesia.[28] Although older institutions like Walezo survived, emphasis shifted somewhat from relief to rehabilitation.

Christians had no monopoly of charity. Islamic practices spread widely in colonial Africa, as was demonstrated by the tendency for standard Islamic terms for poverty and charity, which commonly had connotations of indigence and ill-fate, to supplant words connoting lack of power, kin, or friends.[29] As in Lagos, however, Islamic charity remained largely uninstitutionalised. In Zanzibar during the late 1950s, for example, the revenue of Islamic institutions was insufficient even to support the mosques and could provide nothing for the poor.[30] There is no evidence of *waqf* endowment for that purpose in tropical Africa, but individual philanthropists occasionally financed such institutions as the almshouses in Mombasa built by Sir Ali bin Salim, the Liwali of the Coast, while in Zanzibar individuals gave rooms in their own houses for aged paupers.[31] The *zakat* tithe, which had been the most institutionalised form of poor relief in Muslim Africa, often lapsed under the rule of Unbelievers. It did survive in some small communities. In Senegal it was sometimes paid to religious authorities for distribution, while others gave it directly to the poor as *sadaka*, as was already the practice in Futa Jalon at the end of the First World War. In south-western Niger *zakat* and *sadaka* fused, while in certain areas, as in the Muslim quarter of Kumasi in the 1960s, *zakat* was generally given not to the poor but to prominent teachers.[32] *Sadaka* merged easily with African traditions of honour and largess. Alhassan Dantata of Kano, founder of the richest African trading family in the continent, slaughtered a herd of cattle for the poor each year at Idd el-Kebir. His son Ahmadu distributed alms to all comers at a city gate each Friday after prayers.[33] The specifically African bodies which grew up within Islam during the colonial period laid special stress on charity. Amadou Bamba, who founded the Mouride brotherhood of Senegal, taught that almsgiving could save the giver from hell, solve his difficulties, protect him against sickness, and achieve his desires, while the brotherhood itself attracted many impoverished people, often former slaves or from low castes, and redistributed wealth among them. In one Mouride village studied, fifteen old and poor disciples received food from their *shaikh* each day and many others were occasional recipients.[34]

Other religions also had charitable traditions. No community was more generous than the Indians of East Africa, who not only provided for their own members by means of out-relief, widows' houses, children's homes, and medical institutions,[35] but also extended charity to Africans. It was from a bequest by a caravan financier, Sewa Haji, that the first free hospital and the first government leprosarium were built in German East Africa during the 1890s. The Social Service League, founded by Indians in Mombasa in 1920 and later extended to other towns, 'had the avowed purpose to assist destitute and unfortunate members of any community regardless of race, colour or creed'. In 1947 Indians inspired the Zanzibar Voluntary Social Welfare Society, which largely financed the most efficient welfare system in tropical Africa.[36] West Africa's Lebanese community also included generous philanthropists. European settlers – and especially their wives – were often active in charitable works, especially in Southern Rhodesia where the Federation of African Welfare Societies, formed in 1936, was in fact a federation of European bodies concerned with African welfare, much of which at that time concerned recreation. In 1952 two pioneer tea planters in Nyasaland bequeathed £232,000 for leprosy work.[37]

Africa's indigenous religions could not match institutional charity on this scale. Like urban spirit possession cults, they probably contributed more by creating networks through which poor people could enjoy individual support. One interesting exception was the Bwiti cult, formed in Gabon early in the colonial period to reintegrate the fragmenting intellectual and moral system of the Fang people, but incorporating also structural features taken from European institutions. Among the eleven major themes identified in Bwiti teaching in the late 1950s was 'the problem of poverty and suffering and the piteous and despairing condition'. The income of a Bwiti chapel (as of a mosque) was devoted first to its upkeep and that of the leaders, the residue being distributed 'to the needy who weekly come forward to make prayers to that effect', grants often taking the form of communal meals or Bwiti uniforms.[38] Another African community practising extensive charity were the Children of the Sacred Heart, who broke away from the Roman Catholic Church in Northern Rhodesia in order to practise a Franciscan ideal. By 1960 they had 22 friars and 7 sisters and had built a Village of Mary, near Kasama, 'from which they go out to give charity to others, and to it they gather the very poor and orphans and other sufferers, and support them there with the gifts from the Copperbelt'.[39] Many rural independent churches attracted the sick, the barren, and the old who often found no place in mission systems, but evidence that they cared specifically for the poor is rare, perhaps because they lacked the resources available to missions.[40] On the present evidence, pre-colonial Africa's methods of poor relief appear to have provided few models of religious institutions on which men could build during the colonial period – in contrast, for example, to the Hindu institutions available to Indian reformers.[41]

Secular institutional charity was a colonial innovation, but it grew slowly. Initially the flow of funds was from Africa to Europe. The first collection for charitable purposes in Dakar appears to have succoured French troops wounded in Tonkin. The first in Nyasaland was for Italians wounded at the Battle of Adwa, while the Nyasaland Charitable Purposes Committee, formed in 1921, collected funds for deserving causes in Britain. This was a common pattern. In March 1918 the British Red Cross was reported to have received over £50,000 from Nigeria.[42] Only gradually was the pattern reversed. The Red Cross, founded in 1863, was the world's first international secular charity and the first to establish itself in Africa, where it appears to have initiated medical work after the First World War. It was especially strong among European communities in French and Belgian colonies. A Kenyan branch was established in 1927. The Gold Coast branch, founded in 1932, was active in child welfare and won much support among the African elite. Red Cross activities at this time appear to have touched only the largest towns.[43]

Colonial Africa was largely closed to secular philanthropic bodies by the entrenched position of missionary societies, the existence of European governments, and the fact that secular overseas charities began only as the great famines of the early colonial period were ending. The situation was well illustrated by the Save the Children Fund, the oldest of modern relief agencies. Created in London in April 1919 to aid destitute children in Vienna, the Fund was not attached to any one religion but was inspired by compassion for children and by the desire, in its founder's words, 'to elevate charity into an exact science'.[44] Like the Red Cross, it saw Africa initially as a source of funds for expenditure in Europe, receiving £45,000 from South Africa in two years. Following the Rand strike of 1922 it began to remit funds in the other direction. In 1929 it appealed for aid during the Rwanda famine – one of Africa's last old-style famines – in which its Belgian counterpart, L'Oeuvre Nationale de l'Enfance, provided relief.[45] The Fund's interest in Africa grew at this time because conditions in Europe were improving, for relief work in the Third World has flourished when Europe has been secure. In 1931 the Fund held an international conference on African children at Geneva, concentrating on infant mortality, education, and child labour.[46] Then the depression intervened, soon followed by war in Europe, and interest in Africa waned. The only exception was Ethiopia, where the Fund met the Italian invasion of 1935 by organising Africa's first modern relief operation, albeit on a small scale, sending food and clothing, appointing a coordinator, supporting children in refugee camps in Kenya and Somaliland, and establishing a children's welfare centre in Addis Ababa which became the nucleus of work among Ethiopian women and children.[47] Yet this was the Fund's last important operation in Africa for two decades. In 1945 it briefly sponsored a child welfare worker in Ibadan. In 1950, with Europe again recovering, it announced that 'SCF prepares to re-enter Africa', but of the two initiatives launched then, a child welfare centre in southern Sudan was closed by political complications and a camp for destitute boys at Hargeisa in Somaliland met many difficulties until handed over to a Somali administrator with Save the Children Fund support.[48] In the mid 1950s the Kenyan branch of the Fund was active in caring for vagrant youths and children orphaned or abandoned during Mau Mau. Yet in 1959, as African independence approached, the Somali worker and a newly appointed Child Care Adviser in Uganda were the only Save the Children Fund staff on the African continent. Oxfam, founded to relieve starvation in Europe during the Second World War, had even less interest in Africa in 1959, except in Algeria. The day of the relief agency had not yet come.[49]

In British colonies governments made little provision for the poor before the Second World War. Officials believed that African families and communities looked after their needy members and that any supplementary care could best be given by missionaries. Government provided general services: increasing control of famine; free but limited public health services; legislation against abuses; rudimentary urban sanitation and control of working conditions. District Officers generally had small discretionary funds to relieve distress. By 1939 most colonies possessed a reformatory, one or more state-subsidised leprosy settlements, perhaps an asylum for the insane, and occasionally a poorhouse in the capital and a sprinkling of clinics for mothers and infants. Not a single British colony in Africa possessed poor law legislation, although Jamaica, for example, had enacted its first poor law as long ago as 1682.[50]

This relaxed attitude began to change during the later 1930s. The depression had created visible unemployment and highlighted the poverty of migrant labourers and their families. Investigation of this problem led Nyasaland to establish a pioneer Native Welfare Committee in 1935. A year later the Colonial Office urged each colony to set up a committee on nutrition.[51] Then in 1937 poverty gained political urgency from riots in the West Indies, where destitution was widespread. In the long term these riots gave rise to a new strategy of development and welfare for the whole colonial empire. In the short term they led to the creation of a Social Services Department within the Colonial Office in March 1939.[52] Four months later each colonial government was asked to create a Social Welfare Committee. At this time the term embraced all social services.[53]

During the 1940s concern with social welfare centred on the West Indies,[54] but the Colonial Office's global perspective ensured that Africa felt ripples from the Caribbean. Thus the appointment of a Committee on Young Offenders in 1940, which coincided with the arrival of European troops in West African coastal cities and the discovery of juvenile delinquency there, introduced African colonies to the new profession of social work and its expensive apparatus of casework, juvenile courts, remand homes, and probation.[55] Social welfare in English-speaking Africa never entirely lost this emphasis.

Yet most British experts on Africa regarded the West Indian model as a snare which diverted attention to a tiny minority of unproductive urban dropouts and away from the continent's real problems, which were economic development and village improvement for the peasant majority.[56] The point was made to the Colonial Social Welfare Advisory Committee in 1946 by Audrey Richards, the anthropologist and expert on African nutrition then working in the Colonial Office:

> *Dr Richards* emphasised that in the past the tendency had been for Social Welfare Officers to concern themselves with the minority of the community

> instead of the majority, and gave as an example the keenness of Social Welfare Officers to cater for the blind or for lepers, and their comparative reluctance to consider the needs of the community as a whole. It should be a rule that the needs of the majority should come first.

Agreeing, the committee resolved that the first priority should be 'Activities to raise the general economic standard of the community', followed by 'Stimulation of community and group activities' and 'Care of the adolescent'.[57] During the next two years this strategy merged with plans for mass adult education (themselves influenced by wartime army experience) to produce the policy of Community Development, later defined as 'a movement designed to promote better living for the whole community with the active participation and on the initiative of the community'.[58] When compared with social welfare, community development had great attractions for British administrators in Africa. It proposed to cater for the rural majority rather than the urban minority. It undertook to stimulate development and generate wealth rather than spend scarce resources on the least productive members of the community. It planned to encourage untrained African initiative rather than rely upon professional European social workers. It was 'constructive' rather than 'remedial', active and vigorous rather than patient and gradual. It promised to work with people rather than for them. And it merged easily into a 'hearts and minds' strategy to wean colonial subjects away from emerging nationalist movements. Community development also offered influential Africans opportunities for self-advancement and patronage, whereas social welfare offered them little but taxes. It must not be implied that community development was misconceived. It was a successful British invention which even the French imitated.[59] But it had a price, and that price was neglect of the very poor, who were those least able to take advantage of its self-help programmes. Although humanitarians insisted that to neglect social welfare was false economy, colonial officials and their African successors knew that a strategy of maximum economic development must push the weak to the wall.

These issues were played out in each British colony during the 'compassionate period' after the Second World War, but with much variation according to local circumstances. Nigeria, for example, had an abiding emphasis on juvenile welfare from the moment when Faulkner created boys' clubs and a remand home, juvenile court, and probation service to rehabilitate the vagrant boys of Lagos. Officers posted to Calabar in 1948 and Onitsha in 1950 immediately reported that 'juvenile delinquency, pauperism, abuse of child labour etc. stand out a mile as the main job'.[60] When Nigeria's three regional governments took control of social welfare during the early 1950s, they maintained the emphasis. 'There has been little variation in the scope of welfare services in Nigeria since the 1940s', a Nigerian scholar wrote in 1984. 'The emphasis has continued to be on family welfare, juvenile welfare, especially youth club organization, and juvenile correction work.'[61] This emphasis did ensure a concern with at least one section of the poor. Admittedly, Faulkner's clubs gradually attracted 'boys with a more solid background' than the original members. Admittedly, Lagos parents falsely accused their own children in order to gain them free vocational training at an approved school.[62] But there were more than enough destitute boys in Nigeria to absorb the energies of Social Welfare Officers.

One reason why this emphasis survived in Nigeria was that community development remained a separate service there. The Gold Coast had a different experience. There, too, social welfare work began during the war with concern for 'juvenile delinquency'. The Secretary for Social Services, appointed in May 1943, defined his priorities as the care of the young and the construction of a community centre in each district. By 1951 there were 28 community centres. Personal casework, initiated at that time, had to be limited in 1954 lest it become unmanageable, but child welfare remained a priority. There was also some provision for leprosy sufferers, the blind, and the disabled, although for the beggars and destitutes surveyed in 1954 the main concern was to remove a public nuisance by institutionalisation.[63] Meanwhile community development began in 1948 and rapidly outpaced social welfare. In 1964 Ghana's community development service employed over 1,000 field staff, including professional social workers, and was regarded as a model for the continent.[64] Sierra Leone experienced a similar transition: a service founded in 1941 'with a strong bias towards juvenile delinquency' expanded through community centres catering for 'the ex-secondary school and teacher class' to concentrate during the 1950s on community development, while direct concern for destitution – which the Social Welfare Officer in Freetown described in 1948 as 'a great problem' – was left largely to the Kissy Institution, where the paupers of Freetown had long found refuge.[65]

The contrast between social welfare for the poor and community development for the masses was even starker in East Africa. At one extreme, Zanzibar Island, small and heavily urbanised, possessed the most effective social welfare organisation in tropical Africa. The Welfare Section of the Provincial Administration, created in 1946, did not need to concentrate on destitute children, who were rare in Zanzibar except where a whole family was destitute, but concerned itself with adult paupers, especially the beggars who flourished in an Islamic environment. Support came from the Walezo poorhouse and the Zanzibar Voluntary Social Welfare Society, which was founded in 1947, largely at Indian instance, to collect funds for the poor and eliminate begging. Aided by government grants, the society gave out-relief to over 200 poor people at its peak in 1954. It also maintained eight almshouses, four rented houses, and numerous rented rooms. The Welfare Department provided craft training for aged and handicapped people, repatriated destitutes, prosecuted mendicants, and taught 'the value of careful case-work in substitution for indiscriminate alms giving'. The result, during the early and mid 1950s, was a welfare organisation genuinely focussed on the poor but confined largely to towns.[66] As political tension increased during the later 1950s, rural community development grew more important and the Voluntary Society's funds declined, so that by Independence in 1963 Zanzibar's social welfare system was in danger of collapse.[67]

While Zanzibar concentrated on the poor, social welfare on the East African mainland developed in other directions. In Kenya municipal authorities took the initiative. Both Mombasa and Nairobi built almshouses by 1944, while Nairobi appointed a woman welfare officer to work with African women and hired a former district commissioner to deal chiefly with juvenile delinquency. 'They are really doing awfully well', Whitehall noted.[68] The pattern changed when the war ended. As part of its demobilisation programme, the government trained numerous ex-servicemen (chiefly from the Army Education Corps) as community development workers. By 1951 it had a unique 'social welfare' organisation, with 8 European officers (mostly former demobilisation officers) who had no professional qualifications and were part of the provincial administration, some 70 African social welfare workers employed by African District Councils, and over 30 community centres. Their main functions were literacy training, education, and recreation.[69] 'Community Development work', the embattled governor observed in 1952, 'can make a very substantial contribution . . . towards the creation of a sound public opinion.'[70] This organisation had won the acquiescence of the European settlers on the Legislative Council, who refused to finance welfare work among Africans and hankered after the South African principle of leaving everything concerning Africans to the Native Affairs Department. The Colonial Office, by contrast, complained that the Kenyan system was unprofessional, racialistic, and provided 'no Government organisation responsible for the welfare of Africans in the towns or settled areas'.[71] The settlers were unmoved. When a Ministry of Community Development was created in 1954 (and entrusted to the only African minister), it was specifically not given responsibility for social welfare. By then, in response to the widespread destitution caused by Mau Mau, government and the Nairobi municipality were building up overlapping welfare systems in the capital. The result was described in 1962 as 'chaotic'. Elsewhere the provincial administration remained responsible for the relief of distress until 1968.[72]

Tanganyika's postwar 'social welfare' was even more idiosyncratic. In 1945 the government obtained £50,000 from the Colonial Development and Welfare Fund to build 42 welfare centres in the main townships in order to provide 'for the returning soldiers a counterpart to the canteens and community life to which they had become accustomed'. When the returned soldiers disappeared painlessly into civilian life, the welfare centres became dance halls for educated townsmen.[73] In 1947, therefore, strategy changed. The former commander of the East African Education Corps was appointed Commissioner of Social Welfare but concentrated on mass education. In 1950 he told the Colonial Social Welfare Advisory Committee that 'he looked upon the work of Welfare as really Community Development, because if one started case work, the whole population needed it'. The truly destitute, he added, could either be cared for by missionary societies or repatriated to their rural homes. Mass education served larger purposes:

> Agitators easily disturbed people who were ill-informed. Social Welfare must put over Government policy and the reasons behind it to the people . . . Mr Dorman [of the Colonial Office] supposed that not all Government policy would be put across but only Rural Development policy? The speaker replied that in his opinion the population should be informed of the reasons for Government laws and actions e.g. suppressing newspapers, &c. Mr Dorman asked further if it was right that the Welfare Officer should associate himself with a policy that might be opposed to the feelings of the population. Would the Welfare work suffer? Mr Blaxland said no. If a chap thinks a thing is right and stands up for it, he will get the respect of the Africans. Mr Dorman asked if he thought that it was always possible to convince Africans that the Government view was right? Mr Blaxland said yes; it should be assumed that Government always has good reason for its laws and actions.[74]

During the 1950s rural community development had considerable success in Tanganyika, especially with mass literacy.[75] Social welfare fell into the background. In 1958 the Social Development Department reported that 'For various historical reasons, dating back to the days when this Department was known as the Social Welfare Department, there remained a number of "welfare" commitments from which it has been necessary to disengage.'[76]

What Kenya and Tanganyika stumbled towards, Uganda did coolly and deliberately. In 1940 Buganda needed a vagrancy law to deport or, failing compliance, to gaol for up to six months the 'unemployed and destitute natives [who] have been collecting at various big centres', yet when a Department of Public Relations and Social Welfare was established in 1946 it promptly announced that 'Apart from the generally low economic standard of the population, destitution in Uganda is not a major problem. The family structure still tends to act for the relief of its own members.'[77] From the first the Department emphasised community development, and was so renamed in 1952. Leprosy sufferers, orphans, and adult destitutes were left to mission or local authority care. In 1953 a Colonial Office committee suggested that 'Government might profitably play a more positive part in organising social welfare work in urban areas. They understood that there were no officers in Uganda trained in case work.' There was no response.[78]

Uganda was a relatively rich and progressive colony whose rulers had firm development priorities. Nyasaland was a poor and stagnant colony whose rulers had long lost hope. They did not respond to Colonial Office initiatives until 1949, when a woman education officer was given charge of juvenile welfare. Two years later a proposal to appoint a Commissioner for

Social Development was rejected on the grounds that 'The conclusions are to spend more money and we have no more to spend', a view described in the Colonial Office as 'defeatist'.[79] In 1954 the Legislative Council refused to finance an administrative officer – 'we have removed any ideas of experts', the Chief Secretary noted – to survey social development needs.[80] In 1957, after further prodding from London, a former district commissioner was made responsible for social welfare. His attention soon concentrated on community centres, women's organisations, and football clubs. 'Owing principally to the fact that tribal traditions have remained substantially intact in the villages', he reported, 'the problems of delinquency, parental neglect, illegitimacy, and the care of mentally and physically handicapped people, etc. have not yet become very real.'[81] Middle-class Africans agreed. As early as 1952 a provincial commissioner complained that local Social Welfare Committees 'are working on the wrong lines. They are organizing "snobs classes" among the "intelligentsia" and their wives, such as knitting classes, basket-ball classes, football teams and such like.'[82] A few years later the trend was positively welcomed. 'Social development work', government reported in 1959, 'is now treated as a positive contribution to the general progress of Nyasaland, and not as a mere palliative (the term "welfare" is confined to personal problems).'[83] 'The womens section cleared the Netball pitch', a social club reported in January 1959, 'and held a meeting to plan activities for February. They passed a resolution to help and visit sick people in and round the Boma and nearby villages. Visits were made and an old sick woman given a shilling.'[84]

Nyasaland was the no man's land between black and white Africa. Northern Rhodesia in the 1940s was part of the white south. African urban welfare was left to municipalities and companies. Lusaka, for example, appointed its first Director of Social Welfare in 1945. He began by organising youth clubs, welfare centres, sports, and literacy classes. He added family casework in 1950, largely from anxiety about juvenile delinquency, but other towns were slow to follow and the 350 grant-aided welfare workers employed by local authorities in 1955 were chiefly concerned with recreation.[85] Meanwhile, rural welfare was left to the provincial administration, orphans were entrusted to missions, and the central government – in accordance with South African principles – provided social welfare services only to non-Africans, chiefly old age allowances and probation services. From 1952 local authorities received 50 per cent government grants for welfare work, but only in the late 1950s did the central government take over African casework, leaving community development to local authorities.[86] This change coincided with increasing urban poverty both among the elderly and among young people seeking employment. In 1964 no less than 11,988 people sought casual relief or public assistance. Of these, 5,769 were work-seekers, 1,588 old or infirm, 964 deserted or widowed, and 835 physically or mentally handicapped. More than half the applications were in Central Province, which meant chiefly Lusaka.[87]

Southern Rhodesia trod in South African footsteps. In 1936 it instituted old age pensions for non-Africans, later adding widows', orphans', and war pensions, but African urban welfare was left to municipalities or voluntary organisations, both of which concentrated on recreation, while regular rural poor relief was in 1938 confined to fewer than ten old or blind people each receiving between 5 and 30 shillings a month, or rations, from the Native Affairs Department, provided that an official certified each year 'that the native has no relatives able, or willing, to assist him'. Six years later provision for handicapped Africans was confined to one mission school for the blind, an old age home in Salisbury with two inmates, and some individual care at mission stations. Apart from small grants to missions, the state accepted no responsibility for African children unless they were delinquent, when it beat or imprisoned them.[88] A plan was prepared in 1944, again on South African lines, for tax-financed welfare services which would have included urban Africans, but the scheme implemented by the Department of Social Welfare (established in 1947) omitted Africans on the grounds that the reserves guaranteed them 'the minimum social security'.[89] Until 1964 the Department's only dealings with Africans concerned juvenile delinquency and a small amount of child welfare. The burden of urban poverty remained with the municipalities, among which Bulawayo, under the enlightened administration of the anthropologist E. H. Ashton, developed an extensive system of welfare and community development which in the late 1960s employed over 200 people and spent over $600,000 a year, financed on South African lines from a liquor monopoly. In 1964 African welfare was transferred from the Native Affairs Department to the Department of Social Welfare, but a year later the unilateral declaration of independence subordinated everything to white survival. During the later 1960s the Department took over public assistance in Bulawayo from the municipality and ran it down on the grounds that jobs were available on farms, although the numbers needing relief remained substantial. The regime also used rural community development to extend its control over the reserves, in a blatant demonstration of the programme's political potential.[90]

In French Africa, as in British colonies, official concern with the poor was chiefly a consequence of the Second World War, but it took a characteristically different form. The first Colonial Social Service was created in France itself in November 1943 to care for colonial subjects and French administrators and their families stranded there by the war. In 1946 it became the Social Service of the French Union, and in 1948 the Overseas Social Service. A section was to be established in each overseas territory to resolve social problems, including 'poverty and public calamities', working outwards from towns to countryside.[91] Yet social service differed from Anglo-Saxon social work. It was an exclusively feminine profession tied to the powerful French tradition of community medicine. All *assistantes sociales* had nursing training. Most saw the mass welfare of mothers and infants as a more urgent priority than the concern for the juvenile delinquents and demobilised soldiers so important to the British. Social service was not born of any such crisis as the West Indian riots of 1937. It was never intended to concentrate on the poor. Moreover, French Africa lacked resources and its postwar planning stressed infrastructural development. Funds for social services were rarely available before about 1953, at roughly the same time as British notions of community development began to influence French thought. Social service therefore grew slowly according to the idiosyncrasy of each colony and its administrators.[92]

The service first took root in Equatorial Africa because its governors-general (notably Cornut-Gentille) were more sympathetic than their counterparts in Dakar. *Assistantes sociales* arrived in each territorial capital of Equatorial Africa during 1948–50. Eventually there were about a dozen there and a similar number in Cameroun. Their task was to create a social centre in the African quarter of each important town as both childcare clinic, kindergarten, and meeting-place. In 1960 there were 29 social centres in Equatorial Africa and 9 in Cameroun.[93] Each colony had its peculiarities. In southern Chad the whole operation was financed by the all-powerful cotton company, while in Gabon the missionaries were so entrenched that nothing was achieved until the first social centre was entrusted to a sister. Broadly, however, as Dr Audibert concludes, 'the territorial colonial administration desired to do a little "social", but not too much, and on condition that it did not cost too dear'.[94]

In French West Africa the operation was even more hesitant. The governors-general of the late 1940s were hostile and the federal Grand Council, with strong settler representation, refused funds for social service, which therefore depended on territorial and municipal budgets. The first field staff arrived in 1951 in Ivory Coast. A year later Cornut-Gentille, transferred from Brazzaville to Dakar, warned territorial governors that international opinion expected them to provide services for mothers, children, and the deprived.[95] Although impoverished Niger and Mauritania left these questions to their medical authorities, the other colonies of French West Africa employed 18 *assistantes sociales* in 1955 and had 47 social centres in 1960. The chief weakness was in Senegal, where alarms over juvenile delinquency in Dakar led to a concentration on probation work within the city, plus some elitist community development activities. The latter tendency was apparent in several other colonies.[96]

For the French, as for the British, one important aspect of social service was to train indigenous staff. Colonial governments quickly realised that in this field Africans could be especially effective without being politically dangerous. In October 1943 seventeen students from British West Africa and one from Zanzibar began training at the London School of Economics. During the next decade several British colonies established training centres, followed later by diploma courses at local universities. The numbers trained were largest in the Gold Coast (with 420 professional staff in 1962), Northern Rhodesia (with 48 African social workers in 1960), and Kenya, while Jesuit missionaries opened a particularly effective School of Social Service in Southern Rhodesia in 1964. In French Africa in 1960 there were 38 African social welfare staff with diplomas gained in France, 103 with local diplomas (66 of them in Ivory Coast), and 237 with in-service training (98 of them in Ivory Coast); most, if not all, were women, often with prior training as nurses.[97]

Yet social service was only one branch of French social policy. The other was social security: retirement and invalidity pensions, accident and sickness benefits, family and maternity allowances. Here French and British practice diverged sharply. In most British colonies, the only benefit available at Independence covered occupational injury, a provision instituted in the 1940s at employers' expense. Most French colonies, by contrast, legislated during the compassionate 1950s to provide sickness, maternity, employment injury, family, and sometimes retirement benefits, generally financed from contributions by employers and workers.[98] These benefits covered only a relatively privileged group – urban workers in large enterprises, rarely more than 10 per cent of the economically active – and therefore did little to alleviate poverty directly, although their 'trickle-down' effects may have been considerable. The generosity of French benefits – to the point of paying prolific Africans family allowances designed to stimulate France's flagging birth-rate – was due to the applicability of metropolitan laws to French citizens (especially public officials) working in the colonies and to the leverage exerted by colonial trade unions. In the Belgian Congo, however, an even more elaborate system was established without significant trade union pressure as part of the general policy of paternalism and the attempt to stabilise Katanga's labour force. Union Minière du Haut Katanga instituted an accident compensation scheme as early as 1928. Most other forms of social security followed in the early 1950s, while in 1957 the Belgian authorities also created the first extensive system of old age pensions in tropical Africa. By 1959 it covered nearly a million workers.[99] Yet the fact that not even in the Belgian Congo were benefits extended to the unemployed, who were most of the new urban poor, illustrated the extent to which social security, even more than social welfare, was captured by the relatively advantaged. The welfare institutions of land-scarce societies had limited relevance to the poor of a land-rich continent.

During the last years of colonial rule the trend towards more specialised philanthropy, already seen in missionary work, also affected secular charity. Apart from leprosy patients, the first group to attract specialised care were generally the blind, owing to the drastic nature of their handicap. Protestant missionaries had long been active in this field. The British Colonial Office was alerted to it by the need to rehabilitate servicemen blinded during the Second World War. Its enquiries in 1946–7 concluded that the greatest problem was in Northern Nigeria, where blind beggars were so conspicuous, and that training and employment schemes and preventive medicine were widely needed. Except for Northern Nigeria, which agreed to experiment with training institutions, colonial governments responded coolly, arguing that limited funds could be better spent on general medical services and that blind people adapted skilfully and productively to their handicap. French officials agreed and did little for the blind except to exempt them from taxation and distribute rations where necessary.[100] The British, by contrast, turned to private charity. With official encouragement, the British Empire Society for the Blind established an affiliate in each major colony during the 1950s to collect funds, encourage voluntary effort, and occasionally open training institutions. In the Gold Coast its daughter society had 27 branches by March 1952 and opened its first training centre two years later, while in Uganda it initiated the training of blind craftsmen and farmers, an approach later extended to other colonies.[101] The Society's investigations also showed that blindness levels were highest not in Northern Nigeria – where the blind were conspicuous rather than especially numerous – but in remote riverine areas, especially in the Volta Basin where onchocerciasis might blind more than one person in ten.[102] This was an important demonstration of the real nature of African poverty, but only a tiny minority of the blind were actually treated before Independence. The less numerous deaf had recourse only to scarce missionary institutions. The most remarkable was a school at Mampong in the Gold Coast founded in 1957 by a deaf Afro-American graduate and preacher, Andrews Foster, and a deaf Ghanaian, Seth Tetteh-Ocloo, who later also graduated from an American university. Their example inspired a similar school with a deaf headmaster at Ibadan.[103]

Little was done before Independence for the crippled, whose prevalence went largely unperceived.[104] One remarkable exception occurred in Southern Rhodesia. In 1948 Jairos Jiri of Bulawayo was about forty years old and a shop assistant when he was moved by the elderly blind beggars in the city streets and took some into his home. Three years later he founded the Bulawayo and Kikita Society, which ran a small home for the blind and also for cripples whom he found in the villages. When neither self-help activities nor his friends could support the numbers concerned, he sought wider African and European assistance. The Jairos Jiri Association began to receive municipal aid in 1952, government grants in 1956, and then overseas support. In 1961 there were 110 crippled, 72 blind, and 18 deaf at the Jairos Jiri Centre in Bulawayo. By 1967 the Association had become a territorial organisation caring for handicapped Africans of all kinds. Jairos Jiri himself, Founder Life President of the Association, reflected at that time that he had become a small cog in a large machine. He was certainly the continent's most famous African philanthropist.[105]

Generally, African generosity was not easily channelled into large organisations of a European kind. An attempt by Africans in Lusaka to imitate the Jairos Jiri Association failed.[106] Smaller organisations often did useful work. Of 67 self-organised mutual benefit societies listed in Accra in 1954, more than half 'extended their concern to the wider public, especially to the socially handicapped. Members visited the sick in the hospitals, inmates of the Child Care Home, the Destitutes Hostel, Prisons, Leper Settlement and the Blind School, taking presents in money and kind, and giving words of encouragement to all they met.'[107] Individuals also created successful institutions, such as the home for motherless babies which Mrs R. O. Solanke, a nurse, opened at Ibadan in 1960. More often, however, African charity remained personal. Isaac Akinyele, senior chief of Ibadan during the 1950s, went incognito into the streets at night to give clothes and money to destitutes sleeping there. Freetown's Creole families made elaborate provision for poor relations and the community's Masonic lodges had almoners and welfare funds, but they did not establish the welfare institutions so often founded by Freemasons in other continents.[108]

African attitudes to poverty also often differed from those of Europeans. The elite were impressed by postwar welfare schemes – 'real, practical vision', said a Gold Coast clergyman.[109] But, except where pre-colonial patterns of charity remained strong, the elite drew a sharper distinction between deserving and undeserving poor than did European social workers. Probation was generally seen as a 'let off' and African-controlled courts rarely awarded it. Approved schools were thought 'to set a premium on delinquency'. Physical handicaps often carried associations of guilt, shame, or danger which led many to think that elaborate care was wasteful and improper. Eastern Nigerians displayed enthusiastic support for local welfare services in the early 1960s, but with a strong emphasis on institutionalising marginal groups.[110] These attitudes were to appear more clearly after Independence.

The difficulty of integrating modern welfare practices with indigenous traditions was best illustrated in Ethiopia. Its charitable customs were everything that European social workers most despised: personalised, indiscriminate, dependency-creating largess. The social workers' impersonal approach was equally offensive to many Ethiopians. It was therefore a major intellectual leap when Ras Makonnen, Governor of Harar in the early twentieth century, responded to pressure from European consuls by asking Roman Catholic missionaries to build a leprosarium outside the town. He made his nine-year-old son, the future Haile Selassie, its protector.[111] Thereafter, imitation of European welfare models accelerated. The first modern government hospital in Addis Ababa was opened in 1910 and several followed in the 1930s. 'It was difficult to explain that what she wanted to do was to improve the life of children in their own families', a welfare worker found at that time. 'The Abyssinian mind, even the most enlightened, always came back to the idea of orphanages.'[112] Always generous to such institutions, but equally determined to control them, Haile Selassie endowed the Haile Selassie Welfare Trust in 1947 'to promote education, to combat disease, to care for the young, the orphaned, the sick, the old and infirm, to establish hospitals, schools and ecclesiastical seminaries, to rehabilitate delinquents'. Some of its institutions, such as an old people's home at Debra Libanos, were imaginatively integrated with traditional charity.[113] The Emperor created a Ministry of Public Health in 1948, a Ministry of National Community Development in 1958, a School of Social Work in 1959, and an Ethiopian Council of Social Welfare in 1964.[114] He also habitually threw bread from the windows of his car and once told an interviewer, 'Rich and poor have always existed and always will. Why? Because there are people who work and others who do not work . . . Every individual is responsible for his own misfortune.'[115] Novel views took firmer root among the western-educated. In 1965 a discussion group under the auspices of the Council of Social Welfare proposed

> that certain national institutions such as the Senbete, Tezkar, etc., in which many people spent a lot of money in providing food and drinks mainly for people that do not need it in memory of the dead or for the salvation of their soul should be diverted to a better use...
>
> Along with this the church should also teach against indiscriminate charity. If this is diverted to an organized welfare agency it could be a good potential resource.[116]

In practice, however, street-boys still sought a patron and much traditional charity survived. State or missionary institutions supplemented it, but, as so often in Ethiopia, were only rarely integrated with it.

As the colonial period ended, tropical Africa had an extraordinary variety of provision for the poor. The proliferating state, religious, and secular institutions and societies represented the manifold strands of European, Asian, or African tradition.[117] In the later 1950s Mombasa alone had nearly 150 welfare organisations.[118] Yet one had only to walk the streets of Mombasa – and still more of Lagos or Addis Ababa – to realise how much poverty remained uncared for. And in the countryside, where 90 per cent of Africans lived, institutional poor relief rarely meant anything other than mosque or mission.

Much responsibility in the countryside had often rested on the chief, but by the later colonial period his role was waning. Among the Kingdoms of the Savanna whose political authorities had especially succoured the poor, a Bemba chief's capacity to feed his subjects collapsed when he could no longer command tribute. Ngoni rulers in Nyasaland had supported aged and needy subjects in the nineteenth century, but administrators reported in 1949 that the aged and infirm in these chiefdoms 'are not entitled to assistance by their own custom from any unit higher than the family'. Basuto chiefs, similarly, ceased to support the poor and became instead merely a burden upon them.[119] Occasionally a chief's welfare functions passed to an institutionalised native administration. In Benin, where royal largess had been spectacular, the native administration in the 1930s maintained Nigeria's only substantial poorhouse. Emirate governments administered welfare services in Northern Nigeria, while native administrations in Northern Rhodesia maintained orphanages, leprosaria, old age homes, and a lunatic asylum.[120] All these were areas where pre-colonial rulers had actively cared for the poor. Historians, however, have neglected native administrations.

Because institutionalised provision was limited, the care of the incapacitated poor fell chiefly on families and neighbours. How far they met these obligations is unknown. That they did so was a matter of faith to officials and anthropologists, in contrast to the diametrically opposite view of early missionaries. 'There are no uncared for children where the strength of African conceptions of kinship is unimpaired', Lucy Mair assured her readers in 1944 when explaining why social welfare was needed only in towns. 'There is no problem of delinquency in a village where the authority of chief or elders is respected and therefore effective, no unemployment or destitution where every one draws his living from the land.'[121] Some detailed enquiries supported this view. In 1936, for example, a perceptive study of insanity in Nigeria found that lunatics were far more numerous than hitherto realised, especially in the countryside, but were generally treated with 'kindly consideration'. Those most likely to go to asylums were the epileptics and chronic maniacs who were most frightening to villagers.[122] Yet other evidence suggested that family care was far from complete. In 1960 more than 40 per cent of the inmates of Tanganyika's main mental hospital were not acute cases but were senile or mentally defective. 'There is an increasing denial of social responsibility on the part of the African people themselves for their dependants', the Superintendent concluded, 'and there is also a tendency to send vagrants, beggars and other social nuisances to mental hospitals as a line of least resistance.'[123] Unusual strains exposed the limits of family care, as in the structural unemployment of the later 1950s, the impoverishment of village women by labour migration or household disintegration, the inability of some Southern Rhodesian families to care for poor relatives after the imposition of the Land Husbandry Act during the 1950s, or the neglect of the sick and aged in equatorial villages denuded of young people by venereal disease and population decline.[124] The occasional famine of the late colonial period could destroy complacency even more brutally. 'There were people in the villages very nearly dead and the village communities doing nothing to assist . . . this came as a great shock to me', a provincial commissioner complained after a localised famine in Nyasaland in 1949. 'I have been 26 years in this country and I never imagined for a moment that the African village community had ceased to look after its own people, and that points to the fact that your old customs of community life are breaking down very fast.'[125]

Even those who had stared into this abyss believed that failures of family care were due to recent collapse of social ties. Just as Victorian England attributed its insane to 'mechanical civilization', so colonial Africa attributed its neglected poor to 'social change', to the 'disintegrated and maladjusted society' which Busia described in Sekondi-Takoradi.[126] Yet there was nothing new either in the fact that families did not always care for everyone or in the fact that most families did care for most of their unfortunate members most of the time. It was the enduring reality of a continent whose patterns of structural poverty were quite sufficiently entrenched to survive a brief period of foreign rule.

12

Leprosy

Leprosy deserves separate discussion for two reasons. First, although not all those afflicted by it were poor, many were. They provide valuable evidence of the nature of poverty in Africa, and their care was a special concern to Africans and Europeans. Second, the treatment of leprosy passed through phases which paralleled approaches to poverty in Africa generally and enable these to be seen more clearly: a diversity of pre-colonial attitudes; neglect or ruthlessness in the early colonial period; generous but ideologically coloured concern between the wars; scientific optimism in the late colonial period; and divergent trends following Independence. Leprosy brings into high relief the scale and tenacity of African poverty, the dedication of those relieving it, and the courage of its victims.

Leprosy is caused by a micro-organism which chiefly affects the skin, eyes, certain peripheral nerves, and the mucous membranes of the nose and throat.[1] It can be transmitted from one person to another, although the means of transmission are unclear. It is not hereditary, but natural resistance may be in part hereditary; this, together with shared environment and opportunities for infection, explains why leprosy seems often to 'run in families'. Natural resistance is high in most adults, so that leprosy is less infectious than many diseases, but a minority of people are susceptible, especially in childhood. The strength of an individual patient's resistance probably determines whether he suffers active lepromatous leprosy, which is infectious, or tuberculoid leprosy, which is not infectious and is the more common in Africa. Leprosy generally develops slowly in the body. Although most infection probably occurs in children, the disease often first becomes apparent in adolescents or young adults. Many deformities attributed to it are not caused by the disease itself but result from ulcers and injuries which the patient suffers because parts of his body cannot feel pain. Leprosy is rarely fatal in itself but weakens resistance to other diseases. It is often self-arresting.

Although leprosy sufferers were most visible when they congregated in towns, the disease was most common in the countryside, especially in remote and backward areas. In this it typified the causes of African poverty. Since such remote areas were often relatively egalitarian and unlikely to see much poverty as a result of lack of access to resources, leprosy was a major cause of poverty in such regions, as has been seen in Igboland.[2] Although the connection is obscure, the disease was especially prevalent in hot and humid areas.[3] Infant malnutrition may also have increased susceptibility.[4] Broadly speaking, leprosy was most prevalent but also least virulent in Africa's equatorial regions. In higher latitudes it was generally less common, but a larger proportion of cases were lepromatous. The highest recorded prevalence is in north-eastern Zaïre. The highest national prevalence is in the Central African Republic.[5] Away from the Congo forest, severely affected regions in the early colonial period included Igboland and its environs, the riverain and lakeshore areas of Northern Rhodesia, the Nile–Congo watershed between the Belgian Congo and Sudan, most regions bordering Lake Victoria, southern Tanganyika, and southern Nyasaland. Up to 10 per cent of the population could be infected in the worst localities.[6]

The extent to which different cultures – and different individuals within them – have stigmatised leprosy and isolated its sufferers has varied greatly and is difficult to explain. Christian Ethiopia's ambivalence[7] was paralleled in Islamic societies. In the nineteenth century leprosy sufferers were excluded from Kukawa, the capital of Bornu, but occupied a separate quarter in Kano, where, however, an early nineteenth-century visitor described the ostracising of an advanced case. Later accounts of Hausaland confirm that attitudes varied with stages of the disease.[8] Some peoples were more tolerant. In southern Sudan, where leprosy was very common, surveys during the 1930s showed that even the most infectious cases mixed freely with other people. Such attitudes often followed from the belief that leprosy was not infectious. A survey in the Kigezi district of Uganda in 1950 showed that only 4 per cent of sufferers lived alone.[9] In other areas, as in parts of northern Ghana, much tolerance went together with elaborate precautions for the burial of leprosy victims.[10] The next point on the spectrum was where sufferers moved among the community but were subject to precise restrictions, as among the Thonga of Mozambique, where they 'live in the village with other people and even attend beer-parties, but they bring their own mugs, whilst every other guest receives a drinking utensil from the master of the village'.[11] Special regulations might govern marriage and offspring. Strangers were often treated more harshly than kinsmen,[12] or treatment might be matched to social status as well as severity of symptoms. This was the case in Igboland and southern Nyasaland, two areas lacking large-scale political organisation and the machinery for consistent segregation.[13] Only in certain African states did anything approaching segregation take place. In Asante, for example, some leprosy sufferers were apparently rusticated to the remote but holy area of Lake Bosumtwi, where twentieth-century surveys showed unusually high prevalence.[14] Kazembe's kingdom on the

Luapula strictly isolated advanced cases.[15] The two most ruthless segregation policies were practised in Buganda and Yorubaland. Ganda – who had a horror of mutilation – feared and ostracised leprosy sufferers, treated them harshly, and had at least one large leprosy settlement on an island in Lake Wamara. 'Where there is a leper present', said the proverb, 'one does not speak in proverbs.' Colonial surveys showed less leprosy in Buganda than in most other parts of Uganda.[16] Yorubaland was also relatively free of leprosy, despite proximity and environmental similarities to Igboland, where the disease was so common. Yoruba commonly expelled leprosy sufferers from their towns.[17]

Modern understanding of leprosy dates from 1874, when the Norwegian scientist Hansen first described the micro-organism. Earlier doctors had known little about the causes or treatment of the disease. In 1862 a commission of the Royal College of Physicians of London had declared it hereditary.[18] Two years earlier Livingstone had ascribed the Lozi king Sekeletu's leprosy to 'mental anxiety' and treated it first with a poultice of cow dung and then with combinations of sulphate of zinc, rhubarb, soda, quinine, calomel, morphia, tartar emetic, nitrate of silver, and ginger.[19] Following Hansen's discovery, however, most European doctors concluded that leprosy was infectious and that, since it was also incurable, patients must be isolated. Isolation was thought to have eradicated leprosy from Western Europe and to be destroying a surviving focus in Norway.

The first European authorities in Africa to adopt a consistent segregation policy were in South Africa. A degree of isolation had been practised there since the eighteenth century, but universal and compulsory segregation was introduced into the Cape Colony only in 1892. The other South African colonies followed after the Anglo-Boer War. For a generation patients were gradually collected from the African rural areas where they were most numerous. Compulsory segregation met strenuous resistance from kinsmen and neighbours who regarded it as a living death. They had reason. Until the First World War all patients (including tuberculoid cases who were not actually infectious) were confined for life.[20] The hastily erected leprosaria were dreadful. The most important was Emjanyana in the Transkei, which housed 255 patients in 1898. Guarded by twenty men of the Cape Mounted Rifles, it saw repeated attempts to escape. Following one, 'all the rooms were carefully searched and a number of sticks, stones, specially sharpened knives and portions of sharpened iron, were found secreted amongst the bedding and clothing in a number of the rooms. The ringleaders, six in number . . . were then and there arrested and conveyed under escort to the Engcobo Gaol, from whence they were removed a few days afterwards to Robben Island.'[21] Emjanyana's death-rate at that time was 20 per cent a year. It was totally segregated by sex, there was no doctor, and the Superintendent reported ten years later that no drug he used had any effect. It is not surprising that only the threat of Robben Island prevented mass escapes. In

1903 the Superintendent of the Pretoria Leper Asylum, also with an annual 20 per cent death-rate, 'asked for barbed wire fences, ten feet high, well laced, and with the top wires projecting inwards', lest 'the natives again prove troublesome'. The wire was still there in 1920, hung with warning bells and crowned by four watchtowers.[22]

Yet the system seemed to work. In 1920 there were 2,248 segregated leprosy patients in South Africa and the known incidence in the total population had fallen by 11 per cent during the previous eight years.[23] Apart from the United States and Norway, South Africa was probably the only country in the world which had both endemic leprosy and the money to segregate all known victims; in the early 1920s the government was spending almost as much on leprosy as on all other human diseases. Unlike the United States and Norway, moreover, South Africa appeared to have no hope of eradicating leprosy at that time except by incarceration. Here too, as so often, its rulers were prepared to impose their logic at whatever human cost.[24] Whether the apparent decline of leprosy was actually due to segregation is uncertain. Effective segregation is extremely difficult because early and infectious cases often show no visible symptoms. Modern opinion is more inclined to attribute the decline of leprosy to the spread of tuberculosis, a related disease which is propagated especially in towns and appears to give immunity to tuberculoid leprosy. There is evidence in modern Africa that leprosy is least prevalent where rates of urbanisation and tuberculosis are highest.[25] Both urbanisation and the spread of tuberculosis were rapid in South Africa during the first half of the twentieth century,[26] which may explain a decline of leprosy. On the other hand, such a decline need not have a single cause. Recent research has confirmed that isolation helped to reduce high levels of prevalence in nineteenth-century Norway.[27] It may have been one factor in South Africa.

By contrast, the ineffectiveness of isolation where funds and ruthlessness were lacking was demonstrated in Basutoland, the only colony to imitate South African practice before the First World War. In 1913 the Basutoland National Council made segregation of leprosy patients compulsory. In February 1914 a government leprosy settlement was opened at Botsabelo, near Maseru, at a cost of £36,375. Within six months the chiefs had sent 657 patients, mostly advanced cases.[28] But in May 1914 there was a serious riot at Botsabelo. Behind it lay the patients' realisation that the chiefs had tricked them into the settlement by promising that they would be cured. Instead 'they found that they were in a prison and not a hospital'.[29] 'It was pathetic', a visitor reported, 'to listen to frequent repetition of the lament that the doctor neglected to give the medicine which was to cure the sufferer's disease, or that the medicine if given had failed to do what the patient had fondly hoped from it.'[30] By the end of 1914 some 245 patients had absconded. The legislation remained but was not effectively administered and Botsabelo's inmates did not regain their 1914 numbers until 1929, when the government decided that the settlement was so expensive that it must be made effective. This time segregation had more public support and success, but the prevalence of leprosy in Basutoland at Independence was anomalously high.[31]

No other colony seriously attempted universal segregation. The nearest approximation was German East Africa, where the law provided for compulsory isolation and 47 authorised leprosy settlements existed in 1912, containing nearly 4,000 patients and often as many healthy relatives. These were only a small proportion of leprosy sufferers, however, and the authorities recognised that they could neither cure the patients nor in practice hold them against their will.[32] Other German colonies also had government leprosaria. Senegal's leprosy decree of 1907 outlined a similar policy, but it was apparently not implemented seriously. Segregation was theoretically compulsory in British Somaliland, but not in practice. Native Commissioners in Southern Rhodesia were instructed to isolate sufferers close to their homes, but without compulsion.[33]

Early in the twentieth century British officials adopted a vigorous policy in Igboland, where the problem was so acute. At Ugboko in 1904, for example,

> The king called a meeting of the town to give them the new laws from the Government and tonight a boy has been going all round the town calling out loudly that those who were lepers were to be taken away. They have been told to clear ground behind the town and the lepers have to live by themselves there. But there are very few even amongst the Christians who confess there are lepers here.[34]

Three years later a missionary in another Igbo area described how 'the policemen take by assault, one by one, each dwelling occupied by lepers', meeting much resistance:

> All ages and castes are jumbled together: the child is beside the old man, the poor accompany the rich. There they are, gathered together in disorder with all their belongings on their heads, that is to say two or three calabashes topped with a few maize cobs and yams.
>
> The blast of a whistle and the lugubrious column sets off, before a large crowd of the curious. In the distance large numbers of people crying. Mutineers attempt another act of violence. The police feel obliged to show their teeth. All the way through the town there are attempts to escape, but resistance is manifestly impossible and, once beyond the houses, the procession moves on without further faltering. The less crippled soon take the front of the column, leaving the others to space themselves out according to their strength and the condition of their feet. Those most ill, laid out on litters, are carried on the heads of their relations.

Altogether 200 of these sufferers were set down in a camp of thatched bamboo huts on the edge of the forest, 10 kilometres from their homes and too far for their relatives to carry food daily. They asked what crime they had committed.[35] Such settlements probably soon collapsed, for the policy was apparently unknown to leprosy experts in Igboland in the 1930s. There is no evidence that it extended to Yorubaland. In Northern Nigeria the British initially provided sanctuaries for advanced and needy cases whom they wished to remove from the streets. Over 1,000 were concentrated into two Native Administration camps in Bornu. Several Hausa emirates maintained similar settlements.[36]

Most other tropical African governments neglected leprosy at this time. In 1918 all government hospitals in Nyasaland together had one leprosy in-patient and two out-patients.[37] Care was left to missionaries. It was Capuchin Fathers who in 1901 accepted Ras Makonnen's invitation to found Ethiopia's first leprosarium outside the walls of Harar. It was Sisters of Cluny who cared for Zanzibar's advanced leprosy patients at Walezo. It was the London Missionary Society that inaugurated Northern Rhodesia's first leprosy settlement at Kawimbe in 1893.[38] Given the lack of a cure, however, all these settlements were no more than sanctuaries for a tiny minority of sufferers.

At the end of the First World War European doctors came to believe that they could cure leprosy with derivatives of the oil of hydnocarpus trees. This substance, known as chaulmoogra, had been used against leprosy in India for 2,500 years; its adoption by European doctors in 1853 was an early use of indigenous remedies. Hydnocarpus was used without success in nineteenth-century South Africa and was the source of hope and disillusionment at Botsabelo, but at that time it was administered orally and was nauseating. Injections were tried in 1894 but were too painful.[39] The breakthrough was the discovery between 1910 and 1920 of less painful methods of injection. This was the joint work of American doctors and a British physician working in India, Sir Leonard Rogers. In 1923 Rogers and others founded the British Empire Leprosy Relief Association (BELRA) to publicise 'the hopefulness of the latest treatments'.[40]

Once the hope of curing leprosy existed, the strategy of treatment changed to a pattern which doctors in India had advocated for decades.[41] Hydnocarpus was thought most effective against early cases; indeed, Rogers asserted in 1925 that nearly every early case could be cured within a few months. The essential, therefore, was to attract early cases. They were probably unknown to chiefs or neighbours and would not be attracted but only deterred by compulsory segregation, which was anyway impracticable in most of Africa and necessary only for a minority of active lepromatous cases. The new strategy, therefore, was to abolish compulsion and rely instead on the hope of cure.[42] To understand how this worked in practice, one must grasp the importance of hope to both leprosy patients and doctors.

Hydnocarpus had its chief impact in tropical Africa, especially Nigeria. There the breakthrough took place at Itu, a Church of Scotland mission hospital inland of Calabar. In 1926 Dr A. B. Macdonald began to inject hydnocarpus into leprosy patients there. As always in Africa, real help attracted unexpected numbers. Within six months Macdonald had 400 leprosy patients. A settlement took shape in the forest.[43] Organised by dedicated missionaries as a largely self-contained community, supported financially by government and native administration, chiefly run by the patients themselves, and centring on regular hydnocarpus injections, Itu became the model for leprosy settlements throughout Africa. It was first imitated elsewhere in Eastern Nigeria and then in the north, where mission settlements replaced refuges for advanced cases during the late 1930s. By 1938 there were some 7,000 leprosy patients in Nigerian settlements.[44] But with a logic repeated many times in Africa, the operation revealed vastly more sufferers than expected. In 1924–5 Nigeria had reported 32,000; its estimate in 1936 was 200,000.[45]

Macdonald's experience at Itu was paralleled by Dr F. H. Cooke at Ho in British Togoland, where hydnocarpus injections also attracted so many patients that a settlement was needed to house them. It became the Gold Coast's major leprosarium. Elsewhere in British West Africa lack of funds prevented action before the Second World War.[46] In eastern Africa BELRA prompted missionaries in Nyasaland to begin using hydnocarpus in 1924 and to seek government aid to open leprosaria. By 1931 these contained 560 patients.[47] In Uganda the Church Missionary Society established two settlements (one for children) in 1930, soon followed by two run by Roman Catholic sisters. Tanganyika moved more slowly, abolishing its theoretically compulsory segregation in 1930, adopting hydnocarpus, and encouraging greater missionary involvement, but otherwise advancing rather little from the German refuges for advanced cases until a settlement modelled on Itu was established at Makete, near Tukuyu, during the Second World War.[48] Zanzibar abolished compulsory segregation in 1936 and established a voluntary treatment centre in Pemba, while arrested and handicapped cases continued to find sanctuary at Walezo. Northern Rhodesia, by contrast, took little notice of the new approach and had no more than 250 leprosy patients in institutions in 1939. Kenya moved even more slowly, for as late as 1950 only some 350 cases were under active treatment of the more than 35,000 estimated to exist.[49] The most spectacular institutional development of the period took place in south-western Sudan, one of the continent's main foci of leprosy. Between 1928 and 1930 over 5,000 leprosy sufferers were concentrated into three huge camps. They were treated with hydnocarpus and large numbers – some 40 per cent by 1935 – were discharged as arrested. These settlements were compulsory government institutions (although many inmates came voluntarily), contained many healthy relatives, and were an amalgam of the old and new methods of treatment.[50]

Even in southern Africa hydnocarpus injections led to a reconsideration of policy. After opening a voluntary leprosarium in 1905, Southern Rhodesia enacted compulsory segregation in 1919 but abolished it again in the early 1930s, under BELRA's influence, and the government leprosarium at

Ngomahuru became a model settlement of the new type. Its Superintendent, Dr Moiser, was Africa's most enthusiastic advocate of hydnocarpus. By 1939 he had discharged 54 per cent of Ngomahuru's patients as arrested cases.[51] South Africa, by contrast, did not abandon segregation but adopted hydnocarpus and discharged arrested cases. Hope of cure transformed morale, prison-like conditions were relaxed, and patients began to volunteer for treatment, so that between 1923 and 1949 the average duration of the disease prior to admission fell from ten to two years. Patients at Emjanyana insisted that hydnocarpus treatment be compulsory.[52] 'Their one desire', the Superintendent reported in 1931,

> is to become healed so that they may return home to their people. They firmly believe in the efficacy of treatment. At one time the suggestion was put to them that certain patients would be returned to their homes where special huts would be built for them, and they would live under a modified form of home segregation. They were enthusiastic about the idea until one man asked where they would get their treatment. When it was explained to them that the District Surgeons would not be able to give them their injections, they turned the whole idea down. They want to be healed and then sent home.[53]

Despite the influx of early cases, the total number of patients in South African leprosy institutions long remained stable. In 1918 it was 2,374; in 1938, 2,265.[54]

Hydnocarpus injections, like community development, were an Anglo-Saxon innovation which convinced even Francophones. By 1924 Albert Schweitzer at Lambaréné was aware that they were the treatment of choice. Systematic treatment began in French West Africa in 1934 with the opening of the Central Leprosy Institution at Bamako, which organized treatment centres in other colonies. By 1936 Senegal had five such settlements, all using hydnocarpus with encouraging results. French Cameroun, with major leprosy concentrations in the south, had 25 settlements with 4,477 inmates in 1936. As everywhere, the search for sufferers revealed daunting numbers. Known cases in French West Africa rose between 1933 and 1937 from 12,924 to 41,045.[55] In the Belgian Congo the Itu model became official policy in 1938. Two years later Roman Catholic missions alone had 120 leprosaria treating 11,111 patients in Belgian Africa.[56]

A great leprosarium was a complex institution. The patients were not uniform. In 1938 Uzuakoli, in the Owerri Province of Igboland, admitted six categories: those needing hospitalisation; educated people who could be trained to treat others; the destitute and infirm; those most infectious; children; and a number, equal to all the others, of able-bodied patients to do the work.[57] Many leprosaria also contained healthy relatives, especially infants, for although this was anathema to specialists, others held that to exclude relatives deterred early cases from seeking treatment and that infants separated from infected mothers generally died. Leprosaria varied greatly. Some were sanctuaries for advanced cases and ranged from the relaxed village atmosphere of Walezo to the depressing Native Authority settlements of Northern Nigeria. By contrast, the most vigorous institutions were large treatment settlements like Itu, where 'the patients are kept occupied mentally or physically from morning to night'.[58] Apart from growing its own food, Itu had palm-oil plantations, made soap and lemon-grass oil, did most of its own building, paid its patients piece-rates for agricultural and industrial work, required adults to attend literacy classes, ran football teams and a brass band, had huge church congregations, and graced its premises with an equestrian statue of Edward VIII in cement. Itu had an elected chief, a court, several policemen, and a flourishing market, apart from its medical facilities.[59]

For many leprosy patients the worst moment was the first realisation of their condition, generally in adolescence or early adulthood. 'I was a leper', one recalled. 'I shall never forget the misery, when I first saw the marks on my body.'[60] 'Sometimes patients were so terrified', a doctor wrote, 'that they hid themselves until signs of advancing disease made their appearance . . . With little to show in the way of physical signs, they found it difficult to believe that the disease was really leprosy, and some patients refused to believe it for weeks or months.'[61] Initial self-hatred gave way gradually to a more or less embittered resignation. In Ethiopia a psychiatrist observed that while most other patients dramatised their illnesses, those with leprosy did not: 'When the leprosy patients were relating their desperate stories in a calm and matter-of-fact voice the tears were often silently running down their cheeks.'[62] The road to the leprosarium could be cruel:

> There was an occasion when I saw a patient sitting a mile outside the settlement with his head bowed and covered with a filthy cloth. Flies were swarming round his head and feet. I spoke to him several times, but he did not move. He remained there all day, and did not move until darkness fell. The next morning he was in the settlement, but in the same attitude . . . He had been shut out by the world, and he was now for his own peace shutting the world out of his life. It took two weeks to get him to talk at all.[63]

Arrival at the leprosarium confronted early cases with the spectacle, in the advanced patients, of what might happen to themselves. To avoid this, several institutions segregated advanced cases into a special camp. 'The psychological effect on the early cases is wonderful', one superintendent wrote.[64] Some patients despaired utterly. 'I was not surprised by their deformities and sores', a nurse remembered of Likwenu in Nyasaland, 'but I was appalled by their apparent dejection and indifference . . . They called themselves The Dead.'[65] A large leprosy institution, even if voluntary, could be difficult to control, especially if patients refused routine work. A proportion were often uncooperative and even violent.[66] Yet others adapted with remarkable flexibility. One common trait was alternation between exaltation and depression, which helped to explain the eagerness with which patients clutched at any new hope of cure and the sullenness with which they abandoned it at each new disappointment.[67] That hydnocarpus evoked feverish hopes was fortunate, because it was often extremely painful. 'We rammed – I fear that is the only word that describes the treatment – we rammed in the oleaginous product of the hydnocarpus wightiana', a nurse remembered, 'causing in some cases more pain and destruction than the lepra bacilli.'[68]

To work in such institutions required a self-abnegation which justly made leprosy workers the humanitarian heroes of their time. W. A. Lambert, who spent sixteen years as a lay worker in several leprosaria, had been a Sunday School teacher, scoutmaster, and wartime medical dresser. 'My first intimation of the need for help for these afflicted people', he recalled, 'came through a broadcast to Toc H and I was so touched and shaken by the appeal that I had no respite until I had determined to take steps toward offering my services. Worldly advancement no longer had any weight.' Itu immediately evoked his sympathy:

> It was very saddening to us to see strapping lads smitten with this terrible disease, and dwelling among the maimed and disfigured. After witnessing such affliction, borne with almost incredible patience and stoicism, whatever of qualms or regrets slumbered in the sub-conscious, were for ever eliminated. Nothing remained but a great compassion, and the growing urge to dedicate oneself to such an afflicted people.[69]

Others restrained the same emotion behind a nurse's training or a coif.[70] At least two missionaries, Father Honoré in Nyasaland and Brother Josué Delcas of southern Sudan, died of leprosy during the 1930s, while in 1948 the Society of African Missions opened a leprosarium at its European headquarters, chiefly for its own staff.[71] Other workers absorbed themselves in the intellectually fascinating problem of defeating the most tenacious of human diseases. Graham Greene's fictional doctor spoke for them: 'I don't want leprosy loved. I want it eliminated.'[72]

Yet the chief burden of caring for leprosy patients did not fall on doctors or missionaries. It fell in part on their African assistants, the dressers and dispensers of whom little is known save the occasional name: Cosmo Mango, chief dispenser at the huge settlement at Peramiho in southern Tanganyika, with 1,556 leprosy patients in 1938; Elizabeth Tolo, Christian matron of the Emjanyana settlement to which she had herself been admitted as a patient in 1898; Harcourt Whyte, the Igbo choirmaster who inspired Uzuakoli for more than a generation.[73] Among Africans, as among Europeans, leprosy attracted self-sacrificing care. Early in the twentieth century John Alegbeleye, a former slave skilled in herbal remedies, sought out sufferers in the Benin region and attempted to heal them. Sixty years later a Yoruba, John Lakin, was so moved by a visit to Abeokuta leprosarium that he returned to care for its inmates and transformed it into a progressive and prosperous settlement.[74] Yet the chief burden of caring for leprosy patients fell on other patients. Many were trained to give hydnocarpus injections, while others inevitably did much routine nursing. Like any stigmatised minority, inmates found support among their own kind. Tribe had little significance for them. A macabre camaraderie was common.[75]

Logically, leprosy sufferers figured among the very poor chiefly when they were not in leprosaria. 'Often enough' in Igboland 'lepers are discharged with every possibility of their diseases remaining stationary, only to find that the people at home will not accept them and they have to live on the borderline of starvation with only one result.' Missionaries in South Africa founded a special colony for them. Elsewhere they often entered refuges like Walezo or asked to be readmitted to leprosaria. Some formed small independent settlements.[76] As leprosy treatment improved, so the number of destitute former patients increased. Yet more sufferers never entered a settlement at all. Many deliberately avoided them. Others could not gain admission. Impoverished Itu required an entry fee of £3, which 'excludes the poorer type of patient'.[77] This was unusual, but the better mission leprosaria turned away many applicants for lack of facilities or money, while the cost of institutionalising more than a small fraction of cases was prohibitive. In the late 1930s Uzuakoli treated less than 2 per cent of the sufferers in its province.[78] Some small colonies, such as Burundi, had no leprosy institutions until the 1950s. In such remote areas as the eastern Congo it was still possible during the 1930s to stumble on forest settlements of advanced leprosy cases driven from their villages to die.[79]

Expense was one reason why the authorities in Eastern Nigeria devised a new strategy during the later 1930s. Another reason was their belief that leprosy was rapidly increasing, even reaching epidemic proportions, when isolated peoples without immunity were suddenly incorporated into the larger world. The immediate impetus came from the Igbo practice of segregating leprosy sufferers in distinct villages, where conditions were often 'appallingly bad', especially for the incapacitated. In 1935 the superintendent of Uzuakoli decided to encourage the formation of leprosy villages as satellites of his leprosarium to receive treatment from dispensaries served by former patients trained to give hydnocarpus injections. A year later this became the centrepoint of Nigeria's anti-leprosy strategy.[80] In practice it worked only in the east, for only there was there local support for segregation villages. There, however, it was immensely successful. Owerri Province alone had 43 out-patient clinics with over 11,000 weekly attenders in 1943.[81] 'The early days of a clinic', the scheme's director reported,

> witness many distressing scenes which would be a revelation to anyone unfamiliar with the situation. On the appointed morning a motley crowd of lepers gathers at the site, unkempt, hopeless, penniless and in rags; many have dragged themselves along with the aid of sticks, their untreated sores an eloquent testimony to their neglected condition. There is little noise, most of the patients exhibiting that apathy common to Ibo lepers, the result of the

> contempt and ostracism with which they are regarded. Nigeria's 'untouchables' are revealed in all their misery.[82]

Only rarely, he stressed, did out-patient treatment arrest leprosy; the point was to check its spread by encouraging segregation and attracting early cases, using hydnocarpus injections as the bait. '*The object of our work is not leprosy treatment, but leprosy control*.'[83]

In 1945 out-patient work passed to a Government Leprosy Service and became the new model of mass treatment, much like Itu twenty years earlier. By the early 1950s experts believed that they had contained and even reversed the spread of leprosy in Igboland. Surveys in the village area of Ndi Oji Abam showed the prevalence rate of active cases to have fallen between 1947 and 1955 from 7.6 to 1.7 per cent, following the opening of a clinic and isolation village. The decline had been especially marked among children. There was no evidence that tuberculosis had replaced leprosy.[84]

Yet by the 1950s it was also widely realised that if leprosy had declined in Eastern Nigeria, this was not due to hydnocarpus. Some workers had never believed that it had any effect on leprosy. Others had been enthusiastic.[85] Energetic advocacy by Rogers and his disciples ensured that the International Leprosy Congress of 1938 recognised hydnocarpus as the best drug available, but American scientists were especially sceptical. There is some scientific evidence that hydnocarpus had beneficial effects, but modern opinion generally holds that they were slight or negligible.[86] Rather, hydnocarpus was an enormous, unintentional, and brilliantly successful confidence trick. Leprosy is usually self-arresting. The point of arrest depends largely on the body's resistance. Many cases treated with hydnocarpus were arrested naturally. Others entered a leprosarium, enjoyed better nutrition, were treated for parasitic and other complaints, and regained hope, thereby improving their resistance. As hydnocarpus injections attracted an increasing proportion of early cases, so the proportion arrested increased. And as the number of active cases institutionalised increased, so their chance of infecting the healthy declined. Hydnocarpus was, literally, a *confidence* trick.

The notion that leprosy was a disease of social change matched interwar ideas of social pathology. The technocratic bias of development and welfare policies in the 1940s and 1950s had a similar counterpart in a new leprosy treatment. The remedies were sulphone drugs, synthetics devised before the First World War, tested on tuberculosis, and applied to leprosy in 1941 by Faget and other American physicians.[87] Some European experts, notably Rogers, found this American innovation difficult to accept,[88] but most leprosy workers quickly recognised that in the commonly used form, dapsone, the sulphones had three great advantages. They were cheap. They could be administered as tablets. And they worked, although they suppressed leprosy rather than curing it.[89] Treatment at last became primarily a medical rather than a charitable enterprise.

It took two decades for dapsone to replace hydnocarpus in Africa's hundreds of leprosaria and clinics. Experiments began at Uzuakoli in 1946 and in South Africa in 1947, but Zanzibar did not use sulphones until 1951. A year later only one patient in six treated in French West Africa received sulphones, while a few remote mission settlements still used some hydnocarpus during the 1960s.[90] Relieved from the pain of repeated injections and once more promised cure, patients again flocked for treatment:

> The miasma of death began to depart as the contagious patients with their hideous nodules showed dramatic improvement. The news of cures spread far and wide. Those who had sat without hope in the village arrived, many former sufferers who had long ago run away now returned. Although not all responded to the tablets, we had at last a weapon with which to fight the scourge.[91]

Most leprosy institutions experienced rapid expansion. Albert Schweitzer spent his Nobel Peace Prize of 1952 on a leprosarium at Lambaréné to handle the influx. Patients at Yalisombo leprosarium near Stanleyville increased from 118 to 1,025 in two years.[92] Soon, however, the numbers again declined as arrested cases were discharged. New admissions to leprosaria in Southern Rhodesia peaked in the late 1950s, but the number of inmates was already declining and Ngomahuru closed in 1971. In Zanzibar discharges exceeded admissions for the first time in 1956. Patients in South African leprosy institutions declined from 2,398 in 1944 to 1,115 in 1968 and only 111 in 1980, although the last figure excluded the Transkei.[93] South Africa continued to institutionalise active cases, but elsewhere dapsone in tablet form encouraged out-patient treatment, which was cheaper and was already becoming fashionable because of its success in Igboland. A mass campaign in Northern Nigeria during the 1950s gradually deemphasised segregation in favour of dapsone tablets distributed by African dispensers at nearly a thousand clinics. Each territory in eastern Africa organised a similar campaign. A programme launched in French Equatorial Africa in 1954 integrated dapsone with the French technique of mass examination by mobile teams, producing one of the most successful anti-leprosy campaigns ever seen.[94] By 1962 one distinguished leprologist was alarmed at the emphasis on 'pills and land rovers'.[95] Yet political independence only accelerated the trend. The most influential project was launched in southern Malawi in 1965 to eradicate leprosy by mobile out-patient treatment with dapsone. It was later extended to the rest of Malawi and imitated in Zambia and Sierra Leone.[96] Several schemes in Tanzania were coordinated into a national programme in 1977. Liberia launched a National Leprosy Control Programme in 1975, Mozambique in 1982. The Mozambique scheme and a similar operation in Sudan were integrated into the general rural health service.[97]

As dispensers and mobile units penetrated the countryside, so they discovered that the need was vastly greater than expected. In 1908 Nyasaland was officially estimated to have 769 leprosy sufferers; in 1921, 2,100; in 1927, 5,000–6,000; in 1950, 30,000; in 1965, 80,000.[98] Yet experts remained convinced that leprosy was being defeated and that total eradication was possible. Powerful evidence supported them. In 1948 Owerri Province had 32,000 leprosy cases; in 1957, 15,000. Surveys in the Gambia suggested that prevalence declined between 1947 and 1977–8 from 2.5 per cent to 0.6 per cent, with an even more rapid decline among children. In 1966 Upper Volta had a prevalence of 3.5 per cent; a survey in 1976 showed only 0.5 per cent.[99]

Where hostility to advanced cases remained strong, traditional leprosaria, with both active and arrested cases, still functioned during the 1980s. More often, the new treatment left behind increasing numbers of disabled former patients needing care. 'A determined effort' in Southern Rhodesia in 1960 '... to clear out non-infectious patients from the Mtemwa Leper Settlement' had to be abandoned because many had nowhere else to go. At some leprosaria, including Itu, arrested but disabled cases became so large a proportion of the declining population that self-sufficiency collapsed. One solution was to convert redundant leprosaria into sanctuaries for 'welfare cases', usually supported by missions, native authorities, or voluntary organisations. In the early 1970s over 80 per cent of patients in Sudanese leprosy colonies were severely disabled.[100] With time, care often lapsed and sanctuaries decayed into pockets of destitution:

> Most of the patients could not count upon the help of their families. They had either lost contact with them, or had married another leprosy patient with problems similar to their own; 70% had remained in the settlements near the institution after discharge. The fear of rejection was advanced by one-third (32%) as a reason for not returning. Of those who did go home 27% soon returned to the settlement because they had been repudiated by their families or communities...
>
> Severe disabilities, lack of support from able family members, and poor land were important factors in the economic stress of patients. 66% had *no* money, poultry, or livestock, and not enough to eat ... Despite their severe deformities most of the patients wanted to, and did in fact, contribute to the support of their households. Only 27% said that they could do nothing but beg. 62% of the severely disabled farmed occasionally, 40% cut wood, 39% cooked, and 15% reported that they carried heavy loads...
>
> The patients had, in general, low levels of skill. Only 8% had ever been employed in jobs other than farming; 86% had received no formal education, and 70% spoke only their tribal language.[101]

Some leprosy sufferers were among the poorest people of post-colonial Africa.

These consequences of sulphone treatment showed especially clearly against the background of Ethiopian tradition. Modern leprosy treatment there fell to missionary societies until 1954, when the state began to take charge, shifting the emphasis from charity to healing and from institutions to out-patient treatment. Dapsone was made available at markets as well as mobile clinics, while health workers on mules carried drugs each month to remote areas. In 1974 some 48,352 patients were under treatment, but estimates of sufferers had also risen from 9,000 in 1950 to 80,000 in 1964 and 180,000 in 1975.[102] Expanded treatment and the closure of many leprosaria left numerous handicapped people bereft of care. They often joined the leprosy communities and 'villages of the poor' which formed near towns, places of pilgrimage, or leprosaria where treatment was still obtainable. In the mid 1970s perhaps one-quarter of those in Hararghe Province who knew themselves to be infected were living in such communities, varying in size from fewer than 10 people to 1,116. Not all their inmates were economically poor. Some ran successful businesses, sent money to the countryside, and had normal families. But about one-half were extremely poor, especially among the older and more disabled whose sole means of survival was begging. They shared a remarkable faith in dapsone. Three-quarters of those interviewed in the 1970s said that they had used it as their first treatment, knowing that nothing else worked.[103]

In 1975 Pearson and others reported numerous cases of resistance to dapsone in lepromatous patients.[104]

During the 1970s, as Africa's eager hopes of Independence waned, leprosy experts also began to doubt their ability to control and eradicate the disease. They still did not know how it was transmitted. They were coming to think that it was more infectious in more cases than earlier specialists had believed. They discovered that in endemic areas the micro-organism was present in far more people than displayed clinical symptoms. They found evidence of infection in several animals, which could make eradication more difficult.[105] Above all, resistance to dapsone threatened the whole technique of out-patient treatment. By the mid 1980s resistance had been found everywhere it had been sought. It was estimated in 1983 that 10 per cent of the world's lepromatous patients were already resistant and another one per cent were becoming so each year.[106]

Standard response to drug resistance was to use several drugs simultaneously. This became recommended policy as soon as dapsone resistance appeared. New and more active drugs were discovered, especially rifampicin. But this raised other problems. Even with dapsone it was difficult to ensure that out-patients took drugs regularly; in southern Malawi only about half of the recommended dapsone was taken. A multi-drug programme would be not only somewhat more expensive but much more difficult to administer, possibly beyond the capacity of medical assistants.[107] In the early 1980s few countries used multi-drug treatment regularly. They were often delighted by the results, but a further problem was appearing. By 1985 leprosy patients were showing resistance to the other drugs, including rifampicin.[108]

Meanwhile, even if Africa's rapid urbanisation may have been acting against leprosy, its economic and political difficulties hindered treatment. The departure of staff at Independence dislocated some programmes. The Congo crisis of 1960–5, the Sudanese Civil War, and especially the Nigerian Civil War (in which Uzuakoli was extensively damaged) harmed treatment systems in especially endemic areas. By the late 1970s drugs were seriously scarce in several regions. Francophone Africa's mobile units lost effectiveness owing to economic decline.[109]

As problems grew, so did evidence that leprosy was becoming more common in certain areas. In 1982 there were an estimated 10,000,000 cases in the world. The number had changed little during the previous twenty years because population growth balanced more effective treatment. Africa, with perhaps 3,500,000 cases, had the highest prevalence and the lowest proportion of cases under treatment.[110] Local studies revealed high levels of prevalence in areas hitherto thought largely unaffected. Other studies showed numbers of previously undiagnosed cases among the young.[111]

Amidst this gloom, however, leprosy workers also had reason for hope. In 1971 Kirchheimer and Storrs at last succeeded in infecting an animal, the armadillo,[112] thereby facilitating experimentation and opening the possibility of preparing a vaccine which, it was hoped, might eventually eradicate leprosy. The World Health Organisation expected trials to show the first results during the early 1990s.[113] Leprosy had once more demonstrated its tenacity. Human ingenuity had once more rekindled hope. In this, as in other respects, the disease epitomised independent Africa's larger problem of poverty.

13

The growth of poverty in independent Africa

Those fighting poverty in tropical Africa during the 1980s shared the mixed disillusionment and hope of leprosy workers. The bad news was that after relative prosperity during the 1960s, Africa suffered economic crisis during the later 1970s and its very poor people increased in number. As in the colonial period, structural poverty changed less than conjunctural poverty. The incapacitated, the aged, unsupported women, and the young were still the bulk of the structural poor. They were supplemented by the new poor of the twentieth century – inhabitants of neglected regions, the unemployed, and especially the ill paid – and by growing numbers who, although able-bodied, were barred from resources by the competition of a growing population or by a more ruthless use of power and wealth. Yet structural poverty remained a cumulative phenomenon and only a minority of the African poor were yet landless, in contrast to their Asian or Latin American counterparts. Conjunctural poverty, by contrast, showed more discontinuity with the colonial period, especially in the return of mass famine mortality after nearly half a century. This in turn brought important changes in the care of the poor.

The good news was of two kinds. On the one hand, the crises of the 1970s and 1980s showed that the poor had lost little of their resilience and capacity for survival. On the other hand, awareness of African poverty grew rapidly at that time. It was realised at last that the poor were mainly rural. It was realised, too, that earlier public policies had contributed to poverty. This awareness opened the possibility of action, but on the whole, in the mid 1980s, the bad news still outweighed the good.

In post-colonial Africa the structural poor changed less than the methods of studying them. The first global estimates of poverty, measured against arbitrary Poverty Datum Lines, rested on such factual ignorance that their detailed findings had little value. Their estimates of those living in poverty varied improbably from 25 per cent in Tanzania to 66 per cent in Sierra Leone.[1] Yet the broad profile of poverty was interesting. Of the world's fifteen poorest countries tabulated by the World Bank in 1984, eleven were in tropical Africa: Ethiopia; Tanzania and Uganda; Togo, Zaïre, and the Central African Republic; isolated and overpopulated enclaves like Burundi and Malawi; and the arid Sahelian states of Mali, Niger, and Burkina Faso – to which Chad and Mozambique might have been added had they produced statistics.[2] Poverty was generally more common in the countryside than in towns. In the extreme case of Zambia in 1980, 80 per cent of rural and 26 per cent of urban households were classed as poor. Urban–rural income differentials were at least twice as wide as in any other continent during the 1970s.[3] Perhaps most revealing was evidence that Africa had more poverty than Latin America in the late 1970s, but about the same amount (relative to population) as Asia. Setting the Poverty Datum Line at the maximum income of India's poorest 45 per cent of people, proportions below that level in 1975 ranged from 35 per cent in Nigeria to 68 per cent in Ethiopia. During the next decade Africa's relative position deteriorated.[4]

Especially disturbing was evidence that Africans were growing poorer. Between 1965 and 1984 average real Gross National Product per head fell by an estimated 0.1 per cent a year in the low-income countries of sub-Saharan Africa. It was the only major region to experience a decline. National experiences varied. Whereas Botswana's real Gross National Product per head rose by 8.4 per cent a year in that period, Ghana's fell by 1.9 per cent a year.[5] Decline was concentrated in the poorest countries, although the chief reason for the most extreme impoverishment was usually prolonged violence.

In many countries income distribution was increasingly unequal, although statistics were especially uncertain. In Zambia, for example, the share of income enjoyed by the poorest 60 per cent fell between 1959 and 1972 from 27.2 to 19.5 per cent, while the share of the poorest 20 per cent fell from 6.3 to 3.7 per cent. There were exceptions to this pattern. In Tanzania income differentials between senior civil servants or urban workers and the rural smallholders narrowed dramatically during the later 1970s, but by impoverishing townsmen rather than enriching peasants.[6] Broadly speaking, the more prosperous a country, the less equal its income distribution, especially if it produced minerals or housed non-African settlers. Even a notable reduction of poverty after Independence did not prevent Kenya from having the highest level of inequality among 36 developing countries studied in 1975.[7]

Non-economic evidence showed a more complex pattern of change. Life expectancy in sub-Saharan Africa was still only 49 years in 1984, but it had apparently increased from 42 years in 1965. The chief reason was declining mortality during the first year of life, which fell between 1965 and 1984 from 155 to 129 per thousand, although these averages concealed variations ranging in 1984 from 77 per thousand in Zimbabwe to 176 in Guinea, Mali, and Sierra Leone.[8] Urban infants generally survived best, because rural nutrition and health care were worse. In Banjul, for example, infant mortality in 1973 was only half that in the Gambian countryside.[9] Overall nutrition probably worsened, for the best of the very unreliable estimates suggested that Africa's food production per head declined by up to 10 per cent during the 1960s and up to 20 per cent during the 1970s. In all low-income African countries in the early 1980s calorie intake was estimated to be 10 per cent less than required.[10] Yet such figures obscured the real incidence of poverty. Detailed research in the Gambia showed that townspeople and rural men were adequately fed, but the calorie intake of rural women and small children was only 60–70 per cent of the norm, while that of pregnant and lactating women in one village during the rainy season was less than half the desirable level. Half the children in this village died in their first four years of life. Undernourished rural women and children formed 35–40 per cent of the Gambia's total population in the later 1970s.[11] Infant malnutrition and mortality were often worst among poor families with uneducated mothers. The very growth of education made illiteracy an important form of relative impoverishment and marginalisation.

The reasons for growing structural poverty probably lay on two planes. At the deeper level, post-colonial Africa struggled – not entirely unsuccessfully – with the demographic expansion which had begun between the wars. In the early 1980s sub-Saharan Africa's population grew at about 3 per cent a year.[12] In no other continent was the birth-rate still rising or population growth outpacing food supply. Moreover, because Africa's population was young, its growth-rates would take long to decelerate. In 1986 the World Bank projected that Nigeria's population would eventually stabilise at about 528,000,000[13] – unless it was reduced either by contraception (rarely practised by more than 10 per cent of women at risk during the 1980s) or by major famine. Most Africans still regarded population growth as desirable. Experts could show that in the twentieth century both China and India had escaped predicted Malthusian crises such as pessimists feared in Africa. Pessimists could reply that Africa's population was growing with unique suddenness and speed, within less productive and malleable agricultural systems, so that available investment could scarcely even maintain existing standards of services.[14] In the 1980s this pressure on investment was probably a more widespread cause of poverty than was pressure on land.

Growing poverty also had a second level of causation in human action. The actors were not only Africans. Although world market prices did not consistently turn against African producers until the late 1970s and could not explain the fortunes of individual countries, nevertheless one econometric study found that export prices correlated more closely than any other factor with the economic performance of sub-Saharan Africa as a whole.[15] Producers of minerals (other than oil) suffered especially. When copper prices collapsed, Zambia's per capita Gross National Product fell between 1974 and 1980 by 52 per cent – a disaster.[16] During the great depression of the early 1980s real copper prices were the lowest of the century and real commodity prices generally were lower than at any time since the Second World War.[17] Meanwhile the fivefold increase in real oil prices during the 1970s devastated transport systems. In 1980 Tanzania spent over 55 per cent of its export earnings on oil.[18] Extensive international aid kept many economies afloat but was less effective in promoting development than in other continents. The econometric study previously cited found no correlation between aid and growth rates. Black Africa's foreign debts rose between 1970 and 1979 from $5.7 billion to $31.8 billion. By 1984 it was the most heavily indebted continent relative to exports or Gross Domestic Product.[19]

Policy failures were probably even more important. The eager hopes of Independence conspired with current economic theory to direct development policy towards unbalanced growth through urban industry and infrastructure, which bred unprofitable enterprises, heavy recurrent costs, unpayable debts, and exploited villagers. Insecure regimes and parvenu rulers tried to preserve their countries and themselves by concentrating wealth and economic power into their hands. Westernised politicians reconstructed peasant agriculture on 'socialist' lines.[20] The result was to convert a respectable economic performance during the 1960s and early 1970s into a serious decline thereafter.

Even where development occurred, it often did not benefit the very poor. Capital investment did not profit those evicted by irrigation schemes in Northern Nigeria, nor the workers made redundant by capital-intensive technology in Kenya, nor the Malawian smallholders whose low producer prices financed large African estates, nor the Ethiopian or Mozambiquan peasants who subsidised unprofitable state farms.[21] 'We are tired of being developed', a village elder in Shaba declared in 1975.[22] The rural poor supported inflated bureaucracies – public consumption in Black Africa as a proportion of Gross Domestic Product rose between 1960 and 1982 from 10 to 14 per cent – while services often deteriorated.[23] Governments fearful of urban unrest deliberately held down food prices. Zambia's rural–urban terms of trade declined by 65 per cent between 1965 and 1980, which meant that rural people had to sell three times as much in order to buy a constant quantity of urban goods. Uganda's coffee growers received 15 per cent of their crop's value in 1976–7, while 66 per cent went in tax.[24] This steady drainage of cash from the countryside was the continent's most pervasive cause of poverty. As in early modern Europe,[25] national economic integration went together with a polarisation of wealth and poverty.

Amidst widespread rural impoverishment, certain individuals, groups, and regions suffered especially. The landless were the most obvious, although their condition was less common than in Asia.[26] Landlessness was most prevalent in Kenya, where only one-quarter of the country was cultivable and many inequalities of ownership survived from the colonial period. In 1976 Kenya's smallholder areas contained an estimated 190,000 landless households, of which between 60,000 and 120,000 were poor.[27] The largest numbers were in the Kikuyu region of Central Province, where in 1974 some 11.5 per cent of householders were landless and in low-income activities.[28] Yet landlessness had decreased since Independence, partly owing to redistribution of European land. In Central Province, unreliable figures suggested that the proportion of rural households which were landless (not all of them poor) fell between 1963 and 1974 from 23 to 15 per cent.[29] More numerous and widespread were smallholders with tiny holdings. In 1976, 30 per cent of all Kenyan landholdings (i.e. 508,000 holdings) were less than 0.5 hectares.[30] Yet their owners were not necessarily becoming poorer. In Central Province the proportion of smallholders below a poverty line fell between 1963 and 1974 from 49.8 to 22.4 per cent. This was because their access to high-value cash-crops and off-farm employment improved. During 1974 the average smallholder household in Central Province owned 2.67 hectares of land and earned Shs. 5,082, whereas in the more remote Western Province it owned 3.27 hectares but earned only Shs. 2,784.[31] This pattern dated from the colonial period and was found throughout tropical Africa: the rural poor were characteristically those without cash-crop or livestock sales or off-farm earnings.[32] Yet the poor were to be distinguished from the very poor, whose condition had other causes. Landlessness was one.

Outside Kenya, population pressure on limited land steadily impoverished Zimbabwe's rural population – between 1962 and 1977 maize production per capita fell by 36 per cent in the reserves – while absolute landlessness became increasingly serious among younger men.[33] Elsewhere these problems were most common in islands of special fertility and population density. Rwanda in the mid 1980s had an 'ever-growing "reserve" of landless and near-landless peasants'.[34] A village near Kampala studied in 1983 included 24 poor smallholders and 24 landless labourers among its 92 household heads. Most labourers were unmarried children of peasants too poor to bequeath them land. Some worked regularly for a richer villager; others hired themselves out for the day, sometimes earning only food. They relied heavily on *waragi*, the local firewater – '*Waragi* is my blanket', they explained.[35] This region was exceptional, however, because land was freehold property. In south-western Uganda the overpopulated Kigezi highlands displayed not landlessness but 'a fantastic degree of fragmentation, a general depletion of soils, widespread rural poverty and ragged children everywhere'.[36] Such fragmentation was much more common than landlessness. In southern Malawi, for example, landlessness was relatively rare but at least one-quarter of peasant holdings were sub-economic and a category of very poor households was emerging.[37] Ethiopia showed similar patterns. There the revolutionary land reform of 1975 ended landlessness and tenancy but not fragmentation, which had become acute in many areas during the twentieth century. In one Sidamo area of southern Ethiopia studied in 1980–1, 51 per cent of landholdings were less than 0.25 hectares.

'The destitute peasant – and quite a good portion of the peasants in our study are in this position – often has a mini-plot and a small hand tool', the researcher concluded.[38] Elsewhere, especially in the West African savanna, competition focussed on the *best* land. In four Nupe villages studied in 1976, the poorest households cultivated over half as much rain-fed land as the richest but less than one-seventh of the desirable valley-bottom land.[39]

As the Kenyan evidence showed, land shortage was a spectacular cause of rural poverty but not the most common. Africa's most destitute areas were its backwaters, remote from transport, bereft of services, unable to market crops or secure local employment, obliged to export labourers, victimised more by neglect than exploitation. In Zambia in 1980 the average annual rural income in regions close to the railway was 34 *kwacha*; in remote regions (with three-fifths of the rural population) it was 5.8 *kwacha*. In Tanzania in 1973 a new-born baby in the most remote region could expect to live little more than two-thirds as long as one born in the capital.[40] Many remote peoples were pastoralists whose welfare declined after Independence owing to drought, violence, marginalisation, and the hostility of non-pastoral rulers.[41] Others were cultivators who survived only by exporting labour. In the early 1980s two packed trains left Ouagadougou each day for southern Ivory Coast. There the real minimum wage in agriculture fell by one-third between 1960 and 1976.[42] Real wages fell 24 per cent on Ghanaian cocoa plantations between 1957–9 and 1970, 20 per cent in Malawian agriculture between 1968/9 and 1976/7, 50 per cent for Liberian rubber-tappers during the 1970s, and 80 per cent in sections of Zaïrian agriculture during the first two decades of Independence. In newly independent Zimbabwe, by contrast, the government fixed the minimum farm wage at more than double the previous average.[43]

Alongside the landless or isolated, many poor countrymen inherited their poverty. Of the stigmatised groups surviving from pre-colonial Africa, none liberated itself as fully as did the Hutu of Rwanda and the Africans (often slave descendants) of Zanzibar. Even the new Hutu order was far from egalitarian: day-labourers remained despised and the Twa pariah group lost the protection of Tutsi patrons and Belgian officials.[44] Elsewhere egalitarian ideals proved difficult to implement. Eastern Nigeria's legislative assembly formally abolished *osu* status in 1956, but much prejudice remained even among Christians.[45] Although Guinea's nationalists championed the serfs of Futa Jalon, Dr Derman found in 1969 that they still had to rent land from Fulbe owners, perform most wage-labour – during 1969 every male adult of serf origin in the village he studied worked for a Fulbe – and suffer cultural domination by Fulbe who held all Islamic offices. Yet Derman also found that many accepted their inferiority. 'Whoever says a Fulbe and a serf are equal, it's true for the blood', elderly serfs declared. 'But for the law, that which Allah has made, they are not equal.'[46]

Such attitudes were tenacious. In the Borgou region of northern Benin during the 1960s the *machube* servile groups prided themselves on dependent status. 'No, we are not equal', a servile group among the southern Tuareg told a party militant. There, however, dependants did gradually secure autonomy, with the support of black sedentary governments, leaving former masters to tend their own herds and starve in the famines of the 1970s. In Ahaggar the Algerian nationalist regime sent *gendarmes* into Tuareg camps to liberate dependants, although lack of assets often left these as casual labourers or paupers.[47] The most tenacious problem concerned the 100,000 black slaves and 300,000 *haratin* of Mauritania, whose Moorish masters regained power at Independence. Urban demonstrations organised by an emancipation body called El Hor induced the regime to decree the abolition of slavery on 5 July 1980, for the third time in sixty years, but its effectiveness remained uncertain amidst prolonged drought and social dislocation.[48]

The stigmatised group best studied were the San of Botswana. There, as in Mauritania, the old rulers regained power at Independence. Tswana prided themselves on incorporating strangers and hoped eventually to assimilate San, but national leaders were also influenced by Christian and liberal ideas, humanitarian pressure groups, and San wishing to preserve cultural autonomy.[49] The result was some ambivalence. While the Remote Areas Development Programme spent considerable sums on San advancement during the 1970s, boreholes opened former San hunting grounds in the Kalahari to wealthy Tswana ranchers. Generally the assimilation policy predominated.[50] Of the roughly 30,000 San in Botswana in the early 1980s, less than 1,000 were independent hunters. At least 5,000 worked on the farms of Ghanzi district as a depressed group, bitter, resentful, and increasingly marginalised by competition from Bantu labourers – 'clawed animals', as San described them – who were paid two or three times as much. Other San either herded cattle for Tswana or Kgalagadi owners, sometimes without payment, or lived poorly in the towns and villages of eastern Botswana.[51] A survey of 10,594 people in and around the Ngwato capital in 1969–71 showed not a single San among the 43 per cent with some education.[52] A decade later another study 'found a San element in and around the village which was totally integrated into the village economy . . . But, whether they were in employment or sold firewood, wild fruit or other produce, the economic situation of the San was very poor.'[53]

There was extraordinary continuity between the poor of independent Botswana and their nineteenth-century predecessors. As in the past, San were only one category among the 38 per cent of rural households thought in 1974–5 to fall well below a Poverty Datum Line.[54] Poorest of all were refugees from warfare in neighbouring countries. Next to them were certain of the 40 per cent of rural households without a resident adult male member.[55] Not all female-headed households were poor; that depended on their members' ages and abilities, their access to wages, and especially their assets. Women over 30 were especially liable to poverty, particularly if they had no supporting child or adult male. One rural survey in 1972 found that

3 per cent of households had no observable means of support whatever. Another, in the later 1970s, showed that about one-third of rural households possessed no employed man of working age.[56] In 1974–5 female-headed rural households without a resident adult male possessed on average cattle worth 439 Rand and 6 acres of land; the equivalent figures for male-headed rural households with a resident adult male were cattle worth 1,322 Rand and 14 acres. Altogether 37 per cent of rural households owned no cattle, the chief form of Tswana wealth.[57]

Botswana's able-bodied poor relied heavily on casual labour. One village study in 1978–9 found that 12 per cent of households had no land of their own, 6 per cent 'were completely destitute living off begging and "piece-jobs"', and 22 per cent 'were very poor having no cattle, no wage earners and harvesting four bags of sorghum in 1978 or less. This group also relied heavily on "piece-jobs" in exchange for food.'[58] Rural wages were only one-fifth of urban unskilled earnings at that time and were often paid in kind. Some 23 per cent of agricultural workers earned no regular wage.[59] Instead, many poor women, children, and San worked for their betters on the *majako* system, cultivating fields in return for food and an unspecified share of the crop:

> There is very little straight forward charity in the village and most of the wealthier households who help poorer people with food do this primarily in exchange for the performance of domestic chores. During the arable season women and children do *majako* often travelling to more fertile neighbouring villages ... in search of such work; men and women destump agricultural fields; whole families may be involved in constructing thorn-bush fences around arable lands ... women usually stamp corn in exchange for the husk which is eaten; they collect the manure and mud for repairing or building houses and assist in this; fetch water, wash clothes, sweep the *lolwapa's* [compounds] – in short, all the more laborious household chores are done as 'piece-jobs' in exchange for food or a few thebe [cents].[60]

Perhaps the most striking indication of continuity was that poor peasants and unskilled urban workers in the 1970s commonly originated from the lower strata of pre-colonial society and came from the smaller western villages where pre-colonial poverty had concentrated.[61]

Hereditary poverty was increasingly common elsewhere. A study of two locations in Kikuyuland in the early 1970s found that families supplying hired labour were often descended from the client groups of pre-colonial Kikuyu society. Their members consumed on average 12 per cent fewer calories per person than members of labour-hiring families.[62] Here, as elsewhere, hereditary agricultural labour was becoming difficult to escape. Workers in southern Cameroun called plantations 'the garbage can of orphans', while Dr Watts's study of a Hausa village in northern Katsina in 1977–8 concluded that lack of inherited access to the best land, off-farm skills, and extra-village contacts was creating a class of poor peasants barely self-sufficient even in good years, unable to practise risk-averting strategies, and forced to sell their labour-power in order to survive. Dr Kohnert found the same in neighbouring Nupe, where a family's prosperity in 1976 closely paralleled that of its ancestors 50 years earlier.[63] Yet not all observers were convinced. During the 1960s and 1970s Dr Hill studied two Hausa villages in great detail. One, Batagarawa, had ample land; the other, Dorayi, adjoined Kano city and had little. Yet both had numerous poor people – 24 per cent of farming units in Batagarawa and 27 per cent of men in Dorayi[64] – who lacked grain, manured land, or off-farm skills and were forced to sell labour, collect bush products, or practise unrewarding crafts. Poor men found it increasingly difficult to escape their condition, but Hill nevertheless insisted that hereditary classes were not yet formed because a rich man's wealth dispersed among his numerous sons at death, personal enterprise was vital to success, and the insecurity of the savanna environment and the risk of disease could still determine men's fortunes.[65] In Sierra Leone, similarly, accident or sickness, especially at a peak farming season, was an important cause of poverty.[66]

The rural poor were indeed heterogeneous. Eritrean guerrillas divided them into three main categories: those who lacked the equipment to cultivate independently; those who lacked land because they were young or recent immigrants; and 'those who own land but have no labour power', characteristically orphans, widowers, old men, and solitary women.[67] Unsupported women were numerous among the very poor everywhere. Roughly one-quarter of Zambia's rural households were headed by women in 1980; often lacking access to urban wages or kinship ties with other villagers, they were the bulk of the 200,000 weak households which were the core of the country's rural poverty. 'Households of widows plus separated, abandoned and divorced mothers' were also among the poorest villagers in southern Zimbabwe in 1984:

> Many of these are in a state of destitution since they have lost the property and cash accumulated by the household to the family of the children's father. Without cattle or cash income, eking out survival on such informal sector jobs as brewing beer and prostitution these households are closest to total destitution.[68]

The poorest villagers in southern Malawi in the early 1980s were often women whose marriages and kin groups had disintegrated. One 'had gone from place to place trying to find somewhere to stay until she had found a headman who had given her a small plot of land on which to build a house'. A total stranger, her household was chronically short of grain, her four children were malnourished, and she tried to support them by brewing beer for sale.[69] Women were especially vulnerable when land was scarce, for access to it might then be restricted to men. Women were vulnerable, too, where local culture denied them the right to work. In the Hausa village which Dr Watts studied, men did virtually all agricultural work and 12 per cent of householders were chronically poor and unsupported women who did not farm at all but depended chiefly on selling cooked food or receiving gifts from kinsmen.[70] Yet that was an exceptional situation, for the poor could generally still scrape a living by selling labour. Even in Northern Nigeria elderly women could work for wages, sometimes receiving as little as one-sixth of a man's earnings.[71] 'Women at the Chambeshi River, Chinsali District', an observer reported from Zambia,

> were in 1980 doing a day's work in rice harvesting for a small dish of salt, and considered this a good wage as they could resell the salt by the spoonful to their neighbours in exchange for beans, sweet potatoes, groundnuts and the like. At approximately 100 gm weight and a controlled price for salt . . . this is a day's work for . . . one-fifth of the minimum rural wage and slightly over one-hundredth of the urban minimum.[72]

As in the past, the most unfortunate were those too old, sick, or burdened with children to work for wages. They relied heavily on charity. In the Katete area of eastern Zambia in 1968, the poorest rural people obtained 24 per cent of their total income from gifts. During the hungry months before harvest, the poor of the Maragoli region of Kenya relied heavily on food available at funerals.[73] A researcher in Mbere, also in Kenya, recorded the daily movements of a retired policeman, living alone, who had suffered crop failure:

> *9th October* [1972]. Giconjo today was looking if he could get someone to give him food. He was out of cash and he struggled here and there but he couldn't get any. After his struggle he came to sleep. He did not do any work due to hunger.
> *12th October*. When Giconjo woke he went to chase the squirrels (away from sown seed) from sunrise to nine o'clock. Today he had no food to eat, not even a cent had he in his pocket. So he set out to look for one who could give him something to eat. He got some little flour which he prepared as porridge.[74]

Patronage was still the last resource of the rural poor. In a Mende village in Sierra Leone during the early 1980s, where 'those who live in smaller than average households (especially where the individuals concerned are old and/or handicapped or chronically sick)' were especially likely to suffer poverty and hunger, Dr Richards found that patronage relationships were 'buoyant and durable'. 'I once heard the story of a man who died of starvation', he reported. 'It was emphasised, however, that this man was a stranger without a patron.'[75]

Dependence upon patronage inhibited the poor from collective action to advance their interests as distinct from those of community leaders, even if – as was unlikely – they had the political initiative to do so. Poor peasants participated in rural protests, but as members of the crowd. They joined the Agbekoya revolt in Yorubaland in 1968, but its leaders were hunters, tenant-farmers, and middle peasants alienated by misgovernment and rural capitalism, all fighting for 'farmers' kingdom'. Zaïre's rural rebellions of the mid 1960s attacked anyone with visible wealth but shared Pierre Mulele's vision of a two-class society, 'the rich' and 'the poor, or the "popular masses"'. The Eritrean Peoples' Liberation Front claimed that poor peasants were the bulk of its forces, but they fought alongside other peasant categories and joined with them in the land redistribution which political cadres instigated.[76] Arson and machine-breaking took place in northern Ghana, western Kenya, eastern Zambia, and southern Ethiopia, but were the work of 'not the dispossessed so much as the non-joiners, the believers in traditional ways, the non-progressives'.[77] Apart from attacks on merchants' granaries in Sudan, possibly some recruitment of hungry men to rebel forces in Chad, and accounts from Northern Nigeria of migrations eastwards to await the Mahdi, famine provoked remarkably little protest among people anxious to conserve energy.[78] The rural poor were too vulnerable to transform their situation radically by their own efforts.

During Africa's first decade of Independence the urban influx of the 1950s accelerated. Capital cities generally grew most quickly, especially those fed by rural disorder. Kinshasa's population increased from 380,000 to 800,000 during Zaïre's first three tumultuous years of Independence.[79] During the 1970s, however, urban growth changed character. It was still very rapid. Between 1975 and 1980 tropical Africa's towns grew at 5.9 per cent a year, the world's highest rate.[80] Growth was still most dramatic when stimulated by rural disorder. Between 1974 and 1982 civil war swelled Luanda's population from some 450,000 to 1,200,000. One estimate suggested that Salisbury's population might have doubled during the last two years of Rhodesia's liberation war. Drought raised the proportion of Mauritania's people living in towns from 25 per cent in 1970 to 65 per cent in 1981. Dar es Salaam's growth between 1967 and 1978 from 272,821 to 851,522 was probably related to dislocation caused by Tanzania's villagisation programme.[81] Some capitals were still the main growth points. Lagos had something over 1,000,000 inhabitants in 1967 and perhaps 5,000,000 by the early 1980s. But not all capitals were still magnets. There was little net immigration into Nairobi during the 1970s, although many smaller Kenyan towns grew quickly.[82] In Africa generally rural–urban migration was no longer accelerating. Instead, towns increasingly grew by their own natural increase and the fact that immigrants stayed longer.[83] Urban populations became more stable. In 1973 a census first showed a female majority in Lagos. Yet greater stability did not prevent the International Labour Office from estimating that Africa's urban poor doubled during the 1970s.[84]

Governments and municipalities could not cope with urban growth. Between 1964 and 1969 Tanzania's National Housing Corporation built some 6,000 houses, mostly for low-income people, but between 1975 and 1980 it built only 480. Zimbabwe's new government planned to build 115,000 housing units within three years but constructed only 13,500. Abidjan needed 20,000 new housing units a year in 1981 but built only 8,000.[85] Even the cheapest public housing was generally too expensive for the poor. In the mid 1980s only an estimated 7 per cent of Nouakchott's people could afford to rent a one-room house built by the parastatal low-cost housing company.[86] Many authorities scarcely attempted to provide cheap housing. In 1979 Nigerian towns were reckoned to lack 1,000,000 housing units. An official survey in 1971 found that 3.8 persons shared each room in Lagos, as against the legal maximum of 2.0, but unofficial studies suggested as many as 8.7 per room in the Obalende quarter.[87] Working-class households in Lagos generally paid between 30 and 40 per cent of their income in rent during the 1970s and considered rents a greater grievance than overcrowding.[88]

Unable to find or afford formal housing, the poor clustered into the 'informal' or 'squatter' zones which ringed many cities. By the early 1980s these housed almost half of Lusaka's people.[89] Squatter settlements often had an evil reputation. In Mathare Valley – which respectable residents of Nairobi feared to enter – this was justified to the extent that between 60 and 80 per cent of adult inhabitants lacked formal employment during the 1970s, only 14–17 per cent of women were currently married, the median income in the poorest section was less than half the minimum wage, and three women out of four engaged in illicit brewing.[90] Yet this was abnormal. More typical was George, an unauthorised settlement in Lusaka, where in 1973 well over half the household heads were in wage employment and many others were self-employed.[91] Most squatter settlements housed some of the very poor, commonly the unemployed or incapacitated, but they generally had lower unemployment rates than city-centre slums.[92] Most were working-class dormitories built by established wage-earners escaping high rents and overcrowding, 'slums of hope' created by aspiring people proud to own their homes. Where building land was scarce, however, low-income housing could take more exploitative forms. This had long been the pattern in Lagos and Addis Ababa.[93] From 1969 it became especially blatant in Nairobi, where largely Kikuyu housing companies gained control of land in Mathare Valley and within sixteen months built 7,628 rooms, each 10 feet square, in barrack-like rows, constructed of unseasoned wood painted with waste engine oil to repel insects. Rents enabled the companies to recover their capital within twelve to eighteen months. By 1980 three-quarters of Nairobi's 'unauthorised' housing was owned by companies or private landlords, in a pattern comparable to the slumyards of interwar South Africa.[94]

During the 1960s formal employment generally supported a declining proportion of townspeople as urbanisation continued and industry became more capital intensive. The high urban unemployment of the later 1950s was still generally reported, with figures of 12–22 per cent of the potential workforce commonly said to be without jobs.[95] When associated with instability, this could sharply depress earnings. Between 1960 and 1968 Kinshasa's real official minimum wage fell by 54 per cent, while Ghana's declined by some 45 per cent between 1960 and 1970.[96] More commonly, however, the 1960s were good years for urban workers with jobs, as trade unions, minimum-wage legislation, and investment by high-wage multinational corporations added to the unnaturally high earnings of the late 1950s. In Kenya, African real wages outside agriculture more than doubled between 1959 and 1968. Zambia's wage-earners added 32 per cent to their average real earnings between 1964 and 1968, while smallholder incomes rose by only 3.4 per cent. Almost everywhere the differential between skilled and unskilled workers narrowed, while that between formal-sector and other earnings widened.[97] During the 1960s Africa's more fortunate workers began to raise themselves out of general urban poverty.

During the 1970s and early 1980s many returned to it. Depression, inflation, and the destruction of trade union power restored urban wages to market levels. In Kenya, African real wages outside agriculture fell between 1968 and 1978 by 32 per cent in the public sector and 27 per cent in the private sector, while agricultural wages rose by 31 per cent. Tanzania's real minimum wage fell by 43 per cent between 1974 and 1980 to a point 18 per cent below average smallholder incomes, although urban costs (for rent, etc.) were higher. Real unskilled wages in Nigeria roughly doubled between 1964 and 1974 and then halved again by 1979.[98] Yet worse was to come, for the depression of 1979–84 and the abolition of food subsidies demanded by the International Monetary Fund hit urban workers especially hard. Many lost half their real earnings. In the extreme case of Ghana, the minimum wage of 1983 was worth only 13 per cent of its value in 1975.[99]

Reliable data on urban unemployment during the 1970s and 1980s scarcely exist. Estimates ranged up to 50 per cent in Monrovia in 1980, 40 per cent in Dar es Salaam in 1983, 30 per cent in Senegal in 1985, and 12–18 per cent in Zimbabwe in 1986,[100] but most figures were lower. Dr Peil found in Nigeria and the Gambia during the 1970s that between 2 and 9 per cent of men aged over fifteen declared themselves unemployed. Nigeria's national unemployment rate was estimated at 8–10 per cent in the mid 1980s. Nairobi's male unemployment rate fell between 1969 and 1978 from 10 to 6 per cent.[101] There were several reasons for these lower figures. One was less rural–urban migration. Another, in certain countries, was that lower real wages encouraged employers to hire more workers. In Kenya, for example, non-agricultural formal wage employment rose between 1968 and 1978 by 6.3 per cent a year.[102] A more general reason was that the slippery concept of unemployment was defined more rigorously. No longer did it embrace everyone without a formal-sector job, whatever his informal activities.[103] Moreover, observers were increasingly convinced that the unemployed were not the real problem because they were seldom household heads but normally either married women or the young. In Nairobi in 1974, only 19 per cent of unemployed males were household heads, while 80 per cent were relatives of household heads. Poverty correlated less with unemployment than with the low earnings of many household heads in full employment – 'the working poor', as they were described.[104] 'What the poor need', one report concluded, '... is ... not more work, but better work.'[105] This waning of concern with the young unemployed was accompanied by declining provision for 'juvenile delinquents' and a loss of interest by governments in the relief programmes and youth corps which had flourished immediately after Independence.[106]

Another reason for falling unemployment figures amidst depression was an expansion of informal-sector occupations. Growing towns, wealthier African elites, and decaying services and industries all created opportunities for the enterprising, whether as self-employed builders in squatter settlements, repairers of aging vehicles, or pedlars of cigarettes outside the shuttered windows of abandoned modern shops. The greater stability of urban populations and the fact that more were urban-born probably strengthened survival skills. Kenya's informal-sector employment grew by an estimated 10 per cent a year during the 1970s. Nigeria's employed an estimated 72 per cent of the urban labour force in 1978. Proportions were lower elsewhere but invariably increasing.[107] Earnings differed greatly. In the Medina and Pikine quarters of Dakar in 1977 those self-employed in the informal sector averaged 9,960 CFA francs per week, whereas their employees averaged 4,266 and apprentices only 833.[108] Hawkers often earned little more than half as much as unskilled labourers because competition was devastating in an occupation which engaged many married women and otherwise unemployed youths – in 1974, 56 per cent of Lagos street traders had at least six years' schooling.[109] Another entry to urban life for young men was apprenticeship, whose terms of employment appear to have deteriorated as applicants increased. It became quite normal for a young man to begin his working career in an unpaid job. Three-quarters of apprentices in Lagos during the 1970s were unpaid. In Kumasi they averaged about one-fifth of the minimum wage.[110]

Although many economists urged encouragement of the informal sector, African authorities often harried it. 'Deliberate efforts must be made to ensure the highest level of environmental sanitation in Abuja', the Secretary to the Nigerian Federal Government proclaimed when the new capital was opened in 1982:

> Mechanics workshops must not be allowed to mushroom everywhere. Heaps of refuse must not be allowed to disfigure the city. The army of beggars and destitutes that regularly parade the streets of Lagos must be contained within the confines of rehabilitation and welfare centres. Trading activities must be strictly restricted within the locations provided for the purpose and street trading must be absolutely prohibited. The growth of shanty towns must not be allowed.[111]

What tidy minds meant for the poor was expressed by an old woman in Nairobi:

> 'I have always been selling gruel ... and maize and beans. But now this

> government is giving us a lot of trouble. I don't have a license and I have been arrested three times. Last month I was in Langata Prison because I didn't have Shs. 100/- to pay the fine.' She shook her head – 'an old woman like me.' Then she became angry – standing up and shouting, 'I'm not stealing! I've done nothing wrong! Where do you think I could get a hundred shillings?'[112]

The closure of Nairobi's food kiosks in 1980, for fear of cholera, was thought to have left 5,000 people jobless. Four years later an offensive by Nigeria's military rulers against informal activities in Kano deprived an estimated 50,000 entrepreneurs and dependants of their livelihood. Independence and economic decay brought hard times for Accra's market-women.[113]

Repression of the informal sector was seldom effective – Nairobi's shoe-shiners re-emerged after each international conference – but encouraged its tendency to merge with truly criminal activity. Black markets and smuggling created many opportunities for the poor. Open piracy reappeared off Lagos. Political conflict created 'work' for unemployed youths – a Nigerian accused of electoral irregularities in 1964 described himself as 'a daily paid thug'. Personal assaults reported to the Nigerian police increased between 1960 and 1975 from 16,000 to 65,000.[114] Governments replied with draconian legislation. Kenya introduced the death penalty for robbery with violence. Mauritania restored the full brutality of Islamic punishments. In 1984 a Nigerian court sentenced a youth of twenty to death for the armed robbery of two torches and a beret.[115]

Yet the urban poor were not anomic. They had a lively moral economy. Their characteristic protest of the 1970s and 1980s was demonstration against the threat or reality of higher food prices. One such demonstration in Monrovia in 1979 destabilised the True Whig party after 102 years of power, another in Khartoum in 1985 destroyed Nimeiry's government, and many regimes feared similar fates. Like their rural cousins, however, the very poor were probably faces in the crowd, for their vulnerability, ignorance, immediate need, and sense of impotence inhibited autonomous action. The dispossessed of Mathare Valley might riot and loot during an attempted coup. Addis Ababa's shanty-dwellers might purge student 'revolutionaries' when incited by their military rulers. Abidjan's unemployed youths might demonstrate when organised by secondary-school graduates. Ghanaian townsmen might back demands for democracy and social justice articulated by organised labour. Youth protests, with opposition political leadership, might even overthrow a government, as in Brazzaville's *Trois Glorieuses* of August 1963.[116] Left to themselves, however, the poor generally saw themselves realistically as part of the *povo*, the people – a broad populist perspective of 'us' and 'them' which acquiesced in much inequality provided that 'they', the *grands types* as they were known in Abidjan, acquired wealth legitimately and spent it generously.[117] An investigation in two poor Ghanaian townships in 1975 found that 15 per cent of those interviewed were class orientated, 37 per cent populist, and 48 per cent acquiescent.[118]

The most vivid illustrations of popular feeling and its limitations were the street battles which left several thousands dead in Northern Nigerian towns between 1981 and 1983.[119] They were fought by the Yan Tatsine, disciples of an Islamic teacher named Muhammadu Marwa. Yan Tatsine were for once truly the poor in action. Many were young men from the countryside, often *gardawa*, the derogatory term recently applied to the itinerant Islamic students so entrenched in savanna culture.[120] Muhammadu Marwa was said to post agents at railway stations and motor parks to recruit them. Their numbers swollen by land shortage, their casual occupations supplanted by modern technology, their survival threatened by inflation, and their appeals for charity neglected by oil-rich townsmen, *gardawa* turned to a prophet who made them proud of their poverty. 'He condemned affluence', an enquiry reported, 'preaching that anyone wearing a watch, or riding a bicycle, or driving a car, or sending his child to the normal State Schools was an infidel and an unbeliever destined for hell.'[121] Such teachings gave dignity to men like Musa Maikaniki, the former apprentice roadside mechanic who became Muhammadu's successor and led the movement in Yola.[122] An elect community, introverted and paranoid, its members created 'a private republic' in the streets of Kano until destroyed by the army. Yet *gardawa* themselves were not destroyed. They awaited a Shehu Ahmadu.

The care of the structural poor, like the poor themselves, changed only within narrow limits. The family remained their first defence. That Africans cared for their own was a matter of faith and pride, an area of moral superiority over developed nations. Concern for the extended family, the aged, and the infirm was an essential component of Zambian Humanism.[123] Occasionally a westernised politician like Tom Mboya might bewail 'the undesirable situation in which a member of a family whose income increases is suddenly and constantly besieged by demands for support from a large number of distant relatives'.[124] Few were so brash. The new elite as a whole admitted its burdensome obligations.

How far the obligations were met in practice is difficult to assess. Probably, as in the late colonial period, family care generally remained strong, but with identifiable limitations. Family systems varied: Luo recognised wider obligations than Ganda, Gurage than Amhara. Environments differed: duties to kin were more easily and commonly met in an uxorilocal Zambian village than a Copperbelt town. Circumstances differed, as unemployed youths found when they outstayed their welcome or widows discovered when their husband's kinsmen seized his land.[125] Of workers interviewed in Abidjan in 1980–1, 82 per cent claimed to help someone outside their immediate households, but now the city was so dominant that reciprocal aid rarely came from the countryside. Urban crisis could put almost intolerable strains on family care. In 1955 each worker in Kinshasa supported 2.8 people; in 1967, 5.7.[126] In the countryside these strains and limitations were most dramatically revealed during famine, but they were apparent also in daily life. On Kilimanjaro in Tanzania during the 1970s obligations to poorer relatives were met more generously than in a Western society, but 'erosive inroads' meant that 'the poorer Chagga are left largely to fend for themselves in small groups of similarly disadvantaged', while the more prosperous used state or church welfare programmes to shield themselves from 'the chronic drain of the hungry families', who were held to blame for their own poverty. In 1973 some 1,802 Africans in Rhodesia were given pauper burials.[127]

The interaction between family care and institutional provision was especially intricate. Care of orphans was one example. Ideology insisted that institutional orphanages were confessions of moral failure and 'completely foreign to our traditional society'. 'Surely', Zimbabwe's President declared in 1986, 'we must all long for that day when there will be no orphanages because all Zimbabweans will have renewed and rededicated themselves to the sacred traditional values of the extended family that sustained succeeding generations of our founding fathers.'[128] Adoption, too, was seen as alien, in contrast to fostering, which did not alter a child's social identity.[129] These beliefs found practical application in Nigeria after the Civil War, when the authorities returned thousands of Biafran war orphans to their kin or placed them in foster-homes but rejected adoption and made only limited use of institutions. A later survey concluded that those sent to institutions had been the least happy, and other studies of Nigerian orphanages during the 1970s were highly critical.[130] Yet in 1979 there were some 150 homes for motherless babies in Nigeria, for, despite the ideology, orphans had been numerous in many pre-colonial societies and proliferated in the twentieth century.[131] In other independent states, orphanages were generally few but crowded.[132] Child welfare was Africa's most vigorous form of philanthropy.

Elderly people presented a similar, although smaller, problem. Zambia's experience was especially revealing. Shortly before Independence the British established institutions for aged townsmen lacking kin or rural homes. The independent government resolved to use institutions for other purposes and encourage 'the old traditions in Africa of persons looking after their own aged'. Another year in office convinced it that this was impracticable. 'Although the [Social Welfare] Department discourages institutional care of aged persons, in preference to family and community care, in line with the Party and Government policy', it was explained in 1977, 'in practice it has been realised that due to factors such as urbanisation, childlessness and certain cultural taboos connected with ageing, there will always be some aged persons for whom the only mode of care will be in an institution.'[133] There, as elsewhere, the number of elderly people seeking aid grew as the population increase of the 1920s swelled the elderly of the 1980s. For an aged relative to enter an institution implied failure or gross neglect in many parts of Africa, and the elderly often resented it bitterly, but the need for institutions nevertheless increased.[134] A study in Salisbury during 1980 showed great diversity of view among elderly people and a proportion eager for institutionalisation. In that year Tanzania had 43 old people's homes with some 4,000 inmates.[135]

As in colonial times, most Africans, except in Ethiopia and Islamic regions, distinguished sharply between deserving and undeserving poor. Along with the young and old, the deserving generally included the handicapped, although there might be residual feeling that their handicap was due to moral offence. The blind continued to attract dedicated care. In 1980 Tanzania had seventeen schools for the blind and the Salvation Army's remarkable institution at Thika achieved the second-best examination results of any high school in Kenya. The most important attack on blindness was the campaign against onchocerciasis launched by the World Health Organisation in 1975 in the Volta Basin of West Africa, where blindness rates were probably the world's highest.[136]

Blindness had long attracted concern. Care for the crippled, by contrast, was an important post-colonial innovation. Except where begging traditions existed, the crippled, as a Ghanaian put it, 'were kept in the dark corners of village huts'. Southern Rhodesia's census of 1962 showed that the proportion of people unable to use limbs rose from 2.5 per thousand in towns to 5.5 per thousand in African rural areas.[137] Because cripples were often invisible in colonial Africa, little was done for them, and because little was done they were not attracted into the open but remained invisible. Two developments changed this situation after Independence. One was the appearance of epidemic poliomyelitis, which was a major cause of disability. Although early doctors recorded occasional cases, they thought polio rare in Africa until visiting European soldiers contracted the disease during the Second World War – even in 1960 it was said not to exist in Ethiopia.[138] The first small epidemics recorded during the 1950s appeared to attack mainly Europeans. Africans were known to harbour antibodies, so doctors concluded that most Africans suffered mild polio in infancy and thereby acquired immunity. When epidemics appeared among Africans – as in Kenya in 1960 – they were attributed either to new strains of polio or to loss of acquired immunity owing to improved hygiene.[139] 'Paralysed limbs can be seen nowadays in the deepest bush', a doctor remarked in 1975.[140] Epidemics may indeed have been new, but paralysed limbs certainly were not. Polio was known to be widespread in French colonies during the 1950s. The first studies in Nigeria and Ethiopia in the early 1960s showed a proportion of children permanently handicapped by the infantile polio which left the rest immune.[141] It was in fact an endemic disease and studies gradually revealed its scale. One in 1964 estimated that 2,000,000 Africans were crippled by polio. A year later Nigeria alone was thought to have 200,000–300,000 victims. A study there in 1982 reckoned that over 13,000 children were crippled by polio each year, although less than 1,000 cases were reported. Another survey in Zimbabwe found polio to be much the most common cause of lower limb disability.[142] As so often in Africa, a major cause of poverty had gone unobserved until specialists looked for it. Hope, as with leprosy, was pinned on a vaccine.

The search for the handicapped was the second innovation to accompany Independence. It began in Ghana following the enquiry into destitution in 1954. A Ghana Cripples' Aid Society was founded in 1958. Nkrumah's government ordered a survey and rehabilitation programme in October 1959. By January 1964 some 13,325 handicapped people were registered, including 5,326 cripples. Only a fraction could receive vocational rehabilitation at training units, which in 1975 had an annual intake of about 500.[143] But other countries had followed Ghana's lead. Zambia adopted a national programme in 1967, Kenya in 1968, and Nigeria in 1970 with particular attention to rehabilitating Civil War victims.[144] The same motive led Zimbabwe to launch in 1981 the first thorough survey of disability undertaken in any African country. It showed at least 250,000 disabled people, or over 3 per cent of the total population. The most common disabilities were of the eyes (70,000 cases) or lower limbs (60,000). Over half suffered their disability in childhood, nearly half of the identifiable causes were disease, and the overwhelming majority of disabilities could have been prevented. Handicapped children were seriously disadvantaged in schooling, while those disabled as adults rarely remained economically productive. The survey demonstrated how widespread and truly crippling in Africa were the consequences of disease, especially in childhood.[145]

Orphans, aged, blind, and cripples were deserving poor. To the undeserving, by contrast, many independent regimes offered only incarceration. Beggars, in particular, were parasites and symbols of backwardness to modernisers without traditions of religious charity. Nkrumah's regime again set a pattern by launching the *grand renfermement* which colonial governments had hesitated to undertake. In January 1956 it opened a Central Destitute Infirmary at Bekwai. When beggars did not go there voluntarily – and with Independence celebrations approaching – the government sought powers of compulsion. The resulting parliamentary debate revealed the spectrum of African attitudes to the poor. 'Beggars in the streets of many of our main towns have become a public nuisance', the responsible Minister explained, 'and the sight of dirty, sick and often apparently mentally defective persons sitting or lying on the sidewalks of our roads does not reflect credit upon us.' Other members insisted that the destitute were heterogeneous:

> We all agree that begging is a great social evil and should not be allowed to thrive in any healthy society. All the same we would agree that there are real beggars – those who are so infirm and poor that they cannot make their livelihood. Such type of beggars really deserve the sympathy of everybody; we expect our Government which boasts of being a socialist Government, to be sympathetic towards them.

Northern Muslim representatives, by contrast, defended the Islamic tradition of begging and charity. The bill eventually passed, but only when amended to permit 'soliciting or receiving alms, in accordance with a religious or native Custom'.[146] It provoked much hostility in the north and was never fully enforced, but beggars became relatively inconspicuous in Ghana. Bekwai had 69 inmates in 1961 but only 42 a decade later.[147]

Other independent regimes adopted different strategies. Nairobi, always an enemy of the beggar, opened a 'Village of Mercy' in 1965 and concentrated on clearing beggars from the city centre. Zambia created a public assistance programme and claimed to 'proudly count herself among the very few nations with virtually no street beggars'.[148] Nigeria had an especially acute problem to which successive regimes responded with sporadic authoritarianism:

> There have been a number of *ad hoc* rehabilitation centres established by some state governments to cater for the welfare of beggars as well as training them for specific jobs. But these centres have never operated consistently for more than six months. Often beggars are dragged to such centres to clear them from the streets when an important visitor is coming to a particular city or town. After his departure the beggars find their way back to the streets.[149]

These measures won some support in the south, but in northern Islamic regions begging and charity still flourished. Yet even Islamic charity was susceptible to the growth of capitalism. Workers who burned capitalist rice farms in northern Ghana explained that the owners 'like plenty money but they wouldn't give *zakat*'. Yan Tatsine learned the limits of charity in the streets of Kano and Sembene Ousmane imagined them superbly in the last pages of *Xala*, where the beggars of Dakar invaded a bourgeois home and the police prepared their rifles.[150]

'This Africa knows only one law', said the prostitute in James Ngugi's *Petals of blood*. 'You eat somebody or you are eaten.'[151] The ruthlessness was probably no greater than in pre-colonial Africa or poor societies elsewhere, but institutional defences against it were exceptionally weak. Some countries had effective voluntary welfare systems. Zimbabwe, with a settler legacy, had in 1983 some 29 locally based organisations caring for the disabled, employing over 300 professional staff.[152] More often, however, a state had a mass of heterogeneous bodies, inherited from the colonial period and diverse religious traditions, which gave small quantities of aid to the poor in an unsystematic way.[153] Attempts to coordinate them through national councils of social service often created only another committee. Some welfare bodies became important channels for foreign aid. In an extreme case, Lesotho's branch of the Save the Children Fund was in 1984 supplying school meals to one-fifth of the entire population.[154] Leadership of welfare bodies passed increasingly to the African elite, whose philanthropic work merged with the still vigorous tradition of personal largess which was the African counterpart to the institutions of Hindu or Buddhist inspiration which undertook welfare work in India or Sri Lanka after Independence.[155] In 1981 alone, by his own account, the Nigerian politician Obafemi Awolowo gave ₦281,444 in charitable donations. Like their precolonial predecessors, Africa's new rulers understood the uses of philanthropy. The Kwame Nkrumah Trust Fund took over the collection of money for all Ghana's charities. One of Major Mengistu's first actions on gaining power in Ethiopia was to bring lorry-loads of Addis Ababa's destitutes to a feast in the former royal palace.[156]

Official welfare systems had a mixed history after Independence. Social security measures for modern-sector workers expanded to provide for old age, invalidity, widows, and orphans. Additional territories adopted social security legislation – Sudan, for example, in 1975. Ghana created a limited unemployment insurance scheme.[157] Only small and oil-rich Gabon attempted in 1983 to extend a Social Guarantee Scheme to all citizens, although with markedly reduced benefits for those with incomes below the minimum wage 'as an incentive for categories belonging to the modern sector'.[158] Elsewhere, inflation reduced real provision, funds paying immediate benefits like family allowances fell into deficit, and reserves accumulated by provident and pension funds were dangerously attractive to impecunious governments. Many social security schemes verged on insolvency.[159]

Government social welfare departments often expanded after Independence and Africanised their staff. By 1971 Ghana's Department of Social Welfare and Community Development employed 136 people at headquarters and 1,638 in the regions.[160] Official approaches changed remarkably little. Despite much talk of 'authenticity' and the need for even greater stress on development, most social welfare officers continued to spend most time on casework and institutional aid, probably to the benefit of the poor.[161] Francophone territories continued to stress family health. Nigeria still emphasised the young. Yet the demand for aid outpaced the supply. In Zambia applicants for short-term public assistance increased between 1962 and 1969 from 6,008 to 15,105, while those receiving long-term assistance peaked in 1971 at 4,446 before declining to 1,667 in 1978 as economic crisis reduced the funds available. During the mid 1970s suppliers (including state shops) refused the Social Welfare Department's purchase orders, petrol was rarely available for officers' transport, the numbers in state institutions fell drastically, and such essentials as blankets were no longer issued. 'While social problems continued to increase', the Department reported sadly in 1978, 'the machinery to deal with them continued to weaken.'[162]

The growth of structural poverty after Independence was disturbing, but the return of conjunctural poverty in the form of mass famine mortality was terrifying. Famine came in two forms. One resulted from warfare and political conflict. By suddenly uprooting people and preventing them from seeking alternative subsistence, violence could create almost instant famine. Only months after Independence Africa's first modern disaster occurred in the southern Kasai province of Zaïre, where some 150,000 Luba took refuge from ethnic conflict:

> Many of them had been on the road for weeks or months with very little food, and that of the poorest kind. The only food usually available to them was cassava ... About half of the total had settled in an area north-west of Bakwanga, the capital; this area had been practically uninhabited because of poor soil and lack of water . . . The picture which presented itself was one of great helplessness and suffering.[163]

Virtually deprived of protein, these refugees suffered several years of epidemic kwashiorkor. Meanwhile the rebellions of 1964 and their repression brought starvation, disease, and emigration to other regions. Late in 1966, Zaïre was thought to have 500,000 internal refugees.[164]

Three other conflicts surrounding Independence bred numerous refugees during the 1960s. One was the flight of Tutsi pastoralists from the Hutu revolution in Rwanda, followed a decade later by Hutu refugees from Tutsi oppression in Burundi.[165] The second was the Sudanese Civil War, which had driven some 165,200 people into neighbouring countries by 1972. Meanwhile even larger numbers had fled the liberation wars in Portuguese colonies. In 1972, 415,800 refugees from Angola, 81,000 from Portuguese Guinea, and 51,000 from Mozambique were sheltering outside their countries. At that time there may have been about 1,000,000 refugees in sub-Saharan Africa, excluding those internal to Zaïre. Almost all were victims of warfare.[166]

Yet these numbers were already overshadowed by the Nigerian Civil War. An estimated 1,500,000 Igbo refugees returned to Biafra before the war began. Several millions more escaped outwards into federal territory or inwards into central Biafra as Nigerian troops advanced. Central Biafra was a food-deficit region which normally imported 80 per cent of its animal protein. Now kwashiorkor killed tens of thousands of children between May and November 1968.[167] 'People are dying in the gutters', a relief worker reported, 'and the whole area is like Belsen.'[168] International response brought protein-rich foods which dramatically reduced kwashiorkor, but by 1969 Biafrans lacked not only protein but calories derived from grain, which was more difficult to transport. Several thousand people were dying each day when the war ended in January 1970. Nearly 1,000,000 may have died altogether, but there was no mass starvation after the war, nor any major epidemic.[169]

After 1970 Africa's refugees increased until by May 1979 they were thought to number some 4,000,000. Angola remained a major source as its liberation struggle merged into civil war and then into the wider southern African conflict, which by December 1979 had also bred 220,000–250,000 refugees from Rhodesia, apart from those haunting Salisbury's garbage dumps.[170] Violence in Uganda and the expulsion of aliens from Ghana and Nigeria created new refugee problems. But the main trends after 1970 were, first, the merging of political crisis with drought, and, second, the concentration of the refugee problem in the Horn of Africa, owing to conflict between Ethiopia and the Somali, Eritreans, and Tigreans on its borders. By mid 1980 Somalia, with some 1,500,000 refugees, had the worst such problem in the world, while the number from Ethiopia in Sudan was 716,000 in early 1985, when there were probably also over 300,000 refugees from Chad in neighbouring countries.[171]

Most refugees settled themselves in peripheral rural areas and became the poorest of the poor. Those from Angola in Zambian border villages earned just enough by agricultural labour to survive, while the average household income of refugees in Botswana in 1974–5 was one-quarter of the national mean. In 1984 an authority estimated that 12,000,000 people had been 'mass distress migrants' in sub-Saharan Africa during the previous twenty years. Of these, one-half had fled war or persecution, one-third had been famine victims, and one-sixth had suffered both.[172]

The second reason for the return of mass famine mortality was drought. During the 1960s famine due to drought was confined to arid regions of eastern and southern Africa. In 1961 Kenya's pastoralists experienced widespread famine which affected also parts of Sudan and, slightly later, drought-prone central Tanzania.[173] In Kenya and Tanzania this pattern was repeated, less seriously, in the mid 1960s, but on this occasion the worst-hit areas were northern Uganda, central Somalia, and northern Ethiopia, where several thousands may have died.[174] The arid areas of Kenya and Tanzania suffered again between 1969 and 1971. In southern Africa, meanwhile, the rainfall cycle declined during the early 1960s. Children dead of starvation were reported from the northern Transvaal in 1963. Two years later there was destitution from Lesotho to the Cape. From 1966 rainfall improved, but several regions again suffered briefly in 1968–9.[175] Serious fears of desertification were first expressed in independent Africa in 1968 – with reference to the Kalahari.[176]

These fears were soon overshadowed by famine in the West African Sahel. Rainfall faltered in 1968 and then failed throughout the region in 1972 and 1973. Mass famine appeared in certain areas during 1973. One-quarter of the Sahel's livestock may have died.[177] The number of human deaths is unknown and was probably exaggerated,[178] although the Tuareg of the desert edge suffered especially severely. There was no major epidemic disease.

The Sahelian drought extended also into the Horn of Africa and southwards into East Africa. Rainfall in the Wollo region of northern Ethiopia had been low since the mid 1960s and failed seriously in both 1971 and 1972. By May 1973 many were dying.[179] Deaths were more numerous than in the Sahel, possibly 50,000.[180] During 1974–5 drought shifted south-eastwards to the Ogaden border with Somalia, but there the death toll was lower.[181] Rainfall also failed in arid regions of Sudan, Kenya, and Tanzania.

Drought and famine returned to arid Africa during the early 1980s. In the

Sahel the worst-affected countries were Mauritania (which between 1982 and 1984 produced only about 10 per cent of its grain needs), Mali (where pastoralists again suffered most severely), and especially Chad (where civil war so hampered cultivation and relief efforts that some thousands appear to have died of starvation during 1984).[182] Elsewhere in the Sahel, however, the drought was less destructive than that of the early 1970s, while in other arid regions it was almost universal but caused deaths only where exacerbated by violence. In East Africa, for example, Kenya and Tanzania experienced regional food shortages in 1980–1 and 1984, but numerous deaths – one estimate was 30,000 – occurred only in northern Uganda during 1980–1, when drought coincided with violence following General Amin's overthrow.[183] Southern Africa's rainfall cycle also reached its lowest point of the century at this moment, but numerous deaths from starvation occurred only in Mozambique, where warfare exacerbated the situation.[184]

As a decade earlier, the crisis of the early 1980s was most disastrous in north-eastern Africa. Food shortage appeared in northern Ethiopia during 1977 and gradually worsened, but relief work averted a crisis until 1983, when the main rains failed and Ethiopia faced Africa's most terrible famine since the 1920s. The worst-affected areas were Wollo and Tigre, where, as in neighbouring Eritrea, warfare between secessionist guerrillas and Ethiopian troops compounded the problem, so that perhaps half those needing aid early in 1985 were outside the government's control. By then famine was penetrating southern Ethiopia and nearly 8,000,000 people were affected, but thereafter the numbers declined.[185] The crisis lasted longer in Sudan, which had largely escaped famine during the 1970s but was forced by harvest failure to seek aid during December 1984. Eighteen months later some 5,000,000 Sudanese were still at risk, chiefly in the remote western regions but increasingly also in the war-torn south.[186]

The chief reason for most of these famines was drought. After gradually increasing rainfall in savanna regions during the later colonial period, the mid 1950s initiated a decade of instability. In 1961 Lake Victoria rose more than its total range of fluctuation during the previous sixty years and Lake Chad reached its highest level of the century, but a slow downward trend of rainfall was nevertheless already under way in the West African savanna. During the late 1960s this collapsed into acute drought, for reasons which are still unknown.[187] The drought continued with only brief interruptions until the mid 1980s. The Nile flood of 1984 was the worst for 350 years and in the mid 1980s both Lake Chad and the Senegal River fell to their lowest levels of the twentieth century, although by early 1986 Lake Chad was again rising quickly.[188] Africa's drought of 1968–85 was certainly its worst of the twentieth century. Not since the 1830s or possibly the 1740s had it experienced such a catastrophe.

The rainfall sequence might have been calculated to maximise the disaster. Since the 1920s, population growth had encouraged the settlement of marginal land. During the benign 1950s and early 1960s, for example, cultivators in Niger and neighbouring countries pushed northwards into formerly pastoral regions of the Sahel, while veterinary measures, boreholes, peace, and good pastures swelled Niger's cattle herds from 760,000 beasts in 1938 to 4,500,000 in 1970. It was among these pastoralists and frontier farmers that the Sahel famine – like many earlier African famines – was most serious.[189] In Kenya, similarly, the famines of the 1960s and 1970s centred in newly settled lowlands. The Ethiopian famine of 1972–3 was worst in those areas of Wollo province occupied by pastoralists or recently settled by cultivators.[190]

To drought and population growth was added a range of secondary causes, just as the decline of famine mortality between the wars had been due to a combination of factors. One secondary cause was warfare, whose contribution to famine ran from Zaïre and Biafra in the 1960s through northern Uganda, Mozambique, and Chad to the Ethiopian disaster of the early 1980s. Another was declining agricultural production in several regions. In the 24 African states affected by famine in 1984, grain production per head had fallen between 1970 and 1980 by 33 per cent, even after allowance was made for drought.[191] One reason why Sudan suffered so seriously during the 1980s was that agricultural investment had concentrated on exports to the Middle East. Many Ethiopian pastoralists suffered especially during the 1970s because they had lost land to agricultural projects, while the revolutionary government's emphasis on mechanised state farms contributed to Ethiopia's food shortage in the early 1980s.[192]

Many observers believed that a major reason for famine was the breakdown of the devices by which Africans had traditionally averted or survived it. In Hausaland, for example, it was claimed that complex households had disintegrated, local granaries had disappeared, collective institutions had atrophied, rural trade and crafts had decayed, rulers no longer adjusted taxes to grain yields, great men no longer aided the poor, peasants had to sell grain cheaply to repay debts, and the poor lacked the land and resources to practise risk-averting agricultural techniques.[193] These changes were widely reported. Agriculturalists in Senegal in 1973 and pastoralists in Sudan in 1961 and the Sahel in the early 1970s were all said to have survived best where indigenous practices were least changed. Shuwa Arabs in north-eastern Nigeria called the dearth of 1972–4 'The Era of Refusing to Recognise Brotherhood'.[194] Yet against this must be set evidence that survival techniques were practised widely and successfully.[195] In the savanna, as in post-colonial cities, the poor still survived chiefly by their own efforts. Of 74 informants interviewed in a Hausa village after the famine of 1973–4, 68 had intensified a secondary occupation (crafts, trade, etc.), 58 had received support from kin or friends, 52 had borrowed grain or money, 44 had sold assets, 37 had undertaken wage-labour, and 35 had sold livestock.[196] The family was still a first line of defence. In one Mossi village in 1973, household heads responded to famine by taking personal control of grain stores and instituting rationing. Mutual aid flourished in this village: one unfortunate family begged two months' food from kin and neighbours, while distant relatives from other regions received self-sacrificing hospitality.[197] Yet, as always, family solidarity had limits. Men abandoned their families to seek work or food for themselves or pasture for their cattle, to relieve their foodstores of a hungry stomach, or simply to escape dishonour:

> I heard a story of a young mother who had arrived a week before with her four children. She was crying bitterly. When the family had come in sight of the town after two days of walking, her husband had told her roughly to go on ahead with the children. When she looked back he was hanging from a tree at the roadside.[198]

Not only were many traditional forms of famine behaviour practised, but new means of survival existed. The most important were towns. Men moved to towns as migrant workers from the less devastated rural areas, raising from 37 to 75 per cent the proportion of males aged 15–44 absent from one Nigerien village.[199] Families fled to towns as starving refugees. Both in 1972 and 1982 northern Ethiopian villagers converged on market towns and main roads in the ancient belief that power spelled food. Ouagadougou took in over 100,000 refugees between 1968 and 1973. In 1984–5 over 1,500,000 Sudanese were thought to have left their homes in search of food. In December 1984 government repatriated nearly 40,000 of them from Omdurman alone.[200] Elsewhere refugees squatted for years on the flanks of savanna towns, hopeless, bitter, struggling to survive by casual work, begging, and prostitution.[201]

Both old and new means of survival deserve emphasis, for the striking point about post-colonial famines is how few people died in them. Perhaps only Biafra, the two Ethiopian famines, Mozambique, and northern Uganda saw death-rates remotely comparable with earlier 'famines that killed'. Officially, not a single Nigerian died during the famine of 1972–4.[202] The chief reason was that no famine precipitated a major epidemic of disease. There were alarms over measles in Biafra and the Sahel and over cholera in Somalia and Sudan, but the main causes of mortality (apart from kwashiorkor in Biafra) were routine infections acting on malnutrition.[203] This severing of the link between famine and epidemic was one means by which famine mortality was brought under control during the mid colonial period and it was the one that survived best after Independence, probably because it was the easiest to preserve. The other means of controlling famine mortality – effective government, modern transport, large-scale food trade, and generally increased levels of wealth – survived more unevenly in a manner which, along with the incidence of drought and warfare, determined the severity of famine mortality in each region.

Several governments exacerbated famine by refusing to acknowledge its existence or seek international aid, chiefly for reasons of national pride – 'a sign of self-respect vis-à-vis the international community', as President

Lamizana of Upper Volta described it.[204] Deliberate concealment was common in the Sahel during the early 1970s, in Sudan in 1982–4, and especially in Ethiopia during 1972–3. Ethiopia was the one African country that had never established control of famine mortality and in the early 1970s its administration proved incapable of managing relief efficiently.[205] The governments of Niger and Chad also showed themselves incompetent at that time. Nigeria insisted on meeting its less severe famine entirely from its own resources and did so more effectively, although the relief provided was no more than one additional means of survival open to sections of the population.[206] The famine of the early 1980s was generally handled more skilfully. Only in Sudan was there serious concealment. Niger, so badly hit in the early 1970s, largely escaped a decade later owing to improved agricultural policies, while several Sahelian states had built up food stocks.[207] The Ethiopian Relief and Rehabilitation Commission, created in March 1974, grew into a massive organisation – said in October 1985 to have 17,000 field-workers – with greater administrative competence than Ethiopia had hitherto seen. In southern Africa, drought-ridden Botswana was especially successful in preserving control over famine mortality.[208]

Transport was also vital. In Biafra the worst-nourished were often those deep in the bush.[209] By the 1970s higher oil prices and the associated decay of motor transport made the problem still more difficult. Even Nigeria's system experienced bottlenecks, but generally it worked well and farmers there gave better transport as the main reason why the drought of 1973 wrought less damage than that of 1913. Sahelian pastoralists and the remote cultivators of Chad and Upper Volta were less fortunate. Disintegrated transport systems contributed largely to famine in Angola and Mozambique during the early 1980s.[210] Ethiopia's problem was unique, for although a main road bisected the chief famine area in Wollo, feeder roads scarcely existed. 'In those people who could stagger to the [main] road . . . the famine is over', relief workers reported in mid 1974. ' . . . Away from the few roads, both in the north and south of the country, it is not yet known if famine exists, let alone its extent.' 'It's like you have to cross about four or five Grand Canyons to get to where the people are', an exasperated relief coordinator complained in 1985, while a journalist saw 'the uncounted dead in the remote highlands' as the problem which made famine so destructive of life in Ethiopia.[211] In Sudan the problem was different but equally grave, for there the main rail and road routes to the west collapsed entirely during the rains of June 1985 and left millions of people without supplies.[212]

Transport and governmental capacity were inextricably linked with grain markets. In this respect post-colonial famines were of two kinds. At certain times and places there was an absolute shortage of food, as towards the end of Biafra's agony and in northern Ethiopia and the western provinces of Sudan at periods during the 1980s. Elsewhere food was often available, but at prices which many could not pay. On the Nigerian side of the Civil War battle line, for example, 'At some places, even in the war-affected areas, some surpluses of, for instance, beans, maize and rice were available, which the farmers could not sell, in spite of being surrounded by starving refugees who had no money to pay with.'[213] The same was true in Ethiopia and Niger in 1973–4, while peasants in Kano observed that whereas in 1913 there had been money but no food, in 1973 there was food but no money.[214] In reality this was probably not a new phenomenon, for grain prices had soared during famine in nineteenth-century Kano, but the expanded commerce of the twentieth century had reduced regional food-supply variations at the cost of the poor. During post-colonial famines some market systems operated both effectively and ruthlessly. Nigerian entrepreneurs trucked food to the areas of greatest demand, so that a study in July 1973 showed a remarkable uniformity of grain prices throughout Nigerian Hausaland, but at levels which the poor could often not afford.[215] Elsewhere, however, transport was often inadequate, governments had destroyed trading systems, or market mechanisms collapsed under the weight of fears and expectations. When this last process occurred – as in Ethiopia and the Sahel in 1973 and Sudan in 1984 – the price of food could multiply several times in a few weeks and precipitate those dependent on the market (chiefly the poor) into almost instantaneous starvation, especially because the prices of their assets (chiefly stock) generally fell equally fast.[216] This did not make famine more common or severe than in the past, but it did change its character.

Although relatively few people died in post-colonial famines (except in Ethiopia and Biafra), nevertheless suffering and death were probably concentrated more exclusively among the structural poor than hitherto. If this was not quite 'class famine',[217] it approached that. Especially numerous among famine victims were those who were poor because they were remote, as the account of transport has shown. Pastoralists suffered everywhere. In the Sahel their death-rates were several times those of cultivators, while perhaps one-quarter or one-third of the Afar pastoralists of Ethiopia may have died in 1972–4. Among the Mursi of Ethiopia the most vulnerable families were those without cattle to sell. In southern Africa they were those without reliable off-farm income.[218] At Wollo's famine shelters, 'The poorest people came first but small landowners followed, having pawned, sold or simply deserted their holdings to seek work, whilst women and children sought relief. Their number was compounded also by pastoralists from as far as the Danakil desert.'[219]

Among the poor, moreover, those most at risk were the traditionally vulnerable. Wollo's relief shelters in 1974 contained a normal proportion of those aged 15–44 (although with a disproportionate number of women), but those aged 5–14 were over-represented and those aged less than 5 or more than 45 were under-represented, for the very young and the elderly were often already dead.[220] Children were always especially vulnerable. Infants under 5 formed 60 per cent of all those malnourished in parts of Biafra. Among children, girls were often worse nourished than boys. Yet in most famines the death-rate increased most sharply among the elderly – and that meant anyone over 45.[221]

Despite its horrors, the return of mass famine mortality did focus attention on Africa's poor for the first time since the missionary campaigns of the late nineteenth century. The overseas relief agencies were affected first. Although their attention was shifted from Europe to the Third World by the World Refugee Year of 1959 and the Freedom from Hunger Campaign of 1960, it was the Congo crisis of 1960 and the ensuing famine, malnutrition, and refugee problems that first drew them into sub-Saharan Africa. Oxfam's first substantial grant to the region was the £300,000 it sent for immediate relief work in the Congo.[222] Then, after some years of developmental work in drought-stricken areas of southern and eastern Africa, the Biafran crisis of 1967–70 drew the agencies into their first massive relief operation – in 1970 the Save the Children Fund alone was responsible for feeding nearly 1,500,000 people in Nigeria[223] – involved them in intense political controversy, and etched the image of starving African children on Western minds. This experience alarmed the agencies, which would have been glad to return to long-term development projects, but the famines of 1972–85 repeatedly obliged them to concentrate on emergency relief. The famines also greatly expanded their operations. In 1970–1 Oxfam's income, £3,301,450, had scarcely risen for a decade. Five years later, following famine in Ethiopia and the Sahel, it was £6,500,000. In 1984–5, at the peak of the Ethiopian crisis, it was £51,000,000. Oxfam spent £21,700,000 in Ethiopia and Sudan during 1984–5, while late in 1985 some 47 voluntary agencies were delivering relief to Ethiopia and the Save the Children Fund had 540 staff working in Sudan.[224] Meanwhile famine had also brought into Africa the vastly greater resources of the (largely American) food aid agencies. Between 1955 and 1974 only 5–6 per cent of world food aid went to Africa. In 1980–1 the proportion was 52 per cent.[225]

The relief agencies did immense practical good for the African poor. Like Albert Schweitzer, they also validated Western civilisation for a generation of young Europeans. By the mid 1980s they had gone far to convince world opinion of their own confident specific for African poverty and famine, which was small-scale, participatory development projects for the poorest of the poor.[226] The relief agencies also offered an organisational model which some Africans imitated. In Burkina, for example, Captain Sankara articulated a widespread resentment when he exclaimed that 'a bit of us dies with each grain of millet that we receive', but Burkina established its own self-help programmes and voluntary organisations. Sudan set up an Islamic African Relief Agency and a Commission for Relief and Rehabilitation.[227] The latter was probably modelled on Ethiopia's organisation, whose effectiveness was appropriate to the African state with the richest history of institutional care for the poor.

The return of mass famine mortality also restored the poor to an important place in thinking about Africa's economic future, whereas during the 1960s they had still been seen as an urban category interesting only philanthropists and novelists. Even Julius Nyerere, while stressing rural needs, had been silent about the very poor. The impact of famine in the early 1970s coincided with the first modern research into African poverty.[228] As the two revealed the scale of rural misery, first the International Labour Office with its strategy of Basic Needs, then the World Bank under McNamara, and finally in the 1980s African governments altered their development strategies to give at least verbal emphasis to the need to alleviate poverty. By 1986, when a special session of the United Nations discussed it, African poverty was recognised as a critical problem.

Yet it was rarely understood. Men of the left commonly misconceived it as a recent phenomenon due to colonial and capitalist exploitation. Men of the right misconceived it as a recent phenomenon due to the weather or population growth or the incompetence of African governments. Few realised that conjunctural poverty had changed its nature during the twentieth century. Fewer still realised how much of structural poverty had not changed at all.

14

The transformation of poverty in southern Africa

The very poor of twentieth-century Africa showed much continuity with earlier periods. Most were either those made destitute by famine or those unable to work and neglected by others. The able-bodied, even when deprived of land or other resources, generally found work to avert extreme poverty, except at moments of conjunctural unemployment.

In southern Africa, however, new patterns of poverty emerged during the later twentieth century. The very poor of the past survived, but to them were added victims of structural rather than conjunctural unemployment: able-bodied men and women who could not compensate for their lack of resources by working for others, because no such work existed. For them, to belong to a large family could be a reason for poverty rather than a source of wealth as in the past. Southern Africans began to suffer the land-scarce family poverty long predominant in more densely peopled continents. They suffered it especially severely because the South African government sought, with considerable but incomplete success, to remove and confine the poor to the most remote countryside.

The National Party gained power in South Africa in 1948 with a determination to check African urbanisation, redirect labour to farms, and ensure that those Africans indispensable in towns should live not in freehold townships or squatter settlements but in segregated, orderly, and easily controlled locations. This required not merely urban reform but almost total urban rebuilding. The Group Areas Act of 1950 gave power to relocate population groups. The Native Building Workers Act of 1951 broke the monopoly of white construction unions. The Native Services Levy Act of 1952 obliged employers who did not house their African workers to pay a weekly levy to the municipality.[1] In April 1955 Benoni on the Witwatersrand became the first of many towns with an entirely new African township, financed by the National Housing Commission, linked by electric rail to workplaces 11 kilometres away, composed of two- or three-room concrete houses with laid-on electricity, and divided into eight 'tribal' zones with schools teaching in appropriate languages.[2]

The rehousing of African townsmen was a remarkable administrative achievement, but its success varied with place and time. It was most effective in Johannesburg, which had the worst housing shortage and the greatest potential for political disorder. Destruction of squatter camps and freehold townships began in 1955, amid much protest. Their inhabitants were moved to Soweto, 13 kilometres to the south-west, leaving only Alexandra, to the north, as a separate settlement which in the early 1980s housed 50,000–70,000 people in 'one of the most squalid, overcrowded townships in the country', popular with the poor for its low rents.[3] With this exception, the authorities successfully concentrated all Johannesburg's Africans into Soweto, at the cost of enormous overcrowding. In the late 1970s and early 1980s Soweto's 113,000 houses (most with four rooms, some with three or two) averaged ten occupants each. Another 70,000 single people lived in hostels and an estimated 23,000 families in illegal backyard shacks, while many of the poorest occupied scrap car bodies or slept in the streets or under the eaves of churches.[4]

The rebuilding of Durban had a different outcome. Here the authorities' first priority was to destroy Cato Manor, 3 kilometres from the city centre, which in 1958 housed some 120,000 Africans in self-built housing on Indian-owned land. Their transfer to new townships at Kwa Mashu, 18 kilometres to the north, and Umlazi, to the west, was largely completed by 1965, but it failed to eradicate informal housing because urban immigration from nearby KwaZulu was more difficult to control than in Johannesburg. Whereas in 1952 an estimated 200,000 were 'illegally housed in shack slums' in Durban, in 1980 the number inhabiting informal settlements in the Durban Metropolitan Region was at least 300,000, or one-third of the African population, and it was expected to exceed 1,700,000 by the year 2000. A survey of African urban attitudes in the early 1980s revealed exceptional discontent among Durban's squatters.[5]

Cape Town's rehousing was as brutal as Johannesburg's and as unsuccessful as Durban's. In 1952 Cape Town was still the least segregated city in southern Africa, with only one-third of its African inhabitants living in official locations. Thirty years later not only Africans but the entire Coloured population had been removed from the city centre and relocated in arid concrete townships which bred crime and bitter resentment.[6] Yet because the authorities concentrated on rehousing those evicted rather than the population increase, overcrowding was acute. In 1977 the new townships already contained 50 per cent more people than they were designed for, reaching 5.6 per habitable room in Elsies River in 1982–3. At least 120,000 Coloured people were squatters in 1977.[7] The situation was even worse for Africans because Coloured people enjoyed legal preference in employment in the Cape Town area, so that from the mid 1960s no further African family housing was built. The result was a large illegal black population – 43 per cent of the 199,600 Africans in the region, according to official figures in 1981 – perhaps one-third of whom were squatters.[8]

South Africa's squatter settlements resembled the informal housing zones of tropical African towns, except that they were even more illegal. In Cape Town's largest squatter settlement, Crossroads, in only 3 per cent of married couples were both partners legally qualified to reside in the city in 1977.[9] Their shacks were acutely overcrowded:

> The 'average' household in Crossroads [in 1983] . . . will consist of 13 inhabitants spread over 5 rooms, each room measuring approximately 8 to 9 square metres with a ceiling height of 2.1 metres. The six immediate family members of the household head will probably have a separate kitchen and two sleeping rooms. Seven lodgers will occupy the remaining two rooms . . . Most of the lodgers will be related to the household head's family . . . There will be one outside toilet for the entire household, and no running water or electricity.[10]

Yet most residents accepted these conditions. 'Overcrowded, yes', one remarked, 'but my children and I have come to live with my husband.'[11] In 1977, 85 per cent of households had both parents present. They were settled people: the men had averaged eighteen years in Cape Town, the women twelve. They were stable working people: only 6 per cent of household heads were unemployed. A network of male and female committees ran the settlement and organised schools. Observers believed that there was less crime or drunkenness and more satisfaction than in new municipal townships. Yet Crossroads was very poor. The proportion of its households living below the Poverty Datum Line was three times that in a municipal township such as Guguletu.[12]

By the 1980s the National Party's attempt to abolish black slums and squatter settlements had failed in the face of population growth, rural poverty, industrial expansion, and the resourcefulness of the poor. Government had already reduced its building programme in order to concentrate on housing in the African homelands. In March 1983 it announced a new policy of selling existing houses into private hands in order to encourage a black middle class.[13] Many homes constructed during the 1950s were already decaying, but conditions were worse in smaller towns which had not been reconstructed. Of African families in Grahamstown, 60 per cent occupied backyard accommodation in 1978. Beaufort West's 'location' was condemned in 1953 and still housed some 6,000 people a generation later.[14] 'Look at the filth', an old woman told a visitor to Philipstown in the Karoo in 1984,

> look at the way the houses are all almost breaking down. There's no running water in the houses and the state of the common water tap is disgusting, and ten to twelve people live in a room where there isn't space enough to move around. Most of the houses have dirt floors, several are nothing but storerooms. We hardly have any furniture, some families haven't even got chairs and have to sit down on empty cans or broken stones. Fleas and bugs? There are plenty of them. You couldn't live in a worse place than this.

Nearby, when it rained, shanty-dwellers slept in garbage bags.[15]

An observer likened the rebuilding of Cape Town to 'a man with a stick breaking spiderwebs in a forest'.[16] The webs were the networks of kinship and neighbourhood which helped the urban poor to survive. Yet webs could be rewoven. Both ideologically and in practice they were a precious inheritance. 'Reciprocity and sharing is the basic principle underlying neighbour relations', a researcher reported of Grahamstown in 1978, 'and the community claims that nobody goes hungry as long as someone has food.' Any woman there who refused to lend and borrow in a neighbourly manner was dismissed as 'too much of the "English"'.[17] Most immigrants to Grahamstown stayed with a kinsman. The unemployed relied chiefly on family support rather than subsidiary earnings.[18] In a survey of a peri-urban area of Natal in 1982–3, '71 per cent stated they could depend on others, in most cases indefinitely', although other studies suggested, as in tropical Africa, that support had limits. The chronic sick received more care from friends and relatives among Africans and the Coloured people than in other communities.[19]

After their kin, people in Soweto turned first to those from their home areas. 'Homeboy' groups were especially vital to migrant workers.[20] Formal ethnic associations, by contrast, remain obscure. In 1967 the Witwatersrand Shangaan Welfare Association was said to supply food, clothing, and blankets to the aged, to give advice on welfare facilities to the indigent, crippled, bereaved, and incapacitated, and to provide crèches for children needing care, but no other tribal association is known to have done so much and it was perhaps significant that Shangaan were long-distance migrants from Mozambique.[21] By contrast, the fact that Cape Town's shebeens lent money at 30 per cent interest a week[22] helps to explain why rotating credit societies – *stokfel* and *mahodisana* – remained vigorous. A study in one quarter of Soweto in 1972–3 showed that 13 per cent of women belonged to a credit society. Membership was even more common among such lonely people as domestic servants in white areas. In the Langa township of Cape Town only the poorest belonged to these clubs.[23] Burial societies, by contrast, attracted all classes. Half the households surveyed in Soweto in 1972–3 belonged to one, while another 29 per cent held funeral insurance. 'Getting a pauper's funeral is like a dog', one woman explained. 'One must be honoured unto death.' The chief benefit offered by the new trade unions formed after 1979 was funeral benefit.[24] The other widespread self-help organisations were the hundreds of independent churches. In the early 1970s there were some 900 in Soweto alone. Those of Zionist type had an average membership of only 30.[25] More active in welfare than those in tropical Africa, the churches appealed to the poor – of Zionist families studied in the Kwa Mashu township of Durban, 90 per cent were below the Poverty Datum Line – but specifically to 'the upright and respectable poor', especially the elderly, the uneducated, and women, who were three-quarters of their members.[26] Not only did Zionists teach earthly resignation, but their puritanism encouraged wise use of limited funds, they offered cheap healing, they relieved the boredom of poverty, and they provided collective aid. 'They are caring communities', one observer reported, 'where concern is shown for all, but particularly for the sick, the aged, and those in adversity.'[27] In the Nyanga township of Cape Town, for example, 'it is common when a congregant becomes unemployed, for an announcement to be made after the service for others to be on the look out for a job for "Brother So-and-So"'.[28] 'If they do not overcome poverty', another observer commented, 'at least poverty does not overcome them.'[29]

The proliferation of small urban self-help groups matched the inadequacy of formal welfare institutions. When the incoming National Party government amended the Unemployment Insurance Act in 1949 to exclude low-paid African workers it ended South Africa's period of creative welfare legislation. Wage increases subsequently multiplied the number of African contributors to the Unemployment Insurance Fund but also threatened its viability. In the early 1980s only an estimated 0.3 per cent of unemployed Africans drew their main support from unemployment benefits.[30] Old age pensions did remain vital to Africans,[31] as did grants to the blind. Provision for other handicapped Africans was less systematic, despite the enormous burden carried by the state hospital system in sprawling townships like Soweto. A study of non-institutionalised chronic sick in Cape Town in 1974–6 found that only 22 per cent of Africans so handicapped received financial assistance, as against 54 per cent of Coloured people and 66 per cent of whites.[32] The number of elderly Africans, especially elderly men, needing institutional care increased as both rural ties and resistance to institutionalisation weakened, but few institutions existed and such expedients emerged as an organisation in Soweto which recruited younger people to help the elderly and disabled in return for taking over their coveted houses when they died.[33] In 1982 over 5,000 people were thought to be sleeping rough in Cape Town alone. Charitable bodies sought to assist them[34] and relieve many other social needs, but they faced not only the scale of the problem and the inequity of the social order but the obstacles erected by apartheid legislation. Once the Native Affairs Department gained control of African welfare in 1960 it discouraged private white involvement, transferred institutions to the homelands, and in 1966 outlawed multiracial welfare organisations.[35]

The urban poor had to rely chiefly on their own ingenuity. Although the informal sector was smaller than in tropical Africa, apartheid policies expanded it. Separated from white or Asian enterprises, commuters from African townships bought cooked food from Johannesburg's 2,000 coffee carts until the authorities eradicated them during the 1960s.[36] Informal activities also flourished in new townships like Soweto (where they may have provided between one-quarter and one-third of all employment in the early 1980s), in surviving freehold townships like Clermont in Durban (where in

1978 the informal sector employed some 20 per cent of the economically active), and in squatter settlements – during the early 1980s the proportion of people engaged in informal activities was twice as high in Crossroads as in any other African section of Cape Town, partly because official control was weaker in Crossroads.[37] Commonly at least half the informal-sector workers were hawkers, especially 'township aunties' selling fruit and vegetables at very low profits. Women also sold cooked food, while men hawked dry goods (often rather more profitably) and children sold newspapers.[38] Little information is available on prostitution, but unemployed women in Johannesburg used it as a means of survival and Greater Cape Town alone was said to have 26,878 prostitutes in 1970, or 2.4 per cent of the total population.[39] Other important sources of illegal income were drugs – between 1971 and 1976 some 80,000 people were gaoled for selling or using cannabis – and especially liquor, for although marabi was dead and Africans could legally buy alcohol for home consumption after 1961, nevertheless shebeens remained centres of popular culture.[40] In 1975–6, 33 per cent of Clermont's informal-sector workers brewed or sold liquor:

> A man will take his whole week's pay and buy drinks for half a dozen of his friends. 'Fill the table and count the empties', he will say to the shebeen queen. The idea seems to be to live well while you can and face the troubles of tomorrow when they come.[41]

The students who led the urban riots of 1976 made shebeens special targets of attack.[42]

For those evicted from familiar slums, new townships were horrifyingly violent. Murders tripled between 1960 and 1977. In 1972 Soweto averaged 15 murders and 60–80 serious assaults each weekend.[43] Most were committed by the poor against one another. Of 450 deaths by stabbing studied in Cape Town in 1981, 62 per cent of victims were labourers and another 15 per cent were unemployed, 73 per cent died within the area in which they lived, and 85 per cent had alcohol in their blood. Their average age was 29. Another study twelve years earlier showed that 60 per cent of victims knew their assailants.[44] Urban reconstruction destroyed gangs like the Globe but encouraged many successors. In 1982 an incomplete survey counted 280 gangs on the Cape Flats alone, with perhaps 80,000 members.[45] Most were defence gangs, often armed with stolen guns, which sought to control a territory and exploit its resources as a means of survival:

> Many of the gang are BJs [*boere jongs*, farm youths] . . . These upcountry guys get arrested and they're sent to Tokyo [Porter Reformatory, situated in Tokai] . . . Maybe they join a gang in reform. When their time comes they don't want to go back home now . . . So a gang leader he says to them, 'You can stay here by me and get to know the place. I can find you work.' So there he starts, you see. Little jobs – go get some sweets or milk from the shop, sell

> a little garu [dagga (cannabis)] and maybe some buttons [mandrax]. Maybe after a time he can be trusted to pull a job.[46]

South African towns used little child labour, except to sell newspapers. 'A recurring comment by social workers throughout the 1970s was: "Child's father deceased. Whereabouts of mother unknown. The child has no fixed abode. He is 10 years old. Found selling newspapers."' Child poverty, however, was widespread. In 1982 at least one hundred children were thought to be sleeping rough in Cape Town alone.[47] Children's homes revealed a changing pattern:

> Today the emphasis has shifted from the parentless children of some disaster to (almost exclusively) the products of broken families. It is the lucky youths who go to children's homes. Their street brothers – and there are perhaps thousands in Cape Town – scratch out a living by petty theft and selling newspapers, sleeping around the warm air-conditioning pipes of big buildings in the inner city at night.[48]

Better sanitation, medicine, and earnings brought better health. Soweto's infant mortality rate declined between 1950 and 1979 from 23.2 to 3.5 per cent, compared to 13.0 per cent in rural Transkei in the early 1980s. Child malnutrition also fell steadily during the 1970s in Cape Town and Soweto.[49] Yet major differences existed among Africans. In Cape Town in the early 1960s some 70 per cent of victims of gastroenteritis (a major killer of infants) came from households below the Poverty Datum Line. A measles epidemic in Port Elizabeth in 1982–3 was concentrated in impoverished squatter areas. A disproportionate number of malnourished children attending a clinic in Crossroads had single mothers, 58 per cent of whom said they had no income whatever.[50]

The same clinic reported that over 75 per cent of women practised family planning – a proportion probably unique in sub-Saharan Africa. Urban families were becoming smaller, but probably as much in response to prosperity and lower infant mortality as to poverty. Urban malnutrition was most common in large families.[51] Other studies confirmed the evidence from Crossroads that female-headed households were especially likely to be poor. They were also numerous. In 1982 some 25 per cent of mothers surveyed on the Cape Flats were raising a family without a husband, while in older townships 40 per cent of household heads might be women.[52] The difficulty of raising a family while working encouraged young women with children to live with their mothers in three-generation female-linked households. It also made child-minding an important occupation for elderly townswomen.[53] Single mothers had difficulty in obtaining houses – a bogus 'shilling marriage' existed for this purpose in Soweto – and claiming state maintenance grants.[54] Yet many younger mothers preferred to remain single, finding that men were poor providers and wanted large families which urban women found burdensome. In the 1980s more than half the children born in townships like Soweto were technically illegitimate.[55]

Many single mothers were ill-paid domestic servants. In 1970 there were 641,180 African female domestic servants in South Africa. They had largely replaced men during the 1940s by accepting lower wages.[56] In the Eastern Cape in 1978–9 their average wage was R.23 a month plus limited benefits in kind, whereas average African monthly earnings in trade and accommodation services in 1980 were R.149. The 175 domestic servants surveyed in the Eastern Cape averaged 5.53 dependants; 102 were sole breadwinners. They worked an average 61 hours a week, had no legal protection, suffered maddening paternalism, and found extreme difficulty in escaping to another occupation. Two-thirds were daughters of domestic servants and four-fifths had been in service for at least 20 years.[57] 'The predominant response', it was found, '. . . is a sense of being trapped; of having no alternatives; of living out an infinite series of daily frustrations, indignities and denials.'[58]

Other especially ill-paid occupations included catering, the clothing industry, service industries generally, and almost any job which was either filled mainly by women or the young or took place in the homelands.[59] Generally, however, formal-sector wages improved, especially during the 1970s, and began to dissolve the poverty of low wages which had prevailed among townspeople since the 1890s. Real African wages in manufacturing roughly doubled between 1939 and 1951 and increased slowly thereafter. Real African mine wages remained static from 1911 to 1969, but the average paid then multiplied nearly fourfold in eleven years in response to strikes, a high gold price, and declining migration from independent northern countries.[60] Average African real wages outside agriculture and domestic service rose by 89 per cent during the 1970s, then stagnated during the early 1980s.[61] Africans' share of personal income rose between 1970 and 1980 from 20 to 29 per cent. By the late 1970s their industrial wages were higher than those paid in India or Brazil. Government was by then committed to a relatively high-wage urban economy, the recognition of African trade unions and permanent African urbanisation, and an attempt to divide urban workers from the rural poor.[62]

The corollary of higher wages was higher structural unemployment, which now became the chief form of urban poverty. 'Every day' in Soweto in the early 1980s

> large crowds of unemployed workseekers gather outside the West Rand Administration Board Offices in Albert Street, and swarm around any car which slows its progress, in the hope it may be someone offering work. At weekends, hundreds of people stand on roadsides seeking casual labour; some are unemployed, others seek to supplement inadequate wages. The general demeanour is one of defeat, as they stand, hands raised in supplication, as they literally beg for work, as cars speed past, creating the impression of bewildered people who have been left behind by the rapid changes of a capitalist economy.[63]

Unemployment was impossible to calculate precisely, but one authority reckoned that between 1970 and 1980 the proportion of the total labour force unemployed (including underemployment) rose from 12 to 21 per cent.[64] As in tropical Africa, unemployment was most common among women and the young but perhaps most devastating for heads of households:

> It's a terrible situation. When you look at people and they look back at you and you think that they know you're unemployed. People think you're worthless. Any real man can support his family. I used to be a real man now I am worth less than a loaf of bread. Bread is more use to them than me.[65]

Although South Africa's rulers still believed that poverty was chiefly an urban problem,[66] it was estimated in 1981 that in reality only some 7 per cent of the poor lived in cities. Roughly twice as many lived on farms and in small townships on the platteland.[67] There the poverty of low wages survived. South Africa's farm labour statistics are difficult to interpret, but farm employment appears to have risen steadily until the late 1960s and then declined.[68] This suggests that the mechanisation of South African farming – between 1946 and 1973 the number of tractors in use rose from 20,292 to 164,100[69] – did not dramatically reduce the labour force or raise its wages. Instead mechanisation destroyed surviving labour-tenants and replaced them by fully proletarianised workers and their families. Between 1960 and 1983 over one million people were evicted from white farms. Meanwhile urban influx controls virtually bound farmworkers to their employment and destroyed their bargaining power, already weak enough owing to the ban on registered agricultural trade unions and the lack of minimum wages, employment legislation, or protection for strikers.[70] The result was to hold down agricultural wages. In the Eastern Cape, where wages were notoriously low, the average farmworker's household in 1957 earned £8.18.4 a month, or £1.6.8 per head. This was somewhat less than the unskilled wages paid in nearby East London, although better than average income in the Ciskei reserve. Eastern Cape farm wages had just outpaced inflation since 1932. In the central Orange Free State the average farmworker's household income in 1957 was £14.13.4 a month. During the next fifteen years farm wages remained about two-thirds of mining wages and rose only very slowly.[71]

The impact of urban wage increases in the 1970s varied with the degree of agricultural commercialisation. A sugarcane-cutter's basic cash wage multiplied five times between 1969–70 and 1975–6, but a study of the George area of the Cape suggested only a 17 per cent real increase between 1970–1 and 1978. Farm earnings, especially in remote areas, remained well below urban wages. In the early 1980s they were roughly R.60 a month in George and R.80 in the Karoo, against R.189 in occupations outside agriculture and domestic service in 1980.[72] Average farm earnings also concealed especially ill-paid occupations. Many farms made increasing use of the wives and children of permanent workers, often at very low wages. Women were about one-third of all farmworkers during the mid 1970s. Those on northern Transvaal plantations earned only R.20–40 a month during the early 1980s. The lowest regular wages in all South Africa were probably paid to domestic servants in farmhouses. In 1978–9 they averaged R.15 a month on western Transvaal maize farms and R.11 in the Eastern Cape.[73]

In 1981 an estimated 80 per cent of South Africa's poor lived in the homelands.[74] Whatever may have happened to agriculture there before 1948, food production per head undoubtedly fell dramatically thereafter. One estimate suggests that in 1946–8 annual per capita output of maize and sorghum averaged 113 kilograms; in 1955–7, 81 kilograms; in 1971–4, 50 kilograms. In Lesotho the average household produced 21 bags of cereals in 1950 and 9 in 1970. KwaZulu, which in the 1890s had produced much surplus grain, averaged only 30 per cent of its needs between 1960 and 1977.[75] A survey in 1974 found that 67 per cent of Transkeian households had never produced enough to feed themselves. Studies there and in KwaZulu in 1975–7 suggested that average household income was about R.25 a month, or much the same as a domestic servant's wage.[76]

The chief cause of rural poverty was shortage of land. Between the late 1940s and the early 1970s the population of the reserves more than doubled.[77] In 1943 nearly 10 per cent of Transkeian households were landless; in the early 1980s, some 20–30 per cent. In the desperately overcrowded Gazankulu homeland, in the northern Transvaal, roughly half the population had no land in the early 1980s.[78] The proportion of landless households in Lesotho rose between 1950 and 1970 from 7 to 13 per cent and the arable land available per person fell from 1.41 to 0.91 acres.[79] Despite the shortage, however, 20–30 per cent of arable land in the homelands was left uncultivated each year, chiefly owing to lack of access to labour, ploughing teams, or cash to purchase inputs.[80]

Cattle were at least as important as cultivation to homeland economies. Between 1946–8 and 1971–4 their number scarcely changed, but the number of large stock units held by each person fell from 1.50 to 0.66.[81] The proportion of households without cattle was 45 per cent in the Transkei in 1974, 50 per cent in Lesotho in 1970 and KwaZulu in 1980, and 74 per cent among the Tshidi Barolong in 1974.[82]

One means of survival for the rural poor was casual labour, either for neighbours or for white employers. It provided much of the cash earned by rural Zulu women.[83] Yet the few wealthy African farmers could employ only a small minority of the poor. Informal activities were widespread, especially among women, but extremely ill rewarded. Of women undertaking such activities in a poor area of KwaZulu in 1983, 85 per cent earned less than R.30 a month, while a study in the Transkei showed that two common activities, grasswork and collecting firewood, earned 27 and 15 cents an hour respectively.[84]

The rural poor could still rely on much family aid. In KwaZulu in the early 1980s some 67 per cent of those interviewed declared that in need they would borrow food (and 48 per cent money) from neighbours or relatives, while in the Ciskei, where poverty was acute, 'it is only in this burdensome and impoverishing sense that the "extended family" still exists, except in a few anachronistic pockets . . . Consequently few starve, but not many can prosper.'[85] The burden of family aid fell heavily on young women. A survey of 150 households in the Nqutu area of KwaZulu in the early 1970s counted 973 household members of whom only 7 men and 158 women were aged between 22 and 55. Inevitably, therefore, family aid had limits. Even Swaziland had its 'neglected wives, abandoned widows, and women struggling to feed children on inadequate resources'.[86] In less favoured areas such unfortunates suffered malnutrition and disease. A cholera epidemic which affected part of KwaZulu in 1981–2 struck four times as large a proportion of the poor as of the more prosperous.[87] Child malnutrition, too, was especially grave in the homelands, where it had largely replaced famine. In 1976–7 it affected 7 per cent of children in the Nqutu area of KwaZulu, while figures for remote areas – not always easy to evaluate – ranged up to 26 per cent of all children aged from one to five in an isolated part of Gazankulu. Occasionally malnutrition merged into frank starvation, as in the arid Kuruman area in 1968.[88] Nor was hunger confined to children. In the Ciskei in 1980 Dr Thomas described 'a paralysed old woman, persistently scraping the bottom of an empty pot and putting her claw-like hand to her mouth in a despairing *imitation* of eating'.[89]

Dr Thomas reckoned that half the children in the Ciskei in the early 1970s were to some degree undernourished, while of those malnourished – i.e. positively sick – some 80 per cent had been deserted by their fathers and another 10 per cent had fathers who were dead, sick, or unemployed. Some 60 per cent of malnourished children were illegitimate. Only 40 per cent were being cared for by their mothers, 25 per cent by grandmothers, and the rest by others. By contrast, 80 per cent of well-nourished children were legitimate and supported by their fathers, while 95 per cent were being cared for by their mothers. Although sheer poverty caused undernutrition, malnutrition was due to the destruction of family life by migrant labour.[90] Others, however, believed that the problem was more complicated and that poverty was also the primary cause of malnutrition,[91] but they agreed that rural family structures were being transformed. The most dramatic evidence was 'illegitimacy'. Of women with children in Botswana in 1971, 66 per cent of those aged 15–19 and 49 per cent of those aged 20–24 had never married. Illegitimacy rates had increased dramatically during the previous generation.[92] Similar evidence existed in Lesotho, Swaziland, and the South African homelands, where the proportion of children born outside marriage rose between 1960–70 and 1980 from 35 to 43 per cent.[93] Although Africans lamented these 'children of women', in fact a new family structure was emerging to meet the paramount need for migrant labour. Many unmarried mothers were in process of marriage, for the separation of childbearing from formal marriage enabled migrant workers to accumulate the resources needed to establish homesteads while also meeting obligations to aging parents dependent upon their earnings. As a Sotho migrant explained, 'On your first trip to the place of the whites, you support those who brought you up. On your second trip, you take out money that counts as cattle for marrying a wife. On your third trip, you look after everything in your own homestead.'[94] While the young migrant father remained a member of his parents' household, the young mother and her children often remained with her own parents, forming the three-generation household which was not simply a survival from the past but an adaptation to the labour-migration economy. During the 1970s half of Lesotho's households fitted this pattern.[95] If such a household lost its male breadwinner, the result might be a three-generation structure linked by female ties. Some 30 per cent of Lesotho's households were female-headed during the 1970s, compared with 34 per cent in the Ciskei in 1964–5 and 24 per cent in the Transkei in 1968.[96] The difficulties which women faced in obtaining jobs and acquiring and ploughing land meant that the poor included many young solitary women without land and old solitary women without labour.[97]

For such vulnerable households, the key to survival was access to a reliable source of cash income.[98] Two sources existed. One was labour migration, which had replaced agriculture as the economic basis of rural life. In 1982 two-thirds of the Transkei's male workers were absent at any time. Migrants' remittances provided 71 per cent of rural household income in Lesotho and 78 per cent of KwaZulu's total Gross Domestic Product in 1976.[99] Most studies found that migrants sent some 20–25 per cent of their earnings to their immediate families, but they also distributed sums to other kinsmen.[100] Exactly who received the money was a vital question to which nobody knew the answer. Probably most went to the bigger and more prosperous households. In Botswana members of more fortunate households got the better jobs and were possibly more likely to make remittances, but although poorer households received less from migrant labour, the sums they received were relatively more important to them. Among Transkei rural households in 1982, similarly, migrants' remittances provided 67 per cent of income for those earning less than R.500 a year, 46 per cent for those earning R.2,000–3,000, and 13 per cent for those earning R.4,000–5,000.[101] Many poor households were utterly dependent on a single distant labourer. 'I cannot sleep at night any longer', one mother lamented, 'because my son was so ill when he last came home. But I sent him back to work because his is the only income we have. I am being forced to kill one child in order to feed the others.'[102]

The second source of reliable cash income, for those within South Africa, was a state pension. Indeed, the pension system created during the 1940s gave South African poverty a unique pattern. Pensions were paid from general revenue to men over 65, women and veterans over 60, blind people over 19, and other disabled people (including leprosy sufferers) over 16, subject to a means test.[103] When instituted in 1944, maximum pensions paid to Africans were £1 a month in cities, 15 shillings in towns, and 10 shillings in rural areas. (The differentials were abolished in 1965.) During 1946–7 (the first full year) £788,329 was paid to 167,416 old age pensioners.[104] The relative value of the African pension then fell until the 1970s, when its real value increased by 131 per cent, much in the same manner as wages, only to stagnate again thereafter.[105] In 1982 the maximum cash payment was R.49 a month, while the average Household Subsistence Level (the former Poverty Datum Line) was R.242. In 1980 Africans received 560,834 old age pensions and 158,305 disability grants.[106]

To obtain a pension, even at these low rates, was a matter of survival for many poor South Africans. It required a 'book-of-life' (a birth certificate or some substitute), perhaps a letter of credence from a former employer or other responsible person, endless queuing, a means test, the approval of a magistrate, and often months or years of waiting. To obtain the money could then be a bi-monthly ordeal:

> About 40 pensioners slept in the freezing open veld outside the Soweto Council Chambers on Monday night in an attempt to beat yesterday's long queue for their bi-monthly pension payouts . . .
>
> Mrs Elizabeth Morake, who said she believed that her age could be 75, said she had always been an early bird since she had started receiving her pension 10 years earlier.[107]

Elderly recipients might be pushed to the post office in wheelbarrows. Shebeen-owners carefully escorted indebted customers. In the countryside the regular payout attracted traders from far and wide.[108]

By the 1980s pensions vied with local employment as the second source of rural cash income after migrant remittances. In the Transkei in 1982, for example, the poorest 50 per cent of households received about 69 per cent of their cash income from migrant labour, 16 per cent from pensions, and 12 per cent from local employment. The poorest 20 per cent of those households which received nothing from migrant remittances obtained 64 per cent of their cash income from pensions in 1983–4. In Gazankulu in 1984, 45 per cent of all those receiving a steady income were pensioners.[109] By subsidising the elderly, the Government may have hoped to buy the compliance of a group it considered influential. Certainly the elderly enjoyed enhanced status. Often they were breadwinners for whole households. During the drought of 1983 homesteads in northern Natal 'actively attempted to recruit pensioners into their ranks'.[110]

Where subsistence depended on a secure cash income from migrants or pensions, the very poor were naturally those lacking such sources. That the poorest were not labour migrants but households lacking migrants had been noted in Pondoland in the 1930s,[111] but after 1948 it became normal in the southern African countryside. It was the traditional source of African poverty – lack of access to labour – in a modern idiom. This kind of poverty was probably worst in Lesotho, where there were many migrant labourers but no pensions. One study there in 1975–6 showed that migrant earnings provided 71 per cent of all rural income but only 8 per cent of the income of the poorest 27 per cent of households, many of which were female-headed or composed chiefly of elderly people. The same pattern existed in Botswana, where the very poor were the roughly one-third of rural families with no wage-earner in the towns or South Africa. Similar circumstances were reported from KwaZulu and the Transkei during the early 1980s.[112]

Where pensions and migrant earnings were lacking and land was scarce, a large household could be a disadvantage, so that the southern African countryside displayed, perhaps for the first time in rural Africa, the family poverty already familiar in South African towns. This did not mean that poor households were necessarily large. Most contained only an abandoned mother and her child, a widow, an elderly couple, or some other tiny grouping.[113] But it did mean that a minority of large households was very poor. A small study in KwaZulu in the early 1980s found that larger households tended to have lower per capita income. Small households often contained a pensioner. A study in the George area in 1982 showed that the poorest 29 households averaged 8.52 members, against 7.12 for the whole sample, but that the average number of earners was 1.79 and 2.31 respectively.[114] In the desperately overcrowded Ciskei, illegitimate children were often unwanted and neglected. 'Infanticide is a socially accepted and tautly "hushed up" solution', Dr Thomas reported. 'Babies are "delivered" into lavatories, or found and cleared away with the rubbish in the bins in the morning . . . The fabled extended family now usually consists of one old woman, in a hut on a hill, too decrepit to work, who is forced to carry on the backbreaking struggle of caring for small children.'[115]

Differentiation was accelerating in the homelands. Between 1960 and 1980 the per capita incomes of 71 per cent of their population roughly doubled, owing to increased urban earnings. Another 15 per cent received higher absolute but lower relative incomes. A further 10 per cent suffered a deterioration in absolute terms, while a final 4 per cent were destitute in 1980 as in 1960.[116] 'They said that independence has made the rich richer and the poor poorer', researchers reported from Bophuthatswana.[117] Moreover, because the total population rose rapidly, so did the number of poor people.[118] 'The rank and file, the *sans culottes* . . . the people down there, the underdog', as a Transkei politician described them,[119] were more numerous than ever. And the nature of their poverty was changing.

Rural households without a member fit to work in the modern economy experienced a new variant of Africa's traditional poverty. Alongside them, however, was a new category: those willing and able to work but continuously excluded from employment by an absolute shortage of jobs and land. Not only did the proportion of South Africa's labour force unemployed or underemployed increase between 1970 and 1980 from 12 to 21 per cent,[120] but for the first time in South African history the cyclical upswing of 1978–

81 did not reduce unemployment levels. By the mid 1980s structural unemployment had certainly increased further and all projections expected it to grow until the end of the century.[121] Increased wages and mechanisation led even the gold mines to stabilise their labour force by issuing re-registration guarantee certificates to migrant workers on their obligatory annual visits to the reserves. This shut out new applicants. Those outside the Union suffered first. Botswana's labour exports to South Africa peaked in 1976, then fell. Workers from Lesotho employed in the gold mines declined between 1977 and 1983 from some 127,000 to 116,000.[122] As two observers remarked, 'The fact that ablebodied men can no longer assume that they can obtain contracts to work in South Africa is potentially perhaps the most radical change in Lesotho history since its loss of political independence and incorporation into the South African economy at the end of the nineteenth century.'[123] During the late 1970s and 1980s homeland residents who had technically lost South African citizenship also found jobs more difficult to obtain. Transkei's migrant workers declined between 1978 and 1980 from 420,000 to 345,000. Unemployment rates in many homelands were about 20–30 per cent at that time.[124]

In other countries the rural unemployed would have swollen peri-urban shanty towns. In South Africa influx control partly restrained them. Its formal abolition in Namibia in 1977 brought a flood to the towns, as happened also when the police tried the experiment of not asking for reference books on the streets of Pretoria.[125] Unemployment was also concentrated into the homelands by the Government's massive resettlement programme, which between 1960 and 1983 removed at least 3,548,900 people – well over 10 per cent of South Africa's population – from their homes to locations officially considered appropriate to their ethnic identity. Most were resettled in the homelands, whose share of the African population increased between 1960 and 1980 from 39 to 53 per cent.[126]

Resettlement areas varied greatly. The worst were 'closer settlements' in small homelands where hundreds of thousands received little but plots on which to build shacks – areas urban in density of population and lack of agricultural land, but devoid of urban employment or services. Qwaqwa, on the Lesotho border, occupied 48,234 hectares; between 1970 and 1980 its population increased from 24,000 to 300,000. Onverwacht began in midwinter 1979 as a tented camp to accommodate Southern Sotho forced out of a nearby Tswana homeland; three years later it had nearly 200,000 people.[127] The population of Kangwane, the dumping-ground for Swazi, grew between 1970 and 1982 from some 120,000 to perhaps 400,000. Winterveld's population may have been even larger; it consisted of resettled squatters who paid R.3–5 a month to African landowners in Bophuthatswana for a building plot.[128]

As always, poverty in resettlement sites was diverse. Lack of land meant that many residents could not farm. Informal-sector activities scarcely existed in such impoverished agglomerations, apart from some petty retailing.[129] Malnutrition and disease were common. Of the children in the Tsweletswele resettlement area of the Ciskei 10 per cent had kwashiorkor in 1982 and household income was less than one-sixth of the minimum subsistence income calculated for small towns in the region.[130] In the notorious Sada resettlement camp in the north-eastern Ciskei, in 1982, 32.6 per cent of children died during their first five years. Sada had more than twice the national average of Africans aged over 64, two-fifths of its families included grandparents, and at least 10 per cent of its income came from pensions. Those who studied Sada in 1982 reckoned that 50 per cent of its people were on the breadline and another 30 per cent were below it and were absolutely destitute, people who 'live virtually on porridge, are always hungry' – a distinction between poor and very poor which exactly fits the categories used in this book. 'For the very poor in Sada', the researchers concluded, 'survival becomes like a job.' They *hated* it.[131]

Sada was one of the older resettlement sites. Much borrowing and mutual aid took place there among neighbours, 65 per cent were church members, and 32 per cent belonged to burial societies, but there was little organised community action. People were too poor, too dependent on government and the cash economy, too brutally uprooted from homes and kinsmen to organise themselves.[132] Some newer settlements lacked even Sada's degree of social integration. In Winterveld, for example, 'Women do not trust, speak to or help neighbours – "friends destroy marriages" is a typical response.' Winterveld had much wife- and child-beating.[133] In three particularly bad resettlement sites in the Ciskei studied in 1982, only 33 per cent of women were living with their husbands and fewer than 10 per cent of children were cared for by their parents.[134] Crime and violence flourished in 'closer settlements'.[135] So did the exploitation of newcomers by earlier residents. So also did that rare condition among the African poor, despair:

> There are many men in their sixties or older, and men, for whom forced removal, involving physical duress and drastic severance from a familiar social setting has produced psychosomatic effects equivalent to those of a stroke. They sit glassy-eyed and dumb or shuffle round like zombies, and many actually die within weeks or months of the uprooting.[136]

One woman recalled that her husband had been 'a good, brave man . . . he never gave in . . . [But] Here in Elukhanyweni he just gave in and stayed in bed the whole time and then he died . . . I can understand why my husband died. He died of shame and sorrow.' 'People here simply don't care', another resident explained. 'They don't have time to think about these things. During the week they are away at work. During the weekend they are dead drunk.'[137] These were the people who had created marabi culture.

The circular identifying those to be resettled listed first 'the aged, the unfit, widows, women with dependent children'.[138] The transfer of the poor to the homelands was integral to apartheid. As the Minister of Bantu Affairs explained in 1955, 'We want to evolve a system whereby we reinstate the natural obligations of Bantu authorities and Bantu children in regard to their old people, with the support of an equal amount of money to that which we now spend wrongly in caring for them.'[139] This involved closing 'wrongly-situated institutions' and 'devising social and welfare services for the Bantu on their own lines'. Under the first heading, the Bantu Refuge, which had cared for the Witwatersrand's aged poor since 1927, was closed in 1965 and its inmates removed to the homelands. Under the second, institutions for juvenile delinquents were reorganised on ethnic lines and Bantu authorities were initially subsidised to erect 'suitable accommodation for the aged at or near places of residence of Chiefs or Headmen', but during the 1970s this gave way to a simple transfer of modern-style institutions (often run by missionaries) to the supervision of homeland governments.[140] In 1984 Lebowa had two homes for the aged (with 227 inmates) and one for chronic sick (with 79 inmates). It employed 19 qualified social workers. Homeland authorities took over rural health services during the 1970s.[141] Responsibility for pensions was also gradually transferred to them, starting with the Transkei in 1964, although the funds still came largely from Pretoria. In 1980 Africans received 361,269 old age pensions and 71,325 disability grants in the homelands, 199,565 and 86,980 outside the homelands.[142] Homeland control created further bureaucracy and political favouritism. Because there was not enough money to pay all those entitled, pensioners who established their eligibility might be put on a waiting list – for up to five years in Lebowa. KwaZulu was said in 1984 to have 100,000 eligible pensioners not receiving payment. A study in Qwaqwa in 1982 found that at least one-third of those entitled were not paid.[143]

The elderly or handicapped deprived of pensions were one category of the very poor, but South Africa's rulers preserved a nineteenth-century distinction between deserving and undeserving Africans, so that the welfare system scarcely recognised that able-bodied and industrious country-people could be poor and in need of aid as a result of structural unemployment. These new poor were increasingly numerous. As the number of Sotho admitted to work in South Africa fell after 1977, men without re-registration guarantee certificates were 'jammed', as they put it, in Maseru, seeking casual jobs, sometimes sleeping rough and scrabbling in dustbins, waiting in the hope of recruitment. 'I left home with a lot of money saying I am coming here to queue', one explained. 'This money could have been used at home. Now if I go back again, when I get there, the children will look up at me and say, "What has our father brought for us?"'[144] In Botswana some frustrated migrants transferred their poverty to those weaker than themselves by ousting women from the firewood trade.[145] Similar frustrations existed in those resettlement areas which were far from employment opportunities. In remote Qwaqwa in 1982, 'Work-seekers . . . were walking 20 kilometres daily to wait, for the most part hopelessly in a crowd of hundreds' at labour bureaux.[146] 'There's no work', one explained. 'We can't get jobs so that we can work for our children . . . When you want work you go down to the office there and hang around but there's nothing at all, you could wait a year without picking anything up. And the children are being killed by hunger.'[147] Average unemployment in resettlement areas – 24 per cent of both sexes of working age in 1980–3 – was no higher than in the homelands generally, but certain areas had exceptional rates. The highest reliable figure was 38 per cent at Glenmore in the Ciskei, where 31 per cent of families had no wage-worker.[148] These families were the new poor. 'In closer settlements the families of migrant workers are becoming a relative elite', an authority reported. 'They are the ones with brick rather than mud houses, some furniture and more mealie meal to eat.'[149] Some families, especially with female heads, appeared to have no income whatever. 'We beg from our neighbours', one explained, 'and they help us because we Africans believe in sharing.'[150]

In these circumstances, a large family might be a source of poverty. At Mdantsane in the Ciskei, in 1980–1, 'The better-off households (R.81+ per month) tend to be small, their mean size being 3.7 people . . . The poorest households (R.0–25 per month) are generally large, with an average of 8.6 people . . . Quite a few are of extended, three-generational families.'[151] The 25 per cent of people in Elukhanyweni resettlement area in the Ciskei who were then classified as destitute showed the same characteristics: 'Examples: family of 7 with one female in domestic service, family of 4 with a single pension, family of 9 with the remittances of one male migrant, family of 8 with no cash income.'[152] The resettlement site in the Transvaal with the largest average household (modal size nine members) was also the most destitute.[153]

The story of African poverty had come full circle. In the nineteenth-century Tio kingdom, membership of a large family was the very definition of wealth.[154] That was a world where land was abundant and labour scarce, where lack of access to labour was the root of poverty. In South Africa in the 1980s – although rarely as yet elsewhere in sub-Saharan Africa – the world had been turned upside down. Labour was abundant, land and work were scarce, and the great transition which has dominated the history of the poor in every continent was taking place.

Notes

Abbreviations

ANOM:MC	Archives Nationales (Section Outre-Mer): Ministère des Colonies
ASAPS	Anti-Slavery and Aborigines Protection Society
BCE	*Bulletin du Comité d'Etudes Historiques et Scientifiques de l'A.O.F.*
BIFAN	*Bulletin de l'Institut Français [Fondamental] d'Afrique Noire*
BNR	*Botswana notes and records*
BSOAS	*Bulletin of the School of Oriental and African Studies*
CCP	Carnegie Conference Paper (Cape Town, April 1984)
CEA	*Cahiers d'études africaines*
CJAS	*Canadian journal of African studies*
CMS	Church Missionary Society [records in Birmingham University Library]
CMS:UP	Church Missionary Society: Unofficial Papers [at CMS Headquarters]
CNC	Chief Native Commissioner
CO	Colonial Office [records in Public Record Office, London]
CS	Chief Secretary
CSCO	Corpus Scriptorum Christianorum Orientalium, Scriptores Aethiopici
CT	*Chronique trimestrielle de la Société des Missionnaires d'Afrique*
CUL	Cambridge University Library
CWM	Council for World Mission [records in SOAS]
CWM:IL	Council for World Mission: incoming letters [followed by box and piece number]
DC	District Commissioner
DMS	Director of Medical Services
DO	Dominions Office [records in Public Record Office, London]
EAMJ	*East African medical journal*
EDCC	*Economic development and cultural change*
EUL	Edinburgh University Library
IDS	Institute of Development Studies
IJAHS	*International journal of African historical studies*
IJL	*International journal of leprosy*
ILO	International Labour Office
ILR	*International labour review*
JAH	*Journal of African history*
JASPA	Jobs and Skills Programme for Africa
JES	*Journal of Ethiopian studies*
JMAS	*Journal of modern African studies*

JSAS	*Journal of southern African studies*
LR	*Leprosy review*
LWR	*Lagos weekly record*
MC	*Les missions catholiques*
MMS	Methodist Missionary Society [records in SOAS]
MNA	Malawi National Archives
NDT	*Nigerian daily times*
NLS	National Library of Scotland
PC	Provincial Commissioner
RFHOM	*Revue française d'histoire d'outre-mer*
RH	Rhodes House, Oxford
RLJ	*Rhodes–Livingstone journal*
ROAPE	*Review of African political economy*
SAA	Secretary for African Administration
SAHJ	*South African historical journal*
SALB	*South African labour bulletin*
SALDRU	South African Labour and Development Research Unit
SAMJ	*South African medical journal*
SAO	*South African outlook*
SMP	Secretariat minute paper
SN	Superintendent of Natives
SOAS	School of Oriental and African Studies, London
SPP	Surplus People Project
SSM	*Social science and medicine*
TANU	Tanganyika African National Union [records at headquarters]
TNA	Tanzania National Archives
TNR	*Tanganyika [Tanzania] notes and records*
UDSML	University of Dar es Salaam Library
UNECA	United Nations Economic Commission for Africa
WAMJ	*West African medical journal*
ZNA	Zimbabwe National Archives

1 The comparative history of the poor

1 See Polly Hill, *Rural Hausa: a village and a setting* (Cambridge, 1972) and *Population, prosperity and poverty: rural Kano, 1900 and 1970* (Cambridge, 1977); Nigerian Economic Society, *Poverty in Nigeria* (Ibadan, 1976).
2 Listed in the bibliography s.v. International Labour Office, World Bank, and Paul Collier.
3 Available in duplicated form as some 300 Carnegie Conference Papers (Cape Town, April 1984). Copies are in the library of the African Studies Centre, Cambridge.
4 See Peter Townsend, 'Poverty as relative deprivation', in Dorothy Wedderburn (ed.), *Poverty, inequality and class structure* (Cambridge, 1974), ch. 1.
5 See Amartya Sen, *Poverty and famines* (revised edn., Oxford, 1982), pp. 11–17.
6 M. I. Finley, *The ancient economy* (reprinted, London, 1975), p. 41
7 Charles Booth (ed.), *Life and labour: volume 1: East London* (London, 1889), p. 33.
8 Olwen H. Hufton, *The poor of eighteenth-century France, 1750–1789* (Oxford, 1974), p. 48.
9 See p. 41.
10 See p. 275.
11 See ch. 4.

12 A. G. Hopkins, *An economic history of West Africa* (London, 1973), p. 10.
13 *LWR*, 22 March 1913.
14 R. V. Selope Thema in *Bantu world*, 12 May 1934.
15 A. Shawky, 'Social work education in Africa', *International social work*, 15, 3 (1972), 4–5.
16 Jack Goody, *Cooking, cuisine and class* (Cambridge, 1982), esp. pp. vii, 98–9, 206–7.
17 *Ibid.*, p. 194. This is surely not true. The opposite of poverty is non-poverty, i.e. sufficiency.
18 *Ibid.*, pp. 64–5, 191
19 *Ibid.*, pp. 210–12, 193–4.
20 See ch. 4.
21 Jean-Pierre Gutton, *La société et les pauvres: l'exemple de la généralité de Lyon 1534–1789* (Paris, 1971), pp. 51–3.
22 Jean-Louis Goglin, *Les misérables dans l'Occident médiéval* (Paris, 1976), p. 42. See also Michel Mollat, *Les pauvres au Moyen Age* (Paris, 1978), part 1.
23 Georges Duby, 'Les pauvres des campagnes dans l'Occident médiéval jusqu'au XIIIe siècle', *Revue d'histoire de l'église de France*, 52 (1966), 25–9; Léopold Genicot, 'Sur le nombre des pauvres dans les campagnes médiévales: l'exemple du Namurois', *Revue historique*, 522 (April 1977), 273–88.
24 Duby, 'Les pauvres', pp. 30–2.
25 Mollat, *Les pauvres*, pp. 199–200.
26 Keith Wrightson, *English society 1580–1680* (London, 1982), p. 141.
27 Hufton, *Poor*, pp. 11–12, 107–17, 329. But see also Gutton, *Lyon*, pp. 54–8, 111–22; Christian Romon, 'Le monde des pauvres à Paris au XVIIIe siècle', *Annales E.S.C.*, 37 (1982), 729–63.
28 ILO, *Poverty and landlessness in rural Asia* (Geneva, 1977), p. 32; V. M. Dandekar and Nilakantha Rath, 'Poverty in India – I: dimensions and trends', *Economic and political weekly* (Bombay), 6 (1971), 32–3.
29 See the analysis of Shona folktales in Abraham Kriel, *An African horizon* (Cape Town, 1971), pp. 94–7.
30 See Gutton, *Lyon*, pp. 491–2.
31 Wrightson, *Society*, pp. 144–6; Fernand Braudel and Ernest Labrousse (eds.), *Histoire économique et sociale de la France*, vol. 2 (Paris, 1970), pp. 74–6.
32 John D. Post, 'Famine, mortality, and epidemic disease in the process of modernization', *Economic history review*, second series, 29 (1976), 14; Michelle Burge McAlpin, *Subject to famine: food crises and economic change in western India, 1860–1920* (Princeton, 1983), pp. 184–5; Dwight H. Perkins, *Agricultural development in China 1368–1968* (Chicago, 1969), pp. 163–6.
33 See pp. 157–9.
34 For these reasons elsewhere, see Braudel and Labrousse, *Histoire*, vol. 2, p. 76; Post, 'Famine', pp. 14–37; McAlpin, *Subject, passim*; Perkins, *Agricultural development*, p. 166.
35 Braudel and Labrousse, *Histoire*, vol. 2, pp. 76–80. For undernutrition, see p. 160.
36 See Mollat, *Les pauvres, passim*; Gutton, *Lyon, passim*.
37 Hufton, *Poor*, ch. 7.
38 Bronislaw Geremek, *Les marginaux parisiens aux XIVe et XVe siècles* (trans. D. Beauvois, Paris, 1976); Clifford Edmund Bosworth, *The medieval Islamic underworld* (2 vols., Leiden, 1976).
39 J. Michael Mahar (ed.), *The Untouchables of contemporary India* (Tucson, 1972); George De Vos and Hiroshi Wagatsuma (eds.), *Japan's invisible race* (Berkeley, 1966).
40 Hufton, *Poor*, p. 367.
41 A. R. Hands, *Charities and social aid in Greece and Rome* (London, 1968), ch. 6.

42 Edwin Eames and Judith Granich Goode, *Urban poverty in a cross-cultural context* (New York, 1973), ch. 2.
43 See the contrast in Polly Hill, *Dry grain farming families: Hausaland (Nigeria) and Karnataka (India) compared* (Cambridge, 1982).
44 David Clement Scott, *A cyclopaedic dictionary of the Mang'anja language* (Edinburgh, 1982), s.v. *umpawi*; Herbert Barnes, *Nyanja–English vocabulary* (rev. M. W. Bulley, London, 1929), s.v. *umpawi*; information from Dr K. M. Phiri.

2 Christian Ethiopia

1 C. F. Beckingham and G. W. B. Huntingford (eds.), *The Prester John of the Indies* (2 vols., Cambridge, 1961), vol. 1, p. 166.
2 Jerome Lobo, *A voyage to Abyssinia* (trans. S. Johnson, London, 1735), p. 60.
3 W. Cornwallis Harris, *The highlands of Aethiopia* (3 vols., London, 1844), vol. 2, pp. 246–7.
4 *Ethiopia observer*, 9, 4 (1966), 262
5 E. A. Wallis Budge (ed.), *The life of Takla Haymanot* (2 vols., London, 1906), vol. 2, p. 335. For another striking example, see Maurice Allotte de la Fuÿe (ed.), *Actes de Filmona*, CSCO 36 (Louvain, 1958), p. 58.
6 Budge, *Takla Haymanot*, vol. 1, p. 99.
7 Allotte de la Fuÿe, *Filmona*, p. 58; Théophile Lefebvre and others, *Voyage en Abyssinie* (6 vols., Paris [1851]), vol. 2, p. 275.
8 K. F. Schaller, *Ethiopia: a geomedical monograph* (Berlin, 1972), p. 118.
9 *MC*, 42 (1910), 596.
10 R. Giel and J. N. van Luijk, 'Psychiatric morbidity in a small Ethiopian town', *British journal of psychiatry*, 115 (1969), 161.
11 Jules Borelli, *Ethiopie méridionale* (Paris, 1890), p. 247; Frank D. Schofield, 'Some relations between social isolation and specific communicable diseases', *American journal of tropical medicine and hygiene*, 19 (1970), 168 (I owe this reference to Dr G. A. Lewis).
12 Borelli, *Ethiopie*, p. 247.
13 Harm Schneider, *Leprosy and other health problems in Hararghe, Ethiopia* (Groningen, 1975), p. 61.
14 Docteur Mérab, *Impressions d'Ethiopie* (3 vols., Paris, 1921–9), vol. 1, p. 166.
15 Schofield, 'Some relations', p. 168. See also R. Giel and J. N. van Luijk, 'Leprosy in Ethiopian society', *IJL*, 38 (1970), 189.
16 Schneider, *Leprosy*, pp. 105–6; Schofield, 'Some relations', p. 168.
17 See, e.g., Borelli, *Ethiopie*, p. 247; Giel and van Luijk, 'Leprosy', p. 190.
18 Beckingham and Huntingford, *Prester John*, vol. 2, p. 514.
19 See p. 22.
20 Lobo, *Voyage*, p. 119.
21 Giel and van Luijk, 'Psychiatric morbidity', p. 156; Thomas Leiper Kane, *Ethiopian literature in Amharic* (Wiesbaden, 1975), p. 92.
22 *The life and adventures of Nathaniel Pearce, written by himself* (ed. J. J. Halls, 2 vols., London, 1831), vol. 2, pp. 171–2.
23 Arnauld d'Abbadie, *Douze ans dans la Haute-Ethiopie* (Paris, 1868), p. 499.
24 Augustus B. Wylde, *Modern Abyssinia* (London, 1901), p. 231.
25 J. L. Krapf in *The journals of C. W. Isenberg and J. L. Krapf* (reprinted, London, 1968), p. 478.
26 Dexter Lisbon Burley, 'The despised weavers of Ethiopia', Ph.D. thesis, University of New Hampshire, 1976, p. 1.

27 Richard Pankhurst, *Economic history of Ethiopia 1800–1935* (Addis Ababa, 1968), pp. 39–44.

28 Peter Phillips Garretson, 'A history of Addis Ababa from its foundation in 1886 to 1910', Ph.D. thesis, University of London, 1974, pp. 186–202, 224–7; Pankhurst, *Economic history*, ch. 3.

29 Mordechai Abir, 'The Ethiopian slave trade and its relation to the Islamic world', in John Ralph Willis (ed.), *Slaves and slavery in Muslim Africa* (2 vols., London, 1985), vol. 2, p. 126.

30 *Valets de terre inculte*. Wolf Leslau, *Concise Amharic dictionary* (Wiesbaden, 1976), give *čenča* = stony ground (p. 240), *aškar* = servant (p. 471).

31 Mérab, *Impressions*, vol. 3, p. 143.

32 Richard Pankhurst, 'Some factors depressing the standard of living of peasants in traditional Ethiopia', *JES*, 4, 2 (July 1966), 47–8.

33 The administrative head of the church.

34 This was forbidden food.

35 Guèbrè Sellassié, *Chronique du règne de Ménélik II* (trans. Tèsfa Sellassié, 2 vols., Paris, 1930–1), vol. 1, pp. 296–8.

36 *Ibid*., vol. 1, p. 299 n. 3.

37 Garretson, 'Addis Ababa', p. 331.

38 Samuel Gobat, *Journal of a three years' residence in Abyssinia* (2nd edn, London, 1847), pp. 241–2.

39 Richard Pankhurst, 'The great Ethiopian famine of 1888–92: a new assessment', *Journal of the history of medicine and allied sciences*, 21 (1966), 104–8.

40 *Ibid*., p. 122; *MC*, 10 (1878), 437; *MC*, 12 (1880), 212; *MC*, 21 (1889), 63, 328.

41 Charles Johnston, *Travels in southern Abyssinia* (reprinted, 2 vols., n.p., 1972), vol. 2, p. 159.

42 Gobat, *Journal*, pp. 295–6. See also Donald N. Levine, *Wax and gold: tradition and innovation in Ethiopian culture* (reprinted, Chicago, 1972), p. 232.

43 Lobo, *Voyage*, p. 385; Beckingham and Huntingford, *Prester John*, vol. 2, p. 391. Generally, see Steven Kaplan, *The monastic holy man and the Christianization of early Solomonic Ethiopia* (Wiesbaden, 1984), pp. 76–81.

44 Kaplan, *Holy man*, pp. 39–41; Wolf Leslau (ed.), *Falasha anthology* (New Haven, 1951), pp. xxv–xxvi.

45 Goody, *Cooking*, pp. 210–13 (quotation on p. 210); Jack Goody, *Production and reproduction: a comparative study of the domestic domain* (Cambridge, 1976), pp. 110–11.

46 Wylde, *Abyssinia*, p. 258; Beckingham and Huntingford, *Prester John*, vol. 1, p. 171; Pankhurst *Economic history*, p. 46; Lefebvre, *Voyage*, vol. 3, pp. 257–8; Ed. Combes and M. Tamisier, *Voyage en Abyssinie, 1835–1837* (4 vols., Paris, 1838), vol. 2, p. 24.

47 Kurt Wendt (ed.), *Das Mashafa Milad (Liber Nativitatis) und Mashafa Sellase (Liber Trinitatis) des Kaizers Zara Yaqob*, CSCO 41–4 (Louvain, 1962–3), vol. 42, p. 21.

48 Allan Hoben, *Land tenure among the Amhara of Ethiopia* (Chicago, 1973), p. 9.

49 Donald Crummey, 'State and society: 19th-century Ethiopia', in Donald Crummey and C. C. Stewart (eds.), *Modes of production in Africa* (Beverly Hills, 1981), p. 232.

50 Duby, 'Les pauvres', pp. 25–32.

51 Job Ludolphus, *A new history of Ethiopia* (English trans., 2nd edn, London, 1684), pp. 217–18; Donald Crummey, 'Banditry and resistance: noble and peasant in nineteenth-century Ethiopia', in his *Banditry, rebellion and social protest in Africa* (London, 1986), p. 142. Generally, see Pankhurst, 'Some factors', pp. 68–89; R. A. Caulk, 'Armies as predators: soldiers and peasants in Ethiopia c.1850–1935', *IJAHS*, 11 (1978), 457–93.

52 Mansfield Parkyns, *Life in Abyssinia* (2nd edn, reprinted, London, 1966), pp. 66–7.

53 William A. Shack, 'Hunger, anxiety, and ritual: deprivation and spirit possession among the Gurage of Ethiopia', *Man*, NS, 6 (1971), 30–43.

54 Timothy Fernyhough, 'Social mobility and dissident elites in Northern Ethiopia', in Crummey, *Banditry*, p. 163. See also Crummey's chapter in the same volume.
55 Text from Tigre, quoted in Enno Littmann, *Publications of the Princeton Expedition to Abyssinia* (5 vols., Leiden, 1910–15), vol. 2, p. 202.
56 This account is based on Hoben, *Land tenure*.
57 William H. Armstrong and Fisseha Demoz Gebre Egzi, 'Amharic proverbs', *Ethiopia observer*, 12, 1 (n.d.), 56.
58 For their special practices, see Donald Crummey, 'Family and property amongst the Amhara nobility', *JAH*, 24 (1983), 207–20.
59 Richard Holloway, 'Street boys in Addis Ababa', *Community development journal*, 5 (1970), 141.
60 Gobat, *Journal*, p. 315; Lefebvre, *Voyage*, vol. 3, p. 225; Schaller, *Ethiopia*, p. 135; Beckingham and Huntingford, *Prester John*, vol. 1, pp. 107–8.
61 *Ethiopia observer*, 9, 4 (1966), 247–8; Combes and Tamisier, *Voyage*, vol. 2, p. 108; Parkyns, *Life*, p. 268.
62 Mollat, *Les pauvres*, pp. 286–7.
63 E.g. Budge, *Takla Haymanot*, vol. 1, pp. 99–100.
64 See p. 10; Mérab, *Impressions,* vol. 1, p. 162; Lefebvre, *Voyage,* vol. 2, pp. 273–4; Harris, *Highlands*, pp. 246–7.
65 Pankhurst, *Economic history*, p. 46.
66 Duby noted the same in Europe: 'Les pauvres', p. 29.
67 *MC*, 23 (1891), 230.
68 Mérab, *Impressions*, vol. 3, p. 627.
69 Garretson, 'Addis Ababa', pp. 190, 324; C. F. Beckingham and G. W. B. Huntingford (eds.), *Some records of Ethiopia 1593–1646* (London, 1954), p. 82; Pankhurst, *Economic history*, p. 712.
70 Lefebvre, *Voyage*, vol. 3, pp. 225–6; Richard Pankhurst, 'The history of prostitution in Ethiopia', *JES*, 12, 2 (1974), 159–78.
71 Beckingham and Huntingford, *Prester John*, vol. 2, p. 509.
72 Richard Pankhurst, *History of Ethiopian towns from the Middle Ages to the early nineteenth century* (Wiesbaden, 1982), pp. 115–38, 247–64.
73 *Ibid.*, pp. 298–304.
74 Alice Louise Morton, 'Some aspects of spirit possession in Ethiopia', Ph.D. thesis, University of London, 1973, p. 615; Mesfin Wolde Mariam, 'Problems of urbanization', in Haile Sellassie II University, Institute of Ethiopian Studies, *Proceedings of the Third International Conference of Ethiopian Studies, Addis Ababa, 1966* (Addis Ababa, 1970), p. 35.
75 Johnston, *Travels*, vol. 2, p. 149.
76 Eduard Rüppell, *Reise in Abyssinien* (2 vols., Frankfurt am Main, 1838–40), vol. 1, pp. 204–5.
77 J. Boyes, quoted in Pankhurst, *Economic history*, p. 48.
78 J. Baeteman, 'Croquis blancs au pays Abyssin', in *MC*, 44 (1912), 201.
79 Pankhurst, *Economic history*, p. 630.
80 Ignazio Guidi (ed.), *Il 'Fetha Nagast'* (2 vols., Rome, 1897–9), vol. 2, pp. 169, 172.
81 Walter Chichele Plowden, *Travels in Abyssinia and the Galla country* (London, 1868), p. 404.
82 Alaka Imbakom Kalewold, *Traditional Ethiopian church education* (trans. Menghestu Lemma, New York, 1970), p. 16.
83 *Ibid.*, pp. 19–20.
84 *Ibid.*, p. 9; Wylde, *Abyssinia*, p. 164; Schofield, 'Some relations', p. 167; *Journals of Isenberg and Krapf*, p. 238.

85 Borelli, *Ethiopie*, p. 128; Harris, *Highlands*, vol. 2, p. 96; Gobat, *Journal*, p. 25.
86 Lobo, *Voyage*, pp. 55–6.
87 Combes and Tamisier, *Voyage*, vol. 3, p. 193.
88 Plowden, *Travels*, p. 406.
89 *Ibid.*, p. 405; Schaller, *Ethiopia*, p. 115.
90 Plowden, *Travels*, p. 405.
91 *Life and adventures of Pearce*, vol. 1, p. 297.
92 *MC*, 44 (1912), 201.
93 Cited in Pankhurst, *Economic history*, p. 148.
94 Henry A. Stern, *Wanderings among the Falashas in Abyssinia* (2nd edn, London, 1968), p. 83.
95 Combes and Tamisier, *Voyage*, vol. 4, p. 158; Mérab, *Impressions*, vol. 2, p. 13.
96 Simon D. Messing, 'Group therapy and social status in the Zar cult of Ethiopia', *American anthropologist*, 60 (1958), 1120.
97 *Ibid.*, pp. 1124–6; Morton, 'Spirit possession', pp. 575–6, 615–16, 670.
98 Morton, 'Spirit possession', pp. 697, 700
99 Lobo, *Voyage*, p. 61
100 Robert Giel and others, 'Ticket to heaven: psychiatric illness in a religious community in Ethiopia', *SSM*, 8 (1974), 549–56 (quotation on p. 552).
101 William El. Conzelman (ed.), *Chronique de Galawdewos* (Paris, 1895), p. 173; above, p. 12.
102 d'Abbadie, *Douze ans*, p. 499; Harris, *Highlands*, vol. 2, pp. 21–2; Lefebvre, *Voyage*, vol. 1, p. 372.
103 Beckingham and Huntingford, *Prester John*, vol. 1, pp. 224–6. For European practice, see Michel Rouche, 'La matricule des pauvres', in Michel Mollat (ed.), *Etudes sur l'histoire de la pauvreté* (2 vols., Paris, 1974), vol. 1, pp. 91, 107.
104 Combes and Tamisier, *Voyage*, vol. 3, pp. 284–5; Rüppell, *Reise*, vol. 2, p. 124.
105 Stanislas Kur (ed.), *Actes de Marha Krestos*, CSCO 63 (Louvain, 1972), p. 70.
106 Kaplan, *Holy man*, pp. 32, 36.
107 Stanislas Kur (ed.), *Actes de Samuel de Dabra Wagag*, CSCO 58 (Louvain, 1968), p. 5; Enrico Cerulli, 'Il monachismo in Etiopia', *Orientalia Christiana analecta*, 153 (1958), 269.
108 Kur, *Actes de Samuel*, p. 18.
109 Beckingham and Huntingford, *Prester John*, vol. 1, p. 88. The passage in brackets is from a second manuscript.
110 Derek Matthews and Antonio Mordini, 'The monastery of Debra Damo, Ethiopia', *Archaeologia*, 97 (1959), 26.
111 Gobat, *Journal*, pp. 315–16.
112 Beckingham and Huntingford, *Prester John*, vol. 2, pp. 352–3.
113 Combes and Tamisier, *Voyage*, vol. 3, p. 198.
114 Pankhurst, 'Great famine', p. 114; above, p. 12.
115 Pankhurst, *Towns*, p. 130; Richard Pankhurst, 'The history of famine and pestilence in Ethiopia prior to the founding of Gondär', *JES*, 10, 2 (July 1972), 58–9; Bairu Tafla, 'Four Ethiopian biographies', *JES*, 7, 2 (July 1969), 22.
116 G. W. B. Huntingford (ed.), *The glorious victories of Amda Seyon* (Oxford, 1965), p. 11; *Journals of Isenberg and Krapf*, pp. 68, 299.
117 Beckingham and Huntingford, *Prester John*, vol. 2, p. 512; I. Guidi (ed.), *Annales Iohannis I, Iyasu I, Bakaffa*, CSCO 5 (Paris, 1903), pp. 6, 199.
118 Jean Doresse, *La vie quotidienne des Ethiopiens chrétiens aux XVIIe et XVIIIe siècles* (Paris, 1972), p. 79.
119 'The chronicle of the Emperor Zara Yaqob (1434–1468)', *Ethiopia observer*, 5, 2 (1961), 163; Kur, *Marha Krestos*, p. 51.

120 *Journals of Isenberg and Krapf*, p. 103.
121 Guidi, *Annales Iohannis I*, pp. 2, 60; C. Conti Rossini (ed.), *Historia Regis Sarsa Dengel (Malak Sagad)*, CSCO 3 (Paris, 1907), 116–17.
122 H. Weld Blundell, *The royal chronicle of Abyssinia 1769–1840* (Cambridge, 1922), p. 322.
123 Combes and Tamisier, *Voyage*, vol. 2, p. 313.
124 Ludolphus, *History*, p. 394.
125 *Life and adventures of Pearce*, vol. 1, pp. 89, 339; Lefebvre, *Voyage*, vol. 1, p. 181.
126 Gobat, *Journal*, pp. 136–7.
127 Garretson, 'Addis Ababa', pp. 149–50.
128 Kur, *Actes de Samuel*, p. 2.
129 Beckingham and Huntingford, *Some records*, p. 67.
130 Sustained note.
131 Parkyns, *Life*, pp. 273–4.
132 *Life and adventures of Pearce*, vol. 2, pp. 19–20.
133 Richard Pankhurst and Endreas Eshete, 'Self-help in Ethiopia', *Ethiopia observer*, 2, 11 (October 1958), 364.
134 See Guidi, *Il 'Fetha Nagast'*, vol. 2, pp. 166–82.
135 Pankhurst, *Towns*, p. 130.
136 Wendt, *Das Mashafa Milad*, vol. 42, pp. 19–21.
137 See Levine, *Wax and gold*, pp. 228–9.
138 *Ibid.*, pp. 38–41.
139 This may have been especially true of the Shoan tradition of sanctity. The poor seem less prominent in Tigrean hagiographies.
140 Kur, *Marha Krestos*, p. 3.
141 Budge, *Takla Haymanot*, vol. 1, pp. 18, 40.
142 *Ibid.*, p. 67.
143 *Ibid.*, p. 223.
144 Stanislas Kur (ed.), *Actes de Iyasus Mo'a, abbé du couvent de St Etienne de Hayq*, CSCO 50 (Louvain, 1965), p. 37.
145 Budge, *Takla Haymanot*, vol. 1, pp. 224–5.
146 I am indebted to Dr Steven Kaplan for suggestions on this point. Similar relationships are revealed in many early European hagiographies. See Jerzy Kloczowski, 'Les hôpitaux et les frères mendiants en Pologne au moyen âge', in Mollat, *Etudes*, vol. 2, p. 621.
147 See Kaplan, *Holy man*, pp. 45, 69.
148 See M. D. Lambert, *Franciscan poverty* (London, 1961), p. 39.
149 Cerulli, 'Il monachismo', pp. 264–5; Ludolphus, *History*, pp. 259–60; Friedrich Heyer, *Die Kirche Aethiopiens: eine Bestandsaufnahme* (Berlin, 1971), pp. 145–9; Robert van de Weyer, 'The monastic community of Ethiopia', *Ethiopia observer*, 16, 1 (1973), 8–14; Evelyne Patlagean, *Pauvreté économique et pauvreté sociale à Byzance, 4e–7e siècles* (Paris, 1977), p. 62.
150 Emperor.
151 Beckingham and Huntingford, *Prester John*, vol. 2, p. 353. The passage in brackets is from a second manuscript.
152 d'Abbadie, *Douze ans*, pp. 90–1.
153 Mérab, *Impressions*, vol. 1, p. 166.
154 Borelli, *Ethiopie*, p. 247; Schneider, *Leprosy*, p. 75.
155 See esp. Bosworth, *Islamic underworld, passim*.
156 Conti Rossini, *Sarsa Dengel*, p. 81. Combes and Tamisier (*Voyage*, vol. 3, p. 195) say that in the 1830s great men had priests as *aumôniers*, but the French word can also mean a chaplain.
157 Harris, *Highlands*, vol. 2, p. 247.

158 Iobo Ludolfo, *Lexicon Amharico–Latinum* (Frankfurt am Main, 1698), lists *meskin* (p. 12) but apparently not *deha*.
159 Donald Crummey, 'Abyssinian feudalism', *Past and present*, 89 (November 1980), 135.
160 Leslau, *Concise Amharic dictionary*, pp. 318, 438.
161 *Ibid.*, p. 13, gives *läggäsä* = be generous, be charitable.
162 Guèbrè Sellassié, *Ménélik II*, vol. 1, p. 268.
163 Pankhurst, *Economic history*, p. 48.
164 Andrzej Bartnicki and Joanna Mantel-Niecko, 'The role and significance of the religious conflicts and people's movements in the political life of Ethiopia in the seventeenth and eighteenth centuries', *Rassegna di studi etiopici*, 24 (1969–70), 21–2.
165 Crummey, 'Feudalism', p. 137.
166 Goglin, *Les misérables*, p. 226.
167 *MC*, 42 (1910), 502; *Ethiopia observer*, 12, 1 (n.d.), 45; Levine, *Wax and gold*, p. 130.
168 *Life and adventures of Pearce*, vol. 2, pp. 48, 65; Budge, *Takla Haymanot*, vol. 2, p. 336; Harris, *Highlands*, vol. 2, p. 242.
169 E.g. Beckingham and Huntingford, *Prester John*, vol. 2, p. 514.

3 The Islamic tradition

1 Douglas Edwin Ferguson, 'Nineteenth century Hausaland, being a description by Imam Imoru of the land, economy, and society of his people', Ph.D. thesis, University of California at Los Angeles, 1973, p. 145. This is a rearrangement of manuscripts written in the first decade of the twentieth century and published by A. Mischlich, chiefly as *Ueber die Kulturen im Mittel-Sudan* (Berlin, 1942).
2 See p. 215; Roger le Tourneau, *Les villes de l'Afrique du Nord* (Algiers, 1957), p. 22; Haidar Abu Ahmed Mohamed, 'Leprosy – the Moslem attitude', *LR*, 56 (1985), 17–21.
3 Except where onchocerciasis prevailed. See F. C. Rodger, *Blindness in West Africa* (London, 1959), pp. 88–9.
4 Ferguson, 'Hausaland', p. 146.
5 Gustav Nachtigal, *Sahara and Sudan* (trans. A. G. B. and H. J. Fisher, 4 vols., London, 1971–), vol. 2, p. 160.
6 Printed in Mervyn Hiskett, *A history of Hausa Islamic verse* (London, 1975), p. 151.
7 Pol-Pagès, 'Le Mahométisme dans le "Hombori" en 1922', *BCE*, 16 (1933), 401.
8 J. Lacas, 'Quelques coutumes des Malinkés de la Haute-Guinée', *Annales des Pères du Saint-Esprit* (1933), 86. Generally, see Philip D. Curtin, *Economic change in precolonial Africa: Senegambia in the era of the slave trade* (2 vols., Madison, 1975), vol. 1, pp. 31–4; James H. Vaughan Jr, 'Caste systems in the Western Sudan', in Arthur Tuden and Leonard Plotnicov (eds.), *Social stratification in Africa* (New York, 1970), pp. 59–92.
9 See Allan G. B. and Humphrey J. Fisher, *Slavery and Muslim society in Africa* (London, 1970), esp. ch. 1; Irmgard Sellnow, 'Die Stellung der Sklaven in der Hausa-Gesellschaft', *Mitteilungen des Instituts für Orientforschung*, 10 (1964), 85–102; M. G. Smith, 'A Hausa kingdom: Maradi under Dan Baskore, 1854–75', in Daryll Forde and P. M. Kaberry (eds.), *West African kingdoms in the nineteenth century* (reprinted, London, 1971), p. 104.
10 James Richardson, *Narrative of a mission to Central Africa performed in the years 1850–51* (2 vols., London, 1853), vol. 2, p. 265.
11 *Ibid.*, vol. 2, p. 236.
12 Richard Roberts and Martin A. Klein, 'The Banamba slave exodus of 1905 and the decline of slavery in the Western Sudan', *JAH*, 21 (1980), 390.
13 Nachtigal, *Sahara*, vol. 1, p. 324.
14 J. Clauzel, *L'exploitation des salines de Taoudenni* (Macon, 1960), p. 26.

15 Ferguson, 'Hausaland', p. 230; M'Baye Guèye, 'La fin de l'esclavage à Saint-Louis et à Gorée en 1848', *BIFAN*, 28B (1966), 644.
16 Bosworth, *Islamic underworld*, vol. 1, p. 3; Danièle Poitou, *La délinquance juvénile au Niger* (Niamey, 1978), p. 59; Paul Marty, *Etudes sur l'Islam et les tribus du Soudan* (4 vols., Paris, 1920), vol. 2, p. 88. The best account is Neil Skinner (ed.), *Alhaji Mahmudu Koki, Kano malam* (Zaria, 1977), pp. 23–5.
17 Gerhard Rohlfs, *Quer durch Afrika* (2 vols., Leipzig, 1874–5), vol. 1, p. 342.
18 Claude Raynaut, *Structures normatives et relations électives: étude d'une communauté villageoise haoussa* (Paris, 1972), pp. 121–6; Norma Perchonock, 'Occupation and residence in Kano city', duplicated paper, Seminar on the Economic History of the Central Savanna of West Africa, Kano, 1976; S. F. Nadel, *A black Byzantium: the kingdom of Nupe in Nigeria* (reprinted, London, 1969), p. 396; Horace Miner, *The primitive city of Timbuctoo* (Princeton, 1953), pp. 240–2; Nachtigal, *Sahara*, vol. 4, p. 191; Richard Lander, *Records of Captain Clapperton's last expedition to Africa* (reprinted, 2 vols., London, 1967), vol. 1, pp. 192–3.
19 Amadou Hampaté Ba and Jacques Daget, *L'empire peul du Macina: I (1818–1853)* (reprinted, Paris, 1962), pp. 55–6
20 S. M. X. Golberry, *Travels in Africa* (trans. F. Blagdon, 2 vols., London, 1802), vol. 2, pp. 353–4.
21 P. D. Boilat, *Esquisses sénégalaises* (Paris, 1853), p. 320.
22 René Caillié, *Travels through Central Africa to Timbuctoo* (English trans., reprinted, 2 vols., London, 1968), vol. 1, pp. 309, 352, 382, 460.
23 Heinrich Barth, *Travels and discoveries in North and Central Africa* (English trans., reprinted, 3 vols., London, 1965), vol. 3, p. 137.
24 C. E. J. Whitting, *Hausa and Fulani proverbs* (Lagos, 1940), p. 65; Ferguson, 'Hausaland', p. 214.
25 Summary of Ilorin town assessment, 1912, in RH MSS Afr. s. 1586.
26 Caillié, *Travels*, vol. 1. p. 352. See also L. J. B. Bérenger-Féraud, *Les peuplades de la Sénégambie* (Paris, 1879), p. 208. For family structure, see Yves Person, *Samori: une révolution dyula* (3 vols., Dakar, 1968–75), vol. 1, pp. 54–6.
27 Ferguson, 'Hausaland', p. 284; Robert W. Shenton, *The development of capitalism in Northern Nigeria* (London, 1986), p. 128; Abner Cohen, *Custom and politics in urban Africa* (London, 1969), p. 42.
28 M. F. Smith, *Baba of Karo: a woman of the Muslim Hausa* (London, 1954), p. 60; Raynaut, *Structures*, pp. 22–4; Ferguson, 'Hausaland', p. 146.
29 The best accounts are Jerome H. Barkow, 'The institution of courtesanship in the northern states of Nigeria', *Genève-Afrique*, 10 (1971), 58–73; Cohen, *Custom*, pp. 51–66. For the Kanuri parallel, see Ronald Cohen, *Dominance and defiance: a study of marital instability in an Islamic African society* (Washington DC, 1971), pp. 128, 176.
30 Person, *Samori*, vol. 1, p. 142.
31 Sara Randall and Michael Winter, 'The reluctant spouse and the illegitimate slave', in Allan G. Hill (ed.), *Population, health and nutrition in the Sahel* (London, 1985), p. 160.
32 Hill, *Rural Hausa*, pp. 146–9, 190–8; *idem, Population*, ch. 11.
33 Hill, *Population*, p. 7.
34 Michael Watts, *Silent violence: food, famine and peasantry in Northern Nigeria* (Berkeley, 1983), pp. 104–39.
35 Quoted in *ibid.*, p. 122.
36 Barth, *Travels*, vol. 1, p. 512.
37 R. Lander in Hugh Clapperton, *Journal of a second expedition into the interior of Africa* (reprinted, London, 1966), pp. 260–1.
38 Monique Chastanet, 'Les crises de subsistances dans les villages soninke du cercle de

Bakel, de 1858 à 1945', *CEA*, 23 (1983), 12; Tugwell, journal, 21 March 1900, CMS G3/A9/O/1900/25; Nachtigal, *Sahara*, vol. 1, p. 299.

39 Paul Marty, *Etudes sur l'Islam en Côte d'Ivoire* (Paris, 1922), pp. 366–7; *MC*, 35 (1903), 160.

40 M. R. Haswell, *Economics of agriculture in a savannah village*, Colonial Research Studies No. 8 (London, 1953), pp. 7–8.

41 John M. O'Sullivan, 'Slavery in the Malinke kingdom of Kabadougou', *IJAHS*, 13 (1980), 640.

42 Caillié, *Travels*, vol. 1, p. 275; Ferguson, 'Hausaland', p. 377; Charles Monteil, *Une cité soudanaise: Djénné* (Paris, 1932), p. 76; Jean Gallais, *Le delta intérieur du Niger* (2 vols., Paris, 1968), p. 87; Marcel Griaule, *Masques dogons* (2nd edn, Paris, 1963), p. 568.

43 Hill, *Population*, p. 95.

44 Mervyn Hiskett, *The development of Islam in West Africa* (London, 1984), p. 177; Nadel, *Black Byzantium*, p. 131.

45 Miller to Lugard, n.d. [1903] CMS G3/A9/O/1903/25.

46 Hill, *Population*, p. 9; Shenton, *Capitalism*, p. 7.

47 Hill, *Population*, p. 52.

48 David Robinson, *The Holy War of Umar Tal* (Oxford, 1985), pp. 233–40; D. P. Gamble, 'Contributions to a socio-economic survey of the Gambia', duplicated, Colonial Office Research Department [London] 1949, p. 60; Charlotte A. Quinn, *Mandingo kingdoms of the Senegambia* (London, 1972), p. 177.

49 Barth, *Travels*, vol. 3, pp. 273, 420.

50 [L. G.] Binger, *Du Niger au Golfe de Guinée* (2 vols., Paris, 1892), vol. 1, pp. 18–19, 26, 60; Person, *Samori*, vol. 2, pp. 925–9.

51 *MC*, 16 (1884), 561; John Barbot, 'A description of the coasts of North and South-Guinea', in Awnsham and John Churchill (eds.), *A collection of voyages and travels: volume 5* (London, 1732), p. 33; Barth, *Travels*, vol. 2, p. 483.

52 Abderrahman es-Sadi, *Tarikh es-Soudan* (trans. O. Houdas, Paris, 1900), p. 337; *MC*, 4 (1871–2), 683; Nachtigal, *Sahara*, vol. 4, p. 4.

53 Sharon Elaine Nicholson, 'A climatic chronology for Africa', Ph.D. thesis, University of Wisconsin-Madison, 1976, pp. 96, 124, 160, 165.

54 H. T. Norris, *The Tuaregs* (Warminster, Wilts., 1975), p. 84.

55 Sharon E. Nicholson, 'Climatic variations in the Sahel and other African regions during the past five centuries', *Journal of arid environments*, 1 (1978), 9; Akhbar Molouk es-Soudan, *Tedzkiret en-Nisian* (trans. O. Houdas, Paris, 1966), pp. 116–19; Curtin, *Economic change*, vol. 1, p. 110.

56 Nicholson, 'Chronology', pp. 143, 146, 154; Stephen Baier, *An economic history of central Niger* (Oxford, 1980), p. 30; Watts, *Silent violence*, p. 101.

57 Nicholson, 'Chronology', pp. 275–6; Watts, *Silent violence*, pp. 100–4; Chastanet, 'Les crises', p. 32.

58 Ferguson, 'Hausaland', p. 179; *MC*, 9 (1877), 4.

59 Es-Soudan, *Tedzkiret*, pp. 117–18.

60 Lamin Sanneh in *Oxfam news*, September 1973; Barbot in Churchill, *Collection*, vol. 5, pp. 47–8.

61 See Ahmed Beitallah Yusuf, 'A reconsideration of urban conceptions: Hausa urbanization and the Hausa rural–urban continuum', *Urban anthropology*, 3 (1974), 200–21.

62 Dixon Denham and Hugh Clapperton, *Narrative of travels and discoveries in northern and central Africa* (London, 1826), part 2, p. 49; Caillié, *Travels*, vol. 2, p. 56; Roger Pasquier, 'Villes du Sénégal au XIXe siècle', *RFHOM*, 47 (1960), 395.

63 Hill, *Population*, p. 15.

64 Es-Sadi, *Tarikh*, p. 24.

65 P. Alquier, 'Saint-Louis du Sénégal pendant la Révolution et l'Empire (1789–1809)', *BCE*, 5 (1922), 428; *MC*, 9 (1877), 9.
66 Shenton, *Capitalism*, pp. 130–1; above, p. 157.
67 My limited acquaintance with the sources makes this a hazardous statement.
68 One limited description is in William Wallace, 'Notes on a journey through the Sokoto Empire and Borgu in 1894', *Geographical journal*, 8 (1896), 213.
69 Ferguson, 'Hausaland', p. 325; M. G. Smith, *The affairs of Daura* (Berkeley, 1978), pp. 37, 134.
70 See p. 79.
71 Yusufu Bala Usman, 'Some aspects of the external relations of Katsina before 1804', *Savanna*, 1 (1972), 179.
72 Watts, *Silent violence*, p. 413.
73 Caillié, *Travels*, vol. 1, p. 457; G. W. Brooke in *Sûdan Mission, C.M.S. monthly leaflet, no. 13* (1891), in CMS G3/A3/O/1892/13.
74 Barth, *Travels*, vol. 3, p. 210.
75 *MC*, 16 (1884), 453.
76 John Iliffe, *The emergence of African capitalism* (London, 1983), pp. 6–7; Jean Poncet, *La colonisation et l'agriculture européennes en Tunisie depuis 1881* (Paris, 1962), p. 155.
77 Marty, *Soudan*, vol. 3, pp. 357, 360.
78 Majhemout Diop, *Histoire des classes sociales dans l'Afrique de l'Ouest: I: le Mali* (Paris, 1971), p. 61; Ferguson, 'Hausaland', p. 336; Philip James Shea, 'The development of an export oriented dyed cloth industry in Kano Emirate in the nineteenth century', Ph.D. thesis, University of Wisconsin-Madison, 1975, p. 189.
79 Ferguson, 'Hausaland', p. 342.
80 C. F. H. Battersby, 'Journey to Bida May–June 1892', 15 June 1892, CMS G3/A3/O/1892/178; Monteil, *Une cité*, p. 19; [Pruneau de Pommegorge], *Description de la Nigritie* (Paris, 1789), p. 49; Ferguson, 'Hausaland', p. 336.
81 A. W. Cardinall, *In Ashanti and beyond* (London, 1927), p. 107; *MC*, 38 (1906), 210; Paul Staudinger, *Im Herzen der Haussaländer* (Berlin, 1889), pp. 150, 208.
82 Ferguson, 'Hausaland', pp. 65, 62.
83 Staudinger, *Im Herzen*, pp. 282, 602; Rohlfs, *Quer durch Afrika*, vol. 1, p. 346.
84 Lander, *Records*, vol. 1, p. 261.
85 A. Hacquard, *Monographie de Tombouctou* (Paris, 1900), p. 49; Miner, *Timbuctoo*, p. 66.
86 Smith, *Daura*, p. 134; Denham and Clapperton, *Narrative*, part 2, p. 50; Ferguson, 'Hausaland', p. 146.
87 Bosworth, *Islamic underworld*, vol. 1, p. 91; Ira Marvin Lapidus, *Muslim cities in the later Middle Ages* (Cambridge, Mass., 1967), p. 183.
88 Nadel, *Black Byzantium*, p. 102.
89 Shea, 'Dyed cloth industry', pp. 11–15, 218; P. J. Jaggar, 'Kano city blacksmiths', *Savanna*, 2 (1973), 17–18, 22.
90 Ronald Cohen, *The Kanuri of Bornu* (New York, 1967), p. 29; Miner, *Timbuctoo*, pp. 52–4.
91 Denham and Clapperton, *Narrative*, part 2, pp. 56, 63–4; Ferguson, 'Hausaland', p. 146; Robinson, journal, 10 March 1891, in *Sûdan Mission, C.M.S. monthly leaflet, no. 9,* in CMS G3/A3/O/1891/275.
92 Cohen, *Custom*, pp. 42–7. Another account suggests rather less organisation: Anne Bamisaiye, 'Begging in Ibadan, Southern Nigeria', *Human organization*, 33 (1974), 198–9.
93 Barkow, 'Courtesanship', pp. 64–5; Smith, *Daura*, p. 134; Smith, *Baba*, p. 63.
94 Fremont E. Bessmer, *Horses, musicians, and gods: the Hausa cult of possession-trance* (South Hadley, 1983), pp. 21–2, 86.

95 *Ibid.*, pp. 18–19, 26–30; Smith, *Baba*, pp. 64, 262 n. 13; information from Professor M. Last.
96 A. J. N. Tremearne, *The ban of the Bori* (reprinted, London, 1968), pp. 278–9.
97 Lapidus, *Muslim cities*, pp. 144–5.
98 Miller to Baylis, 8 June 1908, CMS G3/A9/O/1908/80.
99 See F. Stambouli and A. Zghal, 'Urban life in pre-colonial North Africa', *British journal of sociology*, 27 (1976), 1–20.
100 Smith, *Daura*, p. 351.
101 Claude Cahen, 'Mouvements populaires et autonomisme urbain dans l'Asie musulmane du Moyen Age', *Arabica*, 5 (1958), 225–50, and 6 (1959), 25–56; le Tourneau, *Les villes*, p. 102; J. D. Y. Peel, 'Inequality and action: the forms of Ijesha social conflict', *CJAS*, 14 (1980), 482.
102 Smith, *Daura*, p. 289.
103 Hiskett, *Hausa verse*, pp. 101–2.
104 Hampaté Ba and Daget, *L'empire peul*, pp. 67–8. See also Robinson, *Holy War*, p. 81.
105 Karl Marx and Friedrich Engels, 'Manifesto of the Communist Party', in their *Selected works* (2 vols., Moscow, 1958), vol. 1, p. 34.
106 Nadel, *Black Byzantium*, p. 145.
107 See esp. Janet L. Abu-Lughod, *Cairo* (Princeton, 1971), pp. 60–5.
108 Miner, *Timbuctoo*, ch. 3; Michel Abitbol, *Tombouctou et les Arma* (Paris, 1979), pp. 165, 170; Barth, *Travels*, vol. 3, p. 128.
109 'Conseil d'Administration: Séance du 4 Mars 1859', ANOM:MC Sénégal XI:42.
110 *Essai de dictionnaire pratique français–malinké, par un Père de la Congrégation du Saint-Esprit* (Saint-Michel en Priziac, 1896), pp. 226, 260, 300, 321. See also Maurice Delafosse, *La langue mandingue et ses dialectes* (2 vols., Paris, 1929–55), vol. 2, p. 176.
111 Abdoulaye-Bara Diop, *La société wolof: tradition et changement* (Paris, 1981), p. 118 n. 5. The Songhay-Zarma use of *talaka* had much the same meaning: see Jean-Pierre Olivier de Sardan, *Concepts et conceptions songhay-zarma* (Paris, 1982), pp. 348–9.
112 Abitbol, *Tombouctou*, p. 159.
113 Ronald Cohen, 'Social stratification in Bornu', in Tuden and Plotnicov, *Social stratification*, pp. 252–3.
114 Abdullahi Smith, 'Some notes on the history of Zazzau under the Hausa kings', in M. J. Mortimore (ed.), *Zaria and its region* (Zaria, 1970), p. 84; James Frederick Schön, *Dictionary of the Hausa language* (London, 1876), part 1, p. 224; R. C. Abraham, *Dictionary of the Hausa language* (2nd edn, London, 1962), p. 845.
115 Schön, *Dictionary*, part 1, pp. 224, 161. See also Charles Henry Robinson, *Dictionary of the Hausa language* (4th edn, 2 vols., Cambridge, 1925), vol. 1, pp. 397, 299.
116 Ferguson, 'Hausaland', p. 286.
117 Goody, *Cooking*, pp. 194–203.
118 Le Tourneau, *Les villes*, p. 44; Afaf Lutfi al-Sayyid Marsot, *Egypt in the reign of Muhammad Ali* (Cambridge, 1984), p. 8.
119 Es-Sadi, *Tarikh*, p. 120; Marty, *Soudan*, vol. 2, p. 102.
120 Mahmoud Kati, *Tarikh el-fettach* (trans. O. Houdas and M. Delafosse, Paris, 1913), p. 211.
121 Marty, *Soudan*, vol. 2, pp. 102–3, 273.
122 For a possible minor exception, see Peter Fuchs, *Das Brot der Wüste: Sozio-Oekonomie der Sahara-Kanuri von Fachi* (Wiesbaden, 1983), p. 219.
123 Paul Marty, *L'Islam en Guinée: Fouta-Diallon* (Paris, 1921), p. 401; Marty, *Côte d'Ivoire*, p. 257; F. Rougier, 'L'Islam à Banamba', *BCE*, 13 (1930), 232, 244.
124 *Waqf* was somewhat more common on the East African coast, although the revenue was usually absorbed by the upkeep of mosques. See J. Spencer Trimingham, *Islam in East*

Africa (Oxford, 1964), pp. 84, 155. Nineteenth-century Zanzibar also had the only rudimentary hospital in Islamic tropical Africa. See *MC*, 15 (1883), 54.

125 J Spencer Trimingham, *Islam in West Africa* (Oxford, 1959), p. 74 n. 2. See also Marty, *Côte d'Ivoire*, p. 257.

126 W. Heffening, 'Wakf', in *Encyclopaedia of Islam* (1933), p. 1099.

127 Smith, *Daura*, p. 37; Skinner, *Alhaji Mahmadu*, p. 101; Shenton, *Capitalism*, p. 42.

128 Robert Mantran, *Istanbul dans la seconde moitié du XVIIe siècle* (Paris, 1962), p. 173.

129 Le Tourneau, *Les villes*, p. 102.

130 Caillié, *Travels*, vol. 1, p. 460; Rougier, 'L'Islam', p. 223; Marty, *Soudan*, vol. 2, pp. 241–3; Marty, *Guinée*, pp. 322–4.

131 J. Schacht, 'Zakat', in *Encyclopaedia of Islam* (1929), pp. 1202–4; T. H. Weir, 'Sadaka', in *ibid*. (1934), pp. 34–5.

132 M. Mauss, *The gift* (trans. I. Cunnison, London, 1954), p. 15; Miner, *Timbuctoo*, p. 139.

133 Mahmoud Kati, *Tarikh*, pp. 180–3; Miner, *Timbuctoo*, pp. 130–1.

134 M. G. Smith, *The economy of Hausa communities of Zaria* (London, 1955), p. 84

135 Milum to Kilner, 24 October 1879, MMS 272/A/69.

136 Smith, *Daura*, p. 129.

137 Mahmoud Kati, *Tarikh*, p. 261.

138 Weir in *Encyclopaedia of Islam*, p. 34.

139 Caillié, *Travels*, vol. 2, p. 56.

140 Fisher, *Slavery*, p. 48.

141 Uthman ibn Fudi, *Bayan wujub al-hijra ala 'l–ibad* (trans. F. H. el Masri, Khartoum, 1978), p. 144.

142 El-Hadji Mouhamadou Sakhir Gaye and Assane Sylla (eds.), 'Les sermons de Seydina Mouhamadou Limamou Lahi et de son fils Seydina Issa Rohou Lahi', *BIFAN*, 38B (1976), 396.

143 Marty, *Soudan*, vol. 2, p. 229; Marty, *Côte d'Ivoire*, p. 283.

144 Hiskett, *Development*, p. 162.

145 A. D. H. Bivar and M. Hiskett, 'The Arabic literature of Nigeria to 1804', *BSOAS*, 25 (1962), 124; Uthman ibn Fudi, *Bayan*, p. 133; Bosworth, *Islamic underworld*, vol. 1, p. 12.

146 Rougier, 'L'Islam', p. 236; Hiskett, *Hausa verse*, p. 192.

147 Es-Sadi, *Tarikh*, p. 77.

148 Rougier, 'L'Islam', p. 236.

149 Marty, *Soudan*, vol. 2, p. 229.

150 *Ibid*., p. 72; Marty, *Guinée*, pp. 305–6; David Robinson, *Chiefs and clerics: Abdul Bokar Kan and Futa Toro, 1853–1891* (Oxford, 1975), pp. 16, 46, 97, 108.

151 Smith, *Daura*, pp. 114, 127–8, 271; Murray Last, *The Sokoto Caliphate* (reprinted, London, 1977), pp. 103, 186; Watts, *Silent violence*, pp. 137–9; Ian Linden, 'Between two religions of the book', in Elizabeth Isichei (ed.), *Varieties of Christian experience in Nigeria* (London, 1982), p. 81.

152 Marion Johnson, 'The economic foundations of an Islamic theocracy – the case of Masina', *JAH*, 17 (1976), 486–8; Trimingham, *Islam in West Africa*, pp. 146–7.

153 Robinson, *Holy War*, p. 201.

154 Person, *Samori*, vol. 2, pp. 875–7.

155 Uthman ibn Fudi, *Bayan*, p. 161.

156 Hampaté Ba and Daget, *L'empire peul*, p. 48.

157 Robinson, *Holy War*, p. 33; Mervyn Hiskett, 'The "Song of the Shaihu's miracles"', *African language studies*, 12 (1971), 71–107.

158 See, e.g., Mungo Park, *Travels in Africa* (ed. R. Miller, revised edn, London, 1969), pp. 138, 151, 202.

159 Yaya Wane, 'Le célibat en pays toucouleur', *BIFAN*, 31B (1969), 728–9; G. Le Goff, 'Les Noirs se suicident-ils en A.O.F.?' *BCE*, 21 (1938), 132.
160 Whitting, *Proverbs*, pp. 135, 177.
161 Marguerite Dupire, 'The position of women in a pastoral society', in Denise Paulme (ed.), *Women of tropical Africa* (trans. H. M. Wright, Berkeley, 1971), p. 84; Paul Riesman, *Freedom in Fulani social life* (trans. M. Fuller, Chicago, 1977), pp. 180, 186, 231.
162 Marty, *Guinée*, p. 515.
163 Charles Henry Robinson, *Specimens of Hausa literature* (Cambridge, 1896), p. 56.
164 *Ibid.*, p. 42.
165 Marty, *Guinée*, pp. 324–5; Abba Ashigar, 'Mallamti settlements: some aspects of their role in the history of Borno', BA thesis, Abdullahi Bayero University, Kano, 1977, p. 39; Hiskett, '"Song"', p. 97.
166 Ferguson, 'Hausaland', p. 183; Trimingham, *Islam in West Africa*, pp. 178–83; Caillié, *Travels*, vol. 1, p. 125.
167 Carson I. A. Ritchie, 'Deux textes sur le Sénégal (1673–1677)', *BIFAN*, 30B (1968), 319; Nott to Baylis, 8 April 1898, CMS G3/A3/O/1898/60; J. S. Birks, *Across the savannas to Mecca* (London, 1978), p. 88; Marty, *Guinée*, p. 309.
168 Boilat, *Esquisses*, p. 482; John Ralph Willis, 'The Torodbe clerisy: a social view', *JAH*, 19 (1978), 197.
169 N. Levtzion and J. F. P. Hopkins (eds.), *Corpus of early Arabic sources for West African history* (Cambridge, 1981), p. 290; G. W. Brooke in *Sûdan Mission, C.M.S. monthly leaflet, no. 18* (1892), in CMS G3/A3/O/1892/86.
170 Weir, 'Sadaka', in *Encyclopaedia of Islam* (1934), p. 34; Robinson, *Specimens*, p. 70; Isichei, *Varieties*, p. 2.
171 Es-Sadi, *Tarikh*, p. 82.
172 *Ibid.*, pp. 67–8, 84.

4 Poverty and power

1 Ray A. Kea, *Settlements, trade, and politics in the seventeenth-century Gold Coast* (Baltimore, 1982), pp. 13–14, 40, 292–5, 320; R. E. Bradbury, *The Benin kingdom and the Edo-speaking peoples of south-western Nigeria* (London, 1957), p. 30. But see also William Bosman, *A new and accurate description of the coast of Guinea* (English trans., 4th edn, London, 1967), pp. 120, 124.
2 Godefroy Loyer, 'Relation de voyage du royaume d'Issyny' (1714), in Paul Roussier (ed.), *L'établissement d'Issiny 1687–1702* (Paris, 1935), p. 203.
3 Kea, *Settlements*, p. 19
4 *Ibid.*, pp. 5, 295–8.
5 *Ibid.*, p. 297.
6 *Ibid.*, pp. 309, 313.
7 *Ibid.*, p. 291.
8 Bosman, *Description* , p. 158.
9 Kea, *Settlements*, pp. 293–5.
10 *Ibid.*, pp. 19, 134–5; Bosman, *Description*, pp. 212–15, 449.
11 Kea, *Settlements*, p. 300.
12 Bosman, *Description*, pp. 140–1.
13 Kea, *Settlements*, p. 244.
14 De Marees, quoted in J. D. Fage, 'Slaves and society in western Africa, *c.*1445–*c.*1700', *JAH*, 21 (1980), 308.
15 Northcote W. Thomas, *Anthropological report on the Edo-speaking peoples of Nigeria* (2 vols., London, 1910), vol. 1, p. 97.

16 Kea, *Settlements*, pp. 102, 121.
17 Barbot in Churchill, *Collection*, vol. 5, p. 368.
18 De Marees, quoted in Fage, 'Slaves', p. 308.
19 Barbot in Churchill, *Collection*, vol. 5, p. 256.
20 Kea, *Settlements*, p. 304.
21 *Ibid.*, pp. 304–6.
22 *Ibid.*, p. 303.
23 A local word for both poor and commoners.
24 Kea, *Settlements*, p. 307.
25 Adam Jones (ed.), *German sources for West African history 1599–1669* (Wiesbaden, 1983), pp. 4–5.
26 Wrightson, *Society*, pp. 30–1, 36–7.
27 See p. 51.
28 J. Cuvelier and L. Jadin, *L'ancien Congo d'après les archives romaines (1518–1640)* (Brussels, 1954), p. 135.
29 A grain.
30 Gianuario da Nola to Gio-Battista da Napoli, 6 June 1645, in Louis Jadin (ed.), *L'ancien Congo et l'Angola 1639–1655 d'après les archives romaines, portugaises, néerlandaises et espagnoles* (3 vols., Brussels, 1975), vol. 2, p. 684.
31 John K. Thornton, *The kingdom of Kongo: civil war and transition 1641–1718* (Madison, 1983), p. 10; Joseph C. Miller, 'The significance of drought, disease and famine in the agriculturally marginal zones of west-central Africa', *JAH*, 23 (1982), 22.
32 [J. A.] Cavazzi, *Relation historique de l'Ethiopie occidentale* (trans. J. B. Labat, 5 vols., Paris, 1732), vol. 2, p. 37.
33 Thornton, *Kingdom*, p. 36.
34 Cuvelier and Jadin, *L'ancien Congo*, p. 135.
35 See Anne Hilton, 'Family and kinship among the Kongo south of the Zaire River from the sixteenth to the nineteenth centuries', *JAH*, 24 (1983), 189–206.
36 See Wyatt MacGaffey, 'Economic and social dimensions of Kongo slavery', in Suzanne Miers and Igor Kopytoff (eds.), *Slavery in Africa* (Madison, 1977), ch. 9.
37 Mateus Cardoso, 14 September 1625, in Louis Jadin, 'Relations sur le Congo et l'Angola tirées des archives de la Compagnie de Jésus, 1621–1631', *Bulletin de l'Institut Historique Belge de Rome*, 39 (1968), 418.
38 Luca da Caltanisetta, *Diaire congolais (1690–1701)* (trans. F. Bontinck, Louvain, 1970), p. 7.
39 Thornton, *Kingdom*, p. 15.
40 Jean de Santiago, *Relation de la première mission capucine au royaume du Congo (1645–1648)* (ed. J. P. Wetter, Louvain, 1969–70), pp. 241, 409.
41 Cavazzi, *Relation*, vol. 1, p. 223.
42 Hilton, 'Family', pp. 196–8; Thornton, *Kingdom*, pp. 19, 39–41.
43 Anne Hilton, *The kingdom of Kongo* (Oxford, 1985), p. 80; Cuvelier and Jadin, *L'ancien Congo*, p. 120; Thornton, *Kingdom*, pp. 41–2.
44 Bernardo da Gallo, quoted in Thornton, *Kingdom*, p. 109.
45 André Cordeiro, June 1622, in Jadin, 'Relations', p. 373.
46 Thornton, *Kingdom*, p. 23.
47 Cavazzi, *Relation*, vol. 3, p. 195, and vol. 5, p. 165.
48 The most remarkable is described in Louis Jadin, 'Pero Tavares, missionnaire jésuite, ses travaux apostoliques au Congo et en Angola, 1629–1635', *Bulletin de l'Institut Historique Belge de Rome*, 38 (1967), 271–402.
49 Bentley's Kongo dictionary of 1887 gave one word, *–asukami*, for both poor and destitute (its root, *–suka*, meant 'to come to an end . . . to be done, finished . . . exhausted') and

another, *–akondwa*, for destitute but not for poor (its connotations were: to be deficient, fall short, need, or lack). The earliest Kongo dictionary, composed during the 1650s, does not contain *–asukami* but has *–suka*, meaning to be finished or worn out. It does not include *–akondwa* or any related form. See W. Holman Bentley, *Dictionary and grammar of the Kongo language* (London, 1887), pp. 56, 163, 303, 419; J. Van Wing and C. Penders (eds.), *Le plus ancien dictionnaire bantu* (Louvain, 1928), p. 302.

50 Dionigio Carli da Piacenza, in John Churchill (ed.), *A collection of voyages and travels: volume 1* (London, 1704), p. 633.

51 Cavazzi, *Relation*, vol. 1, p. 230; Karl Laman, *The Kongo* (4 vols., Stockholm, 1953–68), vol. 2, p. 16.

52 Georges Balandier, *Daily life in the kingdom of the Kongo from the sixteenth to the eighteenth century* (trans. H. Weaver, London, 1968), p. 186; Louis Jadin, 'Andrea da Pavia au Congo, à Lisbonne, à Madère: journal d'un missionnaire capucin, 1685–1702', *Bulletin de l'Institut Historique Belge de Rome*, 41 (1970), 434; Laman, *Kongo*, vol. 2, pp. 40, 44–5, 87–8, 112.

53 Hilton, *Kingdom*, pp. 26–8.

54 António Brásio (ed.), *Monumenta Missionaria Africana: Africa Ocidental* (9 vols., Lisbon, 1952–79), vol. 2, pp. 185, 211–14.

55 *Ibid.*, vol. 6, pp. 73, 174.

56 Jadin, 'Relations', p. 431.

57 Jadin, 'Andrea da Pavia', p. 441.

58 From *lukau* (gift, offering) and *nkenda* (mercy, sympathy). See Bentley, *Dictionary*, pp. 8, 92, 328, 344, 382; K. E. Laman, *Dictionnaire Kikongo–Français* (reprinted, 2 vols., Ridgewood, NJ, 1964), pp. 421, 538, 716, 881.

59 O. Dapper, *Description de l'Afrique* (Amsterdam, 1686), p. 354.

60 Garcia V to João VI, 26 November 1813, in L. Jadin, 'Recherches dans les archives et bibliothèques d'Italie et du Portugal sur l'ancien Congo', *Bulletin des séances de l'Académie Royale des Sciences Coloniales*, NS, 2 (1956), 961. There was no missionary in Kongo at this time.

61 Brásio, *Monumenta*, vol. 3, p. 502.

62 *Ibid.*, vol. 6, p. 420.

63 Francisco de Soveral to Urban VIII, 1 April 1631, in Jadin, 'Relations', p. 435.

64 Brásio, *Monumenta*, vol. 5, pp. 527, 529, 531–2; vol. 6, p. 573; vol. 7, p. 444.

65 Girolamo Merolla da Sorrento in Churchill, *Collection*, vol. 1, p. 743.

66 Andrea da Pavia, who was stationed at Mbanza Sonyo in the late 1680s, does not mention a hospital. See Jadin, 'Andrea da Pavia'.

67 Jan Vansina, *The children of Woot: a history of the Kuba peoples* (Madison, 1978), ch. 9.

68 *Ibid.*, p. 237.

69 A. C. P. Gamitto, *King Kazembe* (trans. I. Cunnison, 2 vols., Lisbon, 1960), vol. 2, p. 116.

70 David and Charles Livingstone, *Narrative of an expedition to the Zambesi and its tributaries, 1858–1864* (London, 1865), p. 274.

71 W. G. Clarence-Smith, 'Slaves, commoners and landlords in Bulozi, c.1875 to 1906', *JAH*, 20 (1979), 222.

72 Vansina, *Children*, p. 182; Audrey I. Richards, *Land, labour and diet in Northern Rhodesia* (2nd edn, London, 1961), p. 44.

73 Clarence-Smith, 'Slaves', p. 225; Richards, *Land*, p. 35.

74 Vansina, *Children*, pp. 165–7, 180–1.

75 Clarence-Smith, 'Slaves', pp. 227–30; Gwyn Prins, *The hidden hippopotamus: the early colonial experience in western Zambia* (Cambridge, 1980), pp. 70–7.

76 Richards, *Land*, p. 144.

77 See Horace Waller (ed.), *The last journals of David Livingstone* (2 vols., London, 1874), vol. 1, p. 175.
78 Clarence-Smith, 'Slaves', pp. 226, 232; Vansina, *Children*, pp. 71–4.
79 Jan Vansina, *The Tio kingdom of the middle Congo 1880–1892* (London, 1973), p. 310; Robert W. Harms, *River of wealth, river of sorrow: the central Zaire basin in the era of the slave and ivory trade, 1500–1891* (New Haven, 1981), p. 5; Samuel N. Chipungu, 'Famine and hunger in Bulozi, 1850–1900', *Transafrican journal of history*, 13 (1984), 30.
80 Vansina, *Children*, p. 166.
81 Frederick Stanley Arnot, *Garenganze* (new edn, London, 1969), p. 73.
82 Clarence-Smith, 'Slaves', p. 231; Adolphe Jalla, *Pionniers parmi les Ma-Rotse* (Florence, 1903), pp. 236–7.
83 Vansina, *Tio*, pp. 306, 525.
84 David Livingstone, *African journal 1853–1856* (ed. I. Schapera, 2 vols., London, 1963), vol. 2, pp. 299, 318.
85 Frederick Stanley Arnot, *Bihé and Garenganze* (London [1893?]), p. 62; W. Singleton Fisher and Julyan Hoyte, *Africa looks ahead* (London, 1948), ch. 7.
86 Alfred Bertrand, *Au pays des Ba-Rotsi* (Paris, 1898), p. 198; Emil Holub, *Seven years in South Africa* (trans. E. E. Frewer, reprinted, 2 vols., Johannesburg, 1975), vol. 2, pp. 226–7.
87 Jalla, *Pionniers*, p. 341; Federation of Rhodesia and Nyasaland, *Report on the public health 1959*, p. 11; Prins, *Hippopotamus*, p. 41.
88 G. E. Tilsley, *Dan Crawford: missionary and pioneer in Central Africa* (London, 1929), p. 310; *Echoes of service* (1892), 115, 141.
89 P. Glyn Griffiths, 'Leprosy in the Luapula Valley', *LR*, 36 (1965), 62–3; Jalla, *Pionniers*, p. 341; Northern Rhodesia, *Social welfare report 1962*, pp. 9–10.
90 Dugald Campbell, *In the heart of Bantuland* (London, 1922), p. 105.
91 See V. W. Turner, *The drums of affliction* (Oxford, 1968), and other works.
92 Richards, *Land*, p. 145.
93 David Livingstone, *Missionary travels and researches in South Africa* (new edn, London, 1899), pp. 335–6.
94 Vansina, *Children*, pp. 185–6.
95 Andrew D. Roberts, *A history of the Bemba* (London, 1973), p. 170; Richards, *Land*, p. 214.
96 Livingstone, *Missionary travels*, p. 134.
97 Tilsley, *Crawford*, p. 150.
98 Ian Cunnison, *The Luapula peoples of Northern Rhodesia* (Manchester, 1959), pp. 197–8.
99 Robert Laws, diary, 3 June 1905, EUL GEN 561/1.
100 B. M. Zimbe, 'Buganda and the King', typescript trans. by F. Kamoga, p. 39 (CUL); Walter Rusch, *Klassen und Staat in Buganda vor der Kolonialzeit* (Berlin, 1975), part 2, ch. 2.
101 John Roscoe, *The Baganda* (2nd edn, London, 1965), p. 14.
102 Baskerville to Stock, 13 August 1891, CMS G3/A5/O/1892/50; Walker to his father, 21 September 1898, CMS:UP 88.
103 F. J. Bennett and A. Mugalula-Mukibi, 'An analysis of people living alone in a rural community in East Africa', *SSM*, 1 (1967), 110. Generally, see Ferdinand Walser, *Luganda proverbs* (Berlin, 1982).
104 White Fathers' Bukumbi journal, 2 September 1883, *CT* 23–4 (October 1884), 208; above, pp. 153–4.
105 Rusch, *Klassen*, pp. 110–11; John Mary Waliggo, 'The Catholic Church in the Buddu Province of Buganda, 1879–1925', Ph.D. thesis, University of Cambridge, 1976, p. 210; G. R. Blackledge, *Luganda–English and English–Luganda vocabulary* (London, 1904), pp. 68, 209; R. A. Snoxall (ed.), *Luganda–English dictionary* (Oxford, 1967), p. 233; Zimbe,

'Buganda', pp. 315–16; White Fathers' Buganda journal, 1–5 June 1890, *CT* 50 (April 1891), 373; John H. Orley, *Culture and mental illness: a study from Uganda* (Nairobi, 1970), p. 35; above, p. 216.

106 Roscoe, *Baganda*, pp. 12–13.

107 J. W. Nyakatura, *Anatomy of an African kingdom: a history of Bunyoro-Kitara* (trans. T. Muganwa, New York, 1973), p. 194; Apolo Kagwa, *The customs of the Baganda* (trans. E. B. Kalibala, New York, 1934), p. 15.

108 The following account is based on Claudine Vidal, 'Economie de la société féodale rwandaise', *CEA*, 14 (1974), 52–74.

109 *Ibid.*, p. 60.

110 *Ibid.*, pp. 64–5.

111 Claudine Vidal, 'Enquête sur le Rwanda traditionnel: conscience historique et traditions orales', *CEA*, 11 (1971), 536; *idem*, 'Economie', p. 65.

112 Vidal, 'Economie', pp. 67–8.

113 *Ibid.*, p. 64.

114 *Ibid.*, p. 53.

115 There may have been a small and marginal category of girls enslaved during famine. See Jan Czekanowski, *Forschungen im Nil–Kongo-Zwischengebiet: erster Band: Ethnographie* (Leipzig, 1917), pp. 262–3.

116 Vidal, 'Enquête', pp. 527–8; Vidal, 'Economie', pp. 57–8.

117 Vidal, 'Enquête', p. 536.

118 Czekanowski, *Forschungen*, pp. 261–2.

119 *Ibid.*, p. 265.

120 *Ibid.*, p. 270.

121 Helen Codere, *The biography of an African society, Rwanda 1900–1960* (Tervuren, 1973), p. 211.

122 Czekanowski, *Forschungen*, p. 249.

123 *Ibid.*, p. 263.

124 Rita Vanwalle, 'Aspecten van Staatsvorming in West-Rwanda', *Africa-Tervuren*, 28 (1982), 74–5.

125 Roger Botte, 'Burundi: de quoi vivait l'Etat', *CEA*, 22 (1982), 301.

126 Emile Mworoha, *Peuples et rois de l'Afrique des lacs* (Dakar, 1977), pp. 202–7.

127 Joseph Gahama, *Le Burundi sous administration belge* (Paris, 1983), p. 27.

128 Botte, 'Burundi', p. 278; Roger Botte, 'Processus de formation d'une classe sociale dans une société africaine précapitaliste', *CEA*, 14 (1974), 609–13.

129 Botte, 'Burundi', pp. 301–8 (quotation on p. 305).

130 Gahama, *Burundi*, p. 312.

131 Botte, 'Processus', pp. 605–13.

132 F. Ménard, *Dictionnaire Français–Kirundi et Kirundi–Français* (Roulers, 1909), part 2, p. 230.

133 *Ibid.*, part 2, pp. 133, 179, 230; F. M. Rodegem, *Dictionnaire Rundi–Français* (Tervuren, 1970), pp. 220–1, 311, 432, 599.

134 Botte, 'Processus', pp. 621–3.

135 *Ibid.*, p. 614.

136 F. M. Rodegem, *Sagesse kirundi* (Tervuren, 1961), p. 247.

137 José Kagabo and Vincent Mudandagizi, 'Complainte des gens de l'argile: les Twa du Rwanda', *CEA*, 14 (1974), 79; Codere, *Biography*, pp. 144–5; Botte, 'Burundi', p. 313; Czekanowski, *Forschungen*, pp. 262–3.

138 Codere, *Biography*, pp. 215, 253–4.

139 Ian Linden, *Church and revolution in Rwanda* (Manchester, 1977), p. 98.

140 Mworoha, *Peuples*, ch. 5.

141 Vanwalle, 'Aspecten', p. 73; Johan P. Pottier, 'The politics of famine prevention: ecology, regional production and food complementarity in western Rwanda', *African affairs*, 85 (1986), 222–4.
142 Rodegem, *Sagesse*, p. 53.
143 Botte, 'Burundi', p. 296.
144 *Ibid.*, p. 295.

5 Poverty and pastoralism

1 See R. D. Waller, '"The lords of East Africa": the Maasai in the mid-nineteenth century (c.1840–c.1885)', Ph.D. thesis, University of Cambridge, 1978, p. 73. I am grateful to Dr Waller for access to unpublished work and for ideas concerning pastoralism.
2 This account is based chiefly on Johannes Nicolaisen, *Ecology and culture of the pastoral Tuareg* (Copenhagen, 1963), esp. pp. 10–18.
3 *Ibid.*, p. 431.
4 For southern Tuareg stratification, see Edmond Bernus, *Touaregs nigériens* (Paris, 1981), pp. 72–7.
5 Johannes Nicolaisen, 'Slavery among the Tuareg in the Sahara', *Kuml* (Aarhus), 1957, 107–12; André Bourgeot, 'Rapports esclavigistes et conditions d'affranchissement chez les Imuhag (Twareg kel Ahaggar)', in Claude Meillassoux (ed.), *L'esclavage en Afrique précoloniale* (Paris, 1975), pp. 77–97.
6 J. P. Olivier de Sardan (ed.), *Quand nos pères étaient captifs . . . récits paysans du Niger* (Paris, 1976), esp. p. 19.
7 Edmond and Suzanne Bernus, 'L'évolution de la condition servile chez les Touaregs sahéliens', in Meillassoux, *L'esclavage*, p. 33; Stephen Baier and Paul E. Lovejoy, 'The Tuareg of the Central Sudan', in Miers and Kopytoff, *Slavery*, p. 401.
8 Djibo Hamani, *Contribution à l'étude de l'histoire des états hausa: l'Adar précolonial* (Niamey, 1975), pp. 189–210.
9 Marceau Gast, 'Pastoralisme nomade et pouvoir: la société traditionnelle des Kel Ahaggar', in L'équipe écologie et anthropologie des sociétés pastorales, *Pastoral production and society* (Cambridge, 1979), p. 206; Nicolaisen, *Ecology*, p. 428.
10 Caillié, *Travels*, vol. 1, p. 102. For social organisation, see Constant Hamès, 'L'évolution des émirats maures sous l'effet du capitalisme marchand européen, in L'équipe, *Pastoral production*, ch. 23.
11 Caillié, *Travels*, vol. 1, p. 102.
12 G. Gerhardt, 'Le Trarza', *Revue du monde musulman*, 15 (1911), 492.
13 Caillié, *Travels*, vol. 1, p. 78.
14 *Ibid.*, vol. 1, pp. 76–7.
15 Mungo Park, *Travels in the interior districts of Africa* (London, 1799), p. 153.
16 Caillié, *Travels*, vol. 1, p. 68.
17 Waller, '"Lords"', *passim*, and 'Economic and social relations in the central Rift Valley: the Maa-speakers and their neighbours in the nineteenth century' (unpublished paper, n.d.).
18 Waller, '"Lords"', pp. 61–2.
19 Waller, 'Economic', pp. 24–5.
20 *Ibid.*, p. 25.
21 Waller, '"Lords"', p. 74.
22 *Ibid.*, pp. 77–9.
23 Ludwig von Höhnel, *Discovery of Lakes Rudolf and Stefanie* (trans. N. Bell, 2 vols., London, 1894), vol. 1, p. 260; Waller, '"Lords"', pp. 291–3.
24 Waller, 'Economic', p. 41.

25 See Nicolaisen, 'Slavery', pp. 107–8.
26 P. H. Gulliver, *The family herds* (London, 1955), p. 39.
27 Neville Dyson-Hudson, *Karimojong politics* (Oxford, 1966), pp. 49–50, 85–6; Gulliver, *Family herds*, p. 39 n. 2; Paul Spencer, *Nomads in alliance* (London, 1973), pp. 41, 134.
28 Walter Goldschmidt, *Culture and behavior of the Sebei* (Berkeley, 1976), p. 134; Gudrun Dahl, 'Ecology and equality: the Boran case', in L'équipe, *Pastoral production*, pp. 272–9.
29 Malcolm Guthrie, *Comparative Bantu* (4 vols., Farnborough, 1967–70), vol. 3, p. 138.
30 M. P. Cowen, 'Differentiation in a Kenya location', duplicated paper, East African Universities Social Science Council Conference paper, Nairobi, 1972, pp. 3–5; D. Mukaru Ng'ang'a, 'Differentiation of the peasantry and the development of capitalism in the Central Province of Kenya: 1880–1970s', IDS Nairobi paper no. 84, 1977, p. 5; Hildegarde Hinde, *Vocabularies of the Kamba and Kikuyu languages of East Africa* (Cambridge, 1904), pp. 7, 47.
31 See A. Ruffell Barlow, *English–Kikuyu dictionary* (ed. T. G. Benson, Oxford, 1975), p. 219; T. G. Benson (ed.), *Kikuyu–English dictionary* (Oxford, 1964), pp. 340–1.
32 See p. 91.
33 Richard Elphick, *Kraal and castle: Khoikhoi and the founding of white South Africa* (New Haven, 1977), pp. 83, 94; H. B. Thom (ed.), *Journal of Jan van Riebeeck* (3 vols., Cape Town, 1952–8), vol. 1, p. 46.
34 Elphick, *Kraal*, p. 94.
35 Thom, *Journal of van Riebeeck*, vol. 1, p. 30.
36 Werner Jopp (ed.), *Unter Hottentotten, 1705–1713: die Aufzeichnungen von Peter Kolb* (Tübingen, 1979), p. 120; Elphick, *Kraal*, p. 28.
37 Elphick, *Kraal*, p. 39.
38 H. Vedder, 'The Herero', in C. H. L. Hahn and others, *The native tribes of South West Africa* (reprinted, London, 1966), pp. 175, 207.
39 Ludwig Alberti, *Ludwig Alberti's account of the tribal life and customs of the Xhosa in 1807* (trans. W. Fehr, Cape Town, 1968), p. 77.
40 Henry Lichtenstein, *Travels in Southern Africa* (trans. A. Plumptre, reprinted, 2 vols., Cape Town, 1928), vol. 1, pp. 328, 343.
41 Evidence of Rev. J. A. Chalmers, in Cape of Good Hope, *Report and proceedings . . . of the Government Commission on Native Laws and Customs* (Cape Town, 1883), p. 140.
42 E.g. John Henderson Soga, *The Ama-Xosa: life and customs* (Lovedale [1931?]), p. 385.
43 J. B. Peires, *The house of Phalo: a history of the Xhosa people in the days of their independence* (Berkeley, 1982), pp. 32–3.
44 Eileen Jensen Krige, *The social system of the Zulus* (2nd edn, Pietermaritzburg, 1950), p. 241.
45 Hilda Kuper, *An African aristocracy* (London, 1947), p. 157.
46 Hugh Ashton, *The Basuto* (2nd edn, London, 1967), pp. 212–13.
47 Jack Lewis, 'The rise and fall of the South African peasantry; a critique and reassessment', *JSAS*, 11 (1984–5), 5–6.
48 'An account of . . . Caffraria, by Dr Vanderkemp', *Transactions of the [London] Missionary Society*, 1 (1795–1802), 436–7.
49 Peires, *House of Phalo*, p. 40.
50 Lewis, 'Rise and fall', p. 4.
51 Krige, *Social system*, p. 53.
52 'An account of . . . Caffraria', *Transactions of the [London] Missionary Society*, 1 (1795–1802), 436–7.
53 Sexual requisition by the chief and his followers.
54 Peires, *House of Phalo*, p. 77.

55 Lichtenstein, *Travels*, vol. 1, p. 322; Monica Hunter, *Reaction to conquest* (2nd edn, London, 1961), p. 23.
56 Lichtenstein, *Travels*, vol. 1, pp. 327–8.
57 Alberti, *Xhosa*, pp. 21–2; Stephen Kay, *Travels and researches in Caffraria* (London, 1833), p. 203; Peires, *House of Phalo*, p. 68; J. Philip to W. Philip, 15 January 1842, CWM:IL South Africa 18/3/B/4.
58 Andrew Steedman, *Wanderings and adventures in the interior of southern Africa* (2 vols., London, 1835), vol. 1, pp. 34, 49.
59 Hunter, *Reaction*, ch. 1.
60 Evidence of Rev. T. W. Green and of the Tembu Paramount and Councillors in Cape of Good Hope, *Commission on Native Laws*, pp. 390, 443.
61 E.g. Steedman, *Wanderings*, vol. 1, pp. 46–7; *Mission field*, 3 (1888), 330–1.
62 P. D. Tyson, 'Southern African rainfall: past, present and future', in Madalon T. Hinchey (ed.), *Proceedings of the Symposium on Drought in Botswana* (Gaborone, 1979), pp. 45–52; Peires, *House of Phalo*, p. 8.
63 Lichtenstein, *Travels*, vol. 1, pp. 351–2; Peires, *House of Phalo*, pp. 89–90, 128; John Zarwan, 'The Xhosa cattle killings, 1856–57', *CEA*, 16 (1976), 524 n. 35; William Beinart, *The political economy of Pondoland 1860–1930* (Cambridge, 1982), p. 26.
64 Rev. H. Waters, 10 April 1857, in *Mission field*, 2 (1857), 200–1.
65 Zarwan, 'Cattle killings', p. 527.
66 Quoted in Lewis, 'Rise and fall', pp. 19–20.
67 Cape of Good Hope, *Blue book on native affairs 1880* (G.13–'80), p. 173.
68 Cape of Good Hope, *Commission on Native Laws*, p. 482.
69 Martin Legassick, 'The Sotho-Tswana peoples before 1800', in Leonard Thompson (ed.), *African societies in southern Africa* (London, 1969), p. 116; Adam Kuper, *Kalahari village politics* (Cambridge, 1970), p. 7.
70 Price to Shippard, 28 September 1887, CO 417/16/445.
71 In this instance the term appears to mean Kgalagadi.
72 Robert Moffat, *Missionary labours and scenes in southern Africa* (London, 1842), p. 8.
73 I. Schapera (ed.), *Livingstone's missionary correspondence 1841–1856* (London, 1961), p. 160.
74 John Mackenzie, *Day-dawn in dark places* (London [1883?]), p. 57.
75 See Shula Marks, 'Khoisan resistance to the Dutch in the seventeenth and eighteenth centuries', *JAH*, 13 (1972), 55–80.
76 John E. Yellen, 'The process of Basarwa assimilation in Botswana', *BNR*, 17 (1985), 17; Hamilton, journal, 28 September and 26 October 1820, CWM South Africa journals box 3; S. Passarge, *Die Buschmänner der Kalahari* (Berlin, 1907), pp. 114–19.
77 Moffat, journal, 16 July 1824, CWM South Africa journals box 4; James Chapman, *Travels in the interior of South Africa 1849–1863* (2 vols., Cape Town, 1971), vol. 1, *passim*; Richard B. Lee, '!Kung spatial organization', in Richard B. Lee and Irven De Vore (eds.), *Kalahari hunter-gatherers* (Cambridge, Mass., 1976), p. 92.
78 A Tswana group.
79 Chapman, *Travels*, vol. 1, p. 61.
80 *Ibid.*
81 *Ibid.*, pp. 54–5.
82 *Ibid.*, p. 28.
83 *Ibid.*, p. 74.
84 Mackenzie, *Day-dawn*, p. 63.
85 Wookey to Administrator, 21 June 1887, CO 417/15/586; I. Schapera, *Tribal innovators: Tswana chiefs and social change 1795–1940* (London, 1970), p. 89; M. G. Guenther, 'From hunters to squatters', in Lee and De Vore, *Kalahari hunter-gatherers*, p. 127.

86 I. Schapera, *A handbook of Tswana law and custom* (2nd edn, London, 1955), pp. 32, 250–2.
87 See London Missionary Society, *The Masarwa (Bushmen)* (Lovedale [1935]), pp. 5–7, 10, 25, 27–8.
88 Schapera, *Innovators*, p. 164.
89 *Ibid.*, pp. 89–90; J. D. Hepburn, *Twenty years in Khama's country* (3rd edn, London, 1970), p. 265.
90 Schapera, *Tribal innovators*, p. 164 n. 1; Neil Parsons, 'The economic history of Khama's country in Botswana, 1844–1930', in Robin Palmer and Neil Parsons (eds.), *The roots of rural poverty in central and southern Africa* (London, 1977), p. 119; I. Schapera (ed.), *Praise-poems of Tswana chiefs* (Oxford, 1965), p. 209; Schapera, *Handbook*, p. 121.
91 London Missionary Society, *Masarwa*, p. 5; Mackenzie, *Day-dawn*, p. 59.
92 Moffat to Administrator, 16 April 1887, CO 417/15/582.
93 Thomas Tlou, 'Servility and political control: *botlhanka* among the BaTawana of north-western Botswana', in Miers and Kopytoff, *Slavery*, ch. 14.
94 Lichtenstein, *Travels*, vol. 2, pp. 396–7; William J. Burchell, *Travels in the interior of southern Africa* (reprinted, 2 vols., Cape Town, 1967), vol. 2, p. 473; R. L. Cope (ed.), *The journals of the Rev. T. L. Hodgson* (Johannesburg, 1977), p. 173.
95 Una Long (ed.), *The journals of Elizabeth Lees Price, 1854–1883* (London, 1956), pp. 229–33, 378–80; Edwards to Tidman, 6 August 1847, CWM:IL South Africa 23/1/B/14; Moffat to Burder, 13 November 1826, CWM:IL South Africa 10/1/C/27.
96 Long, *Journals of Price*, p. 469.
97 Solomon T. Plaatje, *Sechuana proverbs* (London, 1916), p. 64; J. Tom Brown, *Secwana–English dictionary* (revised edn, Tiger Kloof [1931]), p. 136.
98 Burchell, *Travels*, vol. 2, pp. 349–50.
99 Margaret Kinsman, '"Beasts of burden": the subordination of southern Tswana women, ca.1800–1840', *JSAS*, 10 (1983–4), 52.
100 E.g. Percival R. Kirby (ed.), *The diary of Dr Andrew Smith, 1834–1836* (2 vols., Cape Town, 1839–40), vol. 2, p. 258.
101 Schapera, *Handbook*, pp. 164–5, 193.
102 Long, *Journals of Price*, p. 438.
103 Schapera, *Handbook*, p. 155.
104 Livingstone, *Missionary travels*, p. 89.
105 Cope, *Journals of Hodgson*, pp. 208–9.
106 Kinsman, '"Beasts of burden"', p. 45.
107 Chapman, *Travels*, vol. 2, p. 169; Schapera, *Livingstone's missionary correspondence*, p. 291; Moffat, *Missionary labours*, p. 465.
108 *MC*, 29 (1897), 325–6.
109 Moffat, journal, 5 August 1821, CWM South Africa journals box 3; Long, *Journals of Price*, p. 279; Ross to Tidman, 28 April 1856, CWM:IL South Africa 30/1/A/4.
110 See esp. Margaret Kinsman, 'Notes on the southern Tswana social formation', University of Cape Town, Centre for African Studies, *Africa seminar collected papers, volume 2* (1981), pp. 185–6.
111 Burchell, *Travels*, vol. 2, p. 544.
112 Kirby, *Diary of Smith*, vol. 1, p. 346; Hamilton and Moffat to Burder, 20 August 1827, CWM:IL South Africa 10/3/A/35. Batlaro were a Tswana group.
113 Pia du Pradal, 'Poverty and wealth in a Kalahari village in Botswana', CCP 284 (1984), 14.
114 Hughes to Ellis, 13 March 1836, CWM:IL South Africa 15/1E/34.
115 Hamilton, journal, 29 November 1818, CWM South Africa journals box 3; J. Tom Brown, *Among the Bantu nomads* (London, 1926), p. 82.
116 Brown, *Dictionary*, pp. 91, 394, 502.

117 *Go senang khumo ga gona lehuma*: Plaatje, *Proverbs*, p. 42. See above, p. 41.
118 Richard Elphick, 'The Khoisan to c.1770', in Richard Elphick and Hermann Giliomee (eds.), *The shaping of South African society, 1652–1820* (Cape Town, 1979), p. 30.
119 Moffat to Ellis, 3 February 1834, CWM:IL South Africa 14/2/F/10.
120 John Mackenzie, *Ten years north of the Orange River* (2nd edn, London, 1971), p. 71.
121 Hamilton to Burder, 15 December 1825, CWM:IL South Africa 9/4/B/41; Moffat to Ellis, 10 January 1833, CWM:IL South Africa 13/4/E/4; R. K. Hitchcock, 'The traditional response to drought in Botswana', in Hinchey, *Proceedings*, p. 92.
122 David Livingstone, *Family letters 1841–1856* (ed. I. Schapera, 2 vols., London, 1959), vol. 2, pp. 14–15.
123 *Ibid.*, p. 76.
124 *Ibid.*, p. 31; Ross to Directors, 2 June 1846, CWM:IL South Africa 22/1/A/7.
125 Hitchcock in Hinchey, *Proceedings*, pp. 93–4.
126 Chapman, *Travels*, vol. 1, p. 179.
127 Cope, *Journals of Hodgson*, p. 14; Cape of Good Hope, *Blue-book on native affairs 1899* (G. 31–'99), pp. 59, 62, 67–9; Ross to Tidman, 1 November 1858, CWM:IL South Africa 31/1/B/20; Ross to Directors, 12 September 1846, CWM:IL South Africa 22/1/A/8.
128 Mackenzie, *Day-dawn*, p. 154.
129 George Thompson, *Travels and adventures in southern Africa* (2 vols., Cape Town, 1967–8), vol. 1, chs. 8–16, 18; Cope, *Journals of Hodgson*, pp. 14, 306; Kirby, *Diary of Smith*, vol. 2, pp. 138–9, 145–6, 171–2, 184–5, 246.
130 Hamilton and others to Ellis, 15 June 1837, CWM:IL South Africa 15/4/D/56.
131 Moffat, *Missionary labours*, p. 12.
132 Truter and Somerville's report in John Barrow, *A voyage to Cochinchina* (London, 1806), pp. 390–1.
133 Mackenzie, *Ten years*, p. 365; Hepburn, *Twenty years*, p. 314; above, p. 37.
134 There are good descriptions in Barrow, *Voyage*, pp. 389–93; Lichtenstein, *Travels*, vol. 2, pp. 373–80.
135 See John L. Comaroff, 'Tswana transformations, 1953–1975', in I. Schapera, *The Tswana* (2nd edn, London, 1976), pp. 71–5.
136 Hamilton and Moffat to Miles, 12 August 1829, CWM:IL South Africa 11/3/D/35.
137 Moffat to Burder, 8 May 1824, CWM:IL South Africa 9/2/B/19; Livingstone, *Family letters*, vol. 2, p. 31; Anthony Joseph Dachs, 'Missionary imperialism in Bechuanaland, 1813–1896', Ph.D. thesis, University of Cambridge, 1968, p. 118.
138 Schapera, *Innovators*, p. 118; Parsons in Palmer and Parsons, *Roots*, p. 140 n. 74; Gwayi Tyamzashe, 'Life at the diamond fields' (1874), in Francis Wilson and Dominique Perrot (eds.), *Outlook on a century* (Lovedale, 1973), p. 21.
139 Long, *Journals of Price*, p. 438.
140 *Mission field*, 44 (1899), 410.
141 Livingstone, *Missionary travels*, p. 14.
142 Schapera, *Handbook*, pp. 69, 192.
143 Mackenzie, *Ten years*, pp. 44–5; Schapera, *Praise-poems*, p. 199.
144 Schapera, *Handbook*, p. 68; K. K. Prah, 'Some sociological aspects of drought', in Hinchey, *Proceedings*, p. 89.
145 Kirby, *Diary of Smith*, vol. 1, p. 344.
146 Cope, *Journals of Hodgson*, p. 124; Hamilton to Ellis, 15 June 1837, CWM:IL South Africa 15/4/D/56. Burchell (*Travels*, vol. 2, p. 544) made the same point.
147 Du Pradal, 'Poverty', p. 28.
148 See pp. 146, 236.

6 Yoruba and Igbo

1 For a more detailed account, with fuller references, see John Iliffe, 'Poverty in nineteenth-century Yorubaland', *JAH*, 25 (1984), 43–57.
2 Doherty, journal, 12 May 1876, CMS C.A2/O.35/11.
3 *MC*, 36 (1904), 398.
4 Three were incapacitated in more than one way.
5 This was not true. See p. 214.
6 *MC*, 23 (1891), 602. There are accounts of Yoruba killing leprosy sufferers: see T. F. G. Mayer, 'The distribution of leprosy in Nigeria with special reference to the aetiological factors on which it depends', *WAMJ*, 4 (1930–1), 13.
7 White, journal, 17 February 1863, CMS C.A2/O.87/65.
8 See Iliffe, 'Poverty', pp. 47–8; *MC*, 26 (1894), 415; *MC*, 36 (1904), 398; Adefunke Oyemade, 'The care of motherless babies: a century of voluntary work in Nigeria', *Journal of the Historical Society of Nigeria*, 7 (1974), 369–71.
9 Doherty, journal, 24 February 1875, CMS C.A2/O.35/8.
10 See p. 85.
11 *Lagos observer*, 4 January 1883.
12 R. H. Stone, *In Afric's forest and jungle or six years among the Yorubans* (Edinburgh, 1900), p. 186.
13 *MC*, 24 (1892), 450.
14 *MC*, 36 (1904), 398.
15 For a general account, see E. Adeniyi Oroge, 'The institution of slavery in Yorubaland with particular reference to the nineteenth century', Ph.D. thesis, University of Birmingham, 1971.
16 Peel, 'Inequality', p. 482.
17 S. Crowther, journal, quarter ending 25 September 1855, CMS C.A2/O.32/61.
18 Samuel Crowther, *A vocabulary of the Yoruba language* (London, 1852), p. 161.
19 Lander, *Records*, vol. 2, pp. 205, 208, 213, 219.
20 Crowther, *Vocabulary*, pp. 30, 218, 225; T. J. Bowen, *Grammar and dictionary of the Yoruba language*, Smithsonian contributions to knowledge, vol. 10 (Washington, DC, 1858), part 2, pp. 102, 118; [Church Missionary Society,] *Dictionary of the Yoruba language* (new edn, Lagos, 1918), part 1, pp. 42, 118, and part 2, pp. 38, 229.
21 Peter Marris, *Family and social change in an African city* (London, 1961), p. 73.
22 *MC*, 15 (1883), 306.
23 Bowen, *Grammar*, p. xviii.
24 V. F. Biscoe, Re-assessment report on Sharagi District, Ilorin Province, 1918, RH MSS Afr. s. 1586.
25 J. Okuseinde, journal, 25 January 1887, CMS G3/A2/O/1888/48; Harding to Baylis, 1 August 1899, CMS G3/A2/O/1899/123; *LWR*, 29 October 1892.
26 *Lagos observer*, 16 March 1882; above, pp. 164–7.
27 Akiele, journal, 25 January 1888, CMS G3/A2/O/1889/130. 'His' refers to Tela Kofoworola.
28 Bamisaiye, 'Begging in Ibadan', p. 198.
29 Akiele, journal, 10 September 1890, CMS G3/A2/O/1891/121.
30 Doherty, journal, 29 May 1876, CMS C.A2/O.35/11.
31 Divinity.
32 Olubi, journal, 10 January 1873, CMS C.A2/O.75/28.
33 See Iliffe, 'Poverty', p. 55; T. King, journal, 18 August 1853, CMS C.A2/O.61/50.
34 Harding to Merensky, 18 October 1888, CMS G3/A2/O/1888/172; William Bascom, *Sixteen cowries: Yoruba divination from Africa to the New World* (Bloomington, 1980), pp. 37–8.

35 W. S. Allen, journal, 9 February 1871, CMS C.A2/O.19/15; C. Phillips Jr, journal, 5 June 1878, CMS C.A2/O.78/21.
36 Crowther to Hutchinson, 10 September 1856, CMS C.A2/O.31/78.
37 See William R. Bascom, *The sociological role of the Yoruba cult-group* (Menasha, Wis., 1944); Vendeix, 'Etude sur les couvents fétichistes au Dahomey', *BCE*, 11 (1928), 640–6; Pierre Verger, *Notes sur le culte des orisa et vodun* (Dakar, 1957).
38 E.g. S. Johnson, journal, 18 September 1883, CMS G3/A2/O/1884/101.
39 Gollmer to Snaith, 4 June 1861, CMS C.A2/O.43/68.
40 Crowther, *Vocabulary*, s.v. *alagbe*; G. J. Afolabi Ojo, *Yoruba palaces* (London, 1966), p. 72.
41 *MC*, 16 (1884), 581.
42 See Iliffe, 'Poverty', p. 57.
43 Young, journal, 9 June 1875, CMS C.A2/O.98/10; J. S. Eades, *The Yoruba today* (Cambridge, 1980), p. 148.
44 G. T. Basden, *Niger Ibos* (reprinted, London, 1966), p. 124.
45 Samuel Crowther and John Christopher Taylor, *The Gospel on the banks of the Niger* (reprinted, London, 1968), p. 426.
46 Taylor, 'Report on the political and spiritual state of Onitsha' [1864] CMS C.A3/O.37/57; Buck, journal, 13 July 1878, CMS C.A3/O.9/9.
47 John Loiello, 'Bishop in two worlds: Samuel Ajayi Crowther', in Isichei, *Varieties*, p. 48; Frances M. Hensley, *Niger dawn* (Ilfracombe [1954]), pp. 45–7; Mary Elms, 'The early days: twenty-five years of medical work in Eastern Nigeria', typescript, n.d., CMS:UP 17; *MC*, 25 (1893), 616.
48 Herbert M. Cole, *Mbari: art and life among the Owerri Igbo* (Bloomington, 1982), p. 160.
49 *MC*, 30 (1898), 196.
50 Crowther, 'A visit to the markets in the interior of Ibo from Bonny' [May 1889] CMS G3/A3/O/1889/87.
51 T. J. Dennis, journal, 9 April 1898, CMS:UP 89/F1; *MC*, 25 (1893), 607.
52 John P. Jordan, *Bishop Shanahan of Southern Nigeria* (Dublin, 1949), p. 15; John M. Todd, *African mission* (London, 1962), p. 127.
53 Victor C. Uchendu, *The Igbo of southeast Nigeria* (New York, 1965), p. 57; *MC*, 33 (1901), 366; M. M. Green, *Ibo village affairs* (London, 1947), pp. 86, 187.
54 Basden, *Niger Ibos*, p. 213.
55 *MC*, 25 (1893), 615.
56 Uchendu, *Igbo*, p. 50; Taylor, 'Report' [1864] CMS C.A3/O.37/57.
57 Northcote W. Thomas, *Anthropological report on the Ibo-speaking peoples of Nigeria* (6 vols., London, 1913–14), vol. 1, p. 17; Sylvia Leith-Ross, *African women: a study of the Ibo of Nigeria* (London, 1939), pp. 93–4.
58 T. F. Davey, 'First report on leprosy control work in the Owerri Province', *LR*, 11 (1940), 124, 126; *idem*, 'Leprosy control in the Owerri Province', *LR*, 13 (1942), 32, 38. For the conditions encouraging leprosy, see above, p. 215.
59 Elms, 'Early days', p. 58, CMS:UP 17; *MC*, 25 (1893), 615–16.
60 T. Frank Davey, 'Uzuakoli Leper Colony', *LR*, 10 (1939), 179.
61 James A. K. Brown, 'Leprosy folk-lore in Southern Nigeria', *LR*, 8 (1937), 157–60.
62 *Ibid.*, p. 159.
63 *MC*, 25 (1893), 616.
64 E. Muir, 'Leprosy in Nigeria', *LR*, 11 (1940), 63; Brown, 'Folk-lore', p. 160.
65 *MC*, 25 (1893), 616; *MC*, 31 (1899), 255.
66 Paul Edwards (ed.), *Equiano's travels* (London, 1967), pp. 7–8; Thomas, *Ibo*, vol. 2, p. 8, and vol. 6, p. 5. For one special form of begging, see above p. 93.
67 Uchendu, *Igbo*, p. 92. He goes on to list other considerations complicating the classification.

68 Thomas, *Ibo*, vol. 2, p. 66; vol. 3, pp. 3–8, 11; vol. 6, pp. 1–6.
69 Green, *Ibo*, p. 88; Simon Ottenberg, 'Ibo receptivity to change', in William Bascom and Melville J. Herskovits (eds.), *Continuity and change in African cultures* (Chicago, 1959), pp. 130–43; Emmanuel N. Obiechina (ed.), *Onitsha market literature* (London, 1972), p. 83.
70 Thomas, *Ibo*, vol. 1, p. 97; Elizabeth Isichei, *A history of the Igbo people* (London, 1976), pp. 27, 79; T. J. Dennis, journal, 6 May 1896, CMS:UP 89/F1.
71 George, journal, 11 March 1863, CMS C.A3/O.18/20.
72 Thomas, *Ibo*, vol. 6, p. 2.
73 *Ibid.*, vol. 1, pp. 17, 63; Uchendu, *Igbo*, p. 86.
74 Thomas, *Ibo*, vol. 1, pp. 13–18. Thomas's figures are inconsistent and unreliable.
75 *Ibid.*, vol. 4, p. 166, and vol. 1, p. 104; T. J. Dennis, journal, 3 November 1910, CMS:UP 89/F1.
76 Uchendu, *Igbo*, p. 22; Thomas, *Ibo*, vol. 1, ch. 10.
77 Leith-Ross, *Women*, p. 94; *MC*, 33 (1901), 366; J. S. Harris, 'Some aspects of the economics of sixteen Ibo individuals', *Africa*, 14 (1943–4), 316–17, 327.
78 Thomas, *Ibo*, vol. 1, pp. 134–5; Isichei, *History*, p. 27.
79 George, journal, 21 January 1866, CMS C.A3/O.18/23; F. M. Dennis, journal, 17 November 1908, CMS:UP 4/F2; T. J. Dennis, journal, 15 March 1907, CMS:UP 89/F1.
80 Leith-Ross, *Women*, pp. 128, 249; Uchendu, *Igbo*, p. 14; Thomas, *Ibo*, vol. 6, p. 3.
81 Quoted in Elizabeth Isichei (ed.), *Igbo worlds* (London, 1977), p. 67.
82 F. M. Dennis, journal, 11 January 1906, CMS:UP 4/F1.
83 See Cole, *Mbari*, ch. 3.
84 See J. H. Hutton, *Caste in India* (2nd edn, Bombay, 1951), p. 144.
85 Basden, *Niger Ibos*, p. 246.
86 S. N. Ezeanya, 'The *osu* (cult-slave) system in Igbo land', *Journal of religion in Africa*, 1 (1968), 40. See also S. Leith-Ross, 'Notes on the Osu system among the Ibo of Owerri Province', *Africa*, 10 (1937), 206–20.
87 Ezeanya, '*Osu*', pp. 38–9.
88 Green, *Ibo*, p. 158 n. 1; G. T. Basden, *Among the Ibos of Nigeria* (reprinted, London, 1966), p. 106.
89 Ezeanya, '*Osu*', p. 38.
90 Thomas, *Ibo*, vol. 1, p. 103.
91 John to Crowther [1878] CMS C.A3/O.22/2; Elms, 'Early days', p. 59, CMS:UP 17.
92 Uchendu, *Igbo*, p. 90; A. J. Fox (ed.), *Uzuakoli: a short history* (London, 1964), p. 17.

7 Early European initiatives

1 John Vogt, *Portuguese rule on the Gold Coast 1469–1682* (Athens, Ga., 1979), p. 51.
2 See p. 51.
3 G. M. Theal (ed.), *Records of south-eastern Africa*, vol. 2 (London, 1898), p. 44.
4 C. R. Boxer, 'Moçambique Island and the "Carreira da India"', *Studia* (Lisbon), 8 (1961), 105–8.
5 Livingstone, *Narrative*, pp. 35–6.
6 *MC*, 22 (1890), 331.
7 António Brásio, 'As Misericórdias de Angola', *Studia*, 4 (1959), 107–16.
8 *Ibid.*, p. 121.
9 Jadin, 'Relations', p. 360; Barbot in Churchill, *Collection*, vol. 5, p. 516.
10 Brásio, 'As Misericórdias', pp. 133–4.
11 *Ibid.*, pp. 135, 139, 149; above, p. 55.

12 Brásio, *Monumenta*, second series, vol. 5, p. 177; Lobo, *Voyage*, p. 113.
13 Brásio, 'As Misericórdias', p. 116.
14 Jadin, 'Pero Tavares', p. 358.
15 Brásio, *Monumenta*, vol. 7, p. 352; J. Cuvelier, 'Le Vénérable André de Burgio et la situation religieuse au Congo et dans l'Angola au temps de son apostolat (1745–1761)', *Collectanea Franciscana*, 32 (1962), 93. (Cuvelier doubted the last statement, perhaps unnecessarily.)
16 Merolla in Churchill, *Collection*, vol. 1, p. 753.
17 Edmund H. Burrows, *A history of medicine in South Africa up to the end of the nineteenth century* (Cape Town, 1958), p. 31.
18 Maria M. Marais, 'Armesorg aan die Kaap onder die Kompanjie, 1652–1795', *Argiefjaarboek vir Suid-Afrikaanse geskiednis*, 6 (1943), 1–4.
19 See Robert M. Kingdon, 'Social welfare in Calvin's Geneva', *American historical review*, 76 (1971), 50–69.
20 Marais, 'Armesorg', pp. 9–12, 22, 27; O. F. Mentzel, *A geographical and topographical description of the Cape of Good Hope* (trans. H. J. Mandelbrote, 3 vols., Cape Town, 1921–44), vol. 1, pp. 128–9, 148–9.
21 Marais, 'Armesorg', pp. 13–21, 61.
22 'Report of J. T. Bigge, Esq., to Earl Bathurst upon Courts of Justice', 6 September 1826, in G. M. Theal (ed.), *Records of the Cape Colony* (36 vols., London, 1897–1905), vol. 28, p. 74.
23 Marais, 'Armesorg', pp. 39–40, 47; Mentzel, *Description*, vol. 2, p. 114; P. F. Greyling, *Die Nederduits Gereformeerde Kerk en armesorg* (Cape Town, 1939), p. 158. (Henceforth referred to as *NGK*.)
24 Gerrit Schutte, 'Company and colonists at the Cape', in Elphick and Giliomee, *Shaping*, p. 189.
25 John Barrow, *An account of travels into the interior of southern Africa* (2 vols., London, 1801–4), vol. 1, pp. 48–9, and vol. 2, p. 390.
26 Charlotte Searle, *The history of the development of nursing in South Africa 1652–1960* (Cape Town, 1965), pp. 34, 39–40.
27 Marais, 'Armesorg', p. 14.
28 Greyling, *NGK*, p. 191.
29 Marais, 'Armesorg', pp. 11, 62–4.
30 Barrow, *Account*, vol. 2, p. 378.
31 Robert Ross, 'The first two centuries of colonial agriculture in the Cape Colony', *Social dynamics*, 9 (1983), 39.
32 R. Collins, 'Journal of a tour to the north-eastern boundary . . . in 1809', in D. Moodie (ed.), *The record* (5 parts, Cape Town, 1838–41), part 5, p. 22.
33 Susan Newton-King, 'The labour market of the Cape Colony, 1807–28', in Shula Marks and Anthony Atmore (eds.), *Economy and society in pre-industrial South Africa* (London, 1980), p. 177.
34 'Report of the Commissioners of Inquiry . . . upon the police at the Cape of Good Hope', 10 May 1828, in Theal, *Cape Colony*, vol. 35, p. 147.
35 Plaskett to Commissioners of Enquiry, 4 December 1825, in *ibid.*, vol. 24, p. 61.
36 'Report . . . upon the police', 10 May 1828, in *ibid.*, vol. 35, p. 147.
37 Read to Burder, 2 September 1827, CWM:IL South Africa 10/3/A/38.
38 Leslie Clement Duly, 'A revisit with the Cape's Hottentot Ordinance of 1828', in Marcelle Kooy (ed.), *Studies in economics and economic history* (London, 1972), pp. 36–8.
39 Edna Bradlow, 'Emancipation and race perceptions at the Cape', *SAHJ*, 15 (1983), 20–3; W. M. MacMillan, *The Cape Colour question* (London, 1927), p. 253.
40 Edna Bradlow, 'Cape Town's labouring poor a century ago', *SAHJ*, 9 (November 1977), 20, 22.

41 Shirley Judges, 'Poverty, living conditions and social relations – aspects of life in Cape Town in the 1830s', MA thesis, University of Cape Town, 1977, p. 53 and appendix.
42 *Ibid.*, pp. 3–4, 12.
43 *Ibid.*, pp. 7, 10, 13.
44 *Ibid.*, pp. 45, 47, 135.
45 *Ibid.*, pp. 73, 86–7; Christopher Saunders, 'Segregation in Cape Town: the creation of Ndabeni', in University of Cape Town, Centre for African Studies, *Africa seminar collected papers*, vol. 1 (1978), 43.
46 Wagenaar's journal, 1 December 1664, in Moodie, *Record*, part 1, p. 283; Theal, *Cape Colony*, vol. 24, p. 354, and vol. 35, p. 146.
47 Colin Bundy, 'Vagabond Hollanders and runaway Englishmen: white poverty in the Cape before Poor Whiteism', seminar paper, Institute of Commonwealth Studies, London, 1983.
48 S. S. Dornan, *Pygmies and Bushmen of the Kalahari* (London, 1925), p. 43.
49 Long, *Journals of Price*, p. 269.
50 Transvaal, *Report of the Transvaal Indigency Commission 1906–08* (T. G. 13–'08), p. 113.
51 Livingstone, *Missionary travels*, p. 67; J. F. W. Grosskopf and others, *The Poor White problem in South Africa: report of the Carnegie Commission* (5 vols., Stellenbosch, 1932), vol. 1, p. 173.
52 Grosskopf, *Poor White*, vol. 1, pp. 193, 228; South Africa, *Report of the Transvaal Leasehold Townships Commission 1912* (U.G.34–1912), pp. 95–6.
53 Percy Ward Laidler and Michael Gelfand, *South Africa: its medical history 1652–1898* (Cape Town, 1971), p. 184. See also Burrows, *History*, pp. 108–14.
54 For the shift of policy, see esp. 'Report of the Commissioners of Inquiry to Earl Bathurst upon the finances', 6 September 1826, in Theal, *Cape Colony*, vol. 27, p. 487.
55 Greyling, *NGK*, p. 159; Great Britain, 'A return of the provision, if any, made by law or otherwise, in Her Majesty's different colonial possessions, for destitute persons', *Accounts and papers*, 1846, XXIX, p. 558.
56 Laidler and Gelfand, *South Africa*, pp. 236–9; Judges, 'Poverty', pp. 34–7.
57 Great Britain, 'A return of the provision', p. 559.
58 For the New Poor Law, see M. A. Crowther, *The workhouse system 1834–1929* (London, 1981), ch. 1.
59 Judges, 'Poverty', p. 29.
60 Cape of Good Hope, *Reports by the Special Commissioner appointed to inquire into the agricultural distress* (G.68–'99) p. 14 and (G.67–'99) p. 2.
61 J. B. Peires, 'Sir George Grey and the Kaffir Relief Committee', *JSAS*, 10 (1983–4), 145–69 (quotation on p. 145).
62 Cape of Good Hope, *Commission on Native Laws*, appendix, pp. 3–4; Transvaal, *Indigency Commission*, p. 139.
63 Laidler and Gelfand, *South Africa*, pp. 88, 259. The Dutch Reformed Church did not regard burial as a religious rite.
64 Great Britain, 'A return of the provision', p. 560.
65 Robert C. H. Shell, 'Rites and rebellion: Islamic conversion at the Cape, 1808 to 1815', in Christopher Saunders and others (eds.), *Studies in the history of Cape Town, volume 5* (Cape Town, 1983), pp. 2–4.
66 Greyling, *NGK*, p. 180; Great Britain, 'A return of the provision', pp. 558, 560.
67 John Philip, *Memoir of Mrs Matilda Smith* (London, 1824), pp. 131–4; Laidler and Gelfand, *South Africa*, p. 121; *MC*, 65 (1933), 278.
68 *Mission field*, 76 (1931), 157; Searle, *Nursing*, p. 149; O. J. M. Wagner, *Social work in Cape Town* (2 vols., Cape Town, 1939), vol. 1, p. 67.

69 Greyling, *NGK*, p. 160.
70 Robert Sandall and others, *The history of the Salvation Army* (6 vols., London, 1947–73), vol. 2, pp. 287–92, and vol. 3, p. 119.
71 Burrows, *History*, pp. 103–5; C. H. Somerset, Proclamation, 14 February 1817, in Theal, *Cape Colony*, vol. 25, pp. 16–18.
72 Great Britain, 'Despatches from the Governor of the Cape of Good Hope', *Accounts and papers*, 1847, XLVIII, p. 449.
73 Laidler and Gelfand, *South Africa*, p. 223.
74 Andrew T. Scull, *Museums of madness: the social organization of insanity in nineteenth-century England* (reprinted, Harmondsworth, 1982), pp. 112–13.
75 Laidler and Gelfand, *South Africa*, p. 222.
76 Cape of Good Hope, *Report from the Select Committee . . . on the arrangements for . . . lunatics, lepers, and chronic sick* (Cape Town, 1855), pp. 17–25; *idem*, *Reports on the Somerset Hospital in Cape Town, and General Infirmary on Robben Island, for the year 1855* (G.12–'56), pp. 10–14.
77 Petrus Borchardus Borcherds, *An autobiographical memoir* (reprinted, Cape Town, 1963), pp. 368–9.
78 Simon A. de Villiers, *Robben Island* (Cape Town, 1971), p. 69.
79 Cape of Good Hope, *Report on the General Infirmary, Robben Island, for the year 1866* (G.8–'67), pp. 4–6.
80 Dr Ebden, in Cape of Good Hope, *Report of the Select Committee . . . on Robben Island Establishment* (A3–'71) (Cape Town, 1871), p. 2.
81 See Scull, *Museums*, p. 240.
82 Cape of Good Hope, *Report of the Commission appointed to inquire into . . . moving the asylum at Robben Island to the mainland* (G64–'80) (2 parts, Cape Town, 1880), part 1, p. 4, and part 2, pp. 8–9, 19.
83 Cape of Good Hope, *Reports on the government-aided hospitals and asylums . . . for 1898* (G21–'99), p. 122; de Villiers, *Robben Island*, p. 93.
84 Cape of Good Hope, *Report of the Select Committee on Robben Island* (1871), pp. 17–18.
85 Dr Ebden in *ibid.*, p. 4.
86 Cape of Good Hope, *Report on hospitals for 1898*, p. 114.
87 Rev. H. P. Bull in Cape of Good Hope, *Report of the Select Committee on Robben Island Leper Asylums* (C2–'09) (Cape Town, 1909), p. 56.
88 Cape of Good Hope, *Report on hospitals for 1898*, pp. 82–3.
89 South Africa, *Report of the Hospital Survey Committee* (UG 25–27) (Cape Town, 1927), pp. 15–16; Laidler and Gelfand, *South Africa*, p. 142.
90 Borcherds, *Memoir*, p. 368.
91 Cape of Good Hope, *Report of the Select Committee on Robben Island* (1871), pp. 4, 7–8.
92 Cape of Good Hope, *Leprosy Commission 1895: volume IV: final report of commissioners* (G.4A–'95) (Cape Town, 1895), pp. 7, 12–13, 82, 86–7, 90; *idem*, *Report of Select Committee on Robben Island* (1909), p. 71.
93 Cape of Good Hope, *Reports on hospitals for 1898*, p. 116.
94 Rev. J. W. Mangin, 'Robben Island', in *Mission field*, 42 (1897), 376–7.
95 James Walsh in Cape of Good Hope, *Report of Select Committee on Robben Island* (1909), p. 147.
96 Cape of Good Hope, *Leprosy Commission 1895*, pp. 96–7.
97 Vaaltuin (or Voortuin: a Thembu) in Cape of Good Hope, *Report of Select Committee on Robben Island* (1909), p. 161.
98 James W. Fish, *Robben Island* (Kilmarnock [1924?]), p. 199.
99 James Walsh in Cape of Good Hope, *Report of Select Committee on Robben Island* (1909), p. 141.

100 Frederick Jacobus Lange in *ibid.*, p. 153.
101 Fish, *Robben Island*, pp. 62, 72, 92.
102 Cape of Good Hope, *Report of Select Committee on Robben Island* (1909), pp. 21, 35, 94–5, 101, 143–4, 159.
103 *Mission field*, 52 (1907), 20.
104 Amanas in Cape of Good Hope, *Report of Select Committee on Robben Island* (1909), p. 162.
105 Mrs Kriger in *ibid.*, p. 166.
106 Frederick Jacobus Lange in *ibid.*, p. 152.
107 Antoine (from Cape Verde) in *ibid.*, p. 163.
108 *Ibid.*, p. 141; De Villiers, *Robben Island*, p. 113; Cape of Good Hope, *Reports on government-aided hospitals for 1908*, p. 51.
109 Miss M. Lamey in Cape of Good Hope, *Report of Select Committee on Robben Island* (1909), p. 170.
110 *Mission field*, 52 (1907), 20.
111 De Villiers, *Robben Island*, p. 93.
112 Great Britain, 'A return of the provision', p. 561; Christopher Fyfe, *A history of Sierra Leone* (London, 1962), pp. 104, 375.
113 Fyfe, *History*, p. 306.
114 *Ibid.*, p. 229; Great Britain, 'A return of the provision', p. 561.
115 Michael Banton, *West African city: a study of tribal life in Freetown* (London, 1957), p. 19; John Peterson, *Province of freedom: a history of Sierra Leone, 1787–1870* (London, 1969), pp. 259–60, 262–3; Fyfe, *History*, p. 171.
116 Banton, *City*, p. 20; Fyfe, *History*, p. 171.
117 Alan Forrest, *The French Revolution and the poor* (Oxford, 1981), esp. pp. 27–30.
118 Golberry, *Travels*, vol. 1, p. 117, and vol. 2, p. 55; Gouin [?] to Schoelcher, 6 May 1848, ANOM:MC Sénégal XI:43.
119 Alquier, 'Saint-Louis', pp. 428–52.
120 'Conseil d'Administration: séances des 25 et 26 Novembre 1856', ANOM:MC Sénégal XI:5.
121 Boilat, *Esquisses*, pp. 34–6.
122 Guèye, 'La fin', pp. 652–3; Governor to Minister, 27 September 1851, ANOM:MC Sénégal XIV:12; Camille Camara, *Saint-Louis-du-Sénégal* (Dakar, 1968), p. 49; François Renault, *L'abolition de l'esclavage au Sénégal: l'attitude de l'administration française 1848–1905* (Paris, 1972), pp. 23–4.
123 'Conseil d'Administration: séance du 20 Avril 1861', ANOM:MC Sénégal XII:8.
124 Baudin to Ministry, 9 November 1849, ANOM:MC Sénégal XI:4.
125 Bour to Minister, 15 March 1887, ANOM:MC Sénégal XI:43.
126 See Georges Goyau, *Un grand 'homme': Mère Javouhey, apôtre des noirs* (Paris, 1929).
127 Adrien Dansette, *Histoire religieuse de la France contemporaine* (2 vols., Paris, 1948), vol. 1, p. 488.
128 Geneviève Duhamelet, *Les Soeurs Bleues de Castres* (7th edn, Paris, 1934), p. 56.
129 *Ibid.*, p. 74.
130 *Ibid.*, p. 210; *Annales de la Propagation de la Foi*, 41 (1869), 110.
131 *MC*, 5 (1873), 519.
132 Gachon to Barillec, 2 April 1882, in *MC*, 14 (1882), 256–7.
133 *MC*, 19 (1887), 424.
134 Duhamelet, *Les Soeurs Bleues*, p. 211. The quotation is from a biography by Briault which I have not found.
135 See *MC*, 19 (1887), 424.

136 Fava to Maupoint, 25 July 1861, in 'Lettre de M. l'Abbé Fava', *Revue d'histoire des missions*, 10 (1933), 115.
137 *Ibid.*, pp. 115–16; *MC*, 1 (1865), 65; *MC*, 17 (1885), 379–80, 389–91; *MC*, 30 (1898), 46–7; *MC*, 38 (1906), 566; *MC*, 42 (1910), 37–8.
138 Anna Hinderer, *Seventeen years in the Yoruba country* (London, 1872), pp. 104–6.
139 Eugene Stock, *The history of the Church Missionary Society* (4 vols., London, 1899–1916), vol. 3, p. 678; Searle, *Nursing*, pp. 135–52.
140 *MC*, 11 (1879), 609; *MC*, 37 (1905), 27.
141 Duhamelet, *Les Soeurs Bleues*, p. 269.
142 *Transactions of the [London] Missionary Society*, 1 (1795–1802), 359.
143 *MC*, 34 (1912), 346. See also Donald Crummey, *Priests and politicians: Protestant and Catholic missions in Orthodox Ethiopia 1830–1868* (Oxford, 1972), ch. 4.
144 See W. P. Livingstone, *Mary Slessor of Calabar* (3rd edn, London, 1916).
145 F. B. Welbourn, *East African rebels* (London, 1961), p. 69.
146 C. F. Andrews, *John White of Mashonaland* (reprinted, New York, 1969), pp. 119, 186.
147 P. A. C. Isichei, 'Ignatius Bamah in Asaba (c. 1900–67)', in Isichei, *Varieties*, ch. 13.
148 Isichei, *Varieties*, p. 5; Anne Luck, *African saint: the story of Apolo Kivebulaya* (London, 1963); *MC*, 41 (1909), 346.
149 *Mission field*, 53 (1908), 81.
150 Elizabeth Isichei, *Entirely for God: the life of Michael Iwene Tansi* (Ibadan, 1980), p. 66.
151 *Annales de la Propagation de la Foi*, 39 (1867), 27.
152 Isichei, *History*, p. 162; Stanley Shaloff, 'The American Presbyterian Congo Mission: a study in conflict, 1890–1921', Ph.D. thesis, Northwestern University, 1967, p. 116.
153 *MC*, 43 (1911), 400; *MC*, 22 (1890), 489.
154 *MC*, 37 (1905), 50; *MC*, 41 (1909), 6–7; *MC*, 42 (1910), 183.
155 *MC*, 43 (1911), 64.
156 Robert Laws, *Reminiscences of Livingstonia* (Edinburgh, 1934), p. 121.
157 Stock, *History*, vol. 3, p. 310.
158 See p. 195.

8 Poverty in South Africa, 1886–1948

1 See pp. 98–9.
2 See pp. 99–100; Judges, 'Poverty', pp. 134–5; John Western, *Outcast Cape Town* (London, 1981), pp. 13–15.
3 Saunders, 'Segregation', p. 45; B. H. Kinkead-Weekes, 'A history of vagrancy in Cape Town', CCP 11 (1984), 5.
4 Quoted in Christiane Elias, 'A housing study: legislation and the control of the supply of urban African accommodation', CCP 157 (1984), 11.
5 Maynard W. Swanson, 'The sanitation syndrome: bubonic plague and urban native policy in the Cape Colony, 1900–1909', *JAH*, 18 (1977), 392–4; Elizabeth van Heyningen, 'Cape Town and the plague of 1901', in Christopher Saunders and others (eds.), *Studies in the history of Cape Town, volume 4* (Cape Town, 1981), pp. 66–107.
6 *SAO*, 52 (1922), 205, quoting *Cape Times*.
7 M. W. Swanson, '"The Durban system": roots of urban apartheid in colonial Natal', *African studies*, 35 (1976), 159–76.
8 Keith S. Hunt, 'The development of municipal government in the Eastern Province of the Cape of Good Hope with special reference to Grahamstown 1827–1862', *Archives year book for South African history*, 24 (1961), 154 n. 59.
9 D. H. Reader, *The black man's portion* (Cape Town, 1961), pp. 12–14; *Christian express*, 51 (1921), 189–90.

10 South Africa, *Report of Native Economic Commission 1930–1932* (Pretoria, 1932), p. 70. See also Swanson, 'Sanitation syndrome', pp. 400–4; *SAO*, 71 (1941), 46.
11 *Diggers' news and Witwatersrand advertiser*, 3 March 1888; Charles van Onselen, *Studies in the social and economic history of the Witwatersrand 1886–1914* (2 vols., Harlow, 1982), vol. 2, pp. 116–18.
12 Van Onselen, *Studies*, vol. 1, pp. 104, 112, 146, 173, and vol. 2, pp. 3, 117–18.
13 Patrick Harries, 'Kinship, ideology and the nature of pre-colonial labour migration', in Shula Marks and Richard Rathbone (eds.), *Industrialisation and social change in South Africa* (Harlow, 1982), p. 159; van Onselen, *Studies*, vol. 2, pp. 127–31.
14 This is the theme of van Onselen, *Studies*, vol. 1, ch. 4, and vol. 2, ch. 2. But see also Christian Myles Rogerson, 'The casual poor of Johannesburg, South Africa: the rise and fall of coffee-cart trading', Ph.D. thesis, Queen's University, Kingston, Ontario, 1983, pp. 121–2.
15 Quoted in Sean Moroney, 'Mine married quarters', in Marks and Rathbone, *Industrialisation*, p. 262.
16 Transvaal, *Indigency Commission*, pp. 117, 120, 136.
17 David Coplan, *In township tonight! South Africa's black city music and theatre* (London, 1985), p. 60.
18 *Mission field*, 58 (1913), 309.
19 Tom Lodge, *Black politics in South Africa since 1945* (London, 1983), p. 93; P. N. Pillay, 'Alexandria: an analysis of socio-economic conditions in an urban-ghetto', CCP 19 (1984), 2; André Proctor, 'Class struggle, segregation and the city: a history of Sophiatown 1905–40', in Belinda Bozzoli (ed.), *Labour, townships and protest* (Johannesburg, 1979), p. 58.
20 Bundy, 'Vagabond Hollanders', pp. 2–3, 10–11; Vivian Bickford-Smith, 'Dangerous Cape Town: middle-class attitudes to poverty in Cape Town in the late nineteenth century', in Saunders and others, *Studies*, vol. 4, pp. 29–65.
21 Grosskopf and others, *Poor White problem*.
22 *Ibid.*, vol. 1, p. vii, and vol. 3, p. 222.
23 *Ibid.*, vol. 1, p. v, n. 1 gives this definition: '"Bywoners": lit. by-dwellers, denotes landless rural persons to whom the resident owner of a farm has given permission, under conditions that vary considerably, to live on his farm. Formerly a sort of tenants, they are today mostly in a position of service.'
24 *Ibid.*, vol. 1, p. v.
25 *Ibid.*, vol. 4, p. 124, and vol. 1, pp. 221–2.
26 *Ibid.*, vol. 1, p. 139.
27 William Miller MacMillan, *Complex South Africa* (London, 1930), pp. 52–3. See also Transvaal, *Indigency Commission*, pp. 3–4.
28 Grosskopf and others, *Poor White problem*, vol. 3, pp. 196–7; vol. 4, p. 127; vol. 5, p. 152.
29 See Stanley Trapido, 'Reflections on land, office and wealth in the South African Republic, 1850–1900', in Marks and Atmore, *Economy*, pp. 355–9.
30 Grosskopf and others, *Poor White problem*, vol. 1, ch. 3 and p. 125, and vol. 2, pp. 121–2; Stanley Trapido, 'Landlord and tenant in a colonial economy: the Transvaal 1880–1910', *JSAS*, 5 (1978–9), 51, 58.
31 Grosskopf and others, *Poor White problem*, vol. 1, pp. 120, 206, and vol. 3, p. 215; MacMillan, *Complex*, p. 54.
32 Grosskopf and others, *Poor White problem*, vol. 1, p. 23.
33 *Ibid.*, vol. 1, pp. 127–8.
34 Wilfred Wentzel, 'Hard times in the Karoo', CCP 38 (1984), 74.
35 J. R. Albertyn in Grosskopf and others, *Poor White problem*, vol. 5, p. 38.
36 *Ibid.*, vol. 1, p. 129; Pieter le Roux, 'Poor Whites', CCP 248 (1984), 3.
37 Grosskopf and others, *Poor White problem*, vol. 1, p. 77.

38 *Ibid.*, vol. 1, pp. vi, 144, and vol. 5, p. 156.
39 Emile Boonzaier, 'Economic differentiation and racism in Namaqualand', CCP 68 (1984), 9.
40 Grosskopf and others, *Poor White problem*, vol. 1, p. 77; Margo Russell, 'Slaves or workers? Relations between Bushmen, Tswana, and Boers in the Kalahari', *JSAS*, 2 (1975–6), 185; *Mission field*, 69 (1924), 104–6.
41 Grosskopf and others, *Poor White problem*, vol. 1, p. vi, and vol. 2, pp. 75–6, 99–101.
42 *Ibid.*, vol. 1, pp. vi, 183, 188–9.
43 Marian Lacey, *Working for boroko* (Johannesburg, 1981), p. 48; Grosskopf and others, *Poor White problem*, vol. 1, p. 190, and vol. 5, p. 12.
44 Grosskopf and others, *Poor White problem*, vol. 1, pp. xix, xxx–xxxi, 174–5, and vol. 5, pp. 115–16.
45 *Ibid.*, vol. 2, p. 46, and vol. 5, pp. 68, 208.
46 Transvaal, *Indigency Commission*, p. 116.
47 Grosskopf and others, *Poor White problem*, vol. 1, pp. 184, 212–19, and vol. 2, p. 213.
48 Quoted in Wilfred Wentzel, *Poverty and development in South Africa (1890–1980): a bibliography*, SALDRU working paper 46 (Cape Town, 1982), p. 49.
49 See Transvaal, *Indigency Commission*, pp. 3–4.
50 O. J. M. Wagner, *Poverty and dependency in Cape Town* (Cape Town, n.d.), pp. 38–41, 53–4, 130.
51 *Ibid.*, p. 120; Edward Batson, 'A contribution to the study of urban Coloured poverty', *Race relations*, 9 (1942), 4.
52 Wagner, *Poverty*, p. 109.
53 *Ibid.*, pp. 12–14, 44–5, 71; Batson in *Race relations*, 9 (1942), 3–4; *Bantu world*, 12 February 1938.
54 South Africa, *Report of the inter-departmental committee on poor relief and charitable institutions* (U.G. 61–'37) (Cape Town, 1937), p. 10; Wagner, *Poverty*, p. 143.
55 South Africa, *Report on poor relief*, pp. 9, 12–13.
56 Grosskopf and others, *Poor White problem*, vol. 5, p. 76.
57 South Africa, *Report of the Social Security Committee* (U.G. 14–'44) (Cape Town, 1944), p. 14.
58 South Africa, *Social welfare report 1937–9*, pp. 15–16; Greyling, *NGK*, p. 197.
59 *The Salvation Army year book 1935*, p. 90.
60 South Africa, *Social welfare report 1937–9*, pp. 17, 94, 97; *SAO*, 86 (1956), 28.
61 South Africa, *Social welfare report 1937–9*, pp. 19–20.
62 Grosskopf and others, *Poor White problem*, vol. 5, pp. 58, 114–20, 126; Wagner, *Poverty*, ch. 13.
63 Grosskopf and others, *Poor White problem*, vol. 1, p. xxxiii; South Africa, *Report of the National Conference on the Post War Planning of Social Welfare Work, September 1944* (bound into DO 11/144), p. 294.
64 South Africa, *Social welfare report 1937–9*, p. 8.
65 South Africa: Department of Social Welfare, *Memorandum on poor relief* (Pretoria, 1941).
66 A. Lynn Saffery and Julian Rollnick, 'Social and economic position of unskilled workers at Kimberley', duplicated [1942?] (Institute of Commonwealth Studies, London).
67 South Africa, *Social welfare report 1937–49*, p. 2.
68 South Africa, *Report of the Social Security Committee, passim*; J. D. Rheinallt Jones, 'Social welfare', in Ellen Hellmann (ed.), *Handbook on race relations in South Africa* (Cape Town, 1949), pp. 418, 421–3. The consequences for Africans are discussed on pp. 141–2.
69 Le Roux, 'Poor Whites', p. 13.

70 *Umsebenzi*, 26 August 1933.
71 Heribert Adam and Hermann Giliomee, *Ethnic power mobilized* (New Haven, 1979), p. 154.
72 *Bantu world*, 21 October 1939; South Africa, *Report of National Conference*, p. 155.
73 *Race relations*, 6 (1939), 120.
74 See Le Roux, 'Poor Whites'.
75 Wentzel, 'Hard times', p. 29.
76 Colin Bundy, *The rise and fall of the South African peasantry* (London, 1979), p. 127; *South Africa 1984: official yearbook* (Johannesburg, 1984), p. 26; above, p. 161.
77 R. W. M. Mettam, 'A short history of rinderpest with special reference to Africa', *Uganda journal*, 5 (1937), 23; C. van Onselen, 'Reactions to rinderpest in southern Africa 1896–97', *JAH*, 13 (1972), 484 n. 72.
78 *Mission field*, 43 (1898), 146; Cape of Good Hope, *Reports by the Special Commissioner* (G.67–'99), p. 8; *idem, Blue-book on native affairs 1899*, p. 104; *MC*, 34 (1902), 351; *Mission field*, 42 (1897), 150.
79 Beinart, *Political economy*, p. 71.
80 Cape of Good Hope, *Reports by the Special Commissioner* (G.67–'99), p. 3; *Mission field*, 43 (1898), 46; Cape of Good Hope, *Blue-book on native affairs 1899*, p. 69.
81 *SAO*, 76 (1946), 78, 87, 183.
82 See pp. 156–9.
83 The essentials of this argument are stated by Monica Wilson in *SAO*, 106 (1976), 41–2.
84 J. B. Knight and G. Lenta, 'Has capitalism underdeveloped the labour reserves of South Africa?' *Oxford bulletin of economics and statistics*, 42 (1980), 160.
85 Charles Simkins, 'Agricultural production in the African reserves of South Africa, 1918–1969', *JSAS*, 7 (1980–1), 260–2, 270.
86 *Ibid.*, pp. 264, 266.
87 Bundy, *Rise and fall*, p. 117; South Africa, *Blue book on native affairs 1910*, pp. 62–4; South Africa, *Native Economic Commission*, p. 21.
88 Osmund Victor, *The salient of South Africa* (revised edn, Westminster, 1946), p. 189; M. E. Elton Mills and Monica Wilson, *Keiskammahoek rural survey: volume IV: land tenure* (Pietermaritzburg, 1952), p. 129; Lodge, *Black politics*, p. 12.
89 D. Hobart Houghton and Edith M. Walton, *Keiskammahoek rural survey: volume II: the economy of a native reserve* (Pietermaritzburg, 1952), pp. 96, 102.
90 *Ibid.*, p. 175; Hunter, *Reaction*, p. 139; Beinart, *Political economy*, p. 161; South Africa, *Report of the Native Affairs Commission 1927–31*, p. 5.
91 Hill, *Dry grain farming*, p. 223.
92 Houghton and Walton, *Economy*, p. 97; Elton Mills and Wilson, *Land tenure*, pp. 41–2, 98 n. 1.
93 Hunter, *Reaction*, pp. 377, 387–8, 429.
94 Bengt G. M. Sundkler, *Bantu prophets in South Africa* (2nd edn, London, 1961), p. 93; *idem, Zulu Zion* (London, 1976), p. 183; Beinart, *Political economy*, p. 73.
95 James Henderson in Wilson and Perrot, *Outlook*, p. 370.
96 Beinart, *Political economy*, p. 95; Knight and Lenta, 'Labour reserves', p. 183; South Africa, *Native Economic Commission*, p. 173; MacMillan, *Complex*, p. 224.
97 M. Harris, 'Labour emigration among the Moçambique Thonga', in I. Wallerstein, *Social change: the colonial situation* (New York, 1966), p. 93.
98 Quoted by Rob Turrell, 'Kimberley: labour and compounds, 1871–1888', in Marks and Rathbone, *Industrialisation*, p. 71 n. 34.
99 See pp. 130–1; Kinkead-Weekes, 'Vagrancy', p. 14.
100 Houghton and Walton, *Economy*, pp. 99, 55 n. 1.
101 Monica Wilson and others, *Keiskammahoek rural survey: volume III: social structure* (Pietermaritzburg, 1952), pp. 93, 107–8.

102 *Ibid.*, pp. 52–60.
103 Beinart, *Political economy*, pp. 149–50.
104 South Africa, *Blue book on native affairs 1910*, pp. 215–24, 232–41, 245–51.
105 Bundy, *Rise and fall*, p. 190; South Africa, *Blue book on native affairs 1910*, pp. 37, 262–5.
106 South Africa, *Blue book on native affairs 1910*, pp. 53, 154, 272–5.
107 *Ibid.*, pp. 266–72.
108 Tim Keegan, 'The sharecropping economy', and Ted Matsetela, 'The life story of Nkgono Mma-Pooe', in Marks and Rathbone, *Industrialisation*, pp. 204, 233; Sol. T. Plaatje, *Native life in South Africa* (London, n.d.), p. 73; Timothy Keegan, 'Crisis and catharsis in the development of capitalism in South African agriculture', *African affairs*, 84 (1985), 390–1; Colin Murray, 'Land, power and class in the Thaba 'Nchu District, Orange Free State, 1884–1983', *ROAPE*, 29 (1984), 39.
109 South Africa, *Native Economic Commission*, p. 51.
110 Hunter, *Reaction*, p. 557.
111 *SAO*, 55 (1925), 251; South Africa, *Native Economic Commission*, p. 317.
112 E. S. Haines, 'The economic status of the Cape Province farm native', *South African journal of economics*, 3 (1935), 61, 69, 71. A study of relatively prosperous farms in the Grahamstown area at the same period showed substantially lower earnings. See Hunter, *Reaction*, pp. 509–16.
113 Wentzel, *Poverty*, p. 86.
114 Haines, 'Economic status', p. 74; Francis Wilson and others (ed.), *Farm labour in South Africa* (Cape Town, 1977), p. 10.
115 Hunter, *Reaction*, p. 518; Lacey, *Working*, p. 164.
116 Hunter, *Reaction*, p. 507.
117 Haines, 'Economic status', pp. 74–5; Hunter, *Reaction*, p. 544.
118 Coplan, *In township*, pp. 94–110; *Bantu world*, 28 May 1932; Can Themba, quoted by Proctor in Bozzoli, *Labour*, p. 49.
119 Eddie Koch, '"Without visible means of subsistence": slumyard culture in Johannesburg 1918–1940', in Belinda Bozzoli (ed.), *Town and countryside in the Transvaal* (Johannesburg, 1983), p. 154.
120 Ellen Hellmann, *Rooiyard: a sociological survey of an urban native slum yard*, Rhodes–Livingstone Papers 13 (Cape Town, 1948), pp. 7–8.
121 *Ibid.*, pp. 9, 11, 15, 17, 21, 26.
122 *Ibid.*, p. 22. A parallel study of the Marabastad location of Pretoria in 1934 stressed the 'feverish activity on the part of almost every member of the family to make what money he can': Eileen Jensen Krige, 'Some social and economic facts revealed in native family budgets', *Race relations*, 1 (1933–4), 95.
123 Hellmann, *Rooiyard*, pp. 25, 26, 28.
124 *Ibid.*, p. 90; Ellen Hellmann, 'The diet of Africans in Johannesburg', *Race relations*, 6 (1939), 8. Other studies made this more doubtful. See *Race relations*, 1 (1933–4), 98, and 6 (1939), 35.
125 Hellmann, *Rooiyard*, pp. 9, 12; above, p. 133.
126 *SAO*, 82 (1952), 42.
127 See Koch in Bozzoli, *Town*, pp. 164–5.
128 Ezekiel Mphahlele, *Down Second Avenue* (reprinted, Berlin, 1962), p. 32, describing Marabastad.
129 *Bantu world*, 27 May 1939; Hellmann, *Rooiyard*, p. 47; Ray E. Phillips, *The Bantu in the city* (Lovedale, n.d.), p. 202.
130 Peter Quennell (ed.), *Mayhew's London* (London, 1951), p. 532; Alejandro Portes, 'Rationality in the slum', *Comparative studies in society and history*, 14 (1971–2), 268–86; above, p. 2.

131 Hellmann, *Rooiyard*, p. 22; South Africa, *Native Economic Commission*, p. 153; Phillips, *City*, pp. 39–40; Ari Sitas and others, 'Trade unions: monopoly power and poverty in Natal's industries', CCP 108 (1984), 15.
132 Sheila T. van der Horst, 'Native urban employment: a study of Johannesburg employment records, 1936–1944', *South African journal of economics*, 16 (1948), 254–5.
133 W. M. B. Nhlapo in *Bantu world*, 7 May 1932.
134 *Ibid.*, 3 March 1934; transcript of interview between Nick Hyman and Philip Matante, Botswana, 1971, in Institute of Commonwealth Studies, London; *Umsebenzi*, 10 November 1933.
135 *Umsebenzi*, 15 May 1931, 1 October 1932, 1 and 15 July 1933.
136 *Bantu world*, 21 May, 20 August, 3 September 1932; above, p. 122.
137 Mphahlele, *Avenue*, p. 84.
138 *Bantu world*, 3 June 1933.
139 Phillips, *City*, pp. 49–50.
140 *Bantu world*, 30 March 1940.
141 Hunter, *Reaction*, pp. 539–40; Miriam Janisch, *A study of African income and expenditure in 987 families in Johannesburg, January–November, 1940* (Johannesburg, 1941), p. 8. Compare the figures for tropical towns on p. 173.
142 South Africa, *Report of the inter-departmental committee on the social, health and economic condition of urban natives* (Pretoria, 1942), p. 25; Reader, *Portion*, p. 91.
143 Saffery and Rollnick, 'Unskilled workers at Kimberley', appendix D; Phillips, *City*, p. 20; Leo Kuper, *An African bourgeoisie* (New Haven, 1965), p. 264.
144 Hunter, *Reaction*, p. 440; Rogersòn, 'Casual poor', *passim*, esp. pp. 8, 219, 282, 305–7.
145 Hunter, *Reaction*, p. 440; Reader, *Portion*, p. 94; Rogerson, 'Casual poor', pp. 142–3; Don Pinnock, *The brotherhoods: street gangs and state control in Cape Town* (Cape Town, 1984), p. 33.
146 *Bantu world*, 16 April 1932; Hunter, *Reaction*, p. 440.
147 Phillips, *City*, p. 18; *Bantu world*, 9 February 1935.
148 Marks and Rathbone, *Industrialisation*, p. 12.
149 Hellmann, *Rooiyard*, pp. 27, 61. See also South Africa, *Report on conditions of urban natives*, p. 12; Hunter, *Reaction*, p. 471; Phillips, *City*, p. 131.
150 Koch in Bozzoli, *Town*, p. 159; Krige in *Race relations*, 1 (1933–4), 96.
151 Modikwe Dikobe, *The marabi dance* (London, 1973), p. 33.
152 South Africa, *Native Economic Commission*, p. 110.
153 Koch in Bozzoli, *Town*, p. 160; South Africa, *Report of Director of Prisons 1935*, p. 11.
154 Koch in Bozzoli, *Town*, p. 161; Proctor in Bozzoli, *Labour*, p. 82.
155 Reader, *Portion*, pp. 120–2, 143–5; *Bantu world*, 17 November 1945.
156 Proctor in Bozzoli, *Labour*, p. 73; Deborah Gaitskell and others, 'Class, race and gender: domestic workers in South Africa', *ROAPE*, 27 (1984), 102.
157 Hunter, *Reaction*, p. 440; Saffery and Rollnick, 'Unskilled workers at Kimberley', p. 11.
158 Except in the Western Cape, where Coloured women servants remained numerous.
159 See Gaitskell and others, 'Class', pp. 86–108; Jacklyn Cock, *Maids and madams: a study in the politics of exploitation* (Johannesburg, 1980), ch. 6.
160 Eileen Jensen Krige, 'Changing conditions in marital relations and parental duties among urbanized natives', *Africa*, 9 (1936), 4; Phillips, *City*, p. 90 n. 37; *Bantu world*, 6 May 1933; Deborah Gaitskell, '"Wailing for purity": prayer unions, African mothers and adolescent daughters 1912–1940', in Marks and Rathbone, *Industrialisation*, p. 349.
161 Gaitskell in Marks and Rathbone, *Industrialisation*, p. 350; Krige, 'Changing conditions', p. 5; Monica Wilson and Archie Mafeje, *Langa* (Cape Town, 1963), p. 79. *Baiskopo* was the cinema.

162 Hellmann, *Rooiyard*, p. 13; Selby Ngcobo, 'The urban Bantu family as a unit', *Race relations*, 14 (1947), 140.
163 Hunter, *Reaction*, p. 482; Hellmann, *Rooiyard*, pp. 77–8, 81; Krige, 'Changing conditions', p. 21.
164 Mphahlele, *Avenue*, pp. 22–7.
165 Hunter, *Reaction*, p. 448; Reader, *Portion*, pp. 110–12; MacMillan, quoted in Cock, *Maids*, p. 33.
166 Deborah Gaitskell, '"Christian compounds for girls": church hostels for African women in Johannesburg, 1907–1970', *JSAS*, 6 (1979), 44–69; Ray E. Phillips, *The Bantu are coming* (London, 1930), p. 113; Gaitskell in Marks and Rathbone, *Industrialisation*, ch. 13.
167 *Bantu world*, 30 July 1932 and 27 July 1940; Hunter, *Reaction*, p. 449.
168 *Bantu world*, 8 May and 27 November 1937 and 29 January 1938.
169 *Ibid.*, 24 November 1945.
170 *Ibid.*, 9 and 16 September 1933; Hilda Kuper and Selma Kaplan, 'Voluntary associations in an urban township', *African studies*, 3 (1944), 178.
171 *Bantu world*, 23 January 1937.
172 Koch in Bozzoli, *Town*, p. 163.
173 Hunter, *Reaction*, p. 449.
174 *Bantu world*, 30 July 1932.
175 Hellmann, *Rooiyard*, pp. 23, 53; Krige in *Race relations*, 1 (1933–4), 97; *Mission field*, 82 (1937), 137.
176 Hunter, *Reaction*, p. 449.
177 See Hellmann, *Rooiyard*, p. 44; Kuper and Kaplan, 'Voluntary associations', pp. 178–86; Julian Y. Kramer, 'Self help in Soweto: mutual aid societies in a South African city', MA thesis, University of Bergen, n.d.; Coplan, *In township*, pp. 102–5.
178 *Phillips' news* (mimeographed), 18 June 1921.
179 Trevor Huddleston, *Naught for your comfort* (London, 1956), p. 90.
180 South Africa, *Social welfare report 1937–9*, pp. 17, 43, 52.
181 *Ibid.*, pp. 64–5.
182 *Ibid.*, p. 71; South Africa, *Social welfare report 1937–49*, p. 43.
183 Pinnock in *SAO*, 110 (1980), 10; Proctor in Bozzoli, *Labour*, p. 74; Koch in Bozzoli, *Town*, p. 162; Coplan, *In township*, pp. 156–60.
184 Louis Franklin Freed, *Crime in South Africa* (Cape Town, 1963), p. 44; Koch in Bozzoli, *Town*, p. 162; Lodge, *Black politics*, p. 101.
185 Philip and Iona Mayer, 'Socialization peers: the youth organization of the Red Xhosa', in Philip Mayer (ed.), *Socialization: the approach from social anthropology* (London, 1970), pp. 159–89; Jonathan Clegg, 'Ukubuyisa isidumbu – the ideology of vengeance in the Msinga and Mpofana rural locations, 1882–1944', in P. Bonner (ed.), *Working papers in southern African studies, volume 2* (Johannesburg, 1981), p. 168.
186 Van Onselen, *Studies*, vol. 2, pp. 54–60.
187 *Phillips' news*, 10 October 1951; South Africa, *Report of the interdepartmental committee on destitute, neglected, maladjusted and delinquent children and young persons, 1934–1937* (U.G. 38, 1937) (Pretoria, 1937), p. 7.
188 Shack.
189 O. D. Wollheim, 'The Cape skolly', *Race relations*, 17 (1950), 48.
190 See p. 188.
191 *Bantu world*, 8 October 1938; Pinnock, *Brotherhoods*, ch. 6. See also the account of Diepkloof in Alan Paton, *Towards the mountain* (London, 1981), pp. 138–205.
192 Van Onselen, *Studies*, vol. 2, pp. 54–60, 171–201; Coplan, *In township*, pp. 62, 109, 162–4; Freed, *Crime*, chs. 5 and 6.

193 Coplan, *In township*, pp. 12–13; Robin Hallett, 'The Hooligan Riots, Cape Town: August 1906', in Christopher Saunders (ed.), *Studies in the history of Cape Town, volume I* (reprinted, Cape Town, 1984), p. 51; Pinnock, *Brotherhoods*, chs. 2 and 3.
194 Rodney Davenport, 'African townsmen? South African natives (urban areas) legislation through the years', *African affairs*, 68 (1969), 98–102.
195 *SAO*, 71 (1941), 46–8; Lodge, *Black politics*, p. 49.
196 Christopher Saunders, 'From Ndabeni to Langa', in Saunders, *Studies*, vol. 1, pp. 202–21; Western, *Outcast*, pp. 36, 48.
197 Gavin Maasdorp and A. S. B. Humphreys (eds.), *From shantytown to township* (Cape Town, 1975), pp. 9, 13–14.
198 *Bantu world*, 22 October 1932; Hellmann, *Rooiyard*, p. 7; Phillips, *City*, pp. xxvii, xxiv.
199 Janisch, *Study*, p. 3.
200 Proctor in Bozzoli, *Labour*, pp. 50, 58, 72, 74; Coplan, *In township*, ch. 6.
201 Pillay, 'Alexandria', p. 2.
202 *Bantu world*, 25 March 1939; Alan Paton, *Hofmeyr* (London, 1964), p. 281.
203 Lodge, *Black politics*, p. 11; *Bantu world*, 21 March 1942.
204 South Africa, *Report on the conditions of urban natives*; J. H. Hofmeyr, 'The approach to the native problem', *Race relations*, 3 (1936–7), 36.
205 Hellmann, *Handbook*, pp. 268–9.
206 South Africa, *Report of a Committee of Enquiry . . . on the Cape Flats* (U.G. 18–'43) (Cape Town, 1943), pp. 6, 14; Pinnock, *Brotherhoods*, p. 23; Lodge, *Black politics*, p. 50.
207 The ration.
208 *Bantu world*, 6 April 1946.
209 Dan O'Meara, *Volkskapitalisme* (Cambridge, 1983), p. 147; *idem*, 'The 1946 African mineworkers' strike and the political economy of South Africa', *Journal of Commonwealth and comparative politics*, 13 (1975), 146–73; Lodge, *Black politics*, pp. 12–15; A. W. Stadler, 'Birds in the cornfield: squatter movements in Johannesburg, 1944–1947', *JSAS*, 6 (1979–80), 93–123.
210 E.g. South Africa, *Report of the Department of Native Affairs 1935–6*, pp. 87, 125, 137, 155, 177–8.
211 South Africa, *Native Economic Commission*, p. 143; *Bantu world*, 14 March 1936 and 14 September 1940; South Africa, *Report of the National Conference*, p. 226.
212 South Africa, *Social welfare report 1937–49*, p. 99; *idem*, *Report of the Mental Hospitals Departmental Committee 1936–1937* (U.G. 36, '37) (Pretoria, 1937), pp. 7, 10.
213 Phillips, *City*, p. 141.
214 Mphahlele, *Avenue*, p. 32.
215 *SAO*, 85 (1955), 20; *Bantu world*, 20 September 1941.
216 South Africa, *Report of the Social Security Committee*, pp. 16, 58. Similar pensions were paid to leprosy sufferers.
217 Paton, *Hofmeyr*, p. 333.
218 South Africa, *Report of the Social Security Committee*, pp. 6, 39.
219 Paton, *Hofmeyr*, p. 380.
220 South Africa, *Report of the Department of Native Affairs 1948–9*, p. 27; above, pp. 271, 276.
221 South Africa, *Debates of the House of Assembly*, 1 April 1947, p. 2094 (Mentz).
222 *Ibid.*, 19 May 1947, p. 4901; Charles Meth and Solveig Piper, 'Social security in historical perspective', CCP 250 (1984), 9–18.

9 Rural poverty in colonial Africa

1 Philip A. Igbafe, 'Slavery and emancipation in Benin, 1897–1945', *JAH*, 16 (1975), 416–19; Bernus in Meillassoux, *L'esclavage*, pp. 40–1.

2 David Ross, 'Dahomey', in Michael Crowder (ed.), *West African resistance* (Londo 1971), p. 161; Roberts and Klein, 'Slave exodus', pp. 375–94.

3 Denise Bouche, *Les villages de liberté en Afrique noire française 1887–1910* (Paris, 1968); F. D. Lugard, *The dual mandate in British tropical Africa* (3rd edn, Edinburgh, 1926), pp. 371–80.

4 K. Poku, 'Traditional roles and people of slave origin in modern Ashanti', *Ghana journal of sociology*, 5, 1 (February 1969), 36; J. Lombard, 'Les bases traditionnelles de l'économie rurale bariba et ses fondements nouveaux', *BIFAN*, 23B (1961), 226–39.

5 Frederick Cooper, *From slaves to squatters: plantation labor and agriculture in Zanzibar and coastal Kenya, 1890–1925* (New Haven, 1980).

6 Félix de Kersaint-Gilly, 'Essai sur l'évolution de l'esclavage en Afrique Occidentale Française', *BCE*, 7 (1924), 474; Bernus, *Touaregs nigériens*, pp. 404–5.

7 Diop, *Histoire des classes*, vol. 1, p. 33; Victor Azarya, *Aristocrats facing change: the Fulbe in Guinea, Nigeria, and Cameroon* (Chicago, 1978), p. 184; Dirk Kohnert, *Klassenbildung im ländlichen Nigeria: das Beispiel der Savannenbauern in Nupeland* (Hamburg, 1982), pp. 104–5; M. G. Smith, *Government in Zazzau 1800–1950* (London, 1960), pp. 223, 255.

8 Melville J. Herskovits, *Dahomey* (2 vols., New York, 1938), vol. 1, p. 103.

9 Olivier de Sardan, *Quand nos pères*, pp. 16, 138–40; Bernus in Meillassoux, *L'esclavage*, pp. 20–6.

10 Jean Malaurie, 'Touaregs et noirs au Hoggar', *Annales E.S.C.*, 8 (1953), 338–46; Jeremy Keenan, *The Tuareg: people of Ahaggar* (London, 1977), pp. 164–8, 173–8; Nicolaisen, *Ecology*, pp. 198–9.

11 Bou Haqq, 'Noirs et blancs au confins du désert', *BCE*, 21 (1938), 482–3; J. L. Boutillier and others, *La moyenne vallée du Sénégal* (Paris, 1962), p. 222; C. C. Stewart, 'Political authority and social stratification in Mauritania', in Ernest Gellner and Charles Micaud (eds.), *Arabs and Berbers* (London, 1973), pp. 375, 390.

12 Claire C. Robertson and Martin A. Klein (eds.), *Women and slavery in Africa* (Madison, 1983), pp. 17–18, 220, 223.

13 See John Price, 'A history of the outcaste: untouchability in Japan', in De Vos and Wagatsuma, *Invisible race*, ch. 1.

14 Augustine S. O. Okwu, 'The mission of the Irish Holy Ghost Fathers among the Igbo of southeastern Nigeria, 1905–1956', Ph.D. thesis, Columbia University, 1977, pp. 78–82, 327; Leith-Ross, 'Notes', pp. 207–9, 216–19; Ezeanya, '*Osu*', p. 41.

15 I. Schapera and D. F. van der Merwe, *Notes on the tribal groupings, history, and customs of the Bakgalagadi*, University of Cape Town, Communications from the School of African Studies, No. 13, 1945, p. 6.

16 Transcript of interview between Nick Hyman and Radiphohu, Botswana, 1971, in Institute of Commonwealth Studies, London; Robert K. Hitchcock and A. C. Campbell, 'Settlement patterns of the Bakgalagari', in R. R. Hitchcock and M. R. Smith (eds.), *Proceedings of the Symposium on Settlement in Botswana* (Gaborone, 1982), p. 157.

17 Guenther in Lee and De Vore, *Hunter-gatherers*, p. 123; CO to Robinson, 29 September 1887, CO 417/15/597; Schapera and van der Merwe, *Notes*, p. 6.

18 Daniel, 'Report regarding "hereditary servants" in the Bechuanaland Protectorate', 5 December 1928, DO 9/13; Cuzen to Government Secretary, 18 November 1926, DO 9/5; Rey to High Commissioner, 30 May 1930 and 3 February 1931, DO 35/358/10371/4 and 7.

19 E. S. B. Tagart, 'Report upon the conditions existing among the Masarwa in the Bamangwato Reserve of the Bechuanaland Protectorate', *Official gazette of the High Commissioner for South Africa*, 12 May 1933, pp. 28–35. Tagart's original report (printed in DO 35/358/10371/27) was more critical of the administration than was the published version.

ort on the Masarwa', 30 October 1937, in ASAPS papers G. 588, RH.
a and van der Merwe, *Notes*, p. 4.
ılshwa Gadibolae, 'Serfdom (*Bolata*) in the Nata area 1926–1960', *BNR*,
30; David Stephen, *The San of the Kalahari* (London, 1982), p. 10.
ilberbauer, *Report to the Government of Bechuanaland on the Bushman*
erone, 1965), ch. 9.
hurch, p. 124; M. Catharine A. Newbury, 'The cohesion of oppression: a cen-
ientship in Kinyaga, Rwanda', Ph.D. thesis, University of Wisconsin-Madison,
. 176–9.
ia, *Le Burundi*, pp. 325–8, 343–5.
ury, 'Cohesion', p. 266; Botte, 'Processus', p. 624.
s Cory, 'Report on land tenure in Bugufi', typescript, 1944, Cory Papers, UDSML; R. Z. Hall and H. Cory, 'A study of land tenure in Bugufi 1925–1944', *TNR*, 24 (December 1947), 28–45.
Vedder in Hahn and others, *Native tribes*, p. 162.
Robin Palmer, *Land and racial domination in Rhodesia* (London, 1977), pp. 24, 38, 68.

9 Terence Ranger, *Peasant consciousness and guerrilla war in Zimbabwe* (London, 1985), pp. 68–77.

30 A. K. H. Weinrich, *African farmers in Rhodesia* (London, 1975), p. 60.

31 John Middleton, 'Kenya: administration and changes in African life 1912–45', in Vincent Harlow and E. M. Chilver (eds.), *History of East Africa, volume II* (Oxford, 1965), p. 340.

32 Luka Wangana wa Wakahangara, in Great Britain, *Kenya Land Commission: evidence and memoranda* (3 vols., London, 1934), vol. 1, p. 185. (I owe this reference to Dr J. M. Lonsdale.) Generally, see Gretha Kershaw, 'The land is the people: a study of Kikuyu social organization in historical perspective', Ph.D. thesis, University of Chicago, 1972, pp. 60–88.

33 See p. 69.

34 Jeanne M. Fisher, 'The anatomy of Kikuyu domesticity and husbandry', duplicated, Department of Technical Co-operation, London, n.d., pp. 268–9; M. P. K. Sorrenson, *Land reform in the Kikuyu country* (Nairobi, 1967), pp. 78–9.

35 Kershaw, 'The land', ch. 4; Sorrenson, *Land reform*, ch. 4.

36 Paul Collier and Deepak Lal, *Labour and poverty in Kenya 1900–1980* (Oxford, 1986), pp. 146–7, 153 n. 22.

37 Holger Bernt Hansen, 'Church and state in early colonial Uganda', seminar paper, Institute of Commonwealth Studies, London, 1981, p. 7; P. G. Powesland, *Economic policy and labour* (Kampala, 1957), p. 27.

38 Nicoll to McLachlan, from Alto Moloque, 26 September 1925, NLS MS 7608/191. The best account is 'Report on native labour conditions in the Province of Mozambique', printed in *SALB*, 2, 2 (July 1975), 14–27.

39 Leroy Vail and Landeg White, *Capitalism and colonialism in Mozambique* (London, 1980), p. 219.

40 Gavin Kitching, *Class and economic change in Kenya* (New Haven, 1980), pp. 144–5.

41 Collard to CS, 3 January 1956, MNA SMP/10029.B/7.

42 D. G. Clarke, *Agricultural and plantation workers in Rhodesia* (Gwelo, 1977), pp. 24, 31, 38, 41, 91–5.

43 Quoted in Paul Parin and others, *Fear thy neighbor as thyself: psychoanalysis and society among the Anyi* (trans. P. Klamerth, Chicago, 1980), p. 88.

44 Baier, *Economic history*, ch. 4; Laurel van Horn, 'The agricultural history of Barotseland, 1840–1964', in Palmer and Parsons, *Roots*, ch. 6; Boutillier and others, *La moyenne vallée*, pp. 106–9, 202, 241–52; Richards, *Land*, pp. 22–6; Gilbert Vieillard, 'Notes sur les Peuls du Fouta-Djallon', *BIFAN*, 2 (1940), 98.

45 Manuel Gottlieb, 'The extent and character of differentiation in Tanzanian agricultural and rural society 1967–1969', *The African review*, 3 (1973), 260.
46 Helmuth Heisler, *Urbanisation and the government of migration* (London, 1974), p. 111; André Vanhaeverbeke, *Rémunération du travail et commerce extérieur* (Louvain, 1970), p. 186; Hill, *Dry grain farming*, p. 223; D. W. Norman, 'Rural economy', in Mortimore, *Zaria*, pp. 139, 146.
47 W. K. Hancock, *Survey of British Commonwealth affairs, volume II, part 2* (London, 1942), p. 210; H. L. Vis and others, *A nutritional survey in the Republic of Rwanda* (Tervuren, 1975), p. 155.
48 Bernus, *Touaregs nigériens*, pp. 404–5; Charles van Onselen, *Chibaro: African mine labour in Southern Rhodesia 1900–1933* (London, 1976), p. 123; Van Horn in Palmer and Parsons, *Roots*, pp. 149–50.
49 Enid Schildkrout, *People of the zongo* (Cambridge, 1978), p. 43; Philippe David, *Les navétanes* (Dakar, 1980), p. 126; Jean-Pierre Chrétien, 'Des sédentaires devenus migrants: les motifs des départs des Burundais et des Rwandais vers l'Uganda (1920–1960)', *Cultures et développement*, 10 (1978), 91.
50 PC Ashanti, 1930–1, in Schildkrout, *People*, p. 73.
51 I. Schapera, *Migrant labour and tribal life* (London, 1947), pp. 42–3, 133–5; William Derman, *Serfs, peasants, and socialists* (Berkeley, 1973), p. 157.
52 D. Crawford in *SAO*, 53 (1923), 15.
53 Shenton, *Development*, p. 129; R. W. Shenton and Louise Lennihan, 'Capital and class: peasant differentiation in Northern Nigeria', *Journal of peasant studies*, 9 (1981–2), 63.
54 R. Galletti and others, *Nigerian cocoa farmers* (London, 1956), p. 403.
55 Cowen, 'Differentiation', p. 16; Iliffe, *Emergence*, p. 55; Ashton, *Basuto*, pp. 131, 175.
56 Daryll Forde and Richenda Scott, *The native economies of Nigeria* (London, 1946), p. 64.
57 Harris, 'Some aspects', pp. 310–11, 316–17.
58 Richards, *Land*, p. 131.
59 Betty Preston Thomson, *Two studies in African nutrition*, Rhodes–Livingstone Paper 24 (Manchester, 1954), pp. 46–7.
60 David Hirschmann and Megan Vaughan, 'Food production and income generation in a matrilineal society', *JSAS*, 10 (1983–4), 86–99; Eddy Lee, 'Export-led rural development: the Ivory Coast', *Development and change*, 11 (1980), 633.
61 Hill, *Population*, ch. 12.
62 See p. 126.
63 Audrey I. Richards (ed.), *Economic development and tribal change* (revised edn, Nairobi, 1973), p. 292; Audrey I. Richards and others (eds.), *Subsistence to commercial farming in present-day Buganda* (Cambridge, 1973), pp. 189, 191; C. C. Wrigley, *Crops and wealth in Uganda* (Kampala, 1959), p. 79.
64 Archie Mafeje, 'Social and economic mobility in a peasant society: a study of commercial farmers in Buganda', Ph.D. thesis, University of Cambridge, 1968, p. 128.
65 This section is based on Bennett and Mugalula-Mukibi, 'Analysis', pp. 97–115.
66 Joan Vincent, 'Colonial chiefs and the making of class: a case study from Teso', *Africa*, 47 (1977), 151; Shenton, *Development*, p. 35.
67 Boutillier and others, *La moyenne vallée*, p. 209; Vieillard, 'Notes', pp. 171–2.
68 James C. Scott, *The moral economy of the peasant* (reprinted, New Haven, 1978), p. 98.
69 A. L. Malley, 'Dagharo Gharghara', seminar paper, University College, Dar es Salaam, n.d.; Philippe Leurquin, *Le niveau de vie des populations rurales du Ruanda-Urundi* (Louvain, 1960), p. 252.
70 Eliane de Latour Dejean, 'Shadows nourished by the sun', in Martin A. Klein (ed.), *Peasants in Africa* (Beverly Hills, 1980), p. 138.
71 Above, p. 129; Peter B. Hammond, *Yatenga* (New York, 1966), p. 104.

72 Raynaut, *Structures*, p. 231. Identical processes are described in Sandra Wallman, *Take out hunger: two case studies of rural development in Basutoland* (London, 1969), pp. 64–6.
73 Yusufu Bala Usman, 'The transformation of Katsina, c.1796–1903', Ph.D. thesis, Ahmadu Bello University, Zaria, 1974, p. 144; Polly Hill, *The Gold Coast cocoa farmer* (London, 1956), p. 58; L. P. Mair, *An African people in the twentieth century* (London, 1934), p. 153.
74 Nadel, *Black Byzantium*, pp. 311–12; K. A. Busia, *Report on a social survey of Sekondi-Takoradi* (London, 1950), p. 36.
75 W. H. Beckett, *Akokoaso: a survey of a Gold Coast village* (London, 1944), pp. 50, 54.
76 Polly Hill, 'The study of individual poverty', CCP 296 (1984), 5.
77 Shenton and Lennihan, 'Capital and class', p. 62; Shenton, *Development*, p. 136. See also Gavin Williams, *Inequalities in rural Nigeria*, University of East Anglia, Development Studies Occasional Paper 16, 1981, pp. 45–7.
78 R. D. Pearce, *The turning point in Africa* (London, 1982), p. 12; John Iliffe, *A modern history of Tanganyika* (Cambridge, 1979), p. 343; David Huston Groff, 'The development of capitalism in the Ivory Coast: the case of Assikasso, 1880–1940', Ph.D. thesis, Stanford University, 1980, p. 338; Bernard Founou-Tchuigoua, 'Salariat de fait dans le Gesira Scheme', in Samir Amin (ed.), *L'agriculture africaine et le capitalisme* (Paris, 1975), p. 86.
79 Patrick Braibant, 'L'administration coloniale et profit commercial en Côte d'Ivoire pendant la crise de 1929', *RFHOM*, 63 (1976), 564 n. 25.
80 Senegal, 'Rapport économique 1950' (p. 85) ANOM:MC Affaires économiques 915/7; above, p. 149.
81 B. Jewsiewicki, 'The great depression and the making of the colonial economic system in the Belgian Congo', *African economic history*, 4 (Autumn 1977), 158; A. A. Oldaker, Kondoa District annual report 1931, TNA Library 967.823.
82 Shenton, *Development*, p. 101; Jewsiewicki, 'Great depression', pp. 153–76; C. Coquery-Vidrovitch, 'Mutation de l'impérialisme colonial français dans les années 30', *African economic history*, 4 (Autumn 1977), 141.
83 Nicholson, 'Climatic variations', pp. 13–14; Iliffe, *Modern history*, p. 70; Nicholson, 'Chronology', p. 116; A. T. Grove, 'Desertification in the African environment', in David Dalby and others (eds.), *Drought in Africa 2* (London, 1977), p. 57.
84 I am following G. Farmer and T. M. L. Wigley, *Climatic trends for tropical Africa* (Norwich, 1985), *passim*, esp. pp. 45–50, 78. Others believe that the whole colonial period was unusually dry. See Sharon E. Nicholson, 'The methodology of historical climate reconstruction and its application to Africa', *JAH*, 20 (1979), 42.
85 E.g. Henri A. Junod, *The life of a South African tribe* (2nd edn, reprinted, 2 vols., New York, 1962), vol. 2, p. 89 n. 1; T. J. Dennis, journal, 26 November 1893, CMS:UP 89/F1.
86 Above, pp. 12–13; Gamble, 'Contributions', p. 65; van Onselen, 'Reactions', p. 473; Iliffe, *Modern history*, p. 124; Jill Dias, 'Famine and disease in the history of Angola, c.1830–1930', *JAH*, 22 (1981), 374.
87 Oscar Baumann, *Durch Masailand zur Nilquelle* (Berlin, 1894), pp. 31–2.
88 Kershaw, 'The land', p. 211.
89 Quoted in Marvin P. Miracle, 'Economic change among the Kikuyu, 1895 to 1905', IDS Nairobi Working Paper 158 (1974), p. 20. See also Marc H. Dawson, 'Smallpox in Kenya, 1880–1920', *SSM*, 13B (1979), 245–50.
90 A. Retel-Laurentin, *Infécondité en Afrique Noire* (Paris, 1974), pp. 50–7, 72; K. R. S. Morris, 'The movement of sleeping sickness across central Africa', *Journal of tropical medicine and hygiene*, 66 (1963), 59–76.
91 Shenton, *Development*, p. 132; G. Jan van Apeldoorn, *Perspectives on drought and famine in Nigeria* (London, 1981), p. 35.
92 A. C. G. Hastings, *Nigerian days* (London, 1925), p. 111.

93 Bob Shenton and Mike Watts, 'Capitalism and hunger in Northern Nigeria', *ROAPE*, 15 (May 1979), 53–62.
94 Pankhurst, *Economic history*, p. 220; McAlpin, *Subject to famine*, p. 187; Gerhard J. Liesegang, 'Famines, epidemics, plagues and long periods of warfare: their effects in Mozambique 1700–1975', in University of Zimbabwe: Department of History, *Conference on Zimbabwean history* (2 vols., Harare, 1982), vol. 1; May to Resident Commissioner, 9 September 1914, CO 417/545; Dias, 'Famine', pp. 374–5.
95 Bernard Lugan, 'Causes et effets de la famine "Rumanura" au Rwanda, 1916–18', *CJAS*, 10 (1976), 347–56; Iliffe, *Modern history*, p. 269.
96 Gilles Sautter, *De l'Atlantique au fleuve Congo* (2 vols., Paris, 1966), vol. 2, pp. 849, 859–62; Catherine Coquery-Vidrovitch, 'Population et démographie en Afrique Equatoriale Française dans le premier tiers du XXe siècle', in Christopher Fyfe and David McMaster (eds.), *African historical demography* (Edinburgh, 1977), p. 339.
97 Watts, *Silent violence*, pp. 305–12; Chastanet, 'Les crises', p. 27.
98 Leurquin, *Le niveau de vie*, pp. 31–3; Gahama, *Le Burundi*, pp. 168–71; André Salifou, 'When history repeats itself: the famine of 1931 in Niger', *African environment*, 1, 2 (April 1975), 22–48.
99 Ethiopia: Relief and Rehabilitation Commission, *The challenges of drought* (Addis Ababa, 1985), p. 74; Charles A. Wood, 'A preliminary chronology of Ethiopian droughts', in Dalby and others, *Drought 2*, p. 71.
100 Pottier, 'Politics', p. 218 n. 39; Pierre Bonte, 'Pasteurs et nomades: l'exemple de la Mauritanie', in Jean Copans (ed.), *Sécheresses et famines du Sahel* (2 vols., Paris, 1975), vol. 2, pp. 76–7; Chastanet, 'Les crises', p. 27; Watts, *Silent violence*, pp. 329–36.
101 See p. 156.
102 See p. 6.
103 Leurquin, *Le niveau de vie*, pp. 32–7; above, p. 123.
104 Salifou, 'When history repeats itself', pp. 27–9, 38–41.
105 Joan Vincent, *African elite* (New York, 1981), pp. 43–4, 71.
106 Ph. Leurquin, 'Economie de subsistance et alimentation au Ruanda-Urundi: quelques cas concrets', *Zaïre*, 12 (1958), 3–4, 31; Gahama, *Le Burundi*, pp. 175–83.
107 Liesegang in University of Zimbabwe, *Conference*, vol. 1.
108 Kim Mulholland, 'Cholera in Sudan', *Disasters*, 9 (1985), 247; Iliffe, *Modern history*, p. 315.
109 Albert Schweitzer, *More from the primeval forest* (trans. C. T. Campion, London, 1931), p. 97; John Iliffe, 'The poor in the modern history of Malawi', in K. J. McCracken (ed.), *Malawi: an alternative pattern of development* (Edinburgh [1985]), pp. 258–9.
110 Leurquin, *Le niveau de vie*, pp. 33, 39, 71; Gahama, *Le Burundi*, p. 163.
111 Van Apeldoorn, *Perspectives*, pp. 37–8; Shenton, *Development*, pp. 133–7; Watts, *Silent violence*, pp. 309–10, 322. See also Paul Clough, 'Grain marketing in Northern Nigeria', *ROAPE*, 34 (December 1985), 16–34.
112 Jacques Richard-Molard, 'Essai sur la vie paysanne au Fouta Djalon', *Présence africaine*, 15 (1953), 198.
113 'Meeting of the headmen and indunas at Bulawayo, 5th January, 1897', ZNA LO/5/6/8/33.
114 British South Africa Company, *Reports on the Company's proceedings and the conditions of the territories within the sphere of its operations, 1896–1897* (n.p., n.d.), pp. 91–3; Gielgud to CNC, 3 April 1897, ZNA LO/5/6/9/47.
115 Masterman to Administrator, 23 October 1912, ZNA A/3/18/22/152.
116 This account is based on examination of the monthly or annual reports, or both, of all Native Commissioners for each famine year. I hope to document the account more fully elsewhere.
117 Above, p. 6; McAlpin, *Subject to famine*, pp. 19–20; Sen, *Poverty and famines*, *passim*.

118 See Megan Vaughan, 'Famine analysis and family relations: 1949 in Nyasaland', *Past and present*, 108 (August 1985), 177–205.
119 Es-Soudan, *Tedzkiret*, pp. 117–18.
120 Quoted in Kohnert, *Klassenbildung*, p. 198. On the causes of undernutrition, see also Steven Feierman, 'Struggles for control: the social roots of health and healing in modern Africa', *African studies review*, 28, 2 (June 1985), 99–101.
121 L. Guebels, *Relation complète des travaux de la Commission Permanente pour la Protection des Indigènes* ([Elisabethville, 1952?]), pp. 284–8; Cicely D. Williams, 'The story of kwashiorkor', *Nutrition reviews*, 31 (1973), 334–40; Great Britain: Economic Advisory Council, Committee on Nutrition in the Colonial Empire, *First report* (2 parts, Cmd 6050 and 6051 of 1939: London, 1939); materials (from 1938) in ANOM:MC Affaires politiques 2853/2.
122 A. I. Richards and E. M. Widdowson, 'A dietary study in North-Eastern Rhodesia', *Africa*, 9 (1936), 184; Thomson, *Two studies*, p. ix; M. C. Latham, *Human nutrition in tropical Africa* (2nd edn, Rome, 1979), p. 250.
123 Great Britain, *First report*, part 1, p. 43.
124 See Latham, *Human nutrition*, pp. 62–5, 250.
125 Gahama, *Le Burundi*, pp. 167, 175–81, 213; Vis and others, *Nutritional survey*, pp. 55, 152.
126 Ulli Beier (ed.), *Yoruba poetry* (Cambridge, 1970), p. 89; Paul Collier and others, *Labour and poverty in rural Tanzania* (Oxford, 1986), p. 91; Vail and White, *Capitalism*, p. 219.
127 Clarke, *Agricultural workers*, p. 106. Generally, see Latham, *Human nutrition*, pp. 113–39.
128 H. C. Trowell, 'Prevention of kwashiorkor in children', in Great Britain: Colonial Office, *Malnutrition in African mothers, infants and young children* (London, 1954), p. 319.
129 E. M. Demaeyer, 'Le problème du kwashiorkor au Congo Belge', *Annales de la Société Belge de Médecine Tropicale*, 38 (1958), 393, 397; Zbigniew A. Konczaki, 'Infant malnutrition in sub-Saharan Africa', *CJAS*, 6 (1972), 439; K. E. A. Underwood Ground, 'Kwashiorkor in Basutoland', in Great Britain, *Malnutrition*, p. 52.
130 Mary Theresa Howard, 'Kwashiorkor on Kilimanjaro: the social handling of malnutrition', Ph.D. thesis, Michigan State University, 1980, pp. 35–6, 66, 81, 207; World Bank, *The Gambia: basic needs* (Washington, DC, 1981), p. 99.
131 B. S. Platt, 'Report of a nutrition survey in Nyasaland', duplicated [1940?] MNA Library Q.267.
132 Richards and Widdowson, 'Dietary study', p. 175; Great Britain, *First report*, part 2, p. 39; Forde and Scott, *Native economies*, p. 77.
133 Miller, 'Significance', p. 22.
134 The figures, but with a different explanation, are in D. N. Beach, 'Zimbabwean demography: early colonial data', duplicated, Conference on the Analysis of Census Data from Colonial Central Africa, Milwaukee, August 1986. (I am indebted to Dr Beach for a copy of this paper.)
135 James W. Brown, 'Increased intercommunication and epidemic disease in early colonial Ashanti', in Gerald W. Hartwig and K. David Patterson (eds.), *Disease in African history* (Durham, NC, 1978), p. 202.
136 Anne Retel-Laurentin, *Un pays à la dérive* (Paris, 1979), p. 175; Feierman, 'Struggles', p. 88.
137 Sautter, *De l'Atlantique*, vol. 2, pp. 983–6, 1016.
138 See p. 148.
139 A. R. Kururagire, 'Land fragmentation at Rugarama, Kigezi', *Uganda journal*, 33, 1 (1969), 59–64; Henri Enjalbert, 'Paysans noirs: les Kabré du Nord-Togo', *Cahiers*

d'outre-mer, 9 (1956), 139; Uchendu, *Igbo*, p. 31; Jean Hurault, 'Essai de synthèse social des Bamiléké', *Africa*, 40 (1970), 20–1.

140 See Margaret Haswell, *The nature of poverty* (London, 1975), and the references therein.

141 *Ibid.*, p. 188.

142 *Ibid.*, p. xv.

10 Urban poverty in tropical Africa

1 'Colony of Lagos: report of the Superintendent of the Census for the year, 1901', CO 147/157/336.

2 J. M. Rowland, 'Report on the work of the Medical Department for the year 1894', CO 147/99/251; Report of the Commission on Infantile Mortality, encl. in MacGregor to Chamberlain, 20 April 1901, CO 147/155/121.

3 Morgan, journal, 10 October 1858, CMS C.A2/O.71/35; Oroge, 'Slavery', pp. 295–8.

4 Johnson to Fenn, 1874, CMS C.A2/O.56/56a; *LWR*, 29 August 1896 and 5 January 1901; 'Lagos: report on the blue book for 1887', *Parliamentary papers*, 1889, LIV, 73–4; Glover to Cardwell, 11 March 1865, CO 147/8/177.

5 Pickels to Colonial Secretary, 21 September 1903, encl. in MacGregor to Lyttleton, 24 November 1903, CO 147/167/262; *LWR*, 8 September 1906.

6 Hausa petitioners to Elgin, 7 September 1906, CO 520/37/234; *LWR*, 25 September 1897.

7 'Lagos: annual report for 1891', *Parliamentary papers*, 1893, LIX, 45–7.

8 *LWR*, 11 July 1896; 'Lagos: report on the blue book for 1887', *Parliamentary papers*, 1889, LIV, 71–7.

9 'Lagos: report on the blue book for 1887', *Parliamentary papers*, 1889, LIV, 28–30.

10 Willoughby, journal, 29 July 1870, CMS C.A2/O.95/15; *LWR*, 22 May 1897; *Lagos standard*, 11 January 1899, quoted in Fred I. A. Omu, *Press and politics in Nigeria, 1880–1937* (London, 1978), p. 107.

11 *LWR*, 4 May 1895, 24 September 1898, 1 July 1899, 18 August 1894.

12 *LWR*, 8 September 1894.

13 Pratt, report, 27 June 1888, and Moloney to Knutsford, 31 August 1888, in CO 147/65/371 and 314, and other papers in this file.

14 Grant to Officer i/c Secretariat, 30 April 1885, CO 96/174/72.

15 Evidence of Baladino Santos, 2 July 1888, CO 147/65/426.

16 Cole and others to Knutsford, 16 July 1888, CO 147/65/342 (italics in original).

17 *LWR*, 6 July 1895, 21 January 1899, 1 October 1904.

18 Sylvia Leith-Ross, *Stepping stones: memoirs of colonial Nigeria 1907–1960* (London, 1983), p. 83.

19 Diana H. Patel and R. J. Adams, *Chirambahuyo: a case study in low-income housing* (Gwelo, 1981), p. 5; S. von Sicard, *The Lutheran Church on the coast of Tanzania 1887–1914* (Lund, 1970), p. 172; Medical Officer to Senior Health Officer, 18 September 1931, MNA M/2/16/1/4.

20 See Kenneth Gordon McVicar, 'Twilight of an East African slum: Pumwani and the evolution of African settlement in Nairobi', Ph.D. thesis, University of California at Los Angeles, 1968, pp. 8–12; Claude Meillassoux, *Urbanization of an African community: voluntary associations in Bamako* (Seattle, 1968), p. 8.

21 H. F. Smith, 'A report on certain phases of the public health situation in Monrovia', typescript [early 1930s] Howells papers, RH; Philip D. Curtin, 'Medical knowledge and urban planning in tropical Africa', *American historical review*, 90 (1985), 603.

22 See Marris, *Family, passim.*

23 Ladd Lind Johnson, 'Luanda, Angola: the development of internal forms and functional patterns', Ph.D. thesis, University of California at Los Angeles, 1970, pp. 120–4, 155;

Jeanne Marie Penvenne, 'A history of African labor in Lourenço Marques, Mozambique, 1877 to 1950', Ph.D. thesis, Boston University, 1982, pp. 285–8; Elliott P. Skinner, *African urban life: the transformation of Ouagadougou* (Princeton, 1974), p. 144.

24 Sautter, *De l'Atlantique*, vol. 1, p. 398; Meillassoux, *Urbanization*, p. 9; 'Notes on building plots in the native quarter of Dar es Salaam' [1931] TNA SMP 12589/1/130; Bruce Fetter, *The creation of Elisabethville, 1910–1940* (Stanford, 1976), p. 73.

25 Iliffe in McCracken, *Malawi*, p. 261.

26 René Gouellain, *Douala: ville et histoire* (Paris, 1975), pp. 130–42; Raymond F. Betts, 'The establishment of the Medina in Dakar', *Africa*, 41 (1971), 143–52.

27 A. L. Mabogunje, 'The problems of a metropolis', in P. C. Lloyd and others (eds.), *The city of Ibadan* (Cambridge, 1967), p. 265.

28 Richard A. Joseph, *Radical nationalism in Cameroun* (Oxford, 1977), p. 160; Raymond F. Betts, 'The problem of the Medina in the urban planning of Dakar', *African urban notes*, 4, 3 (September 1969), 5–15.

29 See McVicar, 'Twilight', pp. 19–25; Eric Gargett, *The administration of transition: African urban settlement in Rhodesia* (Gwelo, 1977), p.19.

30 Skinner, *Ouagadougou*, p. 27; Anthony O'Connor, *The African city* (London, 1983), p. 90.

31 Penvenne, 'Lourenço Marques', p. 481; Coquery-Vidrovitch, 'Mutation', p. 137; Paul Raymaekers, *L'organisation des zones de squatting* (Paris, 1964), pp. 4–5.

32 Akin Ogunpola and Oladeji Ojo, 'Housing as an indicator of urban poverty', in Nigerian Economic Society, *Poverty*, p. 112; Samir Amin, *Le développement du capitalisme en Côte d'Ivoire* (Paris, 1967), p. 35; Laketch Dirasse, 'The socio-economic position of women in Addis Ababa: the case of prostitution', Ph.D. thesis, Boston University, 1978, p. 115.

33 L. Thoré, 'Dagoudane-Pikine', *BIFAN*, 24B (1962), 155–98.

34 Norman Calvin Rothman, 'African urban development in the colonial period: a study of Lusaka, 1905–1964', Ph.D. thesis, Northwestern University, 1972, pp. 115–16, 151–9.

35 O'Connor, *City*, p. 82.

36 Fetter, *Creation*, pp. 34–6.

37 Quoted in Elikia M'Bokolo, 'Peste et société urbaine à Dakar: l'épidémie de 1914', *CEA*, 22 (1982), 15.

38 Fetter, *Creation*, p. 82.

39 Arnold Hughes and Robin Cohen, 'An emerging Nigerian working class: the Lagos experience 1897–1939', in Peter C. W. Gutkind and others (eds.), *African labor history* (Beverly Hills, 1978), pp. 39–43; Richard Jeffries, *Class, power and ideology in Ghana* (Cambridge, 1978), p. 28; Penvenne, 'Lourenço Marques', pp. 363–70.

40 Fetter, *Creation*, p. 126; R. van Zwanenberg, 'History and theory of urban poverty in Nairobi', *Journal of eastern African research and development*, 2 (1976), 179.

41 Nigeria, *Report of the committee ... to enquire into the question of unemployment*, Sessional Paper 46 of 1935 (Lagos, 1935), pp. 1–4.

42 Penvenne, 'Lourenço Marques', pp. 380–2; Bruce Fetter, 'African associations in Elisabethville, 1910–1935', *Etudes d'histoire africaine*, 6 (1974), 215; Rothman, 'Lusaka', p. 235; Jeff Crisp, *The story of an African working class* (London, 1984), p. 58; Claire C. Robertson, *Sharing the same bowl: a socioeconomic history of women and class in Accra* (Bloomington, 1984), p. 36.

43 See Crisp, *Story*, pp. 56–65; Iliffe, *Modern history*, pp. 310–11, 353.

44 E. R. StA. Davies, 'Some problems arising from the conditions of housing and employment of natives in Nairobi', 18 March 1939, Davies Papers, RH.

45 Idi Salim to CS, 9 August 1936, TNA SMP 22444/1/96.

46 Jacques Guilbot, 'Les conditions de vie des indigènes de Douala', *Etudes camerounaises*,

27 (1949), 221; T. Killick, 'Labour', in Walter Birmingham and others (eds.), *A study of contemporary Ghana* (2 vols., London, 1966–7), vol. 1, p. 141.

47 Crisp, *Story*, p. 76; David William Throup, 'The governorship of Sir Philip Mitchell in Kenya, 1944–1952', Ph.D. thesis, University of Cambridge, 1983, p. 262.

48 Joseph, *Nationalism*, pp. 63–8; Robin Cohen, *Labour and politics in Nigeria 1945–71* (London, 1974), pp. 159–64; Richard Sandbrook and Robin Cohen (eds.), *The development of an African working class* (London, 1975), pp. 41, 61–5; Southern Rhodesia, *Report of the Secretary of Native Affairs . . . for the year 1948*, p. 46; J. Suret-Canale, 'The French West African railway workers' strike, 1947–1948', in Gutkind and others, *Labor history*, ch. 5; Penvenne, 'Lourenço Marques', pp. 462–3; Jack Arn, 'Political economy of urban poverty in Ghana: the case of Nima, Accra', Ph.D. thesis, University of Toronto, 1978, p. 306.

49 Guilbot, 'Les conditions de vie', p. 221; Killick in Birmingham and others, *Study*, vol. 1, p. 141; Throup, 'Governorship', ch. 7.

50 Collier and Lal, *Labour and poverty in Kenya*, ch. 2 (esp. p. 49).

51 Marion Wallace Forrester, *Kenya today* ('s-Gravenhage, 1962), pp. 121, 128.

52 B. Thomson and G. Kay, 'A note on the Poverty Datum Line in Northern Rhodesia', *Rhodes–Livingstone journal*, 30 (December 1961), 48–9; David G. Bettison, 'The Poverty Datum Line in Central Africa', *ibid.*, 27 (June 1960), 22, 25.

53 Caroline Hutton, *Reluctant farmers? a study of unemployment and planned rural development in Uganda* (Nairobi, 1973), pp. 17–21, 73; Collier and Lal, *Labour and poverty in Kenya*, p. 58; W. T. Morrill, 'Immigrants and associations: the Ibo in twentieth century Calabar', *Comparative studies in society and history*, 5 (1962–3), 436.

54 Peter C. W. Gutkind, 'The poor in urban Africa', in Warner Bloomberg Jr and Henry J. Schmandt (eds.), *Power, poverty, and urban policy* (Beverly Hills, 1968), p. 365; Congo Belge, Direction du Travail, 'Urban unemployment in Africa south of the Sahara', *Inter-African Labour Institute bulletin*, 7 (1960), 10.

55 Merran Fraenkel, *Tribe and class in Monrovia* (London, 1964), p. 39; A Hauser, 'Les problèmes du travail', in M. Sankale and others (eds.), *Dakar en devenir* ([Paris] 1968), p. 360; Peter Kilby, *Industrialization in an open economy: Nigeria 1945–1966* (Cambridge, 1969), p. 208; Killick in Birmingham and others, *Study*, vol. 1, p. 149.

56 Amin, *Le développement*, p. 39; O'Connor, *City*, p. 159; Thoré, 'Dagoudane-Pikine', p. 175; Raymaekers, *L'organisation*, p. 55.

57 Collier and Lal, *Labour and poverty in Kenya*, pp. 238–9; above, p. 192; J. I. Carlebach and others, 'Report of the Panel of Survey of Social Welfare on social services and housing in the City of Nairobi', duplicated [Nairobi], 1962, appendix 5.

58 Hutton, *Reluctant farmers?* pp. 39, 302; Raymaekers, *L'organisation*, p. 89; Etienne van de Walle, 'Chômage dans une petite ville d'Afrique: Usumbura', *Zaïre*, 14 (1960), 347–9; Joyce Sween and Remi Clignet, 'Urban unemployment as a determinant of political unrest: the case study of Douala', *CJAS*, 3 (1969), 472–4; André Lux, 'Le niveau de vie des chômeurs de Luluabourg', *Zaïre*, 14 (1960), 33.

59 Guy Bernard, 'L'Africain et la ville', *CEA*, 13 (1973), 583; Georges N. Nzongola, 'Les classes sociales et la révolution anticoloniale au Congo-Kinshasa', *Cahiers économiques et sociales*, 8 (1970), 377; Richard Sandbrook and Jack Arn, *The labouring poor and urban class formation: the case of Greater Accra* (Montreal, 1977), p. 43.

60 Meillassoux, *Urbanization*, p. 39; Kenneth Swindell, 'Farmers, traders, and labourers: dry season migration from north-west Nigeria, 1900–33', *Africa*, 54 (1984), 1–19; Heather Joshi and others, *Abidjan: urban development and employment in the Ivory Coast* (Geneva, 1976), p. 45.

61 Barbara Lloyd, 'Indigenous Ibadan', in Lloyd and others, *Ibadan*, p. 71; Y. Mersadier, 'Les niveaux de vie', in Sankale and others, *Dakar*, p. 248; Joshi, *Abidjan*, p. 45; Manfred

Bienefeld, 'The informal sector and peripheral capitalism: the case of Tanzania', *IDS bulletin*, 6, 3 (February 1975), 57.

62 Skinner, *Ouagadougou*, p. 71; Banton, *City*, p. 34; East African Statistical Department, Tanganyika Unit, 'Interim report on budget survey of African consumers in Dar es Salaam 1956/7', July 1957, V. M. Davies papers, RH.

63 Margaret Peil, *Cities and suburbs: urban life in West Africa* (New York, 1981), p. 234; Robertson, *Sharing*, p. 176; Suzanne Comhaire-Sylvain, 'Le travail des femmes à Lagos', *Zaïre*, 5 (1951), 182.

64 Peil, *Cities*, p. 234; Fraenkel, *Monrovia*, p. 176; Pankhurst and Eshete in *Ethiopia observer*, 2, 11 (October 1958), 357.

65 Sankale and others, *Dakar*, pp. 82, 268, 288; Vis and others, *Nutritional survey*, pp. 102–7; Platt, 'Report', ch. 10, pp. 22, 24; Lux, 'Le niveau de vie', p. 33; Bettison, 'Poverty Datum Line', p. 39.

66 Ioné Acquah, *Accra survey* (London, 1958), p. 63; Collier and Lal, *Labour and poverty in Kenya*, p. 71.

67 Schildkrout, *People*, p. 57; Skinner, *Ouagadougou*, p. 47; O'Connor, *City*, p. 146.

68 Penvenne, 'Lourenço Marques', pp. 196–200; Aidan W. Southall and Peter C. W. Gutkind, *Townsmen in the making: Kampala and its suburbs* (Kampala, 1957), p. 57; Yusuf, 'Reconsideration', p. 207.

69 Peter Kilby, *African enterprise: the Nigerian bread industry* (Stanford, 1965), p. 71; P. T. Bauer, *West African trade* (reprinted, London, 1963), p. 22.

70 Rowena M. Lawson, 'The supply response of retail trading services to urban population growth in Ghana', in Claude Meillassoux (ed.), *The development of indigenous trade and markets in West Africa* (London, 1971), p. 380; Marris, *Family*, p. 68.

71 Andrew A. Beveridge and Anthony R. Oberschall, *African businessmen and development in Zambia* (Princeton, 1979), pp. 56, 62; Stephen Thornton, 'The struggle for profit and participation by an emerging African petty-bourgeoisie in Bulawayo, 1893–1933', *Seminar papers on the societies of southern Africa* (SOAS, London), 9 (1977–8), 79; Penvenne, 'Lourenço Marques', pp. 184–6, 195.

72 Robertson, *Sharing*, pp. 106–17; Andrew Hake, *African metropolis: Nairobi's self-help city* ([London] 1977), p. 179.

73 Uchendu, *Igbo*, p. 30; Nachtigal, *Sahara*, vol. 2, p. 232; Atsé Léon Bonnefonds, 'La transformation du commerce de traite en Côte d'Ivoire', *Cahiers d'outre-mer*, 21 (1968), 399.

74 Walter Elkan and others, 'The economics of shoe shining in Nairobi', *African affairs*, 81 (1982), 247–56; Holloway, 'Street boys', p. 140.

75 Archibald Callaway, 'Nigeria's indigenous education: the apprenticeship system', *Odu*, 1, 1 (July 1964), 62–3; Kenneth King, *The African artisan* (London, 1977); Beveridge and Oberschall, *Businessmen*, p. 79.

76 O. Y. Oyeneye, 'Apprentices in the informal sector of Nigeria', *Labour, capital and society*, 13, 2 (November 1980), 71; Callaway, 'Indigenous education', p. 68; Claude de Miras, 'Le secteur de subsistance dans les branches de production à Abidjan', *Revue tiers-monde*, 21 (1980), 358; King, *Artisan*, p. 51.

77 Peil, *Cities*, p. 106; Donald Faulkner, *Social welfare and juvenile delinquency in Lagos* (London [c.1950]), pp. 6–7; S. V. Sethuraman (ed.), *The urban informal sector in developing countries* (Geneva, 1981), pp. 73, 85–6, 92.

78 Callaway, 'Indigenous education', pp. 68–9; King, *Artisan*, p. 50; Roland Devauges, 'Le neveu et l'apprenti', in Isabelle Deblé and Philippe Hugon (eds.), *Vivre et survivre dans les villes africaines* (Paris, 1982), pp. 208, 212–13; Kilby, *Industrialization*, p. 216.

79 De Miras, 'Le secteur de subsistance', pp. 359–60; Faulkner, *Social welfare*, p. 7; Arn, 'Political economy', p. 191.

80 Ibrahim A. Tahir, 'Scholars, sufis, saints and capitalists in Kano, 1904–1974', Ph.D.

thesis, University of Cambridge, 1975, p. 294; Jean-Jacques Guibbert, 'Survie et dépendance des petits producteurs urbaines à Dakar', in Deblé and Hugon, *Vivre*, p. 70; William J. House, 'Nairobi's informal sector', IDS Nairobi Working Paper 347 (1978), p. 11; Peil, *Cities*, p. 109.

81 Peil, *Cities*, pp. 106, 109; Southall and Gutkind, *Townsmen*, p. 145; King, *Artisan*, pp. 111–12.

82 Housden, 'Report on the homeless boys in British Somaliland', February 1950, CO 859/221/12500/7/2/50/2.

83 Penvenne, 'Lourenço Marques', pp 163–4.

84 See W. Clifford, *Crime in Northern Rhodesia*, Rhodes–Livingstone Communication 18 (Lusaka, 1960), p. 80.

85 *Anglo-African*, 22 July and 28 October 1865.

86 See *NDT*, 26 April 1935, on the 'archgangster' Alabi, or Smith (*Baba*, p. 184) on 'Aeroplane'.

87 Alison Izzett, 'The Yoruba young delinquent in Lagos', B.Litt. thesis, University of Oxford, 1955, p. 122; Throup, 'Governorship', pp. 44–6, 264–6, 300.

88 Anne Bamisaiye, 'The spatial distribution of juvenile delinquency and adult crime in the city of Ibadan', *International journal of criminology and penology*, 2 (1974), 65–83; Marshall B. Clinard and Daniel J. Abbott, *Crime in developing countries* (New York, 1973), pp. 17–18, 141–64.

89 Georges Balandier, *Sociologie des Brazzavilles noirs* (Paris, 1955), pp. 181–2; Miner, *Timbuctoo*, pp. 250–1; J. Lombard, 'Cotonou: ville africaine', *Etudes dahoméennes*, 10 (1953), 195; Bernard, 'L'Africain', p. 583; Clinard and Abbott, *Crime*, p. 97.

90 Banton, *City*, chs. 9 and 10; Kenneth Little, 'The role of voluntary associations in West African urbanisation', *American anthropologist*, 59 (1957), 579–96; Peil, *Cities*, pp. 217–18.

91 Fetter, 'Associations', pp. 205–23.

92 Rothman, 'Lusaka', pp. 231–3.

93 Above, p. 107; S. A. Akintoye, *Revolution and power politics in Yorubaland 1840–1893* (London, 1971), p. 80.

94 Fraenkel, *Monrovia*, pp. 68, 70, 81, 108, 148–9, 151–2.

95 M. Clarkson, 'The problem of begging and destitution in urban areas of the Gold Coast', *Proceedings of the Fourth Annual Conference of the West African Institute of Social and Economic Research, Ibadan, 1956* (reprinted, 1963), pp. 143–4.

96 Iliffe, *Modern history*, pp. 389–90; 'Report of the Native Commissioner, Bulawayo, for the year ended 31st December 1947', ZNA S/1051; Acquah, *Accra survey*, p. 87; Zanzibar, *Social welfare report 1949*, p. 7; Leonard Plotnicov, *Strangers to the city: urban man in Jos* (Pittsburgh, 1967), pp. 68–71.

97 Pankhurst and Eshete in *Ethiopia observer*, 2, 11 (October 1958), 358–62; Acquah, *Accra survey*, p. 107; Zanzibar, *Social welfare report 1950*, p. 10; Plotnicov, *Strangers*, p. 69; Pauline H. Baker, *Urbanization and political change: the politics of Lagos, 1917–1967* (Berkeley, 1974), p. 83.

98 Danielle Pontié, 'Les Moba de Lomé', *CEA*, 21 (1981), 53–65.

99 Peil, *Cities*, pp. 6, 220–9; Audrey C. Smock, *Ibo politics: the role of ethnic unions* (Cambridge, Mass., 1971), pp. 136–9, 146–7.

100 David Parkin, *Neighbours and nationals in an African city ward* (London, 1969), pp. 153–5.

101 Adrian J. Peace, *Choice, class and conflict* (Brighton, 1979), ch. 2; Sautter, *De l'Atlantique*, vol. 1, p. 392; Sankale and others, *Dakar*, p. 207.

102 Frank Furedi, 'The African crowd in Nairobi', *JAH*, 14 (1973), 281; Sankale and others, *Dakar*, p. 411; McVicar, 'Twilight', p. 202 n. 1.

103 Suzanne Bernus, *Particularismes ethniques en milieu urbain: l'exemple de Niamey* (Paris, 1969), p. 75; Acquah, *Accra survey*, p. 68.
104 O'Connor, *City*, p. 121; Penvenne, 'Lourenço Marques', pp. 161–3; Rothman, 'Lusaka', p. 207.
105 Andrew G. Onokerhoraye, *Social services in Nigeria* (London, 1984), pp. 282–3; Penvenne, 'Lourenço Marques', pp. 163–6.
106 Ousmane Silla, 'Persistance des castes dans la société wolof contemporaine', *BIFAN*, 28B (1966), 762, 765; Burley, 'Weavers', p. 63.
107 Diop, *La société wolof*, pp. 69–70, 96–103; Margaret Strobel, *Muslim women in Mombasa, 1890–1975* (New Haven, 1979), p.18.
108 Messing, 'Group therapy', pp. 1124–5.
109 Fraenkel, *Monrovia*, pp. 158–68; John V. Taylor and Dorothea A. Lehmann, *Christians of the Copperbelt* (London, 1961), p. 297; J. Akinyele Omoyajowo, *Cherubim and Seraphim* (New York, 1982), p. 173; Izzett, 'Young delinquent', p. 28; Janet Anne Seeley, 'Praise, prestige and power: the organisation of social welfare in a developing Kenyan town', Ph.D. thesis, University of Cambridge, 1985, pp. 235–6.
110 G. Forrest Johnston, 'Welfare organisations in Mombasa', Mombasa Social Survey Papers (1956–8), RH; John Iliffe, 'A history of the dockworkers of Dar es Salaam', *TNR*, 71 (1970), 146.
111 Gutkind in Bloomberg and Schmandt, *Power*, p. 380; Arn, 'Political economy', p. 308.
112 *LWR*, 2 September 1893.
113 *LWR*, 10 August 1895, 31 July 1897, 13 May 1911.
114 Wole Soyinka, *Aké: the years of childhood* (London, 1981), ch. 14; Isichei, *History*, pp. 151–5; Andrée Audibert, 'Le service social en Afrique francophone dans une perspective de développement (l'époque coloniale)', 2 vols., Thèse pour le Doctorat du spécialité en sciences sociales du travail, Université de Paris I, n.d., vol. 2, p. 434; Robertson, *Sharing*, p. 82.
115 M'Bokolo, 'Peste', p. 42; Banton, *City*, p. 101; Eric Stanley Gargett, 'Welfare services in an African urban area', Ph.D. thesis, University of London, 1971, p. 49.
116 *LWR*, 7 November 1896; *Tanganyika standard*, 12 August 1955; Lansiné Kaba, *The Wahhabiyya* (Evanston, 1974), pp. 206–13.
117 Richard Sandbrook, *The politics of basic needs* (London, 1982), pp. 146–7; Sandbrook and Arn, *Labouring poor*, p. 6.
118 Above, p. 170; Gutkind in Bloomberg and Schmandt, *Power*, pp. 377–8; Sandbrook and Arn, *Labouring poor*, p. 45.
119 Sandbrook, *Politics*, pp. 171–2; P. C. W. Gutkind, 'The energy of despair: social organization of the unemployed in two African cities: Lagos and Nairobi', *Civilisations*, 17 (1967), 389.
120 Amilcar Cabral, *Revolution in Guinea* (trans. R. Handyside, revised edn, London, 1971), p. 51.
121 P. C. Lloyd, *Power and independence: urban Africans' perceptions of social inequality* (London, 1974), pp. 174–83; Peil, *Cities*, pp. 7, 261–5; Jean-Marie Gibbal, *Citadins et paysans dans la ville africaine: l'exemple d'Abidjan* (Paris, 1974), p. 383.
122 Above, p. 172; Izzett, 'Yoruba young delinquent', pp. 257–8.
123 Peil, *Cities*, pp. 114–15; Holloway, 'Street boys', pp. 139–40; Marris, *Family*, p. 70.
124 Lloyd, *Power*, pp. 119–21; Janet M. Bujra, 'Proletarianization and the "informal economy": a case study from Nairobi', *African urban studies*, 3 (Winter 1978–9), 47–66.
125 See Balandier, *Sociologie*, p. 262; Peil, *Cities*, pp. 140–1; A. L. Epstein, *Urbanization and kinship: the domestic domain on the Copperbelt of Zambia, 1950–1956* (London, 1981), p. 192.

126 Marris, *Family*, p. 36; Robertson, *Sharing*, pp. 207–8; Gibbal, *Citadins*, pp. 223, 127.
127 P. C. Hiza to J. S. Chombo, 3 August 1938, TANU 2. (For the reference, see Iliffe, *Modern history*, p. 578.)
128 Margaret Peil, *The Ghanaian factory worker* (Cambridge, 1972), p. 164; Hutton, *Reluctant farmers?* p. 56.
129 Quoted in Gutkind, 'Energy', pp. 197–8. See also A. Schwarz, 'Solidarité clanique, intégration urbaine et chômage en Afrique noire', *CJAS*, 3 (1969), 380–1; Robertson, *Sharing*, pp. 218–22.
130 P. Stopforth, *Survey of Highfield African Township, Salisbury* (Salisbury, 1971), introduction.
131 Gutkind in Bloomberg and Schmandt, *Power*, p. 374; Jeffries, *Class*, p. 182; Heisler, *Urbanisation*, p. 113.
132 Margaret Peil, 'The unemployment history of Ghanaian factory workers', *Manpower and unemployment research in Africa*, 1, 2 (November 1968), 12; Izzett, 'Yoruba young delinquent', p. 258.
133 Gibbal, *Citadins*, pp. 119, 215–44.
134 See, e.g., Busia, *Report*, p. 20; Epstein, *Urbanization*, p. 54.
135 Gibbal, *Citadins*, pp. 139, 120–1.
136 P. O. Sada, 'Urban poverty – the case of Lagos', in Nigerian Economic Society, *Poverty*, p. 103; C. and J. Houyoux, 'Les conditions de vie dans soixante familles à Kinshasa', *Cahiers économiques et sociaux* (Kinshasa), 8 (1970), 105–17.
137 David Parkin, *The cultural definition of political response* (London, 1978), p. 89; Holloway, 'Street boys', pp. 140–1.
138 Susanne Comhaire-Sylvain, 'Migration', in University College of Addis Ababa, *Social survey of Addis Ababa 1960*, duplicated, n.d., p. 53; *Ethiopia observer*, 9 (1966), 247; Dirasse, 'Socio-economic position', p. 117.
139 Carlebach, 'Report', appendix 5.
140 Philip Curtin and others, *African history* (London, 1978), p. 566; M. Di Giacomo and S. Stanley, 'Family structure and demography', in University College of Addis Ababa, *Social survey*, p. 62.
141 Epstein, *Urbanization*, pp. 119–21; Houyoux, 'Les conditions de vie', pp. 102–7.
142 Elizabeth Mandeville, 'Poverty, work and the financing of single women in Kampala', *Africa*, 49 (1979), 43, 45. See also Robertson, *Sharing*, p. 224.
143 Mandeville, 'Poverty', p. 49.
144 Acquah, *Accra survey*, p. 68; Robertson, *Sharing*, pp. 15–17.
145 Alf Schwarz, 'Illusion d'une émancipation et aliénation réelle de l'ouvrière zaïroise', *CJAS*, 6 (1972), 201, 210–11.
146 Dirasse, 'Socio-economic position', pp. 127, 130.
147 Comhaire-Sylvain, 'Le travail', pp. 478–82.
148 Nici Nelson, 'Some aspects of informal social organization of female migrants in a Nairobi squatter neighbourhood: Mathare Valley: paper II', seminar paper, SOAS, 1975, p. 2; D. G. Bettison and P. J. Rigby, *Patterns of income and expenditure – Blantyre-Limbe, Nyasaland*, Rhodes–Livingstone Communication 20 (Lusaka, 1961), p. 19.
149 Epstein, *Urbanization*, p. 35; Comhaire-Sylvain in University College of Addis Ababa, *Social survey*, p. 14; Banton, *City*, p. 204; Robertson, *Sharing*, p. 62.
150 J. Hinderink and J. Sterkenburg, *Anatomy of an African town* (Utrecht, 1975), p. 330.
151 Nici Nelson, 'Female-centred families: changing patterns of marriage and family among *buzaa* brewers of Mathare Valley', *African urban studies*, NS, 3 (Winter 1978–9), 85, 89–90; *idem*, 'Some aspects of informal social organization of female migrants in a Nairobi squatter neighbourhood: Mathare Valley: paper I', seminar paper, SOAS, 1975, p. 14; Coralie Rendle-Short, 'Study of the social background of mothers attending an M.C.H.

centre in Addis Ababa', *Ethiopian medical journal*, 6 (1967–8), 52; Robertson, *Sharing*, pp. 200–1.

152 Marris, *Family*, p. 50; Nigeria, *Social welfare report 1961–2*, p. 7; Robertson, *Sharing*, p. 191.

153 Di Giacomo and Stanley in University College of Addis Ababa, *Social survey*, p. 62; Rendle-Short, 'Study', pp. 49–52.

154 Nelson, 'Some aspects: paper I', p. 13; Dirasse, 'Socio-economic position', p. 9; Balandier, *Sociologie*, p. 186.

155 Ethiopia, and perhaps Rwanda, were exceptions.

156 Jean S. la Fontaine, 'The free women of Kinshasa', in J. Davis (ed.), *Choice and change* (London, 1974), p. 99; above, p. 34.

157 Jean Rouch and Edmond Bernus, 'Note sur les prostituées "Toutou" de Treichville et d'Adjamé', *Etudes éburnéennes*, 6 (1957), 231–42.

158 Luise White, 'A colonial state and an African petty bourgeoisie: prostitution, property, and class struggle in Nairobi, 1936–1940', in Frederick Cooper (ed.), *Struggle for the city* (Beverly Hills, 1983), ch. 5; F. J. Bennett, 'The social determinants of gonorrhoea in an East African town', *EAMJ*, 39 (1962), 337–40.

159 La Fontaine in Davis, *Choice*, p. 90.

160 Hufton, *Poor*, p. 317.

161 The best account of this is Luise Susan White, 'A history of prostitution in Nairobi, Kenya, circa. 1900–1952', Ph.D. thesis, University of Cambridge, 1983.

162 Above, pp. 17, 108; Strobel, *Muslim women*, p. 140; van Onselen, *Chibaro*, pp. 178–82.

163 Colette Piault, *Contribution à l'étude de la vie quotidienne de la femme mauri* (n.p., 1965), pp. 125–33; la Fontaine in Davis, *Choice*, p. 94; Schwarz, 'Illusion', pp. 195–6.

164 Rouch and Bernus, 'Note', p. 237; Yakou Ba, 'Some elements for a debate on juvenile "prostitution" and its suppression', *African environment*, 14 (1980), 247 (quoting Inna Diallo).

165 Raymaekers, *L'organisation*, pp. 165–7; Marijke Vandersypen, 'Femmes libres de Kigali', *CEA*, 17 (1977), 114; Poitou, *La délinquance*, p. 56.

166 Hake, *Metropolis*, p. 195; Janet M. Bujra, 'Postscript: prostitution, class and the state', in Colin Sumner (ed.), *Crime, justice and underdevelopment* (London, 1982), p. 147; Julius Carlebach, *Juvenile prostitutes in Nairobi* (Kampala, 1962), pp. 4, 11–13, 30.

167 See the papers in CO 859/224/5.

168 Quoted in Dirasse, 'Socio-economic position', p. 38. See also Pankhurst, 'Prostitution', pp. 167–77.

169 Dirasse, 'Socio-economic position', pp. 1, 50–1.

170 Compare the figure for Cape Town on p. 265.

171 The subject obsessed Ethiopian writers. See Kane, *Ethiopian literature*, pp. 41–8; Reidulf Knut Molvaer, *Tradition and change in Ethiopia* (Leiden, 1980), pp. 157, 224–5.

172 This paragraph is based on Dirasse, 'Socio-economic position', *passim* (quotation on p. 149).

173 As pointed out in *ibid.*, p. 2.

174 Enid Schildkrout, 'The employment of children in Kano', in Gerry Rodgers and Guy Standing (eds.), *Child work, poverty and underdevelopment* (Geneva, 1981), pp. 86, 93–4.

175 Penvenne, 'Lourenço Marques', p. 354; Crisp, *Story*, p. 75; M. Bekombo, 'The child in Africa', in Rodgers and Standing, *Child work*, p. 128.

176 Acquah, *Accra survey*, pp. 76–7; Comhaire-Sylvain, 'Le travail', p. 174.

177 Schildkrout in Rodgers and Standing, *Child work*, p. 84; Esther N. Goody, *Parenthood and social reproduction* (Cambridge, 1982), p. 140; Izzett, 'Yoruba young delinquent', p. 83.

178 Nigeria: Eastern Region, *Social welfare report 1956–57*, p. 4; Balandier, *Sociologie*, p. 64; Hake, *Metropolis*, p. 195.

179 See Goody, *Parenthood*, *passim*; Nici Nelson, 'Is fostering of children on the increase in central Kenya?' duplicated, Conference on the History of the Family in Africa, London, 1981.

180 Busia, *Report*, p. 92.

181 Comhaire-Sylvain in University College of Addis Ababa, *Social survey*, p. 55; Nelson, 'Fostering', pp. 7–9; Southall and Gutkind, *Townsmen*, pp. 39–40; Izzett, 'Yoruba young delinquent', p. 76.

182 Busia, *Report*, p. 36.

183 Eighteenth-century French housemaids were rural girls aged twelve and upwards: Hufton, *Poor*, p. 26.

184 Nigeria: Eastern Region, *Social welfare report 1956–7*, pp. 3–4; *West Africa*, 21 April 1956, p. 201; Jonathan Derrick, *Africa's slaves today* (London, 1975), p. 207. There is much material on this subject in the papers of M. L. Belcher, RH.

185 *LWR*, 9 December 1916; Izzett, 'Yoruba young delinquent', p. 107.

186 Quoted in Poitou, *La délinquance*, p. 96.

187 Nigeria: Northern Region, *Social welfare report 1955–6*, pp. 5–7; Jean Hochet, *Inadaptation sociale et délinquance juvénile en Haute-Volta* (Paris, 1967), p. 188.

188 Holloway, 'Street boys', p. 142; Acquah, *Accra survey*, p. 54.

189 *The war cry*, 2 June 1934; M. D. Kenny, 'Report on remedial social welfare in Kenya', 4 June 1948, CO 859/220/12500/2/51/2; *The world's children*, 35 (1955), 32.

190 *The world's children*, 34 (1954), 183–4.

191 Hake, *Metropolis*, p. 206.

192 Iliffe, *Modern history*, pp. 62–3; *Mission to the Central Sûdan: letters from Mr G. Wilmot-Brooke. No. 1* (1 April 1889), CMS:UP 82/F4.

193 *Nigerian pioneer*, 16 July 1926; Banton, *City*, p. 182 n. 1; Commissioner of Police to CS, 2 June 1938, TNA SMP 21963/I/55; Gargett, *Administration*, p. 59.

194 Faulkner, *Social welfare*, p. 1. The remainder of the paragraph is based on this pamphlet.

195 Rennie to Edmonds, 2 June 1944, CO 859/122/12810/6A/44/7; Gold Coast, *Social welfare report 1946–51*, p. 18; Uganda, *Public relations and social welfare report 1951*, p. 16.

196 Audibert, 'Le service social', vol. 2, pp. 471–3.

197 Hochet, *Inadaptation*, p. 20; F. Y. St Leger, 'Crime in Southern Rhodesia', *RLJ*, 38 (December 1965), 36.

198 Collier and Lal, *Labour and poverty in Kenya*, p. 59.

199 See Hochet, *Inadaptation*, *passim*.

200 Poitou, *La délinquance*, pp. 208–9, 219.

201 Clinard and Abbott, *Crime*, p. 36.

202 Poitou, *La délinquance*, p. 49; Holloway, 'Street boys', p. 141.

203 Uganda, *Community development report 1956*, p. 29; Izzett, 'Yoruba young delinquent', p. 262; Comhaire-Sylvain, 'Le travail', p. 483.

204 Izzett, 'Yoruba young delinquent', pp. 82, 278. See also Alison Izzett, 'The fears and anxieties of delinquent Yoruba children', *Odu* (Ibadan), 1 (January 1955), 26–34.

205 Benjamin H. and G. Winifred Kagwa, 'Juvenile delinquency in Uganda', *EAMJ*, 46 (1969), 379; Poitou, *La délinquance*, p. 170.

206 Izzett, 'Yoruba young delinquent', pp. 13, 108–9, 129–30, 277; Hochet, *Inadaptation*, pp. 84, 91–3.

207 Hochet, *Inadaptation*, p. 159; Poitou, *La délinquance*, pp. 67, 152; Epstein, *Urbanization*, p. 158.

208 Paul Raymaekers, 'Pre-delinquency and juvenile delinquency in Leopoldville', *Inter-African Labour Institute bulletin*, 10 (1963), 329–57; J. S. la Fontaine, 'Two types of youth groups in Kinshasa', in Mayer, *Socialization*, pp. 191–213.

209 O'Connor, *City*, p. 82.

210 Rothman, 'Lusaka', pp. 325, 330; Guebels, *Relation*, pp. 136–7.
211 Gouellain, *Douala*, p. 220; "Gouvernement Général de l'A.O.F.: Circonscription de Dakar et Dépendances: rapport annuel 1944', ANOM:MC Affaires politiques 3450/11.
212 *LWR*, 13 May 1911; Nigeria, *Annual report on the Colony 1932*, p. 14; Sierra Leone, *Social welfare report 1954*, p. 8.
213 Bamisaiye, 'Begging', p. 202 n. 3; Francis O. Okediji (ed.), *The rehabilitation of beggars in Nigeria* (Ibadan, 1972), p. 27.
214 *LWR*, 2 April 1921; Cohen, *Custom*, p. 46; Sada in Nigerian Economic Society, *Poverty*, p. 98.
215 Bamisaiye, 'Begging', pp. 199, 202 n.3.
216 The following is based on Gold Coast, *Report on the enquiry into begging and destitution in the Gold Coast 1954* (Accra, 1955); Clarkson, 'Problem'; Acquah, *Accra survey*, p. 81.
217 Ebow Mensah, 'A note on the distribution of beggars in Zaria', *Savanna*, 6, 1 (June 1977), 73–6.
218 *Ethiopia observer*, 9, 4 (1966), 265; Giel and others, 'Ticket', p. 555.
219 *Ethiopia observer*, 4, 2 (January 1960), 53–4.
220 Schneider, *Leprosy*, p. 77.
221 *Ibid.*, p. 70
222 E.g. *Nigerian pioneer*, 24 June 1927; *Tanganyika opinion*, 24 September 1937.
223 George Simeon Mwase, *Strike a blow and die* (ed. R. I. Rotberg, Cambridge, Mass., 1967), p. 27.
224 Hake, *Metropolis*, pp. 55, 189.
225 SN Bulawayo to CNC, 22 September 1933, ZNA s/1542/P/1; Southern Rhodesia, *Report of the Secretary of Native Affairs 1949*, p. 7; 'Report of the Native Commissioner, Victoria District, for the year ended 31st December, 1960', ZNA 71881/16 (temporary file number).
226 W. Clifford, *Physical handicap amongst Africans in Broken Hill* (Lusaka, 1960), pp. 9, 12–15.
227 Valdo Pons, *Stanleyville* (London, 1969), p. 223; Robertson, *Sharing*, p. 211
228 Gutkind, 'Energy', p. 392. See also Abel G. M. Ishumi, *The urban jobless in eastern Africa* (Uppsala, 1984), p. 41.

11 The care of the poor in colonial Africa

1 Baker, *Urbanization*, p. 39.
2 *LWR*, 23 February 1901.
3 *LWR*, 10 August 1895.
4 *LWR*, 3 January 1903.
5 *Nigerian pioneer*, 24 June 1927.
6 Johnson to Lang, 12 February 1885, CMS G3/A2/O/1885/81.
7 *LWR*, 26 June 1897.
8 'Lagos: annual report for 1891', *Parliamentary papers*, 1893, LIX, 22; above, p. 166.
9 Ralph Schram, *A history of the Nigerian health services* (Ibadan, 1971), p. 104; *Lagos observer*, 2 March 1882; *LWR*, 8 September 1894, 25 June 1898, 24 March 1900; *Lagos times*, 13 September 1882.
10 *LWR*, 4 January 1896 and 23 November 1895.
11 *NDT*, 11 May 1936; *Lagos observer*, 1 May 1886.
12 E.g. *LWR*, 12 June 1897.
13 *Lagos observer*, 28 August 1884; *LWR*, 14 October 1893 and 9 October 1897.
14 Enclosure in MacGregor to Chamberlain, 23 February 1901, CO 147/154/49; *LWR*, 15 February 1902 and 4 March 1905.

15 *Annales des Pères du Saint-Esprit* (1931), 142; Zanzibar, *Medical report 1933*, p. 56; above, ch. 12.
16 Jean Pirotte, *Périodiques missionnaires belges d'expression française 1889–1940* (Louvain, 1973), pp. 249–52.
17 This is a personal impression from reading *Les missions catholiques*.
18 See the comment on Schopenhauer in Albert Schweitzer, *Reverence for life* (trans. R. H. Fuller, London, 1970), p. 26.
19 *Idem, Out of my life and thought* (trans. C. T. Campion, reprinted, New York, n.d.), p. 94.
20 Don Cupitt, *The sea of faith* (London, 1984), p. 108. (I owe this reference to Professor S. W. Sykes.)
21 Albert Schweitzer, *On the edge of the primeval forest* (first published 1921: trans. C. T. Campion, reprinted, London, 1955), pp. 124–5.
22 See Guebels, *Relation, passim*.
23 *MC*, 79 (1947), 104–5, 141.
24 Margaret Mary Nolan, MMM, *Medical Missionaries of Mary, 1937–1962* (Drogheda, n.d.), pp. 124–5.
25 *Ibid.*, p. 93.
26 See Paul B. Rich, *White power and the liberal conscience* (Manchester, 1984), ch. 1.
27 *Salvation Army year book* (1955), 75; *ibid.* (1981), 119.
28 Hochet, *Inadaptation*, pp. 129–41; Federation of the Rhodesias and Nyasaland, *Public health reports*, 1958 p. 17, 1962 p. 21.
29 See Frederick Johnson, *A standard Swahili–English dictionary* (reprinted, Oxford, 1959), pp. 212 (s.v. *-kiwa*) and 262 (s.v. *maskini*); Delafosse, *La langue mandingue*, vol. 2, pp. 507 (s.v. *misikine*) and 720 (s.v. *talaka*); Olivier de Sardan, *Concepts*, pp. 22, 348–9.
30 Zanzibar, *Social welfare report 1958*, p. 8.
31 Kenya, *Report on the incidence of destitution among Africans in urban areas* (Nairobi, 1954), p. 8.
32 G. Rocheteau, 'Mouridisme et économie de traite', in G. Ancey and others, *Essais sur la reproduction de formations sociales dominées* (Paris, 1977), p. 44; Marty, *Guinée*, pp. 305–7; Olivier de Sardan, *Concepts*, p. 403; Schildkrout, *People*, p. 110.
33 *West Africa*, 29 October 1955, p. 1020; C. S. Whitaker Jr, *The politics of tradition* (Princeton, 1970), p. 333.
34 Fernand Dumont, *La pensée religieuse d'Amadou Bamba* (Dakar, 1975), p. 233; Donal B. Cruise O'Brien, *The Mourides of Senegal* (Oxford, 1971), p. 96.
35 Zanzibar, *Social welfare report 1949*, p. 7; Surendra Mehta and G. M. Wilson, 'The Asian communities of Mombasa', Mombasa Social Survey Papers, RH.
36 David F. Clyde, *History of the medical services of Tanganyika* (Dar es Salaam, 1962), p. 10; Otto Peiper, 'Die Bekämpfung der Lepra in Deutsch-Ostafrika', *Lepra*, 14 (1914), 192; Mehta and Wilson, 'Asian communities', Mombasa Social Survey Papers, RH; above, p. 202.
37 Percy Ibbotson, 'Federation of Native Welfare Societies in Southern Rhodesia', *RLJ*, 2 (December 1944), 35–9; Nyasaland, *Medical report 1952*, p. 5.
38 James W. Fernandez, *Bwiti: an ethnography of the religious imagination in Africa* (Princeton, 1982), pp. 542, 433.
39 Taylor and Lehmann, *Christians*, pp. 107–8, 167.
40 M. L. Daneel, *Old and new in southern Shona independent churches* (2 vols., The Hague, 1971–4), vol. 2, pp. 201–9; Monica Wilson, *Communal rituals of the Nyakyusa* (London, 1959), p. 192; M. L. Daneel, 'The growth and significance of Shona independent churches', in M. F. C. Bourdillon, SJ (ed.), *Christianity south of the Zambezi, volume 2* (Gwelo, 1977), p. 181.

41 E.g. C. A. Bayly, *Rulers, townsmen and bazaars: North Indian society in the age of British expansion, 1770–1870* (Cambridge, 1983), pp. 125–39.
42 Governor to Minister of Marine, 28 July 1885, ANOM:MC Sénégal XI:46; *Central African planter*, August 1896; G. H. Adams, 'The Nyasaland Charitable Purposes Committee' [19 February 1947] MNA SMP/13629/1; *LWR*, 2 March 1918.
43 Audibert, 'Le service social', vol. 1, p. 278; Seeley, 'Praise', p. 92; P. S. Selwyn Clarke, 'The British Red Cross Society on the Gold Coast', *WAMJ*, 7 (1932–3), 117–19.
44 *The record of the Save the Children Fund*, 2 (1921–2), 119.
45 *Ibid.*, pp. 6, 217; *The world's children*, 10 (1929–30), 8, 29–30.
46 Evelyn Sharp, *The African child* (London, 1931).
47 *The world's children*, 16 (1935–6), 84, 156; *ibid.*, 18 (1937–8), 3, 117; *ibid.*, 19 (1938–9), 69; *Ethiopia observer*, 4, 2 (January 1960), 45.
48 *The world's children*, 25 (1945), 83; *ibid.*, 30 (1950), 136, 155–7; *ibid.*, 34 (1954), 150; *ibid.*, 43 (1963), 37–8; papers in CO 859/229/12592/11/52; 'Note of account by Mr Chinn of his tour . . . January–March, 1953', CO 859/372/4.
49 *The world's children*, 35 (1955), 32, 52, 121–2; *ibid.*, 39 (1956), 46; Benedict Nightingale, *Charities* (London, 1973), pp. 218–21.
50 'Poor law in the colonies, etc.' [December 1939] CO 859/38/12802/40/1; Gloria Cumper, *Survey of social legislation in Jamaica* ([Mona] 1972), p. 58.
51 Nyasaland, *Report of the committee appointed . . . to enquire into emigrant labour* (Zomba, 1936); above, p. 160.
52 D. J. Morgan. *The official history of colonial development* (5 vols., London, 1980), vol. 1, pp. 64–7; Robert Pearce, 'The Colonial Office and planned decolonization in Africa', *African affairs*, 83 (1984), 78.
53 Richards, minute, 27 December 1941, and Jeffries to Burns, 30 January 1942, in CO 859/75/12810/8/43.
54 There is an excellent summary of current thinking in L. P. Mair, *Welfare in the British colonies* (London, 1944).
55 'Juvenile welfare in the colonies: draft report of the Juvenile Delinquency Sub-Committee of the Colonial Penal Administration Committee, 8th October, 1942', CO 859/73/12770/43.
56 See Mair, *Welfare*, p. 109.
57 'Colonial Social Welfare Advisory Committee: minutes of the 27th meeting', 3 December 1946, CO 859/158/12531/47/2.
58 Quoted in Peter du Sautoy, *Community development in Ghana* (London, 1958), p. 2.
59 Audibert, 'Le service social', vol. 1, pp. 31–2.
60 Swaisland to Darlow, 5 February 1950, CO 859/221/12500/12/50/2.
61 Onokerhoraye, *Social services*, p. 165.
62 'Youth work in Lagos: summary of a talk by Mr D. E. Faulkner', 18 September 1950, CO 859/221/12500/12/50/6; Nigeria, *Social welfare report 1961–2*, p. 8.
63 'Social Welfare Department development plan', 1945, CO 859/112/12500/11/45/30A; Gold Coast, *Social welfare reports*, 1946–51 p. 43, 1954 p. 7; above, p. 190.
64 United Nations Economic Commission for Africa: Social Development Section, *Patterns of social welfare organization and administration in Africa* (New York, 1964), p. 19.
65 'Colonial Social Welfare Advisory Committee: draft minutes of the 36th meeting', 27 September 1948, CO 859/158/12531/48/18; James Midgley, *Professional imperialism: social work in the Third World* (London, 1981), p. 163; Sierra Leone, *Social welfare report 1954*, p. 8 and appendix B.
66 Zanzibar, *Social welfare reports*, 1949 pp. 6 and 10, 1953 pp. 9 and 13–14, 1954 pp. 8 and 15.
67 *Ibid.*, 1957 pp 12–13 and 27–8, 1961 p. 3, 1962 pp. 2–4.

68 Kenya, *Report on the incidence of destitution*, p. 4; 'Record of a meeting held at the [Nairobi] Town Hall', 16 June 1944, Rennie to Edmonds, 2 June 1944, and minute by Darlow, 21 July 1944, all in CO 859/122/12810/6A/44.
69 'Social Welfare Organisation, Kenya Colony: 1948 annual report', CO 859/220/12500/2/2/50/4; *Commonwealth survey*, 30 March 1951, p. 27.
70 Quoted in a paper for the Committee on Mass Education (Community Development), 29 October 1952, CO 859/477/7.
71 Typescript memoirs (first version) of T. G. Askwith, RH; 'Extract from draft minutes of the 45th meeting of the Colonial Social Welfare Advisory Committee', 28 May 1951, CO 859/220/5/3.
72 Kenya, *Community development reports*, 1955 p. 1, 1968 p. 12; Carlebach and others, 'Report', p. 28.
73 Tanganyika, *Social welfare report 1947*, pp. 2, 5.
74 'Mr Blaxland's talk on social welfare in Tanganyika, to the Reports Sub-Committee, 20th January, 1950', CO 859/220/12500/4/50/3.
75 See H. Mason, 'Progress in Pare', *Corona*, 4 (1952), 212–19.
76 Tanganyika, *Social development report 1958,* p. 21.
77 Dundas to Lloyd, 31 January 1941, CO 859/79/12836/2/41/1; 'Activities of social welfare', 19 March 1947, CO 859/220/12500/3/50/1.
78 Uganda, *Public relations and social welfare report 1949,* p.1; Uganda, *Community development report 1951*, pp. 21–2; 'Advisory Committee on Social Development, Reports Sub-Committee, minutes of the first meeting', 21 September 1953, CO 859/476/2.
79 Minute 5 by CS, 27 November 1951, MNA SMP/20273; 'Advisory Committee on Social Development, minutes of the first meeting', 19 October 1953, CO 859/467/2.
80 Minute 85 by CS, 22 April 1954, MNA SMP/20273; CS to Marnham, 21 July 1954, MNA SMP/20273/29.
81 H. McK. Tasker, 'Factual report on social welfare activities and amenities in Southern Province', 1957, MNA SMP/32641/1A.
82 PC Southern to SAA, 11 March 1952, MNA SMP/20925/23.
83 'Social Development Branch. Annual report, 1959', T. D. Thomson papers, RH.
84 W. D. S. Talbot, 'Southern Province: January 1959, monthly report social development', MNA SMP/20933/30A.
85 Rothman, 'Luṣaka', pp. 73–4, 260–3; Northern Rhodesia, *Social welfare report 1955*, p. 3.
86 Northern Rhodesia, *Social welfare reports,* 1950 pp. 3–5, 1959 p. 9.
87 *Ibid.*, 1964 p. 19.
88 Southern Rhodesia, *Report on social security by the Social Security Officer* (duplicated, 2 vols., n.p., 1944), vol. 1, pp. 28–30, 34, and vol. 2, pp. 196, 199; Gargett, *Administration*, pp. 59, 72–3; papers in ZNA S/1542/P/1.
89 Southern Rhodesia, *Report on social security*; Ernest W. Kachingwe, 'Social welfare services for urban Africans in Zimbabwe', Ph.D. thesis, University of Iowa, 1979, p. 25.
90 Gargett, 'Welfare services', pp. 45–6, 143, 145–8, 152–4, 157–62, 182; Rhodesia, *Labour and social welfare report 1973*, pp. 22, 35.
91 Audibert, 'Le service social', vol. 1, pp. 15, 254–6.
92 *Ibid.*, vol. 1, pp. 26, 31, 205–7, and vol. 2, pp. 350, 469.
93 *Ibid.*, vol. 1, pp. 23, 262, 301–5, and vol. 2, p. 586.
94 *Ibid.*, vol. 1, pp. 278–9, and vol. 2, pp. 532, 581. The missionary obstacle also faced Belgian *assistantes sociales*: see Guebels, *Relation*, pp. 726–8.
95 Audibert, 'Le service social', vol. 1, pp. 281–4, 287, 341–4.
96 *Ibid.*, vol. 1, pp. 23, 296–7, and vol. 2, pp. 376, 477–8, 586; UNECA, *Patterns*, pp. 63–4.
97 'Social welfare in West Africa' [1943–4] CO 859/75/12810/8/43/25; Midgley, *Professional imperialism,* pp. 59–68, 117; UNECA, *Patterns*, p. 26; Northern Rhodesia, *Social welfare*

report 1960, p. 2; A. J. Dachs and W. F. Rea, SJ, *The Catholic Church and Zimbabwe 1879–1979* (Gwelo, 1979), p. 195; Audibert, 'Le service social', vol. 2, pp. 547–69, 586.
98 See Pierre Mouton, *Social security in Africa* (Geneva, 1975), pp. 4–8.
99 Guebels, *Relation*, p. 573; ILO, 'La sécurité sociale en Afrique au sud du Sahara', *Afrique-documents*, 63 (May 1962), 102–3.
100 Great Britain: Colonial Office, *Blindness in British African and Middle East territories* (London, 1948), pp. iii, 5, 20–1; papers in CO 859/159/12590/C/2/1/48; Audibert, 'Le service social', vol. 2, pp. 522, 527–30, 544.
101 *Advance* (Accra), 37 (January 1963), 8; Gold Coast, *Social welfare report 1954*, p. 6; Clutha Mackenzie, 'Pilot project for the rural blind in Uganda', *International social service review*, 7 (October 1960), 45–53.
102 Rodger, *Blindness*, pp. 88–9, 93; John M. Hunter, 'Progress and concerns in the World Health Organization onchocerciasis control program in West Africa', *SSM*, 15D (1981), 261.
103 *Advance*, 37 (January 1963), 2, and 51 (July 1966), 3–4; Schram, *History*, p. 386.
104 See pp. 247–8.
105 *Oxfam news*, August 1967 and November 1975; Federation of the Rhodesias and Nyasaland, *Public health report 1961*, p. 37.
106 Northern Rhodesia, *Social welfare report 1960*, p. 5.
107 Acquah, *Accra survey*, p. 89.
108 *The world's children*, 44 (1964), 30; Ayokonnu Ogunranti, 'Pastor and politician: Isaac Akinyele, Olubadan of Ibadan', in Isichei, *Varieties*, p. 135; Abner Cohen, *The politics of elite culture* (Berkeley, 1981), pp. 72–3, 107–8.
109 'Meeting of the Central Welfare Committee', 17 January 1945, CO 859/112/12500/11/45/30.
110 Nigeria: Northern Region, *Social welfare report 1956–7*, p. 5; Busia, *Report*, p. 102; Sylvia Walker, 'The disabled in Ghana', Ed.D. thesis, Columbia University, 1978, pp. 2, 60–4, 120–1; Nigeria: Eastern Region, *Report of the first conference of Eastern Nigeria Councils of Social Service* (Enugu, 1965).
111 *MC*, 43 (1911), 257; *MC*, 44 (1912), 16.
112 Pankhurst, *Economic history*, p. 650; *Ethiopia observer*, 2, 4 (March 1958), 151; *The world's children*, 16 (1935–6), 156.
113 *Ethiopia observer*, 2, 4 (March 1958), 151; Heyer, *Die Kirche*, p. 148.
114 Schaller, *Ethiopia*, p. 95; UNECA, *Patterns*, pp. 44, 47; *Ethiopia observer*, 9 (1966), 245.
115 Oriana Fallaci, 'Straft Gott die Faulen und macht die Fleissigen reich?' *Afrika heute* (October 1973), 35.
116 *Ethiopia observer*, 9 (1966), 269.
117 This point is especially well made in Seeley, 'Praise', p. 129.
118 G. F. Johnston, 'Welfare organisations in Mombasa', Mombasa Social Survey Papers, RH.
119 Richards, *Land*, pp. xv, 258–63; Iliffe in McCracken, *Malawi*, pp. 246–7, 266; Ashton, *Basuto*, p. 173; David Rooney, *Sir Charles Arden-Clarke* (London, 1982), pp. 58–9.
120 'Poor law in the colonies, etc.' [December 1939] CO 859/38/12802/40/1; R. Cunyngham Brown, *Report III on the care and treatment of lunatics in the British West African colonies: Nigeria* (Lagos, 1938), p. 64; Northern Rhodesia, *Social welfare report 1950*, pp. 5–6; Cunnison, *Luapula peoples*, p. 188.
121 Mair, *Welfare*, pp. 109–10.
122 Brown, *Report*, pp. 12–14, 25, 29, 31, 38, 57.
123 Cyril G. F. Smartt, 'Problems and prospects of psychiatry in Tanganyika', *EAMJ*, 37 (1960), 482.
124 Above, pp. 181, 152; 'Annual report of the Native Commissioner, Bulalima Mangwe

District for the year ended 31 December 1960', ZNA 71881/37 (temporary file number); Retel-Laurentin, *Un pays*, pp. 231–2.

125 PC Southern, 1950, quoted in Megan Vaughan, 'Poverty and famine: 1949 in Nyasaland', University of Malawi Social Science Conference paper, July 1982, p. 9.

126 Scull, *Museums*, p. 228; Busia, *Report*, p. 117.

12 Leprosy

1 Convenient modern accounts are W. H. Jopling, *Handbook of leprosy* (3rd edn, London, 1984), and John M. Hunter and Morris O. Thomas, 'Hypothesis of leprosy, tuberculosis and urbanization in Africa', *SSM*, 19 (1984), 27–57.

2 See p. 90.

3 Hunter and Thomas, 'Hypothesis', pp. 36–41; James Ross Innes, 'Leprosy and leprosy work in East Africa', *IJL*, 18 (1950), 367.

4 See L. M. Irgens, 'Epidemiological aspects and implications of the disappearance of leprosy from Norway', *LR*, 52 (1981), supplement 1, p. 154; Halvor Sommerfelt and others, 'Geographical variations in the occurrence of leprosy', *IJL*, 53 (1985), 530.

5 J. A. Cap, 'The epidemiological situation in Africa', *LR*, 52 (1981), supplement 1, p. 57; Hunter and Thomas, 'Hypothesis', pp. 36, 39.

6 Davey, 'First report', p. 124; E. Muir, 'Leprosy in Northern Nigeria', *LR*, 11 (1940), 18–21; O. F. H. Atkey, 'Leprosy control in the southern Sudan', *IJL*, 3 (1935), 74; Innes, 'Leprosy in East Africa', pp. 366–7; Innes to DMS, 30 April 1950, MNA DC Blantyre MD/12/1; Hunter and Thomas, 'Hypothesis', pp. 36, 39.

7 See p. 10. On this subject generally, see Nancy E. Waxler, 'Learning to be a leper', in Elliot G. Mishler and others, *Social contexts of health, illness, and patient care* (Cambridge, 1981), ch. 7. (I owe this reference to Dr G. A. Lewis.)

8 Lethem to Oldrieve, 11 February 1926, MNA S1/512/I/24/17; Ferguson, 'Hausaland', p. 146; Lander, *Records*, vol. 1, pp. 218–19; Ailon Shiloh, 'A case study of disease and culture in action: leprosy among the Hausa of Northern Nigeria', *Human organization*, 24 (1965), 143.

9 A. J. Sowden, 'Report of leprosy survey in the Amadi district', *LR*, 12 (1941), 42; Médecin-Capitaine Longe, 'Note sur la prophylaxie anti-lépreuse dans le cercle du Sine-Saloum (Sénégal)', *IJL*, 6 (1938), 52; James Ross Innes, 'Leprosy in Uganda: a survey in the Kigezi district', *EAMJ*, 27 (1950), 281.

10 M. B. D. Dixey, 'Work in the Gold Coast', *LR*, 1, 2 (April 1930), 27.

11 Junod, *Life*, vol. 2, p. 477.

12 Mayer, 'Distribution', p. 14.

13 Above, p. 90; Robert Howard, 'General description of the diseases encountered during ten years' medical work on the shores of Lake Nyasa', *Journal of tropical medicine and hygiene*, 13 (1910), 67.

14 M. B. D. Dixey, 'Some observations on leprosy in the Gold Coast and British Togoland', *WAMJ*, 5 (1931–2), 3; E. Muir, 'Leprosy in the Gold Coast', *LR*, 7 (1936), 185–6.

15 Griffiths, 'Leprosy', pp. 62–3.

16 Orley, *Culture*, p. 35; draft autobiography of A. B. Fisher, book 4, p. 2, CMS:UP 84; Walser, *Luganda proverbs*, no. 0708; Innes, 'Leprosy in East Africa', p. 364.

17 Above, p. 83; Mayer, 'Distribution', pp. 13–14.

18 Patrick Feeny, *The fight against leprosy* (London, 1964), p. 99.

19 J. P. R. Wallis (ed.), *The Zambezi expedition of David Livingstone, 1858–1863* (2 vols., London, 1956), vol. 2, pp. 260–1.

20 Above, pp. 105–7; E. J. Schulz and H. H. L. Pentz, 'Leprosy control in South Africa', *LR*, 41 (1970), 15–16; *The Cowley evangelist* (1917), 267.

21 Cape of Good Hope, *Reports on the government-aided hospitals and asylums*, 1898, part 2, pp. 59–61; *ibid.*, 1908, pp. 52, 54.
22 *Transvaal Administration reports for 1903: part II: administration*, section 1, pp. C3–4 and C10; *Mission field*, 66 (1921), 37.
23 *Memorandum regarding the medical policy of the British Empire Leprosy Relief Association*, encl. in Devonshire, circular despatch, 8 January 1924, MNA S1/512/I/24/1.
24 P. D. Winter, 'South African leprosy laws and control policy', *IJL*, 17 (1949), 255; *SAO*, 55 (1925), 150; Cape of Good Hope, *Report of the Select Committee on Robben Island Leper Asylums*, p. 179.
25 See Hunter and Thomas, 'Hypothesis', *passim*.
26 E.g. Peter Buirski, 'Mortality rates in Cape Town 1895–1980', in Saunders and others, *Studies*, vol. 5, pp. 151–4.
27 Irgens, 'Epidemiological aspects', p. 162.
28 May to Resident Commissioner, 18 May 1914, CO 417/545; R. C. Germond, 'A study of the last six years of the leprosy campaign in Basutoland', *IJL*, 4 (1936), 219.
29 [N. M.] Macfarlane, 'Basutoland Leper Asylum 1914–1922', ZNA A3/12/9.
30 May to Resident Commissioner, 18 May 1914, CO 417/545.
31 Germond, 'A study', pp. 219–20; Hunter and Thomas, 'Hypothesis', p. 50.
32 Peiper, 'Die Bekämpfung', *passim*.
33 H. Delinotte, 'The fight against leprosy in the French overseas territories', *IJL*, 7 (1939), 539–40, 544; E. Muir, 'Leprosy in British Somaliland', *LR*, 10 (1939), 96; Michael Gelfand, *A service to the sick: a history of the health services for Africans in Southern Rhodesia* (Gwelo, 1976), p. 35.
34 F. M. Dennis, journal, 8 December 1904, CMS:UP 4/F1.
35 *MC*, 40 (1908), 2–3.
36 A. Schultze, *The Sultanate of Bornu* (trans. P. A. Benton, London, 1913), p. 75 n. 103a; W. A. Lambert, 'My life with the lepers', duplicated, n.d., p. 11 (CMS:UP 118).
37 Nyasaland, *Medical report 1918*, pp. 36–9.
38 *MC*, 43 (1911), 257–60; *MC*, 38 (1906), 566; Griffiths, 'Leprosy', p. 63.
39 Feeny, *Fight*, pp. 106–7; above, p. 106; May to Resident Commissioner, 23 June 1914, CO 417/545.
40 Feeny, *Fight*, pp. 108–10; Leonard Rogers, *Happy toil* (London, 1950), pp. 189–90; Oldrieve to DMS, 26 November 1926, MNA S1/512/I/24/11a.
41 Cape of Good Hope, *Leprosy Commission*, p. 85, citing *Indian Leprosy Commission report* (1893), pp. 6, 9–11.
42 Leonard Rogers, 'A memorandum on the prevalence of and prophylaxis against leprosy in the British Empire', 1925, MNA S1/512/I/24/5a.
43 Andrew B. Macdonald, *In His Name* (London, 1964), pp. 93–4.
44 Muir, 'Leprosy in Nigeria', pp. 53–69; Nigeria, *Medical report 1938*, p. 9.
45 Rogers, 'A memorandum', 1925, MNA S1/512/I/24/5a; Muir, 'Leprosy in the Gold Coast', p. 187.
46 F. H. Cooke, 'History of the Ho Leper Settlement', *LR*, 2, 1 (January 1931), 8; E. Muir, 'Leprosy in Sierra Leone', *LR*, 7 (1936), 195.
47 Murray to Bowring [1924] MNA M/2/5/12/4; Nyasaland, *Medical report 1931*, p. 10.
48 E. Muir, 'Leprosy in Uganda', *LR*, 10 (1939), 31–46; *idem*, 'Leprosy in Tanganyika Territory', *ibid.*, 58–80.
49 *Idem*, 'Leprosy in Zanzibar', *ibid.*, 81–4; *idem*, 'Leprosy in Northern Rhodesia', p. 19; Innes, 'Leprosy in East Africa', p. 363.
50 Atkey, 'Leprosy control', pp. 73–9.
51 Gelfand, *Service*, pp. 35–8; B. Moiser, 'Leprosy in Southern Rhodesia', *LR*, 9 (1938), 110–11; E. Muir, 'Leprosy in Southern Rhodesia', *LR*, 11 (1940), 36.

52 E. Muir, 'Report on leprosy in the Union of South Africa', *LR*, 11 (1940), 45–7; Winter, 'South African leprosy laws', p. 260.
53 A. R. Davison, 'Anti-leprotic treatment at the Emjanyana Leprosy Institution', *LR*, 2 (1931), 149.
54 Muir, 'Report', p. 49.
55 Schweitzer, *More from the primeval forest*, pp. 16, 74–5; Delinotte, 'Fight against leprosy', pp. 540–1, 546; Aussel, report of 22 February 1936, ANOM:MC Affaires politiques 628/4.
56 Guebels, *Relation*, pp. 587–94; *MC*, 72 (1940), 96.
57 Davey, 'Uzuakoli', p. 173.
58 J. A. Macdonald, 'Itu Leprosy Colony', *LR*, 4 (1933), 20.
59 E. Muir, 'Leper institutions in Nigeria', *LR*, 7 (1936), 178–9; A. B. Macdonald, 'Rehabilitation – the industrial and social work of a leper colony', *LR*, 19 (1948), 46–53.
60 Quoted in Macdonald, *In His Name*, p. 10.
61 'A Medical Man', 'The stigma of leprosy – a personal experience', *LR*, 43 (1972), 83.
62 Giel and van Luijk, 'Leprosy', p. 188.
63 J. A. Kinnear Brown, 'Foundation of the leper settlement', in Fox, *Uzuakoli*, pp. 108–9.
64 Russell L. Robertson, 'Garkida Agricultural–Industrial Leprosy Colony', *LR*, 3 (1932), 55.
65 Electra Dory, *Leper country* (London, 1963), p. 40. (I owe this reference to Dr M. A. Vaughan.)
66 See, e.g., Williams to Medical Director, 1 May 1921, ZNA A/3/12/9/117; 'Annual report: Health Department: Pemba: 1949', Tallack papers, RH.
67 E. Muir, 'Some mental aspects of leprosy', *LR*, 10 (1939), 118.
68 Dory, *Leper country*, p. 44.
69 Lambert, 'My life', pp. 1, 4.
70 Dory, *Leper country*, is an outstanding account.
71 Ian Linden, *Catholics, peasants, and Chewa resistance in Nyasaland, 1889–1939* (London, 1974), p. 69; *MC*, 65 (1933), 126; *MC*, 81 (1949), 11.
72 Graham Greene, *A burnt-out case* (London, 1961), p. 20.
73 Muir, 'Leprosy in Tanganyika', pp. 63, 68; *Mission field*, 67 (1922), 108; S. G. Browne, 'Leprosy', in E. E. Sabben-Clare and others (eds.), *Health in Africa during the colonial period* (Oxford, 1980), p. 73.
74 Elizabeth Isichei, 'Christians and martyrs in Bonny, Ora and Lokoja', in her *Varieties*, p. 76; *The forty-fifth annual report of the British Leprosy Relief Association, 1968* (London, n.d.), p. 3.
75 Lambert, 'My life', p. 12; 'Report of the first annual meeting of the Leprosy Board held at Morgenster: September 1st 1922', ZNA A/3/12/9; Robertson, 'Garkida', p. 60.
76 James A. K. Brown, 'Leprosy in Southern Nigeria', *WAMJ*, 9 (1936–7), 14; *The Cowley evangelist* (1917), 267; Zanzibar, *Medical reports*, 1935 p. 15, 1936 p. 50.
77 Muir, 'Leprosy in Nigeria', p. 61.
78 Brown in Fox, *Uzuakoli*, p. 110.
79 Gahama, *Le Burundi*, p. 270; Browne in Sabben-Clare and others, *Health*, p. 76.
80 Brown, 'Leprosy in Southern Nigeria', p. 13; E. Muir, 'Leprosy in East Africa', *IJL*, 7 (1939), 389; Davey, 'Uzuakoli', p. 184; E. Muir, 'Leprosy in Nigeria', *LR*, 7 (1936), 158.
81 R. G. Cochrane, 'Report on visit to Nigeria', *LR*, 24 (1953), 46; T. F. Davey, 'Leprosy control in the Owerri Province', *LR*, 14 (1943), 54.
82 T. F. Davey, 'Leprosy control in the Owerri Province', *LR*, 13 (1942), 34.
83 *Idem*, 'Leprosy control in the Owerri Province', *LR*, 14 (1943), 57.
84 *Idem*, 'Decline of leprosy in a group of Nigerian villages between 1941 and 1956', *IJL*, 25 (1957), 333, 335; Hunter and Thomas, 'Hypothesis', p. 32.

85 E.g. P. D. Strachan, 'Leprosy and leprosy treatment in Basutoland', *IJL*, 2 (1934), 436–9; Moiser, 'Leprosy in Southern Rhodesia', pp. 110–11.

86 Charles C. Shepard, 'Experimental chemotherapy in leprosy, then and now', *IJL*, 41 (1973), 307; A. B. A. Karat and K. Ramanujam, 'A century of progress in the therapy of leprosy', *ibid.*, 382; M. Hooper, 'The search for new drugs for the treatment of leprosy', *LR*, 56 (1985), 59; *Encyclopaedia Britannica* (13th edn, 1970), vol. 13, p. 981.

87 G. H. Faget and R. C. Pogge, 'Treatment of leprosy with Diasone – a preliminary report', *LR*, 18 (1947), 17–23.

88 Rogers, *Happy toil*, p. 210.

89 Jopling, *Handbook*, pp. 85–6.

90 John Lowe and Michael Smith, 'The chemotherapy of leprosy in Nigeria', *IJL*, 17 (1949), 181; *LR*, 26 (1955), 127; Zanzibar, *Medical report 1951*, pp. 9, 11; *LR*, 25 (1954), 206; *LR*, 37 (1966), 131.

91 Dory, *Leper country*, p. 186.

92 George Seaver, *Albert Schweitzer* (6th edn, London, 1969), p. 176; Browne in Sabben-Clare and others, *Health*, p. 78.

93 N. F. Lyons and B. P. B. Ellis, 'Leprosy in Zimbabwe', *LR*, 54 (1983), 48; Zanzibar, *Medical report 1956*, p. 11; Schulz and Pentz, 'Leprosy control', p. 17; South Africa, *Report of the Director-General for Health, Welfare and Pensions 1980,* p. 81.

94 Schram, *History*, p. 361; R. Cheneveau, 'La lutte contre la lèpre en A.E.F.', *Médecine d'Afrique Noire*, 5 (1958), 535; Browne in Sabben-Clare and others, *Health*, p. 70.

95 J. Ross Innes, 'Editorial', *LR*, 33 (1962), 170.

96 B. D. Molesworth, 'Malawi leprosy control project', *Society of Malawi journal*, 21, 1 (January 1968), 58–69; *LR*, 45 (1974), 334; A. H. Drake and C. McDougall, '"Mobile" leprosy control in the Eastern Province of Zambia', *LR*, 41 (1970), 107; *LR*, 45 (1974), 80.

97 E. van Praag and S. A. Mwankemwa, 'A prevalence survey . . . in Muheza district, Tanzania', *LR*, 53 (1982), 28; *LR*, 48 (1977), 43; *LR*, 53 (1982), 314–15; A. C. McDougall, 'Leprosy in the Sudan', *LR*, 46 (1975), 226.

98 Michael Gelfand, *Lakeside pioneers: socio-medical study of Nyasaland* (Oxford, 1964), p. 294; Nyasaland, *Medical report 1923*, p. 10; F. Oldrieve, 'Memorandum on leprosy work in the Nyasaland Protectorate', 19 May 1927, MNA M/2/5/12/52a; Innes to DMS, 30 April 1950, MNA DC Blantyre MD/12/1; Molesworth, 'Project', p. 64.

99 *LR*, 29 (1958), 6; H. J. R. Meesters, 'Leprosy control in the Gambia', *LR*, 51 (1980), 215, 219; H. Sansarricq, 'The general situation of leprosy in the world', *Ethiopian medical journal*, 20 (1982), 99.

100 'Annual report of the Native Commissioner at Mtoko for the year ended 31st December 1960', ZNA 71881/33 (temporary file number); Schram, *History*, p. 358; Haidar Abu Ahmed, 'Leprosy in the Sudan', *LR*, 46 (1975), 219.

101 Thomas F. Frist, 'A developing country, leprosy conrol, and the severely disabled', *LR*, 44 (1973), 92 (referring to central Tanzania).

102 K. F. Schaller, 'Zur Epidemiologie der Lepra in Aethiopien', *Zeitschrift für Tropenmedizin und Parasitologie*, 10 (1959), 91, 93; S. G. Browne, 'Leprosy control in Ethiopia', *LR*, 45 (1974), 78; *Ethiopia observer*, 9 (1966), 263; Schneider, *Leprosy*, p. 61.

103 Schneider, *Leprosy*, ch. 5; Father Nicholas and R. Giel, 'A spontaneous leprosy settlement in Ethiopia', *Tropical and geographical medicine*, 23 (1971), 289–93.

104 J. M. H. Pearson and others, 'Sulphone resistance in leprosy', *Lancet*, 12 July 1975, pp. 69–72.

105 Jopling, *Handbook*, p. 1; G. Weddell and Elisabeth Palmer, 'The pathogenesis of leprosy', *LR*, 34 (1963), 59; D. L. Leiker, 'On the mode of transmission of Mycobacterium leprae', *LR*, 48 (1977), 9; *IJL*, 52 (1984), supplement, p. 678; Hunter and Thomas, 'Hypothesis', p. 41.

106 S. R. Pattyn and others, 'Prevalence of secondary dapsone-resistant leprosy in Upper Volta', *LR*, 55 (1984), 367; J. M. H. Pearson, 'Dapsone-resistant leprosy', *LR*, 54 (1983), 87.

107 T. W. Meade, 'How effective is the treatment of leprosy?' *LR*, 48 (1977), 6; A. D. Askew, 'Managerial implications of multidrug therapy', *LR*, 56 (1985), 97; *IJL*, 52 (1984), supplement, p. 742.

108 H. Sansarricq, 'Recent changes in leprosy control', *LR*, 54 (1983), 125; Ji Baohong, 'Drug resistance in leprosy – a review', *LR*, 56 (1985), 273.

109 Richard C. Browne, 'Death and rebirth of a leprosy service', *LR*, 47 (1976), 69–70; Ahmed, 'Leprosy in the Sudan', p. 222; *LR*, 42 (1971), 6; *LR*, 51 (1980), 89; *IJL*, 52 (1984), supplement, p. 742.

110 Sansarricq, 'Recent changes', pp. 10, 14; *LR*, 47 (1976), 145; Sansarricq, 'General situation', pp. 92, 95.

111 M. Ziedses des Plantes and others, 'Leprosy in Kenya', *EAMJ*, 45 (1968), 371–7; Van Praag and Mwankemwa, 'Prevalence survey', pp. 31–2.

112 W. F. Kirchheimer and Eleanor E. Storrs, 'Attempts to establish the armadillo ... as a model for the study of leprosy', *IJL*, 39 (1971), 693–702.

113 Sansarricq, 'Recent changes', p. 13.

13 The growth of poverty in independent Africa

1 ILO/JASPA, *Basic needs in danger: a basic needs oriented development strategy for Tanzania* (Addis Ababa, 1982), p. 88; Franklyn Lisk and Rolph van der Hoeven, 'Measurement and interpretation of poverty in Sierra Leone', *ILR*, 118 (1979), 721, 723.

2 World Bank, *World development report 1986* (New York, 1986), p. 180.

3 ILO/JASPA, *Basic needs in an economy under pressure* (2 vols., Addis Ababa, 1981), vol. 2, p. 53; Dharam Ghai and Samir Radwan (eds.), *Agrarian policies and rural poverty in Africa* (Geneva, 1983), p. 10.

4 Ghai and Radwan, *Agrarian policies*, p. 13; Montek S. Ahluwalia and others, 'Growth and poverty in developing countries', *Journal of development economics*, 6 (1979), 302–4; Reginald Herbold Green and Hans Singer, 'Sub-Saharan Africa in depression', *World development*, 12 (1984), 284.

5 World Bank, *World development report 1986*, p. 180.

6 Assefa Bequele and Rolf van der Hoeven, 'Poverty and inequality in sub-Saharan Africa', *ILR*, 119 (1980), 384; ILO/JASPA, *Basic needs in danger*, pp. 256, 258, 270, 273.

7 Frances Stewart, *Planning to meet basic needs* (London, 1985), p. 81; Ahluwalia and others, 'Growth', p. 333; Collier and Lal, *Labour and poverty in Kenya*, p. 277.

8 World Bank, *World development report 1986*, p. 232.

9 World Bank, *The Gambia*, p. 20.

10 Great Britain: House of Commons, *Second report from the Foreign Affairs Committee: session 1984–85: Famine in Africa*, House of Commons Paper 56 (London, 1985), pp. x, 154.

11 World Bank, *The Gambia*, pp. v, 27, 49, 52, 82.

12 World Bank, *World development report 1986*, p. 228.

13 *Ibid.*

14 One estimate suggested that in order to maintain services at existing standards, 4 per cent of Gross National Income must be invested for each 1 per cent of population growth. See Etienne van de Walle, 'The relationship between population change and economic development in tropical Africa', in John C. Caldwell and Chukuka Okonjo (eds.), *The population of tropical Africa* (London, 1968), p. 361.

15 David Wheeler, 'Sources of stagnation in sub-Saharan Africa', *World development*, 12 (1984), 1, 4. See also David Fieldhouse, *Black Africa 1945–80* (London, 1986), p. 104.

16 ILO/JASPA, *Economy under pressure*, vol. 1, p. xxv.
17 Green and Singer, 'Depression', p. 290; Great Britain, *Famine in Africa*, p. 155.
18 World Bank, *Accelerated development in sub-Saharan Africa* (Washington, DC, 1981), p. 18; Stewart, *Planning*, p. 185.
19 Wheeler, 'Sources', p. 5; Fieldhouse, *Black Africa*, p. 106; Great Britain, *Famine in Africa*, pp. 149, 196.
20 For these trends, see Tony Killick, *Development economics in action* (London, 1978); Thomas M. Callaghy, *The state–society struggle: Zaire in comparative perspective* (New York, 1984); William I. Jones, *Planning and economic policy: socialist Mali and her neighbors* (Washington, DC, 1976); Fieldhouse, *Black Africa*.
21 Tina Wallace, 'The Kano River Project, Nigeria', in Judith Heyer and others (eds.), *Rural development in tropical Africa* (London, 1981), pp. 301–2; Steven Langdon, 'Multinational corporations, taste transfer and underdevelopment', *ROAPE*, 2 (1975), 12–35; J. G. Kydd and R. E. Christiansen, *Structural change and trends in equity in the Malawian economy 1964–1980* (Zomba, 1981), pp. 95–6; Great Britain, *Famine in Africa*, pp. 202–3; Philip Raikes, 'Food policy and production in Mozambique since independence', *ROAPE*, 29 (1984), 101–4.
22 Brooke Grundfest Schoepf, 'Food crisis and class formation in Shaba', *ROAPE*, 33 (August 1985), 39.
23 Fieldhouse, *Black Africa*, p. 242; ILO/JASPA, *Economy under pressure*, vol. 1, pp. xxvi–xxvii.
24 ILO/JASPA, *Economy under pressure*, vol. 1, p. xxvi; J. R. Bibangambah, 'Approaches to the study of rural poverty in Africa', in Fassil G. Kiros (ed.), *Challenging rural poverty* (Trenton, NJ, 1985), p. 39.
25 Keith Wrightson and David Levine, *Poverty and piety in an English village: Terling, 1525–1700* (New York, 1979), p. 7.
26 See Charles Elliott, *Patterns of poverty in the Third World* (New York, 1975), *passim*, esp. pp. 20, 60.
27 Collier and Lal, *Labour and poverty in Kenya*, pp. 79–80.
28 Paul Collier and Deepak Lal, *Poverty and growth in Kenya*, World Bank Staff Working Paper 389 (Washington, DC, 1980), p. 26.
29 Collier and Lal, *Labour and poverty in Kenya*, pp. 146–7, 153 n. 22.
30 Diana Hunt, *The impending crisis in Kenya* (Aldershot, 1984), p. 176.
31 Collier and Lal, *Labour and poverty in Kenya*, pp. 80, 261.
32 See Collier and others, *Labour and poverty in Tanzania*, pp. 76–7, 95, 105–6; Jonathan Kydd, *Measuring peasant differentiation for policy purposes* (Zomba, 1982), pp. 137–8.
33 Michael Bratton, *Beyond community development: the political economy of rural administration in Zimbabwe* (Gwelo, 1978), p. 9; Ranger, *Peasant consciousness*, p. 304.
34 Pottier, 'Politics', p. 236.
35 Mahmood Mamdani, 'Analyzing the agrarian question: the case of a Buganda village', *Mawazo* (Kampala), 5, 3 (June 1984), 49–58.
36 E. S. Clayton, 1967, quoted in his 'Agriculture and rehabilitation in Kigezi, Uganda, 1946–66', duplicated, Workshop on Conservation in Africa, Cambridge, 1985.
37 Iliffe in McCracken, *Malawi*, pp. 276–7.
38 Dessalegn Rahmato, 'The Ethiopian experience in agrarian reform', in Kiros, *Challenging*, pp. 209, 214.
39 Dirk Kohnert, 'Rural class differentiation in Nigeria', *Afrika spectrum* (1979), 307.
40 ILO/JASPA, *Economy under pressure*, vol. 1, pp. 13–14; *idem*, *Basic needs in danger*, p. 320.
41 For a striking example, see Richard Hogg, 'The politics of drought: the pauperization of Isiolo Boran', *Disasters*, 9 (1985), 39–43.

42 *West Africa*, 6 April 1981, p. 735; Eddy Lee, 'Export-led rural development: the Ivory Coast', in Ghai and Radwan, *Agrarian policies*, p. 113.
43 N. O. Addo, 'Employment and labour supply on Ghana's cocoa farms', *Economic bulletin of Ghana*, 2, 4 (1972), 45; Ghai and Radwan, *Agrarian policies*, p. 15; *West Africa*, 15 April 1985, p. 735; René Lemarchand, 'The politics of penury in rural Zaire', in Guy Gran (ed.), *Zaire: the political economy of underdevelopment* (New York, 1979), p. 247; A. K. H. Weinrich, *African marriage in Zimbabwe and the impact of Christianity* (Gweru, 1982), p. 31.
44 Vidal, 'Economie', p. 66 n. 1; Kagabo and Mudandagizi, 'Complainte', p. 87.
45 Ezeanya, '*Osu*', p. 45; Okwu, 'Mission', p. 646.
46 Derman, *Serfs*, p. 247.
47 Bernd Baldus, 'Responses to dependence in a servile group: the Machube of northern Benin', in Miers and Kopytoff, *Slavery*, ch. 17; Jones, *Planning*, p. 290; Bernus, *Touaregs nigériens*, pp. 111–12.
48 'Slavery in Mauritania in 1980', *Anti-slavery reporter*, seventh series, 13, 1 (December 1981), 15–17; *West Africa*, 12 July 1982, pp. 1817–18.
49 Liz Wily, *Land allocation and hunter-gatherer land rights in Botswana* (London, 1980), pp. 5, 88–9, 98; Richard B. Lee, *The !Kung San* (Cambridge, 1979), pp. 424–6.
50 Stephen, *San*, pp. 11–13; Yellen, 'Process', pp. 19–20.
51 Stephen, *San*, p. 13; Lee and De Vore, *Hunter-gatherers*, pp. 20, 123, 127; Robert K. Hitchcock, 'Tradition, social justice and land reform in central Botswana', in Richard P. Werbner (ed.), *Land reform in the making* (London, 1982), p. 7.
52 Lucy Syson, 'Social conditions in the Shoshong area', *BNR*, 4 (1972), 49, 52.
53 Stephen, *San*, p. 14.
54 Barbara Watanabe and Eva Mueller, 'A poverty profile for rural Botswana', *World development*, 12 (1984), 116.
55 Christopher Colclough and Peter Fallon, 'Rural poverty in Botswana', in Ghai and Radwan, *Agrarian policies*, p. 136; Sherrie Kossoudji and Eva Mueller, 'The economic and demographic status of female-headed households in rural Botswana', *EDCC*, 31 (1982–3), 832.
56 Pauline Peters, 'Gender, developmental cycles and historical process', *JSAS*, 10 (1983–4), 116–17; Kossoudji and Mueller, 'Economic status', pp. 838, 843–4; Hoyt Alverson, *Mind in the heart of darkness* (New Haven, 1978), p. 54; David Cooper, 'An overview of the Botswana urban class structure', University of Cape Town, Centre for African Studies, *Africa seminar collected papers*, vol. 2 (1981), p. 152.
57 Kossoudji and Mueller, 'Economic status', p. 845; Colclough and Fallon in Ghai and Radwan, *Agrarian policies*, p. 146.
58 Du Pradal, 'Poverty', pp. 3, 16.
59 Dave M. Cooper, 'An interpretation of the emergent urban class structure in Botswana: a case study of Selebi-Phikwe miners', Ph.D. thesis, University of Birmingham, 1982, p. 351; Watanabe and Mueller, 'Poverty profile', p. 126; Jack Parson, 'The working class, the state and social change in Botswana', *SALB*, 5, 5 (January 1980), 54 n. 14.
60 Du Pradal, 'Poverty', p. 28.
61 Cooper, 'Overview', pp. 139–41.
62 Cowen, 'Differentiation', p. 4; Collier and Lal, *Poverty and growth in Kenya*, p. 27.
63 Jeanne K. Henn, 'Peasants, workers, and capital: the political economy of labor and incomes in Cameroon', Ph.D thesis, Harvard University, 1978, p. 280; Watts, *Silent violence*, pp. 448–59; Kohnert, 'Rural class differentiation', pp. 310–11.
64 Hill, *Rural Hausa*, p. 61; Hill, *Population*, p. 113.
65 Hill, *Rural Hausa*, ch. 13; Hill, *Population*, ch. 11.
66 Paul Richards, *Coping with hunger* (London, 1986), pp. 116–17.

67 Jordan Gebre-Medhin, 'The Eritrean Peoples Liberation Front and the rural poor', *Mawazo*, 5, 3 (June 1984), 81.
68 ILO/JASPA, *Economy under pressure*, vol. 1, pp. 18, 118, and vol. 2, pp. 76, 124; Roger Leys, 'Drought and relief in southern Zimbabwe', in Peter Lawrence (ed.), *World recession and the food crisis in Africa* (London, 1986), pp. 263–4.
69 Hirschmann and Vaughan, 'Food production', p. 98.
70 Watts, *Silent violence*, pp. 404, 413.
71 Sam Jackson, 'Hausa women on strike', *ROAPE*, 13 (May 1978), 24.
72 ILO/JASPA, *Economy under pressure*, vol. 1, p. 23.
73 Elliott, *Patterns*, p. 34; Joseph W. Ssennyonga, 'The Maragoli population trends', University of Nairobi, IDS Paper 107, 1978, p. 19.
74 Hunt, *Impending crisis*, p. 81
75 Richards, *Coping*, pp. 115, 117, 128.
76 Christopher Beer, *The politics of peasant groups in Western Nigeria* (Ibadan, 1976), pp. 160, 189, 222; Renée C. Fox and others, '"The second independence": a case study of the Kwilu rebellion', *Comparative studies in society and history*, 7 (1965–6), 95; Gebre-Medhin, 'Liberation Front', pp. 77–87.
77 Jack Goody, 'Rice burning and the Green Revolution in northern Ghana', *Journal of development studies*, 16 (1979–80), 151. See also Collier and Lal, *Poverty and growth in Kenya*, p. 29 n. 1; Jan Kees van Donge, 'Understanding rural Zambia today', *Africa*, 55 (1985), 71; René Lefort, *Ethiopie: la révolution hérétique* (Paris, 1981), p. 154.
78 Jay O'Brien, 'Sowing the seeds of famine: the political economy of food deficits in Sudan', *ROAPE*, 33 (August 1985), 31; Jean-Louis Ormières, 'Les conséquences politiques de la famine', in Copans (ed.), *Sécheresses*, vol. 1, p. 144; Michael Mortimore, 'Famine in Hausaland, 1973', *Savanna*, 2 (1973), 106.
79 Benoit Verhaegen, *Rebellions au Congo* (2 vols., Léopoldville, 1966–9), vol. 1, p. 20.
80 O'Connor, *City*, p. 17.
81 *West Africa*, 25 January 1982, p. 269, and 12 July 1982, p. 1818; Patel and Adams, *Chirambahuyo*, pp. 1, 37; Ishumi, *Urban jobless*, p. 22; O'Connor, *City*, p. 49.
82 Michael Watts and Paul Lubeck, 'The popular classes and the oil boom', in I. W. Zartman (ed.), *The political economy of Nigeria* (New York, 1983), p. 131; Collier and Lal, *Labour and poverty in Kenya*, p. 87.
83 O'Connor, *City*, pp. 53, 62, 68.
84 Olanrewaju J. Fapohunda and Harold Lubell, *Lagos: urban development and employment* (Geneva, 1978), p. 27; Watts and Lubeck in Zartman, *Political economy*, p. 131.
85 ILO/JASPA, *Basic needs in danger*, p. 126; *Moto* (Gweru), 45 [May 1986] 6; Kouamé N'Guessan, 'Devant et derrière les murs', in Philippe Haeringer (ed.), *Abidjan au coin de la rue* (Paris, 1983), p. 453.
86 *West Africa*, 27 May 1985, p. 1043.
87 ILO, *First things first: meeting the basic needs of the people of Nigeria* (Addis Ababa, 1981), p. 13; Onokerhoraye, *Social services*, pp. 239–41.
88 J. O. C. Onyemelukwe, 'Urban slums in Nigeria', *Journal of environmental management*, 13 (1981), 112, 116.
89 O'Connor, *City*, p. 185.
90 Nici Nelson, 'How women and men get by', in Ray Bromley and Chris Gerry (eds.), *Casual work and poverty in Third World cities* (Chichester, 1979), p. 286; Nelson, 'Some aspects: paper I', pp. 3–4; Nelson, 'Some aspects: paper II', p. 2.
91 Ann and Thomas Schlyter, *George – the development of a squatter settlement in Lusaka* (Stockholm, 1979), pp. 26, 29.
92 Margaret Peil with Pius O. Sada, *African urban society* (Chichester, 1984), p. 283.

93 Susan T. Barnes, 'Migration and land acquisition: the new landowners of Lagos', *African urban studies*, 4 (Spring 1979), 59–70; F. J. C. Amos, 'Housing and town-planning', in University College of Addis Ababa, *Social survey*, p. 108.
94 See David Etherton (ed.), *Mathare Valley* (Nairobi, 1971), pp. 10, 54–6; Philip Amis, 'Squatters or tenants: the commercialization of unauthorized housing in Nairobi', *World development*, 12 (1984), 87–96.
95 Elliott, *Patterns*, pp. 279–80; Gutkind, 'Energy', p. 191.
96 Houyoux, 'Les conditions de vie', p. 99; Sandbrook and Arn, *Labouring poor*, p. 29.
97 Collier and Lal, *Labour and poverty in Kenya*, p. 64; Robert H. Bates, *Unions, parties, and political development* (New Haven, 1971), p. 73; Elliott, *Patterns*, p. 221.
98 Collier and Lal, *Labour and poverty in Kenya*, p. 92; ILO/JASPA, *Basic needs in danger*, pp. 256, 268; ILO, *First things first*, p. 224.
99 Great Britan, *Famine in Africa*, p. 149; *West Africa*, 24 December 1984, p. 2642.
100 *West Africa*, 13 April 1981, p. 785, and 28 January 1985, p. 184; Katabaro Miti, 'L'opération Nguvu Kazi à Dar es Salaam', *Politique africaine*, 17 (March 1985), 91; *Moto*, 46 [July 1986] 10.
101 Peil, *Cities*, pp. 34, 38; *West Africa*, 14 July 1986, p. 1495; Collier and Lal, *Labour and poverty in Kenya*, pp. 247–8.
102 Collier and Lal, *Labour and poverty in Kenya*, p. 246.
103 Sandbrook and Arn, *Labouring poor*, p. 22.
104 ILO, *Employment, incomes and equality* (Geneva, 1972), p. 9. See also Collier and Lal, *Labour and poverty in Kenya*, pp. 238, 249; Albert Berry and R. H. Sabot, 'Unemployment and economic development', *EDCC*, 33 (1984–5), 111.
105 ILO/JASPA, *Basic needs in danger*, p. 76.
106 Hochet, *Inadaptation*, pp. 129–31, 140–1; E. Costa, 'Back to the land: the campaign against unemployment in Dahomey', *ILR*, 93 (1966), 29–49.
107 Collier and Lal, *Labour and poverty in Kenya*, p. 248; ILO, *First things first*, p. 217; Sandbrook, *Politics*, p. 59.
108 Meine Pieter Van Dijk, 'Les petits entrepreneurs de Dakar', in Deblé and Hugon (eds.), *Vivre*, p. 98.
109 Lisk and van der Hoeven, 'Measurement', p. 720; Sada in Nigerian Economic Society, *Poverty*, p. 99.
110 André Hauser, 'Cent mille personnes devant les grilles', in Haeringer, *Abidjan*, p. 403; O. J. Fapohunda, 'Human resources and the Lagos informal sector', and George Aryee, 'The informal manufacturing sector in Kumasi', in Sethuraman, *Informal sector*, pp. 73, 94, 97.
111 *West Africa*, 11 October 1982, p. 2614.
112 McVicar, 'Twilight', p. 210.
113 *Weekly review* (Nairobi), 18 July 1980, p. 27; Michael Mortimore, *Shifting sands and human sorrow* (Durham, 1985), p. 19; Robertson, *Sharing*, pp. 16–17.
114 *West Africa*, 9 December 1985, p. 2587; John de St Jorre, *The Nigerian Civil War* (London, 1972), p. 30n; ILO, *First things first*, p. 9.
115 Hake, *Metropolis*, p. 202; *West Africa*, 13 October 1980, p. 2045, and 9 July 1984, p. 1417.
116 Kate Currie and Larry Ray, 'State and class in Kenya', *JMAS*, 22 (1984), 570; Lefort, *Ethiopie*, pp. 278–81; Michael A. Cohen, 'The sans-travail demonstrations', *Manpower and unemployment research in Africa*, 5, 1 (April 1972), 22–5; Sandbrook and Arn, *Labouring poor*, p. 6; Pierre Bonnafé, 'Une classe d'âge politique: la JMNR de la République du Congo-Brazzaville', *CEA*, 8 (1968), 327–68.
117 E.g. Arn, 'Political economy', pp. iii, 221–3; Michael G. Schatzberg, *Politics and class in Zaire* (New York, 1980), p. 158; Margaret Peil, *Nigerian politics: the people's view* (London, 1976), esp. ch. 3.

118 Sandbrook and Arn, *Labouring poor*, p. 48.
119 The major source is Nigeria, *Report of Tribunal of Inquiry on Kano Disturbances* (Lagos, 1981). See also G. Nicolas, '"Guerre sainte" à Kano', *Politique africaine*, 1, 4 (November 1981), 47–70; Paul M. Lubeck, 'Islamic protest under semi-industrial capitalism: Yan Tatsine explained', *Africa*, 55 (1985), 369–89.
120 For the changing use of *gardawa*, see Schön, *Dictionary*, part 1, p. 65; Robinson, *Dictionary*, vol. 1, p. 116, and vol. 2, p. 23; Abraham, *Dictionary*, p. 304.
121 Nigeria, *Report of Tribunal*, p. 41.
122 *West Africa*, 12 March 1984, p. 581, and 15 October 1984, pp. 2081–2.
123 *A humanist handbook* (Lusaka, 1976), cited in Schlyter, *George*, p. 57.
124 Quoted in Gutkind, 'Energy', p. 402.
125 Above, p. 181; Peter Stromgaard, 'A subsistence society under pressure: the Bemba', *Africa*, 55 (1985), 50; above, p. 238.
126 Bernard Delpech, 'La solidarité populaire abidjanaise en chiffres et en dires', in Haeringer, *Abidjan*, pp. 551–66; Houyoux, 'Les conditions de vie', p. 99.
127 Howard, 'Kwashiorkor', pp. 210, 216, 246; Rhodesia, *Labour and social welfare report 1973*, p. 36.
128 *Sunday mail* (Harare), 6 July 1986.
129 Onokerhoraye, *Social services*, p. 152; Goody, *Parenthood*, pp. 278–9.
130 D. S. Obikeze, 'What treatment mode? an assessment of alternative childcare methods employed in resettling war-displaced children in Nigeria', *International social work*, 23, 1 (1980), 2–15; Adefunke Oyemade, 'Nourrissons orphelins au Nigéria', *Environnement africain*, 1, 4 (1975), 89–98.
131 Onokerhoraye, *Social services*, p. 151; above, p. 89.
132 Howard, 'Kwashiorkor', pp. 214–15; *Oxfam news*, October 1982.
133 Northern Rhodesia/Zambia, *Social welfare reports*, 1961 p. 4, 1964 p. 5, 1965 p. 6, 1977 p. 12.
134 Onokerhoraye, *Social services*, pp. 154–6; Ada A. Mere, 'Field work instruction in Nigerian schools of social work', *International social work*, 24, 3 (1981), 44.
135 Joe Hampson, SJ, *Old age: a study of aging in Zimbabwe* (Gweru, 1982), pp. 57–63; ILO/JASPA, *Basic needs in danger*, p. 147.
136 ILO/JASPA, *Basic needs in danger*, p. 149; *Salvation Army year book 1981*, p. 117; Hunter, 'Progress', pp. 261–75.
137 J. S. Adoo, 'Services for the physically handicapped', in St Clair Drake and T. Peter Omari (eds.), *Social work in West Africa* (Accra [1963]), p. 93; Southern Rhodesia, *Final report of the April/May 1962 census of Africans* (duplicated, Salisbury, 1964), p. 41.
138 Adrian M. Bain, 'Historical note on poliomyelitis in Uganda', *EAMJ*, 43 (1966), 62; *The world's children* (December 1975), 21; B. Oscar Barry, 'Review of infantile paralysis in Addis Ababa', *Ethiopian medical journal*, 3, 1 (October 1964), 3.
139 A. J. Walker, 'Poliomyelitis in Kenya', *EAMJ*, 33 (1956), 169–80; B. Kaur and D. Metselaar, 'Poliomyelitis in Kenya: the 1965–1966 epidemic', *EAMJ*, 44 (1967), 74–82.
140 *The world's children* (December 1975), 21.
141 Audibert, 'Le service social', vol. 2, p. 530; W. R. F. Collis and others, 'Poliomyelitis in Nigeria', *WAMJ*, NS, 10 (1961), 217–22; Barry, 'Review', p. 10; J. Andre and others, 'Poliomyelitis in Addis Ababa', *Ethiopian medical journal*, 3, 1 (October 1964), 16.
142 *The world's children*, 44 (1964), 25; Schram, *History*, p. 381; T. O. Harry and G. M. R. Munube, 'Residual polio paralysis in urban and rural school children of Lagos State, Nigeria', *EAMJ*, 59 (1982), 833; Zimbabwe: Ministry of Labour and Social Services, *Report on the national disability survey of Zimbabwe* (Harare [1983]), pp. 34, 46.
143 Adoo in Drake and Omari, *Social work*, pp. 93–8; *Advance*, 41 (January 1964), 26; Walker, 'Disabled', p. 148.

144 Zambia, *Social development report 1967*, p. 36; Kenya, *Community development report 1968*, p. 1; Nigeria, *Building the new Nigeria: social services* (Apapa, 1971), p. 23.
145 Zimbabwe, *National disability survey, passim.*
146 Gold Coast, *Legislative Assembly debates, 1956–57*, first series, vol. 3, pp. 484, 496, 776.
147 *Advance*, 37 (January 1963), 14; Adoo in Drake and Omari, *Social work*, p. 95; Sandbrook and Arn, *Labouring poor*, p. 34; Ghana, *Social welfare reports*, 1961 p. 18, 1971 p. 11.
148 City Council of Nairobi, *Social services report 1965*, p. 29; Zambia, *Social welfare report 1972*, p. 8.
149 Onokerhoraye, *Social services*, p. 155.
150 Nicholas van Hear, '"By-day" boys and dariga men: casual labour versus agrarian capital in northern Ghana', *ROAPE*, 31 (December 1984), 53; above, p. 245; Sembene Ousmane, *Xala* (trans. C. Wake, London, 1976), pp. 107–14.
151 James Ngugi, *Petals of blood* (London, 1977), p. 291.
152 Zimbabwe, *National disability survey*, p. 52.
153 The best account is Seeley, 'Praise'.
154 *The world's children* (September 1984), 10.
155 E.g. Nandasena Ratnapala, *The Sarvodaya movement* (Essex, Conn., 1978).
156 *West Africa*, 30 January 1984, p. 243; Ghana, *Social welfare report 1959*, p. 5; Lefort, *Ethiopie*, p. 382.
157 Mouton, *Social security*, pp. 4–8, 38; International Social Security Association, *Sixth African Regional Conference, Cairo, 16–21 October 1978* (Geneva, 1980), p. 194.
158 J. V. Gruat, 'The extension of social protection in the Gabonese Republic', *ILR*, 123 (1984), 457–71.
159 Mouton, *Social security*, pp. 31, 55–7, 84–92; International Social Security Association, *Sixth African Conference*, pp. 110–13.
160 Ghana, *Social welfare report 1971*, p. 1.
161 See Vukani Gaskell Nyirenda, 'Social change and social policy in a developing country: the Zambian case', DSW thesis, University of California at Los Angeles, 1975; Kachingwe, 'Social welfare services'; Midgley, *Professional imperialism*, pp. xiii–xiv, 117, 125, 128, 150–7.
162 Zambia, *Social welfare reports*, 1962 pp. 25–6, 1970 p. 14, 1971 p. 19, 1974 p. 2, 1976 p. 10, 1978 pp. 3, 12, 17.
163 Frank W. Lowenstein, 'An epidemic of kwashiorkor in the South Kasai, Congo', *Bulletin of the World Health Organization*, 27 (1962), 751.
164 *Oxfam news*, October 1966.
165 See René Lemarchand (ed.), *African kingships in perspective* (London, 1977), part 2.
166 Neville Rubin, 'Africa and refugees', *African affairs*, 73 (1974), 298–9.
167 Cato Aall, 'Relief, nutrition and health problems in the Nigerian/Biafran War', *Journal of tropical pediatrics*, 16 (1970), 74; Aaron E. Ifekwunigwe, 'Recent field experiences in Eastern Nigeria (Biafra)', in Gunnar Blix and others (eds.), *Famine* (Uppsala, 1971), p. 144.
168 *The world's children*, 48 (1968), 52.
169 *Ibid.*, 48 (1968), 76–9, and 49 (1969), 4; St Jorre, *Nigerian War*, pp. 125, 208, 230, 404; Ifekwunigwe in Blix and others, *Famine*, pp. 150–2.
170 Aderanti Adepoju, 'The dimension of the refugee problem in Africa', *African affairs*, 81 (1982), 21, 28, 30, 34.
171 *Ibid.*, 26, 30; Great Britain, *Famine in Africa*, p. 246.
172 Robert Chambers, 'Rural refugees in Africa', *Disasters*, 3 (1979), 382, 387; Colclough and Fallon in Ghai and Radwan, *Agrarian policies*, p. 137; Great Britain, *Famine in Africa*, p. 181.

173 M. J. Roberts, *Famine and floods in Kenya 1961* (Nairobi, 1962); Anne M. S. Graham, 'Adapting to water shortage in a year of poor rains: a case study from the Sudan', *Savanna*, 2 (1973), 121–5; Adolfo C. Mascarenhas, 'Resettlement and desertification: the Wagogo of Dodoma District', *Economic geography*, 53 (1977), 377.
174 S. J. K. Baker, 'A background to the study of drought in East Africa', in Dalby and others, *Drought 2*, p. 77; *Oxfam news*, October 1965; Ethiopia, *Challenges*, p. 77.
175 Tyson in Hinchey, *Proceedings*, pp. 49–50; *SAO*, 93 (1963), 146, and 95 (1965), 65; *Oxfam news*, October 1965 and May 1968.
176 *Oxfam news*, June 1968.
177 Jonathan Derrick, 'The great West African drought, 1972–1974', *African affairs*, 76 (1977), 543–5; Hal Sheets and Roger Morris, *Disaster in the desert* (Washington, DC, 1974), pp. 85, 92, 110; Jacques Giri, *Le Sahel demain* (Paris, 1983), p. 128.
178 The figure 100,000, often quoted, was apparently a misunderstanding. See Sheets and Morris, *Disaster*, pp. 1, 49, 133; J. C. Caldwell, 'Demographic aspects of drought', in Dalby and others, *Drought 2*, pp. 94–5.
179 Ethiopia, *Challenges*, ch. 3; D. S: Miller and J. F. J. Holt, 'The Ethiopian famine', *Proceedings of the Nutritional Society*, 34 (1975), 168–9.
180 Figure from Miller and Holt, 'Ethiopian famine', p. 171. The official figure was 200,000: Ethiopia, *Challenges*, p. 77.
181 *Oxfam news*, July 1975; Gunnar Haaland and Willem Keddeman, 'Poverty analysis: the case of rural Somalia', *EDCC*, 32 (1983–4), 855.
182 Jonathan Derrick, 'West Africa's worst year of famine', *African affairs*, 83 (1984), 283; *West Africa*, 22 October 1984, p. 2142, 3 December 1984, pp. 2438–40, and 18 March 1985, p. 540.
183 *The world's children*, December 1980.
184 *Africa emergency* (New York), 5 (November 1985).
185 Robert J. McKerrow, 'Drought in Ethiopia 1977/1979', *Disasters*, 3 (1979), 131–3; Ethiopia, *Challenges*, pp. 146–7, 171–2; Great Britain, *Famine in Africa*, pp. xxv, 13, 83.
186 O'Brien, 'Sowing', pp. 23–4, 31; Great Britain, *Famine in Africa*, p. xviii; *Africa emergency*, 7 (May 1986).
187 Above, p. 156; Nicholson, 'Climatic variations', p. 12; Grove in Dalby and others, *Drought 2*, p. 58; Farmer and Wigley, *Climatic trends*, pp. 58, 106.
188 Farmer and Wigley, *Climatic trends*, pp. 28, 63; Great Britain, *Famine in Africa*, p. 262; *Oxfam news*, Winter 1985–6.
189 Bernus, *Touaregs nigériens*, ch. 20; Giri, *Le Sahel*, p. 121; Leurquin, *Le niveau de vie*, pp. 32, 36–8.
190 Ben Wisner, 'Man-made famine in eastern Kenya', in Phil O'Keefe and Ben Wisner (eds.), *Landuse and development* (London, 1977), p. 195; John Seaman and Julius Holt, 'Markets and famines in the Third World', *Disasters*, 4 (1980), 285.
191 Great Britain, *Famine in Africa*, p. 150.
192 O'Brien, 'Sowing', pp. 29–30; Lars Bondestam, 'People and capitalism in the north-eastern lowlands of Ethiopia', *JMAS*, 12 (1974), 429; Great Britain, *Famine in Africa*, pp. 202–3.
193 Watts, *Silent violence*, ch. 5; van Apeldoorn, *Perspectives,* ch. 11; Mortimore, *Shifting sands*, pp. 20–1.
194 Jean Copans, 'La sécheresse en pays mouride', in his *Sécheresses*, vol. 2, p. 115; Graham, 'Adapting', p. 125; Charles Toupet, 'La grande sécheresse en Mauritanie', in Dalby and others, *Drought 2*, p. 111; van Apeldoorn, *Perspectives*, p. 58.
195 See Caldwell in Dalby and others, *Drought 2*, pp. 96–7; van Apeldoorn, *Perspectives*, p. 58; Mortimore, *Shifting sands*, pp. 11–12.
196 Watts, *Silent violence*, p. 432.

197 Suzanne Lallemand, 'La sécheresse dans un village mossi de Haute-Volta', in Copans, *Sécheresses*, vol. 2, pp. 52–5.
198 *Oxfam news*, October 1973.
199 Ralph H. Faulkingham, 'Ecological constraints and subsistence strategies', in Dalby and others, *Drought 2*, p. 155.
200 S. Belete and others, 'Study of shelter population in the Wollo region', *Journal of tropical pediatrics and environmental child health*, 23 (1977), 15; Christine Messiaut, 'La situation sociale et matérielle des populations', in Copans, *Sécheresses*, p. 73; *Africa emergency*, 3 (July 1985).
201 J. L. Amselle, 'Famine, prolétarisation et création de nouveaux liens de dépendance au Sahel', *Politique africaine*, 1 (1981), 5–22.
202 Van Apeldoorn, *Perspectives*, p. 71.
203 Ifekwunigwe in Blix and others, *Famine*, p. 150; Sheets and Morris, *Disaster*, pp. 85–6, 92, 123; *Africa emergency*, 2 (June 1985); Mulholland, 'Cholera', pp. 247–58; *West Africa*, 25 November 1985, p. 2486.
204 Derrick, 'Great drought', p. 554.
205 *Ibid.*; O'Brien, 'Sowing', p. 31; Ethiopia, *Challenges*, ch. 3.
206 Derrick, 'Great drought', pp. 563–75; van Apeldoorn, *Perspectives*, pp. 44–5, 62, 65, 68.
207 Derrick, 'Worst year', pp. 286–7.
208 Germaine Greer, 'Ethiopia behind the headlines', *The listener*, 24 October 1985, p. 8; John D. Holm and Richard G. Morgan, 'Coping with drought in Botswana: an African success', *JMAS*, 23 (1985), 463–82.
209 Jean Mayer and others, 'Report of the Biafra Study Commission', *Congressional record – Senate*, 91st Congress, 1st Session, 25 February 1969, vol. 115 (33), p. 4372.
210 Van Apeldoorn, *Perspectives*, pp. 36, 151; Sheets and Morris, *Disaster*, p. 86; John Seaman and others, 'An inquiry into the drought situation in Upper Volta', *Lancet* (1973), 777; Great Britain, *Famine in Africa*, pp. 82–7.
211 *The world's children*, June 1974; *Africa emergency*, 3 (July 1985); Greer, 'Ethiopia', p. 8.
212 *Africa emergency*, 4 (September 1985).
213 Aall, 'Relief', p. 79.
214 Miller and Holt, 'Ethiopian famine', p. 170; Ralph H. Faulkingham and Peter F. Thorbahn, 'Population dynamics and drought: a village in Niger', *Population studies*, 29 (1975), 466; Mortimore, 'Famine', p. 104.
215 Mortimore, 'Famine', p. 104.
216 Seaman and Holt, 'Markets', pp. 283–97; Sheets and Morris, *Disaster*, pp. 76–7, 92, 98; Jeremy Shoham, 'Report on a visit to Sudan, November 1984–1985', *Disasters*, 9 (1985), 12–14.
217 As argued in van Apeldoorn, *Perspectives*, p. 3.
218 Victor Piché and Joel Gregory, 'Pour une mise en contexte de la famine', in Dalby and others, *Drought 2*, p. 177; Lars Bondestam, 'Population et capitalisme dans la vallée de l'Aouache', in Amin, *L'agriculture*, p. 320; David Turton, 'Response to drought: the Mursi of southwestern Ethiopia', *Disasters*, 1 (1977), 284; Andrew D. Spiegel, '"Internal" migration and rural differentiation: a field report from the Matatiele/Qacha's Nek region', CCP 51 (1984), 38.
219 Miller and Holt, 'Ethiopian famine', p. 169.
220 Belete and others, 'Study', p. 18.
221 Aall, 'Relief', p. 84; J. P. W. Rivers, 'Women and children last', *Disasters*, 6 (1982), 265–6; Blix and others, *Famine*, pp. 20, 62.
222 Lissner, *Politics of altruism*, pp. 60–5; *Oxfam news*, October 1967.
223 *The world's children*, 51 (1971), 57.

224 *Oxfam news*, September 1971 and August 1976; *Oxfam review*, 1984–5; Greer, 'Ethiopia', p. 7; *The world's children*, December 1985.
225 Pascal Erard and Frédéric Mounier, *Les marchés de la faim* (Paris, 1984), p. 33.
226 See Great Britain, *Famine in Africa*, pp. xxx, 6, 16.
227 *West Africa*, 8 April 1985, p. 666, and 28 October 1985, pp. 2266–7; *Oxfam news*, Winter 1985–6; *Africa emergency*, 4 (September 1985).
228 See p. 279 nn. 1–2.

14 The transformation of poverty in southern Africa

1 Peter Wilkinson, 'The sale of the century? A critical review of recent developments in African housing policy in South Africa', CCP 160 (1984), 10–11.
2 Deryck Humphriss and David G. Thomas, *Benoni* (ed. A. M. Cowley and J. E. Mathewson, Benoni, 1968), pp. 123–34.
3 Pillay, 'Alexandria', pp. 1, 25–8.
4 David Webster, 'The reproduction of labour power and the struggle for survival in Soweto', CCP 20 (1984), 1; *SAO*, 105 (1975), 126.
5 Maasdorp and Humphreys, *Shantytown*, pp. 14, 25, 61; Surplus People Project, *Forced removals in South Africa* (Cape Town: vol. 1, 2nd edn, 1985; vols. 2–5, 1983), vol. 4, p. 198; Gavin Maasdorp, 'Informal housing and informal employment', in David M. Smith (ed.), *Living under apartheid* (London, 1982), p. 161; V. Møller and others, 'Poverty and quality of life among blacks in South Africa', CCP 6 (1984), 18.
6 The best account is Western, *Outcast Cape Town*.
7 George Ellis and others, *The squatter problem in the Western Cape* (Johannesburg, 1977), pp. 6, 15, 24; Pieter Jansen and others, 'Area study of Cape Town: Elsies River', CCP 10c (1984), 11.
8 *SAO*, 111 (1981), 133; Ellis and others, *Squatter problem*, p. 6.
9 *SAO*, 108 (1978), 22.
10 G. Hewatt and others, 'An exploratory study of overcrowding and health issues at Old Crossroads', CCP 14 (1984), 7.
11 *Ibid.*, p. 8.
12 Western, *Outcast Cape Town*, pp. 297–301; *SAO*, 108 (1978), 22; Jane B. Prinsloo, 'A description of income, expenditure and earning patterns from households in Cape Town and Durban', CCP 16 (1984), 13.
13 Wilkinson, 'The sale of the century?'
14 Mercia Wilsworth, 'Poverty and survival: the dynamics of redistribution and sharing in a black South African township', *Social dynamics*, 5, 1 (1979), 18; David Schmidt, 'Beaufort West has many windmills', CCP 35 (1984), 4.
15 Mary-Jane Morifi, 'Life among the poor in Philipstown', CCP 33 (1984), 11, 7.
16 O. Wollheim, quoted in Pinnock, *Brotherhoods*, p. 56.
17 Wilsworth, 'Poverty', pp. 20, 22.
18 C. W. Manona, 'Migration from the farms to towns and its implications for urban adaptation', CCP 30 (1984), 12; Norman Bromberger, 'Unemployment in South Africa', *Social dynamics*, 4, 1 (1978), 21.
19 Julian Hofmeyr, 'Black unemployment: a case study in a peri-urban area of Natal', CCP 123 (1984), 18; Reader, *Portion*, p. 74; B. Dick and others, 'Chronic illness in non-institutionalized persons', *SAMJ*, 53 (1978), 935.
20 Webster, 'Reproduction', p. 6; Philip Mayer, *Townsmen or tribesmen* (2nd edn, Cape Town, 1971), pp. 99–100.
21 *SAO*, 97 (1967), 189; Mia Brandel-Syrier, *Reeftown elite* (London, 1971), p. 48.
22 Wilfried Schärf, 'Street gangs, survival, and political consciousness in the eighties', duplicated, Fifth Workshop on the History of Cape Town, Cape Town, 1985, p. 8.

23 Kramer, 'Self help', p. 132; Eleanor Preston-Whyte, 'Segregation and interpersonal relationships: a case study of domestic service in Durban', in Smith, *Living*, p. 174; Wilson and Mafeje, *Langa*, p. 135.
24 Kramer, 'Self help', pp. 133, 135, 147; Eddie Webster, 'A new frontier of control?' CCP 111 (1984), 10.
25 Martin West, *Bishops and prophets in a black city* (Cape Town, 1975), p. 195; Webster, 'Reproduction', p. 7.
26 J. P. Kiernan, 'Poor and puritan: an attempt to view Zionism as a collective response to urban poverty', *African studies*, 36 (1977), 33–6; West, *Bishops*, p. 195.
27 West, *Bishops*, p. 87.
28 Dinga Sikwebu, 'Area study of Cape Town: profile of Nyanga', CCP 10a (1984), 17.
29 Kiernan, 'Poor and puritan', p. 40.
30 Meth and Piper, 'Social security', p. 41; Jillian Nicholson, 'Problems with the administration of unemployment insurance to Blacks in Natal', CCP 125 (1984), 17.
31 See p. 271.
32 Dick and others, 'Chronic illness', p. 931
33 L. R. Tibbit, 'An evaluation of institutional care of the aged in South Africa', *SAMJ*, 64 (1983), 244; Kramer, 'Self help', p. 127.
34 Kinkead-Weekes, 'Vagrancy', pp. 2, 20–3.
35 South Africa, *Bantu administration reports*, 1960–2 p. 8, 1963 p. 8, 1964 p. 10; *SAO*, 97 (1967), 166.
36 Rogerson, 'Casual poor', p. 291.
37 Webster, 'Reproduction', p. 8; D. Dewar and V. Watson, 'Urbanization, unemployment and petty commodity production and trading', in Smith, *Living*, pp. 132–3.
38 K. S. O. Beavon and C. M. Rogerson, 'The informal sector of the apartheid city: the pavement people of Johannesburg', in Smith, *Living*, pp. 120–1; Nicoli Nattrass, 'Street trading in Transkei', CCP 237 (1984), 11–12.
39 C. N. Ntoane and K. E. Mokoetle, 'Major problems as perceived by the community', CCP 2 (1984), 8; L. F. Freed, 'Prostitution', in *Standard encyclopaedia of southern Africa*, vol. 9 (Cape Town, 1973), p. 156.
40 Pinnock, *Brotherhoods*, pp. 11, 15; Kramer, 'Self help', pp. 47–8.
41 Nat Nakasa, 'Snatching at the good life', in Essop Patel (ed.), *The world of Nat Nakasa* (Johannesburg, 1975), p. 22. See also Maasdorp in Smith, *Living*, p. 157.
42 Andrew Silk, *A shanty town in South Africa: the story of Modderdam* (Johannesburg, 1981), p. 95.
43 Francis Wilson, 'Southern Africa', in Michael Crowder (ed.), *The Cambridge history of Africa, volume 8* (Cambridge, 1984), p. 309; Kramer, 'Self help', p. 24.
44 G. A. Lawrence, 'Epidemiology of stab fatalities in Cape Town, 1981', CCP 185 (1984).
45 Pinnock, *Brotherhoods*, pp. 3–4. They are said to have declined thereafter: see Schärf, 'Street gangs', p. 21.
46 Quoted in Pinnock, *Brotherhoods*, p. 62.
47 *SAO*, 110 (1980), 10; Kinkead-Weekes, 'Vagrancy', p. 24.
48 Pinnock, *Brotherhoods*, p. 69.
49 John Hansen, 'Food and nutrition policy with relation to poverty', CCP 205 (1984), 4, 7; C. M. Ntoane and others, 'Infant mortality in Naphuno', CCP 188 (1984), 8.
50 Buirski in Saunders and others, *Studies*, vol. 5, p. 146; Stewart Fisher, 'Measles and poverty in Port Elizabeth', CCP 172 (1984), 4; Ingrid Le Roux and Nozizwe Nyakaza, 'Philani Nutrition Centre', CCP 217 (1984), 6.
51 Le Roux and Nyakaza, 'Philani', p. 9; Maasdorp and Humphreys, *Shantytown*, p. 69; Hansen, 'Food', p. 8.
52 Pinnock, *Brotherhoods*, p. 58; B. A. Pauw, *The second generation* (Cape Town, 1963), p. 146.

53 Pauw, *Second generation*, pp. 139, 144–5; J. Cock and others, 'Child care and the working mother', CCP 115 (1984), 20–9.
54 Kramer, 'Self help', pp. 126–7; S. B. Burman and J. Barry, 'Divorce and deprivation in South Africa', CCP 87 (1984), 22–32.
55 Virginia van der Vliet, 'Staying single: a strategy against poverty?' CCP 116 (1984).
56 Gaitskell and others, 'Class', pp. 94, 100.
57 Cock, *Maids*, pp. 29, 38, 41, 51, 77, 80; Gadija Berhardien and others, 'Domestic workers in poverty', CCP 114 (1984), 18.
58 Cock, *Maids*, p. 7.
59 Debbie Budlender and others, 'Industrial Council wage rates and poverty', CCP 107 (1984), appendix; SPP, *Forced removals*, vol. 2, pp. 47–53.
60 Francis Wilson, *Labour in the South African gold mines 1911–1969* (Cambridge, 1972), pp. 46, 66; J. B. Knight, 'Is South Africa running out of unskilled labour?' in Wilson and others, *Farm labour*, pp. 43, 50; Merle Lipton, *Capitalism and Apartheid* (Aldershot, 1985), p. 388.
61 Charles Simkins, 'What has been happening to income distribution and poverty in the homelands?' CCP 7 (1984), 5; W. J. Vose, 'Wiehahn and Riekert revisited: a review of prevailing Black labour conditions in South Africa', *ILR*, 124 (1985), 459.
62 Iraj Abedien, 'Public sector policies and income distribution in South Africa during the period 1968–80', CCP 127 (1984), 19; Adam and Giliomee, *Ethnic power*, p. 181; Lodge, *Black politics*, pp. 336–9.
63 Webster, 'Reproduction', p. 5.
64 Norman Reynolds, 'Citizens, the state and employment', CCP 234 (1984), 15, citing the findings of Charles Simkins.
65 Bruce Irvine, 'The psychological effects of unemployment', CCP 126 (1984), appendix, p. 25.
66 Helen Zille, 'Political power and poverty', CCP 83 (1984), 29–30.
67 Francis Wilson, 'Carnegie Conference overview', CCP 311 (1984), 3.
68 Wilson in Crowder, *Cambridge history*, vol. 8, p. 262; Knight in Wilson and others, *Farm labour*, p. 38.
69 Stanley B. Greenberg, *Race and state in capitalist development* (New Haven, 1980), p. 424.
70 SPP, *Forced removals*, vol. 1, p. xxiv; Margaret Roberts, *Labour in the farm economy* (2nd edn, Johannesburg, 1959), pp. 117–18; Nicholas Haysom and Clive Thompson, 'Farm labour and the law', CCP 84 (1984).
71 Roberts, *Labour*, pp. iii, 62; S. J. du Toit, 'African farm labour', *Race relations*, 26 (1959), 77; Knight in Wilson and others, *Farm labour*, p. 50.
72 Knight in Wilson and others, *Farm labour*, p. 47; Laura Levetan, 'Structural shifts in the George economy', CCP 39 (1984), 56, 59; Nomusa Ndaba, 'Nutritional status of adults in Willowmore', CCP 209 (1984), 6; Simkins, 'Income distribution', p. 5.
73 Knight in Wilson and others, *Farm labour,* p. 47; Catherine Schneider, 'Microstudies in Gazankulu', CCP 66 (1984), 11; Patrick Harries, 'Aspects of poverty in Gazankulu', CCP 67 (1984), 6; Michael de Klerk, 'The incomes of farm workers and their families', CCP 28 (1984), 32; Cock, *Maids*, p. 38.
74 Wilson, 'Overview', p. 3.
75 Knight and Lenta, 'Labour reserves', pp. 160, 181; G. Lenta and G. Maasdorp, 'Food production in the homelands', CCP 224 (1984), 3.
76 *SAO*, 107 (1977), 35, and 108 (1978), 148.
77 Knight and Lenta, 'Labour reserves', p. 160.
78 Lodge, *Black politics*, p. 12; J. Baskin, 'Access to land in the Transkei', CCP 45 (1984), 3–5; Elize Moody and Christina Golino, 'Area study of Gazankulu', CCP 252 (1984), 8.

79 Colin Murray, *Families divided: the impact of migrant labour in Lesotho* (Cambridge, 1981), p. 89; Knight and Lenta, 'Labour reserves', p. 181.
80 Lenta and Maasdorp, 'Food production', pp. 11–13.
81 Knight and Lenta, 'Labour reserves', p. 160.
82 *SAO*, 107 (1977), 35; ILO/JASPA, *Options for a dependent economy* (Addis Ababa, 1979), p. 244; Lenta and Maasdorp, 'Food production', p. 13; Jean Comaroff, *Body of power, spirit of resistance* (Chicago, 1985), p. 40.
83 Eleanor Preston-Whyte and Sibongile Nene, 'Where the informal sector is *not* the answer: women and poverty in rural Kwa Zulu', CCP 235 (1984), 3.
84 *Ibid.*, p. 22; Terence Moll, 'A mixed and threadbare bag: employment, incomes and poverty in Lower Roza, Qumbu, Transkei', CCP 47 (1984), 24.
85 Elizabeth Ardington, 'Poverty and development in a rural community in Kwa Zulu', CCP 53 (1984), 142; Trudi Thomas, *Their doctor speaks* (reprinted, Kenilworth, 1982), p. 27.
86 Liz Clarke and Jane Ngobese, *Women without men: a study of 150 families in the Nqutu district of Kwazulu* (Durban [1975?]), p. 26; Margo Russell, 'Beyond remittances: the redistribution of cash in Swazi society', *JMAS*, 22 (1984), 610.
87 Freddy Sitas, 'An investigation of a cholera outbreak at the Umvoti mission reserve, Natal', CCP 151 (1984), 9.
88 *SAO*, 108 (1978), 148; Eric Buck and Cedric de Beer, 'Health and health care in Mhala', CCP 192 (1984), 3; *SAO*, 99 (1969), 187. See also Hansen, 'Food'.
89 Quoted in Human Awareness Programme, 'State pension scheme and private pension funds', CCP 138 (1984), 75.
90 Thomas, *Their doctor*, pp. 11–13; *idem*, 'Life in the Ciskei', *SAO*, 105 (1975), 52–4.
91 Hansen, 'Food', p. 8; T. Vergnain in Hans Steyn (ed.), 'Malnutrition in the Stellenbosch area', CCP 184 (1984), appendix, pp. 4, 14.
92 Cooper, 'Interpretation', p. 90; Colin Murray, 'Migrant labour and changing family structure in the rural periphery of southern Africa', *JSAS*, 6 (1979–80), 145–6.
93 Murray, 'Migrant labour', p. 146; Russell, 'Beyond remittances', p. 606; Simkins, 'Income distribution', p. 17.
94 Quoted in Murray, *Families*, p. 60.
95 *Ibid.*, pp. 104, 110, 173, 176; Cooper, 'Interpretation', pp. 91, 237–8.
96 Peters, 'Gender', p. 113; Murray, *Families*, p. 54; Johann Maree and P. J. de Vos, *Underemployment, poverty and migrant labour in the Transkei and Ciskei* (Johannesburg, 1975), p. 28.
97 Andrew D. Spiegel, 'Rural differentiation and the diffusion of migrant labour remittances in Lesotho', in Philip Mayer (ed.), *Black villagers in an industrial society* (Cape Town, 1980), pp. 121, 128, 149–50.
98 See esp. John S. Sharp and Andrew D. Spiegel, 'Vulnerability to impoverishment in South African rural areas', *Africa*, 55 (1985), 137.
99 Murray, *Families*, p. 96; N. D. Muller, 'Aspects of the political economy of drought and water in Transkei', CCP 149 (1984), 3; Andrew D. Spiegel, 'Changing patterns of migrant labour and rural differentiation in Lesotho', *Social dynamics*, 6, 2 (1981), 2; Roger J. Southall, 'Consociationalism in South Africa', *JMAS*, 21 (1983), 86.
100 Simkins, 'Income distribution', p. 6; Russell, 'Beyond remittances', pp. 597–9.
101 ILO/JASPA, *Options*, pp. 245, 248; Cooper, 'Overview', pp. 131, 139–41; du Pradal, 'Poverty', p. 23; Colclough and Fallon in Ghai and Radwan, *Agrarian policies*, p. 149; Muller, 'Aspects', p. 5.
102 Quoted in Sharp and Spiegel, 'Vulnerability', p. 145.
103 Outline in Human Awareness Programme, 'State pension scheme', pp. 10–15
104 South Africa, *Native affairs report 1947–8*, p. 22; South Africa, *Bantu administration report 1976–7*, p. 112.

105 Ina Brand, 'Public expenditure in the R.S.A. on health, welfare and education', CCP 128 (1984), 2; Brian Kahn, 'The effects of inflation on the poor in South Africa', CCP 134 (1984), 16, 42–3.
106 Human Awareness Programme, 'State pension scheme', p. 13; Simkins, 'Income distribution', p. 3.
107 *Sowetan*, 7 July 1982, quoted in Human Awareness Programme, 'State pension scheme', p. 19.
108 Clarke and Ngobese, *Women without men*, p. 51; W. Naidoo and W. Dreyer, 'Area study of Cape Town: Vrygrond and Lavender Hill', CCP 10b (1984), 3; Preston-Whyte and Nene, 'Informal sector', p. 15.
109 Muller, 'Aspects', p. 5; C. D. Cragg, 'Estimated household subsistence levels for Transkei', CCP 44 (1984), 70; Harries, 'Aspects', p. 7.
110 Peter Derman and Clive Poultney, 'The politics of production and community development in rural South Africa', CCP 226 (1984), 12. See also Dudley Horner and Graham van Wyck, 'Quiet desperation: the poverty of Calitzdorp', CCP 36 (1984), 53; Ardington, 'Poverty', p. 21; Schneider, 'Microstudies', p. 5.
111 See p. 126.
112 Murray, *Families*, pp. 95–7; Cooper, 'Overview', p. 152; Ardington, 'Poverty', p. 39; Moll, 'Mixed and threadbare bag', p. 34.
113 E.g. Wallman, *Take out hunger*, pp. 68–9.
114 Ardington, 'Poverty', p. 41; Moll, 'Mixed and threadbare bag', p. 39; Levetan, 'Structural shifts', p. 83.
115 Thomas, *Their doctor*, pp. 4, 17.
116 Simkins, 'Income distribution', p. 13.
117 Ntoane and Mokoetle, 'Major problems', p. 23.
118 Wilson, 'Overview', p. 5.
119 Cromwell Diko, quoted in R. J. Harris and others, 'The silence of poverty: networks of control in rural Transkei', CCP 48 (1984), 12.
120 Reynolds, 'Citizens', p. 15, citing Simkins. The calculation was in full-time job equivalents. Figures for Africans alone would have been higher.
121 Trevor Bell and Vishnu Padayachee, 'Unemployment in South Africa', CCP 119 (1984), 7; N. D. Muller, 'The labour market and poverty in Transkei', CCP 43 (1984), 17.
122 Cooper, 'Interpretation', p. 15; Motlatsi Thabane and Jeff Guy, 'Unemployment and casual labour in Maseru', CCP 124 (1984), 5. See also James Cobb, 'Consequences for Lesotho of changing South African labour demand', *African affairs*, 85 (1986), 23–48.
123 Thabane and Guy, 'Unemployment', p. 1.
124 *SAO*, 112 (1982), 2, 178; Ardington, 'Poverty', p. 65.
125 David Simon, 'The end of apartheid? Some dimensions of urban poverty in Windhoek', CCP 22 (1984), 18; Zille, 'Political power', p. 20.
126 SPP, *Forced removals*, vol. 1, pp. xxiv–xxv; Laurine Platzky, 'Relocation and poverty', CCP 73 (1984), 2.
127 SPP, *Forced removals*, vol. 3, pp. 148, 161, 164–6.
128 *African business*, June 1982, p. 4; SPP, *Forced removals*, vol. 5, p. 184; Joanne Yawitch, 'Women and squatting: a Winterveld case study', in Bonner, *Working papers*, vol. 2, pp. 199–227.
129 SPP, *Forced removals*, vol. 1, p. 26.
130 R. J. Fincham and G. C. Thomas, 'Nutritional intervention: a Ciskei and Eastern Cape perspective', CCP 213 (1984), 3, 6.
131 SPP, *Forced removals*, vol. 2, pp. 218–29.
132 *Ibid.*, pp. 228, 243, 246.
133 Yawitch in Bonner, *Working papers*, vol. 2, pp. 219–20.

134 G. Ellis and others, 'Ciskei health survey', CCP 189 (1984), 4.
135 Sharp and Spiegel, 'Vulnerability', p. 145.
136 *SAO*, 111 (1981), 155.
137 SPP, *Forced removals*, vol. 2, p. 358; Laurine Platzky and Cherryl Walker, *The surplus people: forced removals in South Africa* (Johannesburg, 1985), p. 365.
138 General circular no. 25, 1967, in Platzky and Walker, *Surplus people*, p. 28.
139 Quoted in Gerhard Maré, 'Old age pensions and the Bantustans', *Work in progress* (Johannesburg), 17 (1981), 17.
140 South Africa, *Bantu administration reports*, 1960–2 p. 7, 1963 p. 8, 1964 p. 9, 1965 p. 7, 1968 p. 18.
141 Moses Bopape, 'Social welfare services in Lebowa and poverty related problems', CCP 65 (1984), 6, 9; Anthony Zwi, 'Piecing together health in the homelands', CCP 187 (1984), 12–16.
142 Simkins, 'Income distribution', p. 3.
143 Human Awareness Programme, 'State pension scheme', pp. 37, 61; Bopape, 'Social welfare services', p. 10; Jillian Nicholson, 'The pension crisis in Kwa Zulu', CCP 143 (1984), 2; John Sharp, 'Relocation and the problem of survival in Qwaqwa', *Social dynamics*, 8, 2 (1982), 17.
144 Quoted in Thabane and Guy, 'Unemployment', p. 12.
145 *The herald* (Harare), 29 July 1986.
146 Sharp, 'Relocation', p. 17.
147 Quoted in Colin Murray, 'Struggle from the margins: rural slums in the Orange Free State', in Cooper, *Struggle*, p. 293.
148 SPP, *Forced removals*, vol. 1, pp. 25–7; Platzky and Walker, *Surplus people*, p. 360.
149 Platzky, 'Relocation', p. 12.
150 SPP, *Forced removals*, vol. 1, p. 26, and vol. 2, p. 337.
151 *Ibid.*, vol. 2, p. 189.
152 *Ibid.*, p. 274.
153 *Ibid.*, vol. 5, pp. 338–9.
154 See p. 57.

Bibliography

Newspapers and magazines

Advance (Accra)
Africa emergency (New York)
African business (London)
The Anglo-African (Lagos)
Annales des Pères du Saint-Esprit (Paris)
Annales de la Propagation de la Foi (Lyon)
Bantu world (Johannesburg)
Central African planter (Blantyre)
Christian express (Lovedale)
Chronique trimestrielle de la Société des Missionnaires d'Afrique (Pères Blancs) (Lille)
Commonwealth survey (London)
The Cowley evangelist (Oxford)
Diggers' news and Witwatersrand advertiser (Johannesburg)
Echoes of service (Bath)
Ethiopia observer (Addis Ababa)
Lagos observer (Lagos)
Lagos times (Lagos)
Lagos weekly record (Lagos)
Mission field (London)
Les missions catholiques (Lyon)
Moto (Gweru)
Nigerian daily times (Lagos)
Nigerian pioneer (Lagos)
Oxfam news (Oxford)
Phillips' news (Johannesburg)
Race relations (Johannesburg)
The Salvation Army year book (London)
South African outlook (Lovedale)
Tanganyika opinion (Dar es Salaam)
Tanganyika standard (Dar es Salaam)
Transactions of the [London] Missionary Society (London)
Umsebenzi (Cape Town)
The war cry (London)
Weekly review (Nairobi)
West Africa (London)
The world's children (London)

Other works cited more than once

Aall, Cato. 'Relief, nutrition and health problems in the Nigerian/Biafran War', *Journal of tropical pediatrics*, 16 (1970), 69–90.

Abitbol, Michel. *Tombouctou et les Arma*. Paris, 1979.

Abraham, R. C. *Dictionary of the Hausa language*. 2nd edn, London, 1962.

Acquah, Ioné. *Accra survey*. London, 1958.

Adam, Heribert and Hermann Giliomee. *Ethnic power mobilized*. New Haven, 1979.

Adepoju, Aderanti. 'The dimension of the refugee problem in Africa', *African affairs*, 81 (1982), 21–35.

Ahluwalia, Montek S. and others. 'Growth and poverty in developing countries', *Journal of development economics*, 6 (1979), 299–341.

Ahmed, Haidar Abu. 'Leprosy in the Sudan', *LR*, 46 (1975), 219–22.

Alberti, Ludwig. *Ludwig Alberti's account of the tribal life and customs of the Xhosa in 1807*. Trans. W. Fehr, Cape Town, 1968.

Allotte de la Fuÿe, Maurice (ed.) *Actes de Filmona*, CSCO 36. Louvain, 1958.

Alquier, P. 'Saint-Louis du Sénégal pendant la Révolution et l'Empire (1789–1809)', *BCE*, 5 (1922), 277–320 and 411–63.

Amin, Samir. *Le développement du capitalisme en Côte d'Ivoire*. Paris, 1967.

Amin, Samir (ed.) *L'agriculture africaine et le capitalisme*. Paris, 1975.

Ardington, Elisabeth. 'Poverty and development in a rural community in Kwa Zulu', CCP 53 (Cape Town, 1984).

Arn, Jack. 'Political economy of urban poverty in Ghana: the case of Nima, Accra', Ph.D. thesis, University of Toronto, 1979.

Ashton, Hugh. *The Basuto*. 2nd edn, London, 1967.

Atkey, O. F. H. 'Leprosy control in the southern Sudan', *IJL*, 3 (1935), 73–9.

Audibert, Andrée. 'Le service social en Afrique francophone dans une perspective de développement (l'époque coloniale)', 2 vols., Thèse pour le Doctorat du spécialité en sciences sociales du travail, Université de Paris I, n.d.

Baier, Stephen. *An economic history of central Niger*. Oxford, 1980.

Baker, Pauline H. *Urbanization and political change: the politics of Lagos, 1917–1967*. Berkeley, 1974.

Balandier, Georges. *Sociologie des Brazzavilles noirs*. Paris, 1955.

Bamisaiye, Anne. 'Begging in Ibadan, Southern Nigeria', *Human organization*, 33 (1974), 197–202.

Banton, Michael. *West African city: a study of tribal life in Freetown*. London, 1957.

Barkow, Jerome H. 'The institution of courtesanship in the northern states of Nigeria', *Genève-Afrique*, 10 (1971), 58–73.

Barrow, John. *An account of travels into the interior of southern Africa in the years 1797 and 1798*. 2 vols., London, 1801–4.

A voyage to Cochinchina in the years 1792 and 1793. London, 1806.

Barry, B. Oscar. 'Review of infantile paralysis in Addis Ababa, 1960/63', *Ethiopian medical journal*, 3, 1 (October 1964), 3–12.

Barth, Heinrich. *Travels and discoveries in North and Central Africa ... in the years 1849–1855*. English trans., reprinted, 3 vols., London, 1965.

Basden, G. T. *Niger Ibos*. Reprinted, London, 1966.

Beckingham, C. F. and Huntingford, G. W. B. (eds.) *The Prester John of the Indies ... being the narrative of the Portuguese embassy to Ethiopia in 1520 written by Father Francisco Alvares*. Trans. Lord Stanley of Alderley, 2 vols., Cambridge, 1961.

Some records of Ethiopia 1593–1646. London, 1954.

William. *The political economy of Pondoland, 1860–1930*. Cambridge, 1982.

., F. J. and Mugalula-Mukibi, A. 'An analysis of people living alone in a rural community in East Africa', *SSM*, 1 (1967), 97–115.

y, W. Holman. *Dictionary and grammar of the Kongo language*. London, 1887.

rd, Guy. 'L'Africain et la ville', *CEA*, 13 (1973), 575–86.

us, Edmond. *Touaregs nigériens*. Paris, 1981.

mer, Fremont E. *Horses, musicians, and gods: the Hausa cult of possession-trance*. South Hadley, Mass., 1983.

tison, David G. 'The Poverty Datum Line in Central Africa', *RLJ*, 27 (June 1960), 1–40.

veridge, Andrew A. and Oberschall, Anthony R. *African businessmen and development in Zambia*. Princeton, 1979.

irmingham, Walter and others (eds.) *A study of contemporary Ghana*. 2 vols., London, 1966–7.

Blix, Gunnar and others (eds.) *Famine*. Uppsala, 1971.

Bloomberg, Warner, Jr, and Schmandt, Henry J. (eds.) *Power, poverty, and urban policy*. Beverly Hills, 1968.

Boilat, P. D. *Esquisses sénégalaises*. Paris, 1853.

Bonner, P. (ed.) *Working papers in southern African studies, volume 2*. Johannesburg, 1981.

Bopape, Moses. 'Social welfare services in Lebowa and poverty related problems', CCP 65 (Cape Town, 1984).

Borcherds, Petrus Borchardus. *An autobiographical memoir*. Reprinted, Cape Town, 1963.

Borelli, Jules. *Ethiopie méridionale*. Paris, 1890.

Bosman, William. *A new and accurate description of the coast of Guinea*. English trans., 4th edn, London, 1967.

Bosworth, Clifford Edmund. *The medieval Islamic underworld: the Banu Sasan in Arabic society and literature*. 2 vols., Leiden, 1976.

Botte, Roger. 'Burundi: de quoi vivait l'Etat', *CEA*, 22 (1982), 277–324.

'Processus de formation d'une classe sociale dans une société africaine précapitaliste', *CEA*, 14 (1974), 605–26.

Boutillier, J. L. and others. *La moyenne vallée du Sénégal*. Paris, 1962.

Bowen, T. J. *Grammar and dictionary of the Yoruba language*. Smithsonian contributions to knowledge, 10, Washington, DC, 1858.

Bozzoli, Belinda (ed.) *Labour, townships and protest: studies in the social history of the Witwatersrand*. Johannesburg, 1979.

Town and countryside in the Transvaal. Johannesburg, 1983.

Brásio, António. 'As Misericórdias de Angola', *Studia*, 4 (1959), 106–49.

Brásio, António (ed.) *Monumenta Missionaria Africana: Africa Ocidental*. 9 vols., Lisbon, 1952–79.

Braudel, Fernand, and Labrousse, Ernest (eds.) *Histoire économique et sociale de la France, tome 2*. Paris, 1970.

Brown, J. Tom. *Secwana–English dictionary*. Revised edn, Tiger Kloof [1931].

Brown, James A. K. 'Leprosy folk-lore in Southern Nigeria', *LR*, 8 (1937), 157–60.

'Leprosy in Southern Nigeria', *WAMJ*, 9 (1936–7), 10–14.

Brown, R. Cunyngham. *Report III on the care and treatment of lunatics in the British West African colonies: Nigeria*. Lagos, 1938.

Budge, E. A. Wallis (ed.) *The life of Takla Haymanot*. 2 vols., London, 1906.

Bundy, Colin, *The rise and fall of the South African peasantry*. London, 1979.

'Vagabond Hollanders and runaway Englishmen: white poverty in the Cape before Poor Whiteism', seminar paper, Institute of Commonwealth Studies, London, 1983.

Burchell, William J. *Travels in the interior of southern Africa*. Reprinted, 2 vols., Cape Town, 1967.

Burley, Dexter Lisbon. 'The despised weavers of Ethiopia', Ph.D. thesis, University of New Hampshire, 1976.

Burrows, Edmund H. *A history of medicine in South Africa up to the end of the nineteenth century*. Cape Town, 1958.

Busia, K. A. *Report on a social survey of Sekondi-Takoradi*. London, 1950.

Caillié, René. *Travels through central Africa to Timbuctoo ... in the years 1824–1828*. English trans., 2 vols., reprinted, London, 1968.

Callaway, Archibald. 'Nigeria's indigenous education: the apprenticeship system', *Odu*, 1, 1 (July 1964), 62–79.

Cape of Good Hope. *Leprosy Commission 1895: volume IV: final report of commissioners*. (G.4A–'95) Cape Town, 1895.

Report and proceedings, with appendices, of the Government Commission on Native Laws and Customs. Cape Town, 1883.

Report of the Select Committee appointed to consider and report on Robben Island Establishment. (A.3–'71) Cape Town, 1871.

Report of the Select Committee on Robben Island Leper Asylums. (C.2–'09) Cape Town, 1909.

Reports by the Special Commissioner appointed to inquire into the agricultural distress and land matters in the divisions of Herbert, Hay, Barkly West, Vryburg and Kimberley. (G.67–'99) Cape Town, 1899.

Carlebach, J. I. and others. 'Report of the Panel of Survey of Social Welfare on social services and housing in the City of Nairobi', duplicated [Nairobi] 1962.

Cavazzi, [J. A.] *Relation historique de l'Ethiopie occidentale*. Trans. J. B. Labat, 5 vols., Paris, 1732.

Cerulli, Enrico. 'Il monachismo in Etiopia', *Orientalia Christiana analecta*, 153 (1958), 259–78.

Chapman, James. *Travels in the interior of South Africa 1849–1863*. Ed. E. C. Tabler, 2 vols., Cape Town, 1971.

Chastanet, Monique. 'Les crises de subsistances dans les villages soninke du cercle de Bakel, de 1858 à 1945: problèmes méthodologiques et perspectives de recherches', *CEA*, 23 (1983), 5–36.

Churchill, Awnsham and John (eds.) *A collection of voyages and travels, volume 5*. London, 1732.

Churchill, John (ed.) *A collection of voyages and travels, volume 1*. London, 1704.

Clarence-Smith, W. G. 'Slaves, commoners and landlords in Bulozi, c.1875 to 1906', *JAH*, 20 (1979), 219–34.

Clarke, D. G. *Agricultural and plantation workers in Rhodesia: a report on conditions of labour and subsistence*. Gwelo, 1977.

Clarke, Liz and Ngobese, Jane. *Women without men: a study of 150 families in the Nqutu district of Kwazulu*. Durban [1975?]

Clarkson, M. 'The problem of begging and destitution in urban areas of the Gold Coast', *Proceedings of the Fourth Annual Conference of the West African Institute of Social and Economic Research, Ibadan, 1956* (reprinted, 1963), pp. 142–8.

Clinard, Marshall B. and Abbott, Daniel J. *Crime in developing countries*. New York, 1973.

Cock, Jacklyn. *Maids and madams: a study in the politics of exploitation*. Johannesburg, 1980.

Codere, Helen. *The biography of an African society: Rwanda 1900–1960*. Tervuren, 1973.

Cohen, Abner. *Custom and politics in urban Africa: a study of Hausa migrants in Yoruba towns*. London, 1969.

Cole, Herbert M. *Mbari: art and life among the Owerri Igbo*. Bloomington, 1982.

Collier, Paul and Lal, Deepak. *Labour and poverty in Kenya 1900–1980*. Oxford, 1986.

Poverty and growth in Kenya. World Bank Staff Working Paper 389, Washington, DC, 1980.

Collier, Paul and others. *Labour and poverty in rural Tanzania*. Oxford, 1986.
Combes, Ed. and Tamisier, M. *Voyage en Abyssinie, 1835–1837*. 4 vols., Paris, 1838.
Comhaire-Sylvain, Suzanne. 'Le travail des femmes à Lagos, Nigeria', *Zaïre*, 5 (1951), 169–87 and 475–502.
Conti Rossini, C. (ed.) *Historia Regis Sarsa Dengel (Malak Sagad)*, CSCO 3. Paris, 1907.
Cooper, Dave M. 'An interpretation of the emergent urban class structure in Botswana: a case study of Selebi-Phikwe miners', Ph.D. thesis, University of Birmingham, 1982.
'An overview of the Botswana urban class structure and its articulation with the rural mode of production: insights from Selebi-Phikwe', in University of Cape Town, Centre for African Studies, *Africa seminar collected papers, volume 2* (1981), pp. 128–56.
Cooper, Frederick (ed.) *Struggle for the city: migrant labor, capital, and the state in urban Africa*. Beverly Hills, 1983.
Copans, Jean (ed.) *Sécheresses et famines du Sahel*. 2 vols., Paris, 1975.
Cope, R. L. (ed.) *The journals of the Rev. T. L. Hodgson, missionary to the Seleka-Rolong and the Griquas 1821–1831*. Johannesburg, 1977.
Coplan, David. *In township tonight! South Africa's black city music and theatre*. London, 1985.
Coquery-Vidrovitch, C. 'Mutation de l'impérialisme colonial français dans les années 30', *African economic history*, 4 (Autumn 1977), 103–52.
Cowen, M. P. 'Differentiation in a Kenya location', East African Universities Social Science Council Conference paper, Nairobi, 1972.
Crisp, Jeff. *The story of an African working class: Ghanaian miners' struggles, 1870–1980*. London, 1984.
Crowder, Michael (ed.) *The Cambridge history of Africa, volume 8*. Cambridge, 1984.
Crowther, Samuel. *A vocabulary of the Yoruba language*. London, 1852.
Crummey, Donald. 'Abyssinian feudalism', *Past and present*, 89 (November 1980), 115–38.
Crummey, Donald (ed.) *Banditry, rebellion and social protest in Africa*. London, 1986.
Cunnison, Ian. *The Luapula peoples of Northern Rhodesia*. Manchester, 1959.
Curtin, Philip D. *Economic change in precolonial Africa: Senegambia in the era of the slave trade*. 2 vols., Madison, 1975.
Cuvelier, J. and Jadin, L. *L'ancien Congo, d'après les archives romaines (1518–1640)*. Brussels, 1954.
Czekanowski, Jan. *Forschungen im Nil–Kongo-Zwischengebiet: erster Band: Ethnographie*. Wissenschaftliche Ergebnisse der Deutschen Zentral-Afrika-Expedition 1907–1908: Band VI: erster Teil, Leipzig, 1917.
d'Abbadie, Arnauld. *Douze ans dans la Haute-Ethiopie*. Paris, 1868.
Dalby, David and others (eds.) *Drought in Africa 2*. London, 1977.
Davey, T. F. 'First report on leprosy control work in the Owerri Province, S. Nigeria', *LR*, 11 (1940), 123–34.
'Leprosy control in the Owerri Province, Southern Nigeria', *LR*, 13 (1942), 31–46.
'Leprosy control in the Owerri Province', *LR*, 14 (1943), 54–65.
'Uzuakoli Leper Colony', *LR*, 10 (1939), 171–85.
Davis, J. (ed.) *Choice and change*. London, 1974.
Deblé, Isabelle, and Hugon, Philippe (eds.) *Vivre et survivre dans les villes africaines*. Paris, 1982.
Delafosse, Maurice. *La langue mandingue et ses dialectes*. 2 vols., Paris, 1929–55.
Delinotte, H. 'The fight against leprosy in the French overseas territories', *IJL*, 7 (1939), 517–47.
de Miras, Claude. 'Le secteur de subsistance dans les branches de production à Abidjan', *Revue tiers-monde*, 21 (1980), 353–72.
Denham, Dixon and Clapperton, Hugh. *Narrative of travels and discoveries in northern and central Africa, in the years 1822, 1823, and 1824*. London, 1826.

Derman, William. *Serfs, peasants, and socialists: a former serf village in the Republic of Guinea*. Berkeley, 1973.

Derrick, Jonathan. 'The great West African drought, 1972–1974', *African affairs*, 76 (1977), 537–86.

'West Africa's worst year of famine', *African affairs*, 83 (1984), 281–99.

de Villiers, Simon A. *Robben Island*. Cape Town, 1971.

De Vos, George and Wagatsuma, Hiroshi (eds.) *Japan's invisible race: caste in culture and personality*. Berkeley, 1966.

Dias, Jill R. 'Famine and disease in the history of Angola, c.1830–1930', *JAH*, 22 (1981), 349–78.

Dick, B. and others. 'Chronic illness in non-institutionalized persons', *SAMJ*, 53 (1978), 892–904 and 928–37.

Dikobe, Modikwe. *The marabi dance*. London, 1973.

Diop, Abdoulaye-Bara. *La société wolof*. Paris, 1981.

Diop, Majhemout. *Histoire des classes sociales dans l'Afrique de l'Ouest, I: le Mali*. Paris, 1971.

Dirasse, Laketch. 'The socio-economic position of women in Addis Ababa: the case of prostitution', Ph.D. thesis, Boston University, 1978.

Dory, Electra. *Leper country*. London, 1963.

Drake, St Clair, and Omari, T. Peter (eds.) *Social work in West Africa*. Accra [1963].

Duby, Georges. 'Les pauvres des campagnes dans l'Occident médiéval jusqu'au XIIIe siècle', *Revue d'histoire de l'église de France*, 52 (1966), 25–32.

Duhamelet, Geneviève. *Les Soeurs Bleues de Castres*. 7th edn, Paris, 1934.

du Pradal, Pia. 'Poverty and wealth in a Kalahari village in Botswana', CCP 284 (Cape Town, 1984).

Elliott, Charles. *Patterns of poverty in the Third World*. New York, 1975.

Ellis, George and others. *The squatter problem in the Western Cape*. Johannesburg, 1977.

Elphick, Richard. *Kraal and castle: Khoikhoi and the founding of white South Africa*. New Haven, 1977.

Elphick, Richard, and Giliomee, Hermann (eds.) *The shaping of South African society, 1652–1820*. Cape Town, 1979.

Elton Mills, M. E. and Wilson, Monica. *Keiskammahoek rural survey: volume 4: land tenure*. Pietermaritzburg, 1952.

Epstein, A. L. *Urbanization and kinship: the domestic domain on the Copperbelt of Zambia, 1950–1956*. London, 1981.

L'équipe écologie et anthropologie des sociétés pastorales. *Pastoral production and society*. Cambridge, 1979.

es-Sadi, Abderrahman. *Tarikh es-Soudan*. Trans. O. Houdas, Paris, 1900.

es-Soudan, Akhbar Molouk. *Tedzkiret en-Nisian*. Trans. O. Houdas, reprinted, Paris, 1966.

Ethiopia: Relief and Rehabilitation Commission. *The challenges of drought*. Addis Ababa, 1985.

Ezeanya, S. N. 'The *osu* (cult-slave) system in Igbo land', *Journal of religion in Africa*, 1 (1968), 35–45.

Fage, J. D. 'Slaves and society in western Africa, *c*. 1445–*c*.1700', *JAH*, 21 (1980), 289–310.

Farmer, G. and Wigley, T. M. L. *Climatic trends for tropical Africa*. Norwich, 1985.

Faulkner, Donald. *Social welfare and juvenile delinquency in Lagos, Nigeria*. London [1950?].

Feeny, Patrick. *The fight against leprosy*. London, 1964.

Feierman, Steven. 'Struggles for control: the social roots of health and healing in modern Africa', *African studies review*, 28, 2 (June 1985), 73–147.

Ferguson, Douglas Edwin. 'Nineteenth century Hausaland, being a description by Imam Imoru of the land, economy, and society of his people', Ph.D. thesis, University of California at Los Angeles, 1973.

Fetter, Bruce. 'African associations in Elisabethville, 1910–1935', *Etudes d'histoire africaine*, 6 (1974), 205–23.
The creation of Elisabethville, 1910–1940. Stanford, 1976.
Fieldhouse, D. K. *Black Africa 1945–80*. London, 1986.
Fish, James W. *Robben Island: an account of thirty-four years' gospel work amongst lepers of South Africa*. Kilmarnock [1924?]
Fisher, Allan G. B. and Humphrey J. *Slavery and Muslim society in Africa*. London, 1970.
Forde, Daryll, and Scott, Richenda. *The native economies of Nigeria*. London, 1946.
Fox, A. J. (ed.) *Uzuakoli: a short history*. London, 1964.
Fraenkel, Merran. *Tribe and class in Monrovia*. London, 1964.
Freed, Louis Franklin. *Crime in South Africa*. Cape Town, 1963.
Fyfe, Christopher. *A history of Sierra Leone*. London, 1962.
Gahama, Joseph. *Le Burundi sous administration belge: la période du mandat 1919–1939*. Paris, 1983.
Gaitskell, Deborah and others. 'Class, race and gender: domestic workers in South Africa', *ROAPE*, 27 (1984), 86–108.
Gamble, D. P. 'Contributions to a socio-economic survey of the Gambia'. Duplicated, Colonial Office Research Department. [London] 1949.
Gargett, Eric. 'Welfare services in an African urban area', Ph.D. thesis, University of London, 1971.
The administration of transition: African urban settlement in Rhodesia. Gwelo, 1977.
Garretson, Peter Phillips. 'A history of Addis Ababa from its foundation in 1886 to 1910', Ph.D. thesis, University of London, 1974.
Gebre-Medhin, Jordan. 'The Eritrean Peoples Liberation Front and the rural poor', *Mawazo*, 5, 3 (June 1984), 77–87.
Gelfand, Michael. *A service to the sick: a history of the health services for Africans in Southern Rhodesia (1890–1953)*. Gwelo, 1976.
Germond, R. C. 'A study of the last six years of the leprosy campaign in Basutoland', *IJL*, 4 (1936), 219–24.
Ghai, Dharam, and Radwan, Samir (eds.) *Agrarian policies and rural poverty in Africa*. Geneva, 1983.
Gibbal, Jean-Marie. *Citadins et paysans dans la ville africaine: l'example d'Abidjan*. Paris, 1974.
Giel, R. and Luijk, J. N. van. 'Leprosy in Ethiopian society', *IJL*, 38 (1970), 187–98.
'Psychiatric morbidity in a small Ethiopian town', *British journal of psychiatry*, 115 (1969), 149–62.
Giel, Robert and others. 'Ticket to heaven: psychiatric illness in a religious community in Ethiopia', *SSM*, 8 (1974), 549–56.
Giri, Jacques. *La Sahel demain*. Paris, 1983.
Gobat, Samuel. *Journal of a three years' residence in Abyssinia*. 2nd edn, London, 1847.
Goglin, Jean-Louis. *Les misérables dans l'Occident médiéval*. Paris, 1976.
Golberry, S. M. X. *Travels in Africa, performed during the years 1785, 1786, and 1787*. Trans. F. Blagdon, 2 vols., London, 1802.
Gold Coast. *Report on the enquiry into begging and destitution in the Gold Coast 1954*. Accra, 1955.
Goody, Esther N. *Parenthood and social reproduction*. Cambridge, 1982.
Goody, Jack. *Cooking, cuisine and class*. Cambridge, 1982.
Gouellain, René. *Douala: ville et histoire*. Paris, 1975.
Graham, Anne M. S. 'Adapting to water shortage in a year of poor rains: a case study from the Sudan', *Savanna*, 2 (1973), 121–5.
Great Britain. 'A return of the provision, if any, made by law or otherwise, in Her Majesty's

different colonial possessions, for destitute persons', *Accounts and papers*, 1846, XXIX, 465–572.

Colonial Office. *Malnutrition in African mothers, infants and young children*. London, 1954.

Economic Advisory Council: Committee on Nutrition in the Colonial Empire. *First report – part I: nutrition in the Colonial Empire*. (Cmd 6050 of 1939.) London, 1939; *First report – part II: summary of information regarding nutrition in the Colonial Empire*. (Cmd 6051 of 1939.) London, 1939.

House of Commons. *Second report from the Foreign Affairs Committee: session 1984–85: Famine in Africa*. House of Commons Paper 56, London, 1985.

Green, M. M. *Ibo village affairs*. London, 1947.

Green, Reginald Herbold, and Singer, Hans. 'Sub-Saharan Africa in depression: the impact on the welfare of children', *World development*, 12 (1984), 283–95.

Greer, Germaine. 'Ethiopia behind the headlines', *The listener*, 24 October 1985, pp. 7–8.

Greyling, P. F. *Die Nederduits Gereformeerde Kerk en Armesorg*. Cape Town, 1939.

Griffiths, P. Glyn. 'Leprosy in the Luapula Valley, Zambia', *LR*, 36 (1965), 59–67.

Grosskopf, J. F. W. and others. *The Poor White problem in South Africa: report of the Carnegie Commission*. 5 vols., Stellenbosch, 1932.

Guebels, L. *Relation complète des travaux de la Commission Permanente pour la Protection des Indigènes*. [Elisabethville, 1952?]

Guèbrè Sellassié. *Chronique du règne de Ménélik II, Roi des Rois d'Ethiopie*. Trans. Tèsfa Sellassié, ed. M. de Coppet, 2 vols., Paris, 1930–1.

Guèye, M'Baye. 'La fin de l'esclavage à Saint-Louis et à Gorée en 1848', *BIFAN*, 28B (1966), 637–56.

Guidi, I (ed.) *Annales Iohannis I, Iyasu I, Bakaffa*, CSCO 5. Paris, 1903.

Guidi, Ignazio (ed.) *Il 'Fetha Nagast'*. 2 vols., Rome, 1897–9.

Guilbot, Jacques. 'Les conditions de vie des indigènes de Douala', *Etudes camerounaises*, 27 (1949), 179–239.

Gulliver, P. H. *The family herds: a study of two pastoral tribes in East Africa, the Jie and Turkana*. London, 1955.

Gutkind, P. C. W. 'The energy of despair: social organization of the unemployed in two African cities: Lagos and Nairobi', *Civilisations*, 17 (1967), 186–214 and 380–405.

Gutkind, Peter C. W. and others (eds.) *African labor history*. Beverly Hills, 1978.

Gutton, Jean-Pierre. *La société et les pauvres: l'exemple de la généralité de Lyon 1534–1789*. Paris, 1971.

Haeringer, Philippe (ed.) *Abidjan au coin de la rue: éléments de la vie citadine dans la métropole ivoirienne*. Paris, 1983.

Hahn, C. H. L. and others. *The native tribes of South West Africa*. Reprinted, London, 1966.

Haines, E. S. 'The economic status of the Cape Province farm native', *South African journal of economics*, 3 (1935), 57–79.

Hake, Andrew. *African metropolis: Nairobi's self-help city*. [London] 1977.

Hampaté Ba, Amadou and Daget, Jacques. *L'empire peul du Macina, volume 1 (1818–1853)*. Paris, 1962.

Hansen, John. 'Food and nutrition policy with relation to poverty: the child malnutrition problem in South Africa', CCP 205 (Cape Town, 1984).

Harries, Patrick. 'Aspects of poverty in Gazankulu: three case studies', CCP 67 (Cape Town, 1984).

Harris, J. S. 'Some aspects of the economics of sixteen Ibo individuals', *Africa*, 14 (1943–4), 302–35.

Harris, W. Cornwallis. *The highlands of Aethiopia*. 3 vols., London, 1844.

Haswell, Margaret. *The nature of poverty: a case-history of the first quarter-century after World War II*. London, 1975.

Heisler, Helmuth. *Urbanisation and the government of migration: the inter-relation of urban and rural life in Zambia*. London, 1974.
Hellman, Ellen. *Rooiyard: a sociological survey of an urban native slum yard*. Rhodes–Livingstone Paper 13, Cape Town, 1948.
Hellmann, Ellen (ed.) *Handbook on race relations in South Africa*. Cape Town, 1949.
Hepburn, J. D. *Twenty years in Khama's country*. Ed. C. H. Lyall, 3rd edn, London, 1970.
Hewatt, G. and others. 'An exploratory study of overcrowding and health issues at Old Crossroads', CCP 14 (Cape Town, 1984).
Heyer, Friedrich. *Die Kirche Aethiopiens: eine Bestandsaufnahme*. Berlin, 1971.
Hill, Polly. *Dry grain farming families: Hausaland (Nigeria) and Karnataka (India) compared*. Cambridge, 1982.
Population, prosperity and poverty: rural Kano, 1900 and 1970. Cambridge, 1977.
Rural Hausa: a village and a setting. Cambridge, 1972.
Hilton, Anne. 'Family and kinship among the Kongo south of the Zaïre River from the sixteenth to the nineteenth centuries', *JAH*, 24 (1983), 189–206.
The kingdom of Kongo. Oxford, 1985.
Hinchey, Madalon T. (ed.) *Proceedings of the Symposium on Drought in Botswana, Gaborone, 5–8 June 1978*. Gaborone, 1979.
Hirschmann, David and Vaughan, Megan. 'Food production and income generation in a matrilineal society: rural women in Zomba, Malawi', *JSAS*, 10 (1983–4), 86–99.
Hiskett, Mervyn. *The development of Islam in West Africa*. London, 1984.
A history of Hausa Islamic verse. London, 1975.
'The "Song of the Shaihu's Miracles": a Hausa hagiography from Sokoto', *African language studies*, 12 (1971), 71–107.
Hoben, Allan. *Land tenure among the Amhara of Ethiopia: the dynamics of cognatic descent*. Chicago, 1973.
Hochet, Jean. *Inadaptation sociale et délinquance juvénile en Haute-Volta*. Paris, 1967.
Holloway, Richard. 'Street boys in Addis Ababa', *Community development journal*, 5 (1970), 139–44.
Houghton, D. Hobart and Walton, Edith M. *Keiskammahoek rural survey, volume 2: the economy of a native reserve*. Pietermaritzburg, 1952.
Houyoux C. and J. 'Les conditions de vie dans soixante familles à Kinshasa', *Cahiers économiques et sociaux*, 8 (1970), 99–132.
Howard, Mary Theresa. 'Kwashiorkor on Kilimanjaro: the social handling of malnutrition', Ph.D. thesis, Michigan State University, 1980.
Hufton, Olwen H. *The poor of eighteenth-century France, 1750–1789*. Oxford, 1974.
Human Awareness Programme. 'State pension scheme and private pension funds – how they affect black people in South Africa', CCP 138 (Cape Town, 1984).
Hunt, Diana. *The impending crisis in Kenya: the case for land reform*. Aldershot, 1984.
Hunter, John M. 'Progress and concerns in the World Health Organization onchocerciasis control program in West Africa', *SSM*, 15D (1981), 261–75.
Hunter, John M. and Thomas, Morris O. 'Hypothesis of leprosy, tuberculosis and urbanization in Africa', *SSM*, 19 (1984), 27–57.
Hunter, Monica. *Reaction to conquest: effects of contact with Europeans on the Pondo of South Africa*. 2nd edn, London, 1961.
Hutton, Caroline. *Reluctant farmers? a study of unemployment and planned rural development in Uganda*. Nairobi, 1973.
Iliffe, John. *The emergence of African capitalism*. London, 1983.
A modern history of Tanganyika. Cambridge, 1979.
'Poverty in nineteenth-century Yorubaland', *JAH*, 25 (1984), 43–57.
Innes, James Ross. 'Leprosy and leprosy work in East Africa', *IJL*, 18 (1950), 359–68.

International Labour Office. *Employment, incomes and equality: a strategy for increasing productive employment in Kenya*. Geneva, 1972.
First things first: meeting the basic needs of the people of Nigeria. Addis Ababa, 1981.
International Labour Office/Jobs and Skills Programme for Africa. *Basic needs in danger: a basic needs oriented development strategy for Tanzania*. Addis Ababa, 1982.
Basic needs in an economy under pressure. 2 vols., Addis Ababa, 1981.
Options for a dependent economy: development, employment and equity problems in Lesotho. Addis Ababa, 1979.
International Social Security Association. *Sixth African Regional Conference, Cairo, 16–21 October 1978*. Geneva, 1980.
Irgens, L. M. 'Epidemiological aspects and implications of the disappearance of leprosy from Norway; some factors contributing to the decline', *LR*, 52 (1981), supplement 1, pp. 147–65.
[Isenberg, C. W. and Krapf, J. L.] *The journals of C. W. Isenberg and J. L. Krapf*. Reprinted, London, 1968.
Ishumi, Abel G. M. *The urban jobless in eastern Africa*. Uppsala, 1984.
Isichei, Elizabeth. *A history of the Igbo people*. London, 1976.
Isichei, Elizabeth (ed.) *Varieties of Christian experience in Nigeria*. London, 1982.
Izzett, Alison. 'The Yoruba young delinquent in Lagos, Nigeria', B.Litt. thesis, University of Oxford, 1955.
Jadin, Louis. 'Andrea da Pavia au Congo, à Lisbonne, à Madère: journal d'un missionnaire capucin, 1685–1702', *Bulletin de l'Institut Historique Belge de Rome*, 41 (1970), 375–592.
'Pero Tavares, missionnaire jésuite, ses travaux apostoliques au Congo et en Angola, 1629–1635', *Bulletin de l'Institut Historique Belge de Rome*, 38 (1967), 271–402.
'Relations sur le Congo et l'Angola tirées des archives de la Compagnie de Jésus, 1621–1631', *Bulletin de l'Institut Historique Belge de Rome*, 39 (1968), 333–454.
Jalla, Adolphe. *Pionniers parmi les Ma-Rotse*. Florence, 1903.
Janisch, Miriam. *A study of African income and expenditure in 987 families in Johannesburg, January–November, 1940*. Johannesburg, 1941.
Jeffries, Richard. *Class, power and ideology in Ghana: the railwaymen of Sekondi*. Cambridge, 1978.
Jewsiewicki, B. 'The great depression and the making of the colonial economic system in the Belgian Congo', *African economic history*, 4 (Autumn 1977), 153–76.
Johnston, Charles. *Travels in southern Abyssinia*. Reprinted, 2 vols., n.p., 1972.
Jones, William I. *Planning and economic policy: socialist Mali and her neighbors*. Washington, DC, 1976.
Jopling, W. H. *Handbook of leprosy*. 3rd edn, London, 1984.
Joseph, Richard A. *Radical nationalism in Cameroun*. Oxford, 1977.
Joshi, Heather and others. *Abidjan: urban development and employment in the Ivory Coast*. Geneva, 1976.
Judges, Shirley. 'Poverty, living conditions and social relations – aspects of life in Cape Town in the 1830s', MA thesis, University of Cape Town, 1977.
Junod, Henri A. *The life of a South African tribe*. 2nd edn, reprinted, 2 vols., New York, 1962.
Kachingwe, Ernest W. 'Social welfare services for urban Africans in Zimbabwe: the role of social work education in the distribution of services', Ph.D. thesis, University of Iowa, 1979.
Kagabo, José and Mudandagizi, Vincent. 'Complainte des gens de l'argile: les Twa du Rwanda', *CEA*, 14 (1974), 75–87.
Kalewold, Alaka Imbakom. *Traditional Ethiopian church education*. Trans. Menghestu Lemma, New York, 1970.
Kane, Thomas Leiper. *Ethiopian literature in Amharic*. Wiesbaden, 1975.

Kaplan, Steven. *The monastic holy man and the Christianization of early Solomonic Ethiopia*. Wiesbaden, 1984.
Kea, Ray A. *Settlements, trade and politics in the seventeenth-century Gold Coast*. Baltimore, 1982.
Kenya. *Report on the incidence of destitution among Africans in urban areas*. Nairobi, 1954.
Kershaw, Gretha. 'The land is the people: a study of Kikuyu social organization in historical perspective', Ph.D. thesis, University of Chicago, 1972.
Kiernan, J. P. 'Poor and puritan: an attempt to view Zionism as a collective response to urban poverty', *African studies*, 36 (1977), 31–41.
Kilby, Peter, *Industrialization in an open economy: Nigeria 1945–1966*. Cambridge, 1969.
King, Kenneth. *The African artisan: education and the informal sector in Kenya*. London, 1977.
Kinkead-Weekes, B. H. 'A history of vagrancy in Cape Town', CCP 11 (Cape Town, 1984).
Kinsman, Margaret. '"Beasts of burden": the subordination of southern Tswana women, ca. 1800–1840', *JSAS*, 10 (1983–4), 39–54.
Kirby, Percival R. (ed.) *The diary of Dr Andrew Smith, 1834–1836*. 2 vols., Cape Town, 1939–40.
Kiros, Fassil G. (ed.) *Challenging rural poverty*. Trenton, NJ, 1985.
Kitching, Gavin. *Class and economic change in Kenya: the making of an African petite bourgeoisie 1905–1970*. New Haven, 1980.
Knight, J. B. and Lenta, G. 'Has capitalism underdeveloped the labour reserves of South Africa?' *Oxford bulletin of economics and statistics*, 42 (1980), 157–201.
Kohnert, Dirk. *Klassenbildung im ländlichen Nigeria: das Beispiel der Savannenbauern in Nupeland*. Hamburg, 1982.
Kossoudji, Sherrie and Mueller, Eva. 'The economic and demographic status of female-headed households in rural Botswana', *EDCC*, 31 (1982–3), 831–59.
Kramer, Julian Y. 'Self help in Soweto: mutual aid societies in a South African city', MA thesis, University of Bergen, n.d.
Krige, Eileen Jensen. 'Changing conditions in marital relations and parental duties among urbanized natives', *Africa*, 9 (1936), 1–23.
The social system of the Zulus. 2nd edn, Pietermaritzburg, 1950.
Kuper, Hilda and Kaplan, Selma. 'Voluntary associations in an urban township', *African studies*, 3 (1944), 178–86.
Kur, Stanislas (ed.) *Actes de Marha Krestos*, CSCO 63. Louvain, 1972.
Actes de Samuel de Dabra Wagag, CSCO 58. Louvain, 1968.
Lacey, Marian. *Working for boroko: the origins of a coercive labour system in South Africa*. Johannesburg, 1981.
Laidler, Percy Ward and Gelfand, Michael. *South Africa: its medical history 1652–1898*. Cape Town, 1971.
Laman, Karl. *The Kongo*. Studia Ethnographica Upsaliensia, 4, 8, 12, 16: 4 vols., Stockholm, 1953–68.
Lambert, W. A. 'My life with the lepers', duplicated, n.d. (CMS:UP 118).
Lander, Richard. *Records of Captain Clapperton's last expedition to Africa*. Reprinted, 2 vols., London, 1967.
Lapidus, Ira Marvin. *Muslim cities in the later Middle Ages*. Cambridge, Mass., 1967.
Latham, M. C. *Human nutrition in tropical Africa*. 2nd edn, Rome, 1979.
Lee, Richard B. and De Vore, Irven (eds.) *Kalahari hunter-gatherers: studies of the !Kung San and their neighbors*. Cambridge, Mass., 1976.
Lefebvre, Théophile and others. *Voyage en Abyssinie exécuté pendant les années 1839, 1840, 1841, 1842, 1843*. 6 vols., Paris [1851].
Lefort, René. *Ethiopie: la révolution hérétique*. Paris, 1981.

Leith-Ross, S. 'Notes on the Osu system among the Ibo of Owerri Province, Nigeria', *Africa*, 10 (1937), 206–20.
African women: a study of the Ibo of Nigeria. London, 1939.
Lenta, G. and Maasdorp, G. 'Food production in the homelands: constraints and remedial policies', CCP 224 (Cape Town, 1984).
Le Roux, Ingrid and Nyakaza, Nozizwe. 'Philani Nutrition Centre: an experiment in nutrition intervention', CCP 217 (Cape Town, 1984).
Le Roux, Pieter. 'Poor Whites', CCP 248 (Cape Town, 1984).
Leslau, Wolf. *Concise Amharic dictionary*. Wiesbaden, 1976.
Leslau, Wolf (ed.) *Falasha anthology*. New Haven, 1951.
Le Tourneau, Roger. *Les villes musulmanes de l'Afrique du Nord*. Algiers, 1957.
Leurquin, Philippe. *Le niveau de vie des populations rurales de Ruanda-Urundi*. Louvain, 1960.
Levetan, Laura. 'Structural shifts in the George economy: underemployment and unskilled labour as conditions of impoverishment', CCP 39 (Cape Town, 1984).
Levine, Donald N. *Wax and gold: tradition and innovation in Ethiopian culture*. Reprinted, Chicago, 1972.
Lewis, Jack. 'The rise and fall of the South African peasantry: a critique and reassessment', *JSAS*, 11 (1984–5), 1–24.
Lichtenstein, Henry. *Travels in southern Africa in the years 1803, 1804, 1805 and 1806*. Trans. A. Plumptre, 2 vols., reprinted, Cape Town, 1928.
Linden, Ian. *Church and revolution in Rwanda*. Manchester, 1977.
Lisk, Franklyn and Hoeven, Rolph van der. 'Measurement and interpretation of poverty in Sierra Leone', *ILR*, 118 (1979), 713–30.
Lissner, Jørgen. *The politics of altruism: a study of the political behaviour of voluntary development agencies*. Geneva, 1977.
Livingstone, David. *Family letters 1841–1856*. Ed. I. Schapera, 2 vols., London, 1959.
Missionary travels and researches in South Africa. New edn, London, 1899.
Livingstone, David and Charles. *Narrative of an expedition to the Zambesi and its tributaries, 1858–1864*. London, 1865.
Lloyd, P. C. and others (eds.) *The city of Ibadan*. Cambridge, 1967.
Lobo, Jerome. *A voyage to Abyssinia*. Trans. S. Johnson, London, 1735.
Lodge, Tom. *Black politics in South Africa since 1945*. London, 1983.
London Missionary Society, South Africa District Committee. *The Masarwa (Bushmen): report of an inquiry*. Lovedale [1935].
Long, Una (ed.) *The journals of Elizabeth Lees Price, 1854–1883*. London, 1956.
Ludolphus, Job. *A new history of Ethiopia*. English trans., 2nd edn, London, 1684.
Lux, André. 'Le niveau de vie des chômeurs de Luluabourg', *Zaïre*, 14 (1960), 1–34.
Maasdorp, Gavin and Humphreys, A. S. B. (eds.) *From shantytown to township: an economic study of African poverty and rehousing in a South African city*. Cape Town, 1975.
McAlpin, Michelle Burge. *Subject to famine: food crises and economic change in western India, 1860–1920*. Princeton, 1983.
McCracken, K. J. (ed.) *Malawi: an alternative pattern of development*. Edinburgh [1985].
Macdonald, Andrew B. *In His Name: the story of a doctor in Nigeria*. London, 1964.
Mackenzie, John. *Day-dawn in dark places: a story of wanderings and work in Bechwanaland*. London [1883?]
Ten years north of the Orange River. 2nd edn, London, 1971.
MacMillan, William Miller. *Complex South Africa: an economic foot-note to history*. London, 1930.
McVicar, Kenneth Gordon. 'Twilight of an East African slum: Pumwani and the evolution of African settlement in Nairobi', Ph.D. thesis, University of California at Los Angeles, 1968.

Mahmoud Kati. *Tarikh el-fettach*. Trans. O. Houdas and M. Delafosse, Paris, 1913.
Mair, L. P. *Welfare in the British colonies*. London, 1944.
Mandeville, Elizabeth. 'Poverty, work and the financing of single women in Kampala', *Africa*, 49 (1979), 42–52.
Marais, Maria M. 'Armesorg aan die Kaap onder die Kompanjie, 1652–1795', *Argief-jaarboek vir Suid-Afrikaanse geskiednis*, 6 (1943), 1–71.
Marks, Shula and Atmore, Anthony (eds.) *Economy and society in pre-industrial South Africa*. London, 1980.
Marks, Shula and Rathbone, Richard (eds.) *Industrialisation and social change in South Africa*. London, 1982.
Marris, Peter. *Family and social change in an African city: a study of rehousing in Lagos*. London, 1961.
Marty, Paul. *Etudes sur l'Islam en Côte d'Ivoire*. Paris, 1922.
Etudes sur l'Islam et les tribus du Soudan. 4 vols., Paris, 1920.
L'Islam en Guinée: Fouta-Diallon. Paris, 1921.
Mayer, Philip (ed.) *Socialization: the approach from social anthropology*. London, 1970.
Mayer, T. F. G. 'The distribution of leprosy in Nigeria with special reference to the aetiological factors on which it depends', *WAMJ*, 4 (1930–1), 11–15.
M'Bokolo, Elikia. 'Peste et société urbaine à Dakar: l'épidémie de 1914', *CEA*, 22 (1982), 13–46.
Meillassoux, Claude. *Urbanization of an African community: voluntary associations in Bamako*. Seattle, 1968.
Meillassoux, Claude (ed.) *L'esclavage en Afrique précoloniale*. Paris, 1975.
Ménard, F. *Dictionnaire Français–Kirundi et Kirundi–Français*. Roulers, 1909.
Mentzel, O. F. *A geographical and topographical description of the Cape of Good Hope*. Trans. H. J. Mandelbrote, 3 vols., Cape Town, 1921–44.
Mérab, Docteur. *Impressions d'Ethiopie (L'Abyssinie sous Ménélik II)*. 3 vols., Paris, 1921–9.
Messing, Simon D. 'Group therapy and social status in the Zar cult of Ethiopia', *American anthropologist*, 60 (1958), 1120–6.
Meth, Charles and Piper, Solveig. 'Social security in historical perspective', CCP 250 (Cape Town, 1984).
Midgley, James. *Professional imperialism: social work in the Third World*. London, 1981.
Miers, Suzanne and Kopytoff, Igor (eds.) *Slavery in Africa*. Madison, 1977.
Miller, D. S. and Holt, J. F. J. 'The Ethiopian famine', *Proceedings of the Nutritional Society*, 34 (1975), 167–72.
Miller, Joseph C. 'The significance of drought, disease and famine in the agriculturally marginal zones of West-Central Africa', *JAH*, 23 (1982), 17–61.
Miner, Horace. *The primitive city of Timbuctoo*. Princeton, 1953.
Moffat, Robert. *Missionary labours and scenes in southern Africa*. London, 1842.
Moiser, B. 'Leprosy in Southern Rhodesia: report of Ngomahuru Leprosy Hospital for 1937', *LR*, 9 (1938), 110–13.
Molesworth, B. D. 'Malawi leprosy control project', *Society of Malawi journal*, 21, 1 (January 1968), 58–69.
Moll, Terence. 'A mixed and threadbare bag: employment, incomes and poverty in Lower Roza, Qumbu, Transkei', CCP 47 (Cape Town, 1984).
Mollat, Michel. *Les pauvres au Moyen Age*. Paris, 1978.
Mollat, Michel (ed.) *Etudes sur l'histoire de la pauvreté*. 2 vols., Paris, 1974.
Monteil, Charles. *Une cité soudanaise: Djénné*. Paris, 1932.
Moodie, D. (ed.) *The record; or, a series of official papers relative to the condition and treatment of the native tribes of South Africa*. 5 parts, Cape Town, 1838–41.

Mortimore, Michael. 'Famine in Hausaland, 1973', *Savanna*, 2 (1973), 103–7.
Shifting sands and human sorrow: social response to drought and desertification. Durham, 1985.
Mortimore, M. J. (ed.) *Zaria and its region*. Zaria, 1970.
Morton, Alice Louise. 'Some aspects of spirit possession in Ethiopia', Ph.D. thesis, University of London, 1973.
Mouton, Pierre. *Social security in Africa*. Geneva, 1975.
Mphahlele, Ezekiel. *Down Second Avenue*. Reprinted, Berlin, 1962.
Muir, E. 'Leprosy in the Gold Coast', *LR*, 7 (1936), 182–90.
'Leprosy in Nigeria', *LR*, 11 (1940), 53–69.
'Leprosy in Northern Rhodesia', *LR*, 11 (1940), 18–24.
'Leprosy in Tanganyika Territory', *LR*, 10 (1939), 58–80.
'Report on leprosy in the Union of South Africa', *LR*, 11 (1940), 43–52.
Mulholland, Kim. 'Cholera in Sudan: an account of an epidemic in a refugee camp in eastern Sudan, May–June 1985', *Disasters*, 9 (1985), 247–58.
Muller, N. D. 'Aspects of the political economy of drought and water in Transkei', CCP 149 (Cape Town, 1984).
Murray, Colin. *Families divided: the impact of migrant labour in Lesotho*. Cambridge, 1981.
'Migrant labour and changing family structure in the rural periphery of southern Africa', *JSAS*, 6 (1980), 139–56.
Mworoha, Emile. *Peuples et rois de l'Afrique des lacs*. Dakar, 1977.
Nachtigal, Gustav. *Sahara and Sudan*. Trans. A. G. B. and H. J. Fisher, 4 vols., London, 1971–80.
Nadel, S. F. *A black Byzantium: the kingdom of Nupe in Nigeria*. Reprinted, London, 1969.
Nelson, Nici. 'Is fostering of children on the increase in central Kenya?' duplicated, Conference on the History of the Family in Africa, London, 1981.
'Some aspects of informal social organization of female migrants in a Nairobi squatter neighbourhood: Mathare Valley: papers I and II', seminar papers, SOAS, London, 1975.
Newbury, M. Catharine A. 'The cohesion of oppression: a century of clientship in Kinyaga, Rwanda', Ph.D. thesis, University of Wisconsin-Madison, 1975.
Nicholson, Sharon Elaine. 'A climatic chronology for Africa: synthesis of geological, historical, and meteorological information and data', Ph.D. thesis, University of Wisconsin-Madison, 1976.
'Climatic variations in the Sahel and other African regions during the past five centuries', *Journal of arid environments*, 1 (1978), 3–24.
Nicolaisen, Johannes. *Ecology and culture of the pastoral Tuareg*. Copenhagen, 1963.
'Slavery among the Tuareg in the Sahara', *Kuml* (1957), 107–12.
Nigeria. *Report of Tribunal of Inquiry on Kano Disturbances*. Lagos, 1981.
Nigerian Economic Society. *Poverty in Nigeria*. Ibadan, 1976.
Nolan, Margaret Mary, MMM. *Medical Missionaries of Mary, 1937–1962*. Drogheda, n.d.
Ntoane, C. N and Mokoetle, K. E. 'Major problems as perceived by the community', CCP 2 (Cape Town, 1984).
O'Brien, Jay. 'Sowing the seeds of famine: the political economy of food deficits in Sudan', *ROAPE*, 33 (August 1985), 23–32.
O'Connor, Anthony. *The African city*. London, 1983.
Okwu, Augustine S. O. 'The mission of the Irish Holy Ghost Fathers among the Igbo of south-eastern Nigeria, 1905–1956', Ph.D. thesis, Columbia University, 1977.
Olivier de Sardan, Jean-Pierre. *Concepts et conceptions songhay-zarma*. Paris, 1982.
Olivier de Sardan, J. P. (ed.) *Quand nos pères étaient captifs ... récits paysans du Niger*. Paris, 1976.
Onokerhoraye, Andrew R. *Social services in Nigeria*. London, 1984.

Orley, John H. *Culture and mental illness: a study from Uganda*. Nairobi, 1970.
Oroge, E. Adeniyi. 'The institution of slavery in Yorubaland with particular reference to the nineteenth century', Ph.D. thesis, University of Birmingham, 1971.
Palmer, Robin and Parsons, Neil (eds.) *The roots of rural poverty in central and southern Africa*. London, 1977.
Pankhurst, Richard. *Economic history of Ethiopia 1800–1935*. Addis Ababa, 1968.
'The great Ethiopian famine of 1888–92: a new assessment', *Journal of the history of medicine and allied sciences*, 21 (1966), 95–124, 271–94.
History of Ethiopian towns from the Middle Ages to the early nineteenth century. Wiesbaden, 1982.
'The history of prostitution in Ethiopia', *JES*, 12, 2 (1974), 159–78.
'Some factors depressing the standard of living of peasants in traditional Ethiopia', *JES*, 4, 2 (July 1966), 45–98.
Parkyns, Mansfield. *Life in Abyssinia*. 2nd edn, reprinted, London, 1966.
Patel, Diana H. and Adams, R. J. *Chirambahuyo: a case study in low-income housing*. Gwelo, 1981.
Paton, Alan. *Hofmeyr*. London, 1964.
Pauw, B. A. *The second generation: a study of the family among urbanized Bantu in East London*. Cape Town, 1963.
[Pearce, Nathaniel.] *The life and adventures of Nathaniel Pearce, written by himself*. Ed. J. J. Halls, 2 vols., London, 1831.
Peel, J. D. Y. 'Inequality and action: the forms of Ijesha social conflict', *CJAS*, 14 (1980), 473–502.
Peil, Margaret. *Cities and suburbs: urban life in West Africa*. New York, 1981.
Peiper, Otto. 'Die Bekämpfung der Lepra in Deutsch-Ostafrika', *Lepra*, 14 (1914), 192–250.
Peires, J. B. *The house of Phalo: a history of the Xhosa people in the days of their independence*. Berkeley, 1982.
Penvenne, Jeanne Marie. 'A history of African labor in Lourenço Marques, Mozambique, 1877 to 1950', Ph.D. thesis, Boston University, 1982.
Perkins, Dwight H. *Agricultural development in China 1368–1968*. Chicago, 1969.
Person, Yves. *Samori: une révolution dyula*. 3 vols., Dakar, 1968–75.
Peters, Pauline. 'Gender, developmental cycles and historical process: a critique of recent research on women in Botswana', *JSAS*, 10 (1983–4), 100–22.
Phillips, Ray E. *The Bantu in the city*. Lovedale, n.d.
Pillay, P. N. 'Alexandria [sic]: an analysis of socio-economic conditions in an urban-ghetto', CCP 19 (Cape Town, 1984).
Pinnock, Don. *The brotherhoods: street gangs and state control in Cape Town*. Cape Town, 1984.
Plaatje, Solomon T. *Sechuana proverbs with literal translations and their European equivalents*. London, 1916.
Platt, B. S. 'Report of a nutrition survey in Nyasaland', duplicated [1940?] (MNA library).
Platzky, Laurine. 'Relocation and poverty', CCP 73 (Cape Town, 1984).
Platzky, Laurine and Walker, Cherryl. *The surplus people: forced removals in South Africa*. Johannesburg, 1985.
Plotnicov, Leonard. *Strangers to the city: urban man in Jos, Nigeria*. Pittsburgh, 1967.
Plowden, Walter Chichele. *Travels in Abyssinia and the Galla country*. London, 1868.
Poitou, Danièle. *La délinquance juvénile au Niger*. Niamey, 1978.
Post, John D. 'Famine, mortality, and epidemic disease in the process of modernization', *Economic history review*, second series, 29 (1976), 14–37.
Pottier, Johan P. 'The politics of famine prevention: ecology, regional production and food complementarity in western Rwanda', *African affairs*, 85 (1986), 207–37.

Preston-Whyte, Eleanor and Nene, Sibongile. 'Where the informal sector is *not* the answer: women and poverty in rural Kwa Zulu', CCP 235 (Cape Town, 1984).
Prins, Gwyn. *The hidden hippopotamus: the early colonial experience in western Zambia*. Cambridge, 1980.
Ranger, Terence. *Peasant consciousness and guerrilla war in Zimbabwe*. London, 1985.
Raymaekers, Paul. *L'organisation des zones de squatting*. Paris, 1964.
Raynaut, Claude. *Structures normatives et relations électives: étude d'une communauté villageoise haoussa*. Paris, 1972.
Reader, D.H. *The black man's portion: history, demography and living conditions in the native locations of East London*. Cape Town, 1961.
Rendle-Short, Coralie. 'Study of the social background of mothers attending an M.C.H. centre in Addis Ababa', *Ethiopian medical journal*, 6 (1967–8), 47–54.
Retel-Laurentin, Anne. *Un pays à la dérive: les Nzakara de l'est centrafricain*. Paris, 1979.
Reynolds, Norman. 'Citizens, the state and employment', CCP 234 (Cape Town, 1984).
Richards, Audrey I. *Land, labour and diet in Northern Rhodesia: an economic study of the Bemba tribe*. 2nd edn, London, 1961.
Richards, A. I. and Widdowson, E. M. 'A dietary study in North-Eastern Rhodesia', *Africa*, 9 (1936), 166–96.
Richardson, James. *Narrative of a mission to central Africa performed in the years 1850–51*. 2 vols., London, 1853.
Roberts, Margaret. *Labour in the farm economy*. 2nd edn, Johannesburg, 1959.
Roberts, Richard and Klein, Martin A. 'The Banamba slave exodus of 1905 and the decline of slavery in the Western Sudan', *JAH*, 21 (1980), 375–94.
Robertson, Claire C. *Sharing the same bowl: a socioeconomic history of women and class in Accra*. Bloomington, 1984.
Robertson, Russell L. 'Garkida Agricultural–Industrial Leprosy Colony', *LR*, 3 (1932), 50–8.
Robinson, Charles Henry. *Dictionary of the Hausa language*. 4th edn, 2 vols., Cambridge, 1925.
Specimens of Hausa literature. Cambridge, 1896.
Robinson, David. *The Holy War of Umar Tal*. Oxford, 1985.
Rodegem, F. M. *Sagesse kirundi: proverbes, dictons, locutions usités au Burundi*. Tervuren, 1961.
Rodger, F. C. *Blindness in West Africa*. London, 1959.
Rodgers, Gerry and Standing, Guy (eds.) *Child work, poverty and underdevelopment*. Geneva, 1981.
Rogers, Leonard. *Happy toil*. London, 1950.
Rogerson, Christian Myles. 'The casual poor of Johannesburg, South Africa: the rise and fall of coffee-cart trading', Ph.D. thesis, Queen's University, Kingston, Ontario, 1983.
Rohlfs, Gerhard, *Quer durch Afrika*. 2 vols., Leipzig, 1874–5.
Roscoe, John. *The Baganda*. 2nd edn, London, 1965.
Rothman, Norman Calvin. 'African urban development in the colonial period: a study of Lusaka, 1905–1964', Ph.D. thesis, Northwestern University, 1972.
Rougier, F. 'L'Islam à Banamba', *BCE*, 13 (1930), 217–63.
Rüppell, Eduard. *Reise in Abyssinien*. 2 vols., Frankfurt am Main, 1838–40.
Rusch, Walter. *Klassen und Staat in Buganda vor der Kolonialzeit*. Berlin, 1975.
Russell, Margo. 'Beyond remittances: the redistribution of cash in Swazi society', *JMAS*, 22 (1984), 595–615.
Sabben-Clare, E. E. and others (eds.) *Health in Africa during the colonial period*. Oxford, 1980.
Saffery, A. Lynn and Rollnick, Julian. 'Social and economic position of unskilled workers at Kimberley', duplicated [1942?] (Institute of Commonwealth Studies, London).

Salifou, André. 'When history repeats itself: the famine of 1931 in Niger', *African environment*, 1, 2 (April 1975), 22–48.

Sandbrook, Richard. *The politics of basic needs*. London, 1982.

Sandbrook, Richard and Arn, Jack. *The labouring poor and urban class formation: the case of Greater Accra*. Montreal, 1977.

Sankale, M and others (eds.) *Dakar en devenir*. Paris, 1968.

Sansarricq, H. 'The general situation of leprosy in the world', *Ethiopian medical journal*, 20 (1982), 89–106.

'Recent changes in leprosy control', *LR*, 54 (1983), 7s–16s.

Saunders, Christopher. 'Segregation in Cape Town: the creation of Ndabeni', in University of Cape Town, Centre for African Studies, *Africa seminar collected papers, volume 1* (1978), pp. 43–63.

Saunders, Christopher (ed.) *Studies in the history of Cape Town, volume 1*. Reprinted, Cape Town, 1984.

Saunders, Christopher and others (eds.) *Studies in the history of Cape Town, volume 4*. Cape Town, 1981.

Saunders, Christopher and others (eds.) *Studies in the history of Cape Town, volume 5*. Cape Town, 1983.

Sautter, Gilles. *De l'Atlantique au fleuve Congo: une géographie du sous-peuplement*. 2 vols., Paris, 1966.

Schaller, K. F. *Ethiopia: a geomedical monograph*. Berlin, 1972.

Schapera, I. *A handbook of Tswana law and custom*. 2nd edn, London, 1955.

Tribal innovators: Tswana chiefs and social change 1795–1940. London, 1970.

Schapera, I. (ed.) *Livingstone's missionary correspondence 1841–1856*. London, 1961.

Praise-poems of Tswana chiefs. Oxford, 1965.

Schapera, I. and Merwe, D. F. van der. *Notes on the tribal groupings, history, and customs of the Bakgalagadi*. University of Cape Town, Communications from the School of African Studies, NS, 13, 1945.

Schärf, Wilfried. 'Street gangs, survival, and political consciousness in the eighties', duplicated paper, Fifth Workshop on the History of Cape Town, Cape Town, 1985.

Schildkrout, Enid. *People of the zongo: the transformation of ethnic identities in Ghana*. Cambridge, 1978.

Schlyter, Ann and Thomas. *George – the development of a squatter settlement in Lusaka, Zambia*. Stockholm, 1979.

Schneider, Catherine. 'Microstudies in Gazankulu', CCP 66 (Cape Town, 1984).

Schneider, Harm. *Leprosy and other health problems in Hararghe, Ethiopia*. Groningen, 1975.

Schofield, Frank D. 'Some relations between social isolation and specific communicable diseases', *American journal of tropical medicine and hygiene*, 19 (1970), 167–9.

Schön, James Frederick. *Dictionary of the Hausa language*. London, 1876.

Schram, Ralph. *A history of the Nigerian health services*. Ibadan, 1971.

Schulz, E. J. and Pentz, H. H. L. 'Leprosy control in South Africa', *LR*, 41 (1970), 15–19.

Schwarz, Alf. 'Illusion d'une émancipation et aliénation réelle de l'ouvrière zaïroise', *CJAS*, 6 (1972), 183–212.

Schweitzer, Albert. *More from the primeval forest*. Trans. C. T. Campion, London, 1931.

Scull, Andrew T. *Museums of madness: the social organization of insanity in nineteenth-century England*. Reprinted, Harmondsworth, 1982.

Seaman, John and Holt, Julius. 'Markets and famines in the Third World', *Disasters*, 4 (1980), 283–97.

Searle, Charlotte. *The history of the development of nursing in South Africa 1652–1960*. Cape Town, 1965.

Seeley, Janet Anne. 'Praise, prestige and power: the organisation of social welfare in a developing Kenyan town', Ph.D. thesis, University of Cambridge, 1985.

Sen, Amartya. *Poverty and famines*. Revised edn, Oxford, 1982.

Sethuraman, S. V. (ed.) *The urban informal sector in developing countries*. Geneva, 1981.

Sharp, John. 'Relocation and the problem of survival in Qwaqwa', *Social dynamics*, 8, 2 (1982), 11–29.

Sharp, John S. and Spiegel, Andrew D. 'Vulnerability to impoverishment in South African rural areas', *Africa*, 55 (1985), 133–52.

Shea, Philip James. 'The development of an export oriented dyed cloth industry in Kano Emirate in the nineteenth century', Ph.D. thesis, University of Wisconsin-Madison, 1975.

Sheets, Hal and Morris, Roger. *Disaster in the desert*. Washington, DC, 1974.

Shenton, Robert W. *The development of capitalism in Northern Nigeria*. London, 1986.

Shenton, R. W. and Lennihan, Louise. 'Capital and class: peasant differentiation in Northern Nigeria', *Journal of peasant studies*, 9 (1981–2), 47–70.

Simkins, Charles. 'Agricultural production in the African reserves of South Africa, 1918–1969', *JSAS*, 7 (1980–1), 256–83.

'What has been happening to income distribution and poverty in the homelands?', CCP 7 (Cape Town, 1984).

Skinner, Elliott P. *African urban life: the transformation of Ouagadougou*. Princeton, 1974.

Skinner, Neil (ed.) *Alhaji Mahmudu Koki, Kano malam*. Zaria, 1977.

Smith, David M. (ed.) *Living under apartheid: aspects of urbanization and social change in South Africa*. London, 1982.

Smith, M. F. *Baba of Karo: a woman of the Muslim Hausa*. London, 1954.

Smith, M. G. *The affairs of Daura*. Berkeley, 1978.

Sorrenson, M. P. K. *Land reform in the Kikuyu country*. Nairobi, 1967.

South Africa. *Report of the inter-departmental committee on poor relief and charitable institutions*. (U.G.61–'37) Cape Town, 1937.

Report of the inter-departmental committee on the social, health and economic conditions of urban natives. Pretoria, 1942.

Report of the National Conference on the Post War Planning of Social Welfare Work, September 1944. (Bound into DO 11/144.)

Report of Native Economic Commission 1930–1932. (U.G.22, 1932) Pretoria, 1932.

Report of the Social Security Committee. (U.G.14–'44) Cape Town, 1944.

Southall, Aidan W. and Gutkind, Peter C. W. *Townsmen in the making: Kampala and its suburbs*. Kampala, 1957.

Southern Rhodesia. *Report on social security by the Social Security Officer*. Duplicated, 2 vols., n.p., 1944.

Staudinger, Paul. *Im Herzen der Haussaländer*. Berlin, 1889.

Steedman, Andrew. *Wanderings and adventures in the interior of southern Africa*. 2 vols., London, 1835.

Stephen, David. *The San of the Kalahari*. London, 1982.

Stewart, Frances. *Planning to meet basic needs*. London, 1985.

St Jorre, John de. *The Nigerian Civil War*. London, 1972.

Stock, Eugene. *The history of the Church Missionary Society*. 4 vols., London, 1899–1916.

Strobel, Margaret. *Muslim women in Mombasa, 1890–1975*. New Haven, 1979.

Surplus People Project. *Forced removals in South Africa*. Cape Town: vol. 1, second impression, 1985; vols. 2–5, 1983.

Swanson, Maynard W. 'The sanitation syndrome: bubonic plague and urban native policy in the Cape Colony, 1900–1909', *JAH*, 18 (1977), 387–410.

Taylor, John V. and Lehmann, Dorothea. *Christians of the Copperbelt*. London, 1961.

Thabane, Motlatsi and Guy, Jeff. 'Unemployment and casual labour in Maseru', CCP 124 (Cape Town, 1984).

Theal, G. M. (ed.) *Records of the Cape Colony*. 36 vols., London, 1897–1905.

Thom, H. B. (ed.) *Journal of Jan van Riebeeck*. 3 vols., Cape Town, 1952–8.

Thomas, Northcote W. *Anthropological report on the Ibo-speaking peoples of Nigeria*. 6 vols., London, 1913–14.

Thomas, Trudi. *Their doctor speaks*. Reprinted, Kenilworth, 1982.

Thompson, Leonard (ed.) *African societies in southern Africa*. London, 1969.

Thomson, Betty Preston. *Two studies in African nutrition: an urban and a rural community in Northern Rhodesia*. Rhodes–Livingstone Paper 24, Manchester, 1954.

Thoré, L. 'Dagoudane-Pikine: étude démographique et sociologique', *BIFAN*, 24B (1962), 155–98.

Thornton, John K. *The kingdom of Kongo*. Madison, 1983.

Throup, David William. 'The governorship of Sir Philip Mitchell in Kenya, 1944–1952', Ph.D. thesis, University of Cambridge, 1983.

Tilsley, G. E. *Dan Crawford*. London, 1929.

Transvaal. *Report of the Transvaal Indigency Commission 1906–08*. (T.G.13–'08) Pretoria, 1908.

Trimingham, J. Spencer. *Islam in West Africa*. Oxford, 1959.

Tuden, Arthur and Plotnicov, Leonard (eds.) *Social stratification in Africa*. New York, 1970.

Uchendu, Victor C. *The Igbo of southeast Nigeria*. New York, 1965.

United Nations Economic Commission for Africa, Social Development Section. *Patterns of social welfare organization and administration in Africa*. New York, 1964.

University College of Addis Ababa. *Social survey of Addis Ababa 1960*. Duplicated, n.d.

University of Zimbabwe, Department of History, *Conference on Zimbabwean history*. 2 vols., Harare, 1982.

Uthman ibn Fudi. *Bayan wujub al-hijra ala 'l-ibad*. Trans. F. H. el Masri, Khartoum, 1978.

Vail, Leroy and White, Landeg. *Capitalism and colonialism in Mozambique*. London, 1980.

Van Apeldoorn, G. Jan. *Perspectives on drought and famine in Nigeria*. London, 1981.

Van Onselen, Charles. *Chibaro: African mine labour in Southern Rhodesia 1900–1933*. London, 1976.

'Reactions to rinderpest in southern Africa 1896–97', *JAH*, 13 (1972), 473–88.

Studies in the social and economic history of the Witwatersrand 1886–1914. 2 vols., Harlow, 1982.

Van Praag, E. and Mwankemwa, S. A. 'A prevalence survey on leprosy and the possible role of village 10-cell leaders in control in Muheza District, Tanzania', *LR*, 53 (1982), 27–34.

Vansina, Jan. *The children of Woot: a history of the Kuba peoples*. Madison, 1978.

The Tio kingdom of the middle Congo 1880–1892. London, 1973.

Vanwalle, Rita. 'Aspecten van Staatsvorming in West-Rwanda', *Africa-Tervuren*, 28 (1982), 64–78.

Vidal, Claudine. 'Economie de la société féodale rwandaise', *CEA*, 14 (1974), 52–74.

'Enquête sur le Rwanda traditionnel: conscience historique et traditions orales', *CEA*, 11 (1971), 526–37.

Vieillard, Gilbert. 'Notes sur les Peuls du Fouta-Djallon', *BIFAN*, 2 (1940), 85–210.

Vis, H. L. and others. *A nutritional survey in the Republic of Rwanda*. Tervuren, 1975.

Wagner, O. J. M. *Poverty and dependence in Cape Town*. Cape Town, n.d.

Walker, Sylvia. 'The disabled in Ghana: status and change in information and attitude', Ed.D. thesis, Columbia University, 1978.

Waller, R. D. 'Economic and social relations in the central Rift Valley: the Maa-speakers and their neighbours in the nineteenth century', typescript, n.d.

'"The lords of East Africa": the Maasai in the mid-nineteenth century (c.1840–c.1885)', Ph.D. thesis, University of Cambridge, 1978.

Wallman, Sandra. *Take out hunger: two case studies of rural development in Basutoland*. London, 1969.

Walser, Ferdinand. *Luganda proverbs*. Berlin, 1982.

Watanabe, Barbara and Mueller, Eva. 'A poverty profile for rural Botswana', *World development*, 12 (1984), 115–27.

Watts, Michael. *Silent violence: food, famine and peasantry in Northern Nigeria*. Berkeley, 1983.

Webster, David. 'The reproduction of labour power and the struggle for survival in Soweto', CCP 20 (Cape Town, 1984).

Wendt, Kurt (ed.) *Das Mashafa Milad (Liber Nativitatis) und Mashafa Sellase (Liber Trinitatis) des Kaizers Zara Yaqob*, CSCO 41–4. Louvain, 1962–3.

Wentzel, Wilfred. 'Hard times in the Karoo: case studies and statistical profiles from five peri-urban residential areas', CCP 38 (Cape Town, 1984).

Poverty and development in South Africa (1890–1980): a bibliography. SALDRU Working Paper 46, Cape Town, 1982.

West, Martin. *Bishops and prophets in a black city: African independent churches in Soweto, Johannesburg*. Cape Town, 1975.

Western, John. *Outcast Cape Town*. London, 1981.

Wheeler, David. 'Sources of stagnation in sub-Saharan Africa', *World development*, 12 (1984), 1–23.

Whitting, C. E. J. *Hausa and Fulani proverbs*. Lagos, 1940.

Wilkinson, Peter. 'The sale of the century? A critical review of recent developments in African housing policy in South Africa', CCP 160 (Cape Town, 1984).

Wilson, Francis. 'Carnegie Conference overview', CCP 311 (Cape Town, 1984).

Wilson, Francis and Perrot, Dominique (eds.) *Outlook on a century: South Africa 1870–1970*. Lovedale, 1973.

Wilson, Francis and others (eds.) *Farm labour in South Africa*. Cape Town, 1977.

Wilson, Monica and Mafeje, Archie. *Langa*. Cape Town, 1963

Wilsworth, Mercia. 'Poverty and survival: the dynamics of redistribution and sharing in a black South African township', *Social dynamics*, 5, 1 (1979), 14–25.

Winter, P. D. 'South African leprosy laws and control policy', *IJL*, 17 (1949), 253–63.

World Bank. *Accelerated development in sub-Saharan Africa*. Washington, DC, 1981.

The Gambia: basic needs. Washington, DC, 1981.

World development report 1986. New York, 1986.

Wrightson, Keith. *English society 1580–1680*. London, 1982.

Wylde, Augustus B. *Modern Abyssinia*. London, 1901.

Yellen, John E. 'The process of Basarwa assimilation in Botswana', *BNR*, 17 (1985), 15–23.

Yusuf, Ahmed Beitallah. 'A reconsideration of urban conceptions: Hausa urbanization and the Hausa rural–urban continuum', *Urban anthropology*, 3 (1974), 200–21.

Zartman, I. William (ed.) *The political economy of Nigeria*. New York, 1983.

Zarwan, John. 'The Xhosa cattle killings, 1856–57', *CEA*, 16 (1976), 519–39.

Zille, Helen. 'Political power and poverty: an examination of the role and effect of influx control in South Africa', CCP 83 (Cape Town, 1984).

Zimbabwe: Ministry of Labour and Social Services. *Report on the National Disability Survey of Zimbabwe*. Harare [1983].

Zimbe, B. Musoke. *Buganda and the King*. Mengo, 1939: typescript translation by F. Kamoga (CUL).

Index